THE
REAPPEARING
AMERICAN

Robert Murray Ricketts, D.D.S., M.S.

WRIGHT & CO. PUBLISHERS
SCOTTSDALE, ARIZONA

THE REAPPEARING AMERICAN

Copyright © 1993 by Robert Murray Ricketts

Library of Congress Cataloging-in-Publication Data
Ricketts, Robert Murray 1920-

　　　　The Reappearing American
　　　　p. cm.

Library of Congress Catalog Card Number 93-70203
ISBN: 0-9635961-0-1
First Edition
1 2 3 4 5 6 7 8 9 10

Printed in the United States of America

WRIGHT & CO. PUBLISHERS
4839 E. GREENWAY ROAD, SUITE 154
SCOTTSDALE, ARIZONA 85254
(602) 443-9431

*This work expresses my affection for mankind,
and is my sign to honor my children and your children
and all the young people yet to come.*

Robert Murray Ricketts

Acknowledgments

Throughout this book I have cited many people who guided and influenced my life. To all those I want to express my gratitude. I have received inspiration from my family, many friends and many colleagues. I have also benefited from the encouragement and practical advice of my entire family, whom I wish to thank for allowing me the time to reflect on many of the ensuing subjects.

Several years ago I wrote an article entitled "Those Wonderful Ladies" without whom many institutions could not thrive. One such to be recognized is my loyal and devoted executive aide, Sallie Coyle. Without her extra time including many week ends and her sage supervision this book could not have been brought to fruition.

TABLE OF CONTENTS

PART ONE

THE DISAPPEARING AMERICAN

A Personal Narrative on
America's Disappearing Culture
and Her Future

INTRODUCTION

This narrative could have had another title. It could have been called "The Life and Distresses of a Twentieth Century Professional". Or it could have been named simply "The Disappearing American", as a sort of narrative on the modern era. Yet people are tired of hearing America being bashed, and "disappearing" might sound negative. Because I am optimistic I have called it "The Reappearing American" with the objective of influencing you, your children, and my children and grandchildren.

It is said that each person is a product of all that he has surveyed. One single person, one single chance experience, one book, may re-direct a person's life completely. This has proven true of numerous encounters in my life. Therefore, maybe my story can inspire, can provoke and stimulate others to utilize that special quality, the human mind.

There may be many who will disagree with some of my conclusions, particularly as they pertain to the future of America and to our earth or world at large. That is not unhealthy, because any teacher can only inspire and challenge, whereas it remains for the individual to learn. Thus, I will try to expose the reader to provoking ideas. If others find food for thought, and perhaps learn something they did not know, my goal will have been accomplished.

The idea for this book germinated for many years. It started in 1958 with the death of my father. With his passing, it appeared to me that he had represented a whole era in "American" culture. His life, almost that of a pioneer in rural America, is taken as an example of the thinking and the processes which I experienced first hand.

Ideas for this book accumulated and were collected during my world travels over the past 40 years. Consequently, it was organized much as my good friend the author and playwright Robert Ardrey suggested, as a three-act play. It was decided to make the first act my experiences as a youth, my observations and some of the characters I knew as a young lad on an Indiana farm.

The second act represents the transformation of America that occurred with World War II, through the first-hand knowledge of the changes witnessed, and the role America was forced to assume following that disastrous world occurrence. It also includes personal experiences in my professional life.

The last act deals with roughly the 1990s and the future -- the "Reappearing American" and the "New Renaissance".

Although the year is now 1993, the present is considered to comprise essentially the past 20 years, or since 1970. We examine the current forces at work in the world, which probably will mold our future, and further make speculations or scenarios regarding our destiny.

Human existence is but a small blip on earth's antiquity. Homo sapiens' supremacy started with the freeing of his hands for signals and the development of the larynx for vocal communication. Imagination and human ability to learn sets man and woman apart. Human endurance by bipedal locomotion and social altruism were other factors in their ascendance. It would seem impossible that while man-like creatures' fossil remains almost ten to fourteen million years old are found, it was only ten thousand years ago that agriculture and the use of animals for energy was evident. It wasn't until six thousand years ago that people grouped into villages and cities. It is speculated that about then the communal building of the pyramids was principally for the unification of the state. The making of paper and printing started only about five hundred years ago.

A mere two hundred years ago marked the industrial revolution as machines came to be used for energy. Manufacturing processes promoted extensive commerce. About one hundred years ago the dental field discovered anesthesia. Only fifty years ago the binary system was adapted to electronics and the cybercultural revolution began which, with computers and television, has restructured societies in the entire world.

Your author, for almost half a century, has been a person working in the health care services. As a scientific investigator in orthodontics, which dealt with craniofacial deformities and locomotor problems of the head and jaws, I have experienced many social aspects of humanity in my work on the human face.

Mankind's face is a window to the world. It attracts or repulses, it shows happiness or sorrow. The head is free of clothing, to see, hear, smell, breathe, eat, smile, talk and, yes, even to engage in love-making. The jaws dominate the face because the upper jaw bones support the eyes. The jaws are barometers of human distress and repressed feelings as tension is released through clenching and grinding. No small wonder, therefore, that a professional person involved with the diagnosis and treatment of such a highly personal component of the body would naturally become a student of human nature and be concerned with social science interfaces.

Most of the lay public may consider the doctor to be somewhat separated from such major problems as politics, economics, and the other aspects of the social sciences. Although the psychologist and psychiatrist delve deeply into problems of human affairs, most professionals would just as soon leave social problems alone and continue to practice the science and the art of their profession.

At the final preparation of this writing I am 72 years old. Perhaps fortuitously but by necessity I delayed a year going to college after high school, and experienced the drudgery and sometimes the social degradation that possibly may accompany those involved in hard manual labor. Because I had a strong body, it appeared that one avenue that I might pursue to get a college education was through football. Although I had been an honor student in grade school, I had pretty much given up hope of ever achieving a college education and neglected high school scholastically. But the experience of poorly rewarded labor drove me into seeking education as an escape from that kind of drudgery.

A secret desire to be a dentist became, in the end, a passion. Due to the commitment and energy and expense involved, I took college education seriously, and very early decided to specialize. Also, my exposure to the plight of the farmer in the great crash of 1929 and the subsequent depression of the thirties made an indelible mark on my attitude or work ethic. After serving in World War II in both the Army and the Navy, I was finally able to pursue, at the age of 27, a graduate education and research which was to occupy my next five years. By chance, this work was in a critical field, and I became exposed in a very short time to virtually all the leaders in the orthodontic specialty as well as other branches of dentistry and medicine.

After my research fellowship was completed, and after about twelve years of private practice, many colleagues sought to learn of the new developments I had made. Due to requests I started teaching private advanced courses in 1963. Some of my students came to label me "the missing link" because of my acquaintance with so many of the older, significant people in the profession, and saw me as a sort of a link with the past and a platform for the present and future.

Throughout my career, despite the intensity of my studies, I have tried to stay abreast of current issues in politics, economics, and social problems in our culture as well as questions in my profession. Many anecdotes grew out of the process of originating and championing ideas and the struggle in gaining their acceptance. Consequently, many of my students, after our discussions lasting into the wee hours of the morning, would ask why I didn't write a personal account and record my experiences. I really didn't think that many outside the profession would have such interest. But in discussing it with laymen it became clear that my point of view and experiences might be of value, at least on a historical basis. I have never been reluctant to express my opinion when I felt it was worth something and when I had done my homework. I therefore debated in my mind just how to write an effective story and still project some of the broader ideas of a professional person. Thus, this book is a personal narrative that includes the life and the experience of others, together with many significant events as they have affected my life, which formed the matrix for this writing.

Look Only Ahead

As with evolution, we can never go backward. The world can never be as it was yesterday. And neither can America. Despite people's hope of going back to "the good old days", we will look to "the good new days".

Throughout my career I have been the eternal optimist. If I had accepted the restrictions, limitations and derision of others, my contributions would never have been made. In fact, negative ideas are not only limiting but completely unhealthful. Positive ideas and altruism are a hallmark for health and longevity. There is an old saying: "Just do it." So I "just did it". Procrastination breeds uncertainty and fosters frustration. I am therefore not pessimistic, and the last section is accordingly called "The Reappearing American".

I ask a pardon for using "American" as synonymous with the United States. Both North and South America are Americas, and no elimination of those friends, both to the North and to the South, is intended.

May this book, therefore, serve to help in my fellow man's happiness and help potentiate goodness and help bring out the best in all of us.

R. M. R.

1

A DISAPPEARING CHARACTER

On the morning of October 14, 1958, at 3:00 A.M., I was awakened by a phone call from "back home in Indiana" informing me of my father's coronary attack. I was immersed in a seminar meeting of the Dental Medicine Institute at Palm Springs, California which each year is headed by leading men of the biologic sciences from the U.S. and abroad. It was only a moment until the full reckoning of the phone call struck me. I quickly gathered myself for a speedy drive back to Los Angeles, phoning my wife to arrange air passage to Kokomo. I kept reminding myself of the good possibilities of recovery in spite of the poor reports on Dad's condition.

Flying Eastward, back over Palm Springs, thoughts of my fellow seminarians passed through my mind. It had been my good fortune to befriend many older scholars in our fields of allied medical research. Most were mellowed with age and had the dignity and sophistication coupled with deep modesty and humility that basic research ultimately yields to the investigator of the life sciences. All were great men. I had often experienced the isolation from everyday problems of life that deep concentration in a chosen profession affords. The shock of sudden reality, of near death to one dear, sobered me from the intoxication brought on by ever-consuming challenges and the necessities of daily routine. By the time we were over the Grand Canyon, I was sufficiently motivated to put down on paper, even if only for myself, my feelings for my father.

A glance over my shoulder revealed one of our country's statesmen (Everett Dirkson) too engrossed in rehearsing a bold-typed speech to even look up. Then my thoughts again turned, by comparison, to my father's niche in life. He, too, in my opinion, was a great American but one who is of a breed that I'm afraid is rapidly disappearing from the American scene.

The life of my father must be pieced together from experiences he told me about during my years of growing up on the farm just south of Kokomo, Indiana. His father had been among the early settlers of Howard County. He boasted of his father's disregard for the frivolities of life and his open woolen shirt in the cold of winter. He recounted the times my grandfather, going to town, allegedly on business, would throw a sack of potatoes on the rear of the buggy for the Browns or the Grays because things "weren't too well" with them. He also mentioned my grandfather's love for a story and the friendship of neighbors which characterized the early Hoosier in those days. Many of these traits were passed on to my father.

Charles Murray Ricketts was born on October 26, 1884. He was born in a homestead log cabin to which through the years had been added occasional rooms, so that it became a rather typical large Indiana farm house. I remember the old place, no running water but earlier an inside pump with a large handle standing at one corner of the old kitchen. This room eventually had to be demolished because it slipped down a hill and pulled away from the old log cabin, exposing the logs. Opposite the pump was a large wood-burning cooking range which we gathered around early on cold mornings to warm our clothes before putting them on. Life had no false pretenses. The chore of cutting wood and stacking it near the range was a daily affair. This had been part of my father's young life, and it was part of mine too, in the same house. The old log cabin stood until it was leveled by a tornado in the 1950s. It was inhabited for more than 100 years.

Dad had a proud inheritance. His grandfather on his mother's side, Joseph Murray, was a brigadier general of the 89th Infantry in the Civil War and first editor of the "Howard Tribune", later to become the present "Kokomo Tribune" newspaper. He was also Kokomo's first lawyer. My grandfather Joseph had a beard, as did many people in that era, and never wore a tie. He also chewed tobacco, the juice of which would freeze in his beard in winter time. He was a farmer and a trader of horses and just about anything else he could make a profit on. He was an extremely good neighbor, and very well liked.

My grandfather came from a large family which produced four Methodist ministers and one girl who wedded Benjamin Harrison, a son of President William Henry Harrison. Dad's great grandfather was sent to Logansport, Indiana by the government to deal with the Indians at about the time Indiana was admitted to the Union in 1816.

When my father was age 14, his father died, leaving him (the oldest of three boys) to be the breadwinner for the family. My father had gone through the first grade of high school. He "allowed" he was the fastest runner and the strongest boy in the school, which he later proved by his activities and stamina as a man throughout his productive life.

Taking over a farm of 120 acres in those days was no simple matter. He recalled that Uncle John Martindale and some old horses were all that he inherited. Uncle John and Aunt Judy were two older black people who had been slaves. They followed some neighbors north into Indiana after the Civil War. Dad often described those days of plowing corn, raising pigs and trying to do a man's job with only Uncle John to help. From that time on Dad always had a soft spot for black people. They called him Mr. Ricketts, with great respect. He always had stories for them and he often remarked there were no others who could laugh like black people.

Dad's mother had become an invalid when he was 14 years of age. At that time she sought a hired girl, and found Eva Ann Jones, who also had an invalid mother and who could care for both older people at once. This hired girl later was to become Dad's wife and my mother.

During my childhood on the farm, it was not uncommon to have friends call uninvited and unannounced. In fact, our doors had no locks and there was not even a door on the privy. When a neighbor or friend dropped in during dinner, Dad would cut off a piece of whatever he was eating and holding it with a fork at arm's length he would greet the visitor with "Here, get your mouth around that and pull up a chair." Then we would sit by the hour, which Dad called "A Ricketts Minute", and listen to stories and that true-to-life slapstick so typical of Hoosier farmers. Some of those conversations would make some of our best comedians hang their heads in shame. I remember laughing until tears filled our eyes.

The family Bible and a Christian faith were common in this small midwest city.

Grandma, who I never saw, had been a steady member at the Congregational Church and had instilled a faith, lasting moral quality, and goodness in my father. The struggle for existence for a large family was manifested in the need for double mortgages on the farm in those days.

So after twelve long years of toil and directly after his mother had passed on, Dad finally married Eva. He sold a whole load of straw to a neighbor for $2.00 so he could get the marriage license. This was on Christmas Eve, 1910. Dad was 26, Mom was 30. They were blessed with six children. I, the fifth, arrived on May 5, 1920. All the others were born in the winter or fall. Mom always said I was her "little spring flower".

Children, the World War I years, a small farm with inadequate tools, and a heavy mortgage brought its problems. However, there was no lack of spirit. In spite of meager surroundings and a dearth of worldly goods, few were happier than Dad and few could count as many friends.

Dad loved to sing. He belonged to a small chorus and later led the choir of Trinity Methodist Church in Southeast Kokomo. Regular attendance was a requirement, even to the Thursday evening prayer meetings. The church social was one of my most pleasant boyhood experiences. Sunday School parties with softball, potato sack races and horseshoe pitching contests were all entered into by Dad. His loud full laugh could be heard above everyone else. A generosity of life, love and friendship became his trademark.

Tragedy struck in 1926 when my oldest brother died of spinal meningitis at age 14 following an infected blood clot in his leg after an accidental kick on the thigh in a basketball game. The church rallied around our family.

By the late 1920s Dad had almost gotten his breath financially. He rented land and hired help and had a stable of work horses. He and his brother, my Uncle Tom (who lived with us) had started a dairy right after World War I and had just about reached financial success when the Depression struck. I was only nine at the time but I remember it in detail. Dad had insisted on getting good basic stock for his herd of Holstein cows and talked about some day turning over a big dairy to "us kids". He had invested all available income back into the business. But, by 1932 he was forced to sell at a disheartening loss. During this time, also, he and Tom had invested in a threshing machine and tractors and led a "threshing ring", which was a sort of cooperative for harvesting grain. One of my jobs as a very young boy was milking 10 of the cows two times daily.

Farming in those "Depression days" was a losing venture. Products could not be sold for the cost of growing them. More crops generated by harder and longer hours led only to greater losses. Being on the farm, we never went hungry but never had much variety most of the time. We raised soup beans and sold them for two cents per pound. People would walk out from town to buy warm fresh milk for eight cents a gallon. Dad prided himself on always giving a little extra. He said, "Never cheat anyone." We used this small income to subsist on. All other profits still went for mortgages and debts accumulated prior to the Depression.

Dad, being a native of Kokomo, had received a Republican discipline. He emphasized the benefits of freedom and free enterprise with the idea that each person was responsible for their own economic welfare and their own moral conduct. He also had a genuine civic interest and a sense of responsibility which eventually led him into local politics. He became a county commissioner in the 1930s. It was a minor post with practically no pay which he held for six years. Later, during the Roosevelt years, he was defeated for County Sheriff, which he thought he could handle through his knowledge of county and local laws.

Through his experience Dad was a butcher, a veterinarian, a mechanic and a dairyman. I remember his going out at cold midnight to tend the cattle during the birth of their young.

I remember butchering hogs and rendering lard. I remember his crawling into a threshing machine with only bailing wire and pliers and in short order having everything humming again. I remember his coming home at night so dirty you wouldn't know him, and tired to the bone. Yet he possessed a spirit and faith in God that seemed to radiate about him. He had a certain quiet confidence that many years of experiences had brought.

Dad was the head of the table. I remember his saying he had the boys sit on either side of him so he could "back-hand" both of us at the same time. But it was never necessary. He had the capacity to be an impartial judge among the children and always seemed to know where the true fault lay in a dispute. He was never quick to stop a fight between my brother Jim and me. I always felt he thought a good spat made men of both of us. Even so, he was a strict disciplinarian. At seventeen I was felled by a blow to the side of the head when I rudely challenged his judgment on one occasion. We all respected him and loved him beyond description. Inside his character he was so generous and so good, no one could dislike him that knew him.

His respect for truth and righteousness were always with him. As children we were never permitted to go to a movie or play cards on Sunday. But he loved the card game Euchre. He could be heard howling over a close hand and would review the play ad nauseam. However, I never knew him to bet on anything. Being a staunch Methodist, he never drank, but he smoked regularly. I can't remember ever hearing him swear in the presence of the family.

My uncle Tom died in 1933 of acute appendicitis. During this bleakest year, it was suggested to my father that he let the farm go by bankruptcy and get a fresh start elsewhere. We were down to almost nothing. We had no tractors and only three mules to tend 80 acres. Dad called my brother Jim and me together and laid everything before us. He explained what a difficult time we would have in "saving" everything. I was just 13 and Jim was almost 12. I honestly believe that serious year, at the age of 13, gave me the fortitude that has since taken me through several crises.

I never saw a man put out so much. Dad worked in a slaughterhouse when he wasn't in the fields. He kept his faith in spite of hours that would break an average man's will. He had one mule (Sam) drop dead in his harness in the field. We were desperate. Dad said he hoped we boys would never have to work so hard again in our whole lifetime. Our family was never so close. We all came through; and that fall Dad made a downpayment on a small tractor.

As time went on we turned to "truck farm" produce. We raised peas, tomatoes, and sweet corn for canning and survived with the old farm still ours. Dad went into politics again in 1938, running for Assessor of the township, and was elected by a wide margin. He stayed in office for 12 years.

I was extremely proud of Dad during those years. This job was not tremendous pay, but it was more than that to which we had been accustomed. Our prayers were with Dad as he took over the work of Assessor with dedication. Through his long life in this beloved community he had seen Kokomo develop into quite an industrial center for a small Indiana town. He remembered meeting Elwood Haynes during the "horseless carriage" era only a mile or so from our home. He remembered the first rubber tire and many new industrial firsts in this small city which came to be known as the "City of Firsts".

Most of all, Dad loved people. He tried to be fair in all his transactions. Through his efforts, assessments on improved property never before taxed were sought and brought in. He was able to reduce the tax rate by fair distribution to everyone. Obvious schemers got nowhere in their efforts to procure unwarranted reductions of their rightful obligations. His acceptance of duty and his ability to carry it out were witnessed by the fact that thirty to forty people worked under him, some of them with college degrees. He had a broad understanding of history and government, and could quote the law to the individual page.

During years while he was in the assessor's office, I graduated from high school and sought my way to college. Both Jim and I played basketball and football, and I'm sure helped realize some of the dreams that Dad had for us. I went on to play football at Indiana University, and during the latter part of my freshman year came home for some advice from Dad. I remember well sitting at the old family table with Mom and Dad discussing whether or not I should try for Dental School. Dad probably gave me the soundest advice I could have had. He said, "Bobby, you have gone through high school and now one year of college. I went to the first grade of high school. This is your choice. It's a question of your ambition. If you want to do it, go after it. Mom and I are behind you all the way, but you know how little we can help. You should be in a better position to judge for yourself than we are. My only advice is to do 'what's right'. We've always tried to teach you and want you to do what's right. If you do that, then we can't expect more."

How much confidence these words gave! It made me search for the kind of effort that just doesn't come naturally. It gave me courage to face my own problems with my Dad choosing now to be in the background as a solid moral support. This was necessary to build the character for my competitive life as a student and scholar in my later life. This deep concern for truth and right, for which I am genuinely thankful, were later to kindle the curiosity that led to my career as a researcher in my chosen profession.

One experience of my father in the last years of his public office, however, brought home to me the intense cruelty of some thoughtless and selfish people. The tax rates in Indiana had been changed by the State Congress and the whole state had to be reassessed and reevaluated. People thought that their taxes would all be doubled, not thinking far enough ahead to see that everyone's evaluation would change, and that all would be fair in the end because all communities would now be evaluated on a par. Inadvertently, one of Dad's deputies made a mistake in one block and overtaxed a group of people. The error was soon discovered and corrected. But some saw fit to use this as a tool to stir up public sentiment and aroused the whole town. Dad was called in the middle of the night by ugly, unkind people. He was sworn at and ridiculed to the point of near breakdown. After almost twenty years of devoted public service where honesty had been his pledge, to have false accusations of this kind made, even though explained in the papers, was enough to break the average person.

Yet Dad forgave. He withdrew from public life, being defeated the following year. For years after, to my recollection, he never had the old fire and spirit and human warmth that epitomized him prior to this public slander.

A rather fortunate event occurred at about this time, however. Kokomo was growing and our farm was in the line of expansion toward Indianapolis. Finally, after about 45 years of mortgage indebtedness, Dad sold a part of the farm, paid off the remaining debt, and had enough left to build a nice small modern home with running water for himself and Mother. Later they were able to make other land sales and Dad and Mom were comfortable in their last years.

The thought occurred to me that here was a real American, a person so typical of the kind of fortitude it has taken to create the America she became. God help me, I prayed, to be such a credit to myself, to my parents and to my community. If it weren't for that background I'm sure I wouldn't have that core of character that I hope I possess and display.

I can't help feeling that our children today are just as anxious to help and just as intent to do right as ever. But are we, as parents and adults, by example leading them the right way? Are we losing the grit and sinew that made America what it is? Is there some way that an allegiance to principle and right can be maintained? Does it take catastrophe or hazard to bring this out in us?

* * *

These were my rambling thoughts as I sat on the airplane going back to Indiana, now crossing Iowa and Illinois. (Remember, these were days before jets and twelve hours were needed for the journey.)

My father will never be listed by the historians in Who's Who or The Country Club Gold Cup Brigade. But he was a living example of a real human being and a real man. Measured by standards of truth, honesty and faith and charity, no one was greater.

In the present day, when our standards for success have been so tainted by prestigious automobiles, large homes and impressive bank rolls, maybe his life will serve to quiet us in our greed for money and its false sense of human worth. The qualities of outgoing love, kindliness and respect for opposite views are indeed everlastingly refreshing. But at the same time the rigid discipline for ideals and the hard core that makes a man a man and a woman a woman are needed to prevent this character from disappearing from the American scene altogether.

* * *

Dad's courage and faith were manifested in his struggle during the next few weeks after his heart attack. He had confidence in his physician and comfort and support from his family, church and friends. He held his own but was, according to the hospital records, in extremely critical condition.

Three weeks later, on November 7, 1958, I again visited Dad at the hospital. His condition was improved, but still special nurses were required. We talked freely at this time, and I had the opportunity, thank God, to express to Dad personally my deep love and appreciation for all that he had done and meant to me.

This visit was immediately following a local and state election. Dad had been defeated for a minor advisory post of County Councilman, which had no opposition in the primary. The Democrats had swept the country by storm and the "right to work" had been defeated in Indiana. The dominance of organized labor was apparent. Always believing in free enterprise and asking for no favors or handouts in spite of living in as hard conditions as faced by anyone, Dad was deeply concerned about the long-term future of our country.

"Did the people really know what they voted for when they did this?" he asked. "What is all this going to lead to? Can't they see this is not our way - but socialism? The more they ask for, the more it's going to cost everyone. How will we ever pay the debt? It's going to bankrupt our country. Taxes will escalate and we will lose foreign trade. Oh! I'm so tired of talking this way, People don't listen. And those workers, all they think about is themselves and strike, strike, strike! It's going to ruin our country as we have known it."

I agreed with Dad and told him he must rest and not think about anything but getting well. We discussed California and his deep-sea fishing trip with me about two years earlier when he had caught a nice yellowtail just off the Coronado Islands. He froze the head and took it back to Indiana as proof of his catch. He recalled that visit to California to see his new grandson, Craig. The fishing, the drive through the Mojave Desert, and the flowers in my community of Pacific Palisades were the most pleasant memories of a trip that he ever had. I was so happy to have shared it with him before it was too late even though it was very short.

* * *

On December 14, 1958, I was again called back to Kokomo for the final visit. Just two months after his bad attack Dad had passed on in his sleep with his arm around Mother.

In turn, Mother, at age 78, had a collapse and was taken to the hospital in complete shock. She couldn't attend Dad's funeral but insisted on being carried to see him before he was buried. Her life was as colorful as was Dad's, as I will describe later.

As many Democrats paid their respects as Republicans, which was token of the esteem they held him in. Catholics, Jews, Gentiles, and black people all showed their regard for him. How many times I heard it said, "I've never heard a bad word about your Dad."

On Dad's grave it should read:

> Here lies Murray Ricketts, a Great American.
> His life characterizes the hard core and strength
> that has made America during the first half of
> the twentieth century. His human qualities of faith,
> love, hope, and charity were an example for
> all to follow.

2

THE SECRET AMERICAN STRENGTH —WOMEN

The Magnificent Lady

There were several instances reflecting love in our family life which I remember. One particular happening that stands out vividly reflected the joy around our "supper" table. In the 1920s we ran a dairy and two or three young men would "live in" and work for their board and room plus a small wage. They would eat with the family which, when all were together, would frequently add up to 13 or 14 eating at the same time. Naturally, the food was simple. Potatoes and gravy, home-cured ham, chicken, pork and beef, and mince pie were popular items in the winter. In the summer it was our own vegetables and canned meats except for chicken.

Jokes would pass back and forth, and every so often we would have a "laughing jag". Have you ever been caught laughing with someone and then got hysterical laughing at the others laughing until tears rolled down your cheeks? Well, we did! I remember one of the helpers who actually fell off his chair onto the floor, holding his stomach in fits of laughter.

Can you imagine a mother planning for and feeding that many people three times daily? Can you further imagine doing it without gas or electric heat, without running water and, most of all, without a refrigerator or even an ice box? Would it not take the deepest love of a woman to repeat that performance day after day without a moment's hesitation and without a word of malice? How could my mother have done it without the strength that love gave her?

* * *

Eva Ann Jones Ricketts

Mom was born in 1880. I asked her one time what she knew about her parents. "Not much," she said. "All I know is that my father was a pauper."

Although I never saw any of my grandparents, I knew that Grandpa Henry Jones once worked at the Pittsburgh Plate Glass factory in Kokomo; he was an unskilled laborer and died in middle age. "What about your mom?" I asked. "Well, she was an ordinary person too." And then she didn't want to go on much about Grandma Jones. Perhaps a little background may explain why.

When I was a child growing up in Indiana there were still Indians (Native Americans) around. They didn't sleep in tepees or live in tribes, but were generally workers on farms. One such was Arch O'Banion, whom I befriended while a boy. He liked to "kid around" and tell me stories.

Arch liked to hunt crow. Most people won't eat crow meat because it's bony and not very tasteful. But he ate almost any wild animal he could catch or shoot. He had a full regalia of feathers and headdresses, and I loved to be with him on a crow hunt. He had an old rifle and had to be very close to a crow to hit it. I would accompany him to the woods where we would lie low in bushes. He would then start calling the crows into range by mimicking one injured. When the crows would land in a nearby tree, curious to see what was the trouble, he would shoot them in the head so he would not damage the carcass.

This old Indian also had a bow and some arrows which I never saw him use. Hung on the walls of his little one-room house were trappings, with buckskins, moccasins and all. What a thrill to coax him into dressing up and doing his "war dance" for me alone, which he did a couple of times. My mother often scolded me for bothering him so much. But I loved the old guy and he loved me. He was always so exciting. I was saddened to learn of the early death of this old friend.

One year the church had a costume party at Halloween. Dad borrowed Arch O'Banion's paraphernalia and painted his face. He did an Indian dance that looked like the real thing and won the contest.

During the early 1900s many people of European ancestry held the Indian people in low regard. This disdain is still depicted in some of the movies of the old West.

One reason Mom never talked much about her mother was that she was part Blackfoot Indian -- a part of the Algonquin nation. My high cheek bones are very dominant and my daughter Gale has teeth very much like those characteristic of the Indian race. Genetics reasserts itself! I'm proud of that small legacy.

If a person had Indian heritage in the 1880s it wasn't exactly a social advantage, even around Kokomo which got its name from an Indian chief of the tribe "Kokomocus". This was when Indiana was first settled and the swamps were drained and the forests were cleared for farming. Indiana had earlier been a part of the French territory. Our street, La Fountaine, was named after an Indian chief named in turn after a Frenchman.

The Native Americans were tough people living in nature and respecting her. Maybe that's where Mom got her resilience and persistence. She only went through the seventh grade in school because she had to stop and go to work. She couldn't travel to high school, so she took the seventh grade twice. When Mom was 12 she became a hired girl at my grandfather Ricketts' farm just three miles south of the center of Kokomo. When she arrived my Dad was only eight years old, and she always said she raised him. My grandfather had acquired about 200 acres of land and had one son by a first marriage. When his wife died he married again and had three more sons, with my Dad the eldest.

Therefore, when Mom came to work as a hired girl, living with the family, she had to care for Murray (age 8), and also Edward (age 5), and Thomas (age 3). After she had worked for some years her father died and her mother became an invalid, so she returned to her home to care for her mother.

In 1898, when my father was 14, his father died and left him as the family's breadwinner. Murray, in the ninth grade, was forced to quit school in order to run the farm. Later his mother, my Grandma Ricketts, became ill. Thereupon, Dad went to get the girl who would become my mother, together with her mother, Grandma Jones, to live with them so that Mom -- who was then 18 years old -- could have a job and care for both the older women.

According to Mom's conversations, Grandma Ricketts never thought a hired girl was good enough for her son. Therefore, as recounted in Chapter One, Dad's courtship with Mom lasted 12 years. In 1910 they got married and proceeded to have six children; I was the fifth, born when my mother was 40.

At the time of their wedding, she was 30 and Dad was 26. Mom swore there was never any hanky-panky in all those twelve years and I believed her. What a contrast today!

Mom -- the Bonding Substance

Life on a poor Indiana farm in those years was not easy. Mom made our soap with fats and lye, churned our butter, canned our meat in the winter and "packed" our fruits and vegetables in the summer. I remember her, dripping wet with sweat, boiling the cottons and linens in the heat of the summer on the old cooking range. She bore and raised us in that environment, as well as cooking and washing for my Uncle Tom and the helpers who lived with us. She could lift a ten-gallon can of milk in each hand at the same time. She was strong! And she could bend over and touch both her palms to the floor at the age of 70.

Mom's life was devoted totally to the family but she would never tolerate any "sassing" whatsoever. I remember the evenings when she would recite poetry to us and read us novels. She was intelligent and wise and often wrote her own poetry. Where she got her knowledge no one knew. We could ask her how to spell almost any word and she would be correct. Teachers must have taught a lot in the first seven years of school around 1890.

Memorable Occasions

Other occasions that stand out in my memory are the cold winter nights around the old pot-bellied stove. Dad would shout, "Who wants popcorn?" We all loved to nibble, but better yet we loved the getting together that the occasion presented. We raised our own popcorn and kept it in tightly sealed barrels to keep out the rats. Dad would get the corn and "shell" it from the cob while my older sisters would heat up a skillet and melt the butter. We would all gather around to hear the happy sound of the corn bursting and the rattle of the popper against the kerosene stove as it was shaken with a rhythm of the whole body. Popping corn was an art. Anyone who left some unpopped kernels or burned the popped kernels just "didn't have it". We didn't stop with a small amount of corn, but only when a large dishpan was filled. Then came the butter and salt and tossing. Finally, and all together, we took it in large serving bowls and sat around a warm stove joking and chomping the corn. Sometimes we had an apple along with it. We often wisecracked and cajoled those who might have fallen short of a perfect popper of corn. Yes, that was family activity and family love. It was joyful no matter how many times it was redone. Mom, through it all, was the organizer and the glue that held us together.

Apparently my mother had inquired from our grade school teachers what books should be read to us children. Our school teachers also taught our Sunday School classes and advised my parents to read as a family. I remember listening to whole books like "Oliver Twist", "The Little Shepherd of Kingdom Come" and "Ben Hur". Mother would read until her eyes would tire in the dim light of the kerosene lamp and then Dad would take over. I remember laughing together at the funny episodes but I remember, too, how Mom would turn the reading over to Dad when her eyes would be too filled with tears to go on over a sad or sympathetic situation.

Playing and Staying Together

We also played games together. Checkers, dominoes, and various card games were well known to us by school age. Mom liked dominoes and checkers but never cards. Our favorite card game was Euchre and we would argue to be Dad's partner. He would always love to "set you" and would bid on almost impossible hands. He would get more fun out of five cards than anyone you ever saw. After each hand, if he lost, he would replay the hand and see what should have been done. Of course he would never confess to making a bad bid in the first place.

We played other card games, but we never considered gambling. This was unthinkable, just as it was unthinkable to ask to play any kind of game on Sundays. That was the Lord's Day. No movies were permitted on Sundays either. However, during the week the whole family might go to "a show" when possibly enough had been saved to do so. Mom never seemed to have enough time for movies, therefore generally when we did go Dad would take us, and even that was a family activity. I remember the scolding Dad got from Mom one time. Dad had taken my brother and me to see "Tarzan and the Apes". This was the one where Tarzan (Johnny Weismuller) fought a crocodile and rode on the back of a rhinoceros. We went early in order to get cheap seats and to return home early. We stayed to see the same picture three times. It was midnight when we got home and Mom was worried. Dad sheepishly explained that "the boys wanted to see it again and get our money's worth."

In the hot Indiana summer evenings, we would sometimes get in the old car and go for a cooling ride with the family. A "ride" consisted of only a few miles, starting out with a look at our crops and going around to see how the neighbors' crops were coming. Sometimes there was a refreshing stop at a flowing well where cold "rotten egg" water was always available.

Even with all this love, however, we knew our limits. We never had to learn respect for authority because it came so naturally. We never had to learn respect for older people because we respected their example and their attention. We never had to learn respect for God because Nature was always a part of our life. We also respected other people's property because we knew how hard it was to come by. We were never permitted to even think about talking back, but we weren't really tempted because we knew that with the love of our parents their thoughts and actions were always in our best interest.

I often wonder what effect the lack of a family will have in the way of love, companionship and mutual respect in our future generations. The father in many urban cultures often comes home to a fast martini as the mother is hurrying to throw a meal together in the microwave, while the kids remain glued to television, learning the latest jingle on junk foods.

* * *

The Country in 1968
On July 31, 1968, ten years after that memorable conversation with my father told in Chapter One, I had just visited my semi-invalid mother in a rest home. We celebrated her 88th birthday with a party at my brother's home, which she attended together with the whole family. As I sat cramped in a loaded jet en route back to Los Angeles, my seatmates -- apparently a man and wife -- were taking turns with continuous cigarettes, the smoke of which clouded our small area. I wondered, as they made a ceremony over the cigarette, with alcohol added, if they realized others were being offended. I thought to myself that non-smokers were as much entitled to clean air on a flight as these people were to choke me with their smoke. There was not even the courtesy of asking if smoke bothered me. (Thank goodness that has changed. For years, as a doctor, I wrote airline presidents regarding being choked by smokers in flights.)

As I reflected on the changes taking place, it seemed the whole country had become extensively selfish and preoccupied with personal comfort and welfare at the price of courtesy and a constructive culture. Here we were, a country ostensibly altruistic toward underdeveloped countries all over the world, but we were losing humanity and grace to those touching our elbow. I wondered further at that time about the future plight of my beloved country. I recalled those concerns and predictions that prevailed in that last conversation with the old "disappearing American" just a decade before.

The country in 1968 was deep in its longest and most controversial war, in Vietnam. Fear of crime and wanton destruction of private property raged in our midst. Inflation was sapping our strength and tearing at the heart of our economy. We had lost our identity to a social security number. The grip of a socialized-like government appeared to be as malignant as a cancer. People demanded services of all kinds. Liberalism and freedom were words used without understanding. Liberalism had come to mean looseness, and freedom was extended to include elimination of compliance with law and order.

The answers to problems of racial and ethnic conflict, a social dilemma in most cultures, were sought only in economic or materialistic gains. "Liberalization" seemed to further imply efforts toward more government control and more socialism. This was leading to heavier and heavier taxation on the public, and truly a greater loss of freedoms while regulations piled up.

Juveniles were rightly rebelling against an older society considered to be hypocritical. Narcotic drugs were being used to what to me appeared an inconceivable and incredible extent. Both young and older age groups had increased alcoholic consumption. We were in the midst of a divorce culture. The "man" at the head of the family was all but lost. Rearing and discipline was relinquished to fawning "Spockian" mothers, or to inexperienced, uninterested or overworked school teachers.

Violence was everywhere -- the traditional ideals of philosophy hammered out of 4,000 years of history were being buried. Religion was a mockery as liberal ministers spread and propagandized socialism in the name of a God who many claimed to be "dead".

Newsworthy was the settling of several strikes. Football players already averaging comparatively high salaries struck for benefits into the year 2000. Steel workers were granted uncontested raises of three to four times more than hourly wages had been twenty years before. We forget that a copper strike cost the United States over a billion dollars in lost taxable revenues in addition to the purchase of 400 million dollars' worth of foreign metal. The Congress limited our personal spending abroad, which meant more bureaucracy.

Worst of all, it had become clear that even the legislators on Capitol Hill had lost control of the government. Even contact with the reality of many movements afoot was not recognized by our Congressmen. The left hand was totally out of touch with the right. Factions prevailed in a "Pentagon struggle", one for withdrawal and defeat in Vietnam, the other for quick victory.

All this was present in 1968! Where was the family going?

* * *

Polarization

By the 1970s, the country was polarizing rapidly, not specifically into political parties but into ideologies. Moves to the extremes seemed to be the direction, with no middle course any longer acceptable. The young working force had "too much pride" to become apprentice laborers. The fear of Communism was a laugh to the youth, but the record spoke cold facts in favor of the freedom fighter. There was a spread of unrest by political agitators at every opportunity. Patriotism and national respect were replaced by scorn, long beards, a dirty shirt and smelly body.

The lustful male and the willing female exemplified society. A sense of frustration and hopelessness permeated the public. At the same time the future was awesome in perspective. "The Pill" had come, and in the mind of the Pope it should have been stopped. Conservatism, as a backlash to liberalism's extremists, was on the rise as people looked for better experience and leadership. The hand of unionization power spread ever more widely over every labor segment. Criminal elements such as the Mafia were known to invest now in legitimate big business in order to camouflage their true character. Jimmy Hoffa, as a leader in the union movement, allegedly was a part of this development. The black race cried for jobs, while the union restricted its members in order to control its wages.

Prudent investments no longer were based on sound principles but rather on the gamble of a frenzied speculative public, aimed at beating heavy taxes. **Pride and perfection in work and a good day's labor were no longer virtues.**

People working in government employment ridiculed the salesman and the business person who "pounded the freeway" to make profits. At the same time educators shouted for more funds and higher taxes for their own interests.

Gold reserves at Fort Knox dwindled. Many foreigners were gleeful at the big U.S. failure in economics and world politics. The Communists were all smiles and rubbed their hands in delight.

Moral Drift

Love was defined as a lay on the beach. In our capital city, one-third of the newborns were illegitimate.

Such was the situation in Johnson's "Great Society". It's true we had economic affluence, but we had raised generations without a culture to be proud of. It was the permissive society. The family as an institution generally in our culture was deteriorating. Family values were scorned by the very people shouting for liberalism.

It was argued that times had changed. Indeed they had. But really, are the instinctual needs of mankind any different than those of 5000 years ago? I think not. Any biologist knows that evolution is very slow. Our psychologic and biologic needs are fundamentally fixed, as I shall explain in later chapters.

It was true, we traveled faster, and relatively more cheaply; we had more comforts at home; we had faster communication and all the problems of the world were laid instantly at our feet. McLuhan defined news as bad happenings while the reporting of the good was considered to be propaganda. We were bombarded constantly by reports of death, accidents, fires, hurricanes, rapes and murders, while the good was often classed as advertisement.

Advertising itself was scarcely believed, and the news medium was no longer trusted. Sensationalism by ambitious reporters and homemade cures for man's social ills by self-appointed journalists led to disrespect of newspapers by readers.

Treatment of Seniors

Yes, times had changed. In the traditional family the father was the wage-earner, and the mother of the household and the children would be free to care for the grandparents. The children would be raised with "Gramps" around and the old would be accepted and enjoyed as a part of the family. Indeed, their wisdom and counsel would be sought. In conditions of greater affluence, maids or help could be afforded and the aging parent could stay with the family under doctor's instructions, sharing the direct love of the family. Under the most affluent conditions, nurses could be afforded in the private home.

However, now the times were different. Houses were not homes. The parents were often both on the freeways or in the factories. The children were on the streets or in school, and Gramps had no role to play. Because domestic help at an affordable cost was not available, "rest" homes by the thousands sprang up. The aged person was no longer a family problem, but "society's" responsibility. Social welfare was the answer. Society paid taxes, government took its cut, the grafters had their chance, and so it went.

Impatience of Youth

And now youth with its inexperience, its lack of property and its limited view for the present, asked for a vote; many sensing its socialistic tendencies supported that demand. Over one-half the U.S. population in 1968 was under 25 years of age. My own 12-year-old son couldn't understand why he wasn't permitted to vote since he was a citizen too. It was difficult telling a 14-year-old daughter that she was not yet a woman of the world.

Youth is often reckless and bent on experimentation. It was true, the young of that generation were exposed to increasing amounts of information, and my children and my neighbors' children were intelligent. They received training and education; but did it follow that they possessed wisdom and judgment? Certainly not, this comes through experience. I was frustrated over the decision to change the voting age, because the majority of young people had spent their lives by age 21 entirely in school, except for the drop-outs who had even less comprehension of society and problems. Many believed mostly what they had been taught by teachers who often clamored for greater extension of government control because they worked for the state or local government. I opted that obligatory military service, as is practiced in many countries, would be a good thing for all Americans.

Anthropologic scientists point out that it is unnatural to delay sexual relations until the ages of most current marriages. Time is spent in sex education in today's complicated and specialized society. No one can argue with its need. But is complete sexual promiscuity the answer to a biologic impulses? In 1968 I had two lovely teen-age daughters, and I hated to think of them as bitch-dogs in heat. Would promiscuity be fair to them, to their future husbands, or to the possible unwanted children resulting from these "enriching" or "maturing" experiences?

Mom's Wisdom

All these ideas were in part the subjects of discussion with my beloved mother, as I visited her in Kokomo. In dazed confusion she asked, "What is the world coming to?"

I must say that I have worked with children of all ages in my profession, and the great majority of them are wonderful. Most of them have great personalities. They are refreshing, honest, intelligent, optimistic and a distinct joy. I have faith in this kind of young person, and their numbers are many. But in 1968 I saw danger signals. I hated to see teen-age girls who are already hardened. Maybe the eyes were clear, but the words were short. Maybe the skin was clean, but the frown and the resentment came too easily. I hated to see unkempt young men carrying chips on their shoulders. Maybe it wasn't their fault. Our generation in 1968 saddled each new child coming into life with a $2,200.00 debt. In America we were certainly not born free!

* * *

Much of this writing was done on that plane ride in a cloud of smoke. My eyes were smarting and my nostrils were burning, and enough was enough. I finally did it! I turned to the people beside me and said, "Do you realize that we are almost five hours in the air and one or both of you have been smoking constantly the whole time? Don't you think others are entitled to breathe clean air?" The woman became quite huffy and indignantly shouted, "If you don't like it, you can move. We were here first!" The man suggested that if I smoked myself I wouldn't be bothered.

Finally, I did squeeze into another seat between a kindly old moustached gentleman and a young, charming school teacher. He was flying West on his way from the East coast where he had visited children and grandchildren. Flying was new to him because he was an old railroad man and the rail line for which he worked had discontinued passenger service. He therefore could no longer get passes to travel. Yes, times were changing . . . .

* * *

Each Spring and Fall in those years I would often be asked to go somewhere in the country to lecture at meetings or schools. I used such occasions to go through Kokomo to visit the family. My sister Esther had tried to take care of Mom, but occasionally she would have hallucinations, and we were afraid for her safety. Fortunately, Dad had left her with enough funds for her care, and after long debates we children recommended she be put in a nice rest home. At first she felt caged, but when she made new friends and found some of her old friends there, she became more adjusted. My sisters, Mary and Esther, and my brother Jim visited her daily.

I tried to give her a whole day of my time on each visit. It was precious to me. I would sit and hold her hand or read to her because her eyes were failing. She remained keen of mind and spirit, but her strong body gradually declined. Even the weight of a blanket on her toe would twist her knee because of the weakness of the muscles of her leg.

On one of my visits I asked her to come and live with us in California for a time. I told her I would be happy to have her, and that I was successful and could take care of her royally. She declined, saying that her friends and the rest of the family were there, and that she belonged where she was. I then asked if there was anything that I could do in any way. She said, "No, there's nothing I need or want. I appreciate your coming when you can."

A few minutes later she brightened and said, "Well, Bobby, maybe there is something -- is there anything you can do for my teeth?"

Reportedly Mom at the age of 22 (in 1902) had extensive dental cavities. At one appointment all her teeth were extracted **without anesthesia**. Rubber vulcanite artificial dentures were made for her. She wore the same set of artificial teeth for the next 44 years.

Mom had episodes of headaches so severe she would become unconscious. Now that's tough. When I was just out of dental school I made her a second set of teeth when she was age 66. To my knowledge she never fainted again. However, her problem could have also been connected with menopause.

When my brother Jim specialized in dental prosthetics, he had taken her dental records to a meeting of his study club, and said, "Look, you guys -- this is not a patient, this is my Mom! Let's do the best job we can do for her. They had done the best they could, but after 60 years of no natural teeth her gums were gone and her muscles were atrophied.

Looking at her lying there, requesting something in my own field, and having to tell her that she already had the best we could do chagrined me deeply.

I also took a lesson soon thereafter. It was lunch time on one of my visits, and I didn't want to sit in her room alone, so I accompanied her to the dining room. I was shocked! First, it was the soft foods and lack of leafy vegetables which required chewing, but second, it was seeing other senior people taking their artificial teeth out and placing them beside their water glasses while they munched the meal with their gums. Two of the old ladies got into a squabble and slapped at each other like children. It was a sad experience and awakened my consciousness of older people's needs.

I recalled at the time a lecture I had heard in 1948 at the Chicago Midwinter Dental Meeting. A physician addressed the group and started with an apology. He and colleagues had conducted a geriatric study in rest homes. After the usual questions and interviews, the older people were asked to respond, stating what they felt was most needed. This physician — a psychiatrist — was shocked to find the most common request was, "I would like most to be able to chew and eat a good meal." The medical doctors were dismayed to find the greatest request was not in their field. After all, what else do they have to look forward to?

Even as Mom was returning to her room that day after lunch, I overheard one of the other older ladies remark, "I wonder what they're going to have for supper."

Unfortunately, Mom was too early. Implants in the bone for support of artificial teeth have now been developed to help some of these older people. What it still shows, however, is the wisdom of caring for the natural teeth.

*   *   *

In 1971, while Mother was still living, I made one of my greatest discoveries in growth of the human jaw. After a six-year computer study I determined that our lower jaw grew on a spiral, like a sea shell. It was thought to be a part of a logarithmic spiral that was employed for the prediction of the growth from a child to a mature adult. In order to generate the arc on a tracing of a profile X-ray of the head of a child, we had developed certain points of reference. I thought I could without objection by any reasonable scientist name a point after my mother, "Eva". This I did, but it was ridiculed publicly by some educators, which disgusted me. At least her name will forever be remembered in the halls of science.

*   *   *

The rest home was just across from a new hospital. Mom had been kept going with vitamins and other supplements and as good a diet as we could manage. Older people eventually lose their immune resistance, and she was no exception. Those not terminating by heart disease or cancer often succumb to pneumonia and infections. Mom developed an infected spleen which did not respond to antibiotics and she died after four days, in June of 1972, at age 92 years and nine months.

The family glue was gone. But there are memories, and she still finds expression in some of the words of this book. Long live her memory.

*   *   *

As an addendum to this chapter, other thoughts seem appropriate. During the 1992 convention the Republicans focused on family values but endured criticism for calling attention to this concept. It's saddening to have a display against virtue and morality. What is egalitarianism all about in the first place? Traditionally, values start with the mother --

a woman! When we think of life, we most naturally are brought to a consideration of home and family. Even an atheist society recognizes the individual strength that comes from the environment of a good home. Home means a mother -- one of those wonderful ladies -- a secret power.

One champion for the role of home in the cause of freedom was President Eisenhower. He often stressed the role of the family in his speeches before a variety of groups and national audiences. Many times he called attention to the importance of the home as the backbone of our country, shown throughout history. The effects of the Eisenhower family life had great influence on "Ike" the Soldier, Educator, President, Statesman, and Philosopher. His family is beautifully depicted in the American Heritage series "The Five Eisenhower Brothers". Bela Kornitzer quotes Eisenhower in an address to the National Catholic Women's Committee in 1954 as follows:

"In our own land it is largely through the family that our character is formed. Americans love fair play, bravery, hard work, and believe in human brotherhood because American fathers and mothers, by precept and example, teach these virtues to their children."

* * *

The Tale of Two Families

Looking back over my personal experiences, I can compare two families: my own contrasted to a neighbor's back in Indiana. This comparison clearly exemplifies the importance of love and the contributions of the home to the life, happiness and even the health of the people involved. It illustrates the well-known view that the psychological problems of many adults can be traced back to their childhood and the family environment.

I remember as a small child being sometimes taken along by my father to visit John, the neighbor in point. I honestly can't remember ever seeing this man smile. He seemed to always have a sneer on his face. I felt he was mean, unkind and dishonest. Circumstances and the graciousness of my father made it necessary to deal with him. The only time I ever saw him visit us was when he wanted to borrow something.

Children remember isolated happenings throughout their childhood, and I remember vividly one such occasion involving this despicable person. I was the water boy during harvest time. I would take a buckboard, a light four-wheeled wagon, a sort of single horse-drawn "pick up truck", to carry some jugs of water, wrapped in wet burlap sacks and stowed under the shade of the front seat, to workmen in the fields. The men would shout or whistle and I would deliver the water often at a gallop.

One day two of John's children, who were almost my age, had completed their chores and were riding with me on the buckboard. We were hailed by their father who was in a rage. For some reason he did not want them with me, and he cursed his own children. He grabbed one of my water jugs and threw water all over them. The children sat shaking in fear of the wrath of their father. I, being a small boy, was scared also, but I secretly wished I were a man so I could "tell him off".

Later, I asked the children why they were treated in this manner. I was appalled to discover their fear of him and his lack of love for his family. They revealed that they actually hated their father and would leave home just as soon as possible.

There were seven children in that family. It is of interest what happened to them. Two of the boys were dead in their early forties. One died of a heart attack while driving a truck. It was rumored that he drank more than a bottle of hard liquor daily. Another shot himself and lay dead for three days before he was found in his own home. One of the girls left home very early and gained a degree in nursing. Another girl joined a convent to get away from her family, but later left it and married. Only one of the boys made it without apparent major hardship incurred.

But hate can run deep, even into the third generation. The residence of one of the grandchildren of the aforementioned neighbor lay alongside a golf course. A fence was erected to protect the crops from being trampled by errant golfers who might knock a ball out of bounds and go after it. One summer afternoon, however, a young boy was looking for lost balls as many of us often did in the hope of getting a few nickels by selling them back to the golfers. A grandson, seeing the other boy in the field, ran for his father's gun and shouted a word of warning, but at the same time let go a salvo of shot and struck the trespassing child. He later said it was accidental, but the kind of irrational thinking that would possess a young boy to grab a gun and fire deliberately at another represents a hate and lack of understanding that frequently runs in a family that exists without love and mutual self-respect.

Children may enjoy happy lives in spite of the wrath of a father. The question is, however, how far could these young people have gone, and would they be alive and healthier, had there been abiding love from the outset?

My Family

What I knew of that family is a vast contrast to my own childhood family and home. As an example of the trust we had for others, our doors were never locked. This was a rural community, but only half a mile from a town of about 30,000 people.

We were originally six children. As I relate elsewhere, my oldest brother died of an infection at the age of 14, when I was six. My oldest sister, Jeanette, became a nurse for a local physician and later married Russell Bozell. They have two children, one of whom is Tom Bozell, a popular commercial actor in New York. Her daughter Brenda married a local school principal. Mary, my second sister, became a legal secretary, later worked in the Assessor's office, and became Comptroller of the City of Kokomo. She married Charles Craig who became the fire chief. Their son James R. Craig is now a college professor in Denver. Esther, my third sister, became private secretary to the personnel manager at Delco Radio, manufacturer for General Motors automobiles. Both my brother Jim and I became dentists, and both of us specialized.

Without the love of a mother and the faith of a father perhaps this contrast in family experience would not have existed. It has been said that behind most successful men stands a strong woman. There are exceptions but we all benefit by a strong start from a good woman. Will our women of the future be recognized? Will they accept this vital role to our society?

3

IMPRESSIONS OF A YOUTH
(1920 - 1930)

Life on the Farm

[Many readers may find some of my experiences "too earthy", but that was the real world I lived through.]

The original part of the house in which I was born and raised was an old log cabin. The land and house were purchased by my grandfather, Joseph Ricketts, in 1871 and my father had been born there 13 years later. The main room was approximately 15 feet square. It had a fireplace equipped with a plastered mantel on the left as the room was entered from the east. The fireplace was used in the spring and the fall for heating of the room, but in the winter it was insufficient. When freezing weather came the fireplace was blocked off and a stove with a stovepipe curling through the attic was used throughout the winter months. Unfortunately, the stove also was inadequate for proper heating during our extremely cold winter weather.

For as long as I can remember, one of my jobs was to bring in the wood or coal. As soon as I could push or pull or saw or wield an axe, I sawed wood and then split the blocks for firewood. We also used coal, which provided greater warmth but was often unaffordable. I remember taking the old Ford flatbed and riding with Dad down to Bedford, Indiana and getting a whole load of five tons of low-grade sulfur-ladened coal for $20.00.

The house probably had been built around 1840. I recall as a small child climbing on the corners of the logs which had been cut and laid together with a sort of mortar. On the inside the logs had been lined with wood slats which in turn were covered with wall paper. But in the wintertime, when the cold wind blew from the west, drafts could be felt coming through the wall. The leaks could be further identified by frost marks where the wind seeped through the wall. Originally on that side there had been an old kitchen, the footings of which had slipped and caused it to be torn down.

The original cabin had been built on a slight slope on the rim of a shallow valley with a stream, approximately 75 yards from the back door. It ran continuously throughout the year due to a feed from a natural spring on a neighbor's property. The floor of the old part, our family room, was covered with linoleum and quite slanted toward the valley.

Indiana Basketball

A wood closet was on the south side of the room just to the right of the fireplace. When I was a small boy I nailed a round rolled oats box on the door and Mom made us a beanbag. We learned to play basketball as soon as we could throw the beanbag high enough to reach the top of the door.

Indiana still is known as a basketball state, and I often wanted to ask my friend Coach Johnny Wooden at U.C.L.A. if that is how he got his start in Martinsville, Indiana. By the time I was in the first grade, or six years old, I was a member of the "Cubs" basketball team, playing in a church league. Because I was the tallest I "jumped center". In those years, after each point was made we came back to the center ring, and the ball was thrown up and we jumped to tip it to a team member again. A tall center became too much of an advantage, and rules were changed. Two hand shots were usually made, and we scooped the ball between our legs in order to get enough leverage to throw it up to the 10-foot-high basket. It certainly was a far cry from the game today. Nobody ever dreamed of "stuffing" a ball.

The log part served as our family room/dining room/kitchen. A large table was located in the middle of the room. On the north-east side sat a cupboard which held the dishes and the few staples where they could be protected from the rats. (Rats were plentiful in the barns and around old farm houses.) On the west side was a kerosene cooking stove which was bordered by another cupboard with a working surface. This unit contained flour and other staples.

A back door to the west was centered in the room. On its left next to the stairs to the attic sat a stand on which a wash basin and the water bucket were placed. The water bucket supplied our drinking water, and a cup with a handle was always available in it. A cotton towel hung on a nail to the right of the bucket and beside the door. No one ever thought about sterilization. Anyone who wanted to take a drink simply took the dipper from the bucket and drank directly from it, and placed it back in the water.

Bathing

On the coldest winter mornings, the first one to come down to the kitchen usually had to break the ice in the water bucket. This would be followed by lighting the kerosene stove to heat water for washing our hands and faces, our "sponge baths". Showers were for rich people who could waste water!

Once-a-week baths were usually Saturday events. Mom would bring in a round wash tub for the occasion. She would heat buckets of water and pour them into the tub, and then cool the water to a comfortable state. We kids would stand in the tub, and Mom with a ladle would dip and pour water over our bodies. The youngest of the children would be washed first, and gradually the same precious warm water would be used to wash the whole family. When we were finished, we would dump the water out the back door and, as we said, "down the hill". Therefore, we had the saying that anything that was to be discarded was going to be thrown "down the hill". I still am tempted to use this phrase when removing refuse.

After our Saturday evening bath, we would receive a clean pair of blue-jean overalls and a clean blue shirt. This was to last us for the next week. Sometimes we would have only one pair of overalls, and Mom would have to wash them and dry them while we stayed in our B.V.D.s or our long johns, which was also our sleeping attire.

Hoosierisms

In Indiana, as in no other state, "Hoosierisms" were ubiquitous. I wish I could remember more because they were always hilarious to outsiders. They were frequently anecdotal and often similitudes that had a sort of esoteric connection. One such, for instance, would be the retort when someone asked, "Where is So-and-so?" The answer would be, "Well, he had to go to the toilet, and the hogs got him." This would usually bring a laugh, but in order to understand this the reader must first understand that on the farm corncobs were a common means of wiping the anus after defecation. And because corn was fed to the hogs, that was the most likely place that a fresh corncob could be found. Therefore, a person had to get into the hogpen with the hogs in order to do his job. Picture, then, the situation!

On the northern side of the family room another part had been added which became our kitchen in the summer. It was constructed from the lumber from the old kitchen which had slipped away from the house and contained a large old-fashioned cooking range that used wood for fuel. Movable metal plates made up the cooking surface, and a water tank was constructed along the side. Centered beneath the fire area was the oven. An enclosed warming shelf was located above the cooking surface. It was a wonderfully warm place for a child to lie behind on cool evenings in the spring and fall.

* * *

It's amazing how much work just simple living required in those years. The old beds were no more than wood beams connected at corner posts with a flat spring supported by bed rails, or slats. Placed upon the open springs was, not a modern mattress, but a "straw tick". It was sort of like a large canvas bag literally stuffed with real wheat straw. When the straw was first placed it could be fifteen to eighteen inches thick. On top of this was the "feather tick". As its name suggests, it was filled with feathers, which explained why we raised the ducks. Each spring the ducks would be rounded up and caught and their feathers would be pulled from their chests for the filling of the feather ticks. I never really cared for duck eggs; the yolk was too thick.

Beds were all refurbished each spring. At the same time, they would be taken apart, because a continuous alert had to be maintained against the multiplication of vermin such as lice and bedbugs. At that time, the rails and slats would be repainted with oil to protect against all sorts of insects, since there was no sterilization available for the feathers and the straw which came directly from the earth. Sleeping on this kind of bed really was an experience in living with nature.

Poor Soap But It Worked

We made our own soap. We saved our fats, mostly from the excesses of cooking pork, and when soap supplies were down we would heat the fats, and put in lye for the saponification to take place. It took a few days, then, for the soap to develop and condense at the bottom of a tub. We would then cut the soap in blocks like a cake. I suppose this is where the term "a cake of soap" came from.

All the linens and the sheets, pillowcases and white clothes were boiled in this soap. Therefore, any white piece of clothing or bedding was surprisingly sterile. This probably accounts for the practice that when someone suffered a wound, a woman would lift up her dress and tear off a piece of a white petticoat to dress the wound. There was a good chance of it being reasonably sterile.

Monday was the washday. On that day we left Mom alone. She would not take guff from anybody, because washing was indeed time-consuming and hard work. We could expect to have bean soup on that day. If any of the children were fussing and fighting, she would simply order them out of the house and out of her hearing distance if they were going to behave that way! So we took extra precaution to protect her at those stressful times.

Tuesday was usually churning day. The churn was a sort of cone-shaped wooden vat with a lid which had a hole drilled through it large enough to emit the handle of a plunger. Cream would be placed in the churn, and an up-and-down motion would provide the agitation. Gradually, the coagulation of the fats would be separated from the cream. The butter would then be placed in a cloth and squeezed and put in a large wooden crock. A paddle then would be used to further amalgamate and condense the butter as a little salt was added for taste. The butter would then be put in the coolest place we could find, which was no problem in the winter. In the summer it was placed into a metal box about two feet square which was buried in the earth behind the back door on the North side of the house. This served as our cooler and yielded the best chance of preserving any food that would soon become rancid with exposure to the summer heat.

Wednesday, as I remember, was the day to hang curded skim milk in bags to drain off "whey" in the processing of cottage cheese.

Natural Gas Depletion

Around 1900 natural gas had been discovered in the area, and on one corner of the old farm a deep gas well had been drilled. It had been connected with other gas wells in the community around Kokomo. The more recent parts of the old house contained gas pipes. It had been used for heating and lighting of the house, because there was no electricity. Gas was thought to be unlimited in supply, but within a few years all the gas had been depleted. Consequently, when I was a small boy our light came from a kerosene lamp or lantern and candles, but the pipes and jets still were there.

The largest part of the house consisted of four bedrooms and the living room. It was connected by an entrance from the porch and had been built on large logs placed on heavy stones as cornerstones. This became our living and entertaining room. On the east side of the living room was an old player piano. At the center of the room was the large heating stove whose pipe served to heat the two bedrooms upstairs.

Plants at Risk

On the south side of the living room was a bay window where Mom attempted to keep flowers. She dearly loved them, as I think most women do. Not too many kinds of flowers would survive a winter in Indiana, so the containers were filled with ferns, and some hanging leafy plants like ivy but also a few blooming plants. I remember one cold morning coming down from the old upstairs bedroom and seeing Mom sitting there in tears because her flowers had all frozen that sub-zero night. I went over and tried to comfort her because anyone can understand what it would mean to see your mother crying. She gave me a wet embrace and said, "Don't let it bother you, Bobby, I'll get over it, I just need time." How many times did I hear that!

Mom was a true pessimist because she did not dare let herself be optimistic and have too much hope. It would only be greater disappointment if she permitted herself to think of a grander scale. It is beyond me how she did it, how she kept things together and survived, because life was really a survival challenge.

Meals and Country Food

We ate three meals a day, all large meals because everyone worked very hard and required much energy. When I was of pre-school age ours was a milk farm with 100 registered Holstein cattle. We always had milk, cream and cottage cheese. Earlier, before we went broke during the Depression, we had mechanical milkers that worked on a vacuum principle. Living with us, and managing the "Ricketts Brothers Dairy", was my uncle, Thomas Cheney Ricketts, who had never married. He was my dad's youngest brother. The hired hands bunked with Uncle Tom in the attic directly above the log cabin. The ceiling of the attic was peaked, and on one side it was barely two-and-a-half feet from the floor, rising to a height of about six-and-a-half feet. Their beds also had to be maintained by Mom. These sleeping quarters were directly over the family room.

Meals were always "family style" with the food set in the middle of the table, and the dishes passed around. Mom did not often sit down with us because she had too much work to do. "I'll eat when you all get finished," was her common expression.

Mom would try to have enough food for everybody's fill. Let me describe the foods in rural Indiana in those years, because much of it was home grown.

Pickles
For example, we made our own dill pickles. On the south side of the old log cabin was a sort of passageway between the cabin and the milk-house, where there was also a work-bench on a one-step platform that had been a part of the construction to keep out the water. Our two pickling barrels were placed there. Each summer when the cucumbers were grown they would be picked, and what couldn't be eaten in a fresh state were pickled. A layer of cucumbers would be followed by a layer of salt, and then dill leaves would be placed for another layer of cucumbers, and so on, until the barrel was filled. Water would be added to the top of the barrel and the lid would be placed for the pickling action to take place. They would be eaten throughout the following year.

Flour, Milk and Meat
After the harvesting each summer, usually in July or early August, the wheat we raised would be taken to the miller and exchanged for flour for the coming year.

Milk was always available from our Holstein cattle.

We butchered hogs for pork and used our young bulls for beef. We would seldom butcher in the summer because there was no way of keeping the meat. Therefore, the butchering was usually done just at the start of the winter freeze.

When I was a child growing up, my favorite meat was pork tenderloin, particularly when it was very freshly butchered. The way tenderloin was produced at that time yielded about as delicious a meat as anyone could desire. It was taken from the back strip of the hog, as the filet mignon is taken from the backstrip of the beef. My next favorite meat was the so-called Swiss steak my mother made. She would cook steak in a skillet until it was brown, and then make a thick gravy to accompany the steak. Served together with mashed potatoes, I always thought it was an exquisite, really rich meal. This would usually be accompanied by green beans or some green food. The problem was, people in those days believed in overcooking everything, perhaps due to the lack of refrigeration and the need for assurance against disease, which is not appreciated today with the prevalence of modern equipment.

Vegetables and Fruits
During the summer we raised tomatoes, string beans, lettuce, asparagus, celery, carrots, together with peas, sweet corn, and butter beans. Regular navy beans were sold as commercial produce and could also be kept for use throughout the year. It seemed we were always canning: vegetables in the summer and meat in the winter.

We also had some fruit trees with apples and pears and peaches and the cherries that I dearly loved. It was always a race to pick the ripe cherries before the birds got them. To this day, cherry pie is my favorite.

When we had time we would make our own ice cream, particularly for Sunday noon dinners. Time did not permit it to be made usually during the week, but on Sundays time permitted the turning of a crank with the container swirling in salted ice. Ultimately the cream would be frozen.

Potatoes and More Potatoes

Two of the staples which seemed to be the most frequently used then were white bread and potatoes. I also dearly loved Mom's corn bread. Potatoes were raised during the summer, and we had four types. Planted very early would be the Irish cobbler, a small white potato, very sweet, which grew fast and developed early so it was usually the first to be eaten. The second type was either what was called a Rural New Yorker, or a Rural Russet. This came on a little later, and more abundantly, and was the most common in use. Another coming still later was called the Idaho Baker which was more mealy and lent itself to baking. We most frequently would have American fried potatoes made in a huge skillet large enough to serve us all. Mashed potatoes were also a favorite dish, and it was usually my job to do the mashing. I had a strong arm, and so it was -- "Bobby, come and mash the potatoes." I would apply the butter and salt, and fresh cream, and work until I was sweating with the old metal potato masher.

Also, at almost every meal, there was white gravy, again made of the flour, milk, fat and a little salt. The fat would be heated, the flour would be added, some salt and maybe a little pepper would be put in, and the flour would sometimes be browned in the skillet, and then milk would be added to make a gravy.

Potatoes, called "taters" by the old Hoosiers, were available to us the year round, and the question arises, How could they survive the winter freezes? In the fall, during the harvest, we would select a flat area of soil and dig a trench about 18 inches deep in the form of a circle about eight feet in diameter. This made a sort of moat. Within the circle, a thick bed of straw would be placed, followed by a pile of potatoes on the straw base. Then, on top of the potatoes, another thick layer of straw would be added. The earth dug out by the formation of the moat would be shoveled on top of that until a large earth mound about five feet high would be built. The outer soil would be about eighteen inches thick. The most severe winter would not penetrate the soil and the straw because the potatoes themselves tended to generate heat. Sometimes one potato would spoil and it would undergo a sort of decomposition and bacterial action which would produce heat and help preserve the rest. As you know, some vodka is made from potatoes. Many vegetables and fruits can be used to make alcohol.

I read somewhere that on a world basis potatoes are the most common food and represent the greatest volume of food consumed. In fact, on one of my many flights, in querying a person who worked for the Green Giant frozen food company, I was surprised to learn that frozen French fries were produced in greater volume than all their frozen foods combined.

The potato was discovered by the Spanish explorers in South America and taken back to Europe. Potatoes could be served as American fried, French fried, boiled with skins on or with skins off, mashed, baked, scalloped, and made into potato salad and potato cakes; they could be used for hash and many other types of combinations.

In a survival situation people can look to potatoes as one of the chief nutrient sources. They grow in most types of soil.

Canning

Canning was also crucial to our survival. Tin cans were not yet popular but I remember the Ball jars and tops that screwed tightly, and little rubber gaskets that were used to create a seal. Ball State University at Muncie, Indiana was founded by the Ball family who manufactured these jars.

In the summertime, canning was done with green beans, vegetables and fruits to be eaten throughout the winter. Cooking would sometimes be done directly in the jars, as they were boiled in a large tub that was used for the washing. Other times the cooking would be done first and the sterilized jars would be filled with the food while it was very hot. Care was exercised in filling the jars so as not to contaminate them, since the food would spoil if live bacteria were trapped in the jar.

Curing

The jars were gradually emptied in the winter, at which time we did the butchering. Beef was cooked and canned, so that we could utilize the containers and have meat in the summertime.

We also cured our hams. We butchered hogs, a process that I helped with even as a young boy. I hated most the killing of the animals. We put them in boiling water to soften the bristles, scraped off the hair, and then cut up the skin and fat for rendering the lard, and finally cut up the carcass. The hams were trimmed, wrapped in a cloth sack, injected with salt, and sometimes pepper, and smoked. For this, we would take corncobs and place them in the bottom of a small hut and start the corncobs burning, which would not burn fast, but give off a lot of smoke. The smoking sealed the outside of the ham and it would last throughout the summer.

We also raised chickens for their eggs as well as their meat. Usually the eggs were gathered by the girls and sometimes we had an excess that we sold to the grocery stores. But most frequently we would have bacon and eggs or ham and eggs and sometimes pancakes for breakfast. Often we would put in two to three hours of work before we were called to breakfast, and by that time the appetite would be pretty good. We ate so much we filtered lots of vitamins and minerals by sheer volume.

Even as a small boy I remember eating six eggs for breakfast, and when I was in high school one morning I ate 32 pancakes. This was in a contest with one of the hired hands who thought he could "out-eat" me. We ate pancakes with Mom doing the cooking. She said, "I'll cook 'em as long as you two idiots will sit there and eat 'em." So I was not going to be defeated. I ate 32, and my competitor, a hired hand, ate 31. He was a red-headed boy named Brown, so we called him Red Brown.

*   *   *

Life on the farm in the early 1920s was almost self-sufficient. While we had no running water, no central heating, no electricity, no inside plumbing, I do remember getting our first telephone. It was a party line, and it truly did change our lives. Our first number, as I remember, was 236X!

Altruism in Farmers

Life on the farm was one of cooperation. This was a factor that left an imprint on the minds of many of the early pioneers. Neighbors were crucial in times of stress and in times of need. Neighbors were respected. During the harvest months, the "threshing rings" mentioned earlier were an example of this. For threshing (to Hoosiers it was always "thrashing") the grain was cut in the field and the sheaves were bound and placed in shocks to protect against the weather and to dry out so that the grain could be separated. Large wagons with strong horses were used for the hauling. The wheat, oats, or rye was loaded onto "hay ladders", where it was then pulled to a threshing machine usually sitting in a barnyard. A tractor with a pulley and large belt was used to turn the machine to separate the grain and blow the straw into a large stack in the corner of the barnyard. It was quite dusty and noisy. The straw stack was then used throughout the winter to feed the cattle and the horses, because it usually contained some of the grain that was missed, which served as a source of food. In the spring we would pick up the remains around the stack which had decomposed and spread it on the land with a manure spreader.

"Fodder" was made by cutting the ripened corn and putting it in shocks which were gathered throughout the winter months. They would then be "shucked" to provide corn for the pigs or pulverized into a mulch for the cows. The raw fodder was also eaten by the cattle and the horses.

When I was six years old we had 18 horses. My little horse, Totsy, was a mare, and I dearly loved her. She was dark red in color with a black mane, and a long black tail. I called her my horse. She would talk to me when I would feed her.

Many stories could be told about the dinners made by the women for the men. The women carried on a little quiet competition to outdo each other at the noonday dinners (our evening meals were called suppers). There was much hard work, but these noon feasts were a joyous occasion. We would lie around and rest a short time after stuffing ourselves. We especially looked forward to the ice cream social at "settling up" time.

Harvests were made during the hot summer months. Naturally the men needed a lot of drinking water, so it fell upon the "kids" to be the water boys. This was usually my job, and my little horse Totsy was ideal for this work. Owning no saddle, I carried a jug of cool fresh water out to the fields in one hand while holding the reins in the other. When larger amounts of water and distances were involved, I would take a buckboard, as described in the preceding chapter.

Work on the farm from sunup to sundown was literally the routine. Sometimes finishing was done with lanterns when the work needed to be completed in a single day. There was a sense of communal cooperation.

Joey

My older brother Joe was born in 1912. He grew to be a strapping youngster. I remember how I loved him so very much. After he was born came three girls, and then I was the next boy. And that might have been the reason for our strong relationship, because he played with me often.

I can remember when he was only 12 and 13, how he rode Totsy. He would grab her mane and while she was in a full run he would drop off to the side and kick his legs completely over the top and come back and kick them back to the other side -- all this while she was in a full gallop. I remember standing on his shoulders and doing acrobatics.

Joe was also a marvelous athlete. I remember one evening he was very late in coming home from school to do his chores. He had stopped to play basketball with some friends. Dad had given him three warnings to get home and not linger with the "brickyard gang" so Joe received a whipping with a heavy rope. I still remember the sorrow and tears for my big brother. To this day -- now, 65 years later -- I get a sinking feeling when I recall hearing him in tears with my father beating him.

Joe was very bright, and he had one of those loving and radiant personalities which everybody liked. He loved to play basketball and would stop and play with anybody at any time. He had a kind of a free spirit. One day, when he was 14, he was accidentally kicked in the thigh while playing basketball. The boys played in heavy street shoes and the bruise was deep. He developed a hematoma (due to a ruptured blood vessel). I didn't understand the problem then. I remember him first limping home with a swollen leg. The next day it was more swollen, and even more painful. We were all concerned, and suffered with him because he started crying with the pain. Mom rubbed and rubbed it. By the third day he had developed a fever. The hematoma had apparently become necrotic (with dead tissue) and infected. There was no puncture, and no original opening, but somehow inflammation had set in. A large abscess opened just above his knee. There were no antibiotics available: sulfa was not known then and penicillin and other antibiotics were not known until decades later. Diseases and epidemics were common. Infectious diseases or infections were dreaded by everyone.

Despite some so-called sugar pills dispensed by an old homeopathic physician, Joe's temperature continued to rise, and I remember him becoming delirious in my mother's arms. He had recently read a book about Tarzan and hallucinated that the apes were chasing him. I remember his screaming. It was a pitiful sight, and totally hopeless. His fever was so high and the symptoms were so severe it was thought he might have contracted typhoid fever. But as he grew worse the symptoms of typhoid were not supported. The infection had gone to his nervous system. He developed spinal meningitis, and died. I still find myself deeply sorrowed, because I was just a lad of six years, and he was my model, my beloved older brother. And here he was, dead in only six days, after receiving a bruise on the leg while playing a sport.

The whole family was in shock. Mother was put to bed for several days in grief over the loss of her firstborn in the prime of his youth. And it was so sudden. I remember kneeling by her bedside, holding her hand, and her words to me: "Bobby, just think, you will never see Joey again."

This was my first encounter with death, when I was in the first grade of school. I had a sense that something was happening to me that I didn't understand.

Passing of the Drive

In his book "The Social Contract" Robert Ardrey referred to a number of studies which suggested that the firstborn male in the family had extra qualities for leadership and dominance in society as a whole. If the firstborn male dies, that quality seems to be given to the next male in line in the family. Maybe it is a sort of godfather complex, but there seems to be something biologic that underlies this extra force. At any rate, with Joe's death, I was the next male in line, but I had no idea of my future.

Most families, particularly with a large number of children, experience squabbles. It's a part of peer competition, it's a part of growing up, and with Joe's death that left me with three older sisters. I became, then, the first boy to pick on, and pick they did. Prior to Joe's death I was buffered by his presence, and he would protect me from the aggression of particularly my two oldest sisters. Almost daily something would happen to annoy me or annoy them. It was almost as if something in nature was at work which I didn't understand. In addition, I was not well liked, or at least I didn't think so, by my Uncle Tom who lived with the family. I was very fair in complexion, I had blue eyes, I had brown curly hair, and I was a dreamer. Like all boys I loved to play, especially with my younger brother, and we scuffled a great deal. But somehow, I always felt that I was his protector because he was my little brother. I could get in a fight, and cuff him around, but if anyone else touched him they had me to whip because I became a tiger! I really love him.

Uncle Tom

Life on the farm was not easy. Injury was common. Eyes were put out, fingers and hands were lost. The silage cutters, binding machines, grain mills, and ordinary harnessing and working of large dangerous animals were not without risk. Uncle Tom carried a deep scar on his upper lip from a stalk of corn thrown from a shredder. When it came to working with the large animals no merciful consideration was given, and life was tough.

One day the cows had broken through a fence, which was one of the old rail fences. Just as in Abe Lincoln's day, many of the fences were of the herring-bone type arrangement, and a cow on attempting to reach grass on the other side might break or displace a rail and jump out of a pasture into a planted field. One day this happened! The cows had broken the fence and were eating the newly grown very delicious knee-high corn which of course would destroy the crop. My uncle, seeing it from afar, called to us boys to run and get the cattle and herd them back into the pasture. My brother ran ahead of me, and I was walking rapidly, but preoccupied with the carving of some object and not impressed with the urgency of the situation. This angered Uncle Tom to the point of violence. He shouted to me to stop right there, and ran from the barn with a whip which was used to control the cattle. It was about three feet in length and was made of woven bailing wire, very sturdy and very painful. He ran up to me and struck me in the back, on my backside and legs several times with this wire whip. Naturally, I passed my brother up in a hurry! But it is a licking I never forgot. I tried to avoid my uncle for quite some time.

I later asked my mother why Uncle Tom didn't like me. She said, "It's not true, he loves all of you. All of the money that is earned by everyone goes directly to the family." Half of the farm was owned by my uncle, but he never took any more money than was necessary for his meager existence.

My father and Uncle Tom had mortgaged the family property in the hope that my uncle could have another farm for himself, and perhaps ultimately marry a woman from Cincinnati named Eva Zaye whom he had known earlier in his life. Therefore, in 1927 Tom mortgaged the 40 acres he had inherited from my grandmother Emma Ricketts, and bought a farm north of Kokomo which also was mortgaged. Tom certainly could not have had too much happiness, and maybe he had the need for someone on whom to vent his frustration and I was it!

Also, I remember great arguments between him and my father which frightened me. Both of them worked from dawn to dusk and beyond, and it was unrewarding financially. The work was vigorous.

In the front yard was a circular driveway in which cars and trucks could turn around, and buggies and equipment could be parked. Adjacent to the house a milk barn and sheds had been constructed. There was a water well there and also a cream separator and a bottle-washer. This is where the milk was strained, canned and bottled for delivery. There was no pasteurizing which was not needed because all the cows were regularly tested and cleared for tuberculosis. Inside there was a loading platform onto which the truck needed to be backed for loading.

One day, as Uncle Tom was backing up the truck, unknowingly my little brother Jim, age three, was knocked down and the front wheel ran over his head. How he survived no one knew, but cinders were ground into the side of his face which left black tattoos. One of the scars was sort of a keloid (a thickening of scar tissue). He almost lost his ear, which was sewed back in place. I remember it so well, even though I was only five.

When Uncle Tom was a young boy, somehow he had taken some dancing lessons. His mother desired a certain amount of culture in the family. Tom was a very handsome fellow and a graceful dancer. I recall him, when he would hear music, putting his arms up and doing the old two-step. He taught my sisters to dance when they were quite young. And so I learned to dance when I was six.

The bottom of the Depression was in 1933. When Tom became very ill that year, even though he was only forty-three years of age, we had no money for doctors. He started vomiting, ran a fever, and finally under emergency was taken to the hospital. He was diagnosed as having a ruptured appendix. When they opened him up he had an abdomen filled with pus and necrotic tissue. It was a massive infection, and four days later he died. This was my second experience with death in the family and I was deeply sorrowed, mostly because I felt that he had not had the opportunity to have a good quality of life. It was the first time I heard my dad talk about the "hereafter". Dad was with Uncle Tom when he died and said he saw him smile and say "Hello, Mom" as he passed on. In my brother Joe's case and in his case, one shot of penicillin would have saved their lives.

Fears of Disease

During those years we had smallpox epidemics, and I was vaccinated when one started. My father thought that he had had smallpox before and rejected the vaccination. Then I witnessed smallpox at first hand, as he and my sisters Esther and Jeannette came down with it, and I saw the terrible disease it was. Sores literally were all over the body, even inside the mouth. They left deep scars. Our house was under quarantine and we children who were healthy lived with relatives for a while.

If someone contracted diphtheria they went under quarantine. If someone had scarlet fever, they went under quarantine. Measles and mumps and whooping cough were common, and no quarantine was made for these diseases, even though measles is a deadly disease quite often, and mumps can become complicated.

After Joe's death, whether it was by rationalization or simple protection of a guilt feeling, I often heard my father explain that it was not uncommon for all of the families to have lost at least one child. Death was a chronic fear. Getting sick was serious business, because we could easily die. I remember deaths occurring from a wisdom tooth impaction. In Indiana I remember seeing women with goiters, which were large swellings on the neck as the result of hypertrophy of the thyroid gland, due to a lack of iodine in the soils and the drinking water. After a cut or laceration we feared blood poisoning, which was a term used for a streptococcus infection.

Certainly we can take issue with some of the aspects of modern medicine, but the complications from infections as they were experienced in those days is something hard to imagine now. Maybe the closest thing to it would be the current fear of contracting AIDS. Everyone now can share in the common feeling that we had in those days because there was no cure for syphilis and there was no cure, really, for gonorrhea. And any social disease that was contracted was feared greatly.

The First Radio

During the late 1920s we acquired a radio which ran on large A and B batteries. It was one of those crystal sets consisting of three dials and I remember the squawks getting WLS from Chicago, and KDKA from Pittsburgh.

After we had the radio, we would often sit around and listen to choice programs. I remember so well "Amos and Andy", "Jack Armstrong, the All-American Boy", "Kraft Music Hall" with Bing Crosby, "Fibber McGee and Molly" and "The Little Theater Off Times Square" with Don Ameche, which would come on Friday nights. Jack Benny also had his continuous diatribe with Ben Bernie who had an orchestra. Al Jolson was a great singer I really loved as a boy. Other programs were eagerly anticipated by the family.

Dogtown

During those years in the southeast corner of Kokomo, there was a large vacant area about a city-block size that was filled with old bricks discarded from the furnaces of the Pittsburgh Plate Glass Company. It was called "the brickyard". In that section of town there were quite a few tough kids. In fact, that is where the best athletes came from for the high school. It came to be known as "Dogtown" because there were a lot of stray dogs around. In walking to grade school it was a shortcut for me to pass through the brickyard. Frequently some of the kids would pick fights. It was not unusual for me to come home a little bloodied. I never picked fights, but neither did I run away from them.

Just south of the brickyard was a large parcel of rented land where my father grazed our milk cattle, which later became a golf course. Its beautiful rolling hills split by the Kokomo Creek were ideal for grazing. The back part of the land was about half a mile away from our house and barn, and therefore it was a delight to get on Totsy and run across these pastures, herding up the cattle. It was a part of my joy as a youth.

In later school years, I ran the whole distance home for lunch and back to Jefferson Grade School. The school was adjacent to a big gas storage tank that can still be seen from a great distance, and which supplied gas for the city. Just getting out in the air and running, particularly up and down the hills, was great pleasure. What children born and raised in cities miss! It certainly gave me a type of freedom and euphoria, especially in the spring and fall when the air was fresh. I can still sense that freedom.

Anecdotes from Farm Life
Watering the Milk

Milking cows by hand was, I think, one of the most boring things I ever did. After the Depression we reduced the herd to 10 or 20 cattle, and sometimes, I suppose to break the boredom, Jim and I would squirt each other with milk in a playful way. One day he got me a couple of good ones right in the face, as I walked by with a half-pail of milk in my hand carrying it to the large can to put it through the strainer which was near the door of the cow barn. In disgust, I doused him with my pail of milk, upon which he rose up with his milk and threw it on me. I then went to the horse tank and filled my bucket with water and came back and doused him really good with a full bucket of water. I thought everything had quieted down and went back to milking the cows, accumulating about three-quarters of a pail of milk again, only to find my brother with a full pail of water dousing it squarely on my head. I threw my milk at him, and we ended up in a fight at the horse tank. We both became completely soaked, with milk and water all over the place.

Suddenly both of us started laughing and wondering what we should do. We knew we would have a shortage of milk. People from town would be waiting with their jugs to buy fresh milk from us. Therefore, I simply took the water out of the horse tank and filled the can up to the usual level, and told nobody. Little did the customers know that they were sharing the horse-water in the milk that day.

Herman

In the cow barn the cows were chained into stalls, where they were milked. They were fed grain and silage (process of anaerobic acid fermentation of fodder in the silo). A cement trench was located behind them to catch their droppings. Sometimes in the coldest part of the winter the cows were left in the barn because there was no food in the pasture which was covered with snow. We could turn the cows out sometimes, and feed them hay on the ground, and carry them fodder to pick on. But the cow barns would have to be cleaned out. The manure was thrown through the windows into big piles which mounted up to ten and twelve feet outside the barn. When the rains came this would become further soaked and slimy. Under the sun the top would harden into a baked crust, while underneath it would be very soft.

I had a friend in town whose name was Herman. He lived about a mile away, and always loved to come out to the farm. He liked me and was always asking questions about the farm. He never offered to help me milk, he was afraid of the cows. One day Herman had been visiting me and we had played around the barn for a little while before I had to start milking the cows and getting my work done. So Herman stayed and talked while I was milking. He finally announced that he had to go home. The barn door was closed, but the window where the manure was thrown out was open. Herman said, "Can I go out through the window this way? Is it safe?" I said, "Oh, yes." He said, "Where should I step?" I said, "Well, you should jump right over there to the right," pointing to the crusted part of the manure stack. He jumped and then I heard him yell. As I looked out the window I saw that Herman was up to his waist in sleazy, stinky cow dung. He lost one of his shoes and had to dig down in the pile in to find it. I ended up taking him to the horse tank and washing him off. Needless to say, I lost Herman's friendship.

Cow Diets

In the spring, the cows would gorge themselves on fresh grass and sometimes get diarrhea. We also had two or three patches of wild garlic, located in one part of the pasture, which we couldn't seem to get rid of. This, too, would be eaten by the cows, and going into the cow barn after they had been in the garlic patches was really an experience in massive garlic breath. The garlic would also come through in the milk, and the cream would be almost green with garlic. If anyone says you are not what you eat, they should drink the milk from those cows. The cream would sometimes be returned by the creamery as unfit for butter, because the butter would taste like garlic. (I suppose there were no "gourmets" to request garlic-butter in Kokomo, Indiana!) But the hogs loved it. So after milking and going to all the work, sometimes we would have to use the milk and cream as hog-feed. That really hurt.

In the springtime when the cows were turned out to pasture in fresh grass, they would also be very loose in the bowels. As they stood in their stalls, we would have to walk at a safe distance when they defecated, because they could squirt three to four feet behind themselves. One day I had a pail of milk and was taking my usual precautions at what I thought was an appropriate distance. I passed by just as one of the old cows, called Frances, was relieving herself. Just at that instant she coughed. The warm, slimy, stinking projectile caught me on the face, on the forearm, and ran down into my bucket of milk. All I could do was just stop dead and realize the situation. And I turned in anger and kicked Frances, the poor thing, out of my frustration!

The Butting Order

Milk cattle in particular meant a lot of work. They had to be fed, herded, and milked, cleaned and groomed. They had to be bred and the calves fed and cared for. Each evening they would have to be rounded up and herded in when they did not respond to a call. But even a herd of domesticated animals had a butting order just as chickens have a pecking order. Every cow knew her place, even though there were a hundred of them.

Our leading cow and milk producer was named "Star". She was a star, but she got her name because she had a star-shaped black mark in her white forehead. Her udders were large. Any other cow that tried to get ahead of her got a real good butting, until she was subdued and located herself back in the pack. We also had the antithesis: this was perhaps the most slovenly cow imaginable. She was picked on by every other cow in the herd. Consequently when the cows were being herded towards the barn she was always the last in line. Hence, she earned the name "Dead Body". It was absolutely amazing how she was always put in her place.

We always kept a prize bull. Dad would select one every three or four years to be our herd bull, and often would exchange a good bull with a neighbor to obtain cross-breeding. We had one particular candidate for our herd bull which was a son of Star. We mated her with a registered Holstein bull from a neighbor. Dad knew that he had, therefore, a tremendous blood line in that male calf.

We lived on old State Route #31 and our barnyard was next to the highway. Dad rented some space for signs to advertisers who hoped to attract people going by in automobiles. I've heard it said that fighting bulls react to movement. I've also heard it said that the color red will anger a bull. I'm not so sure of that, but at least for this one it did. One of the signs was freshly painted red, advertising Prince Albert tobacco. The red can of tobacco was portrayed on the sign. No sooner had the painters departed than this bull started to gore the sign. He couldn't knock down the billboard but he had a good shot at it. The paint left a ring of bright red paint around his face. So we named him "Ring in the Face".

Breeding was a part of the rural life. The bull was pastured with the cows, in order to serve them whenever they came in heat. The testosterone from the heavy testicles made him mean, and when a cow emitted the proper odors a fence would not stop him. Therefore, rings were usually placed through his nose so he could be led, and Dad always placed a chain on one leg to keep him from running and becoming dangerous.

I remember my father was attacked by Ring in the Face and pinned against a gate. He grabbed a short-handled pitchfork which he kept handy for just such occasions. I remember him jabbing the pitchfork into the head and neck of the bull. That evening he announced to the family that old Ring had to go. We therefore sold him for baloney which could be ground and tenderized, because he was a "mean and tough old dude". He had become too mean and we children were in too much danger.

Pecking Order and "Buff"

We witnessed another demonstration of territorial dominance in animals. It was Mom's responsibility to raise the chickens. Most frequently she raised Barred Rock chickens which were black with white speckles. She also raised some smaller Rhode Island Reds. We had one very cocky rooster in particular which she called "Big Red". He dominated the barnyard and also the front yard where sometimes on Sunday afternoons we would sit in a circle of chairs, as neighbors would come to visit.

Mom thought she would change some of her chickens, so one spring she bought some young chicks which were Buff Orphingtons. They were a lovely beige color, and grew to be larger than the Rhode Island Red. We usually butchered the young male chickens for frying, but one prize rooster would be selected to fertilize eggs for the hens. We could see that "Buff", as Mom called him, was getting bigger. On several occasions he had challenged Big Red, and was trounced thoroughly. But Buff kept growing.

One Sunday as we sat in the front yard we witnessed this terrific rooster fight. Buff was now full grown and was holding his own. As the fight continued, Buff began to get the upper hand. The comb of Big Red became bloodied. Soon thereafter, Big Red tried to retreat and tried to get away. But Buff had vivid memories of the several beatings he had undergone. He really wanted to give Red a final lesson. This was the scene as we all, family and guests, watched old Red trying to escape: Red was squawking very loudly and got the attention of all of us as we observed the battle. He ran in between two bushes only to meet a wire fence, tried to get through the fence, but was caught. Buff was frustrated because he couldn't get at Red's head through the fence, walking back and forth in back of him. Suddenly, as if by impulse, he screwed old Red in the rear. Talk about humiliation!

The Mystery of the Missing Pie

As I remember, we got out of grade school at 3:20, and I would run home across the pastures. (This land is very close to a Chrysler plant which now makes transmissions for Chrysler automobiles.) Being a growing boy, I was always hungry. Every day I would wash the pails for milking the cows, but first had to change from school clothes into my work clothes. Very frequently I would look in the old cupboard to see if there was anything on which to snack, because I would have hours of work before we would sit down for "supper".

One day I saw a beautiful pumpkin pie in the cupboard. Seeing nothing else, I cut myself a quarter of the pie, and ate it on the way upstairs to change into my work clothes. By the time I had my clothes changed I had finished the quarter of the pie, which was positively delicious. On coming back down, I passed through the kitchen again, and not being satisfied I cut myself another quarter. I then went out in back of the house and started washing all the pails, preparing to take them to the milk barn which was about 100 yards away. After washing the pails, I came back for a third serving, which of course was again a quarter of the pie. By now I had consumed three-fourths of the pie. I went over and put the cows in the barn and started my chores of milking. The picture of that last quarter was still in my mind. I ran back to the house and grabbed the last quarter of the pie and put the pie pan on the opposite counter.

That evening after dinner Mom started looking in the cupboard for a dessert for the family. I noticed her out of the corner of my eye, because I was wondering what was going to happen. She looked and looked, here and there. Finally she said, "I swear I had a pumpkin pie in here. Has anybody seen the pumpkin pie?" Then she finally looked over on the counter and saw the empty pie pan. She asked, "Did anybody eat that pie?" And of course nobody volunteered anything. So I said, "Well, I had a piece." She said, "Who else had some?" And of course no one replied. "Bobby, did you eat that whole pie?" she asked. And sheepishly, I said, "Well, I reckon I did." "My goodness, how could a kid your size eat a whole big thick pumpkin pie?" I answered, "With my mouth."

She was of course somewhat disgusted, but she went into a storage room in the very center of the house, where the canned fruit was placed, and selected two jars of peaches. She brought them out so the family had peaches and cream for desert that night.

The Rats

I hated rats. It seemed they were everywhere. We had a double corn crib with a roof connecting the two sides and a driveway in between. The cribs would be filled to the brim with ears of corn each year. The corn was ground for the cattle and was available for hog feed. Each spring or early summer when the cribs were emptied, rails and flooring would be exposed to show that it was literally filled with rats who had wintered on the corn. The cats and dogs fed on the rats and mice, but many remained.

Boys would come out from the town and we would go "ratting". One group would go inside the corn crib on one side, lift the rails, jump on the flooring, and the rats would scurry toward the opposite side, where they would be intercepted by another group with sticks and clubs, brooms, and whatever we could lay our hands on. The screaming and hollering was like a hunt. Those that were missed and made it to the crib on the other side would be spotted and the same routine would be applied to the other crib. Only this time we would have to get on both the inside and the outside of the crib, because the rats would try to make their way to other buildings. The whole process would take about 45 minutes, at the end of which time we would have killed 50 to 75 rats. Rats still make me feel squeamish and I jump whenever I see one!

They even invaded our living quarters. My bed was in the upstairs room about four feet from a window. Outside my window was a most beautiful, symmetrical poplar tree. I called it my tree. The poplar has a white bark and a wood grain which is excellent for furniture because it is so straight and easy to handle. There are not many around any more. When the wind blows the leaves rustle, greatly reminiscent of aspens in the highlands of Colorado. I could lie in my bed and look at this magnificent tree and listen to the wind blow through its leaves.

I mentioned earlier that we took our wheat to the miller and exchanged it for flour. We needed a reasonably safe place for the flour, so it was stacked on a board that was laid between two crates, covered with a sheet and kept right beside my upstairs bed. In the middle of one night, I was awakened by the sound of a rat beside my bed. I looked and could see by the light of a bright moon the silhouette of a rat helping himself to our flour. Very slowly and quietly I reached down from my bed and located one of my shoes. After getting a firm grip I threw the shoe at the rat. Unfortunately, it missed the rat but went straight through the window with a tremendous crash. Suddenly, everyone in the house was awakened. Lamps were turned on and sheepishly I had to tell what I had done. As the rest of the family gathered, Mom very candidly explained, "Bobby tried to kill a rat and threw his shoe through the window." The next morning it was my job to clean up the glass splinters and find a piece of wood to cover the window until we could afford to buy a new pane of glass. Therefore, for some time I lost the view of my tree.

Midwest Lightning

It was during the next summer that we had one of those mid-western storms that were so frightful. They were called cyclones and came from the west. Sometimes they would come by day, sometimes by night, and this particular one came about 3 A.M. The air would first be still and quiet, breathless, and suddenly a rush of wind would come, followed by the cyclone with churning black clouds and sometimes containing a tornado. Usually, when a wind of this magnitude came my poplar tree would be bent over and with the wind rustling the leaves would make a roar. It was during the night in one of these storms that lightning hit it. It could not have been over 20 feet from my head. I don't know of anything more frightening than having that flash and clap of thunder so close to me. It shook the house. The next morning, as I looked out the window, I saw the tree was split all the way to the ground, and some of the branches had been knocked off.

The following week my dad and uncle felled the tree away from the house, because they were afraid the next wind would blow the remains onto my room. It was my job to cut up the tree into firewood. It was almost as if I had lost a friend, because I could remember lying in my bed with my dreams and my imagination, looking at the old, beautiful tree. It had been somewhat of a comfort, and something I assumed would always be there. And suddenly I had lost it. I feel sorry when I see any old majestic tree felled!

Paddy

We made a sport of the rats. It was sort of the job of the boys to help rid the area of them if possible. We always had dogs around, which would also assist us in helping to keep the rat colonies down, because they multiply very rapidly. I had a favorite club that I kept handy because it was formed with a knot on one end and made a handy tool to get my revenge on the rats. One day we noticed a path from one of the pigpens to a very large tomato plant that was some 10 yards from the edge of the barnyard. Rats had burrowed under the plant and created quite a nest in the cool soil beneath the shade of the big plant.

One of our dogs had a litter of pups, and I was drawn to one of them as my favorite. I called her Paddy because she had large soft pads on her feet. She was my dog. She was a sweet dog with a slick grey coat, and a white spot in the middle of her forehead. She followed me everywhere and maybe was the only dog I ever truly loved. She became an outstanding ratter. She would go after a rat and bite it in the back and then shake it faster than the eye could follow. And then she would bite it in the head until the rat would stop moving.

One day my brother Jim and I decided to see if we could catch the rats under that large tomato plant. Jim had gone into the corner of the pen and scared up one of the rats, which usually come out at dusk and are not often seen during the bright day. Anyway, I was ready with my "shillelagh" and was waiting for the rat to make it for his hide-away under the plant. I could see him coming, and I took dead aim. Little did I know that Paddy was around. She saw the rat and made a dead run to intercept him at the same time that I lowered my club. They arrived simultaneously.

I crushed her head. I screamed and I cried, I put water on her head to try to revive her. But she was gone. I had killed my dog. My mother comforted me, to no avail. I buried her and made a wooden cross for her grave. Maybe that's the reason I have never taken, really, to dogs since, because I was a long time in getting over that loss. But that made me hate rats even more.

Jiggs

Each spring the sows would give birth to piglets. We could tell they were about to give birth when we saw that their udders were filled. At that time they would be put temporarily in small pens. Some of the good sows would have more piglets than udders and some, particularly the younger ones, might not have enough newborn for all their teats. My job was to be around when it was noted that either too many or not enough were delivered by one sow. If the new piglet was just born I could grab it without it squealing and place it at a young sow's nose and she would adopt it.

The sows were big and heavy and sometimes would lie on a new piglet and suffocate it. I was to watch for that. Sometimes I would find one stepped on accidentally and killed.

One particular morning I discovered that old Betsy, our best sow, had stepped on the face of a little male. His face was torn, his snout was broken and displaced to the right side. He was lying there in the pen bleeding and barely breathing. I picked him up, and he was too far gone to squeal. I straightened up his nose as best I could, and pushed the skin and his left eye back into place. I held him close to me to get him warm and put him under my jacket to comfort him. I ran to the house and asked Mom if I could try to save him. At first she said No, but when I insisted she said, "Well, all right, but you'll have to take care of him if he lives." I called him Jiggs, after the Maggie and Jiggs comic strip.

I found a cardboard box and put some shredded cotton blankets, and laid Jiggs in it, placing it behind the old kitchen range. That night I got up every hour or so and gave him milk with a spoon because he couldn't move his jaw well. The next morning Jiggs was still alive. I kept feeding him milk, and in a few days got a small nipple to feed him with a bottle. He soon started to grow. Each time I fed him I played with him, and he soon became a pet. He started eating scraps from the table. He loved to have his belly rubbed. Very soon he tore up his box and Mom made me take him out of the kitchen. I made a small pen with chicken wire outside the summer kitchen. He began to grow faster. When I came into view he would start grunting for attention. Soon he had torn up the pen and ran loose in the back yard. His face was always crooked.

Pigs are tough. Jiggs would get under our feet and would be kicked to get him away. He thought it was play and would come back for more. He surely loved us all and became a family pet.

One afternoon I came home from school and as usual went to the back yard to greet Jiggs, but he wasn't there. I inquired where he was. He had followed Mom to the highway to get the mail from our box and had run across the road in the path of a car which struck him and killed him. Dad had refused to just bury him. He was good meat, so Dad skinned Jiggs and dressed him and Mom was cooking him in a big roast pan. Needless to say, I didn't help eat Jiggs, but they all said he was delicious.

* * *

Church

The church we belonged to was called Trinity, and was a Methodist church. Trinity stood for God the Father, God the Son, and God the Holy Spirit. My father had been raised a Congregationalist which was not too different, as far as I could see, from some of the other Protestant denominations. The Protestant movement declared that each individual have his own personal relationship with God rather than go through a mediator such as a priest or a bishop.

In a rural community, with the lack of affluence and other interests, the church served many functions. First, of course, it was a formalized means of worship and even with our meager means a portion of it went to the Lord. With so many uncertainties in health and economics, it was almost as if some sort of an organized crutch was needed. It appeared to me that some people -- maybe for the cause of self-preservation -- went to church for the purpose of some sort of insurance. But many were devout believers and through the church teachings I certainly learned the difference between good and evil and right and wrong.

We were all singers, and my father became the choir leader, which took one of his evenings each week for practice for the songs to be sung on Sunday. I can't say that we were among the greatest devotees of the church, but as a young lad I remember going to Sunday School at 9:30 in the morning on Sunday, which was followed by church. And then there was a young people's meeting called the Epworth League at 6:30 on Sunday evening, where we had lessons from the Bible. At this time we also had the opportunity to socialize with other young people in the church environment.

The church also offered an opportunity for entire family socialization. On Thursday evenings there was usually a scheduled prayer meeting. On Wednesday evenings quite frequently there would be some sort of a social function for the church, of many kinds. Sometimes we would have "penny suppers". Everyone would bring different dishes of food, and each would be charged a penny for each serving, which would put a little money in the church coffers.

We also had basketball leagues made up of different age groups for games in the city among the different Protestant churches. The competition was quite keen, and we had an opportunity to meet other children within the church environment. Thus it was that working on the farm, going to school, and participating in the church constituted our life.

I was told I had a beautiful boy soprano voice. At the Christmas functions I would usually sing a solo for the church, usually one of the carols; "O Little Town of Bethlehem" was the most frequently requested. Even after my voice changed, I still had a good voice and was a part of the Glee Club at the high school and sang a solo ("At Dawning") in a concert with the band.

Probably the activity that we all cherished most was to save our pennies to go to a church retreat in the summertime at one of the lakes in Northern Indiana. We couldn't always do it because we didn't have the money, but it still only cost $5.00. We stayed in cabins and met other children from other cities in the Methodist Church's Epworth League. We had the opportunity to swim, fish, go out in row-boats, play softball, and just mingle. We were carefully watched by the ladies in the church who would go as chaperones. Every morning at breakfast one of us was responsible for a passage from the Bible, or a Psalm, or the giving of our own personal prayer. It sort of was an ice-breaker for each of us to talk in front of the group, and was indeed an opportunity for growth.

Miss Jessie

Fortuitously, among those teaching classes in the Sunday School were some of the teachers that I had in grade school, which was only one block away. Two of these were Miss Martha McGowan and Miss Jessie Albright Coburn. Miss Martha taught the high school age class, and Miss Jessie taught the adult class. They were really tremendous ladies. I remember Miss Jessie finally getting married when she was 50 years old.

Jessie Albright was to have a profound influence on my life. One day when I think I was only about 12, she stopped me near the school. She lived only one block east, and walking to and from the school had to pass a small vacant lot where we young people played. She called to me and told me she had something that she wanted to tell me. At first I thought I might be in for a scolding, but this time it was serious. I always admired and loved her so much for the dedication, warmth, and love she expressed. She started out by saying how lucky I was to have such caring parents. Then she put her arm around me and said, "You are a very special boy. In all of my experience in teaching you are very unusual. I pray for you to become a minister. You must become a leader and a teacher. You must serve as an example to the other children, because many of them look up to you." At first, I laughed because I didn't think there was anything special about me. But she went on, "You have a sense of sincerity and goodness that will be recognized."

I dismissed it then as only a passing experience, but I must admit I never forgot that short conversation there on the sidewalk on a summer day. That loving, short, plump old teacher still holds a warm spot in my heart after 60 years. I pray we still have such teachers!

Intrinsic Qualities

I have often contemplated, when I have been asked, where I got my drive, where I gained persistence, and how I established my values. It has been said that we learn most of our etiquette and how to get along in kindergarten. Coming from a family of six, we had our own kindergarten and had to learn to give and take because siblings tend not to yield to each other. But when there is a sort of communal job to do, and when survival is at stake, perhaps the experience of altruism is imprinted more deeply. Can we call it American? There is no ethnic privilege! The values, virtues and missions which were established later may well have resulted from my youthful experiences before the age of ten. Being a part of a large family and learning to give and take tends to make a good citizen.

One of the greatest imprints on me was the continual reminding to be truthful. "If you always tell the truth, you never have to remember what you lied about." "Harboring a lie is also unhealthful." Therefore, one of our values was truth. How can it be more evident?

A second value was fairness. We learned not to cheat, and not to take advantage of a situation just because it presented itself. We were taught to help our neighbor, not that there was to be some sort of score, but because it was basically good and a proper thing.

As I later learned in connection with altruism, several studies have shown that the ultimate greatest benefactor is the giver, not the receiver. The giver in particular, in giving his time and his energy, reaps the benefit of good health and long life. It has been said that three great virtues are love, faith and charity. Charity is giving, and particularly of one's energy and time.

One result in doing things for others was a deep-seated desire to be of service, not only in doing something for others, but doing something meaningful and with no ulterior or hidden motive.

What is the ultimate definition of happiness?

4

AN ERA OF DEPRESSION AND ENCOURAGEMENT (1931 - 1940)

The Crash

Up until that dark day in October of 1929, when the stock market crashed, we children had been sheltered from economic problems. The crash happened when I was in the Fifth Grade. At first I didn't know what it was all about. As a boy of nine years, I was interested in the outdoors, playing sports and doing chores and going to school.

I remember a debate in the family in the summer of 1929 about buying a used 1928 Buick sedan. At that time the family owned an old Cleveland car. Many companies made automobiles, and in fact prior to that time one had been manufactured in Kokomo which was called an Apperson Jackrabbit, made in 1903. I remember the speed limit was 30 miles an hour on some of the country roads, but when all the family was in the old car it was difficult to make that speed limit. In fact, when we were to go up a steep hill when loaded we would have to put it in first gear, or sometimes even get out and push. Long distances were out of the question.

We were confronted with the prospect of buying a better car, and I thought it was really "hot" because it had an exposed spare tire on the rear. As I remember, the asking price was $2800. I also recall what a tremendous amount of money that was, and the discussions as to how we were going to pay for it. Dad talked to Mom about taking a loan on the car to be paid over the next three years. We bought the car, but it turned out to be a regrettable hardship.

Stocks and a market "crash" were a mystery, but I realized something drastic had changed among our friends. Suddenly there was talk about the difficulty in getting money. Some people had little to eat.

Why Not Write a Check?

I remember observing my father writing checks from his checkbook, and I marvelled at such a wonderful thing. When Dad was having trouble getting money, I said one day, "Well, why don't you just write a check? Isn't that where they make the money? He had a chuckle then and stopped to explain, "Well, Bobby," he said, "that's not the way it works." Not understanding how a bank worked, not knowing what a stock was, and not even having heard the word "capitalism", a ten-year-old boy needed to have it explained in a way that could be comprehended. I often wonder how people in the former Soviet Union understand it. I think Dad felt that he owed it to the family to explain what was going on, because we could all sense that times were getting desperate.

Capitalism in an Easy Lesson

He tried to explain the workings of money in terms that I could understand, and because we were in the business of producing milk, his conversation went something like this:

"Under a capitalistic system there are many businesses. These businesses make things, sell things or trade things, and are owned and operated to make a profit, which means they receive more from sales than it costs them to make something. With the profit they can hire others to work for them and pay salaries or wages. Therefore, out of their profits, which they use for equipment and supplies, their businesses can grow. New jobs for other people can be made when they succeed.

"Let's take for instance, a company that makes milk bottles like we use. Along with the milk bottle they may also either have another company or another group or business make the caps for the bottles. After use the bottles will have to be cleaned, and so someone else will make the brushes. There will also need to be equipment for the holding up the bottles for the scrubbing. There will need to be coal to heat the water. And we need a truck to deliver the milk to our customers. Therefore a lot of people are involved in either the making of the bottle or its use.

"Now, if one person has a lot of money (or wealth), he and others could make the glass bottles and supply the caps and the equipment together with all the other things required in one organized business. He would have to put together all the materials needed to make glass, all the equipment needed to package it and form a company to sell and deliver it. All that takes much money (or capital). It would take some time for any person to accumulate enough money out of profits in order to grow bigger so that he could make still more profit. His larger company would need more help and sales to make more jobs.

"If his needs are small, he can go to a bank and borrow the money for his business. Banks loan money that other people have loaned them. Banks are a go-between for other people who have savings which they give to the bank to hold for them. They leave money at the bank because it is considered to be a safe place. So the bank in turn has money to loan others. People who make money from their work actually loan the bank their money.

"Within the bank some of the people's money or belongings may be put in a safety deposit for savings. They can also put money into a checking account for the running of their own business, or the buying of goods and food for their home. The bank uses portions of depositors' money for investments as loans to others and therefore pays their depositors interest for such use of their money. Now, when another person goes to the bank to borrow money he must expect to pay more interest for the money he borrows than he would get on loaning the bank his money. This is called the bank's spread! The bank makes money on the difference between the amount they pay others to let them manage their money, and what someone else will pay to borrow it.

"But, a person cannot get money from the bank unless the bank is willing to lend him money. He must be prepared to pay the money back, plus the charge for the loan of the money. The bank management takes a chance when it loans people the money others have lent to the bank. They consequently ask a borrower to put up his property (personal or real) as a hedge or security against a loss. This is called 'collateral', and therefore anyone takes a responsibility when they borrow from a bank, or any lender, or any friend for that matter.

"A person with a larger business may need larger amounts of money. He therefore needs to 'raise capital'. He may want to build a building for his business. But the bank may not want to risk lending him that much. He may therefore borrow from his friends. In order to make it fair for the friends who risk lending him their money, he may give them a part of his business. In this way they 'share' in the risk of running the business. But they also share in the risk of him losing! So he forms a legal 'company' in which he then issues certificates, which are called 'shares'. When, or if, he makes a profit, he divides up the profit from the business with the other owners. This dividing up of the profit is called a "dividend". The income to the holder is based on how many shares of ownership of the "stock" a person has.

"Now when good profits are made, the value of the business increases, and the value of the stock goes up. The business becomes less risky, and as the business grows and prospers the stock continues to become more valuable because profits rise. But when the company or business loses money, the value of the stock goes down. The buyer of the shares or the person loaning out his money for use by the company may lose.

"So when you buy a stock you have a chance to win or a chance to lose, and you put your faith in the person who is running that business. This is probably the reason they say that people 'play' the game of buying stocks."

"But how does the bank get all that money?" I asked.

"Well, for instance, if we sell a load of wheat, the person at the granary pays me for the amount based on the number of bushels we delivered to him. Now the grain keeper could pay us in dollars, but that would mean he would have to carry all that money in cash. We would have to keep the money with us or store it in the house. If the house burned or we were robbed, we would lose it all. So, instead, we put the money from the profits with another party, for safe keeping. That third party is the bank.

"A person in business will want to save from his profits. These are stored away ahead of time, and enough money or savings is put in the bank to cover the cost of running his business. Therefore the person at the granary writes us a check, which legally stands as a promise by the bank for the money that he is to pay us for our wheat. We then receive the check and take it to our own bank. We can cash it for the money, or we can keep a part of it and deposit any excess to our account which then is added to or credited with all our other money. With that money deposited in the bank only then can we write a check."

"Oh, I see!" I exclaimed. "You can only write a check when you already have money!"

Dad went on, "When I have money left over after all my expenses, I may have a profit which adds to my account. But when my expenses are more than my sales to the granary, I lose money.

"In farming, some years we make a profit but some years we don't. When that happens, I may want to borrow from the bank against future profits. I then put my property up as security so that the bank will take the risk to loan me money. If I can't pay the loan, the bank will take my property to pay for the loan and I lose again."

"But what does it mean when stocks crash?" I inquired.

"Well, when large companies such as those who make trucks and tractors form their businesses they need lots of money. They offer stocks or shares in their business for sale. Because they are very large and have so many certificates of stock these are traded, or bought and sold, by other workers in an exchange. There is a large one over in New York, and a large one up in Chicago. In fact, some people may buy stock without even understanding the products that a company makes.

"As a company grows and makes more profit, as I said, the value of the shares goes up. Some people will therefore try to buy stock that has a good prospect and as it increases in value they will sell it. They will make a profit on the difference between what they paid and what they sold it for.

"But when a company has trouble making a profit or selling their goods, they start losing money. When this happens, all the people who had bought stocks immediately want to sell them. They are afraid the value will drop. This drives the stock value down. When enough people try to sell their stock all at once, they start offering it at a lower and lower price and this is what leads to what people called THE CRASH."

"Oh," I said. But at that age I really didn't understand what he was trying to tell me. "But Dad, did you have stock?" I asked him. And he said, "No, I never had enough money to do anything other than raise you kids. We did borrow on the farm to raise money for equipment, and now we have that to pay off. So the lower amount of money we now get for our grain affects us a lot."

"If you borrowed the money at the bank, why are the banks closing down?"

"Well, as I said, when the people loan their money to the bank, the bank loans their money out to other people, and takes their property as security. If the value of the securing property goes down, and the property is not worth what they loaned to people on the basis of its value at the time, then the people who loaned their money to the bank come in and ask for their money back all at once, the bank doesn't have enough money to pay them, and it has to close down its business."

"Well," I said, "the banks must be pretty stupid."

He said, "No, they just get greedy."

As a child I still found it mystifying. I didn't own any stock, I didn't have any money in the bank, and capitalism was beyond me. But I could see times getting tougher and tougher as I went from the fifth to the sixth and the seventh grades in 1930, '31, and '32. I began to understand what it meant to be out of a job and to be poor, and what the "Depression" meant personally to our family.

Consciousness of Diseases and Accidents in That Era

My sister Esther, closest to me in age, was a rather sickly child when she was young. She was the only one of us to have an open bite malocclusion, or crooked teeth. And in these trying years she had appendicitis, which extended to involve her perineum (the lining around her intestines) which even became gangrenous (dead tissue). I recall when she was operated on and a draining tube was placed in her belly and she had an extremely high fever. I remember going to the church together with all the members in special sessions for prayer for her. On another occasion she had pneumonia, which involved both lungs, and almost died again. We were always tussling, and in a struggle with her one time I pushed her through a window and gashed her back deeply. She therefore had a trying experience during her development.

In those years it was not known yet that iodine was needed in the water supply for the normal performance of the thyroid gland. Sometimes the lack of thyroid led to problems which could involve the emotions. My two older sisters had spontaneous crying spells and depression which hurt me greatly and both had thyroid problems. I found out much later that I was hypothyroid, but compensated for it with overproduction by my pituitary gland.

The Knock-Out

Sunday afternoons, when the weather was good, we would occasionally join in church picnics. One of the farmers' pastures would be used. We would lay out a softball diamond and all the able-bodied people would become engaged in a softball game, which was much fun. During one such game, I was standing at what I thought was a safe distance from the diamond on the first-base side when my Sunday School teacher, who was a large man by the name of Mr. Smith, took some vicious swings at the ball. This particular day the bat slipped out of his hands, flew about 60 feet and struck me in the face.

I don't remember getting hit, but I do remember waking up after two hours of unconsciousness. The bat hit me a glancing blow below my left eye, beside my nose, and just above the margin of my lip. I remember hearing my mother describe the accident as I woke up and put my tongue under my upper lip and could feel the tissue all mangled. The old doctor just pushed things back in place, and never repaired or sutured anything back together. So consequently, all my life I have had a drooping upper lip on the left side as it turns inside out on that side when I smile. Needless to say, that stopped that ballgame! I later wondered what good the doctor had been to me.

Other Accidents

Another accident happened when I stepped on a board with a rusty nail that went all the way through my right foot. Mom put a fat bacon rind on it to "pull out" any poison. We never heard of tetanus shots in those years.

I also caught my foot in a barbed wire that was buried in the grass and punctured the joint of my left ankle. Swelling in the joint possibly was the worst pain I can remember. A large hematoma lingered for days.

One day while swimming rapidly I struck my shin on an old metal fender of a car buried in the creek. It hurt plenty and bled profusely and was opened down to the bone. The wide one-inch scar is still visible. We never went to a doctor for such trivia.

By the time I was 12 I was doing a man's work. As I lifted a plow one day I felt a tear in my back which at times has bothered me ever since. This was probably aggravated by my round shoulders and poor posture.

Two other uncomfortable situations were experienced. First, with my light skin I suffered in the hot summers in the field. I tried always to wear a full shirt and broad-brimmed hat, but sooner or later I'd be burned horribly by the sun. In those days sun creams and sun screens were unheard of. I hated to see the hot sun come up in the morning, and I still don't like to lounge in the sun.

The other misfortune was poison ivy. We had cut down much of it along the fences, and I thought it was all dead. One hot afternoon I lay down in the shade of some other fence vines to cool down and rest, and took off my shirt. After a while I realized I was lying in the ivy. The next day I was blistered and itched over my whole back, arms, and face. It is a horrible memory!

But we kids were hearty. Most of us worked on the farm, or had other jobs. Even at grade school age we played tackle football with no pads and no helmets. Our ears and cheeks were often bruised.

Milk Business and Embarrassment

When I was only ten years old, as I remember, it was my assignment to milk ten cows in the morning and again in the evening. To be truthful, I was given some of the easiest cows to milk, but nevertheless I had the job to do. The price for milk kept lowering, and by 1931 we could no longer afford to run the dairy.

We lived a little more than a half mile from the edge of town. People who had very little money would walk to the farm in all kinds of weather, bringing a jug for fresh milk. Some of the people would arrive early for the milk and would sit around in our family room to keep warm while waiting for the milk to be delivered. My sisters didn't like people sitting around the kitchen, so they would come to the front porch and scream over to the cow barn, "Bring some milk over!"

During those days I wore typical farmer bib-overalls. The button holes would usually become worn. These were the days before zippers, and after several washings, the button on the fly would not be secure. Usually I would carry a pail of milk in each hand which I would have to set down as I opened one gate, pick them up again and walk through the gateway, reclose the gate, and go on to a second gate and repeat the motions and then still have some distance to walk to the house. By the time that I would get there I would usually kick on the door and one of the girls would open it so that I wouldn't have to put down and pick up the pails again.

One cold, blowy winter evening I kicked on the door, and walked into the kitchen where my sisters and mother were working. Sitting in front of the stove two people were waiting. As I walked through the door with a pail in each hand, my penis unknown to me was hanging out, and my sister Mary said, "Bobby, what are you doing?" My answer was, "Where do you want it?" thinking she was questioning where I was going to set down the milk pails for the straining and delivery. But then she said, "Look at yourself!" On looking down and seeing my penis hanging out, I blushed and all I could think of was, "Gosh, I thought it was awful cold down there!"

We sold our milk for eight cents a gallon. It probably cost us double that to produce it, and so we became further and further in debt. At a local market a gallon container in 1992 was $2.60, or 32 times what we sold it for.

Totsy

One problem with loving animals is that sooner or later they must depart. Totsy was my little horse, and often I would pet her and hug her head, and she would respond with little nibbles on my face like she was kissing me. I always rode her bareback, and she would respond even to my leaning one way or another. As she grew older, when I was about twelve or thirteen, she had her right hind leg draw into a contracture and fibrosis. When the tendon of the human hand (usually in males) undergoes this condition the fingers can't be straightened out and it's called a Dupuytren's Contracture, after a French surgeon of the 18th century. Totsy could not straighten up her hoof and started walking on the toe. She got progressively worse, as it became sore and she would have to stop moving because of the pain.

One evening as I came home from school I saw a man leading Totsy with a halter up the road. When I got home I ran to Mom and desperately asked her where the man was taking Totsy. Mom was chagrined and shook her head and said, "Oh, I'm sorry you saw that, we were trying to keep it from you. Dad decided to put her out of her suffering and sold her to a company for horsemeat for dog food." I went to my room and sobbed. I hated to see her suffer, but I couldn't bear her being butchered for dogs.

The Real Depression of the Depression

I told about the death of my Uncle Tom in the early spring of 1933. A few weeks later, in order to pay for the surgery and the hospital and to attempt to pay off our debts, Dad arranged for an auction of our cattle. I had grown to love some of the old cows, I had spent so much time with them they were sort of like my friends. Because milk was so cheap most of them were sold not for milk cows but to make bologna and hot dogs. We advertised in the papers and many people came. I remember the auctioneer barking and each cow led into a circle of the bidders. Some of the cows that my father had paid $500.00 for were sold for $25.00.

When it was all totalled up, we had sold 80 cows and calves for an average of $33.00 each. The whole herd with the exception of about ten, that we kept for our own use, brought less than $3000.00 which immediately went to the bank against the mortgage on the farm and for the doctor bills.

After the sale I wandered around in back of the barn and saw my father leaning up against the barn, crying. His heart was broken. He couldn't say a word and all he did was grab me and hug me. I was just thirteen, but I was growing up fast.

Going Caroling

Our church was not too large, my guess is that it had no more than a hundred members, but there were about 20 young people, and we had many good times. With the help of the pianist and a couple of good soprano voices, the choir under Dad's leadership did some pretty good specials, particularly around Christmas time.

I particularly remember the yearly pattern on Christmas Eve. There were always shut-ins, older people, cripples, the bed-ridden, that members of the church would know around the town. The church choir, joined by all the youngsters who were old enough to be on their own, would go caroling on Christmas Eve. Our old bob-sled was used on the farm when the snow was deep. When the streets were covered with snow we hitched up the two big mules, Sam and John, and put chains of tinkling bells over the harness for the occasion. We went into town with the team, blankets and straw, and a lantern on each corner of the wagon. The choir was picked up at the church, plus anyone else who wanted to go along, and off we would go, seeking out those who we thought would appreciate some attention. An insider would tip us off as to the bedroom or the location of the person, and we would surround their windows or their doors and sing our hearts out. Afterwards, it was always "A Merry Christmas and a Happy New Year from Trinity".

I was always glad when there were some girls along, so we could pull them off the sled or the wagon into the snow, and make it more than just a caroling party. We would usually end up back at our house, where for the whole day Mom would have been cooking a huge pot of chili. The grown-ups would have coffee, and we would have hot chocolate with large bowls of delicious chili to top off the evening. Occasionally somebody would try to slip somebody too much chili powder.

Even though it would be remarkably cold sometimes, the old mules would end up sweating, and of course after all of the fun was over they would have to be unharnessed, put in their stalls, and fed some grain and hay for their warmth.

Teachers

For some reason, I can remember almost all of my grade school and high school teachers' names. Many of us have been guided, directed, led or assisted by a source of energy we recognize too infrequently. At first we are influenced by a loving mother (ma - matrix); today they call it bonding. Although bonding may imply a dependency attachment, in fact this bonding is a two-way love that lasts a lifetime when nurtured and healthy. It is acknowledged that we shift in our development slowly, but gradually, up to maturity.

There are many matrix and submatrix situations we continue to experience in our lives. It occurs in our work and further in our continued social encounters. In addition to the bonding with a mother and father there may be a loving grandparent or other relative or even a school teacher. I had many fine school teachers, but the "ladies of principle" who affected me most were Miss Jessie (whom I described earlier) and Miss Martha.

Miss Martha was frail of body. She was my 6th grade teacher through the week and my

Sunday School teacher on Sunday. She made sure she knew me well, and routinely communicated with my parents concerning my welfare. Honesty and morality were virtues, and all of her students were treated with respect. Daily prayer in school was accepted to be of benefit to all. I remember her for her warmth, kindness and inspiration.

Darrow Chapel

By 1932, because we lived just outside of the city, my younger brother and I could no longer go to the city school which cost only a six-dollar transfer fee. We simply did not have the six dollars for each of us. Therefore, after having gone to city schools through the seventh grade, I went to a country school called Darrow Chapel, east of Kokomo, and was bused each day for the eighth grade.

It was an old school, having only four rooms, and four teachers for eight grades. My younger brother Jim was set back half a grade because they only had full grade classes. In my class we had the seventh and eighth grades in the same room. Therefore, I almost had a repetition of my seventh grade that I had had previously, and felt that I was not really getting what I needed.

The teacher was Mr. Horner. He was an extremely principled person and was Amish. He drove a car, but many of his people there in Indiana still rode in buggies, refused to have electricity, and refused to have tractors on their farms. They were very honest and forthright people, and very successful farmers, intelligent and hard-working.

Mr. Horner was a fun man who liked to play baseball with us. Some of the boys in that group were older than I was, and had come from a coarse family. Some smoked, chewed tobacco, and used rough language. I got pushed around pretty well.

One day one of the boys struck a match and put it in the pencil sharpener just as a prank. The shavings in the pencil sharpener almost exploded. The covering of the sharpener was made of a volatile material and almost immediately the window blind on that side of the room was set on fire. Luckily the janitor heard the shouting, came in immediately, and jerked the blind down and stomped out the fire, just at the time that Mr. Horner came in the room. I could see that he was most irate and had turned red. But on the other hand, I could see that he was cool and calculating as to what he was going to do. He made a few inquiries and found the guilty party. He then gave us a lecture on the value of private property and on the value of school property. He reminded us that the school wasn't very much but it was all we had, and that many people had gone through the school and more were still to come.

He then asked the boy to come to the front of the room and bend over his lecture table. In front of both classes, about 60 students, he lashed the rear end of the boy six times with a rubber hose he kept for such occasions. He then had the boy go back and sit down and reminded us again of our need for respect of other people's property. It was a lesson I never forgot, and I have often thought how much it is still needed today, with the defacing of our schools and our property, and the lack of respect for authority, and the riots and looting that take place. Corporal punishment never hurt me!

* * *

The school bus came early. To get up before daylight in a place with no central heating, no running water, no electric lights, and to go out to the road and meet a bus in the dark, cold morning by 6:30 a.m., only to ride for 45 minutes, to make pick-ups, to finally only go about four miles from our house was a dreary and unexciting episode in my life. This was particularly galling when I felt that I had missed junior high school and particularly missed the stimulation that at that time of my life was needed most.

Kokomo - City of Firsts

I don't know whether the sign still stands, but at the border of the city there was a sign stating "KOKOMO THE CITY OF FIRSTS", and then many Firsts were listed that were originated in Kokomo.

There was an old inventor, a metallurgist, by the name of Elwood Haynes who formed the Stellite Company. I was told, as I grew up, that he had invented the first horseless carriage. Certainly it was the first that was known in those parts. Just half a mile south of Darrow Chapel School stood a monument with an inscription. The half-mile road running east from that corner was a stretch of road on which Elwood Haynes had run the automobile for the first time. My mother told the story that when she was only 12, in the year 1892, he had taken her for a short ride in the automobile, as he did with many of the children. I think it was always one of the great satisfactions in her life that she perhaps had ridden in the very first automobile that ever ran. Maybe other people will lay claim to building the first automobile, and maybe several were made without knowledge of others at the time, which is not unusual in science and technology.

At any rate, Kokomo was a proud city. It was the source of the first pneumatic rubber tire, stainless steel, derigold, several things in the Standard Pottery Company, stellite and other semi-precious metals, all made in this little city named after an Indian chief.

The Indianapolis 500

Just in passing, it might be of interest to learn exactly why, with all the places on earth, the Indianapolis "500" automobile race would be the most popular in the world. A lot of Hoosiers were what we might call "tinkerers". They were experimenters, and in the early 1900s everyone tried to build automobiles or different mechanization of some sort. Little machine shops would be set up in different communities in Indiana, particularly northern Indiana. The young men would display their newest developments and get out and compete on the dirt roads. Later dirt, gravel and cinders were used for roadways. As the roads became widened and gravel was changed to concrete, they held illegal races. Ultimately it was decided to formalize the contest. So the old brick racetrack, two-and-a-half miles in circumference in the semi-oval shape, was constructed. It has since been covered in asphalt with the exception of one small strip for remembrance of the history of the old brick track. This race still occurs each Memorial Day, but very few know of the history of the young mechanics and their innovations in northern Indiana.

The old cars were named after the people who designed or built them, or after the city from which they came. These old companies were bought out and this still accounts for the names of the different cars in General Motors, Chrysler and Ford. Many of the old companies dropped by the wayside, being unable to compete. But one which didn't succumb to competition until the 1950s was Studebaker, and later Studebaker Packard, which was located in South Bend, Indiana. The technology and materials were more accessible near the Great Lakes, however, so Detroit, Michigan, just adjacent to Indiana, became the most noted manufacturing area for American automobiles. But I would still like to believe that it all started in Kokomo!

High School

And so I was prepared to enter Kokomo high school in 1934 at the age of 14, in the depth of the Depression. I was about 5' 9" and weighed 140 pounds. One of my three older sisters had graduated in 1934 and another the year before, in 1933. My third sister was two years ahead of me and was already a junior, to graduate in 1936.

My oldest sister, Jeanette, on graduating in 1933, found work in a doctor's office, a Dr. McIndoo. She was hired for $5.00 a week, and worked from eight in the morning until eleven at night. She did the X-rays, the smears, and literally did the job of a nurse. When she came in on Saturday mornings, she made an extra fifty cents. On Saturday afternoons she found work at the local A & P grocery chain store, where she was paid fifty cents a day. There she also met a person who was to become my brother-in-law, Russell Bozell. Russ was a graduate of Northwestern University in business and was an assistant manager at a salary of $13.00 a week. After they were married, Russ became manager of a store in Noblesville, just south of Kokomo, where his salary was $35.00 a week and where for $25.00 a month they rented a two-story furnished house. I remember the house and how nice it was, certainly compared to our old house.

My sister Mary, upon graduating, got a job as a secretary for a lawyer, a Mr. Forehand, also for $5.00 a week. That experience was eventually to lead to the place where she became Comptroller of the City of Kokomo and was asked to run for the office of state Governor.

These jobs, as well as serving as something to help them survive, were a learning process for both of my older sisters. My third sister, Esther, made the best grades of all of us. Upon graduation she also became a secretary and became Executive Secretary for the Personnel Manager of Delco Radio Company there in Kokomo, a branch of General Motors.

But being the next boy in the family after three older sisters wasn't all that easy. When I entered high school I had to determine what course I wanted to take. A preparatory course for college was far beyond anything I could imagine. In fact, my mother told me to get as much out of high school as I could because that would be it. I couldn't see how being an intellectual would help me plow corn, stack hay, or milk cows. I considered many of the courses in English, math, algebra and history to be nonsense.

Flunked French

How I ever got enrolled into a class in the French language I'll never understand. I studied hard in French and got good grades the first semester, and then while playing football and basketball I didn't have the interest to study, and it is the only course I ever flunked in my life, mostly because I quit. Little did I realize then that only 24 years later I would be lecturing to an orthodontic academy in Paris. Indeed, a stimulation at that time could have helped in my career later.

Sports

I had discussed going into sports with my father. He said, "Well, you can play football and basketball, but don't run track." I inquired why, because I had the fastest 440 yard run in the Freshman class. He had heard somewhere that running enlarged the heart, and he associated a large heart with heart disease and felt that by running a boy would burn himself out at a young age. So I was only permitted to play football and basketball.

My sophomore year I weighed 152 pounds, at the age of 15. By age 16 I weighed 174, and my senior year, at age 17, I weighed 185 and was 5' 11". I played guard on the basketball team and after having played half-back my first two years on the football team I ended up as a fullback my senior year.

Depression Worsens in Indiana

During that summer of 1934 the Depression had become even more fierce for the farmers.

The best grade of hogs was delivered to the stockyards and sold for two and a half cents a pound. Imagine buying a whole hog for two and a half dollars! Or a 200-pound prime hog for five dollars! We sold Grade A ripe tomatoes at two cents a pound, but little money could be made. From 18 horses and two tractors in the 1920s we were down to three mules and no tractors.

We previously had owned one horse, of which Dad was particularly fond. He called him "King". He was a very large, Belgian draft horse and was extremely proud. One day I heard my Dad scream as he hurtled a gate and ran to push King away from a wagon. He had stood on his hind feet and somehow reached over the bed of a grain wagon. It was unknown how long he had been eating fresh wheat. By this time my Dad was in tears. He put a halter on King and started walking him. Along the rear side of the large barnyard there was a running stream and a slight hill that went up to a gate leading to the back road. He took King to the hill and kept walking him up and down it. King walked more and more slowly and my Dad would prod him more and more. Finally, King lay down, kicked briefly, and was dead. Dad explained that the fresh wheat in his stomach with the heat would expand very quickly. It would expand so much that it would tear his stomach and intestines apart, and that is what had happened. I was broken-hearted at the loss of this magnificent animal, but I think I was even more moved to see my father's sadness again.

The Droughts

I remember the spring and summer of 1934, before my entry into high school that fall, as comprising probably the hardest work I had done in my lifetime. We had two large black mules my father had bought, called Sam and John. Sam was bigger but it was hard to say which of the two was the stronger. John had fallen down when he was a colt and hurt his front knees, and so his knees popped whenever he walked, and he ran at a very peculiar gait. During a spring storm, lightning had struck Sam, and he was never quite the same. The third mule, only about two-thirds the size of the two big black mules, was a little mule that I, as a young boy, had named "Jocko" when he was born from an old sorrel mare named "Granny". When a female horse is mated to a male donkey, a mule is the hybrid result. A mule cannot give rise to another mule. As a cross between a horse and a donkey, they are very tough, very strong, and sometimes, allegedly, very stubborn.

But Jocko was a wonderful and kind animal, and I loved her very much because we raised her as a colt and she took her place right along with the other two big mules in pulling the wagons and pulling the ploughs and doing the work. During the spring ploughing we had to work the animals from sunup to sundown because they were all we had. One day Sam just died in the harness. We took the other two mules, unhitched them, and pulled Sam over to the side of the field to be picked up by a fertilizer truck. Sadly we went back to work with John and Jocko. Dad had to work these two animals very patiently, because they were doing the work of three.

One day I noticed that two men in business suits had come to the house and Dad had taken them into our front room and had sat down and talked with them for quite some time. After they left Dad called me and my brother Jim to him and said, "Well, boys, those two men were from the bank. They want us to give up the farm. I asked them if they could give me one more summer and fall to see if we could make a go of it. Now if you two boys will help, we're going to put in a tomato crop this year because the prospects of raising some tomatoes might be the best thing we can do." We gave Dad a hug, of course, and said he could count on us. I was 14 and my younger brother Jim was not yet even 13. But work we did, seven days a week. My brother and I hoed out 26 acres of tomatoes by hand since we didn't have a tractor or the animals to work. We also put in a field of peas so our general farming had turned almost to "truck" farming.

What made matters worse was that the year of 1934 was the hottest year on record in the continental United States. The mean temperature for the year was 56.61°. The second-hottest year had been 1921, when it was 56.11°, and in 1990 may be the third-hottest year at 56.06°. All I can remember is the hoe in hand in the hot soil, trying to break the crust to protect the little moisture that was present. The corn shriveled, the blades rolled up, and the ears became what we called "nubbins". The heat and lack of moisture destroyed the corn crop. Tomatoes fared somewhat better because they shaded the ground a bit and while we didn't get a bumper crop we did get a small crop of tomatoes which we picked and delivered that fall.

After the crop was in, my Dad again gathered us together and told us that he had paid what was due on the mortgage and hoped that he never in his life would have to see us work that hard again. He said he had made a down-payment on a new small Farmall tractor and he thought maybe we'd make it now with God's help!

But 1935 and 1936 were also to be bleak years for farming. These were the years of the Kansas dust bowl. Due to the dryness, strong winds raced across the plains of Kansas and picked up the topsoil. Even in Indiana, the sky would be grey with the Kansas dust. The heat was still intense. Our streams virtually dried up, all the water was pumped out of our wells, and the water table dropped.

I can remember hearing about the swamps that were originally present in Indiana. I remember the wooded areas. Even on our own property a swamp was still there until the 1930s. We dug ditches and put in tiles for drainage so that crops could be raised and, of course, check the mosquitoes that were so ubiquitous in the summertime. But now there were no more swamps, and no water. All the farmers suffered.

The Winter of '36

Worst of all, perhaps, was the winter of 1936-37 when I was sixteen and a junior in Kokomo high school. The school was approximately three and a half miles from our home. Although it was far below zero we had managed to get to school. But during one morning the temperature kept going down, and the snow was blown and huge drifts formed. No one talked about the chill factor in those days, but the actual temperature dropped to 36 below zero by mid-day and the wind howled. The schools could not be warmed, so they were all closed, and everyone was instructed to go home. One of my friends took me to the edge of town, because snow plows had cleared some of the city streets. But that was as far as he could go in the car, so about the last mile I had to walk with just a sweater and an athletic jacket and corduroy pants to protect me against the arctic weather. Needless to say, I ran most of the distance and when I reached the house at about two in the afternoon the blizzard was at its most intense.

As I came into the house my mother was frantic. She said, "Pile on all the clothes you can find, and go help your father. He's been out there a long time."

"What is he doing?" I asked.

"Well, Mr. Miller (a neighbor about a mile West) got stuck in a drift and Bob Hillis (our next-door neighbor) tried to pull him out with his truck, but he got the truck stuck too. Dad couldn't get the tractor started so he decided to harness up the mules to pull them out. So he had to get the mules in from the field, harness them up, and get them out there."

My first reaction was "What stupidity! Why not just come in and wait until the storm blows over and maybe pull out the vehicles tomorrow or the next day?" But at any rate, there they were, all out there trying to fight the weather. I put on old clothes and two pairs of gloves and a leather hat, and some work boots.

By the time I got to the scene the wind was raging, the snow was swirling, and the black animals were frosted white. I told Dad to go in and get warm. Without hesitation he ran what would be about three blocks back to the house. They had almost dislodged the truck and I finished getting it out, attached a chain to the bumper of the car and dragged it back to the road going east and west which was still navigable. Since the wind was blowing from the west the snow was not piled up on the east-to-west road, whereas those going north and south were covered with large drifts. We pulled the car out and our neighbor went on his way, back to his home which was a little more than a mile distant.

I then took the mules and tried to get them to walk into the wind to go back to the barn. They refused to do so, because they wanted to put their rears to the wind. I therefore backed them the whole distance finally, into the protection of one of the sheds, whereupon I tried to get their harness off.

But my fingers would no longer work. I pulled my glove off to see that my fingers had frosted and were white. Immediately I ran into the house and started to put them in cold water. I found that I had frozen six fingers and discovered that my ears were starting to hurt. I had frosted the lobes of both ears. Needless to say, they were extremely painful. And even today, more than 50 years later, when I get into extreme cold I can detect which six fingers were frozen.

Despite all that work, Mr. Miller -- who had stubbornly sat in his car waiting for help to pull him out -- ironically contracted pneumonia due to the exposure, and was dead in four days. What complete idiocy! I thought. But such was the mindset of that old pioneer spirit. With the windchill that day I can well imagine that the temperature might have been rated as 90 below zero.

The Wildcats

Kokomo High School stood on the banks of the Wildcat Creek, which ran through the city and ultimately emptied into the Wabash River, a branch of the Mississippi. My guess is that the someone, some time, must have seen wildcats along the creek, and named the stream accordingly. And our teams were called the Wildcats.

During my freshman year tryouts for the year's basketball team were announced. All the candidates would work out or play games in front of the coaches. As cuts were made, the names were posted of those who were to continue. When the third cut was made I did not find my name on the list. I was shocked. But I just ignored it and turned out anyhow. A short time later the coach counted the boys and checked his list. He came over to me and said I had made a mistake and that I had been cut. I told him it was his mistake and that I had played with most of those still on the squad in the church league and I knew I was better than any of them because I was a high scoring player. With that he looked surprised and said, "Okay, go ahead and play." I was the only one to make the varsity my sophomore year!

I had also made the varsity football team. During my sophomore year I foolishly offered my right leg one day for one of my friends to learn to block. The shock hyperextended the knee posteriorly, as it bent backward! It swelled up a little bit, but didn't seem to bother me that much. The ligaments were probably torn and loosened. During my junior year it was reinjured severely when I played halfback against Jefferson at Lafayette. The game was played on the Purdue University practice field where there was no grass. In trying to skirt left end and reverse my field I got trapped and the inside ligaments of my knee were torn. Up until that time I had been a very fast runner, and from then on had to wrap my knee for practice and for games. I never felt that I was the same again.

When I was a sophomore I could easily throw a football 50 yards in the air. One day in making a block with my arm extended I tore my shoulder. Today they would call it the rotator cuff. I was finished as a passer.

The Strike

During my junior year in basketball another very traumatic event in my life occurred. There were three seniors on the team, with the coach, "Peedad" Campbell. He was a very small man who had a claim to fame in that he had held John Wooden at Purdue to a few points below his average in a game with Indiana University. I played guard, and was kind of a playmaker and took a little leadership whenever the need arose. During that year the coach brought up a freshman who was a thin, black young man who could really leap. A good jumper would be a great advantage for the team. He didn't interfere with my position, so I wasn't too concerned. He was quiet and just went about his business of playing basketball.

However, one of the seniors was beaten out and the older team members thought it was unfair that this young man was brought up and given a starting position on the team without having practiced with us or competed with us for his position. Therefore, the three seniors sat down and wrote a letter to the effect that it was a strike. They didn't want to play with the young man and so in an afternoon while school was under way, after having written the letter, they caught me in a hallway and asked me to sign it. Naturally, seeing my teammates and wanting to keep the spirit of the team together, I signed the letter, thinking that it would simply lead to a meeting, so that things could be worked out. One of our varsity team members couldn't be located, but it was almost a unanimous signing of the letter.

After receiving the letter, the coach, who was a little man in many ways, immediately kicked all the signees off the team. He was going to teach us a lesson. We had always been told that the team was important, and not to just shoot every time you had the ball, but to work the ball around for the open person to get the best shot. So basketball was a team game -- yet here was the whole team locked out of the gymnasium, with no discussion and no questions. At that time, athletics were very important to me and it was a blow which I felt was quite unfair. The whole issue was considered a strike and received national headlines.

This incident brought popularity to the coach, but it did little to increase respect for him among the students and the local gentry. Since I was a kind of leader he somehow blamed me! However, I was permitted to come back on the team for my senior year.

Encounters

During my junior year I had my first encounter with a homosexual. I was always friendly to everyone. Even though I had heard of homosexuals it was hard for me to understand them. Many times I would stay on and practice shooting baskets and dribbling a little bit longer, and sometimes find myself the last to leave the locker room. One particular day I was sitting in front of my locker after having come out of the shower, and was drying my feet with a towel. This young man, who was in the class ahead of me, had engaged me in conversation and had sat down beside me while I was drying myself. All at once he grabbed my penis. I was frightened. I hit him in the face with the back of my hand and ordered him out of the locker room and never to be caught in there again.

At about that time I had another episode in the locker room which I couldn't quite understand when it happened. There was one tough kid who apparently wanted to determine his position, sort of the way animals will pursue their position in a hierarchy. This young man, whose name was Karl, had a reputation for being a bully. On a couple of occasions he had burned me pretty well by the flipping of a towel. I had warned him to stop it, but he persisted. This particular day I was in no mood for that kind of treatment, and after he had burned me again I went after him. Here were two naked bodies in a fist-fight right there in the shower room. We were both about the same height, but I was a good bit stronger than he was, and it wasn't long before the coaches and others interrupted the fight. That fight was all it took for us to become good friends. It appeared that this was what he particularly had been looking for, to give me the respect that he wanted to in the first place. It was his idea of the behavior needed to gain respect, and if I had been a wimp I might never have earned his respect. He was the only one that I knew of in our class who died at a quite young age of alcoholism. He had some psychological problems but we came to like each other very much. He came to our house for dinner on several occasions and often sought my opinion.

The Question of Early Marriage

It was a part of the rural tradition that marriage came early. In fact, during our senior year in school one of my classmates and his girlfriend decided to get married. As I remember, any woman who was not married at the age of 20 was considered an old maid, and it actually quite often became a family concern. But from my upbringing in the Methodist Church, I had been taught that sexual relations were sinful, and so going out with a lady was really frightening.

In my freshman year in high school, at age fourteen, I had seen, in another homeroom a little girl by the name of Dede. She had something strange in her mouth; it was the only set of braces I remember seeing in the whole city. Her father was a physician and she traveled to Indianapolis to have her teeth straightened. That was no detraction for me, because I thought she was the most beautiful and charming person I had ever seen. But I was from the other side of the tracks, so to speak. She lived in the plush, west side of town and I was a hick from the farm. All I could do was admire her from a distance, and I am not sure she ever knew how I really felt about her for several years. When I finally was able to get enough courage through the insistence of friends to call her on the telephone, my mouth was so dry that I could hardly speak. By that time she was dating an older boy two classes ahead and refused my invitation for a date, which only verified my limited self-image at that time. But I still carried the torch, quietly, just the same.

I dated other girls, whenever I could, because a date usually consisted of just buying a coke and sitting and talking. Or, if we really had money, it would involve a ten-cent tenderloin sandwich at one of the local hangouts. In the places where we went on dates there were usually nickelodeons and whoever had the nickel would put it in the machine. All of us loved to dance.

Big Bands

From my younger years I remember the start of the big band movement. Paul Whiteman was one of the originators of the swing bands, soon to be followed by the big three, Benny Goodman, Tommy Dorsey, and Glenn Miller. Other names that I remember were Jimmy Dorsey, Glen Gray, Bunny Barrigan, Claude Thornhill, Les Brown, Charley Burnett, and Bob Crosby, and in addition the noted Cab Calloway. These bands would frequently be heard on national hookup radio from one of the big dance pavilions around the country. Bing Crosby and Perry Como were both popular during my high school years.

I am amazed at how innocent we were in that semi-rural community. I mentioned the warnings of the church on a moral basis, but it didn't end there. We were told about social diseases. These were the days before antibiotics and there was no good treatment for syphilis or gonorrhea. Therefore, we were scared. In addition, anyone that got a girl pregnant must immediately marry her, and so it was ill-advised to play around unless you had someone that you loved enough to spend your life with. A little petting was about as far as it ever went, and even that made us nervous and scared.

One evening, on coming home -- not even too late -- I was fearful after my sister's and uncle's experience that I was getting appendicitis. I ached in my belly and my groin, so I woke up my mother, telling her that I was fearful of having appendicitis. She examined my stomach by punching it and then said, "Have you been out with a girl tonight?" I sheepishly said, "Yes, for a while." She said, "Go to bed, you will be fine tomorrow." How embarrassed I was later to find that that was the old-fashioned stone-ache, or what some people call "blue balls". It is a cramping of the muscles and referred pain quite similar to the menstrual cramps that a female will get. But little did I know of that when I was sixteen years old! I'm sure there must have been quite a discussion between her and my Dad at my innocence! Needless to say, it was many years before I had an actual sexual experience.

I think the school did its best to keep things straight. There were about 300 in each class in high school. On Friday afternoons there would be what they called "afternoon hops" in the gymnasium, where music records would be supplied and all the kids could come to dance under supervision by teachers. These were the early days of jitterbug, so things could get pretty wild once in a while.

During my senior year, there was another young lady I fancied, and on three occasions I tried to make a date with her. But each time she refused. It wasn't until 50 years later, at our high school's 50th Year Class Reunion that I discovered why she wouldn't accept my invitation to go out. She had later married and her husband had died, and so I asked her for a dance at the reunion, more or less to get the opportunity to talk to her. During the dance I asked her why she had refused me so many times, and she said, "Well, I know I was pretty stupid, but I thought you were nothing but a dumb football player who would never be anything more than a farmer. And I didn't want to become involved." She said, "I know that sounds terrible, knowing what you have done since, but nevertheless that's the reason." I suppose that is the reason why young ladies of senior high school age are attracted to older men: because they see in them more stability and more sophistication. All the senior boys, meanwhile, look to the freshman girls to get attention.

I too found myself being led to the younger girls, mostly by default of many of the females in my own class. There is something biologic about this, in that women mature earlier and always do the choosing. The job of the male as proven by my experience is to earn rank which then makes him attractive to the female! Certainly, it is true that when you call for a lady in a one-and-a-half-ton flatbed truck, as I had to do, there was not much rank and prestige involved.

The Lesson at the Meat Market

During my junior year in 1937, I got a job at Garrison's Meat Market. I trimmed the scraps off of cuts of meat and was the main person to grind the hamburger. As I recall, we sold hamburger at five cents a pound, and people would come in and buy ten, fifteen and up to 25 pounds at one time. They would buy second-day-old bread, make meatloaf and really have a lot of calories for survival. That, together with beans and potatoes, really sustained many of the poorer families on very little money.

I finally graduated to the place where I could serve customers and this is when I got in trouble with Mr. Garrison. My father had always taught me to give a little extra, whether it was a bushel of vegetables or a sack of food. Thinking that this was everyone's view, I was caught one day undercharging a customer by two cents. The next day I was released from the job and I questioned the owner about it. He said, "That may have been what your father taught you, but my profit is on a very small margin, and you have to be fair to the customer but you also have to be fair to me." With the end of that job I learned that any transaction has to be fair to both sides. I learned to be exact, and that making a profit was necessary for survival.

Lunch Money

I would take fifteen cents to have lunch, which would consist of a hamburger and a bowl of chili at one of the White Castle hamburger stands. By the time I had been up all day, with chores early in the morning, and practiced one of the sports in the afternoon, I would be famished on my way home. When I had a spare ten cents I would stop, on walking home the three miles, at one of the doughnut shops where I could get a dozen day-old doughnuts for ten cents. On several occasions I ate the whole dozen while walking home before doing the usual evening chores. It was pure calories, but at that time I was burning them up.

The Real Injury

At the end of my junior year, although I had sustained an injury, my knee was quite stable. That summer, when I was perched atop a load of hay on a wagon that was being pulled through a ravine, I was thrown some fourteen feet in the air. As I landed at an angle on my right foot, my body was in a twisted position and I heard a rip in my right knee. The pain was excruciating and by evening the knee had swollen far beyond anything I had seen before. In the spring football practice of that year, I had been shifted to fullback, and a new coach had been hired by the school. His name was Tubby Trobaugh. I could see that my whole senior season in football would now be at risk.

I was one of only two seniors on the team, and by mid-season I was finally able to run, only to re-injure the knee again and again. I did regain enough use to play my senior year in basketball, but was never quite the same again in my athletic ability.

I finished the general course in high school and although I had been an honor student in grade school and even in junior high school, now if I had been one step lower I would have been in the lowest third of the class in grades.

The Low Point

Perhaps the lowest point of my life was in June of 1938 after the graduating exercises for school. All my friends were talking about which college they would attend, or what their plans would be for the rest of their lives. I had bid good-bye to so many of my companions, and had dejectedly started my walk home on a very hot and sweaty afternoon. I thought I would take one last look at the old gym, and then make my long sad trek back to the farm. As I was walking by the gym almost with tears in my eyes, one of the assistant coaches, a Mr. John King, was parked in his car waiting for someone to join him. He shouted to me to come over and say goodbye. He commented on how unhappy I appeared. That five-minute conversation is one that I have never forgotten.

I told him how disturbed I was that all my friends were going to college and that I had no hope. I said I didn't think that I could make it as an athlete because of my knee, and that we didn't have any money, and I guess all that I could ever hope to be was a farmer, because I felt that I did know how to do that. He told me that I should not get discouraged. He insisted that I was very bright. He said that I was a leader, and he said it didn't make any difference how I did it, but the way would come for me to go to college. He insisted that I keep my courage up, keep working and saving, and that somehow, something would happen that I could get further schooling if I really wanted it. He brightened my spirit. It was an encouragement that was badly needed at that time. But nothing changed soon.

My self-image was still very poor. Here I was, round-shouldered, with no money, not a very good student, and with a bad knee. I had no particular girlfriend, and many of my friends were leaving. But the one thing that I did have was the love of my family, which filled a desperate need for me at the age of eighteen.

Boys of this age often have conflicts with their fathers, because there is something in the psyche of the young man that is fearless and often ostentatious. It has frequently been joked that it is amazing how smart one's father gets in those years between the son's age 18 and 22.

It will be understood, therefore, that I was experiencing much discontent in going back to farming. So I sought other employment. The first summer I did spend mostly farming, and that fall got a job at Delco Radio Factory as a repairman for the push-button part of the automobile radios. As I recall, my wages were twenty cents an hour. Working across from me on the other side of the assembly line were about 30 people, one of whom was a person who had spent one year in college and regretted having quit. He also encouraged me to try to get some advanced education. But the experience of working on an assembly line wasn't all that terrible for me, because I took the opportunity to learn something about electronics and the manufacturing process and assembly line techniques. I could see there was very little to be gained in the long run, because even if I made Supervisor of one of the lines, I was still only going to make twenty-five cents an hour, and in effect be stuck. As I said, my sister worked in the Personnel Office and even the plant manager didn't do too well, according to my thinking.

My Steel Mill Experience

During the winter of 1938 and spring of 1939, I played church league basketball and my knee gradually built up some strength. I felt encouraged to pursue perhaps some further athletic adventures. In the spring I got a job in a steel mill because of the higher pay. I had already joined the union, very reluctantly because I didn't want to give a part of my meager wages, particularly to people who I felt were in it for their own benefit and not necessarily for the cause of the workers.

There was always competition for jobs so I started out in the "slag pits". In the processing of steel most of the melting of the metal is done in an open hearth. The open hearth is lined with bricks which are highly resistant to heat. There are impurities in the metal which when the scrap is melted come to the top. These impurities are skimmed from the top of the molten metal and pushed into a funnel and dropped into a pit. After some cooling, the slag -- which resembles very heavy cinders -- is placed in baskets, lifted and carried off as refuse. And there is a lot of it. This is extremely dirty and hot work.

After the furnace has been used for a number of times it is cooled and must be broken down. Before it is completely cooled, again workers are asked to enter the furnace in asbestos suits and crowbars in order to tear the bricks apart so that the base of the furnace can be reconstructed for use again. The temperature was much hotter than that of a normal sauna and the steam of your sweat would start to burn after about 15 minutes of exposure. I remember one day of that summer coming out of the open hearth and seeking some fresh air that seemed very cool, although it was 106° outside.

Later that summer, I got a more or less steady job in the wire mill. Large ingots of metal are rolled in a rolling mill and heated up to a bright red temperature and in this state rolled on a series of rollers which starts to extend them into a long rod. They go through a series of mills until they are rolled down to approximately the size of the forefinger. They are further processed and pulled through a drawing mill. When they reach this state they are cut into long lengths and the wires then placed into what are called bales, or a coil. Then they are put in the tempering furnace, heated to a proper temperature, and permitted to be cooled so that the wire is softened. Various sizes of wires are coiled, because it is from such material that bolts are made. With further drawing and a series of softenings the size is reduced down for nails and finally to barbed wire.

I couldn't understand why we were making so much barbed wire. This was in the summer of 1939 and although fighting was going on in Europe, Pearl Harbor was not to come until two years later. But here we were making room after room of barbed wire!

Chuck and Ray

On my first day in the wire mill I was taken to a large room with four wire mills in action. It was here that I met Chuck and Ray. The coils were placed over a large peg and the wire was inserted into the drawing mill where it was processed. On asking what it was I was supposed to do, I was told that the bale had to be separated from a group, picked up and put on the peg which was about shoulder height. After this the main operator would take one end and guide it into the mill and make the necessary attachments. That seemed simple enough as I watched Ray do it a couple of times. Both of them were black people. Chuck was a man I would judge to be about six feet two, very large and strong. However, Ray could not have weighed over 170 pounds and was about 5'7". So I remember them standing by and snickering after they had described to me what to do. I was to pick up the coil, walk it over and place it on the peg, and turn the coil in such a manner that the wire could be fed into the machine in the proper way. They had made it look easy.

So I went over to the coil and started to pick it up -- and nothing happened. I then backed away, hitched up my pants a little bit, and grabbed it again. But it still didn't move. I then asked, "Well, how much does this weigh?" They laughed and said, "Oh, three to four hundred pounds." And I said, "And you expect me to handle this myself?" They both nodded in agreement. So after they let me struggle for some time unsuccessfully, I asked them to demonstrate it again. They first lifted only one side and placed their knees under the coil. The second move, then, was to lean backward and at the same time lift the front end of the coil so that now they stood with the legs apart and the coil on the legs. Then from that position, instead of lifting it with the back they walked it across the room with it lying on the thighs. When they arrived at the machine, it was an easier trick, then, to get both arms under it and lift it up so that it could be engaged over the peg.

This job lasted through the spring and summer. Many chewed tobacco, allegedly to help with the dust and grit. Big splashes of brown expectorate were all over the floor. It was obvious to me that this just couldn't be my future life. I had to do something. I was at a low point in my life when all that I knew how to do was work. I worked the night shift at the mill and during the day I worked on the farm for my keep at home.

Back to Football

In late summer of that year I went to see my old high school coach and said that I felt that I was ready now, that my knee might be strong enough for me to go and try to make a college football team. He had received inquiries from the University of Kentucky. So three of us went to Lexington, Kentucky to try to make their squad. Because I had played halfback and fullback in high school and had a knee injury I thought that maybe it would be safer for me to play quarterback, which at that time was a blocking back. Once in a while the quarterback would go out on a pass and on defense he would be a line backer. Nevertheless, I thought that this would maybe save my knee, so I tried out for a position in which I had no experience. Still, I made it to the last cut. It came down to the cost of an in-state or an out-of-state scholarship, and I lost out.

Again I was very disheartened. I came back to Kokomo in a desperate condition. I went back to Coach Trobaugh who after a few minutes said, "Get some clothes and get in the car." He then drove me personally from Kokomo to Indiana University at Bloomington, Indiana, and presented me to Coach Bo McMillan. My brother, the night before, had quarterbacked our Kokomo High School team and had intercepted a pass in the end zone and had run 106 yards for a touchdown, which made the Indianapolis newspapers. So my brother's clipping helped me to get in college.

Coach Trobaugh explained the situation. I had saved just under $200 for my year's work after high school. The athletic jobs paid $30 a month and if I made the squad I received my tuition and books free. It was my opportunity. If I had to be a gladiator, so be it! I didn't want to go back to the farm, to the assembly line, to the steel mill or the meat shop. I felt I deserved something more. The university scholarships and jobs had all been given out to other students.

Coach McMillan told me that inevitably one of the young men given scholarships would not make it. Boys would get homesick, studies would be too stressful, or they would find that they were simply not college material. If I could stick out a couple of months, and survive I possibly could get one of the jobs. It meant that I had to compete for one. Thus, I found myself in college one year late, but now resolved to stay there no matter what the sacrifice.

Not knowing anything else to do at the time, I enrolled in the physical education department and decided that I would be a coach. Prior to that time I had had interest in being a veterinarian. In fact, while I was a senior in high school I had written to various schools and found that Ohio State had the most prominent veterinarian's school in the midwest. I liked animals, particularly horses. And I even imagined myself as a fancy horse doctor at a racetrack. However, that would have to wait, because now the main issue was survival. My self-image was also miserably low. How could a round-shouldered dumb football player be attractive to a decent young lady? I had my work cut out for me.

So I started taking courses in English and other subjects in the Liberal Arts College. (I had a lot to learn: I remember not understanding the word "augment".) My attitude then was to just get started in something. I came to love Indiana University and in order to get the cheapest rate I stayed in a boarding house with other athletes where we got our breakfast and lunch and a room for, as I remember it, $10.00 a week. I boarded there with two or three older players on the Varsity Squad. Freshmen at that time were still not permitted to play on the Varsity. They became good friends, and quite helpful. Now I can honestly say that these were very happy moments and very stimulating and exciting days for me there in Bloomington, Indiana.

The Moment of Truth

My objective was to get an education but it was also to make the football team, which I viewed as a method to stay in school. By now I had learned a few of the tricks for the position of quarterback, and after about two months into the season we came to the night before Homecoming, and the infamous "Rhiney" game. A Rhiney is a freshman, and in the fraternities they are sometimes forced to wear Rhiney pods, or little green caps to indicate that they are green, dumb freshmen.

The alumni would return on the Friday before the big homecoming game on Saturday. On the Friday evening, inside in the Field House, the freshman squad would be divided up and the teams would be pitted against each other, to see what kind of prospects the alumni could expect for the following year. In fact, we were told that a number of us would not be asked back for the next year and that a good bit depended on our performance on this game. As far as I was concerned, this was it!

In our Physical Ed courses we were tested for muscle strength. Such things as freehand rope climbing, standing jumps, and what today are called bench presses were used in order to check our progress in physical performance. As I recall, I lifted almost 800 pounds with my legs, which was second only to one black athlete who had gone to 825 pounds. I was certainly the strongest white person in the freshman class. I credited my experience in the steel mill with building up this kind of muscle. At any rate, when the game came I was ready.

I don't remember much about the happenings in offense except for a few good blocks. But I do remember the display I put on in defense. I made several ferocious tackles. One particularly regrettable experience was a head-on tackle I made on one of the very fast halfbacks that they were grooming for big things for the next year. His name was Gerstenhaver, and he had gone around left end and was cutting back against the grain where I met him head on. I caught him mostly on his right leg and pulled his hip out of the socket. He screamed in agony, and I was deeply sorrowed for him. After that injury they called off the game, because it was simply a demonstration anyway for the pleasure of the alumni, and the evaluation by the coaches.

Needless to say, the next week when I went to the office and told the coach that I was out of money and needed a job, he said there was no question about my being asked back, and that I had made the squad. It was to me a great achievement, and the satisfaction of a goal. But it was also very sad to me that someone got hurt in the process. Yet I reminded myself that playing football was a part of my survival, and injury was a risk to be taken when anyone puts on the pads and buttons up a helmet.

In those days we had no face masks or bite blocks and even the headgears were not well designed. Having some Indian and Scottish genes in my background, I had high protruding cheekbones which were usually raw from abrasions from the time the season started until it ended. Two weeks after the freshman game I got into a pile-up and somehow bent my left thumb backward, breaking it in the first joint. The fingers are considered long bones in the body and contain an epiphysical bone plate underlined with cartilage so growth can occur under pressure. It was almost as if the cartilage plate had not quite closed, although I was 19 years of age, and that part of the finger was still slightly soft. Years later I was to learn that males at 19 years of age are essentially mature in their facial skeleton. But in 1939 my season was over a couple of weeks early, and I could start turning my attention to studies in a more deliberate manner.

Real School Days

As I said, I was happy at Indiana University. At that time there were only 6000 students. At the middle of the year I found a room with two older people closer to the school, and cheaper. It was also not too far from the sorority house where Dede was in residence. By now Dede had become the beauty queen for the university, and was very much in the limelight. Many of my friends from Kokomo had also enrolled at I.U. and I had the opportunity to renew some friendships.

The Kinsey Report

I don't remember whether it was in the Psychology Department or the Sociology Department, or even the field of Biology, but during my Freshman year in college a professor by the name of Kinsey had established a project for studying sexual behavior in males, and he chose to study the students at Indiana University. He was a kindly, white-haired gentleman, who carried a small black briefcase. He had structured a form for recording questions that had been pretty well standardized. He interviewed on a personal basis literally thousands of subjects before writing his very famous *Report*. I was the youngest of the three students sharing a single room right beside a small restaurant called Stone's. Many of the students would come in and hang out talking over coffee or a coke. Many of us had a chance to talk as it was just next door.

I don't remember most of Kinsey's questions, but I do remember several questions circling around homosexuality. He wanted to know the first time that we had been engaged in sex, how many episodes we had encountered, how frequently, how much masturbation we exercised, certain of our attitudes with regard to both our parents, when we first felt that we had fallen in love, if we had, what kind of sex education we had had in the home and in our school, what our attitude was about women, whether we wanted to raise a family -- general questions of this nature which now have become commonplace but which at that time were unacceptable on a public basis.

After the interview he would frequently leave a questionnaire with a little measuring device in which we were supposed to measure the size of an erection. Naturally, some of the students made a joke out of it and some sent in sizes that would even embarrass a horse. Some years later, as I recall, they also did a survey on women in an effort to determine the nature of their sexual behavior.

I was the last to be interviewed in our room. One room mate, John Marlowe, was in his thirties. Dale Thatcher, the other, was in his mid-twenties, but I was barely 20 and had had no sexual experience at that time. Because Kinsey seemed like a knowledgeable person and was quite scholarly, I shared with him some of my inner feelings.

The first two years of college particularly were very difficult for me from an emotional and a sexual point of view. It was extremely difficult for me to concentrate because I was chronically horny. I would lapse into dreams and fantasies of not just one girl but many. More than on a weekly basis I would wake up in the night with a wet dream. Sometimes there would be no dream at all but I would simply awake to find that I had ejaculated in my pajamas to the point of disgust.

It is said that a young boy between 15 and 20 has his most active sexual years. I can certainly believe it, because that time was difficult. In older cultures, and some primitive cultures even today, young men by the age of 16 and 17 were married because life expectancy at the time of the Romans, for example, was no more than 30 - 35 years.

All that is necessary is to visit a locker room and observe athletes to reach the conclusion very rapidly that all men are not created equal. I am sure that I got an extra share of testosterone. It would certainly be an interesting study to determine the relation of testosterone production to general drive and ambition and perhaps even study this particular physiology in criminal cases.

Jocko's Death

There is an old saying that "You can take a boy out of the country but you can't take the country out of the boy". From time to time I would visit the family at home by hitch-hiking from Bloomington to Kokomo. It was comforting to go back to the farm and enjoy some of Mom's cooking and also to get some rest from my toils.

One week end in the spring I was home and was driving to see a friend when I noticed little Jocko, our mule, hitched with two big horses to a neighbor's plow. Furthermore, the neighbor was whipping her. I stopped and shouted at him to stop beating her. When I returned home I asked Dad what she was doing there. "Well," Dad replied, "Milt wanted to borrow her for his plowing." I said, "But she's not in shape and he was beating hell out of her. What do you mean letting him do that?" His answer was, "He's a neighbor and how can you refuse him?"

I was disgusted that anyone would take advantage of my father's friendship. That evening when Milt brought Jocko home her head was hanging low. Her fire was gone. The next day she died. I wanted to kick hell out of Milt but -- that was farm life in Indiana and the Mid-west.

Crude and Aggressive

I must have been a brute. I had a girlfriend named Norma from Kokomo who was in the Tri Delta sorority. One night I gave her a big squeeze when I bid her good night. She said it hurt her, and I thought she was kidding. The next day she phoned from the infirmary that she had been X-rayed and found to have a broken rib! I felt terrible, but I hadn't realized I had hugged her that vigorously. Very soon I was dropped, and she became engaged to a guy with money and a car.

My Great Roommates

It was highly stimulating to have older roommates, two people in their fourth year of school. Dale Thatcher was also from Kokomo, in his last year of Physical Education and lamenting the fact that he felt he had almost wasted his four years in school because he didn't feel he was prepared for very much except for the teaching of physical education maybe in a high school. John Marlowe, who was 35, had gone back to school after having worked a number of years. He was married and was in his first year of medical school. We would sit around occasionally and rap, and they both observed that I was struggling with my classes.

One day I confessed that I deeply wanted to be a dentist. I had never told anybody, and I stressed that I thought it was beyond my capabilities, that I didn't have any money, and I didn't have the brains. Both Dale and John immediately jumped on me and criticized me greatly. They both said that I was stupid in thinking that I was limited. John in particular sat down with me then and said, "Okay, what's your problem?" I said, "Well, right now, for instance, I'm struggling in English. I'm supposed to write this composition and my grades are very poor."

"Why don't you let me help you?" he asked. "What's your subject?"

As I recall it had something to do with education, but I don't remember exactly. Anyhow, he started pointing out my mistakes. He finally said, "Let me re-write it for you and see what we can do. Do you want an A, a B, or a C?"

"Well," I said, "they'll suspect that someone is helping me if I get an A, so why don't we go for a B?" So with John's help I got a B on that composition. He made it all so easy. After that he helped me with some of my other subjects.

John was so excited about what he was learning in medical school that I couldn't believe it. He became a most important factor in my career. Finally, about a month before the school year was to end, I made an appointment with the Dean of the School of Dentistry, Dr.

William J. Crawford. He was another person who was to influence my life at an important turning point.

Because I was helped, I have always tried to encourage young students all around me. Even though I met discouragement at home, I had those almost-by-chance contacts with other people and their encouragement and actions, without which I might not have attempted to do what I have done since.

The chance meeting with Coach King at my lowest moment, the taking of things in hand by Coach Trobaugh, at his own expense escorting me and insisting that I be given a chance, the encouragement, stimulation and enthusiasm of John Marlowe and Dale Thatcher, and finally the big push by Dean Crawford -- all combined to send me on my way, and none asking for anything in return. Their spirit has stayed with me all these years, and I have never forgotten, even after more than half a century. Young people certainly need encouragement and some achievements to build their confidence.

The Learning Base

By now I had probably learned more than I recognized. I had learned that each person needs to respect himself, and that it must be earned. Today, many people call it identity. One must have pride and stand up for himself. I have often thought about the human mind, why among boys there is always a leader, why among gangs there is always one boss -- it is a sort of unwritten principle.

What further lessons could I take from that experience from grade school to college? I learned that everyone is involved in a depression, but I also learned that we can all survive. Work and jobs had started on the farm. Then cutting meat, driving a delivery truck, working on an assembly line in electronics, working at hard labor on a road construction gang, and working in heavy labor at a steel mill all taught me that every job was an opportunity to learn. It further taught me toughness, courage, persistence and fearlessness. It taught me truth, and its importance. It taught me fairness and honesty with all concerned.

It was thus that I became dedicated to a life in the pursuit of dentistry, changing my curriculum and essentially throwing away a full year of college trying to find myself, as so many young people must do. Luckily, I found myself by the age of 20. Others are not so fortunate.

The Drums of War and the Economy

But by now the drums of war were beginning to beat heavily. Roosevelt had been elected and had adopted the Keynesian philosophy of economics. During this time in my life, starting with the great crash of October 24, 1929, an entire decade of my life had witnessed the failure of 85,000 banks and 25% of the population out of work. Whether or not the retention of the free enterprise as described by Adam Smith in 1776 would have seen the country through those times, at least from these ashes the Keynesian philosophy emerged and massive spending was started.

We saw the Works Project Administration (WPA) and the picture of men leaning on their shovels not quite understanding what to do. We saw the Civilian Conservation Corps (CCC) camps opened for young people going out into the country on conservation programs. This was in contrast to Adam Smith's projections in his "Wealth of Nations", where he said that the human was drawn by ego and selfish motives for self-preservation and survival, and that we should, further, not deem self-interests and ambitions as vices, but rather virtues. If a person worked hard and achieved prosperity, he should be left alone. Labor and capital would be put to work in the free marketplace and competition would act as an invisible hand. The best quality at the best price would be produced by such freedom, or "laissez-faire." This was a classical theory for economics, but one that had failed on a world basis.

Scholars during this time (roughly during my junior high school and high school years) were trying to sort out where things had gone wrong. The invisible hand of competition had not shown itself in 1929. The reason for this was that money had leaked out of the free enterprise system. These leaks were from savings and accumulation of wealth, taxes and the entry of foreign goods. Therefore, to put the economy back into balance the government had to borrow, the government had to spend by putting tax money back into the economy, and had to make greater exports in order to counter the imports. If these matched, an equilibrium was produced. This became known as the Keynesian Process.

I had heard these arguments, although I did not understand them. Because my family had always been Republican I felt that I could survive by hard work. Why couldn't others?

By 1940, a recovery was becoming obvious. One possibility which I never hear mentioned much was the fact that we were probably selling goods to foreign countries in preparation for their war effort against Hitler. We knew that young people my age were being trained with guns and regimented in Germany. But the average American chose to look upon this with curiosity rather than involvement. I knew the recovery was under way when I got a job in Bloomington, Indiana in 1940 behind the counter in the meat department of the Kroger Company and was paid forty cents an hour. Imagine working a ten-hour day and getting four whole dollars! Yes, indeed, times were improving.

*   *   *

These were the times as I turned 21 in 1941. Little did I know what lay ahead. If there is one message to pass on from this decade of my life it pertains to the inestimable value of encouragement and respect for young people.

5

THE DISCOVERY OF IDENTITY
(1941 - 1945)

America's Mainspring

In his book "The Mainspring of Human Progress", Henry Grady Weaver started with these words:

> "For 60 known centuries, this planet that we call Earth has been inhabited by human beings not much different from ourselves. Their desire to live has been just as strong as ours. They have had at least as much physical strength as the average person of today, and among them have been men and women of great intelligence. But down through the ages, most human beings have gone hungry, and many have always starved . . . .

> "The Roman Empire collapsed in famine. The French were dying of hunger when Thomas Jefferson was President of the United States. As late as 1846, the Irish were starving to death; and no one was particularly surprised because famines in the Old World were the rule rather than the exception.

> "Down through the ages, countless millions, struggling unsuccessfully to keep bare life in wretched bodies, have died young in misery and squalor. Then suddenly, in one spot on this planet, people eat so abundantly that the pangs of hunger are forgotten.

The Questions

> "Why did men die of starvation for 6,000 years? Why is it that we in America have never had a famine?

> "Why did men walk and carry goods (and other men) on their straining backs for 6,000 years - then suddenly, on only a small part of the earth's surface, the forces of nature are harnessed to do the bidding of the humblest citizen? . . .

"Why did men, women, and children eke out their meager existence for 6,000 years, toiling desperately from dawn to dark -- barefoot, half-naked, unwashed, unshaved, uncombed, with lousy hair, mangy skins, and rotting teeth -- then suddenly, in one place on earth there is an abundance . . .?"

Weaver went on to explain that the incredible switch from candles to electric lights, from caves to air-conditioning, from epidemics to health, and from oxcarts to airplanes was due not to harder work but to a simple answer -- the use of energy. In addition, Weaver insisted that "a decision to act and the action itself are always under your own control".

Weaver pointed out that freedom cannot be separated from responsibility. In addition, he stated, "Man has the ability to change himself as well as his environment. He has the ability to progress and to keep on progressing."

Yes, America is, or was, a land of opportunity like nothing ever before.

Experiences in Social and Economic Developments by the 1940s

The 1930s had been called the "swinging years" with the big bands, and the rise of radio. The image that America had of itself started to change with the rise of the labor movement, and the accepted philosophy of economics. Our country roads were turned into highways. News for the rural areas was no longer just covered by local papers or party telephone lines. Radio had a much greater impact, perhaps, than people realized. The medium of radio came to be taken for granted. Even the farmers on their tractors, working in the fields, were now equipped with a radio.

One good thing about radio, aside from giving the news and people's exposure to information, was that it required an imagination. I remember the jingles and the advertisements that filled our airways.

In the beginning, the saying was "Go West, Young Man!" West Virginia was west of Virginia, and Ohio was west of that. Then came Indiana and Illinois. So the saying was generated from the East Coast. It earlier referred to the tremendous Mississippi Valley. That, together with the plantations west of the eastern seaboard, gave agricultural America a distinct advantage in world economics. Later, for instance, the agricultural products produced in a 400-mile radius from Iowa City were literally capable of almost feeding the world. It was the "great American breadbasket". And it was accessible, by water transport on the Mississippi River, with its branches, the Missouri, the Ohio, the Wabash, and some even farther west.

What the Mississippi Valley was to agriculture the Great Lakes were to industry and manufacturing. We had iron, we had coal, we had minerals, we had Edison and Ford, we had ingenuity and imagination, and we could not imagine an end. The Rocky Mountains made us rich with gold, silver, and copper, and the entire southwest was underlain with oil. It was so plentiful it gushed out of the ground. How could we, above all people, have had a depression?

Yet now, in the late 1930s, we were in an obvious stage of recovery. Through radio Roosevelt had his "Fireside Chats". We were changing, but didn't realize it. The work horse on the farm had begun to disappear. The construction of dams and the production of electricity when combined with coal and gas gave us a degree of energy for the production of work that had never been seen before. Our innovations and our applications of technology had made us the envy of the world.

And above all, our Christian-Judaic ethic and altruistic motives were still basic to our culture. Inherently, we wanted to be loved by our neighbors and loved by other countries while selling them our goods, and accumulating our wealth. We sought a national identity. We were becoming proud again.

Together with that, one of our richest resources was immigration. Ambitious people, willing to work hard, contributed to that work ethic. All had an opportunity. It was just there for the taking, and we were all taught to be responsible for ourselves. Since America was a land of opportunity, success was thought reachable by any person dedicating himself sufficiently to reach goals on his own. Each was to make his own silver spoon rather than being born with it in his mouth.

* * *

We became aware of the "drums of war". Television had not yet arrived, but we learned much via the news media. Movies were another industry that had found its heyday in the depths of the Depression, and had grown to be another medium of communication. Therefore, we all looked forward to the news reports of "Pathe News" at the movies, in black and white.

In 1940 a good Ford, Chevrolet or Plymouth was still around one thousand dollars. The motor could not be dependable for much more than 30,000 miles, so the trade-in after one to two years was the expected pattern. Because of that, Detroit was more production-conscious than quality-conscious. . . "keep it cheap enough that the many families can have a new car regularly, and keep changing the design each year to keep the market booming."

The attitude about automobiles tended to infiltrate the attitude in the whole country. The old artisans who came from Europe and Asia were still around, so there was an underlying quality-consciousness that still existed among artists and tradesmen.

When it was all put together, America literally had it all, or certainly most all of it. Certain metals such as aluminum, some copper, platinum, chromium, manganese, magnesium, and rubber had to be imported. But the things our country possessed could be obtained in abundance. We had good train and ship transportation, we had energy, we had the forests in the Northwest supplying us lumber. We had seaports and a fishing industry, and we had the stock market. The insurance business was booming. Finally, we had democracy and free enterprise and the free marketplace. How could we ask for more? We were great!

My Challenge in 1940

As explained before, during my first year at Indiana University, I made the decision to try for Dental School. On going through my credits, I could see it was almost as if the last two years of my life had been wasted from an academic standpoint. First, I had stayed out of school and worked to save money. Secondly, many of the subjects I had taken were not in science, or not with sufficient background for entrance into Dental School. Consequently, in my sophomore year I found myself taking comparative anatomy, English, and psychology.

I had made the squad in football, and I had joined the Alpha Tau Omega fraternity. In order to pay my fraternity dues and get my food at the fraternity, I washed dishes and waited tables there. I also did my share of janitor duty. Since I was on the football squad, we had one evening meal which was given us by the athletic department. Practice was an every-day affair, and lecture sessions were routine even when workouts were not scheduled. With all this activity, in work, study, and football, I can't remember when I wasn't tired and most times exhausted.

Football in 1940

In college football in 1940 we had gone from the old "T" and the "shifted T" to what was called a set "single wing". The halfback was usually the player who threw the ball or was the passer. The fullback either blocked for the halfback or was a strong runner who usually went through the line on power plays. The game rules were also those from the days before specialization. If a player was in the game he played both offense and defense. Therefore, the halfbacks were usually also the defensive backfield, and the fullback or quarterback or the center became the line backers.

During my sophomore year there had been good competition at the quarterback spot. The position was held by an experienced senior. The school had acquired Lou Saban, a freshman who ultimately was to become an all-pro with the Cleveland Browns and later one of the all-time leading coaches in the National Football League. They therefore asked me if I would use my talents to become a guard. Because the quarterback most frequently blocked down the line, the assignments sometimes were similar to block linemen or to go around the end and stop a line backer. My main goal was to stay on the squad and keep my library job, on which I spent time, mostly out of guilt for taking $30.00 a month for just playing football. I washed windows in the library and helped with the packing of books that were to be transferred to other libraries around the country (which I learned was an exchange program).

I learned both guard positions, right and left, offense and defense, and made the traveling squad my sophomore year. When we went out of town, for half of our games, travel was by bus or on the slow Monon Railroad that ran through Bloomington. It was an overnight trip just to go to Chicago. We played other Big Ten schools, and because our stadium held only about 20,000 people the school made more money playing at the bigger stadiums. So for Michigan and Ohio State, in those years we always played on their field, which seated around 80,000 to 105,000.

Bo McMillan was our coach, and he always referred to us to the press as "his poor little boys". It was true we were not very big, and there certainly were not very many of us. In fact, we couldn't even field three full teams. So many of us had to learn to play more than one position.

I somehow made it scholastically through my sophomore year with passing grades. But I honestly don't think I could have done it without the help of some fraternity brothers. I didn't realize it at the time, but in that sophomore year I was learning valuable lessons from two different sources.

Personal Identity

One of the problems that most cultures have experienced is psychologic depression that occurs in college-age students. We call them kids, but physiologically they are adults. I will be saying more later about my good friend Robert Ardrey who wrote "The African Genesis", "The Territorial Imperative", "The Social Contract", and "The Hunting Hypothesis". But particularly in his "The Territorial Imperative" he made a brilliant deduction that dealt with the psychological origin of human drives, motivations and human needs. He described how, after the main physiologic needs such as food and shelter are satisfied, the human is driven by three main forces. These are the need or desire for identity, the need for stimulation, and the need for security. But these concepts are difficult to understand unless the antithesis of each one is dealt with, which are anonymity (being a nobody), boredom, and anxiety or fear.

We frequently hear a young person and even older people making the statement, "I want to find out who I am." "I want to get in touch with myself." "I want to have some identity." Young people become confused, frustrated, bewildered and depressed. In extremely low moments of discouragement, even without the depression that drugs can produce, many will become suicidal out of hopelessness. In retrospect, my sophomore year was my own personal critical time, when my self-image became enlarged and my self-confidence was enhanced.

Quite frequently we hear of the hazing that occurs in a fraternity. Perhaps many people, never having been in a fraternity or a sorority, would feel there was a certain amount of mystique as to what the Greek letters could possibly mean. The Greek-lettered fraternities in the end perform a function similar to the adult lodges, particularly Free Masonry as I understand it. In high school I was initiated into DeMolay, which was a junior division of the Masonic lodge, but I never really appreciated the experience, nor did I understand its intent. I always regretted using a belt on some friends for initiation. But at Indiana University it soon appeared to me that the most successful in school and later in life were those who were members of a fraternity.

In my fraternity, Alpha Tau Omega (ATO), at least, there was a hierarchy. And above all, there was a discipline. The first year in the fraternity house freshman were in "the rat-class". As a whole we were treated as dum-dums who knew nothing. They started with us from the ground up. I was taught how to behave socially, how to hold a fork properly, and so on. The upper classmen really took on the role of older brothers, because we were chosen brothers in the fraternity. In the evenings or on appointed afternoons, our dining room was turned into study hall which was supervised by the upperclassmen. And when our grades were not adequate, or when we were caught in some sort of deportment error we got our asses beat with large wooden paddles, and it wasn't light -- we were really pounded! The question was, "Were we men enough to stand up to that kind of discipline?"

In my fraternity there was one week called "Hell Week" during which we did not bathe. Underneath our shirts we were constantly to wear an onion around our neck on a string and a rough gunny sack for an undershirt. We were to discipline ourselves not to smile or laugh. If we were caught laughing by an upperclassman we had to take a bite out of the onion. As I recall, two of the nights during that week we were not permitted to sleep. We had to get down on our hands and knees, scrub and wax all the floors. We were sent on various jobs for the fraternity, and we were to continue our work at school with the same degree of attention as usual. If we didn't measure up we were in danger of being dismissed from the fraternity altogether.

Hell Week was the final test before being admitted to brotherhood in the fraternity. And when that was passed to the satisfaction of the upperclassmen, a student certainly had developed an identity, a self-confidence, and a self-image. A young man was no longer just a nobody, he now had an idea of what he could do under the most trying circumstances, and that gave him an identity and confidence. He also had other people or brothers who really cared. Strangely, the fond memories of the fun and the stimulation that I received in my fraternity life are some of the most enjoyable and lasting of my entire life. Some of the fraternity songs, and some of the sorority songs are immortal. An example is one ATO song which I can still sing is:

> There are those who praise
> the diamond's rays
> or the ruby's blood-red hue,

while others praise
the opal's rays
or the sapphire's deep clear blue.

There are those who delight
in the topaz bright
or the pearl with its quiet gloss,
but brighter far
is each radiant star
that we have in our Maltese cross.

Old Alpha, how we love you,
yes, we do.
And Tau, to you we promise
to be true.
Omega, all our praises are to you,
To Alpha Tau Omega,
to dear old gold and blue.

One of the attachments to a co-ed was the act of giving a girl a fraternity pin for her to display on the campus. This was a sign that she was taken by one of the fraternity brothers. It was a sort of quasi-engagement without that formality, and an indication that it was a steady relationship. When this occurred, it was the occasion for a serenade to the sorority of the girl who was "pinned". I always loved to sing, and we had a group of excellent singers, one of whom was Bob McAfee Davis who later had his own television show in Hollywood. Another good singer was Bob Gaston, so we had a trio. I later met Bob Davis in Hollywood, but I never heard again of Gaston.

When one of our brothers gave out his pin, we customarily would go to the sorority house, after curfew, and put our best singers at the door or underneath the girls' balcony. It would be on a week end, on a Saturday night, and often I was asked to sing a specialty of mine, which was "That Old Black Magic". It truly was great fun, and very exciting to go visit the sorority, to have all the girls appear in their bathrobes and sing their sorority songs back to us as a sort of a mutual linkage between the fraternity and the sorority.

Later in the 1960s there was a movement among several universities to question the value of the fraternities, and in fact some universities made them illegal for fear of what would appear to be a lack of egalitarianism. But when some of the schools discovered that an extremely high proportion of the donations made to the university were from only 10% of the graduates, who had received a fraternity experience in college, needless to say the movement to oust the fraternities did not last long. However, the Hell Week was turned into Help Week, in which the fraternities found things in the community to do and the same sort of extra-curricular civic commitment had to be met. It was the same discipline, but more constructive, and it served the same purpose.

Fraternity Life

To get together with the brothers and sing and have dances at the fraternity house with live dance bands that we had in those years was indeed a thrill I haven't forgotten half a century later. I remember buying my first tuxedo in 1940 from Richman Brothers Clothing Store, brand new for $22.00. I used money I had saved, in dimes and quarters and nickels.

No one ever asks to get into a fraternity. A person must be invited. The good prospects or candidates for a fraternity very frequently are "rushed", and there is a competition among fraternities to get the best prospects. "Rushing" meant that a person would be invited to visit several of the fraternities, meet the members of the fraternity, and see the fraternity house. Most all fraternities were represented at all the different schools and universities -- Pre-medical, Pre-dental, Pre-law, Business, School of Fine Arts, School of Liberal Arts, and Science. Literally all aspects of education were represented in the different fraternity houses, so a student had an opportunity to meet several different kinds of people. Each fraternity liked to have one or two athletes in their house. When I was there there were two of us that represented the football team: myself and Charles Steel who also was a guard. There were also two basketball players who later were on the championship team from Indiana that won the NCAA: Bob Dro, who became Athletic Director at Indiana University, and Herman Schafer, who played many years professionally with the Lakers while they were in Minneapolis.

To this day I still donate to my fraternity, in the hope that other young men will receive the same opportunity for growth and finding identity that I had as a young man. In my opinion there should be even more fraternities than there are, because our schools have become so much larger. For instance, there are now more than 30,000 students at Indiana, five times what it was then, but the old fraternity house still stands and looks the same. The old stadium and the field house at Indiana University are long gone, replaced by newer, bigger and better ones. This was, however, the quiet scene in a southern Indiana college town in 1940 and '41.

My Third Year at College

There were three factors that helped me with my own identity: the first was making the football team; the second was my experience in the fraternity, which I think gave me a fuller, more confident life. And the third was the making of passing grades while still a member of the football squad.

Although I made the traveling squad my sophomore year, 1940, the coaches wanted to "red-shirt" me. Red shirts worn during practice were indications of training for the future squad. Therefore, I didn't play in any games as a sophomore so it would give me one more year of eligibility and I could have the benefits of that much more coaching.

In the Spring of 1941 the coaches determined that with my experience in the backfield and the handling of the ball, and my experiences in basketball, I was a good prospect to play the end position. Playing End required a number of skills because it required both speed and strength. Quickness was also an asset and, of course, a player had to be able to catch the ball. During the summer of 1941 I was told to learn both end positions and both guard positions on both offense and defense. That meant that I literally had to know all the players' assignments on almost every play. With that task I would have been prepared to be a good coach had I pursued some of my earlier intentions. Looking at my professional career, the one thing for sure is that if I had been a coach I would have been innovative.

By September of 1941 I had finished some of my preliminary requirements for Dental School. It was now that I tackled Physics, having had none in high school. Trigonometry, and other required courses such as Organic Chemistry and Biology still lay ahead. But now, playing in some of the games and travelling with the team was ever more demanding. In addition, I was having progressively greater problems with my right knee. It was continuously swollen, and was taped or wrapped for every practice and every game, which was quite restricting of movement as well as being painful. On several occasions, I had it drained with a needle and syringe, because the pressure caused more pain. The fluid would contain lots of blood so there were probably some ruptured vessels in the joint capsule. But I persevered because it was my livelihood -- or at least I thought so at that time.

When the team traveled my books would accompany me. When my teammates would go to enjoy a movie for relaxation on Friday night before the game on Saturday, I would stay in my room and study, or study on the train. Still, we missed school classes. That year we played the University of Nebraska. In order to play the game on Saturday in Lincoln we left on Wednesday, travelled two days and two nights by train, and stopped in Omaha for a practice at Creighton University on Friday, and then went down to Lincoln to play Nebraska on Saturday.

Through football I met many people: the press, and often some prominent individuals. For instance, on our trip to Nebraska when it was learned that I was an Alpha Tau Omega, some of the brothers at Nebraska after the game wanted to meet me. I was delighted to find that they had a dinner planned and that the governor of the state, being a brother in the Alpha Tau Omega fraternity, had also been invited. At that dinner I was requested to sit at the head table immediately beside the governor of the state of Nebraska. Certainly, if it hadn't been for my being an athlete, being on the football team, and being in the fraternity, I would not have had that opportunity and the chance for that experience and for growth in identity as well.

Flunking Out

Despite all my study efforts, by mid-season I was flunking flat out every subject I was taking. There were 300 students in my Physics class, and in the mid-term exam I had the lowest grade in the class, which was an unbelievable 10 out of a possible score of 100. I received pink slips in every course, and I was worn out. After the last game, which was always with Purdue, which that year we had won by a field goal (3-0), I went to see the coach to tell him of my predicament. I knew that on such occasions they had provided tutors and help for students who were deserving, and I begged for some help. What he said surprised me. "Well, Rick," he said, "I don't know whether you know it or not, but the football staff met and planned for next year, and you were voted as the most improved player on the squad. So we want to help you all we can."

That helped with my identity, but it wasn't going to give me grades, particularly in the subjects I was taking. I therefore made appointments with the professors in all of my courses. The one that worried me the most was the one which was a required course, Physics. The head of the department, and my teacher, was a Dr. Mitchell. I asked if I could see him, and was granted the appointment. I tried to explain my situation because I had gotten an F. After listening for just a short time, he stopped me and said, "Look, it doesn't mean a damn thing to me that you are on the football team. We have a cyclotron, one of the three that exists in the country, and we're trying to crack the atom. And I haven't the time to sit here and listen to the tales of woe of a football player." He said, "The final exam will be extremely comprehensive. If you can pass that, I will give you a D in the course, and pass you. If you can't, I'm sorry -- you will flunk." "Good enough," I said. "That's all I wanted to hear."

I had a young female teacher in Trigonometry. One of my problems was that I had been ill advised to take the first part of Physics because it involved mechanics and trigonometry, which I hadn't had, but which were needed to calculate some of the problems. So here I was taking a course in Trigonometry when I was supposed to already know it beforehand. I explained my situation to the teacher, and received some sympathy. She said, "The final exam will cover all of the aspects of trigonometry, and whatever grade you get on the final, that's what you will get."

The athletic department supplied me with tutors for all my subjects. So I continued with the regular courses and went back and started over again from the very beginning with each subject. My final exams would be in January, and so that gave me the month of December literally to get back on track. But in three weeks I found that I was having difficulty even walking. I had tried to stay in shape by playing an occasional game of basketball, and I couldn't jump. It got to the place where I was walking with a bad limp. I went in to see the team physician, and on examining my leg he immediately said, "You've just got to have this knee operated on now."

The Operation

During the Christmas vacation from school, I went to Methodist Hospital in Indianapolis where a Dr. Mumford performed the surgery on my knee. When I awoke from the anesthetic, as I lay in the bed with my books beside me, he informed me that it was the worst knee he had ever operated. He removed many calcified blood clots, and took out seven pieces of fractured cartilage and torn ligaments. He couldn't understand how I could even have walked.

I was in the hospital seven days, and literally in all my waking moments I was studying my books, because I wanted to survive in school.

I returned to Bloomington on crutches and took my examinations. When the results of the finals came out, I got an A, two B's and a C. I got an A in Trigonometry because I had a 100 on the exam. I don't remember exactly what I got on the finals in the other two courses where I got B's, but I do know that I started with F's. When I got my paper back from my final in Physics it was a 90, which was tenth from the top of the class. Apparently Mitchell had split the difference and given me a C in the course instead of a D.

That experience did much to boost my self-image, self-worth, self-confidence and security. I thought at the time, if I can do what I just did, then hardly anything should stop me. Playing football, surviving a serious knee operation and achieving those kinds of grades had required more than just an ordinary ability. That, together with making the team and being told I was the most improved player was an absolutely tremendous boost for my ego. And I felt that maybe I was not only an athlete, but a scholar.

Pearl Harbor Day

I was upstairs in my room in the fraternity house studying on Sunday, December 7, 1941, when I heard the shouting. Japan had devastated Pearl Harbor in Hawaii and sunk some battleships. We had all taken it for granted that Hitler was not our problem. We certainly were aware of the threat to England and the raping of Europe, but we were protected by the Atlantic Ocean. There was also the possibility that America was benefiting by selling supplies and munitions to the allied countries. We had witnessed Mussolini's rise and the partnership of Germany and Italy, and there was truly great concern. But now, it had happened. And from an unexpected source.

We all turned to our radios and listened to Roosevelt talking about this "day of infamy". Most of us in the fraternity were already in the ROTC, the Reserve Officers Training Corps in a state school.

One of the fraternity brothers was the son of a general in the Army by the name of Clark. Before even listening to Roosevelt, he had packed all his clothes and books and left that very afternoon to join his father. Most of us just stood and looked at each other, and sat in disbelief and wonderment as to what the likelihood of our personal involvement would be.

I was then 21 years old, one or two years older than most of the others in my class. Because I was already in Pre-Dental School I was not obliged to immediately go into the service. But essentially all of my fraternity class were sent to Fort Benning, Georgia, and were made second lieutenants in the Army within a matter of two weeks. More than half of them I never saw again. Many others who did come back were not all in one piece.

One of my best friends in the fraternity from Kokomo was Joe Dewberry, who was leading his platoon on Bougaineville and caught a bullet straight in his forehead. Joe always admired me so much because I had made the football team. And he kept a scrapbook of pro football players back in the days before it became a popular sport. In 1940, prior to my getting into the fraternity, Joe had been one of four of us students who were living in a single room. Formerly, as I have described earlier, there had been three. My brother Jim, who had just graduated from high school, together with Joe Dewberry and Glenn Edwards and I, lived in that one room. Glenn and Jim were trying to make it on the football team, and were never quite successful. But after staying out one year and wasting another year before I found myself, now my brother and I were both preparing to go into the same class at Dental School, which we did. The war was waging both in Europe and the Pacific.

*   *   *

In Howard County, Indiana, where Kokomo is located, they immediately listed all of the eligible young men for the draft and had a lottery. You guessed it: my name came up first in the whole county. Only a small percentage of the young men who had to face four years of war in the Infantry survived. If it hadn't been that I had made the decision to go to college, and been in the ROTC, I would have gone to the front lines. Those who stayed in school had even greater motivation not to flunk out because front line duty could mean death.

By the spring of 1942, I was successful in mastering some other heavy courses such as Organic Chemistry, and I had all of my credits for Dental School except for two courses. One was an advanced course in Organic Chemistry, and the other was a foreign language requirement. I decided to get some credits in Spanish.

In Spring football I was first team right end. My knee felt better than it had in years, and I was quick and agile. But now I had to make a decision. Despite a football scholarship which essentially only paid my tuition and books, I still had to live. I loved the fraternity life, and I truly feel that it was an important part of my growth. But I still waited tables and washed dishes for my board. I worked at the Kroger food store, I tended the coke machine in the fraternity house, and I picked up and delivered dry cleaning for many of the brothers in the house. That, together with my library job as a part of my football scholarship, meant that I had five jobs in addition to the taking of heavy academic courses.

Concentration on Dentistry

I was determined to become a dentist. By now, in addition to the knee injury, I had rotator cuff injuries in both shoulders, I had twisted my left ankle, had hip pointers in my right hip, I had broken my left thumb, had teeth knocked loose and a face full of scars.

At the end of my year and spring season, then, in June of 1942, I was frustrated. I can truly say that I gave it just about everything I had. After the spring finals I went back home to the farm near Kokomo to rest. I was too exhausted to go see any friends and I told Mom just to let me sleep. The first day home I slept 15 hours, the next day 14 hours, and the third day 13 hours. I had been spent by all my efforts, and it took that amount of rest for me to consider anything else.

After resting, I made an important life decision. I would go to summer school and drop my career in football for three reasons. The first was that with the rigors of playing Big Ten football and doing all the traveling, there was no guarantee that I would get my final credits to enter Dental School, which had now started a speed-up program because of the war, and which I would enter in January of 1943. I simply couldn't see myself continuing what I had been through all over again. The second part of my decision was that I wanted to protect my hands, because I felt certain that I would become a good dentist, and I had already injured my hands by being stepped on, banging helmets, and falling on them.

The third part of my decision was that I recognized that being in the athletic limelight was an ephemeral thing. How quickly an athlete can become a has-been. While it is rewarding to see your name in the paper, to be interviewed by sportscasters, and have the acclaim of students, there are many stories regarding the catastrophic life of athletes who perhaps are over-impressed with their own importance and feel that society owes them something.

Thus it was that I enrolled in summer school and decided not to continue with the 1942 football team, which incidentally had a great winning season. I didn't have the heart to tell the coaches. I suppose I always figured that maybe if I did get all my credits, I could take some elective courses and maybe still have another fling at football which I loved.

One day I was walking down the campus on my way to the Chemistry Building and I happened to pass Coach McMillan. He was surprised that I was there, and asked me what I was doing. I said that I had decided to go to summer school to get my credits for Dental School and I blurted out, "I'm sorry, I won't be with the team this Fall." At that he stomped, and raved, and asked me if I could come into his office and discuss it. I said, "Absolutely."

The following day I appeared in his office and one of the other coaches was present. He asked, "What is this all about, that you are going to quit?" So I reiterated what I had been through, upon which he reminded me, "Look what football has done for you. You are now at the place where you could do something for the game." I replied, "I do love the game, and have all of the respect in the world for you and the other coaches. It was a most difficult decision," I said. And then I asked him, "How many of the boys who started in pre-medical, pre-dental or pre-law have survived besides me?" He couldn't think of a single one. In the end, they gave me their best wishes, and I think they understood that I was trying to change from a warrior to an intellectual.

Survival Again

I did pass the summer exams and got my credits, and was admitted to the Dental School to start in January of 1943. I had four months to try to get a job that would pay enough so that I could support myself at home and save some money. Jobs were not scarce, because the war effort was by now in full swing. So I obtained a job as a construction worker on the Bunker Hill Naval Station north of Kokomo and close to Peru, Indiana. They were building landing pads for the training of Navy pilots, and out there on the plains in Indiana they were constructing a sea of concrete. As I recall, my salary had now jumped to 65 cents an hour, which I thought was a lot of money at that time.

The Speed-Up Program

An ordinary dental curriculum is four years but taking away vacations and semester breaks, we went through Dental School non-stop in 32 months. My brother Jim and I started out by rooming together in the attic of an old house not far from the medical school there on the campus in Bloomington. We slept together in a double bed, and as I recall, the rent for the room was $2.50 a week. I had saved up $300.00 and I think Jim had saved about

$250.00, so we tried to make it go as far as we could.

Again, I went to Dean Crawford and explained our situation. He said, "Just hang in there." So we did. There was hardly any time for play. We took general anatomy, dental anatomy, physiology, biochemistry and histology with no breaks and no mercy. By the end of the first half-year, one-third of the class had dropped out. Our studies had paid off, for Jim and I were third and fourth academically in the class.

But by the end of the first half-year we were out of money. We looked around to see where we could make ends meet, and found that we could get our meals and get a room in the Pi Phi Sorority House which was just across the street from the dental school. So Jim and I together started living in the basement of the Pi Phi Sorority House. We did do janitor service for the kitchen, washed the dishes, and waited on tables for the girls during a summer school session. There were only about 15 girls going to summer school, so we thought it wouldn't be too much to take that on in addition to our studies.

Living in a sorority house was not as exciting as might be imagined, particularly when you had to be patient and be respectful to a group of young fillies in their bathrobes when they first get up each morning. There was one girl in particular who had me completely flabbergasted. In the afternoons or evenings I was particularly impressed with the deportment and the looks of one young brunette, and I swore that that young lady never came down to breakfast. It took me weeks to finally determine who she was, and I believe that it was honestly the beginning of my great respect for the field of cosmetology. By the time that she put on her false eyelashes, her false boobs, high heels and did her hair and makeup, I did not recognize her as the scroungy, sarcastic and impolite bitch of a person to whom I served breakfast.

When the grades came in for the first semester, the second half of the year, I was called in by the Dean. He started the conversation by asking me how I was enjoying Dental School. I remarked how much I loved it and was enjoying every aspect of it. Then he asked me why my grades had gone down significantly.

I explained to him that we had run out of money, and that Jim and I had taken this job in the sorority house and it had taken a great deal more time and energy than either of us had expected. I told him I didn't think that I was a brilliant student, and that grades only came with extremely hard work. I assured him that I had not lost my enthusiasm. He said, "I can understand fully what the problem is." Then he said something else. "I feel that you have something extra, that you are just the type of student I want." He said, "I have access to funds for outstanding students who can receive some scholarship money merely at my request. It's not much," he said, "but it would be enough to keep you in school. If you ever have your back completely up against the wall do not hesitate to come in and request some help." I thanked him for his earnest interest, and said I hoped that I would never have to do that. I never did.

The ASTP

In a few weeks, things changed. We had been given exemption from the war by reason of being in Dental School. But now the armed services had changed their program, because more medical and dental personnel were needed than had been anticipated. Hence we were to be taken into the service. The program was the Army Specialized Training Program, which was called the ASTP. Another was a program for the Navy Reserve. A few of the students had signed up with the Navy with the idea that upon graduation they would immediately go into Navy service. But the rest of us all became Privates in the Army. We were housed and fed and drilled. We were trained in the use of rifles and to fire a machine gun. For our quarters we were put in the women's dormitory. It was only a short distance from the medical school, and we were housed four in a room.

Southern Indiana can be very hot and sultry in the summertime. Another bad feature is that it doesn't cool down very much at night. The dormitory was not intended to be used in the summer, and it had no air conditioning. During the summer of 1943 I perspired at night so profusely that the mattress became soaked. We would take the sheets off and lay the mattress up on its side to dry. But several nights I went back to bed on a mattress that was still wet.

After the first few weeks of our freshman year in Dental School it was customary to elect officers for the Freshman Class. No one ran for an office, but one day an instructor handed out some paper and said, "You need a President, a Vice-President, a Secretary and a Treasurer. So please vote." Unexpectedly, I was elected President of the Freshman class. I suppose it was due to my enthusiasm and determination, and maybe good will and genuine respect for all the work.

The Singing Class

Our class was called "the singing class". The course was only a few hours old when, while waiting for one of the professors to appear for a lecture, someone started to sing. We didn't know it, but there were several singers present. I suppose most dentists and physicians are a little bit broad in their talents, because we had members who had played in dance bands and in vocal organizations. Immediately the hall was ringing with songs, and over a period of the next few weeks, several were introduced into our repertoire. Obnoxious songs seemed to be the most popular.

In the fall of 1943, when we went to Indianapolis for our Sophomore, Junior and Senior years, we formed a double quartet and performed a couple of times for fund-raisers for the war effort in some of the organizations around Indianapolis. In addition, we formed a small dance band with me as a vocalist. It didn't take us long to realize that most of us were out of practice, and short of experience, and we really couldn't devote the time necessary to make it a real success, but it was fun trying.

Forty years later we had a reunion and 16 of us still sang some of the old songs.

In the class there were many characters, but two of the boys, Jack and Bill, were complete clowns. In our first half-year, they had gone 63 nights without missing having at least one beer. We loved them so much because they were a part of our singers, and they always had jokes and stories to tell. We did our best to keep them in the class. We all ended up helping them with their work.

In the freshman year we did complete anatomy dissection along with the medical students, with particular emphasis on the head and neck and additional emphasis on the human hand. Our outstanding professor was Dr. Robert Hill, who also would occasionally join us for a beer party. He loved to join us in song also. He made anatomy a very enjoyable subject, for which I have been grateful ever since. We were issued cadavers, with five students to each specimen. A cadaver is fixed in formaldehyde and the muscle turns quite dark red; fat still looked like fat. To keep the tissues from drying out, after each session the cadaver is covered with wet gauze and a lid is placed over the specimen.

The Ball and Tommy Dorsey

As Class President, I met with the President of the Medical Class that year. I proposed that we have a Medical-Dental Ball so that we could have something to remember from our days there in Indiana that would be long-lasting. We didn't have much money, but if we combined the classes we might be able to do something more worth while. After some discussion we decided to go for the top band in the country for campuses. At that time the big names were Tommy Dorsey and Benny Goodman. Glenn Miller was just becoming known. Dorsey's music had a lot of hop and was a very popular dance rhythm. This was in 1943, just before Sinatra and the Modernaires joined the Dorsey organization; at least they were not there for this occasion. But Tommy had the immortal Buddy Rich on the drums. I contacted Tommy Dorsey's agent and pleaded with him, on behalf of the cause of medicine and dentistry, for a reduction of his price. And to our complete surprise, he accepted our offer.

Needless to say, there was great excitement. I wanted it to be a Class A affair. An assigned committee decorated the ballroom there at the commons, images of teeth, jaws, scalpels and stethoscopes. Everything was arranged. Everyone was determined to save their pennies for the big bash. We advertised it around the campus, and everyone was to get their best girlfriend. This was a formal affair. As a kid on the farm I had heard about tuxedos and had seen them in movies, but we always called them "monkey suits". But now I had come to respect an effort by society to put its best foot forward, and wore one without feeling self-conscious.

When Dorsey's music echoed throughout the hall, most of our class was there. Most people danced in those years and I suppose this accounts for the huge success of so many of the great dance bands. Not only did we get a bargain price, but when Tommy was about to wrap it up I went up and told him that this would be an occasion that most of us would remember all our lives, that we were just poor struggling students, and could he just play a couple more numbers and particularly feature Buddy Rich again. He looked at me and frowned, and said, "Well, okay." So away we went again. It was a night I'll never forget.

Later we went for a snack downtown in Bloomington. Many of the girls who were there were not on curfew with the local sororities, because they were brought in "from home" just for this occasion. We happened to go into a popular restaurant and sitting at the counter were Tommy Dorsey and Buddy Rich having coffee and a sandwich. I went up and thanked them again, told them how much we appreciated them, and of course told them that they were the best, which they loved to hear. I watched Buddy Rich put his head in his hands a couple of times, with his elbows on the counter, and I could see that he had given us everything he had. I had always liked the drumming of Gene Krupa but from that moment on I was a fan of Buddy Rich. Forty years later, while lecturing in Munich, Germany, I went to see him in a concert with Sammy Davis, Jr. I wanted to go and remind him of 1943, but circumstances didn't permit.

By the Fall of 1943 when we moved to the campus at Indianapolis, only one-half of the class that started had survived. We had been warned in the beginning that one out of three would not make it, but in our class it was one out of two in one year. Much of our basic sciences were now behind us, and we were anxious to get a taste of real dentistry. We had had our share of sculpturing the anatomy of a given tooth as exactly as possible. Given only a knife and a chunk of ivorine plastic material, it was not easy, but when finished it was a true piece of sculpture and a real exhibit of art.

It was at this time that we got our first exposure to pathology. Germs were everywhere, and the mouth was a haven for many varieties of microbes. We were almost afraid to kiss our girlfriends.

Decision for Orthodontics

It was during my sophomore year that I heard my first lecture in orthodontics from Dr.

Thomas Spiedel, who was the head of the department at Indiana. We used Dr. Jacob Salzman's textbook written in the early forties, but there was something about the subject that was overwhelmingly fascinating. Dentistry in many aspects is destructive, because good tooth material often has to be cut away to prepare a cavity properly. And before the days of antibiotics it was risky to do root canals. So many teeth, due to infections and periodontal disease, had to be extracted, which was destructive in my thinking. But now here was an opportunity to be constructive.

I could see orthodontics involved growth and development. It involved deformities of the facial structures. It involved the physiology of the whole head and neck. It involved the function of the jaw joint. Here was an opportunity, I thought, to put all the basic sciences to work in addition to working with the psychology of a human being. I was intrigued.

But clinical orthodontics is not taught at the undergraduate level. One reason is that so much more is involved than just a simple technique. It is really a subject for advanced education, and takes years of time and effort to master. Even after graduate training it takes about five years to be fully competent.

It was after the second lecture in orthodontics, I think, that I asked for another conference with Dean Crawford. I went into his office, and said, "Well, I've made another decision. I want to be an orthodontist and I want to do graduate work." He clapped his hands and stood up from his chair and stamped his foot. "I knew it!" he said. "I knew that you'd want to do graduate work. There are so many opportunities. Right now, on my desk, I have invitations for deanships at three other schools. There is such a dearth of dedicated scholars, and such an opportunity for good teachers." And then he sat down. He said, "Now, if you are interested in orthodontics, there is really only one school that I could recommend, and that is with Allan G. Brodie at the University of Illinois in Chicago. This is really the only school I would recommend, and there is not even a second. So my advice to you is, as soon as possible, to find out what is needed and start preparing yourself for graduate education. I can't tell you," he said, "how happy it makes me that you have made that decision so early."

My First Consuming Love

The second half of my sophomore year I had a catastrophe. I fell in love. I was 24 years old. Through a classmate I accepted a blind date. I had had other girlfriends before, in high school, and had even given my fraternity pin to a girl from Kokomo who was at school in Bloomington. In fact, I had thought I was in love with her. Things were not going too well with her, and one day I smelled smoke on her clothes, and tasted tobacco in her kisses. I accused her of smoking, which she denied because she knew my firm stand against nicotine. One day her purse popped open, and right there inside lay a package of cigarettes. We subsequently had words, upon which she took my pin off and returned it to me. She said she had started dating another boy anyhow. I was shocked, and it took quite an adjustment at the time, but in retrospect it was more of a disappointment and a form of rejection that played on my ego.

I don't know why it is that people fall into love. I don't know exactly how the expression came into being, that we "**fall** in love". Maybe the word "fall" comes from the fact that we have ourselves in an elevated position, and when romantic love enters our lives we come down from that pedestal and place someone else's interests ahead of our own. It wasn't love at first sight. This young lady was the daughter of a minister. She was educated, and she was warm. She wasn't the most beautiful woman that I have known, but she was pretty and cute. At the time, she seemed to fit everything that I needed. It was one of those relationships that multiplied at each date. I became so enraptured with her that she became a preoccupation.

After a few weeks, we had agreed to get married and were thinking about setting the date. I had bought her a modest little engagement ring, to be paid for on time. She worked at an Allison Engine Company. The Allison airplane engine was a marvel of power in its time. It was made in Indianapolis and, if I'm not mistaken, had sixteen pistons. I don't remember what she did exactly, but one of my classmates was dating a girl who worked with her at the Allison plant, and that's how we happened to get together.

About the time we became engaged she made the decision to join American Airlines as a flight attendant. It was quite a thrilling, adventurous prospect for a girl from Indiana, and I couldn't stand in her way. So off she went to Dallas, Texas for training, right at the time of my complete crash for her.

Earlier I had become a member of the Xi Psi Phi dental fraternity. Our group had rented an old house on North Meridian and Sixteenth Street in Indianapolis. We were still in the service, consequently I did not have to work outside to earn money for my keep. And this perhaps was another reason for my preoccupation. But I realized my grades were slipping, because I would find myself thinking about her during lectures. In addition, almost on a daily basis, I would write her love letters. I would like to see some of these letters today, to see what kind of penmanship I had, because it certainly got exercised.

Gradually her letters became more and more infrequent, and shorter in length. It was now late summer of 1944. She had finished her training and was based in Dallas as her assignment with the airline. I knew something was wrong. I was now president of the fraternity and we had planned a dinner dance. Everything was set up for her to come to Indianapolis for the affair. But she stood me up and didn't come. I was heartbroken, and very depressed.

At the first opportunity I hitch-hiked from Indianapolis to Dallas because I wanted to see her. I told her I was coming. When I arrived she was living with four other girls in a rented house, and everyone was most cordial. She had to leave for a trip very soon after I arrived, and I had to wait a day for her return. During that time, I had the opportunity to talk with one of the other girls who became friendly. She told me that the girl wearing my ring was dating one of the pilots. She said she thought I should know it. When my fiancee returned we calmly discussed it, whereupon she returned my ring. What a waste.

I concluded I wasn't doing too well with women. I felt that they could not be trusted, were perfidious, and I was embittered. I did not get over that affair for several years.

There must be some biologic necessity with love. We know that some teen-aged girls get stars in their eyes and go "gaga" quite easily. Perhaps it is estrogen at work, but maybe it goes deeper than that. Studies of lower animals show one fact quite distinctly, and that is that survival of the species must be a very high priority. Another fact abundantly clear is that it is the female that always does the choosing. This is true of lower animals, and it is true for the human.

In lower animals males fight for dominance, not for the female. When a male dominates the female is attracted. A male takes over property while the female seeks the propertied. This is probably also a factor in survival because intuitively a woman might desire her offspring to be well cared for. All of these factors, then, may precipitate her feeling of love and the submission of herself sexually in the process.

But such deep underlying biologic feelings for the male also may be present. It is very clear to me, on reviewing my life, that there are many ladies with whom I could have lived, and been content, if there had been a reciprocal respect and the timing had been right. Therefore, it simply doesn't make sense to say that there is only one person with whom we could really fall in love. What is it that prompts the time when a male is ready for a relationship or ready for a family? What precipitates that particular time when a man is ready to quit looking around, and wants to place his interests and energy with one particular person and a family?

After all, inter-sex relationships are the most frequent subjects of movies, books, and fairy tales. All that is necessary to prove that is to observe Walt Disney's "The Little Mermaid" to see how a love relationship with the prince captures the mind of even pre-school children.

After my break-up I was free to look around, and I loved to dance. It was fun, free, and convenient during the war to go to the USO (United Service Organization), which still exists. A typical date in those days was either to go to a movie or go dancing. If we didn't have a date we could go dancing free at the USO. There would be ladies present, and I always looked for the best dancers. I found them to be Arthur Murray dance instructors who would frequent these spots for the entertainment of the service men. I asked these instructresses for dances. Also, because I needed patients on which to practice, I was always looking for girls with cavities, and therefore I had a supply of patients for myself and many of my fellow students. In this way I had established a sort of connection with several people from Arthur Murray Studios.

Out On Our Own Again

Just as quickly as the ASTP had been formed it was disbanded. We were all given a chance of going in the Army as sergeants in the Medical Corps, or being discharged and left to our own devices to stay in school and finish our degree. Naturally, it was not much of a choice to make, as all of us wanted to finish school. So suddenly we were confronted with the need to obtain outside income. We were discharged from the service and were civilians again, but the war was still on. The object was to find a job that would pay well enough for our support while finishing school which was still under the speeded up program.

My Dancing Career

One day I had one of the Arthur Murray ladies in the chair for some dentistry, and she said she had noticed that I was never at the USO any more. I told her we had been let out of the service and couldn't come there. She then said something surprising to me. She said that I was the best dancer that she had danced with in all the time she was there, and asked why I didn't come down and try to be an instructor with Arthur Murray. I laughed out loud.

"What me? a gigolo?" I protested.

She said, "Sure, why not?"

I said I was a football player, and liked girls, and I couldn't imagine myself in that kind of role.

She said, "It pays $4.00 an hour, and if you re-sell a course, you get a commission."

At that point I really lit up, and I said, "How do I get the job?"

She said, "Well, you'll have to come down and dance with the supervisor. They have a training class that's just starting. If the boss thinks that you have the talent, they will train you for nothing if you want to go through with it."

"What's involved?" I asked.

"The training course is six weeks," she said, "and after that you will be given students to teach, and from then on you're on your own."

I made an appointment to visit the studio, which I had never seen before. I walked in and was pleasantly surprised with the amount of fun and the organization of the business that was demonstrated. So I danced two or three different numbers, and soon found out what I didn't know. But the supervisor said, "Yes, I think you have a good sense of rhythm, and good timing, but you'll need to learn an awful lot in order to teach," -- which I already knew.

So I signed up. The classes were to be four hours each night and six hours on Saturdays. I thought, "Well, okay, I'll give it a shot."

We started out with the tango. The reason for this was to develop body control, but it became very, very monotonous and doing it over and over and over again, hour after hour, just going through the steps and the motions and the timing was a test to find out who had a real drive to learn. It was a discipline, and I could see it. By the end of the first week half of the 36 in the class had dropped out.

We then went to the foxtrot, and then to the rhumba, and then to the waltz. By now a few had also been asked not to come back, and others who were not ready for that kind of discipline quit. After six weeks, and 26 hours of lessons each week, there were only six of us left and I was the only male. In order to be a good teacher, I also had to learn to follow, or take the woman's part. In the end, the amount of lessons that I had received were valued at $3000.00, and this was 1944.

A Different Identity

I thought I was there to teach dancing. And in the course for the students we had essentially 20 steps in each of the different dances. But it was a business. Arthur Murray Dance Studios was the third most successful business to start and develop during the Depression. It is very interesting to speculate on the reason for such success. The reason may be that while the dancing is obvious, what we were really selling was self-worth, self-assurance, self-confidence, and self-image. In fact, we were selling identity.

How can anyone develop any identity unless they have achieved something? If identity is the antithesis of anonymity, Arthur Murray was taking wallflowers and giving them an achievement that they could earn themselves. The dance students came from every walk of life, every socio-economic bracket, and every race, color or creed, it made no difference. The satisfaction that comes with achievement was theirs and no one could take it away.

When I would re-sell a series of courses to a person who had signed up for just a few, I would make an extra commission. I was therefore becoming a salesman, but it took a long time for me to realize that I was selling identity. Gradually, I found that dentistry performed the same underlying service. Certainly, orthodontics serves precisely the same psychologic function for the person. Therefore, I was not only learning a little about salesmanship, but I was also learning a lot about people.

I showed ladies how to stand and walk. I told them how to talk. I explained which clothes were becoming to them. In fact, I was **treating** the whole person, not just showing them how to move their feet or keep on a beat.

And also, I had to dance with men. In fact, I think I was a better teacher for men than I was for women, because I knew what it took to be a strong leader, how to move to make it easier for a lady to follow, and how to be bold and self-confident. I was usually assigned ladies at the start, but many of the lady instructresses would suggest to their male students that they have one lesson with me, because they could always see a difference when they got their students back.

I also had opportunities as a gigolo. You can't dance 20 hours with a person without becoming friendly, and on three or four occasions I was invited to go out of town with ladies of means on a so-called dancing field trip, which I always declined.

One of the extra jobs we had was to put on exhibitions at some of the big hotels in town.

It was sort of an advertisement for the studio, but it was also good for the entertainment of the people, where all of the modern dances could be demonstrated. If there was one thing about World War II, it was that the main portion of the population danced as an outlet for the tensions.

My schedule was hectic. I worked all day at school, left for the studio to be there at six, and taught until ten. I then had a light supper and got to bed by twelve. I got up at 6:30 because classes started at eight and patients started at nine. I was rather a fast mechanical operator and usually would have my clinical requirements finished by 11:30. I would grab a quick sandwich and immediately go to the Library where I had sort of taken license on one of the chairs in the back corner facing a wall, where I could be alone and concentrate on my studies. I knew I only had about an hour or two to get all of my assignments finished. While other students would be playing cards in the recreation room I was studying. Patients started again at 1:30, and I would be finished usually by 4:30. I didn't have an automobile in the beginning, so I had to take streetcars and buses, which took time.

After three months, when dance exhibitions were scheduled, I made extra money doing shows. I had one partner who was a tall slim blonde who was as graceful as a deer. She was bewitchingly beautiful, but quite shy and reserved. I always felt she was a very unhappy person. She declined my invitation to date. Yet although she had everything to offer, apparently something was missing. Five years later I saw her again by chance on an elevator in a hotel in Milwaukee. The owner of the Indianapolis studio also was the owner of the Milwaukee studio, so this lady had moved there. When I saw her my heart went out. She had deep dark circles under her eyes, she couldn't look at me directly, and she appeared to be emaciated. I later heard that she died of a drug overdose. I was shocked.

Sometimes -- quite often -- the girls at the studio would be bored with teaching. Many had almost a whole free day, and therefore not a lot of pressure other than teaching. And as I said, many would go to the USO just for the lark. But the big bands came to the Indiana Roof Garden in downtown Indianapolis, and the girls would entice me to go dancing with them after teaching. It was great fun.

After one such evening, we were invited for some food at someone's home, and seven of us all piled into one car. I was sitting in the back left seat and one of the girls whom I had come to know as just another teacher happened to sit on my lap. Her face was not particularly attractive, but certainly not ugly. She had a full smile. Like all the dancers, she was athletic and had all parts positioned in the correct place, rather generously. We had all been having fun and in the middle of all the laughter she turned over to me and gave me a kiss and a big hug. She could no doubt feel my manhood respond. When we arrived at our destination, she whispered to me, "Why don't we let the others go in?" And so I said, "Okay."

With the others gone, we could stretch out a bit in the back seat and got into some rather heavy petting. Pretty soon she said, "I want you. Do you want me?" I can't imagine it, but at the time I was so gullible, I honestly asked, "What do you want?" And she laughed. She said, "I want you sexually. Haven't you ever had a girl before?" I had to admit that I hadn't. She said, "Well, can I be your first?" I was frightened and shaking, and did the best job that I could.

Afterwards, she told me how great she thought I was. I said, "Did you really enjoy that?" She said, "Oh, yes, what do you think?" I said, "Well, do women really enjoy sex like this?" She said, "I don't know about others, but I certainly do." This was actually a shock to me. I suppose from the Puritan ethic in my upbringing I had somehow gained the impression that sex was dirty, that it could not be enjoyed by a woman, and that it was painful, and that a man was no more than an animal. But now, here I was with my first sexual experience having someone tell me how deeply enjoyable it was, to my complete amazement.

Needless to say, that single episode changed my attitude about women immensely. My reaction was immediate. I have to say I was much more of an aggressor after that experience. But it was still difficult for me to put away all of that conditioning engendered throughout my youth.

With about four months left in school, I could no longer keep up with the pace, because of its demanding nature. I was offered the management of a studio when I graduated if I wanted it, at a very attractive salary. I loved dancing and the entertainment business, but my heart was in dentistry.

My First Orthodontics

During my junior year at dental school the Orthodontic Department would not permit any students to work on patients. Treated subjects were supposed to be only for demonstration. Why they had orthodontic patients in active treatment was a mystery, because we never saw them. In my senior year the department head left to take a deanship in another school. That left the school without a teacher for orthodontics. Dr. Drexall Boyd, the head of the Pediatric Dental Department therefore took over patients in the school since he practiced orthodontics privately on week ends. With a lot of cajoling and insistence, he finally permitted me to work on some orthodontic patients with a full orthodontic appliance which was unheard of before that time.

We finally graduated in the summer of 1945 with 32 of the 67 people who had started. I had been admitted to graduate school, but duty called from the Navy. I had been in school for the entire duration of the war.

*   *   *

The war had caused many changes in society that were obscure. Time would be required for the good and bad alterations in American attitudes to become more obvious. Where were we directed in the postwar era which lay ahead?

PART TWO

THE CHANGING AMERICAN

Introduction

The seeds for the changing of America had been sown. It started with the acceptance by so many, during the Depression, that government or society was to be responsible for individual economic welfare. It was further influenced by the psychologic impact of World War II. It was propelled in addition by the confusion brought on by inflation. It was fueled by the positioning for individual advantage when the rebuilding processes were put in motion. Finally, constant change came to be expected, as old values were discarded and a more liberal thought dominated American society.

I will relate to the main force of change, and associate the psychologic effects that I observed our wars have produced in my lifetime, before continuing personal experiences in a more or less chronological manner.

In retrospect, many of the events of the era leading up to and following World War II may be worth discussing as impacts on my personal attitude and the posture of many others. Most of American society, as I recall it, had in the 1930s suffered an utter complacency.

From the aspect of my life's narrative in the first act of this book, I now turn to analysis of my feelings and reactions to the social, economic, political and scientific changes I sensed at this era of my life.

6

CONTEMPLATION OF THE WARS AND THEIR SOCIETAL IMPACT

For a play during World War I, George M. Cohan wrote a song entitled "Over There". This was part of a Broadway show, "Yankee Doodle Dandy", and was brilliantly performed by James Cagney many years later in a movie. In the 1930s our news media had covered the remilitarization of Germany. We knew about the rise of the Third Reich. The ill treatment of Jews was also rumored, but most people felt helpless.

We Were Separated by Oceans

Most of my generation had learned about World War I as students, but it was mostly vague and not too meaningful. "Over There" was history -- we were separated by oceans, and it was still far away by steamship.

After all, the French had the Maginot Line running along their entire border which allegedly was impregnable by war machinery. It was not our concern. Jet travel had not been invented, television was only a dream, sulfa drugs and penicillin and other antibiotics were not yet heard of. Poliomyelitis was dreaded for its nerve damage because it was a mystery. In the 1930s we had our own struggles trying to come out of the Depression. We were still separated by oceans.

I remember when Chamberlain appeased Hitler and that it served only as an encouragement to the German war machine. We had heard of the horrid inflation in Germany in post-World War I. That kind of an economy would be enough to make people desperate.

I could understand the European people's position. The sense of widespread futility, the warrior personality of a leader and the need for a "fix" of their country by a totally Fascist regime in both Germany and Italy probably did not appear to be a bad alternative in the minds of many at the time. It became more acceptable when viewed on the basis of promises that politicians make in order to assume power.

It was obvious that the United States was not the only country in the world undergoing a great depression. The 1930s witnessed a whole world convulsion. Only a few people had money. In the United States in 1929 more than 90% of the wealth was in the hands of only 29% of the people. Some claim the accumulation of wealth was the cause. Even more tragic, history has continuously shown that economic downfall ends in war.

It was obvious that some changes needed to be made. The Depression was blamed on Hoover, who was a Republican. Consequently, in 1932 Franklin D. Roosevelt, a former governor of New York and a Democrat, was elected to lead the country. Together with a vigorous, cooperative Democratic Congress, he adopted a new theory. The government was to spend money. I witnessed many government institutions being founded in order to administrate the many new federal programs. We had our problems in America, but at that time I -- and others -- still felt separated from Europe.

In 1925 Billy Mitchell was badly treated and ridiculed by the Army brass for suggesting a separate air force and that airplanes were able to destroy battleships. Douglas MacArthur was the lone dissenting vote on Mitchell's court martial. It seemed to me that one bomb from an airplane, if it hit, could knock a large ship out of operation. The United States merchant marine, together with the navy of the British Empire, dominated the seas. A strong navy was desired even by Roosevelt. Maybe there were great financial rewards by ship builders. But Germany, limited to the North Sea, I assumed, had a more limited access to the oceans. We thought we were protected because we were isolated by oceans, and in addition we had a strong navy and a strong ally with an even larger navy.

At the time it was difficult for me to imagine that Hitler was America's problem. When Roosevelt was first elected I was only 12 years of age. When he ran for his second term, I was 16, and an uninspired student in high school. Little did I comprehend that within three years I would be at a draftable age for the U.S. Army. After all, this was 1936, and hadn't the world learned a lesson from World War I, the Great War, as we called it?

The Alarm

When Hitler's dive-bombers and speedy tanks blitzed their way through Poland in 1939 for no reason other than aggression, and when the property of those citizens was confiscated, even in Indiana we became concerned despite Europe's being on another continent.

As a high school student, it was difficult for me to imagine our country standing idly by without helping friendly nations such as France, England, and many others as the war clouds gathered. After all, Canada was our sister, as was Mexico. Even though I was isolated in Kokomo I had an intuitive sense that some day we would be fighting Germany all over again. This time it would be my generation's war rather than the war of our fathers.

From a strategic point of view, as I looked at Europe even as a high school boy, the Maginot Line was a farce. From the study of a map it was plain to see how a military attack could skirt the line by coming around through Denmark, Holland, and Belgium to enter France from the North. In football this is called an end run. When the defense is ganged up in the middle, you simply go to the outside. How simple indeed! Thus, the word "blitz" entered the English dictionaries and was connected with football jargon when linemen rush the passer.

We thought America could survive alone on what she had. Airplanes were amazing, we thought, when they could travel over 200 miles an hour. We could now fly from New York to Los Angeles on a true network of commercial airlines. Highways were improving, and inter-urban railways were being abandoned. In 1936 Lou Meyer won the Indianapolis race at an average speed of 109.069 miles an hour, a new record. I was present to observe the time trials.

* * *

Our Psyche

Historically, America had developed with the idea of neighborly love, friendship, and good will. Many foreigners had come to America seeking religious freedom. After all, Philadelphia was called the City of Brotherly Love. I and most of my friends concluded that the United States was at the top of everything. This gave rise to an intuitive belief that we could "live and let live". But things were changing.

As a person meets new experiences, each occasion makes a small impression. This mental impact is often referred to as being subliminal or sometimes subconscious. When enough of these episodes are encountered, they give rise to an "intuitive perception". Perhaps a part of our "gut feeling" of safety by isolation occurred on a whole cultural basis.

Since 1964 I have come to know many very fine Japanese people, and I respect their culture immensely. But in 1941 I didn't know them. They seemed strange. Even the limited number I had dealt with in any way were relatively silent and reserved, which prompted a feeling of mistrust. I had never, to my knowledge, expressed this sentiment to others and it was hidden in my consciousness. Maybe it was their bowing and their manners which were displayed. I wondered if their politeness was genuine, or just a cultural formality. In other words, I felt there was no way of my knowing when a Japanese was honest or sincere or if it was just a social custom to pretend.

Therefore, as Japan developed its military might and created a modern navy, it was also far, far away and we were separated by the Pacific Ocean -- by even more space than by the Atlantic. Yet the Philippines were a sovereign territory of the United States. We had a garrison at Corregidor.

Japan's population, we heard, crowded onto two small islands, desired more land for their expanding population. At that time a union of Japan and Germany seemed inconceivable. Yet the dismantling of the British Empire was under way. Other nations friendly to us shared a common concern regarding developments in both Japan and Germany. Those two countries, seemingly at opposite poles in culture, geography and economics, were most unlikely brothers but became united as an Axis power on the basis of only one thing: a malice against the United States.

Despite courses in political science, we in America had no schools in statesmanship, we were not prepared to become world-involved. Even though we were obviously helping with war supplies we were still neutral.

A naval student earlier had described the manner in which Pearl Harbor could be approached. And so it came to pass. The world was shocked by such accurate bombing. When we were attacked by Japan we were immediately in the war from each side, across both oceans.

Still, there were many who dissented. Some became conscientious objectors. I often wondered at the time how these objectors would react if someone attacked their wives and their children in their home. The human is a territorial animal. The human desires ownership of property and is inclined to protect it. When that property is threatened, it doesn't take much to arouse the pugnacious instinct in either the male or the female, especially when her brood is threatened.

Therefore, aroused we became. Rumors had it that the Japanese might attack the coast of California. Because many Japanese had immigrated from Japan and remained rather independent in their own culture, could anyone among them be trusted? It seemed imperative to those responsible for the safety of the American population that all these people be gathered together and maintained in a position of safety where they could do no harm. Sadly, this indeed was done. Extraordinary measures were deemed necessary.

As strange as it may seem, our common interests brought about a strange marriage with one of our allies, namely the Soviet Union. I remember that Charles Lindbergh, who had visited the Fascist state of Germany and the Communist state of the U.S.S.R., felt there was little choice between the two. Both were opposed to our way of life and thought. Both were led by a form of dictatorship, one by a madman and his party, many of whom were hand-selected and later shown to have mental problems. The other was ruled by a Communist Party which had only two percent or so of the total population, and survived by police state methods and violence.

Wars and Causes

As a young man while plowing in the fields, thinking time was available. I wondered why nations fought wars. In primitive cultures wars were usually fought over hunting territory. Raids would be made by one tribe on other tribes for women and possessions and retaliation ultimately followed. The Mesopotamian kings made conquests to enlarge their territory, their power and to take slaves. Alexander the Great created a vast Greek empire. Julius Caesar captured territory all the way to England, and Caesar Augustus was made Emperor of the Roman Empire whose constituents all paid taxes to Rome. Countless religious and ethnic wars develop because of religiocentrism and ethnocentrism.

The American Revolution was prompted by taxation without representation. Wars with the Indians were fought purely and simply for territory. The Civil War was for the preservation of the Union and freedom for the slaves. World War I and World War II were fought to eliminate tyrants, to make the world "free for democracy". The Korean War and the Vietnam War were mostly results of the fear of Communism and from fear of subsequent loss of our American freedom.

Thus, sovereign territory, religion, politics and ideology regarding forms of government constitute, as I see it, the main reasons for war conflict throughout history.

In order to fight, man went from clubs and stones to spears and arrows, from swords and daggers to muskets and cannons. World War I was characterized by trench warfare, and the machines of war were improved by the introduction of the airplane and the dirigible. Poison gases were used. World War II advanced war technique with larger battleships, the submarine, bombing by air, tank warfare, rocket propulsion and the atom bomb. The helicopter was improved for Vietnam. The Gulf War was one of advanced technology.

Wars of the future will be different. Who knows the extent to which hate and revenge can lead? Each war has left changes geographically, economically, morally, and culturally. Starvation continues. Fighting seems to have no end! I don't fear a depression as much as I fear the wars that often follow.

My Memory of World War II and My Reactions

The actual conflict started in 1939 with the German invasion of Poland. We saw the dive bombers on news reels. Realizing the threat, Britain and France soon declared war on Germany. Strangely, the U.S.S.R. invaded Poland from the east, and poor Poland was divided between Germany and Russia.

In 1940 German armies blitzed their way through Denmark, Norway, Netherlands, Belgium and Luxembourg, to outflank the Maginot line. We were glad to see a coalition government formed in Britain under Churchill. In May the famous evacuation of allied troops from Dunkirk took place. Italy declared war on the Allies as the Germans entered Paris. The air Battle of Britain began. I was just 20 years old.

I remember how in early 1941 the Germans overran Greece. By December they were also within 25 miles of Moscow, holding Leningrad under siege. At this moment the Russians made their counter-offensive. All this happened before Japan attacked Hawaii and America declared war.

In early 1942 the Japanese took the Philippines as I was entering the Army Dental Corps under a specialized training program. By June the Naval battle of Midway marked a psychological turning point for all of us. In November the Soviets countered at Stalingrad and thousands of Germans surrendered there in January of 1943. By May the German resistance in North Africa was crushed.

Americans became encouraged, and finally after two years of preparation we began an offensive campaign in the Pacific theatre. In Europe the Italians surrendered following landings in Salerno, and the Soviets recaptured Smolensk. Italy in turn switched sides. I remember their brutal treatment of Mussolini.

By 1944 the German U-boat campaigns stemming from protected refuges in Brest, France, had ended. [There was little evidence of the destruction when I lectured in Brest in 1992.] D-Day was in June, as the Allies landed in Normandy. In December the Germans made their last counter-offensive in the Battle of the Bulge.

During February of 1945 the Soviets pushed forward to the German border. Continuous day and night allied bombing of Germany was in full force. In the Pacific theatre we took Iwo Jima. Hitler committed suicide in April. In August, in order to save American lives, Truman made the decision to drop atom bombs on Hiroshima and Nagasaki. Many people declared the horror of nuclear war was unnecessary, but try to tell that to kinsmen of those who made the death march from Corregidor. Dr. William Blueher of Albuquerque, a school mate and colleague of mine, died years before his time, never fully recovering from that death march. Japan was forced to surrender to MacArthur on board the U.S.S. Missouri.

That war had cost an estimated 55 million lives. No one could estimate the total cost of the damage and the rebuilding. It was to change the nature of wars as the value of air power was proven. With the atom bomb, and later the hydrogen bomb, the threat of war took on new meaning. People began to build shelters in their homes; some countries made it mandatory with new homes. We were all frightened by the possibilities of nuclear war.

Lessons from Lack of Allied Preparation

During the war the Soviet Union had many people but little armament, and needed supplies. Whatever our feelings were about Communism it made no difference, Hitler had to be stopped. America had entered the war two years after their conflict had started, and it took Pearl Harbor to engage us. We were all shocked to find ourselves so ill prepared. The losses of the battleships were frightening. Atrocities were rumored, but confirmed only later. It was obvious that it would take years to build and train a modern army, whereas the German and Japanese soldiers had been training since childhood. Would mandatory service be a proper thing for Americans?

Without America Germany possibly could have won, and we all sensed it. There is no end to a greedy dictator's arrogance. Such tyrants are surrounded by those anxious to take advantage of the spoils of victory and accordingly obey their leader's every order. This further inflates the ego of the dictator and leads to an ostentatious attitude and a feeling of invincibility.

Changes After the Big War

From the ashes of World War II it seemed to me that we awoke to find ourselves the most powerful and strongest country on earth. We had spent four years in transforming our industrial might into a war economy.

The Soviet Union was also a victor, and their desire for power and communist influence on world affairs soon became obvious. It was my impression they thought we had delayed our engagement too long, to their detriment. Russia's resistance to a more favorably equipped German force at Stalingrad had displayed her fighting spirit to the rest of the world. I admired that courage. She had lost an estimated 20 million citizens. After World War II was over, the U.S.S.R. desired to exert a domination of her own. Thus we entered into the Cold War. I came to fear her when the curtain was dropped.

* * *

Now America, for perhaps the very first time, was forced to change psychologically. It became more than a struggle between two countries. It was a competition regarding a choice in the form of government and the nature of a whole society. A government-controlled welfare of all the people, similar to the beginning notions of Hitler's Fascism, was opposed to our idea of individual freedom for choice of a job, a place to live, and ambition for success. It was, to me, a matter of individual progress as opposed to the progress of a whole state. People had no identity under communism, and most Americans perceived this condition.

But with the closing of World War II the true objectives of the United States did not seem to be clear. Our indominable spirit to be neighborly and to help others gave rise to consent for massive aid to help rebuild those countries which had been defeated. It soon became a bar room joke, "The best way to have a successful country is to lose a war to the United States."

Probably the greatest change I noted soon after World War II was the attitude of our people regarding government controls. People became impatient with "the government". The so-called "establishment" meant those in power to make the laws, referred to as "they". "They" made everyone now conduct detailed bookkeeping. "They" checked up on personal businesses. It became a game of "you" against "them".

Before the war it was necessary to join a union if you wanted a job. There was a watchdog from the union to make sure a worker did only his assigned or "legal" work. Also, work quotas seemed to become less and less, as if to make some jobs last longer. In my opinion, the union was necessary when owners took advantage of the workers in the sweat shops, and wages were too low. Now, however, the unions emerged from the war in a position most non-unionists considered too powerful. From the top down to the straw boss they were often run by suspicious people. The result was that higher wages had to be passed on to the public. Inflation now became a major concern to everyone who was conscious of all the various changes.

Different attitudes regarding other aspects of American society as a whole were developing. One emerging idea was to "live and let live" instead of taking an interest in a neighbor. Whatever people did was no one else's business. Yet each was still a member of a community and a whole society. Women had become "looser" and in general men's respect for women decreased. Many in business always looked for "angles" in their transactions. People tried to "beat their taxes". Instead of helping others, many people took advantage of others wherever they could. Trust turned to suspicion.

Technology also played a great part in the change of American society. Jets had not been developed, but air travel with turbo props and faster planes were linking our cities. Television also provided national hook-ups so immediate news could be seen, not simply described. Through these mediums of travel and communication, we were being forced into a broader look at the whole world. The Cold War was more constantly before us in the news.

When Truman defeated Dewey in 1948 by identifying himself with helping the poor and supporting the egalitarian viewpoint, the movement among the unions became even stronger. We were bombarded by propaganda from the left. The courts and judges became more lenient. Many in the news media were admittedly left of center. More and more people came to rely on government jobs and voted that way. It was popular to ridicule any big business or business people for making profits. Capitalism itself was often blasted.

Another shift was evident in the social graces. Formal attire was rejected by the young. The big dance bands and "swinging years" which had developed during the 1930s had diminished and now the "Latin beats" moved into popularity. The Rhumba, Tango and some Waltz crowded out the traditional Fox Trot. Partnership dancing and grace, and even good manners, were almost ridiculed.

It started with the break from partnership dances. Rock-and-roll music, which split partners into individual twisting, with each "doing his own thing", was a sign of the times. **Personal survival, a personal identity and being on their own became the mind fix among the younger people.** To hell with anyone else!

Respect for others' private property declined. Hard work, thrift, saving and procurement were not appreciated. Egalitarianism, so championed by Eleanor Roosevelt, was interpreted to mean that everyone should share everything rather than earning it. Movies and television seemed to send the message that everyone was entitled to live as the American rich were portrayed in the screenplays. False expectations arose in the realm of medical cures.

All this gave rise to a general feeling of unrest and frustration, and sometimes bewilderment, regarding what was in store for the future. Consequently, young people became stressed, uncertain and frustrated.

The Korean War

In the settlement of World War II Korea had been divided at the 38th parallel. North Korea had been taken over by communists and South Korea had remained neutral. In 1950 North Korea, supported by China, crossed over the 38th parallel and invaded the south. When the Soviet Union walked out at the United Nations in support of the communist aggression, the U.N. voted to drive North Korea back over the 38th parallel.

Truman was still President and MacArthur was our five-star general in the Pacific. Most of the troops doing the fighting were from the U.S.; America therefore became essentially the communist target. MacArthur wanted to strike into North Korea and establish a firm containment of the Communist domino effect or their plan of tumbling one country at a time. We at the time had vastly superior materiel and technology, and MacArthur was familiar with the situation and the culture. Truman was dealing with the recovery in the U.S. and didn't want to enlarge the conflict. I personally sided with MacArthur and could see that a show of weakness could lead to greater encounters later. I was doing my research fellowship at Chicago when Truman, as Commander-in-Chief, called MacArthur home.

MacArthur returned to a hero's welcome. His famous speech to the Congress was moving, finishing with the words "Old soldiers never die, they just fade away." Many people felt that MacArthur should be given a chance to do at home what he had done for the recovery of Japan. He was put up as a presidential candidate at the Republican convention, but Eisenhower was chosen for the nomination because of his popularity on domestic issues, and the management of the European theatre. He took office as President in January, 1953.

Having campaigned on the basis of settling the Korean War, Eisenhower went immediately to Korea, and the 38th parallel was re-established.

Rueful Vietnam

Only a year later many of the warnings of MacArthur came to pass. North Vietnam invaded South Vietnam with complete support by China. In 1958-59 America again underwent a recession. My first lecturing in Europe was in 1958, and I recall the concern about our economy expressed by Europeans at that time. During the years between 1953 and 1959 the country, in my experience, was stable and without war and was continuing to build under Eisenhower. We were paying our war debt and building surpluses, not deficits. **It was the first time without a war and without a depression that I had witnessed in my lifetime.**

Under the Republican leadership by Eisenhower the infusion of money by the Federal Reserve Board had not been made because it was considered inflationary. However, in the 1960 Nixon-Kennedy debates, Kennedy wanted to get the country "going again" as we had witnessed in the war economy. This, according to the Democratic party tradition, meant new federal programs with greater spending. Nixon supported the Eisenhower policies which put him in an awkward position to argue against change. I remember him saying, "Let's go slowly and not rock the economy too hard." He lost, but it was a remarkably close contest. Pumping money into the economy was the politician's dream of power.

Kennedy won the nomination, but I remember well some who said, "He had better stay out of the State of Texas." He defeated Nixon in a questionable election.

Although the Vietnam conflict had been going on for some time, under the Kennedy administration the firing on one of our ships by North Vietnam in the Bay of Tonkin occurred and the U.S. intervened in 1962. J. F. Kennedy was killed in 1963 in Dallas with many mysteries surrounding the motorcade shootings.

The Vietnam war was immediately escalated further by Johnson who immediately proposed the "Great Society" as if it had been planned beforehand. Many of Kennedy's proposals in his "New Frontier" message to Congress had been considered too much, too fast, and many were viewed with contempt. Johnson, however, pushed major legislation through, possibly voted in as the result of the assassination. These pertained to civil rights, education and alleviation of poverty with no thought to future costs of the plethora of expensive Federal programs thus started.

Possibly no greater loss of respect for the presidency occurred than what I witnessed during the Johnson terms. Goldwater ran a strong race, but his suggestions of attacking North Korea and deciding the issue along the lines of a MacArthur plan were rejected in the election of 1964. Under Johnson, men continued to be sent into only a defensive war, with no plan for winning. Johnson was intimidated by China, and without fortitude he offered to negotiate in 1968. Peace was not gained until 1973 under the Nixon administration.

In March of 1975 North Vietnam overran the south after U.S. aid was withdrawn. In 1976 Vietnam was reunited under Communism. Under Johnson came our first military defeat, it involved 2,500,000 U.S. troops, it cost 58,000 lives and 100,000 alleged suicides. Worst of all, it destroyed respect for our military. Our service people came back to public ridicule after having been drafted and sent there by the government in the first place. Gross change in respect to many aspects of society followed.

Attention to the Middle East

Another war impact, although maybe not as obvious or direct to Americans, was the conflict in the Middle East. Zionist aims in Palestine produced difficulties as far back as 1913 when the Balfour Declaration was made. After World War I anti-Zionist riots led to an Arab revolt and a British commission recommended partitioning of Palestine in 1936. This was approved by the U.N. in 1947 but rejected by the Arab League. Their differences led to five wars: the first in 1948, the year after the creation of the state of Israel; the second in 1956 at the same time as the Suez Crisis in which Eisenhower attempted to prevent a great war; the third in 1967 (the "Six-Day War"); the fourth in 1973; and the fifth in 1982.

Deficit Spending and the Demanding Public

By now, as predicted, the Federal government had grown to vast proportions. Federal regulation increased with each Congress. Each new project called for a new Federal building and taxes escalated. It was not just to pay the war debt. Ironically, there was a great deal of frustration because the America we had known before had now become altered. My generation sensed it vividly.

To enjoy continued freedom in a free economy and a democracy, individual citizens must assume responsibility. This responsibility is in three major categories. The first regards a **personal economic welfare**, and the second relates to **personal moral conduct.** People must be honest! Perhaps the third is less obvious. It relates to a situation with regard to world affairs, which means a **personal responsibility for education**.

These great personal issues and responsibilities were not clear to many people at the close of World War II. The idea to live and let live still dominated. Crime continued to increase, because people seemed not to care -- they were busy "making theirs". There was lessened respect for the private property of other people. Many began to laugh at positive values and missions.

* * *

Perhaps it would be well at this juncture to review the Preamble to the Constitution:

We, the people of the United States, in order to form a more perfect Union, establish justice, insure domestic tranquility, provide for the common defense, promote the general welfare, and secure the blessings of liberty to ourselves and our posterity, do ordain and establish this Constitution for the United States of America.

and the Declaration of Independence:

We hold these truths to be self-evident, that all men are created equal, that they are endowed by their Creator with certain unalienable rights, that among these are life, liberty, and the pursuit of happiness. That to secure these rights governments are instituted among men, deriving their just powers from the consent of the governed. . . .

It should be noted that there is no guarantee of happiness for everyone. Happiness is attained by pursuit. The word pursue, as I recall, means to follow with the hope of overtaking. So it was intended, with our form of government, to give the individual a chance to pursue, to follow with the hope of someday overtaking an objective, a goal, or something which will ultimately constitute happiness or quality of life for that individual.

Notice also there was no guarantee of financial independence, no guarantee of economic freedom, and no guarantee of social welfare. However, the United States has always stood for helping others, and this means helping its own.

Yet, it should be realized that some people must be in a position to help other people. Someone has to finance and create jobs. There must be profits which provide salaries to be paid, working places to be maintained, and taxes paid. When greed replaces altruism, democracy is doomed.

Ideology Confrontation

If there was an objective for America, it was perhaps nothing more than an intuitive perception by the people who sensed that our form of government was the best choice available. In the famous "kitchen debate" between Krushchev and Nixon, when Krushchev exclaimed loudly that the world would live in Communism in the future, Nixon countered with the conviction that the world would "live in freedom".

This famous argument, which I remember vividly, implied more than just the words. It was the difference between opportunity or freedom for the individual vs. living in a complete police state. In Communist forms of government all the neighbors performed as police-persons. If one person obtained a slight advantage he was reported to the hierarchy and punished. The objective of most Americans was to maintain freedom of choice. But, we had no major world plan. There was no international objective. There was no long-range goal. There was no organized aim in American society. We were adrift. Yet that was in the nature of freedom itself.

Immediately after the second World War I still felt much fear. There were those in many of our institutions who claimed that it was "better to be Red than dead". Yet, there were also those who exhibited that this was not the case. How many died trying to scale the Berlin Wall? How many countries put up barriers to hold their people in like prisoners rather than barriers to keep people out with immigration laws?

It became quite obvious to me at the close of World War II that we needed statesmen. After World War II, Eisenhower, together with a cooperative Congress, set about to rebuild America. Many of the enactments and aid pertained to national roads and highways. Eisenhower had seen the benefits of the Autobahn in Germany, and felt that transportation was one of the manifestations of internal strength. He was supported by Nixon. Perhaps Nixon was elected later not solely on the basis of a Republican ticket, but because of the need in the country for statesmen.

Kennedy was a statesman, perhaps even more than a leader. His Alliance for Progress in South America was still respected decades later. But for all his faults, Nixon was perhaps, until Ronald Reagan and George Bush, the most successful international statesman-president the United States has known in the modern era. It was Nixon who opened the door to Russia and to China and he was greatly admired and respected in Europe. Diplomacy, particularly with the Secretary of State, is perhaps the most under-respected aspect of our western world. Consequently, after World War II there was cause for frustration.

Economics and Taxes

I have listed, from the effects of the three large wars in my time, several psychologic changes that I detected. Not all those changes could be blamed on the wars, and maybe the wars were used as a scapegoat. One day I received a call from Washington inquiring as to whether or not I needed any research funds. Under the Johnson administration, a large sum of money had been set aside for literally all kinds of research. One of the bureaus in

Washington felt that if they didn't make use of the money they had been allotted it would not be funded in the next go-round.

I had always funded all my own research, and felt that certainly I could use some help. But I didn't feel it honest to use research funds for conjuring up projects, or taking time out of my practice at that particular time to do more research because I was tremendously involved in those years in practice and writing, which my many publications in the 1960s would confirm. I therefore declined the offer, but it seemed to me that a lot of money was being put into research without direction, and it would inevitably be wasted.

By now, in the 1960s, I was beginning to witness some financial success. I worked very hard and also attempted to curtail a heavy pay-out for taxes. As a part of that program, a colleague presented me with the opportunity of investing in some oil drilling in Texas in which I engaged. If I had not had the taxation on my shoulders I certainly would have rejected the whole opportunity. There is an old saying that no good oil deal ever leaves the Petroleum Club room in Midland, Texas. Therefore, all of the speculative investments are put out for people who are more gullible and who do not really know the business. The oil drilling investments in the Sprayberry Trend in Texas have a record of high output initially, which appear attractive, but then the production falls off very quickly. With loss of flow, pumps have to be paid for, and soon after that the available oil is depleted and a process known as water flooding must be used, which is more expensive and risky.

I took a small interest in some wells. We had some successes with drilling and it looked as though maybe we would get our money back and then a respectable income over a period of time. When I was presented with the opportunity to obtain quite a large share in one well, wouldn't you know this one would be a dry hole! All of the small profit that I had accumulated was now gone, and then some. I then did something I should have done before taking the advice of a friend. I went to Texas to observe some of the properties and some of the wells in which I had invested. I was shocked to find, after I had taken the bait, that it was more or less a scam. In the end I had invested heavily in the oil venture in some sixteen wells, and when I got through, considering the fact that it had been done with tax dollars over a period of three years, I lost less, but certainly that money could have been put to much more creative and productive use. In addition, the investment took too much of my time.

Maybe the risk in exploration is the reason why the government permitted tax deductions on such investments. Improvement of farm land and forests and other investments would potentially help society in the long run. A realization struck me that taxes were a major concern. Taxes are a part of the problem of running any business, even a simple professional practice.

For a moment, look at the kind of taxation that is mandatory. First of all, there are Social Security taxes, and then there are withholding taxes to be funded and calculated for all of the employees. If a pension plan is provided there are pension deductions that must be made from the total business revenue. Workmen's compensation has to be calculated and kept current. Then there is, of course, sales tax. On top of that there is state income tax, and on top of everything there is Federal income tax collected by the Internal Revenue Service.

Particularly confounding is the fact that every Congress or state legislature that comes along changes the tax laws. What is allowed in one year is not allowed in the next, and even the Internal Revenue Service agents sometimes are confused. I remember Reagan holding up a mass of paper almost five inches thick in disdain of the complications and controls. This is the reason why many people will challenge when they are audited by the I.R.S. It is impossible for me to believe that a Federal agent can be neutral in such a situation and not take a tax challenge personally.

Several years ago I had a friend whose daughter became a black-jack dealer in one of the casinos in Las Vegas. I knew her very well and one day I engaged her in a conversation regarding her feeling when people would lose, or when people would win. She said that despite the fact that it made no difference whatsoever in her salary, whenever she had someone on a winning streak she would tend to take it personally, and often try to beat them. It is pretty well known that when someone is winning at a gambling table, the dealer or the operator of a particular table will be changed in the hope of breaking the streak.

It would appear to me that also, despite the fact that it makes no difference in the salary of an I.R.S. agent, a person saving every penny in attempting to conserve against taxes would have some competition with that individual agent.

Controls and Regulations

In a system of free enterprise and in a system of democracy or a republic, ethics dictate that certain laws be made so that most people will be treated fairly. In fact, this is the essence of making laws so that order can be maintained. For example, in a culture with automobiles, ethics demand that primitive instincts like speeding, double parking, running red lights and all of the measures in traffic, be brought under control. Therefore, in a free economy a right to freedom carries with it a responsibility.

When citizens insist on being unfair, or when business practices of one group encroach on the business of another, then certain controls are instigated, and put into law for protection of the honest. **All laws are in this sense controls.** The truth of the matter is that not all people have discipline. Many people try to take advantage of others who are more honest and forthright. Laws for fairness to all concerned must be made.

Each new law means that enforcement must become a problem, and consequently more regulatory personnel need to become involved. Therefore, a new agency is established, all of which costs more money, and consequently more revenue is needed for its support. If citizens are not voluntarily good and honest, then controls must be widespread. And such was the widening pattern in the 1960s.

Dr. W. P. Shoftstall, Dean of Students at Arizona State University wrote an article in 1965 explaining the 10 fatal delusions of youth. They were as follows:

1. There is no eternal truth.
2. Physical survival is the highest goal.
3. Right and wrong are relative.
4. The individual has no right to property.
5. I am not my brother's keeper.
6. Loyalty to people is stupid.
7. Physical environment determines all.
8. The majority determines right.
9. We should treat everybody the same.
10. Material change is progress.

There was in that decade also a willingness on the part of most people to urge the government to tax the successful, in order to share it with the unsuccessful. But many resented it and tried to do their utmost to beat the tax game. In Europe, there was a hidden economy in which the black market thrived. In addition, many deals were organized "under the table" in some of the European countries. People cheated because they felt that they had to, in order to remain parallel with their competitors.

Another manifestation of looming problems was the liberalization of the courts and the judges. When it was discovered that people could be sued for having a slick sidewalk after the rain and that any accident in your home could end up in a suit by a friend who was an invited guest, the law schools became jammed with applicants and everybody looked for reasons to sue anyone else. This too might be classified as a moral breakdown, and it added to the stress of life, the stress of doing business. This was particularly true because there were always those intent on carrying on practices at the borderline of the law. Lawyers build practices by defending both sides of the law.

Cultural Shifts

In 1958 I was on the planning staff for the U.C.L.A. School of Dentistry. There had been a study and a report put together by a committee which was called the Western Interstate Commission on Higher Education. Based on the curves of growth that had been projected for that time, obtained from population estimates, rate of cavity formation, and estimated dental work that would be required, within ten years there would need to be a new dental school for every one then in existence or the output of each dental school would need to be doubled, in order to supply the manpower required for the estimated needs in dentistry. I didn't think that a growth curve could continue as the projections were, and I identified several factors that entered into the error of that prediction.

Three main factors were extremely significant in effecting an alteration of those projections. The first was the development of the "pill". In late 1958 and 1959, it was just coming into use, and other methods of contraception such as the I.U.D. were being proposed. In connection with the lowering of the birth rate, the laws were changed with regard to abortion, and it would be difficult to ascertain the number of abortions that were performed. There is no question that there was a drop in the birth rate from 5,000,000 new births a year to about 3,500,000 a year, about a 30% drop.

A second factor was the shift in the economy that took place in 1958 and 1959 as we began to experience a recession. The result of that was that many couples wanted to postpone the starting of a family. The age for marriage became delayed by most females into the twenties and thirties. Therefore, economics played a part in the production of smaller families. The anticipated costs of education, as the rapid inflation was developing, also made an impact. Economics definitely affected the culture.

The third major factor which influenced the projections for dental schools was the advent of fluorides in city water supplies. But perhaps not quite as well appreciated was the fluoride in the dentifrice or the tooth paste. In connection with the lowering of decay and the lowering of dental needs, there was still the better education in oral hygiene and perhaps even the changing of the stickiness of certain foods containing cariogenic or decay-producing factors. All of these made for a change in American culture ever so gradually.

* * *

Still another factor to alter our culture was the advent of drug abuse, which I will talk more about later. But there seemed to be a very strange psychologic situation, because it was in these years of the '50s and '60s that the so-called flower children started to become evident.

The effect of the wars (World War II, Korea and Vietnam) had in my intuitive senses damaged America more greatly than most recognized. We had experienced a collective moral drift, an economic slide, and the prospects of an avalanche to follow.

The lowest point in American confidence was reached during the Iran encounter when they captured our embassy. We were helpless and embarrassed in our military attempt to mount a rescue. Carter and the Congress had so focussed on the domestic problems that our armed forces were inept.

We regained some pride when Reagan put his foot down in Granada, and Bush boldly stopped Iraq's takeover in the Middle East. Working under the limitations of the United Nations Security Council was still unsatisfactory to some citizens. The Cold War was finally terminated. We learned a lesson on staying prepared that I hope will not be forgotten in the future.

But let us consider post-war attitude changes and circumstances in more detail.

7

BEAT THE BURSTING OF THE BUBBLE
(1946 - 1950)

The Aftermath of World War II

When World War II ended, the jubilation was more short-lived than I would have expected. The major gratitude was for the stopping of further bloodshed and loss of lives, because most of us had lost friends. There was a relief because the fear of foreign invasion still persisted as long as either war, in Europe or Asia, was still active. The reduction of the tremendous expense and the useless outlay of raw materials and destruction of natural resources was a relief. We could start thinking about ordinary life and family again.

Germany had been pounded. As the atrocities came to light, most German people were ashamed. The British Empire was crippled. In fact, much of Europe was destroyed, first by the German blitz and dive bombers and then by the Allies. Aside from the absolute havoc of the atom bomb on Hiroshima and Nagasaki and the bombing of Tokyo, the Japanese homeland had emerged surprisingly well. Although quite lacking in raw materials, Japan had a tremendous treasure in its culture and its resilient people.

A New Fear

The Marshall Plan had helped Europe survive, but the fear of Hitler had turned into the fear of Stalin. The conflict really had not ended. Many still remembered the warnings that Communist totalitarianism might be a poor alternative to a Fascist dictatorship.

America had survived unscathed physically, but the war had left scars. It had left engrams in the brains of many Americans, which were not immediately apparent. The changes which that world conflict had thrust upon us would be evidenced later.

As the war crimes came to light, many cried for umbrage. In our modern times many found it difficult to conceive just what there was about man's psyche that would lead him to be so cruel to his fellow man. What was there in the basic nature of man to want to destroy, to demand and then seek revenge?

After the capitulation of Japan, MacArthur set about to establish order in the Far East. Having been isolated there for many years, he was far removed from contact with the American people. But MacArthur was a scholar. He had a great knowledge of history and also had an understanding of economics, politics and government. The programs he suggested and instituted for Japan were exactly those needed. History proved how correct, indeed, he was in the decisions made for that country.

After the war there was a tendency for Americans to look down on the Japanese and perhaps this sense spurred the Japanese onward, particularly in their drive for education and manufacturing. Great pressure was put on their children for learning.

Job Not Completed

The events at the end of the war caused a general mistrust of the Soviet Union and particularly the Communist Party. There still remained the cleaning up of the military bases and the replacement of personnel who had been in service for years.

When the post-war world leadership was thrust upon America we found ourselves ill-prepared. Many felt guilty. There was a sort of paranoia that spread across America, a fear of not being liked, and a fear of not doing what was right. We exported much of our key technology. We helped others to build up what had been torn down and also helped make them self-sufficient -- in fact, opening the door for them to be economic competitors in the future.

Greed

While this was going on I witnessed in our culture a widespread state of frustration and greediness that I hadn't seen before. This, perhaps, resulted from the need to get back into a mode for personal economic survival and further restoring a personal security for the raising of a family.

During the total of six war years there had been a tremendous increase in science and technology as spin-offs from war manufacturing. Rocket power had developed, antibiotics had been discovered, and television communication was ready to explode. But now two new factors began also to affect the attitudes in our culture. The first was the tremendous increase in government spending. The second was higher and higher taxes, which was followed by inflation.

Escalation of Income Occured with Increase in Costs

During my high school years in Indiana, a student could buy a hamburger and a bowl of chili for 15 cents. A respectable warm lunch cost 25 cents. Even in the late thirties, salaries were in the range of only 20 to 30 cents per hour. A little arithmetic will reveal how very meager that type of income was for only a 40-hour week. However, many worked 10-hour days, or more, and six days a week or a 60-hour week.

If a person had a job at 20 cents an hour and worked a 40-hour week, that would bring him only $8.00 for a whole week's work! If the person was very fortunate and had a job at 40 cents an hour, it would still only come to $16.00 a week. During that time, however, a new Ford, Chevrolet or Plymouth automobile could be bought for $600, and a nice home would be no more than $10,000. Still, at 40 cents an hour, it represented $800.00 a year unless someone had two jobs. A standard car would cost about one year's wages.

If a year is taken to be 50 weeks, given the usual two weeks vacation, and a person works a 40-hour week, that means there are 2000 working hours per year. As a starting point, given a salary of $1.00 an hour, a person would have an income of $2000 a year. At $10.00 per hour it would be $20,000.

During the war salaries rose to about 65 cents an hour for unskilled labor, while pay for skilled labor was at about $1.00 an hour. Parents of young people in the 1990s now have a difficult time in explaining the dearth of dollars in those years.

Fear of Communists

In the late 1940s the fear of Communism was still present. Many by now had become aware of the nature of Communism, and its theoretical attraction. Power was sought from ideologic conviction, for economic gain and for the need for identity in some individuals.

I remember in the 1940 election Roosevelt had run against Alf Landon who was the Republican candidate. I was playing football at Indiana University at that time, and among the whole squad the team physician and I were the only Republicans who were for Landon. I learned something in that election just standing by and watching. About one-third of the population voted for Landon, which indicated to me that there was probably one-third of the population who were "conservatives". On the other side, there were probably many more who were Democrats who would always vote their ticket. This would mean that there was about a middle 25%-30% that were the "swing voters", an observation that has been borne out as is represented by the election of more Democratic congressmen and governors on a national scale. But somehow, many people feel deep down that some protection is needed from the socialistically inclined Democratic philosophy. This may be one of the reasons why Republican presidents have been elected in four of the last six presidential elections. In fact, since 1865 there have been 26 presidents elected, of whom 17 have been Republicans while only 9 were Democrats.

* * *

My Orthodontic Ambitions

In my sophomore year in dental school in 1943 I decided on graduate education in orthodontics. It was an opportunity to apply all the basic sciences of anatomy, physiology, histology, biology, and above all it was an opportunity to contribute to beauty and esthetics and express art. It would offer me a continuous challenge.

The last two years of my dental curriculum were directed toward the goal of further studies in graduate school. I was understandably disappointed when, as we received our degrees we were immediately called into the service. The interruption of my education was the concern, but it was good to get some general dental experience. In 1945 I went into the Navy as a dental officer. I was excited at the prospect of traveling and seeing the world. It did prove to be two extremely exceptional years.

* * *

Travels

I was 16 years of age before I ventured more than 50 miles from where I was born. At that age, one Sunday some of my friends invited me to drive in an open roadster to Niles, Michigan, just north of the border of Indiana, only for the lark of saying we had been out of the state. We went through South Bend, so while I was in high school I did see the golden dome at Notre Dame University. Later, while on the football squad at Indiana University I had played at Notre Dame, Ohio State, Nebraska, Michigan, Illinois, Northwestern, Iowa, Wisconsin, and Purdue, to which we traveled by bus or by train. But now in the service there was a chance to see more and experience more. And so I entered into another phase of my life as a Lieutenant Junior Grade, a Navy officer in uniform, with a feeling of some prestige - perhaps really for the first time.

My Duty Assignments

My tour of duty, together with that of my brother Jim, started at the Jacksonville Naval

Air Station in Florida. We soon learned how we must think and practice in the service-oriented environment. It was in Jacksonville that I experienced my first hurricane. We were warned of its coming and told to secure our quarters. I knew little of hurricanes, but I soon learned about the "eye". The air moves in a large circle. First the palm trees were bent in one direction, but as the storm moved there followed a still period — we were in the eye. Shortly afterward the trees bent equally in the opposite direction. It was frightening, but no more so than some of the cyclones bearing tornadoes that I had witnessed in the mid-west.

After one month we were transferred to Camp Perry, Virginia, just outside of Williamsburg, which later became a camp for the C.I.A. I had, from my earnings as a dance instructor, bought an old 1936 Ford which I had driven to Florida. On our way between these two duty stations we came back through Indiana, where my brother Jim got married. Surprisingly we received simultaneous orders to transfer. I therefore escorted Jim and Mary Lou on their honeymoon with all three of us packed in that small two-door Ford. It was quite an experience to be associated with someone else's honeymoon.

At one point in the Appalachian Mountains en route to Camp Perry we were on a downhill road which made a slight left turn, only to be faced suddenly with a one-lane bridge and an oncoming car fast approaching. The brakes in those old cars didn't last very long, and mine were weak. There was no way I could stop in time despite even pulling hard on the emergency brake. The oncoming motorist, on seeing our plight, speeded up his car quite noticeably. We entered the bridge by nicking only one of the stone abutments. I often thought how Providence had smiled on us. That narrow escape still makes me shudder.

Camp Perry was a "boot camp", where young sailors get their boots and are indoctrinated for about three weeks. There were 30,000 recruits in camp, and each week 10,000 left and 10,000 new ones arrived. During the time that they were in camp they were also supposed to be made battle-ready. We had 300 dentists aboard and only 100 dental chairs.

Some of the inductees came from the hills of Pennsylvania and West Virginia, and had never seen a dentist before. Many had never owned a toothbrush. It was not uncommon that one recruit could need 10 to 20 fillings, plus extraction of teeth too far gone to be saved. We were instructed to do silver fillings for the back teeth, and porcelain type restorations for the front teeth. We tried to do a good job under the circumstances.

These were the days before the modern high-speed drills; the technique was slow, and we did most of the routine dentistry without anesthesia. There was a general requirement to perform about 20 fillings a day. I was rather confident, often doing 30 or 40 fillings per day because I saw so much need. I tried to save as many teeth from extraction as possible, many times against the rules.

I was agonized during my first rotation through the surgical duty. The surgical wing consisted of four chairs. The practice was to not ask questions but remove any teeth condemned by other dentists on the line. Novocaine was injected to four patients in a row, then the teeth were removed, and the routine was then repeated. My first day I extracted 95 teeth, many of them the first permanent molars. In retrospect, I believe many of them could have been saved under different circumstances. My arm and hand were sore from the extractions, but worse was the psychologic pain of having to extract savable teeth and the concern I felt for the future welfare of those young men.

Life in the Service

Camp Perry was 10 miles or so from Williamsburg and near Jamestown. There was much history there, especially at Williamsburg which was in the process of being rebuilt in 1945. This effort had, of course, been limited by the war.

Having no friends when we arrived, we had little social life at first. But the local Officers Club seemed to be the hub of most of the social activity. It was there that most of the eligible bachelors -- as I was -- and some of the young married men without their wives had a chance to get acquainted with some William and Mary coeds and some of the local ladies.

I saw one girl at the Officers Club, a most attractive lady whose father, I later learned, was a physician in the Philadelphia area. I saw her from a distance, and having obtained her name from a friend found an opportunity to phone her, and finally arranged to take her to dinner with our group. I became very keen on the pursuit of a romance. I discovered also that she was wearing orthodontic appliances, so I had a chance to observe the type of treatment that was being employed. I would have married her if things had worked out. When I visited her family, however, I sensed that I was not yet ready for the Philadelphia Blue-Book society. And further, my whole graduate career was ahead of me. But I made other marvelous friends and we had many good times. I often wonder what happened to them.

I couldn't help observing that some of the horniest men on the various bases where I served were those who were married and accustomed to having regular sex. They seemed to me even more frustrated than some of the bachelors who had never picked up that practice as a routine.

Lessons from the Military Experience

As I look back on my time in the service, there were very memorable things I learned. When later I had time for contemplation I found that most of the officers, men and women, wanted to get out of the service and get on with their lives in order to obtain financial security. This was a part of the frustration that was felt by many at the time. Our families had gone through the Depression in the Thirties, which left an indelible scar. We had gone through a vigorous speed-up program in school, to the level of a test for survival. Now we found ourselves in the service, where we were still under control, and many were frustrated. An attitude of resistance to authority was developing. It was a feeling of being dominated. We also intuitively feared the economy could collapse, and our pockets were empty. Therefore, as the saying goes, there was a "bubble" that could burst. The economy was beginning to take off, and many wanted to be a part of it. The need for the production of many goods and services made abundant opportunity outside the service.

Dentists often selected the profession so that they could be their own boss and have freedom. Now, being taken into the service, against their interest and after the war was over at the very least led to frustration.

The Party

I had a very educational experience in the service. Two of our fellow-dentists were being discharged. After having served three or four years these men were anxious to get back into the world of private practice. It seemed appropriate that those of us being left in the military should give them a send-off. Therefore, since I was a kind of organizer, I arranged a dinner party at the Officers Club mostly made up of the ring of friends that we had developed.

A wonderful evening was enjoyed by several of us, which ended about ten o'clock. But apparently it was not enough for some of those in the party. At eleven the club was closed down and I had gone to bed. But some continued on to the Officers Quarters with the party. Two of them became quite inebriated. One got a fire extinguisher and started spraying others. Someone threw a tire through the flimsy plaster-board wall of our quarters.

The next day I got up to go to work and saw the mess. That afternoon eight of us who had been at the dinner were brought before the Commodore. He wanted to know whose idea it was to arrange such a party. I spoke up and said, "Mine. But I had no idea that it would get out of hand, I had nothing to do with that." The Commodore retorted, "Since you arranged the party you are responsible. The Officers Club will be off limits for you for 30 days."

There were other military bases in the area in and around Norfolk, and I was not off limits at these clubs. This was fortunate because they were our social world. After this restriction I received calls from friends wondering where I was going to go for entertainment that night. Many of the members supported me and went where I went. It prompted me to look around for nice restaurants in the area and catch some of the local culture also, although that was harder on the pocketbook. So in taking the hit for them, I became endeared to them, and kept an association with some of them for many years.

A Taste of Socialism

After I left the service, I looked back and associated it with a massive social program. We had to check in and check out, go where we were told. There was no advantage for advancement by a performance of excellence. It was a matter of spending time. A person was at the mercy of a superior officer. Was it any different from the block controller in a socialistic police state?

When I later visited the socialized countries of Scandinavia and talked to some of the people, it dawned on me that massive socialization is much like being in the armed services.

One of the advantages of such a system was that after the day was over the job was finished, and there was no lingering responsibility because someone else took over. Maybe that advantage is worthwhile to many people who are not willing to accept responsibility for their economic condition.

In the service I detected an undercurrent of resentment which would come and go depending on the circumstances. Despite having some great enjoyment, most of us looked forward to the day when we could get back into the regular world. Yet, some elected to become permanent officers in the service. Many, after serving twenty years, could be put on a sort of furlough and a pension, and still go out and practice later which they thought was a good plan.

My Last Athletic Fling

While at Camp Perry I noticed on a bulletin board an announcement of try-outs for the service basketball team. Although I had played basketball since I was five years old, I hadn't been on a court for five years because of the demands of dental school. But my legs were like wire because of the dancing that I had done. I suppose out of boredom rather than anything else I thought, "Why not make an attempt to make the team?" And so I started practicing.

There were 200 young men who tried out for the team. The coach was an officer from Indiana who also lived in our Bachelor Officers Quarter. Several of the members on the team had played on winning teams in college, and three of them had played professionally. There had been a change in the game during the years that I hadn't played. I could always push the ball with one hand and pass, and so the one-handed shots and hook shots that were now popular fit in with my ability. Amazingly, I made the team. We travelled around on the East Coast, playing different service and college teams. I had always felt that I would have been a much better college athlete had I not injured my knee as a junior in high school. I had also injured my back at the age of 12, helping my father lift a plough. And so I had episodes of back spasms which were probably further associated with my round shoulders, which made me appear shorter than I actually was.

I was having a great time. I did my dentistry in the morning and practiced basketball in the afternoon. I kept up my requirements despite the fact that I was only there half time. We won our first ten games. I had developed into a point-guard type of player because I had learned to dribble the ball very well as a young boy. Although I was only 5'11", I could "stuff a ball" although it was not commonly done. On the run I could jump up and touch the rim of the hoop which was ten feet from the floor. In about January of 1946 I again tore up my knee while practicing basketball. I had jumped very high to reach for a rebound and on coming down I was bumped off balance. Through the years my knee had become strengthened, and I had become careless and did not have it wrapped or protected. As I was bumped off balance in my descent I came down on my right leg and felt the ligaments tear in my right knee. I heard a "pop". I lay there on the floor realizing my whole future in sports was over.

It was the worst knee injury I had ever experienced. It swelled up and became very painful. Since I couldn't walk and couldn't stand and do my dental work, the orthopedic surgeon on the base examined me and ordered me to the hospital simply to rest the knee. After one week I was transferred to the General Hospital at Portsmouth, Virginia, which is across the bay from Norfolk.

* * *

Portsmouth Hospital

In retrospect, it could almost be believed that everything happens for a cause. While in the hospital I began to beef up, eating three big meals a day and not having much activity. I grew slovenly and could hardly get enough sleep. I learned that too much sleep could be a bad habit.

At Portsmouth Hospital there was an entire section for birthing for the wives of Navy personnel. Several young physicians were based there. I took meals with them and got acquainted. Because I had nothing to do I asked if I could observe their techniques and problems of delivery of newborns and some of their principles of surgery that might come into use for me later in my orthodontic career. I didn't think it would hurt to enhance my knowledge. This was particularly true since I was dealing with the growth of the head and jaws, and I hadn't been previously exposed to forceps delivery of a baby and the possible head and jaw damaging effects involved in birthing.

With their willingness to teach me, and after being surgically scrubbed and with sterile gown, I finally assisted in one delivery, just for my own enlightenment, but not the surgery. This experience also gave me the opportunity to discuss the medical aspects of childbirth. I learned that much depended on not letting the newborn emerge too fast. Control lessened the chance of tearing the orifice, but -- if that was likely -- there were different theories of episiotomy, which they explained. As I observed the operation with its deep layer reconstruction, little did I realize that the technique would come into use for me within less than a year in caring for accidents of the face.

After two months I was assigned duty to Norfolk Naval Base, which I came to enjoy. There was an epidemic of trench mouth, which is necrotic (dead tissue of the gums) and is quite painful. It occurred on board one of the large ships, and I conducted some experiments to determine which drugs or which treatment approach would yield the most effective cure.

One day I was doing routine examinations for one of the groups when I looked on the chart to find a sailor with the same first and last name as mine, and even the same middle initial. His middle name was Morton, however. Since that time I have often wondered, as the earth becomes increasingly populated, if it will ultimately be proper to use both names more often. This is particularly important when credit ratings are affected, and people running out on bills can mar someone else's credit rating. I was once refused credit in Arizona, many years later, because of the default of someone else with the same name. Maybe we will need eventually to have four names, as has been common in the Spanish culture for centuries.

From Entrance to Exit

Just as I was getting into the study of the mouth disease and looking forward to the outcome of the work, I was again transferred, despite the efforts of my senior officer. This time I was sent to Camp Shelton, Virginia, which was a separation center.

At Camp Perry I had seen new recruits. At Camp Shelton they were leaving the service. Each mouth had to be examined and charted. It was a marvelous opportunity to observe human occlusions. How rare indeed is the normal perfect bite!

One day while at work in the separation process I heard from the next building a call from Dr. Phillips, one of my physician friends, who was making his own examinations. "Ricketts, come over here -- you've got to see this!" he shouted. I scurried over immediately, to find a thin sailor standing there naked. He had been drunk at one time and along with some friends had been tattooed. He had a heart form placed around each nipple on his chest and a very large red arrow was engraved all the way down to his pubic hair. Along the arrow was printed "love meat". What an embarrassment for that boy in his future life. Tattoos are essentially permanent.

Key West

I helped close down that base after about three months' duty and was then transferred to Key West, Florida, to the submarine base. I had been to Jacksonville before and knew that Florida was a delightful location. Key West is only 90 miles from Cuba and is the southernmost tip of the United States. I still had my 1936 Ford Tudor, and so I packed up and for the first time drove south through the Carolinas and Georgia and down through the Keys to my new assignment.

The first shock I had when I arrived at Key West was my impression that some service personnel thought it was the end of creation. The island held 20,000 in the armed services and only 6,000 civilians. However, it was exciting to me that Hemingway had lived and produced some books there. Key West, with its almost tropical climate, was also a budding art community before the war. I was sent there as a replacement for two dental officers who were finishing their service time. The dental facility was very adequate, affording me an opportunity for broader application of dentistry than simply routine silver fillings or extractions. In the end, I was the only practicing dentist, as the Commanding Officer, who did only book work, was a career person who hadn't practiced for years.

I still carried my textbooks and studied several times each week. I also abstracted articles from orthodontic journals.

There were two officers clubs in the area. One was at an air base at Boca Chica, and the other at the Army base at Fort Taylor. One small civilian band rotated playing at the clubs for dancing on specific nights. My choice of female companions was quite limited in such a small town. We were not permitted to take junior female personnel to the officers clubs, even though there were some beautiful women Navy personnel on the base.

In the beginning I danced with officers' wives and some of the nurses who were also officers. I was sought out, however, by officers and wives who had sisters or relatives visiting, because I was a willing and able escort. Within three or four months I had a collection of coeds and friends who would revisit on week ends and take holidays on the island. Because I had still another six months in the service and realized I was going to be very deeply engrossed in graduate school later, I felt that now was my time to have a fun time if ever I was to have one. Therefore, I really enjoyed my duty there, with trips to Miami and fishing on the Keys. I also was permitted to use one of the "long boats" in which I took the corpsmen and their wives out for fishing in the waters just off the base.

Among other things, I was required to rotate duty for medical emergencies. Fortunately, there were four good corpsmen as assistants in the clinic. One evening while at Fort Taylor at a dinner dance, I received an emergency call from a young medical colleague who had a young sailor patient present with a facial injury.

The holds, or living quarters of submarines, were equipped with "hatches" which were elevated by a rim of metal about 10 inches high for receiving a watertight lid at the time of submergence or rough weather. Metal ladders for entering and leaving descended at a slight angle and became slick with use. Young men would learn to slide downward on the hand rails rather than backing down facing the ladder. This particular sailor had slipped while in the forward position and the weight of his fall had caught the rim of the hatch with his mouth open slightly. Because his hands were engaged on the rails he couldn't put them up for protection. He had caught his lower lip and torn about a two-inch gash completely through it, knocking out two lower teeth. However, the greatest damage was in the upper jaw. He also had a three-inch split in his upper lip and crushed eight upper teeth, together with the upper jaw bone, and displaced the fragments up near the floor of his eye sockets. The young medical officer was quite shaken with the tooth situation and therefore called me. It was a chance to apply some of the techniques of deep suturing and repair I had observed at Portsmouth but never actually used before.

I anesthetized the areas, cleaned up the debris from the wound, picked out bits of broken teeth and splintered bone, and restored the soft tissues to normal position with tiny sutures starting from the inside just as I had witnessed following a vaginal tear in childbirth. Ironically, the young man had never had a cavity or a filling and had a normal bite before the injury.

The accident had occurred in early November. After he had healed, in about three weeks, we replaced the missing teeth with upper and lower artificial dentures. When he went home for a Christmas holiday leave his parents detected no scars and did not recognize that he had lost his natural teeth. The service experience, therefore, afforded me a certain kind of opportunity and helped me understand better some of the procedures for the surgical repairing of cleft lips and palates which I encountered later in my career.

The Little White House

It may be recalled by some readers that President Harry Truman made Key West his "Little White House". He loved to vacation there while still protected by the base, as President Carter did later at Camp David in Maryland. Truman would appear with some of his cronies and under the pretense of going fishing, as I observed, enjoyed some card games on board the small yacht. We would all stand at attention in the exercise yard of the base at seven in the morning during our daily calisthenics when the party would board the boat.

We enjoyed having Truman on the base because the newest movie releases from Hollywood would be flown in, and we were invited to attend. He insisted that we need not stand at attention when he entered the theater, but how could any citizen remain seated when the President of the United States entered the room?

The Secret Service people stayed in our bachelor officers' quarters whenever Truman was there. They also swam in our pool. However, we were not permitted to be around when the President went swimming for exercise. Truman also took brisk walks around the base. Because the Secret Service was there, and a part of the government, and because I became acquainted with them, they asked me to perform some dental work. They paid privately for the materials for any gold or ceramic work, and it also afforded me the opportunity to practice other than routine Navy dentistry.

Out of respect for my extra effort on their behalf, they asked me one day if they could help me in any way. At first I declined, but then I thought that they might help me get a free flight with the National Air Transport Service (NATS) that delivered top brass people around the country. Since my intended leave was close to their departure back to Washington, one of the agents saw to it that my papers were prepared in three hours instead of the usual three weeks so that I could accompany the President's party the very next day.

It was a feeling of exhilaration to be in civilian clothes, and with a S.S. band on my arm walking in front of the line of officers and personnel standing at attention en route to board the presidential party flight. I was not actually on President Truman's plane. The Secret Service and reporters and assistants to the President were on a chartered flight from United Airlines at that time. We went through some very rough weather, and it was interesting to observe what goes on behind the scenes in the functioning of the President's office.

* * *

One of my fellow dental officers whom I liked very much was being released and needed transportation for his wife and baby back to his home state. He therefore made an offer for my old Ford. Because I knew I couldn't afford a car in Chicago I sold it to him for what I had paid for it two and a half years before, which was $150.00. Because I still needed to get around the base and the Clubs and wanting not to be restricted, I requisitioned a bicycle from the motor pool. By this time I had three girl friends for social activities. I was probably the healthiest and in the best condition of my life, just turning 27 years of age. The bicycle which I pedaled daily, was also used to help recondition my injured knee.

During my two-year tour of duty I had taken only one week of leave. I therefore accumulated some time and was discharged about one month early. This was in July and gave me about two months before my graduate class was to start. I felt it would be good to go back to Kokomo, spend some time with the family, play some golf, and continue to study, particularly anatomy.

My Graduate Plans

The previous winter I had experienced a shock. I had assumed that by being admitted to the Illinois graduate school in 1945 I would automatically be in the class of 1947. However such was not the case. With many dischargees from the service and the concern for the future of general dentistry with fluorides in the drinking water, the competition for orthodontic graduate school was now much stiffer. I was informed in February that I was only an alternate and would get in only in the event of a cancellation. I therefore wrote to my alma mater at Indiana University, knowing Dr. J. William Adams had been released from Army duty and had taken over as a new head of the Orthodontic Department. He had been trained under Dr. Brodie and Dr. William B. Downs, as well as Dr. Abraham Goldstein and Dr. Ernest Myer at the University of Illinois, and represented their philosophy. After some insistence and maneuvering and after he had examined my record at the school, I was accepted at Indiana as a graduate class of one. I decided to train there at Indiana with him. I made plans to study with Dr. Adams and visited him in his office. I observed some of the techniques which he had learned and which came into use later in my career.

We were both anticipating a great year. But approximately two months before I was to start with him I was informed that a place in the class at Illinois had opened up. I therefore phoned him to discuss the situation. He was disappointed but recommended that I accept the opportunity to study with Brodie and particularly with Downs who, at that time, was developing the descriptive facial analysis with the oriented lateral head X-ray. So in September of 1947 I re-entered the "Halls of Ivy" for a new learning experience and a whole new episode in my life.

Romantic Experiences

Probably this writing would not be complete without reference to some affairs of the heart during my last year of service. As I was invited to escort some ladies I became involved with a coed from Nebraska. She was a dancer and sang and played the piano. In fact, when I was home in Kokomo, she came to visit me, and marriage was discussed, which she rejected.

I had another affair during the Key West duty with a beautiful Chief Petty Officer who worked in the Supply Department of the Navy. I met her playing golf. She was very lovely, very wholesome, but I didn't realize at the time how much we cared for each other. It was a year later when she finally expressed herself, and it saddened me. By that time I was busy at the school in Chicago, maybe four months into my graduate work and was in my usual exhausted state, when I received a phone call from her from somewhere in Pennsylvania. She said, "I have been proposed to by a man and I am confused. If there is a chance for us I will wait for you to finish your schooling. I have found that I truly loved you." We had never engaged in sex, but had experienced some heavy petting, and I felt very near to her. I was completely stunned by her call out of the blue. I actually became very nervous. I finally replied, "My life is too uncertain, and I really don't know how long it's going to be this way. I'm into some deep research and I can't see when it will stop. If you have a man who really cares and who will make a good father and a good provider, maybe you had better go ahead and accept his proposal. We both know we care for each other, but now I'm stuck in Chicago and I don't know where it will end."

After I put the phone down I was depressed. If only she had expressed such deep feelings earlier it would have made a difference. I know that before we met she had been dating others, and she was transferred to Norfolk before I left Key West. On my way home from Key West I had visited her in Virginia, but we weren't able to spend enough time together.

That night as I lay awake with memories passing through my mind I realized two things. First, if someone has feelings, maybe they should be expressed before it's too late. Secondly, by now in my life there had been at least six ladies, even one engagement, that could have proceeded to marriage if both partners had been ready at the moment. I was only 27 years of age. What did it take for that big serious step? I could have perhaps been happy with any of them. Does a successful partnership really require being "in love"? Why did arranged marriages by families in some cultures end with such happy situations? Maybe it is the continued enjoyment of each other's company, the sharing of intimate feelings, the continued respect and kindness and mutual goals in life that supersede the heated passion in the long run.

Two of my serious girl friends died quite young -- both of cancer. Three went on to have families and to my knowledge never divorced. With the others I completely lost contact.

Graduate School and Life as a Research Fellow (1947-1952)

Having gotten out of the service early, I arrived on the scene two weeks before my class started. The previous graduating class (of 1947) was still there, finishing up their projects. I met one of them who was particularly helpful, Dr. Allen C. Brader, of Allentown, Pennsylvania.

Brader was working with the field of tomography, which was the forerunner of the CAT scan, and trying to prove its scientific accuracy. He was using a brand of machine called the Laminagraph which was made by the Kelley-Koett Company. This is a tool that permits a body section X-ray or a layer or slice (or lamina) through a structure to the exclusion of parts that lie in front or in back of the section. A picture or film could be produced with such X-ray technique at a prescribed depth and a prescribed thickness. This method particularly lent itself to the structure of the jaw joint which is surrounded by the heavy bone within and around the ear. This joint later became quite well known as the TMJ (temporomandibular joint).

Brader pointed out to me that if a head-holding device could be constructed to fit the laminagraph bed table, which was a medical unit, proper cuts could be calculated. This area would be a remarkable opportunity for research.

The jaw joint (in front of the ear) is the area where growth adjustment is made and i contributes to the size and form of the face. There was a question of whether or not it could be influenced by treatment with braces, and whether indeed the growth of the face could be altered by treatment.

It was, therefore, in this area that I decided to set my spade and start digging. Also, at the same time and with this method, Dr. Milton Engel was attempting to determine the effect of juvenile arthritis on the growth of the jaw, which destroys the cartilage and stops the growth of the lower jaw. When a layman sees a person with a remarkably small lower jaw he can assume it is probably due to a disease of this joint.

Within a period of two weeks I had made measurements on skulls, constructed head-holding device from materials purchased at a hardware store, and had worked out technique for obtaining routinely superb sections through the jaw at the desired level. It wa also necessary to develop the proper exposure factors and determine the correct movement of the machine for the best results. By the time the other members of my class arrived I ha initiated a protocol for research, worked out the techniques for the study, and had already started collecting data.

"Pru"

Also prior to the starting of our course, I met a classmate named Dr. Samuel Pruzansk (whom we called "Pru"), who was later to have a significant effect on my life. When I firs saw him he was sitting at the large library table with his head lowered into a book as h peered through heavy glasses. My first impression was that he was one of the book-worm and perhaps only a library researcher. I went over and shook his hand, and after passin some pleasantries, and good wishes, he returned again to his reading, and I was on my wa about my own business. Pru had a previously obtained master's degree in bacteriology fc which he had studied the oral environment underneath artificial dentures. He had graduate from the University of Maryland, which was one of the first dental schools in the Unite States, and allegedly was the place where anesthesia was developed.

The Class

Orthodontics became the first specialty in dentistry. In fact, it was debated at one time whether or not orthodontics should be a part of dentistry or part of medicine, because many of the people practicing the art were physicians with a high degree of mechanical aptitude. The first orthodontic society was formed with no more than half a dozen men, in about 1904. The early orthodontic graduate schools and specialized training programs were short. They came to be two to three years in duration. That, of course, is after already completing four years of dental school. Thus, our class assembled, consisting of ten people. It was made up of Dr. Douglas Walter, Dr. Guy Wood, Dr. Aaron Schafer, Dr. Elbert King, Dr. Robert Kincaid, Dr. Stanley Rogge, Dr. Samuel Pruzansky, Dr. Robert McGonagle, Dr. Edmund Wong, and myself.

There was a great amount of tradition at that school, and also quite a strict discipline. The course was patterned after the old Edward H. Angle School of Orthodontia in Pasadena, California, which was a private teaching institution. Angle had been a pioneer in the field, developing much of the materials and technique of the specialty. He also created the principal classification of "malocclusion" or bad bite, which still stands 100 years later. Angle had started in Minnesota, gone to Northwestern, to Pennsylvania and to St. Louis, and ended his career in Pasadena. Actually, a group of his graduates combined in funding the school so that no curriculum fee was charged to the students, and none of the patients paid for the treatment! The students were obliged only to furnish their supplies and the materials required for the treatment of their patients.

Thus, Angle commanded a tremendous amount of respect and loyalty from his students. Perhaps a letter written to Dr. Brodie when he applied to the school would be representative of the sternness of "the old man", Angle. (See copy of letter of December 2, 1925 at end of chapter.) He could be very particular about who he accepted as a student, and wanted to be sure that his time would not be wasted with slow or inferior learners.

It was the students who took care of the Angle School clinic. They were requested to scrub the floors, wash the windows, polish the desks, and even to dust the picture frames. Each Friday afternoon was clean-up time. Dr. Brodie had been trained there, and at the invitation of Dr. Noyes, who was the Dean of the University of Illinois Dental School and who had taught with Dr. Angle, Dr. Brodie was chosen to carry on Angle's teachings.

After having explained the discipline that he had received under Angle to one of his early classes, Dr. Brodie was requested by the students that they please be treated in the same manner so that they would have the opportunity for maximum growth and maximum benefit from the teaching. There was almost a military discipline at the school, as will be seen in some of the experiences to be described.

Our class first came together in the rather luxurious Library on the 14th floor of the Tower at 808 South Wood Street in Chicago. The 13th floor was the clinic and the 12th floor was the floor for pediatric dentistry. In the Library there was one rather large seminar table adequate to accommodate about 18 people. Books, journals and past Master's theses were kept on the shelves. On the opposite side of the bookshelves were the windows facing downtown Chicago. At the back of the Library on the right side was a darkroom with mounted tracing tables holding X-ray view boxes for tracing of the X-rays of the head and making measurements. At the other side of the Library was an entrance into the museum, which contained a replica of Dr. Angle's workshop in Pasadena, with many of his tools and equipment he had used in designing so many of the appliances that still were in current use. This workshop is currently in the Smithsonian Institute in Washington, D.C.

As we assembled in the library Dr. Brodie entered, accompanied by the staff that we were to have for the next two years. He was dressed in a traditional white lab coat as were most of the other professors. He laid out the program that was planned for us. He gave the ground rules for our conduct and behavior in the laboratory, the library and the clinic, and what would be expected of us. He talked about the Angle tradition and introduced each one of the professors and described his role. He then reviewed the discipline that would be expected and required.

He said that based on the past history, one of us would not make it through the course. He said that one would either drop out on his own or be asked to leave, and that they didn't require an excuse, it might be simply because they did not like the way we tied our tie. There would therefore be no questions asked if we were asked to leave, and discontinue our graduate education.

At that moment, all the students began to look around the table at each other. I was sitting at a back corner of the table. I was wearing a bright yellow sport coat with a loud tie, and brown trousers, which were not quite in keeping with the classic Ivy League dress. We were reminded that each of us should be prepared to recite the subject matter of each assignment.

The important role of anatomy was discussed. Each morning we were to be assigned one bone of the head and a student would be selected at random to go to the board, draw and describe the bone in three planes of space, after which it was to be discussed with reference to the role of skull architecture by Dr. Brodie. In this way we would build up the complete head. After the descriptions and discussions, we would then be requested to go to the laboratory bench and sit down with wax, a burner, and a wax spatula, and create the bone in wax down to the smallest details.

The mechanical techniques were to include the bending of wire, the exercises on detail of filing metal, soldering techniques, and general exercises in the skillful use of the hands. With that introduction, he wished us all well and told us that he was looking forward to a very successful class. He then gave us our first seminar assignment, which was to be the detailed discussion of the anatomy and function of a basic cell, to be followed by a discussion of the various tissues of the body. He and the staff departed, leaving the class together in the Library.

None of us knew anyone very well and, of course, we were all anxious to see what each other's reactions would be to our first meeting. I seized the opportunity to take the initiative and so I asked, "Okay, which one of you people is not going to be here at the end of the year?" Everybody laughed, of course, and there was further small talk. And then I suggested to the class that when Dr. Brodie entered the room we all stand in respect for this great teacher, as well as in respect for our profession. This man was going to be our leader for the next year, and I said I personally was going to stand when he entered the room. I thought that I had to do something to counter the fact that everyone had been looking at me and sensed a jovial spirit or probable playboy who would not take the work seriously. And I wanted further to explain the fact that I had waited for so long to get here that I was not going to let the class down.

Everything that Dr. Brodie had promised came true, and more. When I started in the course after having had some of Mom's home cooking, I weighed 196 pounds. But there was not much time now to sit around eating, nor was there money for big dinners. When I went home for Christmas, four months later, I weighed 165. I had lost 31 pounds without trying. I also had symptoms which I thought might be ulcers, but all I needed was some relaxation, and the symptoms disappeared rapidly when I took a week's rest.

In addition to carrying the load of the material presented to the class, I was gradually accumulating data by taking tomograph X-rays of all kinds of conditions requested by professional people at the school. It had become known that I had a particular X-ray tool and also the technique to procure such visibility of detail in the film of the temporomandibular joint (TMJ).

Each evening was spent with my friend Dr. Brader, who was in the class ahead of us, which afforded the chance almost to be privately tutored by him. I asked him any questions that came to mind. He owned one of those old Studebakers that looked as if it could go in either direction because the hood was very similar to the trunk of the car. Many times we went to the Ricketts restaurant there on Chicago Avenue, which was quite near the old water tower. Allegedly this was where the cow had kicked the lantern over and started the great Chicago fire. I enjoyed talking with Brader so much because we were both young, and both tremendously excited about orthodontics, which was really our life. It was a most exciting and in-depth experience and it was stimulating to share it with a wonderful friend.

Dr. Brodie had the most exceptional proclivity to instill in his students a sense of the importance of orthodontics to their lives and to our whole culture in general. He expressed a love and respect for the profession that I had never experienced before. There was total immersion and total concentration in the job at hand; even when a couple of us would go out on occasional dates, the ladies would complain that they didn't get any attention, and that all that we could talk about was orthodontics.

Probably the best stimulus for us to learn came from the example of Brodie himself. At that time he was president of the Federation Dentaire International. He was chairman of International Dental Research organization, he was Dean of the School, he was Head of the Department, he supervised all the research, and two half-days a week he conducted a private practice. In addition he was a co-founder and manager of the Midwestern Dental Medicine meeting each year. Finally, he frequently made addresses to different societies and national meetings.

In 1948 he called together a reunion of his past students at that time, who numbered over 100. His seminars were inspirational, as he would bring many of the aspects of biology, archaeology and even geology into discussion with the students. He was a master of the anecdote, and in a weak moment liked a drink of Scotch. He would begin his lectures by coming in and thumping a Pall Mall cigarette on the table, light up, and start the discussions. Behind his back we called him "The Chief" but to his face it was always Dr. Brodie. To his close friends he was known as "Steve", apparently a name that he acquired somewhere because of the famous Steve Brodie who tried to go over Niagara Falls in a barrel. It was understandable why we would stand in respect and gratitude when he entered the room in response to the effort he was making on our behalf.

Controversy

Having sort of a head start, and having a tool with which I could expand the inquiry into the growth of the face, within six months some of my findings were beginning to emerge with regard to the human jaw joint. In the brashness of my youth and with the intensity of the situation, I presented some of these ideas to Dr. Brodie, perhaps on a premature basis. Many of these observations were indeed contrary to his teaching. I therefore found a stronger wall of resistance than I imagined or anticipated. I was instructed to go back and accumulate control samples of individuals, and enlarge my data base. I could immediately sense that I was not going to finish my program with the rest of my class. So I began to gird myself for staying on somewhat longer and getting into research much more deeply. During the next year, after diagnosing patients with a breakdown in the jaw joint, I began to treat them on an experimental basis.

I had taken beginning joint X-rays on all the patients in our class and all the patients in the subsequent class. I then attempted to diagnose the jaw joint conditions and the joint behavior of each one of our patients during the course of treatment. This turned out to be an absolutely monumental task. I remember some nights actually sleeping on the lab bench in the laboratory with a thick anatomy book as my pillow.

More Controversy

It seemed as though in everything I investigated I found discoveries that were at odds with much of the prevailing thought. There was some natural conflict that developed between myself and the staff and even some of my fellow-students. I had the choice of bending my observations in keeping with the conventional thought or standing behind my findings and championing the cause of truth as I saw it to be. As a young scientist I was not prepared to handle the stern opposition to so many of my findings. Should I react with expediency and concentrate on those findings which I was sure would pass -- or should I stand on the principle of truth?

In fact, I was so bothered by the situation that I prepared a small paper entitled, "Is There a Place For Politics in Science?", which was a sort of editorial that I never published because I didn't think I had sufficient stature. But nevertheless, I was awakened to the fact that there was an element of truth in the question. It didn't bother me that people would object to findings on a scientific basis, but when my integrity was questioned, or when my morals were questioned, or my detail of measurement was questioned which involved my very character, I understandably had a tendency to react.

Thus I was considered to be controversial -- a term applied to a person disputed or opposed or unapproved in a profession.

Cleft Palate Work

In 1948 a Federally funded cleft palate team was initiated at the University of Illinois. The idea was to bring many disciplines together and establish a coordinated approach to the treatment and management of the cleft palate child. Formerly, most of the attention had been given to plastic surgery. Certain heroic surgical procedures made in babies inhibited the growth in the mid-face. The condition in time was much worsened rather than helped. The research team was composed of surgeons, ear-nose-and-throat specialists, speech pathologists, psychologists, orthodontists, and myself and Dr. Samuel Pruzansky as growth investigators.

Following that experience in 1948, Dr. Pruzansky became devoted to cleft palate investigation and became if not the leading authority at least one of them in the development of the cleft palate condition. He stayed on and chaired a newly formed congenital deformity department for the rest of his life, and was a most unique investigator.

With the initiation of that group, Dr. Brodie asked me to be the orthodontist for the crippled children service for the state of Illinois. With the laminagraphic X-ray, I could therefore investigate different sections of the head through the upper jaw in all three dimensions. My research took on even greater significance as I became involved in the study of the basic vegetative function of breathing, speech and swallowing.

Team-mates of a Different Sort

Aside from the three members of our class who were accompanied by their wives, the rest of us lived in the local YMCA. Immediately in front of the hospital was a place called The

Greek Restaurant, where on rare occasions we would stop and have a sandwich. One evening, during the winter, I was sitting with a friend talking when I was pounded on one of my shoulders. I looked up and saw three smiling faces of people I thought were giants. I now weighed only about 165. Suddenly two of them lifted me by my arms out of the chair, took me up to the bar and sat me down. They were three athletes who I had played football with at Indiana University and who had recognized me. One was Howard Brown, an all-pro guard with the Detroit Lions, one was Bob Zimney, who was on a championship Chicago Cardinals team, and the other was Ed Bell, a popular tackle with the Green Bay Packers. They had all now grown to the 250-300 pound range, and I of course had gone the other way. I had seen them play on the field, but I hadn't had a chance to talk with them for about eight years, and it was a truly wonderful experience to review old times and find out about their careers and their families and experiences. I never have seen them since then.

Get It Before the Bubble Bursts

In the latter part of 1948 many of my classmates were leaving to get started before there came the "bursting of the bubble". By mid-1948 I could no longer afford to live in the YMCA and so that summer I moved out, into a flat in an area where the buildings had been condemned by the state for expansion of the research and educational facilities. The old flats had been evacuated but during the time before they were to be destroyed they were rented out to students at $30.00 per month. I shared a flat with Aaron, a medical student, which meant that my rent was $15.00 a month, or fifty cents a day. We had no refrigerator, but we did have running water. We didn't have time to cook anyway, so most of our meals were sandwiches and salads. Aaron was doing research with Dr. Ivy who was at that time chairman of Internal Medicine in the Medical School. He was investigating the factors that produced ulcers. As part of his training he was also undergoing psychoanalysis. This therefore afforded me the opportunity to learn the theories and the practices of psychoanalysis and to discuss many things at a deep level, among them the factors that produce a balanced personality and the psychologic development of schizophrenia and other mental disorders.

Some of those things that I learned from this medical student were to serve me later in my career in dealing with disturbed patients with facial pain and temporomandibular joint conditions -- a further illustration of my belief that each person is a product of all of his past experiences and each contact contributes to a future.

The idea of the bursting of the bubble was a part of the post-war fear among many of my generation. The mark of the 1930s was indelibly imprinted in our minds. There was a concern that a relapse in the economy could occur at any time. The impulse was tugging at me to get into the practice side of my profession in order to pay off the borrowing that I had done for my education. In addition, I wanted to put something aside for that ultimate rainy day.

Research Progress and Problems

My research, however, was highly stimulating. Through it I was beginning to meet older colleagues and many of the leaders in my specialty. The University of Illinois, by reputation, had become the crossroads of orthodontics and dentistry on a world basis. At that time a telephone teaching program was initiated which was transmitted all over the country. I had a small hand in its organization and at one time was one of the contributors to the broadcast. Many of the leaders in the dental and medical profession were located in the Chicago area. It was a very fortuitous experience, and so I became resigned to devoting the extra time needed to complete my research and get the most out of the educational encounter that the opportunity afforded.

It was at about this time that I was visited in Chicago by my old dean at Indiana, Dr. William Crawford, who had now taken the post at the University of Minnesota. He was in town on business and invited me to have dinner with him, which I immediately accepted. We dined at the Stockyards Inn, and discussed his experiences in his career with the taking over of a new school. I shared with him many of the findings that I had made.

On our way home, in the taxi, Dean Crawford said, "Well, Rick, what do you think of academia and research, now that you are in it?" I said, "Well," I replied, "it's very exciting and extremely stimulating. Economically, of course, it's a disaster. But the thing that bothers me most is that I work hard to formulate a proper kind of study, go through the steps necessary to satisfy a scientific method, but then as I present my findings I am put down and ridiculed." With that he reared his head back laughing and said, "Well, that's something you're going to have to get used to. You shouldn't let it bother you at all. Any person who does original work and makes original findings is going to be suppressed and derided. You can expect it. But if you are correct, in the end people will ultimately know it. And the truth should be your only underlying motive."

"Well, that makes me feel a lot better," I said. "I don't like to run away from a fight, particularly when I'm convinced that I'm right." He had explained to me that Pruzansky and I, out in the educational field, were coming to be called "the Gold Dust Twins" and indeed, we were making a golden effort. Dr. Pruzansky had been working in the field of electromyography, which is the study of muscle function. I was studying the movements of the jaws with the aid of the section X-rays, and we studied patients together. Pru and I agreed that one day we would write articles together, but the combined opportunities for writing never came. It seemed that we were still always studying.

Marshfield Manor

In the Fall of 1948, when I had already run out of money and was borrowing from my parents and banks to stay in school, the opportunity arose to rent another flat. It was one of the condemned flats on Marshfield Avenue, not too far from a local elevated train stop there in the hospital area. Dr. Elbert ("Eb") King stayed on to complete his research in the growth of the throat area. As a result, Dr. Pruzansky, Dr. King and myself decided to fix up one of the old flats. I went to Kokomo and borrowed my dad's old International pickup truck. Pru and Eb and I drove down to Geneseo, Illinois to an auction of some sound but terribly old furniture and household goods. I think we entirely filled the truck for something around $25.00. At that time I was dating Patricia, who was later to become my first wife. She had been a decorator with Barker Brothers in Los Angeles, and offered to help us with our color schemes and the selection of some of our wallpaper. I seemed to be the only one who had ever laid linoleum or papered walls, or done any plumbing. So the three of us together scrubbed and painted and decorated, and from it we had a living room, a family room, a kitchen, and each of us had our own bedroom.

Probably the most memorable aspect of our relationship was our snacks at 3:00 A.M. We would work until 2:00 or 2:30 and then usually sit down and have a salad or some other food before retiring at about 3:30. This gave rise to the opportunity for a discussion of the day's activities and findings, but it also served as an opportunity to get to know each other very well, and learn of each other's background.

I was a Republican and an Eisenhower-Taft supporter. But I was progressive and was not against change. Pruzansky was the son of a pawn-shop owner, born and raised in New York City, and was Jewish and a staunch Democrat. He had gone to a Jewish school, had gone through the bar mitzvah and was indeed very, very proud to be a Jew and appreciated his heritage. He was a very intense student, a marvelous writer, and stood up for his principles to the point of emotion. I had come from a large mid-western family. Eb was an only child whose parents had divorced before he was an adolescent. We therefore had very contrasting backgrounds, and consequently some differences in our feelings, sentiments and responses.

But just as we worked hard, we played hard. "Marshfield Manor", as we called it, became known to the entire medical complex. It became a hang-out for the orthodontic students, and when we had the occasional party, it would be almost impossible to walk through the flat. Pruzansky was the only person I ever heard of who could make a concoction of plums jelled in pure wine. He turned out to be a master gourmet cook. We took turns in preparing meals, with mine usually some different variety of beans, which became a standard joke.

In 1952 during the national election campaign in which Dwight D. Eisenhower ran against Adlai Stevenson, from Illinois, the three of us had many intense debates regarding the differences between the Republican Party and the Democratic Party. There was also an issue of labor unions at the time, for which the Taft-Hartley Bill had been proposed to put something of a brake upon the power of the unions. We had many opportunities to argue about the most appropriate welfare of the country.

After the experience in World War II, Eisenhower campaigned to get things stabilized. He seemed to display a remarkable leadership even though he was not the greatest orator. Adlai Stevenson was an intellectual and had many excellent ideas with regard to the role of government, and would have been an excellent president. The people, however, seemed to have more confidence in Eisenhower. The start of the Eisenhower Years, after he settled the issue in Korea, gave rise to the greatest stability, without a war, that I had seen in my lifetime. These were truly golden years, with Nixon as Vice-President, lasting for two elected consecutive terms.

The Colossal Chagrin

After two years of working with my research material, I felt it was about time to start finalizing some of the findings and at least completing my master's degree. So from the welter of material that I had accumulated I decided to write the thesis on the anatomic variation of the structures of the jaw joint. The actual title was "The Anatomic and Physiologic Variation of the Temporomandibular Joint as Revealed by Cephalometric Laminagraphy". That was a mouthful for most people but very simply, it was the use of the body section X-ray on normal subjects as a control to be compared to the same method of study in patients with malocclusions of the teeth and problems in the structure of the jaws.

I followed a normal protocol, and tried working up the material. I had written and re-written several times to arrive at the best that I could do with the subject. I finally concluded that it was in a state that I could show it to Dr. Brodie to get his criticism.

It was customary for Dr. Brodie to take such papers home with him on week ends, and go over them at his leisure, usually on Sunday. He lived in Park Ridge, north of Chicago and commuted by train, sometimes poring over the students' writing in the train to and from Chicago. Another unique quality of Dr. Brodie that we all recognized and appreciated was that he never put his name on research papers that were done by his students. He would advise them, and in effect rewrite many of the papers that were published in the students' names. But he always felt that it was a form of identity for the students, a mark of their achievement and a factor in their growth, and a propulsion for their career. He never asked the student to share it with him. Such is not the case with the heads of many graduate schools. Many professors, in order to sustain research grants, to fulfill their own objective to the institution and their research careers, will end up putting their names first on papers with the student or the person who actually did the work somewhere down the line in a series of contributors.

Therefore, it was routine after handing in a paper to Dr. Brodie that within one week he would come back and have a private conference with the student. He would go over the paper, making suggestions as to the research or to the construction of the manuscript. When the conference was to be held there would be a sign posted outside the Library: "Conference at such-and-such hour" which was a signal for everyone else to vacate the Library at that particular time, and it would be a one-on-one proposition with Dr. Brodie and the student.

And so I finally handed in my work, leaving it with Miss Bess Faust who was Dr. Brodie's secretary in the department. After a week had gone by I inquired as to the situation with my paper, and she said Dr. Brodie was still working on it. The second week she informed me that Dr. Brodie wanted to see me at 2:00 on Wednesday afternoon, presumably for my paper, and I was quite excited. At 2:00 I sat alone in the Library awaiting this important moment. Finally, at 2:20 the door opened and Dr. Brodie came in with a frown on his face. Of course I stood up, but he didn't sit down. We both remained standing. He laid my paper down on the Library table, and stood looking at it. He said, "This is perhaps the worst piece of writing I have ever been asked to struggle with." He said, "I spent two week ends on it, and only got halfway through it. There it is, you can do with it as you please." And without another word, without a smile, he turned and walked out of the Library, leaving me standing alone with my disillusionment.

To say that I was disappointed, that my pride was destroyed, and that I was mortified, dismayed and ashamed would be to put it lightly. I sat down, wounded. I had seen others, including my own classmates, who had attempted to get theses accepted, and ended up quitting and simply leaving the school to do routine clinical orthodontics. If I had turned in something that had not had my best effort I might have had an excuse, but this was the best of my capability. I had long since recognized my difficulty in writing and in mastering academic English. I had been through dental school, but realizing the weakness of my vocabulary while in the service I had posted at my dental chair ten new words each day in order to enhance my knowledge. Two years of graduate work were now behind me. And yet here I was, stunned by failure.

I began to recall that my father had not encouraged our reading to any degree. Mother and Father had read good books to us as children, but in my later years he frowned on us sitting around reading. He saw it as a mark of a lazy person. He believed that in order to make a place in life you should get out and work. While I had all the love and all the attention that any child could want, I could see that my lack of scholarship in English had come back to really haunt me at this time.

I also understood the attitude of Dr. Brodie. I sensed that it was possible he saw in me something other than the typical student and was challenging me. What was I to do? Was I to give up and simply leave and start a practice? Or was I to continue and learn to express myself in a manner that would be consistent with the amount of effort already expended for the production of the research?

Brodie's attitude followed the tradition of Angle. It was never to congratulate a student for accomplishing anything that he was supposed to do correctly in the first place. To compliment would breed complacency and stunt the further growth of that student. I realized all this as well.

After sitting there alone in the library with my thoughts for a few minutes, I became angered and somewhat vengeful. I was going to show him. I suddenly vowed that I was going to be a better writer than Brodie himself. I remembered that there was a night school down on Michigan Boulevard called Roosevelt College. I decided to start from the beginning and go through the basics again. I enrolled that evening in two courses in English composition, 101 and 101a.

In the next three months I rewrote the material again and again, maybe twenty times, and finally re-submitted it. The second time, as I sat in the Library after one week's holding of my paper, Dr. Brodie appeared in the room, on time, with a smile on his face, and said, "Now you're talking. I didn't change a word."

English First

In college I had always resented having to look up a word in the dictionary. I seemed always pressed for time. So I ended up skipping over big words. Now, however, I kept a dictionary and Roget's Thesaurus in my briefcase. Much later I found, in some reading, that the one underlying consistent characteristic of successful people was the possession of a good vocabulary. As Harakawa said in the introduction to his book on semantics, "Language is a tool of thought. The greater the capacity for words, the more the thinking power."

The paper that I wrote was submitted in an essay contest for the American Association of Orthodontics and won second prize. It was beaten by a work on muscle analysis by Dr. Robert Moyer who was later research director for the Growth Center at the University of Michigan in Ann Arbor.

Further Searching

By the third year of my graduate studies I had accumulated many jaw joint X-rays of patients who had developed arthritis and degeneration. (If the suffix "itis" is added to a word, it means inflammation of.) There were two types; the most serious was called rheumatoid, and it appears to be a disease in which the body's ability to differentiate its own tissue is altered. The jaw joint has a propensity for this disease, particularly as it occurs in the juvenile age, when it stops the growth of the lower jaw completely.

The second type is called osteo-arthritis, meaning that the bone is involved. It is also called hypertrophic arthritis because the joint starts to flatten out and form overhangs, or lips of bone. It is further called degenerative joint disease, and even sometimes avascular necrosis, or aseptic necrosis. All types are destructive.

I became interested in the causes of these conditions, whether they were due to some peculiar fit of the teeth with over-loading in the joint or whether they were due to the inability of the body and the joint to withstand the normal stresses of function. There was also the possibility that they were due to overloading due to psychic stress resulting in clenching and grinding of the teeth for relief of anxieties. Actually all three factors were revealed to be involved, but in order to study the patients, I needed knowledge in biochemistry and particularly endocrinology and the study of the hormones, because it was a female's disease more than a male's.

On consulting with some of my medical colleagues, I was referred to the work of Dr. Hans Selye on stress. Selye had started out in his research to study female hormones. He found that his preparations were not pure and that they stressed his animals. As a consequence, he ended up describing the biology of distress. He found physical, chemical, thermal or psychological stress all produced identical results.

To my thinking, Selye's work opened new vistas in clinical practice for both medicine and dentistry. I studied his work with great interest. Little did I realize then, in 1948, that we would become friends and that 28 years later (in 1976) I would interview him on television in New York City for the Foundation for Orthodontic Research.

Getting back to reality, a further joy in 1950 was that the bubble had not yet burst and I could safely pursue my research, and hope that good times would continue long enough for me to become solvent.

* * *

DR. EDWARD H. ANGLE
1035 NORTH MADISON AVENUE
PASADENA, CALIFORNIA

December 2, 1925
Dr. Allan G. Brodie
434 Roseville Avenue
Newark, N.J.

My dear Dr. Brodie,-

Your favor of November 25 has been carefully considered. Dr. Dunlap has written me favorably concerning you, and in reply to your letter I would say that I shall be glad to receive you as a member of the next class, provided you are properly qualified. I wish, however, to make plain and emphatic the fact that you will be expected to know the anatomy, embryology and histology of the head and neck (exclusive of the brain) far, far better than the average dental student knows these subjects on graduation. There will be no exceptions made and no 'just slipping in', but you must KNOW these subjects because of their essentiality and daily practical application in the study and practice of orthodontia.

Also, we shall expect you to have your mind reasonably well stored as the result of the broad reading of good literature, for only men of this type seem to have minds sufficiently disciplined to be able to grasp and correlate facts in the diagnosis and treatment of cases of malocclusion, and to take in the world the place that a real scientist should take.

We shall also expect you to be reasonably dextrous and skilful with your fingers, for the clumsy fingered man is so seriously handicapped we feel it wrong to encourage him.

In fact - and you will readily understand the reason - I do not want to take on the burden and responsibility of the long hours of necessary personal effort with each student unless he is of promising timber.

All of the above I wish to emphasize on general principles and especially as the next class is probably the last in which I shall take the strong personal, individual interest that I have always heretofore done.

If you come the middle of this month you will have six weeks in which to demonstrate your fitness to enter the school. But I would certainly recommend you to devote every spare moment from now on to preparation, by no means omitting the seventh edition of my book and the articles I have since written that have appeared in the DENTAL COSMOS, and Black's Dental Anatomy. We expect you to be very familiar with all these subjects.

Trusting to see you soon, and promising you, if you are prepared, every opportunity and every assistance to study orthodontia in the most thorough and practical manner, I am,

Very truly yours,
(signed) EDWARD H. ANGLE

8

BUSINESS AND THE PROFESSIONAL WORLD
(1951-1960)

After my formal residency was completed in 1948, I still worked as a research fellow for long hours, seven days a week. I had borrowed to my limits. Therefore, in 1950 I asked Dr. Brodie, the Dean, for permission to take one or two private patients in the isolated cleft palate clinic we had established. His answer was, "It's absolutely against the rules of the University. However, in your case it's a little different. You'll be unnoticed. What's more, I will send you a patient needing special attention. But, if anyone asks, I'll tell them I told you you couldn't do it."

It was June, 1950, and I was 30 years old. The patient was a 20-year-old very overweight Italian lady with a much oversized lower jaw that required surgery for its reduction. She had already lost four permanent teeth, two of which were upper molars on one side. In addition, she had sixteen cavities needing attention. Hence, my first private patient's dental needs, the records of which I still maintain for teaching purposes, were remarkably complicated. I contracted with her father, an insurance agent, for a total fee of $500 for her complete care -- one-third of my yearly salary as a research fellow.

This patient was to become a hallmark in the science and the art of surgical planning. I took special head X-rays, made detailed three-dimensional tracings of the skull, together with X-ray sections (tomographs) through her jaw joints. I planned the tooth movements and surgical sections on paper. The plan was presented to her and her parents, and also to the surgeon. This procedure was the first of its kind and later was labeled a Surgical Treatment Objective (STO). Ultimately it became a standard procedure for plastic and maxillo-facial surgeons and orthodontists. Thus, I began my private career with this kind of challenge.

Early Recognition of Nutrition

My first thought in this patient's case concerned her life-style and nutritional habits. She was a secretary to Dr. Morris Fishbein, editor of the Journal of the American Medical Association, in Chicago. The physicians there had obviously ignored her dental condition and her total health welfare. Carts with snacks circulated the corridors of the building where she worked at break times mid-morning and mid-afternoon. She had acquired the habit of munching pies, cakes and cokes (heavily loaded with fats and sugar). This contributed to the overweight condition and the advanced decay of her teeth.

Major changes in her living pattern were indicated in order to achieve the most successful orthodontic-surgical results. Her upper left wisdom tooth required movement of over half an inch. I formulated a diet chart with which she was to comply before I would start the major corrections. All cavities were filled and good oral hygiene had to be demonstrated. The presurgical work took about six months. I fixated her teeth and jaws to satisfy our objectives while she was under anesthetia. Her total treatment lasted about twelve months. At each visit I tried to build up her self image, self-esteem and personal confidence.

The result was stunning. She turned out almost exactly as planned. She lost more than 30 pounds. It was only a matter of months until she fell in love and married a drummer in one of the leading dance bands in Chicago. Her father was so pleased he gave me a bonus which was the down payment on a $5000.00 insurance policy. I would call it a happy success. It bolstered my confidence as a clinician.

With that experience, as well as others early in my career, I became convinced that if I needed to change the life styles of patients it would be easier if I avoided consultations with physicians. Medical practices, it appeared, were disciplined to be focused on healing of disease after it occurred rather than on prevention.

Patients even in the 1950s were becoming skeptical of quick fixes with surgery, drugs, or simply advice to change their environment when stress was encountered. In 1950, as well as 1990, for all the brilliant achievements, many Americans felt that many allopathic medicine practitioners had lost touch with the individual person. Fortunately, that is beginning to change.

Naturalism

Looking back on my professional development during those early years it was obvious another realization was being recognized. I found myself moving toward a more "naturalistic" or "holistic" approach to clinical regimes. However, I came later to reject the word "holistic" because so many undisciplined people had adopted the label. The concept of holism proposes that the individual components (or parts or organs of the body) do not contribute as much separately as when they are combined in the whole and function together. This is proven when the right and left brains are sectioned at the midbrain corpus collosum which is the connection.

Nature often needs to be given a chance, as seen in the body's ability to adjust and compensate through its own processes for the re-creation of a lost balance or equilibrium. This reaction to produce a health balance is called "homeostasis". Such balances have occurred in nature on a major scale. Sometimes equilibrium is reestablished with only a placebo or the patient's faith in a drug or confidence in the doctor alone.

Life Changes

Seriousness about the real world developed when I first married, in 1950, and increased when children came along. My first wife, Patricia, was a California girl who was a flight attendant with American Airlines. She was soon pregnant, and we needed larger quarters. The University authorities rented some condemned flats to students and I located one on the second story of a building on Marshfield Avenue, only four blocks from the Cook County Hospital complex. When the rooms had been fumigated I swept up a gallon coffee can heaped with cockroaches. The people living there before had made wine in the basement, leaving grape hulls piled knee deep in one corner.

After much scrubbing, we separated the old kitchen and bedroom and plumbed in a separate bath to make a second small apartment which we then rented out. The old dining room was converted into a family room with the dining table used as a study desk. After painting, plastering and plumbing, papering walls and laying linoleum, it became acceptable. We heated during the winter with oil stoves, storing the oil in the basement for both our apartment and the one I rented to a student, Dr. Alex Jacobson, who was from South Africa and later became head of the Orthodontic Department at the University of Alabama. By the time I had paid for the materials for the renovations made, it was an even deal. Many years later I sold my Pacific Palisades practice to Alex's son, Rick Jacobson, who was born when they returned to South Africa.

The American Prerogative -- To Move

When water slowly drips on granite, eventually it can make a hole. With a wife persistently bringing up the prospects of a better life in California, and with the constant reminder of the opportunities there, it was difficult to resist. Before we were married I had flown to California as her guest and met her family in Brentwood, staying with her relatives in Pacific Palisades in 1949. I liked everyone I met and was therefore in no position to argue about the advantages in California. This was particularly true when compared to bitter experiences in Chicago.

One summer evening in 1949 I borrowed Pru's car to pick up Pat at the "El" station near our flat. She was coming over for dinner from South Chicago. An armed guard was stationed at the stop to escort nurses to the Presbyterian Hospital dorm just 3 blocks away. I had checked inside and saw the guard in uniform, and went out to wait in the car curbside. The window was rolled down on the driver's side, and I suddenly looked up to see a black man with a handgun. He stuck it right at my forehead. I should have been frightened, but I honestly was more enraged. I started to get out of the car but he instructed me to get back in and asked me for my money.

I quickly gathered my thoughts and began to talk. I explained it wasn't my car and that I was just a student, that I had no money, and that he would only get in trouble if he thought otherwise. I told him to look elsewhere. A car suddenly turned onto the street with its lights falling on him, and for some reason he put his gun under his coat and walked slowly toward the station. I immediately got out went around to the other side of the car. I wanted to get my hands on him, and in my frame of mind I honestly think I could have killed him. Foolishly, I then acted as if I had a gun in my pocket and asked him to throw his gun down, whereupon he ran into the shadows under the elevated train tracks. I ran into the station and asked the guard to go get this "stick-up" man. He said he couldn't leave his post, so I asked him to lend me his gun and I'd go get the S.O.B. myself. I was still mad and shaking. He told me to cool off, saying that man might not be alone and I had better slow down!

When I got back to the house I called the police to report the incident exactly as it happened and give them a description of the man. They told me how stupid my reaction had been, and related a similar occasion only one week before when a victim had been shot and killed. I was lucky. I concluded that the man who attempted to mug me was on drugs because his expression was not normal.

On another occasion in 1951, while walking little Robin, our first daughter, in a baby carriage on the sidewalk in front of our flat, Patty was propositioned by a stranger. She was quite frightened and terminated her walks with the baby.

Consequently, in 1951, I made application to take the California Dental Board Examination. I went to California early and spent six weeks reviewing the dental procedures taught at the

University of Southern California. I practiced on relatives or friends in a colleague's office. The techniques in general dentistry had changed somewhat in the five-year hiatus since I had practiced in the Navy but I passed successfully and had no reason not to start planning a future in California.

Robin Renee Ricketts (now Machette, of Piedmont, California) had come along in late 1950. By moving time to California, in May of 1952, Gale Ann Ricketts was on her way and came in August.

Frustrations in California

Despite all the promise of California, it was still difficult for me to leave my roots in the midwest and face many uncertainties. I had always heard that a person should start a practice in a place he desired to live and that if a superb job was performed success would follow. However, it was not a practice alone that I anticipated. I also wanted to stay in the academic environment and continue my research.

Academic Politics

The dental school at the University of Southern California was then the only one in the area. The orthodontic techniques they taught were different from those I had learned and vastly different from the techniques I was developing. I inquired regarding a teaching position there. Despite being invited by one of the professors in General Dentistry, I was rejected by those in the Orthodontic Department.

Dr. Robert McNulty, the Dean at U.S.C., was trying to run a smooth ship. There was a history of conflict in 1928 between Dr. Spencer Atkinson, who was the department head there, and Dr. Angle when he had taught in Pasadena. Because my mentor was Angle-trained and I was his follower, it was assumed I would represent the "Angle tradition". Consequently I was unwelcome. Thus, another realization stuck me: The professors in many institutions have little territories that they defend, sometimes bitterly. Struggles for identity can be vicious. Since Southern California could not be considered for teaching and research, I looked to Northern California.

University of California at San Francisco

Dr. Wendell Wylie was Chairman of the Department of Orthodontics at the University of California medical complex in San Francisco. He had also been a favorite student of Dr. Brodie. I had met Wylie at the reunion meetings, and also at other meetings. I was impressed by his research and his keen mind. So I asked him if there was a spot available for teaching in his school in San Francisco, and was immediately accepted.

I became very excited and went to the "Bay Area" to look for a place to live and practice. I decided on San Jose, for a number of reasons. It was projected to be a hub of future business activity and together with the "Silicone Valley" it has fulfilled that prophecy. In addition, it was next to the prosperous Santa Clara Valley, and I still had a little farming instinct in me. I made arrangements to set up a small office and was ready to start a practice in San Jose. I planned to commute one or two days a week to San Francisco to continue my research and teaching. I went back to Chicago to close out my affairs.

Just before I was to return to California, I received a letter from Dr. Wylie telling me that there was no place for me. He said that his school had no tomograph machine, which was my tool of investigation, and that it probably wouldn't work out to my advantage to be there. I felt crushed, rejected, and put down. I couldn't understand his original enthusiasm, the high excitement about my coming to the University of California, and then suddenly a letter of the "Dear John" kind. Wylie did suggest, however, that I go to Southern California and set up near Westwood because a new dental school was being planned at U.C.L.A. which I might consider.

I didn't learn until almost eight years later that Dr. Wylie's letter was not a rejection but that he had other plans for me. He was being considered for the Deanship of the new school at U.C.L.A. If a staff member was in one of the other branches of the University of California, he could not be transferred to a new school within the system. If I had started at San Francisco, I would not have been able to go with him to U.C.L.A. He had in mind, if he was to become the Dean, for me to be Chairman of the Orthodontic Department. He confided these facts to me years later, but I certainly wish that he could have brought himself to tell me at the time. It would have saved me much grief.

In the end I took his advice. After considering many areas in Southern California, and wanting to be reasonably proximal to U.C.L.A., I decided to start a practice in Pacific Palisades. Information from the Chamber of Commerce indicated approximately 30,000 people were served by the Palisades Post Office. This included the area from the Riviera Country Club all the way to the ocean. Almost half the population was still of school age, and I reasoned this would be a good place for me to go. Several people advised me against it because Pacific Palisades was really hardly more than a bulge on Sunset Boulevard. In order to travel from the ocean to the bluffs it was necessary for people to "climb the hill". Some of the dentists whom I consulted doubted that many people would make the effort. But Westwood was crowded with orthodontists, Beverly Hills and Santa Monica had many, and this seemed the most prudent spot for me.

My father-in-law, Harry Rickert, was a contractor, and was working on a little building called "Sunset Medical Center" with an address at 15247 Sunset Boulevard. I became the first tenant, and rented a small office of 525 square feet on the second floor.

The Big Move West

After arranging a first and last month's rent for the office, I returned again to Chicago to make plans to move. I bought a pick-up truck for my father-in-law that I would deliver to him personally and also use to haul our belongings from Chicago to Los Angeles. From the dental clinic at the University of Illinois I bought some old, used chairs that were obsolete. I also located an Army field X-ray unit made by the Picker Company that had been used in the war. We had in addition accumulated a refrigerator and the usual household goods.

An ordinary pick-up truck is designed to carry about 1000 pounds, or half a ton. I had overload springs added and bought heavy-duty oversize tires for the trip. I made a rack of oak wood and bolted it to the bed of the truck. With the two dental chairs and their hydraulic lifts, the X-ray machine, together with my book collection, beds, dressers and furniture, I had over two tons on the half-ton pick-up. It was compactly loaded and strapped into an almost solid mass.

When it was learned that I was going to drive to California my sister Esther and a friend asked if they could go along. This made three people in the pick-up's cab. We enthusiastically took leave of Kokomo around the first of June, 1952, to find "old Route #66", a song Nat King Cole made popular. As I remember, some of the words were:

"If you ever plan to travel west, travel my way, take the highway that's the best. Get your kicks on Route 66. It goes from Chicago to L.A. more than 2000 miles away. Get your kicks on Route 66. Now you go through St. Louie,

Joplin, Missouri, Oklahoma City is mighty pretty, you see Amarillo, Gallup, New Mexico. Flagstaff, Arizona, don't forget Winona, Kingman, Barstow, San Bernardino -- etc., etc."

We were just out of St. Louis when it first happened -- that all-too-familiar bump, bump, bump of a flat tire. How could that be? I thought, with brand new tires and a new truck. Stopping beside the highway, I discovered, sure enough, the right rear tire was flat. Having one of the smaller tires as a spare I put it on and proceeded slowly to the next station where I had the tube repaired.

Forty years ago innertubes were used and the wheels had "lock rims" to hold the tire in place. These may still be found on bicycles and farm equipment, but today automobile tires are tubeless and designed to hold compression as they wedge airtight into a solid cast wheel. I didn't know it at first, but with the heavy load the tube was squeezing between the tire and the rim and perforating with little blips all around the tube.

I hadn't gotten on my way much farther when to our dismay the left rear tire went bump, bump, bump -- another tire to change. Slowing down significantly again, I reached another service station, bought tire-patching materials and a hand pump for emergencies along the stretches of highway between cities. It was with about the sixth flat that a station attendant explained to me what was happening. After buying two new tubes, I asked if stronger ones were available, but none were made in a heavier grade. One suggestion was to store a part of the load and return for it later, but that was out of the question. I was really becoming quite efficient in jacking up the loaded truck and repairing and changing rear tires. The surprise was that the little ordinary tire was holding up better than the heavy duty variety.

The weather was fine all across the plains. We finally met rain in the mountains around Flagstaff, Arizona, and early in the morning crossed the border into California. But we were still plagued by more flat tires. With my sweat (resulting from making the tire changes) together with two unbathed females in a small cab for three days, the odors left little for the imagination.

On the final leg of the trip, in California, we had three more flats. By the time we arrived at Los Angeles we were marking down the number of flat tires, and it totalled fourteen. After four days of lifting and juggling tires, my arm muscles had developed noticeably. The whole truck seemed to be getting lighter!

When we finally drove up the hill to Pacific Palisades, we looked like genuine desert rats. We had rented an apartment on Sunset Boulevard across from where now stands a Synagogue. We couldn't wait to take showers and put on fresh clothes. I think I slept about eighteen hours straight. The girls stayed for two weeks and swore they never would come to California again, and they didn't!

After unloading the furniture and equipment, I set about to paint and polish the old chairs and the X-ray unit. I designed some cabinets and dividers for the small office, made a down payment on waiting room furniture and office desks and was ready for business. Forty years later I still use the original desk I purchased then; it now holds a copy machine and supplies.

The Real World of Business

On July 1, 1952 I received my first California patient, a crippled boy who had fallen and knocked out his two upper front teeth. I moved his two upper lateral incisors together in the midline and made crowns for them to substitute for the larger central incisors. I still have the before-and-after models of that little boy in a display cabinet in the Pacific Palisades office.

I was suddenly in private practice in the real world. I had to pay bills, pay rent, pay for the telephone, pay for utilities, buy supplies, pay salaries, balance the books, buy insurance, and pay taxes. I soon reached the realization that I could not practice my art without exercising proper business practices, which I had yet to learn.

Earlier, in Chicago, I had met Dr. Cecil Steiner of Beverly Hills. He had been taught by Dr. E. H. Angle in the old Angle School in Pasadena where he himself later taught. Steiner was perhaps the leading orthodontist in Southern California, among many good ones. The Southern California societies further extended all the way into Arizona, and included another noted orthodontist, Dr. Charles Tweed from Tucson, as well as a celebrated Pasadena orthodontist by the name of Dr. Hayes Nance. These, together with many others, were at the time among the most important leaders in the specialty of orthodontics in the whole country.

Dr. Steiner gave me very good advice. In fact, he felt that I was so promising that he offered to hire me in his office as an associate. I accepted enthusiastically, and we arranged for work to start. When I saw his techniques on his patients, I found that many of his procedures were those that I had previously discarded as now being obsolete. He saw me frown when I observed some procedures being used on his patients. At the end of the first day we met in his private room to discuss the situation. He quickly volunteered, "Rick, it isn't going to work, is it?" I said, "No, Cecil, I'm afraid not. Rather than having a conflict with you, I think we had better not try it." He replied, "Well, you just go ahead and develop a practice in Pacific Palisades, and I'll send you some patients to help get you started."

The first patient he sent was a cleft palate case with a lower molar that was fused with the lower border of the jaw which took me years to correct. But Steiner also introduced me to the plastic surgeons at Children's Hospital near Hollywood, and to the practice of another colleague, Dr. Hopkins, who had become ill. Five young men worked one day each week to hold that practice together. The office was located in the Baldwin Hills area. After some discussions, I took the whole practice and with my new methods condensed it into three days. The other three days of each week I was working on building my own practice in Pacific Palisades. Within two years, still working there only three days a week, I had doubled Dr. Hopkins' practice. I worked for $50.00 a day, which to me was a lot of money, even though Dr. Brodie had paid me $75.00 a day for just checking up on his patients in Chicago when he went on vacations. The man I worked for was realizing much more money from his practice by not working than he had ever produced on his own. It was, however, an opportunity for me to learn some of his older techniques. That experience was rewarding, and was to fit in later in my career.

When I asked him for a $25.00 raise, after working for the same pay for three years, he decided to return to his practice. I had changed his practice so much he now needed me to teach him the newer methods I had introduced.

Before I went to California I also knew some colleagues who had graduated from the University of Illinois and who had preceded me to the West Coast. Noted among these was a very scholarly orthodontist by the name of Dr. Lawrence Furstman, who also practiced in Beverly Hills and became a great comfort and friend. When he was almost sixty he went back to U.C.L.A. to conduct research and received his Ph.D., which I think is most remarkable. Thirty years later, I still use some of his work in my lectures.

Slow Development of a Private Practice

My practice in Pacific Palisades developed slowly. I had spent years in study and had published some articles by 1953. I was told by a colleague that research and publishing would help get a professorship, but it would not help build a private practice. However, I wasn't convinced. Consequently, with reprints in hand I started visiting dental offices. I made a particular point of learning the names of the doctors, but even more I wanted to meet the receptionists who directly deal with the public so they could know me and feel comfortable in sending patients. After having visited as many offices as I could, I finally began to see results. In addition, I gave talks before parent-teacher groups on facial deformities and also became chairman of the speakers bureau of the dental society for fluoridation of the city water supply.

The ILLIWASH Club

Dr. Alton Moore, one of my first teachers at Chicago, had become Head of the Orthodontics Department at the University of Washington in Seattle. He had trained several groups and when I arrived in California two of his students had started successful practices in the Los Angeles area. They had formed a study club they called ILLIWASH (Illinois-Washington), which I was invited to join. From the four originals (who were Dr. Philip Klein, Dr. Alfred Baum, Dr. Harvey Cole, and Dr. Robert Lande) it finally grew to ten members, and lasted for about fifteen years. Drs. Gerald Borden, Ted Windorff, Larry Furstmann and Ernest Myer became members later. We were all quite compatible, with similar backgrounds. We took up every aspect of the profession we could imagine as subjects for study on a clinical basis. We formed the first formal written mutual protection arrangement for our practices and our patients in the event of sickness or death. We were to cover each other free of charge, which I felt was an example of brotherly love.

Our agreement was only two years old when Dr. Philip Klein contracted poliomyelitis and never breathed again without an iron lung. We held his practice together until Dr. Jerry Fein, another Illinois graduate, could take it. In 1959, I myself came down with ulcers and took one month off entirely, utilizing the services of these colleagues and friends with great respect and thanks.

Paying Debts

I had to make friends and influence people. Also, I needed to "catch up" and pay off my accumulated debts. In addition, I had no tomographic X-ray machine and although I had designed one for dentistry and presented it to both General Electric and Westinghouse, I had been turned down because of sales uncertainty. I therefore set about to build one on my own. I had previously drawn up a plan for an apparatus to be employed with the patient sitting upright in a natural posture. I took it to a relative, Mr. Loren Wilson, for the requisite mechanical engineering. By the time I had taken all of the time and money that had gone into producing detailed drawings for engineering of the apparatus, procuring the parts, assembling the components, testing the machine, and going through four models, six years had passed, the cost reached about $150,000.00, most of which, of course, I had borrowed. I called it the "Sectograph".

Early in the game I had obtained a good line of credit from the local Santa Monica Bank. As with any business, bankers are in business to make a profit, and to stay in business. Bankers can be quite helpful, particularly when personal investments are needed and if the borrower has the capacity to pay them back. Mr. Aubrey Austin and Mr. Joe Walling at the local Santa Monica Bank were of great assistance to me, and became lifelong friends. It didn't hurt to have them vouch for me occasionally with some of the ventures in which I ultimately participated. These included the building of my own medical building, La Colina Professional Building on Monument Street just off Sunset Boulevard.

Success With Prediction of the Human Face

While I was a resident at the University of Illinois, at the suggestion of a mentor, Dr. W. B. Downs, I successfully developed a technique of forecasting facial growth for a two- to three-year period from the head X-ray. A rendering on paper also included the establishment of treatment objectives for the placement of teeth and the esthetics of the facial profile. The procedure resulted in the designing of treatment sequences to produce the objectives planned.

In my practice in Pacific Palisades I also continued to work on new mechanical techniques. Experiments were designed to measure forces on the teeth. Results were diligently documented by proper treatment records.

Personality Conflicts

I was often asked to address some of the local societies. Unfortunately, I ran into numerous personal problems with other colleagues and teachers bent on maintaining old, "tried and true" methods. In my enthusiasm for the new ideas I was interpreted as trying to tell everyone else how they should practice. I was convinced of the benefits of early treatment, having discovered that much could be accomplished in less time and expense when done early, thus making orthodontics more accessible to the poor.

The interpretation of the X-ray with "prediction" of facial behavior under treatment was a basic part of my approach. I tried to explain tomography (later to be part of the "CAT scan") and demonstrated the method for growth forecasts. Many objections and derisive statements, as always, came back to me. In fact, after one lecture to a local group, as I walked down the hall people turned their backs so they would not have to say something derogatory to me. It was partly xenophobic, but partly my over-ambition and superior confidence which led to profound hostility. Those first ten to fifteen years took a great deal of patience with a good bit of soul-searching. I did not want to appear ostentatious or misleading to anyone, only to see the profession I loved to go forward.

It's Their Problem

One experience particularly stands out in my memory. I had prepared some new material and worked out some new ideas and demonstrated them with good records. One evening I shared the new ideas with members of the study club. Each member, it seemed, had taken issue with my conclusions. I was accustomed to some rankling, but this was more intense because my conclusions were such a threat to their beliefs. When I arrived home at 1:30 a.m. and went to bed I couldn't sleep. I rolled and tossed until Patty woke up and asked what my restlessness was all about. I burst out, "Oh, it's those people in the club. They object to everything. Here I exhaust myself preparing the material and lay it out on a platter and all they do is find fault. If **they** don't understand what I'm doing, how can I ever get new ideas over to the rest of the profession?" She thought a minute and said, "You know, that's not your problem. If you are correct, sooner or later they will find it out. If you are wrong, then it's a mistake. But if they refuse to learn, it's their problem and not yours. Now go to sleep!"

I thought about it and said, "You're right. Why should I assume their anxieties?" That little lesson assuaged my frustrations on many occasions thereafter.

* * *

Having devised the growth forecasting and planning principle, I worked and re-worked it for six years before it was published. I presented my first 55 cases treated with the philosophy. The records indicated a 96% success rate for effective prediction of the lower jaw. Yet there was no interest by others in pursuing these successes, and many at the meeting objected to the idea. I was told by one colleague not to mislead because sooner or later someone might take me seriously. Another advised me to go back and learn to trace and measure X-rays properly because what I demonstrated was impossible. The procedure was thought to be too complicated. However, clinically it was successful, and most of the theories were working superbly.

I kept my fees for treatment quite reasonable because I realized the value of a dollar, and still the work was of as top quality as I could deliver. I didn't want any child not to be helped because of financial problems in the family.

Pacific Palisades was a very unusual community because it was composed of business people, professors and lawyers, people in the entertainment field, and executive-type families. Parents and children alike were engaged in many activities. This made it quite difficult in many instances to gain interest, cooperation, and sustained compliance with instructions. I therefore had to turn into a psychologist of sorts.

Nature of the Orthodontic Specialty

Of all the different divisions in the field of medicine, there is possibly no closer relationship made between professional people and their patients than that of an orthodontist. Treatment may start at as early an age as three, or even younger in cleft palate conditions. The plan may be to accomplish some correction of the malocclusion with the use of natural growth. The early phase is "preventative", in order to mitigate the involvement of the permanent teeth. Therefore, intermittent treatment can continue over a period of years. Even after maturity a person is never dismissed because the doctor may want to monitor the result and perhaps even make small corrections from time to time during adulthood. The teeth of an individual never are absolutely stable, as facial changes and muscle tensions continue during the mature life. Therefore, the orthodontist and staff have an opportunity to exceed the time for personal contact beyond that of almost any other member of the health professional field. It is an opportunity to guide and help mold a child's life.

Motivation and Psychology

Another unique factor is the need for patient cooperation. The patient must wear the appliances, must keep the mouth clean, must meet appointments regularly, and comply with the instructions for the success of the whole venture. The problem arises in continuing to make a sometimes awkward situation into a pleasant experience. It is a challenge to maintain a friendship while at the same time undergoing a trying prolonged relationship.

When I was a graduate student and later was teaching in the university, patients were accepted as teaching cases, and the fee was significantly less than that which would be paid to a professional. There was an available threat that if the patient didn't cooperate, they could be transferred to a private practitioner at a greater fee. There was the old saying they were to "shape up or ship out". However, for someone trying to maintain a private practice and pay bills, and attract a following, that was a horrible policy. In fact, in the late fifties and early sixties, complete meetings or conventions were held to address the problem of motivating patients without offending them.

Training vs. Wisdom and My Faults

When I left the university I actually reasoned that I was perhaps the best-trained and the best-informed orthodontist that had ever entered into practice. Before entering graduate school I had continued to review the literature for four years prior to graduate school. Then I completed a graduate course which held the best reputation of any school in the world at the time. I had stayed on to serve as a research fellow. I investigated many aspects of the profession. Further, I had developed new approaches to treatment based on that research. I consequently felt quite secure technically, perfectly competent with the mechanics.

However, all that training in biology and the mechanical skill did not equip me with the ability to deal with people. After five years of clinical practice, in roughly 1957, I recognized two major flaws in my preparation. The first weakness was in the psychology of dealing with the public and dealing with adults as well as children. The things that I had said that I shouldn't have, or the things that I didn't say that I should have said, inevitably became problems.

The second fault was in the field of management, bookkeeping and economics and budgeting. In other words, I was not trained as a business person. In addition, I had to budget for taxes, which had never been a problem previously because I had never before made any money.

Iatrogenics and Placebo

In the clinical management of patients, there is a word for the professional's effect on a patient that might be damaging, and that word is "iatrogenic". It means the genesis of or adding to a medical problem caused by the actions or even words of the doctor or an assistant or nurse. It is usually associated with an uncalculated effect on the treatment. It may cause anxiety to the patient, which of course is usually inadvertent. It is the exact opposite of a reaction to a placebo. Ironically, it can be something that the doctor said or even the expression on his face perhaps during the examination, or his flinching or his reaction maybe to someone else's work which he did not understand and on which the patient's word was taken. Such circumstances have led to litigation when one clinician waxes as a pompous authority in judgment of another.

An example of an awkward situation which arose and which I didn't discover until maybe 10 years later is the following:

I had worked up the records on an adolescent female, and made a case presentation to both her parents. In my usual way I had shown that the child's face was likely to grow vertically more than it would horizontally, and that she was a linear type (ectomorphic) in body and head. I said, "There are different body types, some patients are short and very strong with very square jaws. Other people are tall and to be in harmony with the body, the face is long, but the proportions can be quite beautiful -- just another type." And then I further explained, "For instance, the draft horse is very strong and his body is square. And he is built for power, and is not a racer. But the thoroughbred is longer and more linear and built for speed, rather than the pulling of a plough. Now your daughter is the tall racy type. We have to take this into account in her future growth and deal with the problem accordingly. And you can see by the prediction in her case that this arrangement is our goal, and the result will be quite nice for her." I thought that I had done a good job of explaining exactly what the problem was, and how we were to deal with it, but I failed to make the sale. With all of my detailed effort, they rejected my plan and went elsewhere.

About ten years later I was at the Riviera Country Club on a social occasion and was introduced to a group of people through other friends. Suddenly I recalled that one couple was the mother and father of that patient I had seen several years before. There had never been any ill feeling on my part because it is understandable that everyone has a choice, and that no one is going to appeal to the total population. But I was inquisitive regarding this particular family. When the opportunity arose, I asked the mother really why some years ago she had rejected my presentation. She said, "Oh, you're the man who told us our daughter looked like a horse face." Needless to say, I never used that method of explaining body type again. I had been referring to the beautiful sleek body of a racehorse which has captured the fancy of many an artist, but she only heard that her child looked like the face of a horse.

There is an old expression that out of the mouths of babes comes truth. As I was enjoying my work, I would often hum or sing and it became a characteristic. Some patients liked to hear me sing because they felt I was in a relaxed mood, and everything was smooth and pleasing and enjoyable -- that is, if they liked my singing, which was also the brunt of many jokes. One day I had been working on a young boy of about twelve when he put his hand up and stopped me and said, "Look, Doc, I don't mind your singing, but I can't stand your breath." What could I say, except to apologize and reach for the breath mint.

Halitosis and Social Problems

Now that the subject has been brought up, perhaps readers would be interested in bad breath because "even your best friend won't tell you". One key to knowing is when people back off a bit in a close conversation. I wonder how many romances have been "nipped in the bud" by bad breath.

Halitosis is more of a social problem than most people recognize. It has several causes and in fact in old time country medicine, the doctor sometimes could make the diagnosis just from the smell of the room of the patient, as he was making a home visit.

Everyone has morning breath, and can identify with that problem. During the day the glands in the nasal and oral cavity normally secrete mucous. The secretions keep the walls of the nose moist in order to help moisten the air as it is channeled to the lung. In the oral cavity there are glands that produce saliva, and also minor secretory glands. As a person sleeps, there is a reduction of the normal flow from the mucous membranes, and a person will slightly dry out both cavities, particularly if he or she is a mouth breather. Due to the contents of certain protein molecules and enzymes that are secreted in the mucous, they produce -- as these dry out -- the classic breath emanating from the oral cavity.

However, the same process occurs in the bronchial tubes which also need to be kept moist, and when these dry out they can also produce a rather putrid odor. Therefore, the typical person will, upon awaking, brush the teeth and freshen up the mouth, and clean out the nasopharynx in the throat. Usually within a few minutes, they are reasonably free of an offensive odor.

I personally like to put my face in the shower and let some water enter my nose and gargle fresh water in the process. For decades I have also kept a tooth brush and fluoride toothpaste in the shower, at which time I brush my teeth, shave and shampoo all at one shower session. People laugh when they hear that I shave with a razor in each hand! Yes, I commonly shave with two razors at once in order to save time and water in the shower.

Other factors entering into halitosis are certain disease states. A person may have diseases of the gums. Anyone watching a toothpaste advertisement will be acquainted with gingivitis, an inflammation (redness) or bleeding of the margin of the gum around the teeth (called the gingiva). When the disease extends down the root to the deeper structure it becomes periodontitis and a certain amount of death of tissue occurs. When this happens, an exudate further complicates the halitosis. In addition, the tongue may be coated because the surface of the tongue is pitted and rough and can contain debris of food as well as the normally shed cells of the membrane itself. This may give rise to an unpleasant odor which the person himself has become conditioned to and is unaware of. The tongue also can be brushed and scraped for alleviation of this condition.

Perhaps the most offensive odors of all come from conditions in the nose rather than the mouth. On each side of the nasal cavity and below the eye are the sinuses. These are lined with membranes which normally produce fluid and have a natural cleansing potential of their own to drain into the nasal cavity which is then drained into the throat cavity. The sinuses can also become infected. As the air circulates through the nasal cavity it picks up the rotting material within the sinus. Even the changing of the head posture, the tipping of the head down, can empty some of the contents of the sinus into the nasal cavity, which immediately produces a very offensive halitosis. Both the oral cavity and the nasal cavity are therefore sites of some of the noticeable bad breath that leads to social embarrassment and much rejection.

There are still other types of halitosis which might be even more serious, and these can emanate from the lung and stomach. One of the most offensive to me is from the chronic smoker which all non-smokers recognize. The normal function of the lung is to make air contact with the lining of the lung so that oxygen can be transferred to the blood. But the impurities in the blood are released in the breath when exhaling. Particularly in older people certain health problems might be present, in which they give off "keytones" which are products of incomplete digestion. Thus, chemicals circulating in the blood can be picked up in the breath. The presence of alcohol on the breath is well known to anyone who has ever been in the presence of a beer-drinker. The same can be said of certain foods, such as onions, garlic, certain types of seafood such as mussels, etc.

The usual function of the stomach is to help break down the food with hydrochloric acid, particularly when there is an excess of acid formation. To a layman the smell is a sour odor, which is an acid smell. Other causes and other odors may be diseases of the throat, diseases of the tonsil, and other types of infections which may leave a particular odor.

Ear, nose, and throat doctors usually will be able to help people with severe halitosis, and in the modern culture should certainly be consulted. Very frequently the dentist may also be consulted with regard to specific conditions offensive to a sex partner and others working in restricted quarters.

The Value of Communication -- Learning to Speak

During my first year in Pacific Palisades I was invited by a local physician to join the Rotary Club. I also became a member of the Chamber of Commerce and other local community groups. As I described earlier, I was a poor writer. But I also found public speaking extremely difficult. In fact, in my first address at a national convention in Lexington, Kentucky, in 1950, where I was to describe the findings of the characteristics of the jaw joint in different major types of facial form and malocclusions, I actually had stage fright. I couldn't utter a sound. People began to clear their throats and I was petrified. Hundreds of people were in the room. I had rehearsed my talk again and again the night before in my room with Patty, and finally I was able to blurt out to her, as she sat in the second row, "Help me!" "Well," she said, "why don't you just tell them what you told me last night?" So with that I got started, and everything thereafter went smoothly. I found speaking publicly to be a strenuous challenge. I further recognized any teacher owed it to audiences or students not to impose on their time and energy by being a poor communicator.

Very soon after I arrived in California I heard about Toastmasters International, which is an organization, still going strong, designed to help public speakers in a sort of self-improvement, personal, club experience. The plan for each member is organized into twelve lessons. I recommend it highly for any teacher, any speaker, or any leader. As fast as I could, therefore, I went through the twelve lessons in Toastmasters to help become an effective speaker and teacher and to gain personal confidence.

The next year I delivered an address at a national meeting in Chicago where several of my past students were in attendance. After my talk, two or three approached me and one of them remarked, "My God, what has happened to you? You have become a tremendous speaker. I can't believe the difference!" I thanked them and told them about the Toastmasters Club and advised them to go through it. I had hoped my transition to better speaking would be noticed, and it was! It was well worth the effort.

UCLA and Incompatibilities

Plans were under way in 1952 for the medical and dental school at U.C.L.A. The offices were in Quonset huts where the parking structures now stand. I made contact with Dr. Dowdy and received an assignment with the X-ray Department in the School of Medicine, which was planned first. Through work with cleft palate patients, I later taught in the Ear, Nose and Throat Department of the Medical School, as well as the Plastic Surgery Department and also Pediatrics. When the time came, later, for the Dental School to be planned, I worked with Weldon Beckett's architectural firm in laying out the teaching modules and the plans for the orthodontic, pediatric dental and X-ray departments. When the staff for U.C.L.A. was put together, I became the first Orthodontic Department Chairman.

I also assisted in working out the first curriculum for the dental school. I found, however, that I was having political problems with some of the others on the staff and differences with regard to a teaching philosophy. When Nixon ran for Governor, I placed his stickers on my automobile but they were continually torn off when I parked on the campus. I appeared to be the only conservative around.

I was accused by other people on the staff of having no "social consciousness", which disturbed me. It took some contemplation for me to determine the differences between my thinking and theirs. I concluded that it was certainly not a matter of altruism or wanting to do things for other people. It was a matter of wanting to do things **correctly** for the individual. In my particular field of orthodontics it is often better not to do anything rather than try to do a little and have it relapse, which then results in a total waste.

It was not a matter of social consciousness, it was a **conscience** regarding the dignity and rights of each individual rather than the masses. Man or woman, infant or child, in my opinion, should not be treated as a number, a statistic, or simply as a part of a total group. I had given more free time to the actual care of crippled children than any of those on the staff who were pointing a finger at me. I had set up and was then contributing to three cleft palate centers in the Los Angeles area without any thought of pay: at U.C.L.A., at St. John's Hospital in Santa Monica, and at Children's Hospital in Hollywood. Yet here I was being accused of having no social consciousness.

The committees wanted me to teach all dental students a full course in orthodontics, which is difficult even at the graduate level. They would not accept that there was no quick magic in the specialty. It simply takes hard work and time to learn. Each student has to start out at zero. No one can simply be injected with knowledge. But they wouldn't accept that.

All specialists have conflicts with general practitioners. The orthodontist was accused of guarding his secrets and not telling the general practitioner the details of the profession, as if there were a few clandestine keys to the whole specialty.

One day as the staff was having lunch at U.C.L.A., one of the members remarked, "Hey, Ricketts, what are you orthodontists going to hold over us when we learn everything about cephalometrics?" Well, I didn't like that sort of quip and its innuendo, and so laughingly I said, "Well, I guess we'll have to find some other new fields to pioneer and be the first to originate some other new methods for you." His expression changed immediately, because he realized that he had stepped out of bounds. It nevertheless represented the inner feelings and the conflict that had always been and perhaps always will be present between generalists and specialists in all healing arts.

It is interesting that general dental practitioners are anxious to learn everything about the specialty in a few lessons, when in fact graduate schools have extended courses to two- and three-year residencies, because of the sophistication that has developed in the field. But that doesn't mean to me, certainly, that lines of communication should be severed, or that the general dentist is inept or should be treated in any other way than with respect. A true student will continue to learn in all aspects of a profession.

Realizations of Professional Weaknesses

But now other of my faults surfaced. It took me ten years to pay back what I had borrowed. By age 40, after earning enough for living expenses, with a home and three children in school, I finally had something left over for investment for the future. I realized that retirement provisions and protection against ill health were my personal responsibility. I had developed a busy practice, and worked hard, but there was no guarantee of my health or continued good economic times. Future security for me and my family meant good investments and some risk-taking. My friend Dr. Lawrence Furstman gave me a book, "The Intelligent Investor" by Benjamin Graham, as a Christmas gift in 1956. Graham stated, "An investment operation is one which, upon thorough analysis, promises safety of principal and a satisfactory return. Operations not meeting these requirements are speculative." Risk could not be avoided, but by bearing good principles clearly in mind I might succeed in reducing it.

In 1958, after being in California only six years, I was elected president of the local dental society. I observed dentists coming to our meetings directly from work, blood drained from their faces and bodies slumped with fatigue. They would immediately go to the bar for a drink for an artificial stimulus. After I was elected, before I took office, I made a study of dentists in the United States. They had the highest suicide rate of all professionals. It was revealed (in 1957) that by age 60 ninety per cent (90%) of the practicing dentists were insolvent. They had acquired more debt than they had assets. In other words, only one in ten could retire at age 60 even if they chose to do so. That was a shocking realization. As it turned out, I found that most had made poor investments, only a few being lucky. These were hard facts for me to accept.

After studying the statistics I contacted one of the mutual fund companies and made arrangements with one of the managers to start a dental group fund so that dentists could set aside only $25.00 per month which in twenty to thirty years with profits and capital gains reinvested could mount up to something very substantial. Not one dentist was interested. They preferred to gamble for big stakes!

I observed that dentists and probably physicians had been short-changed in our education process with regard to how to deal with the business of the real world. I therefore embarked on a long-term study in business and management psychology and particularly the new field of socio-biology, which I will share with the reader later.

Failures

A further realization was that a few of the patients that I had so delicately and carefully finished were relapsing somewhat. Most had acceptable long-term results, relapsing only a small amount, as expected. The word "relapse" means to lapse or fall back into a previous state after an apparent improvement. No one relapsed completely, but when reversion happened after five years it was disappointing, to say the least. I therefore felt that although I had been ten years in the specialty there was still much more to be learned.

Some of the relapses were found in patients where I had already extracted teeth after assurances from older colleagues that reduction of teeth in the arch was almost a certainty in solving the problem of crowding. I found this was true sometimes but not always. I felt that I had to go back and re-examine many of the principles that I had been taught. Further, solutions were needed to problems which nobody to my knowledge had adequately addressed. It meant more research at a level different from the university environment where long-term records usually were not kept.

Speaking engagements around the country led to many questions. The nature of my work and the conclusions reached were explained, together with the resulting techniques and practices that the research in mechanics and biologic theory had directed. Many changes for the profession were recommended. One was the movement for application of preformed bands and prefabricated modules worked out with Rocky Mountain Orthodontics, Inc. of Denver, Colorado.

Europe For The First Time

My first European lecture tour was in June and July of 1958, when I was 38 years of age. I had been invited to address the European Orthodontic Society in Copenhagen on the subject of functional problems of the head and the jaws. Having some Scottish ancestry on both sides of my family, I thought it would be nice to see Scotland first. My wife and I flew overnight, arriving at Glasgow's Preswick Airport early in the morning.

Upon arrival we rented a car, and I had to learn to drive on the opposite side of the road. We wanted to recheck the flight schedules and reconfirm our later passage to London and tried to locate an office for that purpose, driving round the streets of Glasgow. I had assumed that conversing in English would be no problem, but this was not the case. I stopped one very courteous Scottsman and asked for directions to the British Airways office. He directed me with a wave of his hand, "Just over there a couple of blocks on Makini Street!" I asked him to repeat the street and heard again what I interpreted to be "Makini". After roaming around for 10 minutes more we finally found the office we wanted on Buchanan Street.

While I went into the office to confirm our schedule, Patty lay down in the seat to nap because we had lost a night's sleep. When I came out there was a crowd around the car all thinking she was very ill. I explained as nearly as I could, speaking slowly, that we had just arrived from the U.S. with no sleep, and she was resting. We laughed a lot over that episode.

Driving from Glasgow in about an hour we arrived at Edinburgh around 10:00 a.m. Never will I forget looking up through the mist and beholding that old, old castle in Scotland, a reminder of so many stories and songs about its history. What a thrill to see things that I had only heard and read about, and witness first-hand the changing of the guard, and get goose-bumps at the sound of the bagpipes.

We drove around Scotland on roads that world-wide are called "macadam roads", as it was a Scottish engineer, John L. Macadam (1756-1836) who had invented the base design.

The process is one of rolling successive layers of small broken stones on a dry earth roadbed. They later received asphalt paving.

My middle name is Murray, which is a Scottish family name, so I bought a Murray clan blanket, which I still have, and tie which I wear occasionally for the sake of curiosity.

We drove back to Glasgow, enjoying the flowers around the homes and especially the bougainvillea on the old stone walls, and then flew to London. It was particularly interesting to review the history of Britain because Ricketts is an English name.

I was shocked to find in London many areas remaining just as they were after having been bombed in World War II with the debris not yet cleared away. There were insufficient funds for the rebuilding of Britain. This was quite sobering. Yet when we got to Scandinavia, France, and other parts of Europe in 1958 there was little evidence that the war had been so devastating. Why, we wondered, was England dragging in her recovery when the countries that had been defeated were apparently so much better off? There were two reasons: (1) London was bombed more devastatingly than Scandinavia or France, and (2) as previously pointed out, the U.S. rendered more practical aid to her former enemies than she did to her allies.

In London I visited Jack Tulley at the Orthodontic Department at Guys Hospital, where we discussed the English system of health care which was a major disappointment in terms of quality service. I was the house guest of a colleague of Dr. Ron Emslie who had trained in periodontics at the University of Illinois when I was there a decade before and had married an American lady.

While in London I was treated for tennis elbow. Previously I had built a home just over Temescal Canyon in Pacific Palisades, and being without money I tried to do some heavy work myself. I built a retaining wall of cement block and in handling the materials I pulled a tendon in my right elbow. Now, carrying the heavy bags in traveling aggravated it to the point I couldn't shake hands with anyone. The doctors at Guys Hospital were accustomed to such injuries in dock workers and injected it with cortisone. After the anesthetic wore off it was so painful I couldn't sleep. I carried my arm in a sling for the next three days, which interfered with my enjoyment of the trip. The elbow bothered me for years thereafter until I treated it with ultrasound following my experience with the use of that technique for the jaw joint.

From London we traveled to Belgium to visit the Brussels World Fair. I thought it was most remarkable in view of the fact that the war had only been over for 13 years. I was particularly taken by the unique glasswork from Czechoslovakia and the engineering of the French pavilion. We stayed in a very exclusive hotel which had a large mirror the size of the bed fastened to the ceiling over the bed. I thought at the time that Europeans must take greater pleasure and practice more ritual in sex than we Americans.

From there we went to the European Orthodontic Society meeting in Copenhagen where my good friend Dr. Arne Bjork was chairman of the department at the Royal Dental College. We had met previously in Chicago 10 years before. The Society meeting went smoothly and was very exciting. I made many friends. Europeans were quite unfamiliar with the developments I had made in the field, even though I had a number of publications. Little of my previous work was covered in that congress. It was then, for the first time, that I realized my work must be communicated on an international basis and given a new label.

Inger Pedersen, wife of P. O. Pedersen (the dean of the school at Copenhagen), was assigned to be my hostess. She spoke perfect English, as many in Scandinavia do. It was mostly the French that I had trouble with in communicating. They love their language so much and prefer speaking it to English. It was obvious the French were regretting that

English was becoming the world's more common language, thus displacing French which, under what I assumed was the influence of Napoleon, had become the international medium of communication.

English Language Domination

One evening I apologized to my hostess that I didn't know her language, and she laughed. She told me how she resented the hours she had spent in learning so many languages, and that English was the coming international language. She advised me against taking time and neglecting my research just to learn other languages.

I have heard it said that with about 400 words a person can communicate adequately in English. I also learned that in many European countries there were so many dialects that people within the same borders have trouble communicating with others only a mile away. I sensed that maybe the common language of English in the United States may have been more of an advantage than we credit it with. Until recent years, most of the immigrants who have come to the United States have proudly learned English.

Rotary Courtesy

After leaving Copenhagen we became just plain tourists. We visited Paris, which still to me after all these years is perhaps the most exciting city anywhere. We went to Zurich and then to Rome. While in Rome we walked the streets to see as much as possible. I went back to one shop three times to view some alabaster busts of the goddess Diana and the god Apollo which I thought were magnificent. At the third visit the proprietor approached and said he had noticed me there before and asked if I liked them. I replied that I did, but that I had no money. He looked at my lapel and noticed my Rotary button, and said, "You're a Rotarian, aren't you?" I said, "Yes, of course, Pacific Palisades Club near Los Angeles." He said, "Give me your card and I'll send them to you. You can pay me whenever you get the money."

That was my second experience on that trip with Rotary courtesy. We had taken a side trip to Oslo while in Scandinavia, and I had visited the offices of some colleagues I had met at the meeting in Copenhagen. I decided to make up a meeting at a local Rotary Club. On learning I was American, they conducted the whole meeting in English for my benefit. I was very much impressed and flattered.

We went from Rome to Madrid and then to Lisbon where I learned much about the Spanish and Portuguese culture. In Lisbon we went to dinner at 10:30 p.m. and the restaurant was empty. When we finished at midnight it was almost full and people were still arriving. I wondered if they had their clocks set wrong.

The Challenge and the Burn-out

When I returned from Europe, I realized for the first time that my work could make a difference. Most of my theories and practices had been verified to my satisfaction, but I needed to convince the scientific community. I therefore embarked on a whole series of studies with resulting papers leading to several publications in the 1960s.

By 1958 in addition to a busy practice, I was lecturing around the country, and conducting major clinical research. I was also innovating changes in materials with Rocky Mountain Orthodontics, the manufacturers of our appliances. In addition, I was helping to plan the U.C.L.A. dental school. My son Craig was born in 1955. I had built a home and, as mentioned earlier, was planning a medical building, the La Colina Professional Building, completed in 1962.

Without realizing it, I had become overloaded and experienced a complete burn-out. I could not force myself to even look at a patient's X-ray. In addition, my father had died in 1958, and I was apparently grieving his death more than I realized. In 1959, after delivering an important paper in Colorado Springs, Colorado, on skeletal changes possible in the young patient, I went to the bathroom and vomited blood. On returning home, I was diagnosed to have ulcers. It was then that I utilized some of the help from my study club. I took a month off. I vacationed in Acapulco, Mexico, in an effort to change my environment and recuperate if I could. It was almost a full year before I was my old self again. I witnessed at first hand the effects of excessive distress on the body's reserves. I was a proven case for Hans Selye's stress triad.

In addition, subconsciously, I was undergoing a bit of distress with my first wife, although I had three children that I loved as intensely as any father possibly could. I bought a boat and some property at the Salton Sea in California, took time to go fishing, water skiing, and tried to take more time off for golf as a member of the Riviera Country Club.

Rotary Affiliation Advantages

While practicing, researching and teaching was going on, I was also enjoying very much my Rotary Club affiliation. Rotary is an organization formed as a service club for business and professional people. Its history began in 1906 when a group of young business people were brought together in Chicago by a young lawyer, Paul Harris, in order to help each other in their vocations and to get acquainted. There were only six, so they met once each week, and rotated the lunch in their different offices. From this rotation, it acquired its name, the Rotary Club. As time went by others joined the group, which soon became too large to meet in the waiting room of a private office. Hence luncheons came to be held at restaurants and clubs.

As the Rotary Club members began to help each other they recognized that they represented a more complete community. After they had helped each other and developed a club atmosphere with friendship and business support, they began to step forward with projects in the community and do things for others. For instance, it was the Chicago Club #1 that was responsible for ridding the city of its street latrines in the first decade of the twentieth century.

Ultimately, Rotary members would transfer to other cities and the movement became extended and finally went to other countries. It thus became an international association with more than 25,000 clubs in 184 different countries and a 1992 membership of 1,156,174.

Our club met at Riviera Country Club in Pacific Palisades, and after a pleasant lunch with friendship and business, we would routinely hear a speaker on some subject or some important issue of the day. I have always said that Rotary was my realistic contact with the world outside of my profession. I could sit one day with a lawyer, one day with a principal of a local school, another day with a member of the clergy, another day with the president of the bank, or representatives of many other facets of business. It gave me the opportunity to ask questions and also to take notes and grow further intellectually. I proceeded up through all the offices, became president, and served on most of the committees. Despite all of the other work and travel, I managed to keep my membership and stay active in the Rotary movement until I moved to Scottsdale, Arizona in 1987.

One objective of Rotary International was to wipe out smallpox on the face of the earth. Rotary International gives as many scholarships as almost all of the other service organizations combined. Ronald Reagan is an honorary member of the Palisades club because he lived there. He was one of our speakers on a number of occasions, and I always felt he was one of the most decent people that I ever knew.

By invitation I gave about a dozen addresses to our local club on a variety of subjects. When I went on lecture trips to other countries, I would write up my observations and experiences and send them back to our little weekly communication which was called "The Breeze-Shooter".

One of the greatest functions of Rotary is the opportunity to make up a missed meeting at other clubs around the country and around the world, thus fulfilling the requirement for regular weekly attendance which is excused only by death. Each club has a greeting committee which will try to seat a visitor with someone in his profession or someone that an individual might request to meet. Thus, the Rotary Club was truly an opportunity for service, and is extremely worthwhile. Through it I felt I was in contact with the community and with the world at large. Also, the Rotary International publications were distributed on a world-wide basis. Thus, through Rotary, I remained in touch with economics, politics, various sciences, and even religion.

Free Enterprise - The Chance to Win or Lose

My first office in Pacific Palisades was in the little Sunset Medical Center over what is now the Santa Monica Bank. Frequently I would look out over the roof of the adjacent building and across the street to the corner of Monument and Bestor, and see a vacant piece of property with three California oak trees located near the center of the lot. There was a group of about six lots running up to Sunset Boulevard with three houses, and three empty lots. I envisioned a small medical building situated on the corner and set about to see what it would take to rezone the land and erect such a building. In the meantime, I needed a larger office and took 1000 feet in the Ross Building on Via de la Paz for five years.

In 1957 when I contacted the owner of the corner lot I found that it wasn't for sale, but the books revealed that he had paid $8000.00 for the lot. I offered him $12,000.00; he finally asked for $13,000.00 so we settled for $12,500.00, giving him a profit of $4500.00, a good profit for him at that time. Complete houses along the street were selling for around $20,000.00, so it was a fair price for a lot just for building a home. It was a small lot at that, only 50 feet wide.

Another reason for paying that amount was that I planned to rezone the whole block, which would be necessary for the construction of the building. I contacted the other property owners, explained what I was planning, and secured their support. Before re-zoning could be accomplished I had to get the agreement of all the property owners within a certain radius of that location. It was necessary for me to go from door to door explaining what I wanted to do, and show a drawing of a building, so that they would have little or no objection. At first many were very reluctant. I explained that a medical building would improve the area, and also would add significantly to the value of their own property. That did it! I was as tactful as I could be and honest in not trying to pull a fast one on anyone.

As I got into it further, after obtaining neighbors' permission to proceed, I found it would be necessary to widen the street. In addition, I needed to get an easement from the adjacent property on Embury Street in order to exit the parking garage that I planned to place underneath the building. Therefore, I negotiated and bought the house adjacent to the property so that I could give an easement to the building myself. It was then, too, that I had my introduction to City Hall in Los Angeles and, further, to the multitude of requirements and restrictions for this project.

By 1960 I had the whole block re-zoned. Of course others immediately took advantage of the re-zoning, and the value of the property rose sharply. However, I had no money for constructing the building, and had to borrow or raise the capital by financing through the Santa Monica bank. I had established credit on the basis of the prompt payment of loans that I had made before. I was considered a worthy risk, and therefore financing was granted, with the finished building to be put up as security. Because I could then evaluate the finished building, and use the lot as initial security, I was able to proceed with building.

I hired a friend, an architect-designer named Dwight Pollack, who was a student of Frank Lloyd Wright, to develop a modern-type building. We procured a builder (Murray Coleman) and a parking expert (Carlysle Manaugh) and together built La Colina, the first steel-framed building made in the Pacific Palisades area. It was about 11,000 square feet and as much as was allowed on the small lot.

I considered it to be quite a risk to take, and I immediately started contacting colleagues to see if they would be willing to take space in the building. Some of them had indicated that they wanted to expand and I thought it would be good for the community to have many health professionals together. I made verbal agreements for occupancy with a number of colleagues at what I thought was a reasonable and fair rental charge, and then went ahead with construction of the building.

Learning the Hard Way

The first move was to clear the lot. I hired someone to cut down the trees and stack the wood neatly so I could take it to my home for firewood. The saws drew some local attention. The next morning, with my son to help, I borrowed a pick-up to go get the wood. But late the evening before the local people had decided to help themselves. It was almost a riot. Wheelbarrows in hand, they had cleared every stick of wood except a stump which was too big to be put in a fireplace. That was my introduction to neighborly respect! I should have put a fence around it as is common practice.

During the construction I had two other ugly experiences. The first was with my local colleagues. Behind my back they had met together and agreed that they would not sign a lease at the previously agreed figure. Whether it was from jealousy or envy, or just grouping together to strike the best deal, I was crushed by their attitude. I wanted to make it a nice medical-dental complex. I had imported some lovely matched cut marble from Portugal, and thought it would be a building that we and the community could be very proud of. Because I wanted my own private toilets I had arranged to have a private bathroom in each suite. They felt that the building should provide the toilet and that it should be a communal type so that they would not have to pay rent for the extra five-foot square that would be needed for a bathroom and sink! How cheap indeed!

Because I was a specialist and depended on their referrals and good will, they had me over a barrel. I was, therefore, forced to negotiate rentals downward. As a result, with the financing and the cost of all the services, I was just able to meet mortgage payments with no remaining profit from the building. This left me with no remuneration for my risk and for the long hours spent in rezoning, going through the city government and the planning and construction of the building. I consequently got a taste of dreadful business problems. Had I not been one of them, and a specialist, I of course could have held out and told them to take a jump. Human nature can be nasty when money is involved!

The second event happened while the building was still not quite completed. I had designed a small section for filing cabinets to hold my treatment records which I had measured exactly. But the framers had left an extra space of about four inches, thus causing an empty space. Rather than having a wall rebuilt, I decided to take some walnut paneling material and fill in the extra space on my own to create a built-in appearance. The very night before I planned to make this slight alteration, I had pulled the drawers of the files out of the cabinets and had them resting on the floor of my previous office on Via De La Paz there in the village of Pacific Palisades. I also had several panels of the art work, that I had done at the expense of tremendous time, sitting on the floor in preparation for a move within the next day or so. On arriving at the office in the morning I found that for some unknown reason a pipe had burst and the office was completely flooded. I was shocked to the point of tears, because records like that are irreplaceable. I called a friend in the Fire Department and men came to drain the place, and we saved what we could.

After gaining my composure in the afternoon, I proceeded to the new building with some tools and panelling in hand and was in the process of filling in the extra spaces for the cabinetry. I was very disturbed and depressed. As I was on my hands and knees doing some fitting I looked up and saw a large man asking me what I was doing in very broken English. I explained that a mistake had been made and I was attempting to correct it. Whereupon he said, "I can't let you do that." I said, "What? What do you mean? This is my building." He said, "You're not a member of the union. Have you got your union card?" With that, and on top of my loss with the flood, I was incensed. I said, "This is my building, I'll do anything that I want to in it." He said, "Your builder has a contract with us, and you're not to touch it." I grabbed him by the overalls, lifted him up although he was about four inches taller than I, and shook him, and in a rage shouted, "You get out of here and get to work, or we'll see who can do what to somebody else." He turned white, because I must have been white too. I told him I was paying him for a job to be done right, and it was his mistake that I was trying to correct. "Now get out of here," I said, "and don't let me hear a word from you again." He reported it to the builder, and when the builder talked to me I was enraged all over again. I said, "Next time I'll take a club. You go ahead and get that building finished and let's be done with all this stupid nonsense."

This was my second first-hand experience with a labor union. The first, as I mentioned, was when I was in high school and wanted to get a job in construction. I had to borrow to pay union dues in order to acquire the job. I paid more than I thought was fair and reasonable in dues. Certainly I can find no fault with the idea of a labor union as a part of fair business practice. However, I was beginning to feel that they had become just as guilty of greed as the management side. They were beginning to throw around their power actually to the detriment of progress in our society as a whole.

Politicians seeking office will cater to the unions for their support. I found it extremely amusing that a person running for office in England on one occasion said that he wouldn't stop until all of the union workers had "better than an average salary", not realizing that as they raised the salary the average would rise as well. How gullible he must have thought most people to be.

Public Attitudes in the 1950s -- Reflected by the Economy

When I arrived in Pacific Palisades the business center was just a few small buildings along Sunset Boulevard, and it had one public school, a Catholic school and some churches. The community had originally been developed as a retirement center for Methodist ministers, and the hill north of Sunset Boulevard toward the Santa Monica mountains where Easter sunrise services were usually held, called Peace Hill, became covered with houses. Some of the area was still in lemon groves, however, and it resembled a rural community. The Riviera section where later President Ronald Reagan had a home, just above the Riviera Country Club, still had many vacant lots. Access to downtown Los Angeles was at least an hour by car. Only one freeway was in existence in Los Angeles, the Arroyo Seco (now Pasadena).

Santa Monica, adjacent to the Palisades, was also a quiet town. The old founding fathers had tried to keep it free from large buildings and developments. Just above the Pacific Ocean, the bluff rose some 75 feet. Through the years we were bothered by earth slides. From Sunset Boulevard to Santa Monica Pier was about three miles. In my jogging days -- until I wore both my knees out -- I ran it about five times a week.

The great majority of my patients in California were absolutely delightful, and I loved them. They were intelligent, cheerful, enthusiastic and cooperative. But I soon learned I had competition with the hairdresser, the music teacher, the ladies' meetings, and other local attractive occasions. I also was in competition with long vacations, skiing in the winter and foreign trips in the summer. When the surf was up or the sun was out it was easy for them to forget their appointments. But those were all forgivable. However, I had my share of other problems.

It became obvious that some of the children deliberately did not cooperate, and made difficulties. They calculated that I would make an issue of their problem to the point that it would be an attention-grabber with the parent who was too busy to take an interest in the child. All children need love and attention and, indeed, recognition. When this doesn't come naturally they will seek out methods -- and sometimes bizarre methods -- in order to achieve it. I had to learn how to recognize and handle such problems.

Experience in the Eisenhower Years

During his two terms Eisenhower was conscious of budgets and payment of debts of World War II together with the rebuilding of Europe and Japan. The French requested military support against the communist expansion in Vietnam (Indochina). General Westmoreland was sent there to investigate conditions. After a study he pointed out to Eisenhower the difficulty of the terrain and the nature of the logistic problems. According to the writings of David Halverstram, we were informed at that time that air power could not be employed to the same advantage as in Europe's cities and countryside. Westmoreland predicted a need for up to one million troops to stop the communists from North Vietnam who were supported by China. Fresh from the experiences in Korea, Eisenhower rejected the French request. He wanted America not to be drained any further, and to give our citizens a freedom of choice, and a chance to become strong ourselves.

By 1958, however, we were suffering a recession. People in Europe inquired about our economic situation when I first went there. I could definitely feel the recession in my practice. The war economy and the post-war rebuilding, together with the working of free enterprise, had caused a boom. We were spoiled and expected it to last forever. Many still remembered the conditions in the 1930s and feared an even more severe slip.

Eisenhower found it easy to gain a second term in the election of 1956. Yet, somehow by 1960 the attitudes about less control by the Federal government had shifted. Many became dissatisfied, and I sensed that the majority wanted the Federal government to do more. We were so prosperous the cost of a major increase in Federal spending was not opposed. The rich could afford it -- just tax them more! If the economy was slipping, many assumed it was due to the President. They had to blame somebody.

Nixon was nominated by the Republicans because he was known and had served as Vice-President with Eisenhower. As I remember, Eisenhower's support for Nixon was rather assumptive and complacent. The young, aggressive John Kennedy captured the imagination of the public with the idea of more and more programs to "get the country moving again". His insistence on reaching the moon also captured attention. It was difficul for Nixon to win by defending Eisenhower's programs. I remember the debates in whicl Nixon warned about moving into Federal programs too fast.

It was only after a hard and extremely bitter campaign against Johnson that Kennedy ha(won the Democratic nomination in Los Angeles in 1960. Further, it was evident tha Kennedy would need to win the states of Texas and Illinois in order to beat Nixon. Needles to say, there were some strong-arm manipulations with Bobby Kennedy as campaigı manager to convince Johnson to be Kennedy's running mate. There was little cordialit; between Johnson and Kennedy. Johnson had his own ambitions.

Other Events in the Fifties and Sixties That Shook America

While I was occupied with developing my practice and going through the good as wel as the trying experiences in California, many events were taking place which were to effec change in America. These changes would affect Americans which ultimately would affec my profession.

For instance, in 1958 the E.E.C. was formed in Europe. In 1958 in the name of agraria) reform (taking away land from landowners and giving it to the people), Fidel Castro tool over Cuba in a revolution from the Batista dictatorship. However, in a short time h(converted it to a communist dictatorship. He was immediately subsidized by the U.S.S.R Cuba is only 90 miles from Key West. While I was stationed at the submarine base in Ke; West in 1946 I visited Havana twice as a temporary medical officer on the "Gryphon" submarine. Havana was a thriving city with beautiful boulevards, many resorts an(nightclubs. The communist government caused many to flee in fear of their lives. The: escaped to South Florida, which changed that economy, the social conditions and cultur(in Miami. The Casto influence permeated many areas of Central and South America whicl affected the U.S. as a whole.

During this time many of the colonial holdings of England, Belgium, France and othe countries were breaking up in Africa. World Book Encyclopedia (1992) lists 52 independen countries on that continent. New countries were formed, and with them came nev problems. An example of this was the Mau-Mau uprisings in Kenya. While Africa was fa removed from the U.S., the changes there affected our previous trade, our alliances, ou foreign aid programs, our foreign policies and, of course, our taxes.

The average politician and the majority of citizens had lost a sense of realism regardin; taxes and where the government was to spend its returns. Tax evasion was easier t(prosecute and convict than a charge of murder. The country was on a major upward swing and few cared about the rest of the world except for the conflict with the U.S.S.R. and th Cold War.

In addition to Castro in the Americas and revolutions in Africa, the Berlin Wall wa erected in 1961. It was claimed to be nationalistic but was in fact communist-inspired, historical development by the East German communists was dictated by the Kremlin i, Moscow. The wall was a signal of an imprisonment of the people in a totalitarian state b a communist dictatorship. They wanted absolute control of the news, and the media wer employed as an outlet for propaganda. In effect, they not only locked their own people ir but locked the rest of the world out. The more secretive they became, the more secretiv and covert we Americans felt compelled to become. How could they be trusted? We feare(the unknown. After all, they had put up Sputnik in 1957 and Vostok, the first manned spac ship later. America was behind in space technology which could be employed for war.

In retrospect, it is difficult to believe how we were drawn into the Vietnamese War, whic

olved not the one million troops of Westmoreland's estimate but 2.5 million, ended with
e than 100,000 casualties and a still unconfirmed number missing in action 30 years
r, and resulting in America's first defeat in war. We had offered aid to the South
tnamese with training and equipment. The Gulf of Tonkin lies east of North Vietnam
there one of our Navy ships was stopped. I remember the incident and the fear of the
ses of Chinese. Millions of them could be killed which would have little effect on their
ulation. Our anxiety further increased when we discovered that the U.S.S.R. had
eloped their own atomic bomb. Such was my reaction to the situation and stress in
erican society as we entered the 1960s.

9

HEGEMONY BY PRESSURE OF CIRCUMSTANCES
(1961 - 1970)

Hegemony is a term from Greek which means the exercising of leadership or dominant influence, usually referring to one state over another as in a confederation. When certain circumstances prevail, a country and a person or group within a society may find themselves hegemonical.

The North Atlantic Treaty Organization was formed in 1949 with the U.S. as a member along with European countries. It was soon apparent that the protection of these countries would depend upon the strongest element. With the dissolution of the British Empire, from two wars, and the destruction of much of Europe in World War II, as Americans we could feel the pressure toward measures for our own national security for economic and political reasons. America, therefore, by necessity, came into a position of hegemony.

By 1955 the Eastern Block nations had formed the Warsaw Pact. This in effect set up the Communist Party as hegemonic in that confederation. In essence that move sealed the conditions for the Cold War which began to thaw only 20 years later with detente and the SALT I and SALT II treaties during the terms of Nixon and Carter.

It was during this time, ironically, that I found myself in a position of hegemony with the dental profession. For leadership a statesman is needed, and good politics should be practiced. My problem was that I was led by the truth gained from my research findings and also by the desire to see my profession progress. I wanted to be liked, but did not want to make myself appealing by always saying what others would be most delighted to hear.

It was under these circumstances that I entered into the 1960s. In retrospect, I should have had a manager. But it is doubtful that I could have been managed by anyone, because some tried, to no avail.

* * *

In 1960 I was challenged by the raising of a family. We had, in 1955, built a Frank Lloyd Wright-type house on a knoll projecting out over the Presbyterian Conference grounds in Temescal Canyon in Pacific Palisades. The house can still be viewed from the curve on Sunset Boulevard. Temescal, I learned, was the name for heated rock saunas employed by

Native Americans who had once inhabited the area. Leveling of the lot uncovered remains of old burned vegetation. I had heard of fires that denuded those Santa Mor mountains. I planned, therefore, for a light aggregate combed cement roof which later in fact, save the house during a devastating brush fire that took a neighbor's home in 19

Just below the house the school district later built an olympic-sized pool and a prac field for use with the high school which was erected just south of Sunset Boulevard c site where before had stood the secluded home occupied by Eddie Fisher and Deb Reynolds when they were married. I frequently jogged up the canyon or on the prac field. In 1960 Robin was ten, Gale was eight, and Craig was five. They had access to t area and freedom to roam. I felt it was good for them to be close to nature.

Confrontation with a Communist

In the early 1960s I was privileged to give a series of lectures in Mexico City. (particular evening I was invited to a private home. Several professional people wer attendance. After some cocktails I was introduced to a local plastic surgeon who, I had b told, had recently been to Cuba and was a communist. I had no animosity nor o particular feelings, and remained friendly. He, however, soon began to launch int dialogue about how rotten the United States was. Every problem in the world was our fa Among other things I was told that the Chrysler Automobile Company was build thousands of tanks for a world conquest by the U.S. I told him I was unaware of such a th although I tried to stay informed on events in our country. That wouldn't do at all for h it only antagonized him further. I was beginning to become upset, but reminded myself t I was in a foreign country and that arguing with someone whose mind was so fixed wo be of no avail. Here I was, an American citizen, supposedly above average in educati representing our profession abroad and confronted by a communist making accusations which I had absolutely no answer.

I came back from Mexico determined to learn something about communist ideolog bought and read several books, among them "Masters of Deceit" by J. Edgar Hoover, " Naked Communist" by Cleon Skowsen, and "You Can Trust the Communists To Exactly As They Say" by Dr. Fred Schwartz.

I also read the history of socialism and communism, going back to ancient times, and pact made by some of the Pilgrims in settling the New England coast in 1620 as the f socialistic experiment in America. At that time confusion and discontent developed young men found no reason to work for other men's wives and children without compensati In no way was it accepted that the strong and hard working should have a like condition the weak and non-productive. Instead of enjoying a Thanksgiving feast, by 1622 the gr was suffering from starvation, a collapse of morale and an absence of good will, suspicion and mistrust ubiquitous. When the governor at last "gave way that they sho set corn every man for his own particular" and assigned parcels of land to each fam success of the community was achieved. Therefore, the feast of 1623 was a celebratio deliverance from socialism!

Further, I attended discussion groups concerning a communist plan to take over world. They would first convert China, take Korea and Indochina (Vietnam), and cla down on Japan. They would infiltrate and cause unrest in Central America, take o Mexico and destroy the United States from its soft underbelly. The U.S. by then would so divided in ideas and disillusioned that a small well-organized group could do in United States what had been done elsewhere.

It was as if communism was a fanatical religion to many converts. What I heard in Mex vas a calculated and rehearsed "communist line" but at the time I was too ignorant to ecognize it. We were the capitalists and therefore their enemy.

These major events -- the Cuban Revolution, unrest and inflation in South America, the conflict in Korea, the Berlin Wall, Soviet development of the atom bomb, the Soviet tanks rushing the uprisings in Czechoslovakia and Hungary -- all signaled the massive spread and power of communism. It was a world conquest by an ideology that was gaining success.

It is small wonder, therefore, that the citizens of the U.S. would go along with a Congress that tried to contain communism in Korea and Vietnam. We were already playing the role of a world police force. We had to support bases as a buffer against attack from the U.S.S.R. We supported a force in Frankfurt to keep the longest era of peace in Europe in 200 years.

Career Momentum in 1960

I'm a great believer in momentum. When a rocket is fired much force is needed for the propulsion, but once it is in motion the momentum can carry it far without further energy. Momentum is seen in sports when one team gets "on a roll". Players seem to make no mistakes and reach an emotional "high". Other teams seem not able to "get it together" or "get going again" and thereby lose unless the momentum shifts. This can happen often with a single success. The same is true of a whole economy.

My successes in the 1960s were due to the momentum and confidence built in the 1950s. Several publications added to my momentum. The papers were on head growth and its prediction, on the skeletal alteration of the face with orthodontic treatment, and also on function of the jaws and problems of function within the oral environment.

I had also studied speech and the airway spaces in the nose and throat in my previous research which now continued. In 1960 we took 20 patients to U.C.L.A. and in conjunction with Dr. Elise Hahn, Robert Sloan and Dr. Dowdy in the X-ray department made a study of motion radiography in speech and swallowing. The result was a classification of different types of swallowing behavior.

The reader should be aware that the airway through the nose, while being above the mouth which is the foodway, actually reverses position at the back of the throat. The esophagus, a collapsed tube, lies in back of the trachea which is an open tube ringed by cartilage which lies in front. Respiration (breathing) and mastication (chewing and swallowing) constitute two vital basic vegetative functions. These systems cross over each other just behind the tongue. The study led to an hour-long movie still in the U.C.L.A. film library and is still employed for teaching 30 years later.

First Trip to South America - 1961
Uruguay

In 1961 I was invited to attend a Pan American Congress in Uruguay. Most of the professionals in South America were quite cordial and I was indeed treated with respect. However, one day with a camera on my shoulder and searching for memorable sights to photograph, I was walking down the street in Montevideo minding my own business when a group of younger men, on seeing me coming towards them, went four abreast to occupy the whole sidewalk. I stood aside to let them pass, and one intentionally elbowed me into the gutter. I quickly concluded that they didn't like North Americans. I was concerned that we would have leftist problems in all of South America.

Argentina

From Uruguay we crossed over the immense Rio de la Plata into Argentina, which is a very large country extending from Bolivia to the southern tip of South America.

Buenos Aires (which means Good Air) showed evidence of a past era of glory. They produced much beef for export mostly to Europe. The large cattle ranches were tended by gauchos who were excellent horsemen and were also responsible for the invention of a dance. When they came into the fiestas taking long strides in their high boots, their movements became formalized as the tango.

I was a guest for lunch at a restaurant where an Argentine steak was ordered. When it came it was two inches thick and over a foot long. I thought it must surely be a roast for the whole table. But it was for me alone. I asked, "How do you expect me to eat all that?" The answer came back: "Slowly. We have three hours."

Orthodontists there had been exposed mostly to the European methods. They were shocked when I showed data just accumulated from a German orthodontic practice, representing a four-year treatment experience, which revealed that forcing the lower jaw forward did not increase its growth as they had been taught. They were upset because they had their "boat rocked".

While in Buenos Aires at a Sunday brunch I was informed of a firestorm near Pacific Palisades in California. I called and found, to my great relief, that the family and our home were safe.

Chile

From Argentina we crossed the Andes to Santiago, Chile. I had a contact there, a physician who was doing research in one of their institutions. I had previously arranged to give a talk at one of the hospitals on cleft palate and care for congenital deformities. The reception was cold. I found a resistance to anything or anybody from the U.S. The head of the hospital said they were doing their best with a meager staff and funds. I remember the burned child patients. It was reported that 20% of the children died of some cause before two and one-half years of age.

My friend there in Santiago had concluded that a revolution was imminent within five years, and that it could be bloody. Actually, in three years a Christian-Democratic party formed a new government.

Later, in 1970, the first democratically elected communist government took power. A program of massive socialist reform occurred. One of my colleagues told of spending a full day in line just to buy a tire for a car. Every purchase required standing in line, and no one prospered. It took four years for the Chileans to find they had made a poor choice. The government was overthrown by the military. Chile accepted a military dictatorship in order to combat the Communists. In 1990 they again had free elections. With freedom of choice restored the country started moving.

Peru

From Chile we flew north to Lima, Peru, and to one of the most interesting parts of the world I have ever seen. It very rarely rains along the coast of Peru. An enormously deep trench in the Pacific brings a cool flow from the Antarctic along the continent. Clouds bypass the coast and dump heavy precipitation in the mountains separating Peru and Brazil. This water gives rise to the Amazon basin. The water flows thousands of miles completely across South America to the Atlantic. We took a train and bus to the famous Machu Pichu ruins in the most glorious mountains to be found anywhere on earth.

Bolivia

From Lima we doubled back to La Paz, Bolivia. We flew over smoking volcanoes and landed at an airport at an elevation of 12,000 feet. It was interesting to watch fellow passengers as we walked from the plane to pick up our luggage. Their noses and ears turned purple. Reaction times slowed noticeably, because of the altitude. I cashed a twenty-dollar bill and received so many bills (some as large as 100,000 pesos) that I could not put them all in one pocket. I was told that the average life expectancy in this South American city was only 26 years.

At one location I visited shops lining a street along a steep hill. I was near the top and noticed a large rug moving up the hill from far below. All I could see were two skinny legs underneath it. I marveled at the sight and waited. A very small man carried it straight up the hill and delivered it to a shop near where I was standing. After the man had been paid for its delivery and had left, I went into the shop to look at the rug. I inquired how it was that so small a person could carry such a big load so far uphill at that altitude. The answer was that he was chewing coca leaves from which cocaine was processed. I sensed then the use of cocaine by athletes in competitive sports.

From La Paz we went to the nearby shores of Lake Titicaca, which is one of the highest and largest lakes on earth. It was immense, maybe the size of all our Great Lakes combined. I saw people in small reed boats, fishing. I learned that fish canneries were located along the shore to commercialize the huge trout harvested from the lake. I was surprised to find a steamship of ocean size docked there for our overnight travel by water to the opposite side. To my amazement I learned that the steamship had been transported from the coast up through the mountains, piece by piece, by mules and then reassembled on the lake -- unbelievable!

Traveling by train from Titicaca to Cuzco was an experience in contrasts. The train stopped in the villages to take on passengers or produce. At one stop I looked out the window and saw a man severely beating a woman. I rapped on the window and was shouting at him to stop when the conductor reminded me I should mind my own business. I was told that apparently she had come down from the hills against his instructions or wishes, and he had caught her in the act. He was teaching her a lesson. He didn't stop after he had knocked her down, but continued to kick her while she was lying on the sidewalk. She was vomiting, bleeding, and urinating on the platform beside the train. I was irate, but what could I do in such a strange country and such a foreign culture?

From that experience I could imagine the male dominance in many cultures of the past. It is well known that women, like animals, were once considered as private property and in fact were traded for animals. Shakespeare's "The Taming of the Shrew" has long been a popular play. There is also a parallel in the contemporary problem of battered wives in the American culture.

Some people, of either sex, can become very violent under the influence of drugs or alcohol. Some spouses have very sharp tongues and may push their companion to the limit of tolerance. In fact, statistics reveal that many homicides are actually committed within the family or by a close neighbor.

Many different communities along the railway to Cuzco carried their distinction by wearing peculiar hats. The population around Cuzco which is high in the mountains wore derbies. One shocking sight was the people in the markets who wore no shoes. The weather at night was near freezing and still they had no shoes. I observed their feet with awe. The skin was hypertrophied and it looked as if they had formed a half-inch-thick pad on the soles of their feet.

My experiences in South America in 1961 further entrenched my fear of the communist movement afoot. I was now concerned about all of Latin America.

Professional Conflicts - 1962

The year 1962 was highlighted by three memorable happenings.

I had been requested to contribute a chapter to a book ("Vista in Orthodontics") being edited by Dr. Bertram Kraus and Dr. Richard Reidel to honor Dr. Alton Moore at the University of Washington in Seattle. My chapter was to be entitled "Clinical Research". I accepted the invitation out of my respect for my friend Dr. Moore and spent three months in completing a paper on the many aspects of research on living patients. It included almost 100 references to work performed in our field.

After sending in the manuscript I received a conference call with both Dick and Burt on the phone. They thanked me for the paper but said that it wasn't what they had wanted. They wanted the evolution of my personal research, how it started and how I developed my conclusions. For a moment I was silent. "Do you mean you want a completely different paper?" I asked. Burt said, "Yes, the other paper is very good, but it will not fit in with our plan. We want your particular work in morphology, growth, diagnosis and treatment that you have conducted, especially on the temporomandibular joint."

"You're asking, then, for a scientific paper to be written in the first person, is that true?" I inquired.

"That's exactly right," was the answer.

"Well, okay," I said, "but it may take a while."

"We have a deadline in three months. Do you think you can do it in six weeks?" they asked, and I replied, "Okay -- I'll give it my best shot."

The deadline was met and came out to be 30 pages in length. It was a compilation of my first fifteen years in the profession. The whole book represented the status of knowledge in the profession in 1962 together with a summary chapter. Twenty-seven authors contributed, on a wide range of subjects.

Some weeks later I received a thank-you call from Richard Reidel who remarked that mine was the only manuscript he received that required no editing. I was therefore pleased by the effort, as the book came out in August of 1962, published by Lea & Febiger in Philadelphia.

In October of 1962 I received a "crank call" from a Dr. Rodney Mathews in San Francisco. It went something like the following:

"Hello, Rick, this is Rod."

"Hello, Rod, how are you doing?"

"Not very well. I'm disgusted as hell."

"Why?"

"It pertains to your chapter in Kraus and Reidel's book."

"What's the problem?"

"You are the most conceited ass I have ever known."

"What makes you say that? I'm sorry you feel that way."

"Well, I counted in your chapter where you used "I" 29 times. No one else referred to themselves like you did. What makes you think you are so much smarter than anyone else? You are for the shits!"

"Wait a minute, Rod," I said, "that's the second version I wrote for them and they specifically requested me to write it as I did. They wanted the evolution and sequence of my ideas as they developed. They asked that it be in the first person."

"That's bullshit and everybody knows it. I just wanted to get it off my chest. Good-bye."

After this call I felt very hurt and deflated. My egocentrism had been pointed out before. However, I considered myself far from self-centered. I did admit to a preoccupation with the issue at hand which was often interpreted to be a lack of concern for others. I vowed to try to improve and try harder to make Rod a friend.

A few years later Rod was in the audience in Reno, Nevada, where I was on the program speaking on the developments in understanding growth and findings with the computer. After my talk he nailed me again.

"You know, I just can't stand to listen to you lecture. Your 'know-it-all' attitude is more than I can bear."

"Why didn't you leave, then?" I asked him.

"I wanted to listen to others take you apart."

"You really have a problem, don't you, Rod?" I said.

He was still going on and didn't listen. One of my colleagues had offered to carry my briefcase back to my room because I had my hands full of slides, and this bothered him also. So we proceeded out the door of the lecture hall back to the hotel.

"You know, I've done as much research as you and I don't ask people to follow me around like you do. I wouldn't carry your briefcase for you."

I don't remember exactly what I said -- I tried to be funny and offered some jokes. But Rod Mathews still persisted, saying, "You may be okay to sit down and have a beer with, but when it comes to science you are a very poor scientist who likes to deal only in averages."

"You're wrong there," I told him, "I know just as much about curves of distribution, probability and correlation as you. The difference is I believe you must have a starting point for reference rather than groping in inordinate bewilderment."

With that we parted. Thereafter I considered him to be beyond the bounds of a gentleman. A few months later I heard he was ill.

Some time later I had been asked to give a whole day's program for the Angle Society from Northern California that was meeting at the famous old Coronado Hotel in San Diego. The day before I was to talk I asked if Rod was in attendance. Finding that he was, I purchased a six-pack of beer and put it up under the rostrum where I was to speak.

When I started my lecture first thing in the morning I pulled out the beer and opened two bottles. Rod was in the back row and I took one to him and set it down in front of him on the table. The other I left on the podium, and took a long drink myself. I explained to the group that Rod enjoyed drinking beer with me but didn't appreciate my lectures. Therefore, I would consider this a beer party. There was much laughter! I used the beer in place of water, and everything was received graciously. It was the only time I ever drank beer while teaching.

That was the last I saw or heard from Rod. He was a hard worker. He died about two years later. I hope he was happy in the end. Unfortunately, behind my back he did me irreparable damage with my colleagues and the reception of my ideas in Northern California as well as in the Northwest.

* * *

The second important occasion in 1962 was at the annual meeting of the American Association of Orthodontics in May, which happened to be held in Los Angeles. In the previous years I had worked on preformed-prefabricated orthodontic bands for the teeth and had designed preadjusted attachments. Previously each band had been custom formed and fitted, and required lengthy chair time for the patient. This added to the cost of orthodontics. Even with skill and efficiency, it was not unusual to require two hours for this construction. Many orthodontists had waiting lists, due to lengthy appointments for the appliance construction. I worked with the progressive manufacturer Rocky Mountain Orthodontics in Denver, and by changing the composition of the alloy material, improving the designs, making the correct sizes available, and working out a system for integration, I devised a method whereby the fitting and placement was accomplished in 15 minutes of chair time in my hands.

Most clinicians could not believe it. One of my close friends, however, arranged for me to demonstrate the procedure on live television before the American Association of Orthodontics at their annual meeting. We set up two of my office chairs and accessories in an ante room adjacent to the grand ballroom of the Statler Hilton Hotel. Before 750 members of the society, with the help of two of my trained assistants, I fitted and cemented a full mouth, in 20 minutes, taking time to explain every step as I went along.

Within three years the profession had shifted to the new technique. By that time we all were hearing of the diminished number of waiting lists. The real benefactor was the public, because we held the line on orthodontic fees while rapid inflation was occurring throughout our economy. I felt good about this kind of contribution to society.

The third exciting adventure in 1962 was the move into La Colina, my new building. Spanish names of streets were popular and this name was for "the hill", as people from Santa Monica termed climbing Chatauqua Boulevard. I had developed a plan of placing six chairs in a circle with the heads inward and the feet pointing outward. This cut down the need for movement between patients and brought us together in a family atmosphere which I liked. It was easier to manage the work, and everyone helped everyone else. A private room was available for consultation and those requiring privacy. I found, however, that most adults enjoyed being with the children. I treated one lady who was 76 years old in a chair right beside a three-year-old. It was great entertainment for us all.

In the new office I had supplied a teaching room. A large seminar desk was used for conferences with visitors as well as teaching. Patients became accustomed to proudly showing their progress to visiting orthodontists or professors from all parts of the free world. However, the visitors finally became an imposition and it was time for a reassessment concerning visitors, clinical observation, my efficient clinical operation and explaining what I was doing.

One of my new sectographs was installed in the new office. Each morning and each afternoon I took one new TMJ patient. I was therefore carrying on two types of practice at once. More than once professionally I was disappointed because X-ray diagnosis was rejected and continued to go unheeded by the general field of dentistry. Perhaps it was due to two reasons: firstly that there was no proper equipment available to most clinicians, and secondly many dentists had a preoccupation with teeth alone rather than a consideration of the patient as a whole.

Unforeseeable Ventures - 1963

The year 1963 was both alluring and an abomination. I had moved into the new office and was developing some new routines and experimented with lighter forces for orthodontic treatment. In 1962 I had started to write a textbook on the newer methods and curtailed other publications. I made several talks across the country, one being to the alumni at the University of Michigan. Dr. Robert Moyer, from there, had visited Pacific Palisades and felt that my findings and methods should be taught at the graduate level at the university. Therefore, with his recommendation, I put on a two-day seminar in Ann Arbor.

It was Dr. Robert Aldrich and his study group who persuaded me to conduct an advanced course. Several others had inquired about advanced exposure and finally I decided to arrange a seminar for about ten specialists.

I had always abhorred that kind of teaching outside a university, and the thought of private courses. I arranged for the seminar to be given under the auspices of U.C.L.A. Under the arrangements with the school, however, most of the funds were absorbed and after two weeks of solid intensive teaching I had no profit and was exhausted.

That concentrated course, however, turned into a profound discipline for the students. I had no idea of how much there was to offer until it was put together. I spent many long hours in planning and preparing a syllabus. My first private advanced seminar in orthodontics was given in February of 1964.

Poor Investments

The unpleasant part of 1963, however, was problems with three outside investments. In order to lower my taxes I had taken risks, always at the suggestion of personal friends. All, in retrospect, were carrots dangling in front of my face.

The first was in an oil drilling scheme, as mentioned previously, in the Sprayberry Trend in Texas. It had a poor history, which I was to learn about later. It was a neat come-on enticement to make an easy profit and get deduction from taxes. A fellow dentist had become an operator and he and his partner "operated" on many of us.

The second sad investment was in a local laundromat. Until the time I invested never, out of hundreds established, had one been repossessed. Mine was a losing operation which I turned over to a relative. I finally had to abandon it because rent, amortization, and upkeep totals were more than returns.

The third outside interest was in a roofing industry. Southern California is fraught with periodic brush fires. Also, a wood shingled roof was popular. But during the hot Santa Ana winds they dry out and almost explode when hot cinders from fire storms strike. A friend came to me with the deal. They had developed an artificial shingle, more economical to apply than natural and completely fireproof. Samples had been in place for three years and were proven. To someone standing on the street it looked like a natural shingled roof. What a good thing, I thought. I therefore invested moderately in it, but before long I was financing a factory, hiring a manager and starting a production line.

I thought the product was a complete success so I put time and capital into it. We started a night shift to make the material and shipped final product from California all the way to Florida. However, within two years the material became faulty and started to decompose. The cement, if made properly, was stable, but the process they had sold me for mass production did not completely set. It soon became slightly water soluble. I had brought in three orthodontic colleagues with investments, and with the replacement of product at my expense the company had to go out of business. We together lost half a million dollars. A larger roofing firm in the San Francisco area lost twelve million.

I was sued by my friends, even though my risk was major and theirs were minor. I awoke at night in a cold sweat during this trying time. If the product had been stable, our expectations were better than a million dollars in profit per year, the majority of which I had planned to use to build a research institute. But instead I had to work harder than ever to pay off those losses in the next two years. **Thus, in free enterprise it should be understood that there is the chance to win, but also an even greater chance to lose.**

Kennedy's Assassination and Johnson's Megalomania

Many people had originally feared Kennedy's ambition. However, even those who wer suspicious admired his resistance to union pressure and his leadership. But regardless o politics, when an American president was assassinated in 1963 we all rallied, and the whole country mourned the loss. Because in America we have freedom of speech and freedom o ideas, it may sometimes get rather nasty. But whoever orchestrated or masterminded the killing may have had a motive for retaliation or for opportunistic value, or both. In orde to protect the world reputation of our system during the Cold War, no one dared to question the Warren Commission's report which was to be sealed until the year 2039.

Possibly out of sympathy for their murdered president, Congress began to pass many o the bills that Kennedy had recommended. A power-hungry Johnson seized the opportunity and adopted those programs, labeling his movement "The Great Society". It was concluded by many, and talked about publicly, that it was Johnson's ambition to outdo Roosevelt with his "New Deal". He became a champion of human rights, as he also wanted to outdo Lincoln. Those who didn't want to go along with the programs out of feeling for Kennedy were further pressured and strong-armed by Johnson. Some were tempered by Johnson' movement to gain more civil rights for the blacks, which was noble. The Civil Rights bill was really the only program that I could respect Johnson for, and at the time I wondered whether it was a true conviction in his heart, for political expediency, or an expression o his megalomania.

Johnson, in my opinion, was the poorest president we have had during my lifetime. His programs were the launching pad for inflation which ultimately separated our society ever more. He certainly did not represent the best in character that the country had to offer. The Vietnamese War, started under Kennedy, was further complicated by Johnson who seemed completely lost and afraid.

In the 1960s many could feel the whole country slipping as a result of the indecisions and unfairness in asking our young men to go and fight a war on the other side of the earth whose objective was not to win, but simply to "contain communism", which was spreading in Asia like an octopus. Many did not appreciate that we were actually, in fact, conducting wars o attrition. Just as Truman had stopped MacArthur, Johnson put the clamps on the generals in Vietnam. The majority did not heed the words of Goldwater in 1964 when he tried to oust Johnson, despite the fact that there was a mess in Washington greater than anything in our history. With the decay in the national leadership there was also an alarming decay in the attitude of our citizenry toward our own country. No one dared to dig into Johnson's political practices because of the layers of protection he had devised.

Australia - 1964 and the Debates

In 1964 I was invited to go to Australia to lecture at a congress in Perth and conduct a private course as well as performing a critique on the research in their dental schools. The private course was to be for only about 25 clinicians and teachers, as there were not many specialists at that time in the entire country which had a population of only about 10 million

In travelling we made a circle to reach western Australia. It was my first trip through Japan. The specialists then numbered only 20. From Tokyo we went through Hong Kong and visited Macao and then to Bangkok, Thailand, where I lectured at one of the schools We then came through Singapore where I learned of the existence of three sections: one Chinese, one Indian, and one European. I was surprised to see the families watching American TV shows such as "Bonanza" with "voice overs" in their language.

We arrived at Perth during their winter. I was quite taken by the friendliness and the haracter of the Australians. They were loving, energetic in sports, and intent for progress n their country. I have had the opportunity to study the aborigines, who have different jaw nd dental structures from the Caucasian. They are black but are not classified with the lack race.

At the meeting in Perth I had an interesting encounter with Dr. Ballard, who was there rom the Eastman school in England. I had been on a program with him in Copenhagen six ears before. He was steeped in the doctrine of limitations and dogmatic in his stand. Inglish orthodontics, in their socialized scheme, consisted of primary attention to the lignment and position of the upper front teeth only. I could understand the English roblems after the war. Their idea was to do something to enable their population to "get y socially" rather than to aim at any perfection for the individual.

In the end, however, they argued that this was as good as anything that could be done. strongly rejected that proposition. Ballard therefore argued the cause for a simple emovable retainer-like appliance for the mass population. I, on the other hand, defended ull orthodontic correction, growth forecasting, possible skeletal change, depression of eeth in their sockets, and the possibility of changes in oral function.

We clashed rather dramatically. He visited different cities, addressing local groups, mphasizing what couldn't be done. Within days I followed, telling and showing the xciting possibilities. I had no malice, it was just a matter of disagreement without ersonality disapproval. Almost 30 years later these debates are still legendary in Australia.

By the time I reached Sydney, after Perth, Adelaide and Melbourne, the news of the rovocative disagreements had preceded me. I had stopped in Adelaide to visit the school nd laboratories of Dr. Brown and Dr. Barrett who were studying the Aborigine, and I also pent time with Dr. Raymond Begg in his office. Begg had made some interesting daptations to a particular attachment and was treating patients rapidly. I had met him reviously in Washington, D.C. in 1960. But I found a conflict because of the high ncidence of extraction of teeth proposed by his ideology, again based on the limitation octrine. Now I had two people to debate.

I also stopped at the University of Melbourne and spent time with a well known bone esearcher, Dr. Eldon Storey, and with an orthodontist who had visited my office, Sir Kenneth Adamson.

The Australian population at that time had an appalling incidence of decay. Most children ad lost their first permanent molars before age 10. The schools were dominated by oral urgeons and prosthedontists to make artificial teeth. Function of artificial teeth requires ilateral contact during chewing movements, but the natural teeth should not, according to he studies of our best scholars. They had adapted the prosthetic idea to the natural teeth n their teaching and practice. This prompted, therefore, still more debates among the eneral dentists and even among the professors.

Prediction of the Profession

Australians like competition. Almost every orthodontist in Sydney turned out for my ecture and a banquet. When I had finished the questions were explosive. At the conclusion, Dr. Thornton-Taylor, also an old friend, who had visited me in California, asked me where thought the profession was going in the next two decades. Among other things, I said that ome interested person would come along and adapt all our ideas to the computer! We had ot taken advantage yet of the technology available and I thought its time had come.

The very next year, 1965, I broke through my own anxiety with this tool and used it for esearch. In 1959 we had started a study at the Prosthetics Department at Wadsworth

General Veterans Hospital in West Los Angeles on age changes in the human face and jaws. They had a large computer with statisticians from U.C.L.A. working with them. We were permitted to share time and we set up some data processing which was my first computer experience. This computer experience with W. Dixon and F. Massey became a springboard to other more advanced application of the computer.

Professional Foot-dragging - 1965

In 1965 I was asked to present a program on the clinical implications of the jaw joint, again at the national meeting which was being held in Dallas. I tried to explain the regressive changes that occur with degeneration of this joint located just in front of the ear. I further showed how it could be affected by abnormal clenching even in children. I was still trying to bring this joint to the routine consciousness of the profession. The applause was kind but unenthusiastic. As I left the hall, one colleague stopped me and said, "That was one of the most brilliant lectures I ever heard on the subject." "Thank you very much," I replied. But he went on. "There's only one problem -- you were the only one who understood what you were talking about." "Thanks a lot," I said, "that makes me a lousy teacher, doesn't it?" I published the paper in 1966, and more than 25 years later it's still ahead of its time.

Also by the 1965 convention, I noted that most orthodontists no longer talked about waiting lists. Custom construction of the appliances had given way to having a variety of bands supplied by manufacturers. I had likened the orthodontist's clinic now to the store where -- unlike the old shoe cobbler's store -- a person could be fitted for shoes once an adequate supply was available in sizes and shapes. This and other developments were forces that made orthodontics more feasible, affordable by much more of the population, and a giant step in our culture. Preformed bands for the front teeth have since given way to bonding directly to the tooth.

The Master Study

Another hallmark year was 1966. Through the emplacement of metal implants, Dr. Arne Bjork of Copenhagen had demonstrated different patterns in growth mechanisms in the lower jaws. With his work as a frame of reference I developed some new anatomical landmarks for use in diagnosis and forecasting. The idea emerged that a major research project be conducted on growth of children. Dr. Robert Sloan (whom I had worked with at U.C.L.A.) had located a mathematician at Hughes Aircraft, Mr. Robert Shulhof. He had also located a computer programmer, Mr. Jack Chew.

I committed financially to a pilot study to test some of the new anthropologic points and planes I had promulgated. Acquiring computer data on a group of 20 children, we found the measurements supported a larger and more intensive study.

With the availability of the computer (and a team), a major research project was envisaged. We needed cephalometric X-rays on a significant sample of untreated growing children. We wanted to study the make-up of the skull and face but also determine the best method to describe the structures, measure its growth and test forecasting methods. All this was necessary before we could consider offering computerization as a commercial laboratory.

I inquired regarding the availability of growth X-rays from six institutions, but no one would risk lending their material. I was forced, therefore, to look back through our personal files to see what could be found from a personal collection. Some patients recorded years before had elected not to be treated. Others were found not to be candidates for treatment at young ages. Some were my own children and relatives who had had no treatment.

I sent out letters to parents of children requesting that they come back to the office at no expense but simply for research purposes. We were able to accumulate records on 70 children. From these we selected 20 males and 20 females for the large study. The 40 subjects had, on average, five years of development. Thirty is considered by most statisticians to be an adequate sample and ten more were added as a safety factor against potential ridicule.

The Financing of Research

My personal funds had been exhausted with my losses in investments as mentioned. Financing was needed to obtain the information and record it on punch cards (as was the computer state of the art then). This would take a technician and money for computer time, over several months. We needed a sponsor. And after a search, Mr. Martin Brusse, President of Rocky Mountain Orthodontics, against the opinion of his advisors, decided to support the project to the extent of $300,000.

I personally traced all the lateral and frontal X-rays at the beginning and final times and rechecked them in great detail. Tracings for measurement included the skull, teeth, nose, lips and chin, and the vertebrae of the neck. Three hundred sixty-two (362) calculations were made on each patient, made at the beginning and at the end of a growth period (totalling 724). The differences in the values between the start and the end were also determined by the computer.

The data was received from the computer on mat-sized computer sheets assembled in a book that was four inches thick. In all, there were 400,000 measurements to consider that took months to analyze. In addition, after the data was available, I rectified all of the measurements with any previous studies reported in the literature, which took several more months to process.

Climbing the Mountain and Being Hauled Down

The years 1966, 1967, and 1968 were spent in that search. In order to precipitate conclusions in late 1968, I needed to be alone. Earlier in that decade I had built a small chalet at Lake Gregory which is near Lake Arrowhead up in the mountains above San Bernardino. I called it the Rick-Rack. I enjoyed getting away and relaxing with the children, but this time I had to be alone. Therefore, provisioned with cold cuts, cheese and sourdough bread, a large can of coffee and some fruit, I proceeded to the mountains. I laid out all the material on the floor of the living room, and concentrated for three days almost without stopping. That program as developed has stood for over 25 years.

The famous Blue Book on "Introducing Computerized Cephalometrics" was presented in May of 1969. The national meeting of the American Association of Orthodontists at The Fountainbleau in Miami Beach, Florida. We had formed a company, trained a cadre of analysts, purchased the necessary equipment, and had started a laboratory service. Subsequently much of my time and energy was spent in the development of programs and adaptation of the computer.

I had previously consulted colleagues regarding the feasibility of such a contribution for the profession and was, in general, supported. Therefore, I was not at all prepared for the onslaught of broadside condemnations resulting from the introduction of the tool for clinical use. I collected, through friends and through conversations, two pages of statements deriding the procedure. Editorials were written in journals condemning the movement. It was a "gimmick for suckers", it was "the greatest hoax ever perpetrated on the profession", it was "meant only for weak minds", it was "a reduction of all society to a number", and it was "one person telling the rest of the profession exactly what they must do". Most ungenerous of all, I was branded a "commercial whore".

All of these statements, of course, were made out of ignorance. As I learned later, hostility is a product of feelings of inferiority. Colleagues lacked the understanding of the actual working of the process. What was really accomplished was the providing of an access to information regarding a patient's skull in three dimensions that had never been available before. It contained new trustworthy methods of measurement and a new higher information base. It was, however, the victim of xenophobia. I concluded they may have intuitively considered this movement a threat to their own interest in teaching the fundamentals.

Europe Again and the Mediterranean - 1967

While the computer research was going on my work was, to my surprise, being noticed in Europe. In 1967 I was invited for a series of lectures. I had not been there for nine years. The invitation and planning was engineered by Dr. Juan Canut, a dear friend in Madrid. This became a planned trip, and I made it the opportunity to take my family for an educational tour. My wife and two daughters, Robin and Gale, preceded me for two months on a church group trip. They visited many sites in Europe. Craig, now twelve, attended a summer camp in Colorado. We therefore leased out our home at the end of Rimmer Avenue in Pacific Palisades and I moved into the Riviera Country Club for two months while the rest of the family was away. During that time I had the opportunity to practice golf almost daily for a short time, and lowered my handicap down to 6. I was shooting regularly in the 70s, which for me was a major accomplishment.

During those two months I was also very busy preparing lectures for courses in Madrid, Copenhagen, Stockholm and Paris. I was to wind up my tour in London.

The five-day course in Madrid was at a private club. There were about 40 in attendance, and this is where I met Winston Senior from Manchester, who has been a dear friend ever since. I sent a syllabus in advance for translation into Spanish. Organization for the whole trip, together with the research projects, left little time for relaxation except for occasional golf practice.

We planned previously to start a family vacation on a cruise ship through the Greek Islands and up through the Dardanelles to Istanbul and the Bosporus. I would recommend this highly to anyone, because it is the bed of our modern culture.

Greek Islands and Ephesus

I flew with Craig to Athens to meet the family and Barbara, a friend of Robin's, and together the six of us embarked the next morning on the "Argonaut". I had studied the cultures, history, and geography of that area in the past. The Minoan culture, centered on Crete, had dominated the Mediterranean at one time (about 3000 B.C.) Eruption of the volcano that formed Santorini had changed the area in a 500-mile radius. Rhodes was the destination of many of the knights during the Crusades. I enjoyed the uniqueness of the markets and the mosques in Istanbul. But the most memorable single experience was at Ephesus in Turkey, near the coast just below Izmir.

I almost missed it. We had travelled to Turkey from Rhodes, docked, and boarded a bus to visit the ruins at Ephesus. My stomach was slightly upset for some reason, and I almost stayed on the bus, but after some consideration I thought I would feel no worse by going through another ruin. We walked around a large hill and approached the ancient city from its top. How elated I was! Looking downward I could see the deeply grooved marble steps all the way to the city's center. From the attrition of the street I could imagine the traffic, the people together with their donkeys. On each side were terraces where it was said that homes once stood. Ephesus was once a center for thousands.

As we proceeded down the old streets, the remains of old buildings became more evident. On the left or west side was the courthouse, or the state officials' building, and the library. Immediately across from it was the brothel. What a convenient location and cosy arrangement that was! In its walls could be seen the niches with still-visible carbon from the lamps. On the floor were inlaid marble mosaics still brilliant in their colors. The street was paved in marble and sunken between the buildings. Further down and to the west at one block's distance were the crumbled pillars of the large marketplace. I pictured in my mind this once thriving trade center. Continuing another block, on the east side of the street we came to the amphitheatre which could seat thousands. The marble seats were still present. I climbed the stairs to the stage and stood there transfixed for the moment. Here was where the Apostle Paul had preached to the Ephesians, later writing them letters trying to win them away from their gods and goddesses and telling them more of the life and teachings of Christ.

It was completely sobering. I was drawn to stay for a while. I sent Craig up to the last row in the amphitheatre and he could hear me plainly as I talked with a normal speaking voice. It was"beatae memoriae".

Supposedly Mary, the mother of Jesus, was buried at Ephesus on a small mountain just above the old ruins, where now stands a church. I wondered how such a prosperous city could have existed 30 miles inland. The answer was found. At one time, the city had been a port on a harbor, and ships could dock there. However, major storms in Asia Minor had filled the harbor in with silt. Swamplands formed, mosquitoes had brought malaria, and the town was abandoned. It further experienced the ravages of earthquakes and desert sands.

Successes

After concluding our tour, and there was much more that could be reflected on, the children were sent home to return to school, and my teaching began. I tried to impart the knowledge I had accumulated in research, experimentation and innovation.

While in Europe for the next two weeks, I tried to formulate a plan for a two-hour talk in London. I remembered my two confrontations with Dr. Ballard in 1958 and 1964. It was he who represented much of the English thinking. How was I to manage that limitation dogma based on what I had been taught myself as a graduate student 20 years before? Finally, I was prompted by my experiences in Ephesus, which gave me a cue. The spectacle of crumbling pillars of the buildings and the marketplace was used as a symbol for the crumbling pillars of canons, maxims and rules I had been taught as the bedrock in my profession. I listed 28 basic beliefs that I could no longer accept and, starting my lecture with these "crumbling pillars", addressed each point as I went along.

The meeting was in a hospital, and the room was one of those old-style theatres where each row is narrow and stacked almost like a balcony over the one in front. As I addressed the full room it was necessary to look upward at a wall of shoulders and faces mostly set in defiance with their arms folded and a grim look on their faces as if to say, "Show me." Impress them I did. Convince them I did not.

The Professional Split

On returning to the U.S. from Europe I realized that a separation would have to be made between my thinking and the disciplines in which I had been trained. Later on, I divided the field of orthodontics into three distinct groups, the oldest being the so-called Functional Group, or the idea of Functionalism. Opposed to that was the "traditional" ideology which was an outgrowth of the fixed appliance movement that started in the 1920s. With it was a movement to wait until age 10 or later or until the permanent teeth were present. Manipulating of all the teeth at one time was to be conducted with rapidity. This gave rise to the practice of removing some teeth in a high percentage of patients. The third was our movement, labeled Bio-Progressive, which had its roots in 1950 when I had been compelled to make a departure from both of the earlier ideologies. Parts of both had a place in our new philosophy.

The public was becoming confused by the different dogmas. Further, one practitioner utilizing one belief would become emotional and deride his fellow-colleague. In that conflict, it became an open door for litigation, to the delight of all the lawyers. I could see it all coming.

In 1968 I wrote a two-part paper on public and professional relations for the specialty. The purpose was to help clear the air and to try to lead the profession in a more common direction. In effect, without saying it in so many words, I had to divorce myself, not from my personal relations with many of my colleagues, but from many of their theories and ideas on a professional basis.

The tendency in any kind of divorce is toward hard feelings, and difficulty in understanding. After that meeting, many friends phoned, requesting me to come to their societies to defend my views. In fact, I was asked to document results several times more completely than they were accustomed to documenting for the traditional views.

In those years, as always, orthodontics was claimed to be very expensive. However, my overhead was 80-85% when I added the expense of all of the study that I was doing. Robin, my older daughter, worked part time and made the statement at our dinner table one evening, "Mom, you might as well go ahead and spend some of Dad's money, because if you don't he'll spend it all for research."

I suppose I became a little huffy at times, and somewhat stern in my opinions, because I had put forth so much effort and was being challenged by people who spent no time in research. However, I was also challenged by many of the intellectuals in the schools, and it was necessary to do the best job I could accumulating statistical data for the defense of the new findings.

The Foundation for Orthodontic Research

During the 1950s the "baby boomers" (children born after the war from 1945 to the early 1950s) were growing into the age for orthodontics. I was working often at U.C.L.A. planning the new Dental School. In view of projections of population, to reiterate, on the basis of five million new births each year, within the next two decades we would need to build a new dental school for each one then in existence, or double the output of each then existing. National meetings were held to discuss handling the anticipated problem. It was agreed by committees on education to start preceptorship programs. However, I was almost a lone dissenter.

I had looked at the population curve in 1958, and it didn't look possible for its continuation. This feeling was based on my experiences with biologic growth curves. I was also aware of the potential increase in productivity of each office with only part of the new technologies. I wasn't concerned about orthodontists' abilities to handle larger numbers of patients. My efforts were in a direction to persuade the profession to diagnose better, to treat earlier and more efficiently, and to finish with a higher quality.

Abruptly, and once again reiterating, four things happened almost simultaneously. First, the country went into a recession in 1959 and young couples couldn't afford children. The second change was the development of the pill and the I.U.D. The third was the trend in the 1960s, on a social basis, to delay marriage and put off raising a family. In other words, there was a change in the attitude toward a larger family. The fourth change to affect new births was the looser view on abortions. All these made a remarkably sharp alteration in the direction of the birth curve. It had been headed toward the five million level but instead of continuing to rise, it started to decline toward the three million new birth range.

Preceptorship Training

Preceptorship training programs were adopted. Some clinicians with little advanced training took younger dentists into their offices as seemingly cheap labor. To train an orthodontic specialist properly takes time away from a practice. Nevertheless, in 1959 I agreed to accept a young man under a preceptorship, Dr. Ruel Bench, in an attempt to train him with some in-depth exposure. I developed his program by starting with the basic sciences of anatomy, physiology, histology, embryology and growth and development of the head and neck. This plan became known to others in the profession, and one day I received a call from Dr. George Hahn from San Francisco who was chairman of the Pacific Coast committee on preceptorship education. He asked me to train others in preceptorship programs in Los Angeles and give them the proper background since I was already conducting a course for Bench. I agreed and composed a syllabus and took eight others for every Thursday until I felt they had completed a decent requirement. Each was to work up the bones of the skull well enough to give it at a recitation in order to appreciate the make-up of the human face and skull. Some seemed to resent such instruction as an imposition. -- After all, "learning science does not move teeth".

When later in 1963 groups of practicing clinicians asked me to put on special advanced training courses for them I already had much of a syllabus or outline developed. The preceptorship program was dropped in 1962 when training was moved into the different Dental Schools, opening up Orthodontic residencies for post-graduate education.

Each of my advanced classes had from 15 to 25 people. After the first five classes people wanted more information. A work-shop was organized in 1967 where about 90% of all the previous students were assembled. In 1968 we met again, and the Foundation for Orthodontic Research (FOR) was organized in San Francisco, and has been ongoing since.

One year the group approached $100,000 in donations to various schools or institutions for research. In addition, in 1990 almost $70,000 was collected to maintain, expand, and house more efficiently my library and collection of research materials. Here is a preamble I wrote for the group, which may have some far-reaching implications:

"An organization worth forming should be planned to endure. Man always looks for a leader to dispense the last word on matters of interest and there is no shortage of egoists desiring an army of followers. The result is a cult with the slightest deviation from the master's mind a strict taboo. These die in the shadow of a dominant character because individual dignity demands a share of identity.

"The real man can never follow another blindly by continued second guessing. A teacher cannot measure his success until his students surpass him. Do his students creatively think, write and talk? -- each becoming himself, on his own initiative, a friend to join in search for truth?

"Through the development of this kind of thought, a movement will extend to heights undreamed. Human energy will abound from the immense power generated by the desire of man to serve man out of love, conscience, and gratification of higher principles. This increases personal potentiality for awareness, perception, and consciousness -- the foundation for continued success and progress."

Nixon's Victory in 1968

In the 1968 election, foreseeing the handwriting on the wall, considering his health and possibly in fear of his own personal welfare, Johnson decided not to run. Hubert Humphrey from Minnesota was put up as the candidate to run now against Nixon, who was running for the presidency a second time. The cloud of suspicion around Kennedy's death, and a possible Johnson connection, continued. Bobby Kennedy probably would have been nominated, and elected, but he also was killed, possibly by a crackpot. Historians say, however, that Johnson hated Bobby even more than he hated Jack Kennedy. Why he wasn't protected better, no one knows.

In 1968 the U.S.S.R. stamped out a liberal reform movement in Czechoslovakia. This was after a cultural revolution had taken place in China. The war in Vietnam was still dragging on. Johnson was of little help to his Vice-President, Hubert Humphrey, and Nixon was nominated by the Republicans a second time in 1968. Nixon had previously dealt with the Chinese and perhaps was the only one in a position to relate to them now. While Humphrey was quite popular in the Congress and very personable, he was in the position of having to defend the existing Johnson record which people felt left much to be desired. Johnson had stripped Humphrey of as much influence as possible. I felt an undercurrent in the country that again a shift in leadership was wanted. By now Nixon had suffered two losses (one in California for governor and one to Kennedy by some very questionable votes from Texas and Illinois), and he seemed ready to play hardball. He won.

The Computer Introduced Commercially

By the spring of 1969 we introduced the computer as a commercial enterprise which disturbed still further many in the field. Like so many new developments it was different and shocking to many. But I had to persist; after all, I was accustomed to criticism and derision.

* * *

At the beginning of the 1960s, when my children were younger, whenever I would sing in public or be friendly to a stranger they would be embarrassed and tell me to stop. When they asked a question and I would answer with an in-depth explanation they would be impatient for a simple reply. "Don't give us a lecture, Dad, just give us the answer," they would say. But ten years later Robin was 20, Gale was 18 and Craig was 15. They still had questions, but now when they asked it was, "Dad, give us the **real** answer." They wanted to know about history, they wanted to know reasons for the answer. They had grown intellectually and were free to think. This was the family and professional climate and American society in preparation for the 1970s.

10

CULTURAL DETERIORATION AND FRUSTRATION
(1971 - 1979)

Introduction

As a biologic scientist of sorts, I continued to be interested in all the sciences. I posed questions in the 1970s regarding where research was taking mankind in biology, nuclear science and electronics. Arguments stemmed from issues of morality, environment, peace of mind, war and peace, and even individual survival. Great focus was also put on social problems which often were biologic in nature, such as population control, drug abuse, biologic warfare, genetic alteration, and degradation of the environment.

The title for this chapter was selected because of my observations and impressions during those years from a perspective of conditions shaping American society. The stage for that decade is perhaps best expressed in a February 1970 editorial in *The Christian Science Monitor* on "The Impact of Research". To quote:

> "It is good that natural scientists are increasingly concerned about their impact on society. Some forty sessions of the American Association for the Advancement of Science were devoted to the relation of the sciences to the community. In earlier years there was much less heed: power plants were developed, factories built, without thought for air or water pollution. The new biology council aims to post warnings all along the path of today's scientific revolution.
>
> "The day of the withdrawn, isolated scientist is past. He is moving into the political arena and into the brotherhood of concerned people."

Many major situations had caused emotional responses and affected our country, with a kind of Alvin Tofler culture shock in reverse. These were: (1) drug abuse and the drug economy; (2) the Vietnam War continuation, the defeat, the lie and the splitting of society; (3) the start of the living room war through live television; (4) Watergate and the ideologic embarrassment; (5) hostage-taking and exposure of our military vulnerability; (6) the oil shock, gas lines, and the government's ineptness; (7) inflation combined with a slow economy (stagflation); (8) the rebellion of students against affluence and bigness; (9)

continuation of the Cold War; (10) the economic emergence of Japan and Germany; (11) the start of decline of blue-collar jobs; (12) the public recognition of an American work police force; (13) suffering of an empire complex which obscured reality; (14) the "Yom Kippur War" in 1973 which further deepened the Cold War; (15) the Shah's fall and American outrage over incidents at our embassy in Iran; (16) abortion law disagreements (17) changing attitudes with the temptation to place blame on others rather than ourselves and (18) the emergence of peace movements.

I shall attempt to discuss my concerns and what I learned in some of these areas. Some are essentially scientifically correct and some claim poetic license for teaching purposes

Society Defined

The writings of Robert Ardrey have been more fascinating to me than perhaps those of any other author. In 1970 he published his third major work, "The Social Contract", where he took issue with the conclusions of Jean-Jacques Rousseau whose writings were published in 1762, one century before Darwin's time. Ardrey faults Rousseau's vision of primal man as asocial. Rousseau, first of all, could not know of the contributions of the natural sciences in the 20th century. His second major mistake was the assumption that in a state of nature man was always happy and good. He further could not have known that the desire to own private property was not an "invented curse" but an animal imperative far antedating man. Ardrey wrote,

"The catastrophe is not that Rousseau was wrong but that after two centuries we are wrong; that biological advances since Darwin's time have penetrated our thinking not at all; that fashions of thought today are as firmly grounded in the Rousseau fallacies as if the natural sciences had never existed."

Ardrey also stated:

"Order and disorder are intimately entwined. Without that degree of order which only society can provide, the vulnerable individual perishes. Yet without that degree of disorder tolerating and promoting to fullest development the diversity of its members, society must wither and vanish in the competitions of group selection."

Ardrey further defined society as "a group of unequal beings organized to meet common needs". He reasoned that inequality must be regarded as a first law of social material in human or other animal societies. The second law should be equality of opportunity, in that "every vertebrate born is granted equal opportunity to display his genius or to make a fool out of himself". Finally, Ardrey explains,

"The just society, as I see it, is one in which sufficient order protects members, whatever their diverse endowments, and sufficient disorder provides every individual with full opportunity to develop his genetic endowment, whatever that may be. It is this balance of order and disorder, varying·in rigor according to environmental hazard, that I think of as the social contract."

Also in 1970 Alvin Toffler published "Future Shock", in which he analyzed many of the forces at work in the world at large in science and technology.

Culture Defined

"Culture" may be considered to be an improvement or a refinement of the mind, the morals, the taste or the complete enlightenment of a civilization. Cultural traits are the features of a given group transmitted by habit patterns or learned behavior rather than by genetic determination. If lower animals can learn from adults in their groups it can be said, to that end, even they have cultures. It is strange that elephants seem to cover their dead with branches as if in a burial ceremony. But most scholars consider culture to be distinctly human. Conceptually the function of "culture" has served for the production of order and the progression of a people toward civilization. Otherwise the rule of the jungle would lead to destruction.

If mankind developed on the savannahs of Africa in competition with other animals several factors had to operate if they were to find a meal without becoming a meal for another predator. Man had to be an aggressor. He had to be a killer. He needed the protection of a group for the gathering of seeds, nuts and roots. He was forced to display altruism. He had to be cooperative. He had to communicate. He had to be taught to make tools. Finally, he needed some sort of order in his society.

Primitive societies are becoming rare as we approach the 21st century. But we can learn about basic cultural characteristics from what is thought to be the most primitive, the Australian aborigine. They were nomadic and could survive in independent families for weeks at a time. But they came together in their parties, called "oshibori", and decorated their bodies with ochre and made their music with a "digeradoo" as they danced around fires near the "billabong". They were therefore social from the start. Early Africans and early Native American Indian cultures had their art which has been used to differentiate periods in the past.

Cultural anthropology is the study of the sum total of the attainments and activities of a specific group in a specific period which includes the tools, the handicrafts, the architecture, the agriculture, economics, music, the language and to some degree the mythology of a period. Records of these remain in the physical features of the land and in the artifacts which are of human origin. Thus physical anthropology, cultural or behavioral anthropology and archeology are somewhat allied. Society as a whole for each culture can be divided, for study, into the social sciences and into philosophy, art, and science.

The Present and Prediction of the Future

In order to predict the future it is best to understand the principles that have worked in the past, and also be able to determine and analyze the trends of the present. If I can draw on developments in my profession and perhaps apply them to society as a whole, we may consider the present as the era between 1970 and 1990, or thereabouts.

Attitudes can be changed overnight by the mass media of television and radio. Satellites encircle the planet, and today we have the capability of instant communication with hundreds of TV channels from every developed country on the face of the earth. Telephone viewing is just around the corner. Newspeople continuously seek out extraordinary happenings, and indeed do their bit to shape public opinion by way of their own commentary.

At the present moment, shortly after the clock has turned to 1993, I can reflect that I have within the past year lectured in the major sections of the United States, I have put on courses in Mexico and Canada, I was in Europe four times on lecture trips, and spent almost two months teaching in Australia. I also engaged in courses for two groups of students from Japan. All this has helped me to be in the unique position of not being just a tourist for idle amusement, but has promoted intimate contact with people in many different communities around the world.

A World Sickness

As I write this there is a sickness of the economy on a world basis. Everywhere I have been the politicians out of office, or in the minority of a political system, are blaming the party or person in power for their country's condition. I found it true of England, other parts of Europe and Canada. I was present when Hawke was battling Keating in Australia. It seems as though, as history has shown, occasionally the whole world tends to get sick. It is as if the world economy goes on a spending binge and, like the over-indulged alcoholic, vomits. We are not yet to the retching stage but maybe the world economy will have to undergo it before it will get well.

Perhaps it was this world condition that attacked the weakest systems first, hence communism and socialism were the first to suffer and became the most ill.

But economics, while major, is only one part of a culture. Language, education, philosophy, sociology, the attitudes of people, politics, government and religion together with resources are also included. In addition, art and science are a definitive part of culture. Today the role of women in society has also taken a dramatic change.

Thus, when cultural "deterioration" is considered, almost 30 different subjects become involved. It would be impossible for this author to cover all of these, even with just his own impressions, without the help of experts. I am not a historian, nor an economist, nor a politician, but I am an educator, and in order to be the best that I can be I think it is prudent to keep my feet on the ground and employ my peripheral vision to its maximum to see where education relates to the whole state of local and world affairs.

Drugs May Kill

During World War II, probably as a measure to reduce tension, alcohol came into a more noticeable usage in America. It was not only beer and wine, but also hard liquor that found use in abundance. This was a growing habit that became excessive. Traffic deaths are America's most senseless killer, and statistics show that essentially one-half of fatalities are connected to drunken driving. Younger people in the age range of 16 to 24 are more frequently involved in fatal crashes. As if that were not enough, by the 1960s other drugs were entering the scene, possibly as a result of the affluence of the country.

In 1939 to 1941, when I was playing football at Indiana, drugs and steroids were never seen. But in 1970 they were popular. The tragedies of heroin addiction were well known. Use of marijuana was becoming the "in thing" and more commonplace. Marijuana was more cumulative in the body, and perhaps the eventual boredom with it led to a lowering of resistance to other drugs. LSD had been a drug experimentally used in medicine, as had been the barbiturates, for relieving people's anxieties. But despite the fact that cocaine damage and addiction had a long history, which I had learned about in undergraduate school, many insisted that cocaine was not addictive and was, in fact, a useful drug. Worst of all, perhaps, was the incidence of juveniles being exposed to the availability of illegal drugs in the school environment.

By the late 1960s I sensed a change in some of my local young patients. It involved their self-respect. They were more uncooperative, their mouths would be dirty, they would come in dressed in slovenly attire, and they had become very passive in their personalities. I really became concerned when some of these children of the finest families in Pacific Palisades began to take their lives, or to lose their lives under the influence of a variety of drugs.

In 1968 I had a consultation in my office with Jon, a young lad of eight or nine years of age who was there with only his father. After I had presented his case, and the course of treatment had been laid out, the terms of payment had been agreed upon, I turned to the boy and said, "Now, son, whatever you do, don't think you're going to get smart and start playing with all of these drugs." I was moved to say this because just an hour before Harriet Reisser, my office manager, had placed on my desk a newspaper clipping announcing the death of a young man of 20 who had taken his life in a state of depression after having taken drugs. He left a note to that effect, so there was no doubt that he had been using drugs.

I showed the clipping to Jon and further explained, "I treated this boy when he was just your age, when he was just as sweet and just as innocent as you are. And his orthodontic problem was even similar to yours. Now he's dead. He took his own life. How do you think his father and mother must feel?"

I knew his parents well, in fact his father was a member of our Rotary Club. They were prominent members of the community. So it wasn't because this boy had a poor family environment. Rather, it was the fact that he had gotten caught up in the culture.

With tears in my eyes I then turned to the father, and said, "Now this is the twelfth child that I have lost that I have treated. I didn't lose any to the Vietnamese War, I didn't lose any to the Korean War, but I've now lost twelve to the drug war. What do you think is the most serious?"

The father, Mr. Henry Greenberg, then responded, "Can that be really true?" I said, "It sure is." He said, "Well, you didn't know it, but I am the medical editor for the *Los Angeles Times*. I am the only member of Alcoholics Anonymous who was never an alcoholic. I go there so I can write articles and explain to the readers what goes on and help in any way I can. Maybe there is something we could do together in this regard."

So I asked, "You are a resident here in Pacific Palisades?" I said, "Would you like to become a member of the Rotary Club and see if we can work on a project for the community on drug abuse?" He said, "I'd like to learn more about it." I said, "Will you be my guest next Tuesday?" He looked at his book and said, "Yes, I think I can make that." And with that I proposed Henry Greenberg as a member, which was quickly effected, and we set about to establish a project.

Mr. Robert Abernathy, who was anchor newsman for Channel 4 for NBC, was also a member of the Club. I had treated his daughter, and we were good friends. The three of us met in my office as a committee and made the decision to attempt to produce a pamphlet or booklet that would inform young people regarding the nature of drugs and their biologic actions upon the nervous system and the body in general. Henry went to U.C.L.A. and with the help of Dr. Wallace Winters, a pharmacologist, wrote the text. Frank Armitage, who had helped me earlier with illustrations for a movie on swallowing, did the art work. Our pamphlet, produced in 1971, outlined the different drugs, and drawings by Armitage of nerves and the brain helped explain the varying ways the drugs work. In some drugs, when there is an over-stimulation of the nerve, the cell body can actually be blown out and be destroyed. And some drugs are, in fact, a slow chemical suicide.

Our Rotary Club produced 20,000 of these little books for distribution to local schools. I sent them to several other clubs for exposure to other schools.

Action of Drugs

Because drugs have become so much a part of our culture and because there is so little understanding among laymen about them, I feel compelled, as a teacher, to share with the reader some simple facts about drugs. Perhaps it would be informative to briefly overview the actions of some of these drugs.

To fully understand the drugs it is necessary to understand the parts of the body on which they act, primarily the nerves.

The tissues of the body, in general, consist of four types. The first is **epithelial**, which makes up the skin, nails, hair, enamel of the teeth and lining of the glands. The second is **connective tissue**, which composes the bones and joints and the fascia together with a strata which contains fluids to carry oxygen and nutrients to all the cells. A third tissue is **muscle**, which powers the limbs and body, gives elasticity to the vessels and gut, and pumps the heart. But all are dependent on the fourth tissue, the **nerve**, which links all the others and provides the master control in the brain and ganglia.

Most laymen think of the brain as a part separate from the nerve, and are only concerned when a headache is experienced. The nerve is considered to be something like a wire carrying an electric charge which connects the various parts of the body with the brain. Some even think of it only for functioning of the sensation of pain, such as a pin prick, a tooth cavity or a cut or bruise. They realize the nerve is more than that when a foot goes to sleep or a nerve is banged with a "crazy bone" as the elbow is hit. But the nerve is a living organism -- a cell.

The brain is a massive connection of little nerves itself. Like any other cell, the nerve has several components. These consist of an outer membrane, a nucleus containing its genetic material, a fluid, mitochondria, for the production of energy and other units for its life and function. Any cell is therefore a sack within a sack -- sort of a water-filled balloon within a water-filled balloon.

We have individual cells in our body that are transported in our blood, one of which is called the neutrophil (short for polymorphonuclear leukocyte) which wander around as scavengers looking for debris or foreign material to engulf and destroy. Therefore, each cell can be in this sense an independent animal, and we are each a massive assembly of independent living organisms. How are they connected? How do all these little individual animals (or cells) know what the others are doing? Well, this is where the nerve comes in!

Many of the animals (cells) have a short life and are replaced by the development and growth of new cells. This takes place through a series of cells developing from a primitive type transforming into a more mature type, the forerunners being called "progenitor" cells. Therefore when some cells, such as skin or connective tissues, are injured or die as a result of their normal lifespan, they are replaced as a natural process. This is how a cut heals and the normal skin is shed, which is seen grossly in the healing of sunburn.

The nerve vastly differs in this process, however, because after the first few months of life **it cannot replace itself**. Once this tiny animal is killed it is not replaced! But the nerve is also quite different in other aspects. Its membrane is pulled out into a long, long thin "tube" with a sort of delta-shaped end with finger-like formations on one end, like the delta at the end of a river. Somewhere along the nerve it bulges out into a "body" to contain the "nucleus", together with the life or "guts" for the little animals' function.

Each nerve produces its own energy and serves as a tiny battery to produce an electrical charge. Its electricity is produced by chemistry. Certain minerals are used for electrolyte balance for the normal function of the nerve. Inside the nerve (tube) there are certain chemicals such as sodium (Na), chlorine (Cl) and protein materials (amnions). Each nerve is surrounded by a thin layer of fluid which contains potassium (K). The balance between the fluid on the outside with that of the inside maintains the physical equilibrium of the cell.

The nerve has sensitivity at its nerve ending. It has the capacity to become excited and when stimulated it starts a change in the chemical balance of the cell. Some sodium electrical charges leave the cell as potassium charges enter. This carries an electrical charge in a wave along the nerve like a burning fuse. The nerve is therefore a "conductor" of electricity (physics), but this is accomplished with chemicals (chemistry). Thus, the nerve tube also transports chemicals. Nerves therefore have sensitivity, conductivity, and transportability.

The nerves are connected into a "nervous system". Each nerve has a receiving end and a dispatching end. The antennae (receiver) end picks up (senses) signals and transports them to the next nerve in a network. To hand over the information it goes through a "switch" called the synapse. This is not a direct connection but is a close contact like the clasp of hands in a handshake. It is a wet handshake, because between the nerve endings is also a fluid containing chemicals which act as a tiny pump to push the information through to the receiver in the next nerve.

Some large nerves going to the legs and arms may be long and covered or "insulated" like a hot water pipe wrapped in a foam-like material. These are called A fibers. Other nerves (B type) are smaller and are unprotected. Other nerves are very fine (C type) and conduct sensations much more slowly. But at the end (on its axon, meaning axis, away) it spreads out like fingers to connect with other nerves.

In this manner, the nerves are connected in one network, the central nervous system, which is also connected to a second, the automatic system called "autonomic". Everything, so far, is relatively simple until the brain is reached. Here the same nerve plan is present but the nerves are shorter and each nerve is connected with several other nerves in a computer-like arrangement of ten billion cells. These are independent little animals connected to each other sort of like a bee hive or an ant hill. (Insects are connected chemically with substances called pheromones. The brain cells are connected both physically and chemically.) When all these animals work together they can record and remember ten thousand million million or ten quadrillion bits of information. This is a massive physical-chemical plant, and with its fluid only weighs three to four pounds.

Naturally, such a vital and important part of the body must be protected, and therefore it is entirely encased in bone (the skull). The base of the skull has one large hole for the exit of the spinal cord and some smaller holes for blood vessels and for channels for the cranial nerves to the eyes, nose, mouth, face, tongue, and one of these cranial nerves extends all the way to the stomach. The same bones that support the brain form the superstructure for the face, which holds the sensory organs -- the ears, eyes, nose and mouth.

The brain has two hemispheres which are connected at the center by a small body of nerves which cross from the two sides called the corpus callosum (a thick -- or callused -- body of tissue). Each half is roughly divided into three large functional sections. At the center, for purposes of simplification, is the "control system". Information is received or sensed in one system which is the "conscious" part of the brain at the outer layers called the "cortex" that is about the thickness of a U.S. quarter. Information is directed into the central part from the outer part where it was processed. From the central part, after the information is sorted, instructions are transmitted to the base part which is called the sending part, or "motor" system.

Residing in the central part is also a section called the "limbic system". This part contains the primitive imprints thought to have accumulated with evolution -- sometimes also called the reptilian complex. This area is thought to be the "deep-seated" portion connected with habits such as smoking.

The brain is exquisitely sensitive. It needs a constant source of oxygen and is amply supplied by a large carotid artery and jugular vein. Lacking oxygen, serious brain damage can occur in seconds in a fetus before birth and minutes in an adult. The brain burns sugar for its energy.

The brain is also very sensitive to nutritional conditions. All tissues need oxygen, proper nutrients, provision for waste elimination, acid-base balance and particularly in nerves an electrolyte balance. Allergies to certain foods and allergies to drugs have been identified as disturbing these balances.

Our fantastic brain can be overstimulated or understimulated. Rock stars and even abusers of portable cassette players like the "Walkman" may lose some of their hearing, as the nerves in the ear can also be damaged by explosions of sound. Direct viewing of the sun will burn out some nerve components of the eye.

A growing child needs physical and mental stimulation for the ideal development of the brain connections.

Stimulation, Physical Activity and Brain Growth

A child sitting in front of a television set receives no physical stimulation and the thinking facilities stimulate little mental growth. Some experts think a measurable degree of retardation presently exists in 30% of all American children. Television serves for entertainment and communication, but according to Joseph Chilton Pearce it may be causing generations of limited intelligence. In fact, experiments conducted on rats proved physical and mental stimulation produced greater growth of the size of the brain.

Because the brain is so vital, Nature does her best to protect it. There is a blood-brain barrier which seems to buffer the brain or select the appropriate contents from the blood to pass through for use for the brain physiology. Taking from the sources of nutrients, minerals, hormones, and enzymes, the brain also produces its own chemicals. These are called endorphins and enkephalins.

Ecological conditions (excess positive ions), fear, emotional states, stress and senses of pleasure all produce different brain effects. The brain in this sense is the major controller, a hormone affector itself, and in fact the pituitary gland (often called the king gland) is under the direct control of a portion of the midbrain. This explains the dominant effects of psychologic states on the whole body. Norman Cousins focused on this apparatus and stated that in various combinations thousands of chemicals are brain-produced.

Certain drugs cross the protective barrier and alter the normal brain's function, its balance, and therefore the balance of the entire body. Certain drugs or chemicals work on the brain in a specific way. For instance, observe a child or children immediately after a high dose of sugar from a candy bar or dish of ice cream. High stimulation to the brain will result from hyperglycemia (too much sugar in the blood), with consequent over-activity and sometimes hyperkinetic conditions, and the loss of ability for the child to concentrate in school. The child may become unruly, uncontrollable simply because of sugar!

Smokers tell me they like to smoke because they get a pick-me-up. This probably is due to artificial stimulation of sugar from glycogen in the liver, but nicotine also affects the limbic system in the brain, alerting it to a degree for "fight or flight". Consequently, a nicotine habit is among the most difficult to overcome.

Coffee and tea through caffeine are known to overcome drowsiness. This is a mild form of stimulation of the neurons in the brain. It therefore is a "waker-upper" the first thing in the morning. Some people say they "can't get going" in the morning without coffee, and many often combine it with a cigarette to obtain a double-whammy artificial stimulation for the day ahead.

A normal nerve stimulus is recorded on a machine called the electroencephalograph (EEG) which displays waves that can be measured. These are more quiet when we sleep and the spikes or height of the marks in a recording serve as a base line for comparison. The normal waves are the result of 20 million years or more of human evolution. The chemicals in the brain inhibit (slow down) or stimulate (speed up) and direct the body to stop or go.

Drug Actions

With the foregoing background, we are in a position to understand how mind-altering drugs can work. There are "uppers" and "downers." The brain and body are either speeded up or slowed down.

One of the "downers" is one of a group of chemicals labeled barbiturates. These in small amounts are used by doctors and dentists for anesthesia, for example: pentothal for a tooth extraction or other minor surgery. They block the transmission along the nerve by stopping the exchange of sodium and potassium for the stimulus conduction; thus, the excitability of the nerve is impeded. Mild doses of barbiturates were also used to slow people down who had ulcers and other nervous disorders.

When taken in excess they produce a progression from sedation to sleep, to light coma, to coma, to deep coma, to death. This is due to the inability of impulses to reach the control centers of the brain. These are the "downers".

There are many drugs which excite the brain -- the "uppers". Some are the amphetamine group:

     Benzedrine (bennys)
     Ephedrine
     Methadrine and others

However, the following are also profound stimulants:

     LSD
     THC (tetrahydrocannibinol) found in marijuana and hashish
     Mescalin
     PCP (phencyclidine)
     STP
     Organic solvents
     Alcohol

These do not all act in the same way, yet the result of each is a speed-up of nerve activity. Some may say that some of these drugs are depressants. At the brain level they are **excitants to the electrical activity** which increases relative to amount taken.

When an animal is studied with the use of a powerful excitant, Metrazol, the stages of effect on the brain can be followed by a single dose. These stages are:

Hyperexcitation (increase of movement)
    Euphoria (a high)
       Hallucination (distortion of perceptions)
          Catalepsy (fixed, bizarre portions black out)
            Convulsions (body seizures)

Some of these drugs used in controlled amounts will develop hyperaction, euphoria and hallucination, but in excess, overdose (OD), they lead to catalepsy, convulsions and death. Even THC when altered with other drugs has produced these profound actions.

When **benzedrine or amphetamines** are taken intravenously they **penetrate the blood-brain barrier** and keep on exciting the brain, particularly its central control, to faster and faster pace until a balanced protection is passed. **Motor control keeps going despite no sensory input.** Loss of consciousness and pain lead to accidents and injury. The brain is in overload. The euphoria that started leads to misinterpretation of the environment and coordination is lost in the scramble.

With sodium trapped inside the nerve it takes less stimulation to cause it to fire more and more rapidly. The nerve begins to swell as water is drawn into the cell by the sodium. Nerves may become so swollen that the cell body bursts and dies. The longer the cell is swollen, the greater the chance of permanent brain damage.

LSD works by upsetting the cell membrane and the passage at the synapse. It likes the visual system. It overloads the brain with visual irrelevant patterns. But under an LSD condition the brain cannot guide and protect the individual. Thus, hallucinations indicate a brain dysfunction at the chemical and electrical level.

THC (marijuana) is an excitant to the brain even though at the same time the body may be inactive. It simulates the effect of alcohol in small doses and simulates LSD in higher doses. A usual dosage falls between the high of euphoria and hallucination or similar to alcohol. But heavier use results in brain overloading. Yet even moderate usage may result in **recent memory loss** and also marked impairment of perception and judgment. In addition, the ingredients of marijuana tend to be stored in fat and other connective tissues for long periods of time. Therefore, taken over time it requires less by the smoker to reach the euphoric state. Some may adapt and lose the kick and in time end up combining THC with other drugs which becomes progressively easier with a loss of inhibition.

Heroin, like morphine or opiates, comes from the poppy and like other stimulants produces at the beginning a euphoric feeling. It also operates on the nerve membranes and particularly on the chemistry within the nerve. It replaces some of the nerve chemicals in the nerve and henceforth the person becomes dependent on the heroin even for normal transfer of information or the normal sensations and organ functions.

Tolerance to heroin soon sets in and more is needed for the "kick" but also for just the basic control of the glands. At this point the person is addicted! The victim requires increases for the habit to obtain the high, but worse yet the brain and nerve transmission cannot function without it and the person becomes imprisoned by the drug. A ritual becomes imprinted in the mind for the injection procedure, and any reminder of any part of the technique evokes a craving for the drug. It is most difficult to break the habit or to stop taking any of the opiates.

Cocaine has had a long history in dentistry. Earlier in the present century it was used to inject around the tooth for anesthesia. Dentists would padlock their offices in fear of theft by "cocies" who were addicted. In the early 1970s I argued with one of my children who had read that cocaine was not addictive. This was before several well-known professional athletes repeated again and again a cocaine drug dependency. Movie stars and many noted persons are chemically entrapped; any young person, particularly those with money and looking for excitement, became an easy mark for the pusher.

Cocaine acts at the synapse. The tiny pump in the synapse that transmits the chemical transfer to the next nerve is altered. The message normally propelled gets distorted and the sensation is reduced (as for pain reduction in cancer) and in addition the inhibitions are suppressed, which yields the feeling of freedom and a "high". Thus, a free feeling or euphoria results. The user also wants greater and more frequent dosages and therefore becomes dependent and loses judgment. **This reaction arises because of the interruption of the normal nerve flow from the sensory through the central control section of the brain to the motor output portion.**

Personal Observations

One of my personal observations with some patients whom I suspected of indulging more than casually with excitant drugs was a condition I perceived to be a personality change. They would, as I described before, come in dirty, disheveled and with a non-caring attitude. Their oral hygiene would be neglected and compliance with instructions for their treatment would be nil. They would appear slovenly, unambitious and quite lazy.

My impression also has been that too much free sugar also acts as a drug. When too much sugar is consumed it is absorbed in the stomach and goes directly to the blood stream, causing a condition of "hyperglycemia". When this artificial stimulant burns off, the body's adjustment to compensate doesn't "kick in" and the blood sugar levels drop, producing "hypoglycemia", whereupon the person becomes tired, sleepy and weak. But with excitant drugs, after the rise in blood levels they do not go below normal levels because significant amounts are not manufactured in the body. There are, however, certain similarities in body-produced morphine-like chemicals. Yet we observe the ill effects of prolonged use of excitant drugs, for example: epilepsy, psychotic reactions, paranoia, continued hallucinations, psychic depression or stupor or dulled senses, and apathy, and even laziness.

Glue, aerosol sprays and solvents like Tolvene act in the brain in a way similar to stimulant drugs. However, these chemicals are used commercially to dissolve grease spots and attack fat. Fat in fatty tissue is used to protect or insulate the nerve and without this protection in the brain the nerves become exposed to injury, and some nerves may die. Also, breathing the chemicals shuts off oxygen which damages brain cells. Deaths from these poisons are frequent.

All drugs taken in sufficient amount are poisonous to the body tissues and the organs together with the nerves. Diseases and poisons are said to produce a "toxic" state in the body. These poisons may act fast (acute) or act in long term (chronic). But differences in response may occur in one individual as compared to another, or even the same individual under different biologic states. A safe dose to one person may not be safe a day or two later. Also, the "detoxification", usually in the liver, may be slow and the drug may accumulate. Even an ordinary dose of THC or barbiturate may produce a giant toxic reaction on an acute basis.

Tolerance is the opposite to acute reaction, as greater and greater doses may be used to produce a "high" such as desired by the heroin addict. When drugs are discontinued withdrawal symptoms can be ghastly. This is explained, in part, by the fact that motor nerves to the internal organs do not carry the normal impulses for instructions for normal function of the glands due to faulty transmission. People may not be aware that nerve alteration is not just on the sensory side. Therefore, the withdrawing patient can become quite ill due to lack of proper function of the stomach, liver, kidney, lung and endocrine glands. They need a fix just to feel decent again, not just to get a high, as was the practice at the start of the habit. They are now in the condition of chemical dependency.

The Truth Regarding Drugs

Twelve common truths regarding drugs are recognized (as expressed by Winters and Greenberg):

1. Drugs are not foods.
2. Drugs affect nerve tissue but also affect other parts as well -- it may "blow your mind" but it blows vital organs as well.
3. Any drug taken in sufficient amount is toxic or poisonous.
4. Drugs can be cumulative if the body cannot detoxify them. Excessive alcohol turns to formaldehyde which is used as a preservative of dead tissue.
5. Drugs affect the individual cells' function and when enough cells become sick the person becomes sick.
6. Oftentimes the effects of a drug are unpredictable.
7. Tolerance to a drug is a part of the addiction physiology.
8. Drugs can disassociate the taker from reality (being "bombed"), and separate the taker from judgment ("stoned").
9. With damage to the impressive pathways an ability to learn and remember may be impaired **forever**.
10. Addiction may have two sides, a physical dependency and a psychologic dependency.
11. Most people have no idea of the potency of street drugs since there are no manufacturers' controls.
12. Drugs lead to other disease consequences including epileptic fits, different neurotic and psychiatric states such as depression, confusion and suicide.

* * *

One of my patients "under the influence" walked out of a third-storey window, thinking he could fly. As a result, instead of spreading his wings he spread his brains on the sidewalk below. Another patient while despondent took his life, unable to deal with the shattering experiences he had undergone while under the influence. Another turned his car over and killed himself on a curve on Sunset Boulevard while under the influence. Other patients have accidentally overdosed, especially with barbiturate or heroin.

Other diseases connected with drugs are blood vessel destruction and death in cells of the liver and kidneys which is fatal with methodrine users. Another is well known: leather-like cirrhosis of the liver from aldehydes from alcohol.

But users are more exposed to hepatitis and AIDS from a dirty needle or sexual transmission with gonorrhea, syphylis and chancroid as well as genital warts and herpes with the indiscretion that drug influences produce.

Probably worst, in my opinion, are the persons who damage their brains and still claim freedom in society. Heavy users have been observed to have markedly changed personalities and often do not recover even after discontinuing the drug. Sadly, they have destroyed the brain that makes them human, yet they continue to demand their share of human rights.

Loss of Human Quality

It seems to me that most normal individuals are born with a genetic predisposition for survival of the race and the capacity to get along by showing kindness to others. A "conscience" and respect for others is thought to lie in the control seat of the brain. Without that conscience a person can batter another or kill a neighbor without remorse. Hence the battering of a wife when the mean husband is under the influence.

As Henry F. Greenberg so eloquently stated, "Deep within the cells of the brain, in the synapses and the membranes where electrical discharges take place, a person may no longer possess the power to instruct himself to go or to stop. In a real sense, he is a victim of "chemical insanity".

Much of the effort in drug control is aimed at education of children. Traffickers and dealers may be young blacks, Hispanics, or whites and all may be privileged. Their customers, however, are not poor neighbors. They are white people cruising by in expensive cars looking for a "nickel" ($50.00) package of drugs. **We let the user off with a slap on the wrist for possession and put the kid in jail for dealing. Are our laws backward?**

Outlook for the 1970s

Despite the drug concern, my outlook for the '70s was bright. Everyone told me that if I didn't quit working so hard I would die of a heart attack. I therefore decided for my 50th birthday in May of 1970 to throw my own party. I invited about 200 friends, hired a dance band, and had a sit-down banquet at The Beach Club on the Pacific Coast Highway at Santa Monica. We danced until midnight while a brush fire was burning in the Santa Monica Mountains. I wanted to make it certain to everyone that I was not yet on my way out. I sang a couple of numbers with the band just for kicks.

Pacific Palisades, and our practice as well, was growing. Many of my projects were falling into place. Students were coming for courses and organizations were becoming enthusiastic. I had expanded my office by taking over an adjacent suite in La Colina and had converted it to a research area and teaching center. Dr. Bench and I hired Dr. James Hilgers as an associate to free me to expand research and teaching which was increasingly demanding.

On a national scale, the Cold War was deepening and now included a fear of China together with the U.S.S.R. The Vietnam War was separating the country. Nixon was now president, and it was a relief to be rid of Johnson. We had hope for a settlement of some kind, whether it be good or bad. After all, the whole issue was to contain communistic expansion in the first place.

This was our local and national condition as we set course for the next decade.

Professional Developments

It would seem likely that the first 25 years of my career would bring forth more challenges than the latter 25. However, such was not the case. The pace merely quickened.

No sooner was all of the computer application work put in motion than we began to find "spin-offs" from that research. In fact, I listed 40 benefits from that work that could be used for the advantage of the profession.

In 1970 I contributed a chapter on growth and development of the head and jaws for a "Dental Science Handbook" from the National Institute of Health in Washington, D.C. My chapter represented the concepts of growth in 1969, at that moment in time when it was formulated. Little did I know that my views on growth would change radically within the next year.

Arcs in Nature

One of the spinoffs of the computer studies was the discovery of a curve for the growth of the lower jaw. Prior to that time, researchers had presumed the human lower jaw to grow in length by melting of the bone on the front of its vertical portion (or ramus) with additions occurring on the back border of the lower jaw just below the ear. The lower jaw (mandible) has an L-shaped form with various prongs on it called processes. Previously, for our predictions of jaw growth in a child we made straight-line additions in roughly the horizontal and vertical directions. This sufficed for accuracy for a period of two years; however, anything longer than that could be unreliable with those methods.

It was clear that the lower jaw bent as it grew and therefore developed on some form or an arc. Further work made it obvious that it was growing on a spiral quite similar to the growth of the Nautilus seashell. This shell is beautiful because it has a recurrent rhythm that displays a great harmony. The human lower jaw was found to have this unique curve as well. Many, many arcs and curves exist in nature, such as the ram's horn, flowers, rodents' teeth, the tail of a comet, and beaks of birds.

In addition, we had discovered that there were certain shapes that tended to be maintained throughout the growth period. This characteristic enables the part to enlarge during growth without a change in form. Keys to growth behavior were found located at the entrance of nerve and blood vessel bundles into facial cavities. For the first time in my experience the growth of the human face could be forecast in a child to its form and size at maturity with amazing regularity, though not absolute certainty. The growth of the human face, and jaws and head for that matter, was no longer the mystery that it had always been presumed to be.

It was further shown, within useful clinical limits, that the impaction of a lower third molar (or wisdom tooth) could be predicted by age six. Further, there were techniques to apply so that the lower third molar could be aborted. With proper care, the whole human population could avoid the necessity of digging impacted lower wisdom teeth out of the jaw at an adult age. These discoveries were made in 1971, almost exactly 200 years after the first theory of growth of the jaw had been described by Hunter, an Englishman, in 1771.

Dissention

As with the development of the computer, the reaction against early germectomy of the wisdom tooth was immense, despite the fact that in the early 1930s a surgeon in London by the name of C. Bowdler Henry had performed an early operation on the lower third molars in 5000 children. The only differences at this time, however, was that we now had a better means of prognostication.

Again, editorials were not slow in coming. A year or so later a self-appointed committee held a national meeting on the subject, to which I was not invited, and went on record condemning the idea. I was even censored by my local society in California for suggesting it, after it reached national news media following a presentation at the American Association for the Advancement of Science. This was despite the fact that "tooth germectomy" had been practiced in about 500 grateful patients of our own. Naturally, there was some awkwardness when we were first developing the techniques, as with any new idea, but from the time the principles were all worked out there has been no single problem to my knowledge.

Back to Nerves Again

From 1970 to 1973 I was engaged in working out these concepts and improving on the prediction for the rest of the face. It was recognized that the growth of the face was connected in some discreet way with the distribution of the nerve supply, in a process called "neurotrophism" which means the blood and nerve supply going to a part to feed it. It was the site of the nerve entrance into a cavity that became the point of reference.

During 1971 I had recalled hundreds of patients whom I had treated at least ten years before, with two objectives. One was to check the stability of their orthodontic treatment. The second was to test and later to show the accuracy of the new long-range predictions.

* * *

Other technologic events in these years were of significance. In 1970 the first microprocessor for computers was developed. In 1971 Mariner 9 circled Mars. In 1972 Pioneer 10 was launched which passed Jupiter in 1973 and by 1983 had passed the asteroid belt of our solar system.

* * *

Dangerous Trip to Africa

In 1971 I received an invitation from the committee of the bicentennial meeting of the Dental Society of South Africa to be held in 1972. It was to be an international congress with speakers from all over the world. I was one of only two Americans invited to attend.

Never having been to Africa before, I felt it would be educationally productive to take the family. The children were 15 to 21 years of age, and I hoped would be prepared to remember such a long trip. We were accompanied by Dr. Robert Washbon and his wife, Suzie, from Newport Beach, California.

The preparation and anticipation of such a long trip (six weeks) was exciting. Little did I realize the risks that we were to experience during that time. Our itinerary was to take us through Egypt, Uganda, Kenya, Tanzania, the Serengeti and the Olduvai Gorge, and down through Rhodesia (Zimbabwe) en route to Johannesburg. We were then to come back through Rio de Janeiro, Brazil, where I would lecture again and renew acquaintances in South America. While in South Africa, I also was to put on a one-week course for the orthodontists, and this meant extensive planning.

We left in June, 1972. We had heard rumblings of the problems in Uganda with Amin, but the State Department felt that there was no risk for Americans, and we were given visas to visit that country. I had read that Uganda had been the pride of England as a developmental accomplishment.

For each of the six weeks I agreed to report my observations and reactions to the countries and the life of the people to the Rotary Club. I also sent the reports of these observations to Mr. Ronald Reagan who was then Governor of California.

Egypt

Egypt was made by the Nile River. While in Cairo I met two Egyptologists, a Dr. McFall from Michigan State and Jim Jenning from Wheaton College, who were on an expedition to study the tombs and artifacts. We had a private showing of the contents from King Tut's tomb, and I also was permitted to examine some of the mummies. Years later I studied some of the X-rays of the skulls taken by Dr. James Harris and colleagues from the University of Michigan. For those interested, man is essentially the same as he was 4000 years ago.

The preservation of the hieroglyphics, the absolutely symmetrical obelisk made from one solid piece of granite 87 feet high, and the perfection of the dovetailed, fitted stone work remains in my memory to this day.

In the Delta of the Nile, flowers were grown whose crushed petals produced perfume oils for the French industry. It was difficult to imagine Egypt supporting a modern army when life along the river, with its use of donkeys, had in many places changed little since the days of the Pharaohs.

Uganda

From Cairo we went to Uganda where we were to spend five days traveling overland to Murchison Falls and the game reserves along the upper Nile. Landing in Entebbe, we were concerned though not alarmed at the tension in the country. My first apprehension arose when our hired guide was not at the airport to meet us. We went to Kampala, the capitol, and found a modern hotel with good service and food.

Our guide met us at the Kampala hotel and was disturbed that he had missed us at Entebbe. Someone had deliberately misinformed him, he remarked. We had paid double for our taxi with a black driver. He reimbursed to us the difference from our agreed price. The next morning we excitedly left to go on our excursion in a Land-Rover. Uganda borders Lake Victoria, and the scenery and witnessing the life of the animals was magnificent. The native men expressed anger regarding our cameras so we had to be discreet. We went fishing on the Nile near a falls, but had no luck.

When we returned to Kampala five days later the city was silent. I inquired about the dearth of activity and the guide shrugged his shoulders and said maybe they had declared a holiday. That very night my son Craig, then 15 years of age, came down with an African fever. He was delirious. I had no thermometer but his temperature had to be in the danger zone. I kept him sponged with wet towels and gave him some antibiotics which I had taken along for such an emergency. They worked well and rapidly on those strange microbes.

The next morning, we were doubly concerned for by now all the businesses were closed. Multi-story steel building crews were not at work. No Asian Indians were to be seen in our hotel whereas before they had been the clerks and waiters.

We rushed to try to find taxis and get to the airport. All the help had been changed to black people. The Indians, whom I was told had run the major industries, were being kicked out by Amin. I helped the new cashier exchange my money and calculate our bill. He was new and apparently couldn't add or subtract very well. They didn't know how to operate the cash register and had all the money thrown loosely in a drawer.

When we got to the airport, more than an hours' drive, there was only one lone airplane still there. Now I was triply concerned. Fortunately, I had reconfirmed our flight when we first arrived and we were able to board without delay. We discovered that it was the very last airplane to leave before Amin's final clamp on the country. The next few years were tragic for all whites, all Indians, and many blacks in Uganda. We were apparently the last to get out.

Kenya

From Entebbe we went to Nairobi, Kenya, staying in beautiful hotels and one night at the Safari Club, built by the actor Bill Holden just below Mount Kenya. It was truly magnificent. We met Bill just outside our cabin for a chat one evening and learned the history of the Safari Club and the changes taking place in Kenya. Holden had started going to Kenya in 1958. During the intervening time of fourteen years the population of Kenya had more than doubled, growing from five million to eleven million. Many people, particularly children, formerly had starved, died of infections or been wiped out by warfare. Now, with antibiotics, sanitation and stabilization, the new problems were roads, schools, food supplies and clothing.

From Nairobi we went to Ambocelli, the Serengeti, Morongoro Crater and the Great Rift.

I was particularly pleased to visit the Olduvai Gorge, called the Grand Canyon of anthropology and archaeology, where Mary Leakey had found the famous Australopithecus specimen called "Lucy".

Rhodesia (Zimbabwe)

I found Salisbury in Rhodesia to be a clean, modern city with prize beef herds in the country. Suppression of the blacks had occurred and the 350,000 whites, most of them born there, were concerned about being run out of the country and losing their farms if the 5,000,000 blacks took over. We took an excursion into a native village. Later most of the whites were indeed forced to leave. The whites who have remained have a good standard of living but are unable to take their money out. They work with the blacks (who have the political power) and make of Zimbabwe the most hopeful country in Afica--the only one where blacks and whites work together.

South Africa

We were in Johannesburg twelve days and I lectured on eleven of them. I didn't visit the reserves or get down to the Cape, but the family did. While we were there, Bob Washbon came down with malaria which he apparently contracted in Uganda.

Johannesburg houses a museum with a collection of Australopithecus skulls, one of which was the first discovery, the juvenile skull found by a student and analyzed by Raymond Dart, the anatomist at Wittswatersrand University. It was the missing link! After his death he was replaced by Dr. Philip Tobias as Curator and Investigator of that material. Tobias conducted a graduate school with many students in a continuing research effort. He was to be the first speaker at the Congress, describing the head, jaws and the occlusion of the Australopithecus. I, being the second speaker on the program, was charged with the contrasting of that to present-day man's occlusion and function of the jaws.

The debates at the meeting, however, centered on the role of chewing forces as a beneficial or detrimental effect on the health of the teeth. I also gave another address at the same meeting on the current developments in orthodontics.

Having just published, in 1971, an article on the arcial growth of the mandible, I was anxious to study the lower jaw of the Australopithecus skulls and see if it had the same human characteristics I had found in current children. It did.

In addition, I was interested in the temporal bone -- named by anatomists as the "time bone" because the human grays "at the temples" or over this bone. It is also the hardest bone of the body, holding the semicircular canals for equilibrium, containing the organs of hearing, protecting the artery to the brain, and housing the jaw joint just in front of the ear. That very primitive bone, although changed slightly in orientation, likewise has been modified little since the two million years at which those fossilized specimens were dated.

I was privileged to go to Philip Tobias' school and conduct a seminar on growth forecasting of the lower jaw and also was permitted to examine that unique fossil collection at first hand.

By the time we arrived in Rio de Janeiro on the return trip, my daughter Robin was also sick with a fever of some type. Much had changed in Brazil since I had been there eleven years before. I observed what inflation could do to a country. While I was there in 1961 the cruzerio had risen from 370 to 375 to one dollar in one week. It kept going, to 1/5000 to one U.S. dollar. They printed 100,000 C. bills and then formed a new bill. Many exchanges in business and future contracts were being based on the U.S. dollar.

Other Activities

Also in 1972, I made two lecture trips to Mexico. And later in the year I made my second trip to Japan, lecturing at a large meeting in Nigata. During my first visit in 1964 I had been informed there were few orthodontic specialists in the whole country. On this visit there were 200 in attendance, a ten-fold increase in only eight years.

Thus, in one year I had visited three major producing countries: South Africa which produces gold and diamonds, Brazil which is also is a major producer of precious stones, and Japan which was on her way to modernization of all kinds of manufacturing.

Probably one of the most memorable political moments historically was Nixon's visit to China in 1972 which broke much of the ice of the 20-year cold Sino-American relations. I felt particularly proud of his accomplishments as a world statesman at the time.

In 1973 the advanced courses in Pacific Palisades had grown to four, and people were coming from all parts of the country and from abroad. They say the teacher learns the most, so I must have been really learning.

One memorable occasion was our Foundation meeting in San Francisco where Dr. Raymond Roseman presented his material on personality types and cardiovascular disease. When he described the A type everyone pointed at me. I wondered at the time if there wasn't more to stress production than personality. Another classic paper was given by Dr. Egil Harvold from the University of California. He had taken growing monkeys and stopped up their noses progressively, producing an alteration in the growth of the lower jaw and bite development arising from the imposition of chronic mouth breathing.

Fiasco in London - August, 1973

A world congress was held in London in 1973. Several subjects were to be discussed at the meeting. Committees were assigned for each subject, to invite speakers on the world basis. I was invited to give three papers, and in addition I needed to write the abstracts. It was an opportunity -- which I accepted with gratitude -- to expose some of the work that we had done with the computer and with the forecasting procedure, and our mechanics of treatment.

Dr. Rolf Frankel from behind the Iron Curtain in Swiskow, East Germany, was also on the program. He reported progress with a removable appliance he had developed. I followed Dr. Frankel on the program, and I believe the new findings were accepted as a futuristic type of approach in the profession.

The next day I was scheduled to participate on a panel, together with other speakers from different countries, in a discussion on the use of computers in the future. I had arranged my material for three slide projectors but on arriving found that only two projectors had been provided. This would make my presentation slightly incomplete, but I could still do the job.

When I came into the meeting room, however, I noticed a group of the committee members and some of the other speakers in a huddle in a back corner of the room. Considering all of them to be personal friends, I went over to greet them. But as I approached I noticed that they suddenly quit talking and looked at me quite sheepishly. I suspected that something was going on, and their manner betrayed the fact that I was involved with their conversation.

My understanding was that I would have two hours to present as best I could the work that we had done in the previous eight years. There were students and colleagues in the audience who told me they had come to the meeting specifically to hear what I had to say. As the program started, another speaker went grossly past his appointed time, with no objections raised. After I was introduced, I was hardly into my subject, simply giving the background for the study and the protocol for the research, when my time was terminated by the chairman of the day. This was to my complete dismay and to the shock of many in attendance. Not only did the chairman cut off my talk, but he quickly gave a summary which was uncomplimentary and adjourned the meeting as a whole two hours before it was to have ended.

Being in a foreign country, being tired from having worked very hard for the preparation, and suffering from jet-lag did not leave me in a very good mood. I later confronted the chairman in the hallway and told him how cheap I thought it was, how unscientific, how unscholarly, and even how ungentlemanly such treatment was. A group quickly gathered around me in support, but before an ugly scene developed I thought it best just to let the matter drop.

It wasn't until another eight years later that one of those committee members came up to me at an American meeting and told me he couldn't keep it on his conscience any longer, that there had been a conspiracy to scuttle my work at that London meeting. He said he felt very badly about it, and it wasn't his choice. He did, however, want to let me know that such a plan was put in force and executed in an attempt to prevent my work from being presented at the meeting even after I had been invited and had spent considerable time preparing. The committee in question was composed of Americans, or those trained in America.

Later Mr. Mills, editor of the British orthodontics journal, wrote an editorial repudiating much of what I had done without giving me a chance to offer the data and the information that had been accumulated. This has happened in many scientific circles throughout history, particularly when some people do not want to accept the viewpoint of investigators who show new directions.

New Ideas and Stages

It has been said that new ideas pass through three generations of scholars. The first generation exposed will attempt to dispose of the new idea. They will find fault, and do their best to avoid any changes necessary to their thinking. But if the idea persists the second generation may find it worthy of consideration and gradually find that they are not destroyed or threatened by the new idea, and that it has merit. It is then openly evaluated and criticized objectively rather than subjectively. In the third generation, the idea becomes endorsed and integrated into the pattern of practice and the pattern of thinking.

But every new idea also goes through five personal stages. The first stage is that a new concept is laughed at and considered as a humorous notion or too fantastic to be taken seriously. When laughing doesn't make it go away it is then that the second stage, derision, ensues. This is the stage of xenophobia. Emotional objections are raised because it is now considered a threat. The human psyche would like to maintain the status quo because change brings on stress. But as the idea still persists, it gradually starts to become integrated into people's thinking as the third stage.

In the fourth stage the user will try to maintain his self-esteem and identity and will frequently be heard to make the statement, "Well, I always believed that in the first place." Or the statement may be, "Really, the idea is not new anyway." This is an obvious move to maintain a self-image and bring it into self-actualization. The fifth and final stage with a new idea is that the user, in order to reach a level of personal identity, will say, "Well, not only is it not new, but I've developed a much better way of doing it than the person who originated the idea."

One reason I can write about such developments derives from the witnessing of these events as they happened to me so many times.

Success of Ideas

It doesn't take long to recognize that a new commercial idea, a new technique, a new movement within a field, takes about twenty years from its inception until it finally is made completely useful to the public. One example is XEROX, which ran true to form and took about 20 years from the development of the technique to its integration. Businesses today couldn't survive without a copier, and most are increasingly dependent on the facsimile machine. But in previous days the personnel in the office were accustomed to using the old blue ink ditto machines in which they already had an investment, whose use was acceptable because of habit. As mass production ensues, and as products become more economical, these also prove to be factors in acceptance of a new idea. A product has to be **quicker, cheaper** and **better** -- all three -- in order to be integrated into a useful new idea in industry.

Another example of a new idea is the air bag in the automobile for safety. One can also visualize how long it took to produce disk brakes rather than the older band brakes on automobiles. Seat belts are another example. And a further development is the computerized control of the brake to help prevent skidding in the event of slick pavement.

The Manchester Matching

Immediately after the London Congress caper I had been invited to a more private, three-day course given by Dr. Frankel. Many clinicians were making claims about stretching the lower jaw, and I too was interested in studying his patients' X-ray films myself. Winston Senior, the colleague who invited me, was a friend from Manchester who had taken my five-day course in Madrid six years before. He had followed our developments with the computer and with the forecasting methods. I agreed to come and critique the course if I would be able to trace the headplates and make forecasts for comparison to the actual some years later, in order to evaluate the changes and determine whether or not the predictions matched the actual. This was agreed to and accomplished.

The third day I stood in front of about 150 in the group and showed the predictions which fit the lower jaw precisely in eight out of eight subjects. While short-range alterations were observed, in the end genetics dominated. The group was chagrined yet still unmoved.

The First Big Embarrassment for Americans

During 1973 Nixon negotiated a settlement in Vietnam. It was difficult for me to accept that we had lost a war which we hadn't really tried to win. But many in the rest of the world rejoiced. If there was any positive side, it was only that we took a stand to contain communism. The loss did not curtail our world police effort to prevent aggression against weaker nations. We were still the protective big brother.

Nixon did his best as a statesman to make the most of a sad situation. He tried to mend the division of our society and bolster the country by claiming we withdrew with honor and dignity. Honor is a sense of what is right and something which commands respect and is a cause of esteem. Dignity is the state of being worthy and honorable and a high rank of distinction. I suffered for his efforts when the soldiers who had risked their lives in service were booed by neighbors when they returned.

My deep concern was that Johnson and maybe Kennedy had lied to the American people concerning the war. Honesty means truth, justice, and freedom from fraud. It means virtue and trustworthiness. A review by David Halberstam, who was a journalist based there, clearly reveals that we were given a false picture of the conditions and the progress of that war which cost us 58,000 lives and billions of dollars. In the end it was the Japanese who won the war because we made unnecessary concessions just to keep them on our side in the long conflict.

The whole Vietnam adventure was a source of embarrassment to America on a world scale.

The Second Embarrassment for Americans

It is said, "You fight fire with fire." As the U.S.S.R. became secretive we played the same game. As Johnson and others were clandestine, Nixon also "played hard ball". When it had been discovered that wire-tapping and break-ins were conducted, all Nixon needed to do was admit that they were exercised for national security. This would have looked bad to the world, but for our democratic way he would have been seen to be defending us against Krushchev. Through his office he tried to cover it up and failed. Right or wrong, the foregoing was my impression in 1974. There were still many Nixon haters and some who wanted the notoriety of purity, it seemed. Why make it such a big issue when we had major problems in the country already?

Watergate was, then, the second embarrassment and frustration to America in a two-year period. Friends called from abroad and asked me what was going to happen. Ford had already replaced Agnew, which was a more minor embarrassment. All this was a sign of deterioration of all political positions. To save impeachment, Nixon resigned bitterly and Ford took office.

For Brodie and Steiner With Love

Meanwhile, I was fully occupied professionally in 1974. A large meeting was organized in Houston where I was to interview my old mentor, Dr. Allan G. Brodie, and my old friend Dr. Cecil Steiner. They had been two stalwarts in our field. Steiner had been one of Brodie's instructors in the old Angle School of Orthodontia in Pasadena in 1928. As a commentator, I took them back through many of their experiences. It was a touching moment and there was not a dry eye in the room. As far as I know, it was their last time together.

The Letter

In 1974 two other non-professional events were disruptive to my life and would affect it thereafter. The first I will call "the letter".

I was working late one night when I received a midnight phone call from Grant Butler. He was a friend, a writer, and a reader at the Christian Science church, and a golf buddy. He had been based in Saudi Arabia and was a lecturer on the Middle East. After the Israeli attack on the airport in Lebanon he had written a letter to the *Los Angeles Times* regarding the United States' unilateral support for Israel and the danger of losing our friends in the Arab community. He read the whole letter to me over the phone and its argument seemed reasonable. Among other things I remember his statement that we were oblivious to the possible consequences. I was shocked when he asked if he could sign my name to it. He was then a public relations representative of Pan American Airlines and felt he could not involve his company. He felt my reputation would give it some attention but that I would not be damaged. Like a fool, I finally consented, thinking it wasn't really noxious in the first place and only another viewpoint.

I have never been anti-semitic. When I was in college the Hebrew fraternity was next door to our ATO house in Bloomington, Indiana. I was the only one I knew of from our fraternity who went next door to play basketball with their guys. I had several Jewish buddies in dental school. I had Jewish friends in the service. My very best friend an roommate in graduate school was Sam Pruzansky. I found myself conversing everywher with Jewish colleagues because they were the most intellectual and research-conscious. had several Jewish employees through the years.

The blaming of the failure of an economic system on the Jews by Hitler was the mos fiendish injustice ever known. Some of the greatest thinkers in recorded history were Jew. They proudly maintain their beliefs. I believe in freedom for all religions. Therefore, I ha no reason to take sides on a religious issue. My first interest was in America.

The letter was not published as originally written. Only excerpts were printed whic appeared inflammatory. The following morning it was in the "Letters to the Editor" sectio under my name. Soon it was obvious that a phone campaign had begun. Eight mothers cam immediately and took their children out of my practice. Orthodontists and Jewish dentist copied the "Letters" column and sent it to friends in other cities and even abroad. Man good friends called and wanted an explanation, which I gave. I became an outlet for Jewis frustration and a target for their energy. I was branded through no fault of my own excep wanting to help a friend. When I lectured in New York one group arose as a unit and mad a scene by walking out of my lecture as a show of rejection. If I ever had any cause to b anti-semitic it was then. But I understood their feelings. I deplore racism in any form.

I have never been able to overcome the resentment. My position is still for America' interest first. That doesn't mean I'm against anyone. Maybe that makes me a patriot. I sti can't see that's so bad. If people prefer another country, let them live there in peace.

A Conflict Without Hate

The second non-professional event was my marital separation. My Christian upbringin had taught me that a divorce was a serious offense. Mothers were to be honored an respected. I had no problem with this view. However, people do not always develo together. After 20 years I found problems. First of all, Patty had grown steadily closer t her religion. My circle of friends was reduced, and while I liked most of her friends in th church, our social life was limited to her friends. I couldn't see spending the rest of my lif in that philosophy. Secondly, I still was looking to the excitement of my practice an research. She wanted me to quit. I had interests that no longer matched hers. The childre were grown up. I felt restricted at home, but there was no hate. I finally decided to try separation, which was more traumatic than anticipated.

Naturally, I sought some companionship and things happened. It's a long story tha extended over seven years, and I'm not prepared to share the details. Its only significanc is that for some years I was separated and finally divorced in 1978. Very soon thereafte I married Bunnie, my present wife. The reason I'm sharing it now is to help describe th drama as I entered 1975.

The Ketchum Award

At the national meeting of the American association in 1975 Dr. Tom Graber and I wer both given the Ketchum Award, the highest honor the profession can bestow on a membei Perhaps it would be informative to share only a small part of my acceptance speech wit the reader:

> "Orthodontics may seem small and in the total scheme of things may appear
> insignificant, but we perform a unique function for mankind. We contribute
> to man's comfort, to his happiness, and to his sense of well-being. We touch

the very heart of modern culture, for man is a gregarious animal; he clusters together for security in groups for stimulation with all his fellows; his face, eyes, mouth and teeth help him to relate to and communicate with others and, more important, to establish his own identity. This, in turn, leads to happiness, to love, and to a sense of accomplishment and purpose, which, in the final analysis, is the very essence of existence. Good orthodontics is a contribution to the welfare of another human being. It has an element of immortality. Its spirit is good and its purpose is just."

The Backlog

Whenever I became upset or frustrated, I was the type of person who buried himself in work. This would indicate a warrior personality. I had a good memory and the capacity to concentrate which sometimes carried me through awkward times. Some practitioners feel proud to have one good publication in a whole career. In 1975 alone I had six. The troubles in my domestic life had slowed down my writing, but the backlog of papers had accumulated.

I finished many papers because I was traveling less but at the same time still carrying a large practice which I enjoyed immensely. By 1975 the first personal computer was produced and direct digitizing into a processor was possible. I could see the steady improvements in computers. Although smaller they had greater capacity, they were faster and progressively easier to use.

It was at an important meeting in Sardinia, Italy, where I took on some Americans who claimed growth prediction was a fraud. I was disturbed by the negative attitudes of many of my fellow educators. Dr. Franco Magni from Genoa was my interpreter. I think I made him a convert. He has remained a long-time friend.

My Friend Bob

Earlier I have referred to the writings of Robert Ardrey. I had written letters with questions to him and received cordial answers, and knew that he lived in Rome. After my course in Sardinia Bunnie and I were staying with friends in Rome when I suddenly had an impulse to see if he was listed in the phone book. He was. I therefore without hesitation dialed his number and his wife answered. She talked to him and it appeared that he was reluctant to accept a lunch invitation from a stranger. In my own way I told him I was one of his most avid students, that I was lecturing on his books, and he couldn't afford not to have lunch with me! He finally agreed it would be all right if it was a short one.

We met at his home and walked down a hill about two blocks to Romolo's Restaurant, the patio of which backs up against an Ancient Roman wall in Trastevere. I had studied all three of his books and was loaded with questions. Despite his ill health, our lunch lasted until 6:P.M. I found his knowledge completely consuming. We parted with my vow to bring him to the U.S. to give us some lectures at our Foundation meeting. This was later arranged for New Orleans in 1977. I have two and one-half hours of video with him in an interview.

Snafu in Spain

In July I returned to Europe for the European Society of Orthodontics meeting in Tenerife in the Canary Islands. I came through Madrid, and on arriving at Tenerife found that my luggage had not made it. We started tracers, to no avail. Luckily I had brought my slides in hand luggage, but the only clothes I had were on my back and I had traveled overnight. The next morning I borrowed a shirt and some swim trunks and sat by the pool most of the day. That evening with still no word on my luggage, I went shopping to buy a suit and some essentials to get by. Still no word. I was to be there for five days, so friends understood why I was always dressed the same. It became a joke.

The third day I was to speak. I had started my lecture and had shown about two slides when pop! a bulb burned out. I assumed that an extra was available and told some anecdotes while waiting. I was finally informed that none could be found in the whole city. "Well," I said, "I'll just tell you what the slides showed." Some said it was one of the best lectures I had ever given.

The last day as I was paying my bill a bellboy came in with my suitcase. The tag had rubbed off and it had gone to La Palma, a different island, and had been sitting there for five days. I didn't even open the case. I had bought another small one for the extra duds and simply put a new tag on the old one and took it back, through Madrid, to California.

In October, I spoke at a national meeting in Maui, Hawaii. Those were still my jogging days and the beach was beautiful. It was an interesting meeting, and I rediscovered something I already knew. Professional people follow trends: if a little idea comes along and two or three convincing people give it some credence, a propaganda line takes over. It then becomes a movement and almost a fad. If a colleague doesn't embrace it suddenly he's not current. In Maui it was management of one tooth, the upper second molar. Not only was it a rage, but they were advocating doing it entirely inconsistent with nature. I was disgusted.

Thus, 1975 was a great year. I had been awarded my profession's most prestigious prize and I had met Robert Ardrey, a true philosopher.

Stress Without Distress

In April, 1976, the Foundation for Orthodontic Research meeting was in New York. I gave three papers and was privileged to interview on television Dr. Hans Selye, the discoverer of the physiologic actions of stress. Most dentists are interested in stress because patients under duress often clench or grind their teeth and overload their jaw joints.

I had started studying Selye's work almost 30 years before. I had attended his lectures and met him personally a few times at dental-medicine meetings. He had discovered that any kind of stress produced a specific body response. The disturbance was ulcers in the stomach and an involvement of the adrenal, thymus and lymph glands. He then discovered that the body went through an adaptive process but if the challenge was continued without letup it could lead to exhaustion and death.

Selye in his later years became, to many scientists, a philosopher regarding the human experience. It was that philosophy of life that I wanted to bring out in my interview. A certain amount of stress can serve as a stimulation. It is only continuous, heavy stress that leads to distress. This was his message.

The French Society

A most pleasurable trip to France took place in June of 1976. Through Dr. Carl Gugino a Ricketts French Society had been formed. The meeting was in Bordeaux. Dr. Vikas Sassouni was also on the program. We were given the key to the city with a medallion: I cannot now be arrested for being drunk in Bordeaux.

Cultural Spasm

In August of 1976 I gave an address to the local Rotary Club in Pacific Palisades on the subject of inflation. I had studied the William Rees-Mogg book called "The Crisis of World

Inflation — The Reigning Error" together with other books on inflation and its results from a historical perspective. My look at the South American countries had shown that inflation is disastrous to pensions and to savings of those who have put money aside for their old age. The problem with inflation, because of the printing of unsecured money, is that politicians find it impossible to stop. Following is the essence of that talk given in 1976. The principles apply ever as much today and beyond. I labeled it at the time "Cultural Spasm".

My purpose is to talk about today's economics! Perhaps it is presumptuous for an orthodontist to speak on so vast a subject as economics. But there is a need for all of us to be informed about economic aspects because they are of concern to the average citizen as he goes into debt, pays taxes, and worries about the value of his earnings and -- most important -- his future.

I have read and asked questions and taken courses in an effort to find some of the answers so that I may stay out of financial trouble. What I see and what I read and what I hear, I don't like.

Major Observations

First, I see vast differences of opinion among the economic specialists. Economics is thought by some to be only a half-science. Economists seem to be polarizing into two camps -- those who like gold and stabilization of a currency as opposed to those who are champions of continued deficit enlargement.

Second, most ordinary people vote on the basis of their **immediate economic condition**. They select what would appear to be short-range economic advantage rather than contemplate the long-range implications of the decision they make in the voting booth.

Third, society today is beset with major problems perhaps never before encountered in the United States, the main one being a recession and inflation simultaneously here in the early 1970s.

There is the concern about socialization of all medical services. Many in the health services feel that socialization of medicine may be nothing more than the start of a long chain of events leading to massive socialization in many areas of society. I'm appalled at the grade of service rendered in socialized programs and the willingness on the part of the public to accept anything that is free.

Ironically, while that thought is being entertained by the public, we are faced with increased malpractice suits. Many people expect perfection in all things. It is very difficult, with the existence of "human error" in technical matters, to always supply perfection.

Further, let us look at "society" and the change in public attitude. A few weeks ago my office manager exclaimed with dismay that she just could not understand the attitudes of some of our newer patients. They come in with chips on their shoulders; they have doubts before they even get started. They are ready to argue before we make a presentation or explain the problems. We are suffering a public loss of respect for those in the professional field as well as for our public servants. The folk hero image that once existed has vanished. This is true for doctors, teachers, policemen, lawyers and even for judges. It has become popular to mock public officials. Someone is needed to blame, and the politicians are the ones who are faulted most frequently.

A loss of loyalty is obvious as people are confused with values, tastes, their religious views and even with their concept of what amounts to virtue. There is corruption and dishonesty at all levels. If many aren't avoiding taxation, they border on deliberate evasion. In fact, some say if you aren't examined quite often you are not pushing your tax avoidance to the limit. Johnny Carson cuts up everyone.

A progressive increase in the cost of operation is witnessed. Management problems are more difficult. There is frustration, indecision, disillusionment and a feeling of helplessness to do anything about it. This particularly concerns big government and plethoric bureaucracy.

This is further exemplified by the many people in our society who are seeking answers to stress. Many books are being written on the subject. There is a clamor for retaining freedom. There is a search for a sense of well being. Many people are basically frustrated.

All these things are signs and symptoms of a greater problem. They may be signals of a social disorder of a nonspecific nature, a disease of major implications. Inflation, I believe, is one of the major underlying causes of what I might call a "cultural spasm".

What is Inflation?

There are many definitions of inflation, but they all stem from the same thing: an increase in the amount of money in circulation without a base of reference or asset backing. Quite simply, it means counterfeit money issued by government and licensed to banks or institutions.

Why is inflation so bad? Well, many think that it's good, particularly those who speculate, and are lucky, or those who have power for industrial bargaining or power for manipulation. It is informative to quote from the "Newsgram" of *U.S. News and World Report* of May 31, 1976. "Wages are rising for most workers, even after inflation. The average private-industry employee took home $170.41 weekly in April against $159.22 a year before. Feed in higher prices and taxes, and it's still a jump of $5.52." So, during inflationary times there is (apparently) an advantage.

But, if we look at the February 2, 1976 issue of the same magazine, we see what is happening to the cost of housing, and we see where the average person in the U.S. paid $21,000 for a home in 1966 which jumped to $40,800 in November of 1975. Anyone who has priced a home in Pacific Palisades within the last six months can certainly appreciate what I am talking about!

What are the really bad features of inflation? First, inflation basically is immoral. It is unfair, unjust, and particularly so to those who work on insurance programs, pensions, long-term leases, long-term lenders, bond-holders, or anyone who is prudent and has been saving. These people are penalized for their thrift!

Second, inflation produces psychologic trauma. It is a disease, as Rees-Mogg has described, of inordinancy. There is a loss of freedom; there is an insane increase in limitations; it is a breach of order. **It undermines authority and makes society vulnerable to short-term gratification.** It leads to cultural deterioration and gives rise to the faddists and cultists. In addition, when boundaries are lost, people resort to blame-pinning!

Inflation requires a government to make greater seizure of personal assets. This is normally done by taxation, but taxation causes an uproar and ends in revolution when it is strong enough. Therefore, governments camouflage their program by legally counterfeiting money and appropriating it to produce the blissful illusion of helping society (Johnson's Great Society). But the delusion is always uneven and it brings a false sense of profit. It is intended to redistribute wealth but is received by the appropriated first, ups prices, so that consequently those at the other end have prices rise before they get theirs. It separates tiers in a society even further.

Inflation certainly distorts business calculations. In accounting, fixed assets are usually entered at their cost at the time of procurement, but replacement cost becomes far greater than that on the books; hence business tends to seriously overstate its profits. A business may actually be consuming capital, thinking it is profit.

In taking a course in accounting only six months ago, I was told that any accounting procedure that was adopted prior to 1972 would now be obsolete. A return on invested capital must be current and up-to-date to be accurate.

Illusory profits and cost calculations during inflation lead to a sellers' market **with a decline in the quality of goods or services**. People opt for poorer quality rather than a rise in prices for good quality.

Inflation causes people to become enamored with "get rich quick" schemes. They come to discard sober effort, thrift, honesty, and fair dealing. Debt is encouraged as the effort is made to pay back at cheaper money in the future.

Finally, inflation destroys the security of all classes of people, but it is particularly ruthless with the weakest. It divides society, it is certainly an enemy of altruism, it produces discord, and it tends to promote extremism.

Can it happen in America? Rees-Mogg has said that inflation goes through several major processes. First there is the delusion which gives a false sense of progress because wages rise faster than prices can react. The second phase is one in which prices rise faster than the money supply can be printed.

In the first phase, people tend to postpone buying until prices come down. But, prices don't come down, so they feel they must hurry and buy before prices go up even further. This pushes inflation even faster. New money supply is then required; as governments print more, inflation skyrockets even faster. Finally, the third phase is reached in which people must get rid of their money for some real assets so they will trade it for almost anything. People undergo panic spending and governments topple.

Let us look at some of the factors that are producing inflation right now in this country. **The United States alone is not responsible.** It is an international problem, but we can look at several specific causes right here.

Certainly, we cannot avoid the cost of the wars and the cost of financing foreign aid and the cost for defense. Our dwindling natural resources and balance of payment deficits are also examples of severe capital losses as a country.

We have built-in social services and subsidies, and these require progressively more money. We are dealing with automatic bureaucracy in which there tends to be eternal justification of programs once they are initiated.

We are dealing with massive control by labor. Conditions for inflation worsen as continuous employment and higher wages are demanded.

One of the factors that very few people recognize is the danger of uncontrolled credit extension. This relates to international banks and multi-national corporations who issue pseudo receipts.

Another factor is the increased **velocity at which money moves**. There is an accelerated pace of life; there is a more rapid exchange of money, mostly through the use of computers.

As a biologist I recognize the explosion of the world's population. It is true that more money is needed progressively as more people are born and the population grows. Please read Jonas Salk's *Survival of the Wisest* in which he refers to Epoch A in the past and Epoch B in the future.

Possible Answers

What might be some of the answers? One that seems always to be suggested is, of course, price control. There is a book by Frank Slaughter titled *Constantine* from which I would like to quote. This is a dialogue going on between Constantine and Diocletian. Diocletian, who is trying to ascertain the wisdom of Constantine, asks him:

"With four great armies to maintain and borders to guard, more money must always be found to pay the prices charged by the merchants. The emperors who went before me steadily debased the precious metal in our coin but that only made matters worse. What do you think would be the effect of an edict setting all prices and wages at their present levels?"

"I can see the advantage of fixing the amount of precious metal in the coinage, but I don't think setting prices and wages will be effective."

"Why? I'm only trying to bring order out of what is now a chaos of rising prices and wages."

Constantine replies, "Then do it by fixing the amount of gold and silver in the coins at a higher level than is in them now and making the change permanent. Those who work will then be better paid for their labor and will not demand more. And those who sell will get more for their goods and thus will not be tempted to raise prices."

"How can you say that? All merchants are greedy."

"It is because they're greedy that I believe your plan will fail. If you set the price of everything, merchants will hold goods off the market until they become scarce, then sell them under the table for more than the price set by the government."

"And risk flogging or death?" asks Diocletian.

"Men will risk anything for money. We hardly have enough soldiers now to keep back the barbarians on our frontiers. How will you defend them when your armies are busy arresting merchants, who make more profit than they are entitled to, or artisans who refuse to work for the wages you set?"

"How would fixing the value of the coinage prevent all those evils?"

"Not all merchants sell the same thing for the same price now," Constantine points out. "Someone is always willing to decrease his profit in order to sell more. If left alone, the price of goods will come to a fair level, so long as no one can claim that all money does not have the same value."

This is an interesting viewpoint on price fixing in the third century! There seems to be only one answer that makes sense, based on history. As a start we could return to the gold or some kind of stable standard!

An article in *Business Week* (August 23, 1976) entitled "Stabilizing Economies Clobber the Gold Bugs" may serve as a clue. There is an effort to make gold a simple commodity. This is a vast error in the thinking of the person who wrote because he points to the fact that "the superinflation of 1974 is happily no longer with us, and may not return in our generation." Now, anyone who would accept that belief in an effort to make gold of no value is totally inconsistent with history. Does anyone seriously believe that inflation is going to stop in the United States? [NOTE: look what happened in 1979. Note the value of an average home in America in 1992 was over $100,000.]

In my mind, there was one president who perpetrated the greatest wrong on the country. It was Johnson when his "war on poverty" program was enacted as the Economic Opportunity Act of 1964. This began as a $31 billion expenditure the first year. To date -- twelve years later -- it has been a $860 billion program and is approaching one trillion dollars ($153 billion per year was spent on that project in 1975.)

The food stamp program was originally intended to take care of the indigent, the really poor, those who were really starving, which any decent person supports.

If the first solution is to return to a gold standard, the second solution is simply to limit our massive social services to the absolute needy. A third answer would be, perhaps, the curtailment of some of the international credit, the local credit, some of the pseudo-receipts and the offering of money which is inflationary without sufficient collateral **such as the Savings and Loan programs**. I suppose all of us must share some of the blame because we as individuals are not well informed. [Note: look at the savings and loan scandal of 1990.]

The politician's survival is contingent upon an acquiescence to his voters. The public has become conditioned to expect luxury services, at the expense of the rich ... they hope. Self-interests, group interests, even ethnic interests take precedence over national interest. The numerous factors which cause inflation when uncontrolled end in corruption, weak social institutions, produce paranoia, set class against class, and destroy governments. We are in a cultural spasm.

All cultures need order. Business requires codes of ethics, religions need commandments, institutions need rules, governments need laws, and certainly **money needs standards**. All these make for orderliness. But given an error in any of these things, if no limitations are imposed, the result is anarchy, tyranny, and the dominance of rulers and loss of freedom. The first year it cost $30 million. Now that program has grown to be $5 billion each year, an increase of 1,650%!

For discussion, there are some points which need further clarification. It is not implied that man should NOT be altruistic. One of the messages in this talk is that as inflation proceeds, people begin to resent others for high prices or "gouging" -- the farmer blames the merchant and middleman, the housewife blames the farmer, and everyone blames someone else. As a result there is a lessening of a "spirit of altruism" in all of society. A spirit of good will and a helpful attitude toward the needy must be maintained by all those in an advanced society.

There may be an attitude of gloom cast from this talk, but there are signs of hope. We still have control of our Congress and the office of the President. Proper control should keep the economy from a complete runaway type of Latin American inflation.

There is major increase in the world's population and there must, therefore, be somewhat more currency for exchange. Each individual is entitled to his share of the goods of the world, and it stands to reason that each new life that is born MUST be provided with an economic basis for accumulation of worldly goods. The world can absorb a certain rate of inflation in this manner.

We are thus in a competition with the rest of the world in inflation control. A proper rate will ensure our survival.

However, the fact still remains that strikes -- actual blackmail by those in power in the labor unions -- will exert their effect in direct proportion to the controls the unions themselves put on their own power.

There should be no limitations to technology or limitations of the extension of knowledge. Man, without a belief in an outside source of power, may set himself up as a final authority. The ruler becomes a tyrant and therefore is not in a position to realize his own limitations.

It is well known that the greatest scholars of science and the best students of philosophy run into some impasses of knowledge as they learn more and more about their subjects. As we become more specialized in any field, **we become more humbled by the extent of knowledge that is required**. We should not impose limitations on our ambitions, on our will to do good, or on our individual or collective attainments.

In conclusion: all humanity needs identity. Boundaries with rules enable identity to exist; otherwise there is no order, no limitation for assessment of values. Values of freedom normally have rested on the economic basis of private ownership. The right of government to take property at will, without competition, to restrict it in its extent of power will destroy that freedom. Paper money is only as good as the men who control it.

Belief in God supplies spiritual authority other than self and tends to limit one's power over others. Anyone is mad who sees no limitations in ruling or dominating mankind. Order is needed. Order when lost must be restored for a society's long-range welfare as well as the welfare of the rest of the free world.

Man, throughout his entire evolution, has shown tremendous ability for adaptation and flexibility. Who can know of the discoveries of tomorrow! There is hope, there is a bright tomorrow!

As I look at the youth of today, their smiles, their ambitions, and their faith and trust, I cannot help feeling that there must be answers to these problems when they are recognized. Perhaps this talk has been one small effort to bring some of these factors to light.

1. Rees-Mogg, William, *The Crisis of World Inflation*, Baxter, Greenwich, Conn. 1975.
2. Toffler, Alvin, *The Eco-Spasm Report*, Bantam Books, New York, 1975.
3. Salk, Jonas, *The Survival of the Wisest*, Harper & Row, New York, 1973.
4. Slaughter, Frank G., *Constantine*, Pocket Books, New York, 1967.

* * *

The Fall of 1976 was depressing. Now, for the third time in recent history, as I recall, a presidential candidate had to defend a previous record. People had had enough of Watergate, and Ford had pardoned Nixon.

I remember the tremendous contest between Reagan and Ford for the nomination in the campaign of 1976. Ford won the nomination only because of a better organization. Carter was put up by the Democrats as their best candidate to run against Ford. Naturally, running on Nixon's record, Ford was defeated. Carter, knowing nothing other than to support the platform and the massive social programs, went back to and continued the programs the Democratic Congress had started.

Thus ended 1976 with frustrations experienced by many Americans but to the delight of many others.

The Doctrine of Possibility

In 1977 I focused on forecasting growth, the use of the computer, the new methods of treatment, and the pathologic conditions of the jaw joint. In addition, I particularly stressed the "Science of Esthetics".

Three outstanding occasions were quite significant. Our Foundation for Orthodontic Research was able to arrange a meeting with Robert Ardrey for February of 1977. We sat for five hours talking in the hotel room in New Orleans. The next day he gave an address, and the following day we videotaped a two-and-one-half-hour session discussing the issues of his writings. He was still pushing for the instinctual force of private ownership.

In April I made my third trip to Japan, for a three-day course. This time the doctrine of possibilities was explained. That was followed by my second visit to Australia in May 1977 for the Seventh Orthodontic Congress at Surfers Paradise in Queensland. I gave four lectures but was disappointed with the acceptance.

The Dissections

Another factor to account for the dearth of research and publications in 1977 was the breaking up of my partnership with Dr. Bench. We had been together for seventeen years. We had started a second joint practice in San Fernando Valley and he lived in that area. He was a Deacon in the Mormon Church and was tired of traveling through the mountains to work. That office needed more attention, so we decided to split things as evenly as possible and everything was cordial.

Remarriage

Probably the most noteworthy happening in 1978 was my divorce and subsequent marriage to Bunnie (Elmyra). She was originally from the Baltimore area and had become, after some modeling and acting, a superb fine arts photographer. She had exhibited in Europe and Los Angeles and received acclaim. I had met her as a patient and we became friends.

The wedding party on October 27 was a smash. I sang to her "And I Love You So" with the band. Robert St. Martin, a dentist, painter, sculptor, pilot, sportsman and philosopher, was my best man. I had first met him in 1960 when he attended one of my courses, and over the years he became one of my best friends.

Thus my life-style was changing. The years were speeding by.

* * *

After having split the practice with Bench I was further dissected with a split of my remaining estate with my former wife. In 1979, at the age of 59 I was making a new start.

Stagflation and Carter

As I started anew there was a new business climate. For the first time I heard the word "stagflation". The economic pump had been primed again and again by putting money int the economy and lowering interest rates by the Federal Reserve Board Too much mone would bring on more inflation, and too little might not stimulate the economy enough When interest rates on money are lowered, people borrow to build homes and establis businesses. When interest rates are high, foreign investment is attracted for a good retur on their money.

A cutback in the military budget was enacted. There was little attention given to moral or performance in the armed services. Hostages were taken in the Middle East, and ou attempt to recover them was an international comedy of errors, and grossly embarrassing the third major one in the 1970s.

Congress had consistently picked on the military, and now it had come back to haun them. Contrary to past trends, interest percentage rates had now climbed close to 20%, an inflation was at an annual rate of 15% under the Carter administration. We were on collision course, and everyone was concerned, both here and abroad, because the dolla which had become a standard world reference was being destroyed.

A student will find that three metal coins have been used for monetary exchange in the history of the world: copper, silver and gold. In times of well-controlled governments and in times of prosperity, the coins historically will have been seen to have superb artistic worl and be made of essentially pure metal of one of these types. When a country starts to decline two things will be noted. One is that the beauty of the coin slips, the pride in th workmanship lowers. The second is that the precious metals will be eliminated and tin o other base metals will be used. It was true of Rome, it was true of the Emperor Constantin in 330. Kennedy half-dollars and quarters and dimes came to have a numismatic valu because of the purity of the silver. But as the silver had greater value than the exchang value of the coin, under that kind of inflation, the precious metal had to be replaced durin the Johnson administration. Our coins became a tin-like copper sandwich. It was a sign o deterioration of our currency, but no one shouted out.

The Pumpline Frustrations

The fourth major U.S. embarrassment in the 1970s was the specially engineered gasolin shortage and the subsequent rise in prices. America had been spoiled. In 1935, when I wa in high school, I remember buying gasoline at the pump for 11 cents per gallon. Ten cent was for the gas and one cent was tax. By 1950 the price was still only 27 cents with 20 cent for the gas and seven for taxes. With Ford-type production lines in Detroit and the oil field of Texas, every American was almost capable of middle-class status, with his own car Even by 1973 gasoline was only 37 cents (26 cents for the fuel and 11 cents for taxes). In 1970, 6.5 million automobiles were produced together with 1.7 million trucks and buse in the United States. The demand for gasoline was evermore increasing.

In 1973, when Egypt struck Israel in the Yom Kippur War, all the Middle Eastern oi nations temporarily united against those who supported Israel., Oil prices per barrel wen from $3.00 to $12.00. Six years later, in 1979, with the fall of the Shah in Iran, price quadrupled to almost $50.00 per barrel. Not only did prices for gasoline rise to the $1.5(range but gasoline was withheld intentionally to raise the prices.

Americans are impatient people, and to take time waiting for a station to have one pump with gas was belittling; everyone who could was putting tanks in their back yards. We were waiting in line at the service stations, with rationing looming, while loaded tankers were visibly anchored offshore at Santa Monica, California. Meanwhile, we were told by Carte that there was an actual shortage and that the earth was doomed to run out of oil by 2010.

whereas in fact there was an actual oil glut and new reserves were being discovered in many parts of the world.

S. I. Hayakawa, who was a Senator from California, remarked that we had been spoiled by low prices, particularly when compared to Europe, and that the really poor didn't buy gasoline anyway. For this he was ridiculed and quickly rejected.

With the fall of the Shah, American interests in the Middle East were awakened. We had helped to arm Iran as a buffer against the U.S.S.R. movement. With his fall and his successors hating us, we leaned toward Iraq and Hussein as the lesser of two evils. We were not informed concerning his war machine, which was being put together in a complicated and subtle manner. The Cold War had distorted our whole perspective.

But historically, the Arab world had fears of Iranian aggression, and the stage was being set for a conflict with Syria with Libya supporting Iran and all the other Arab countries supporting Iraq. The future of oil supplies for the free world economy was involved.

These were the conditions on the American scene in 1979.

Professional Dilemmas

The climactic year of the seventies was busy professionally. In all, I was away from the practice 27 times. Despite the business of the work and the lecturing I still found time to produce six papers and a book in 1979. The book, "Bioprogressive Therapy", was done with other colleagues and included some of my previous writings. It has been a hallmark in the field and has been translated into Spanish and German.

It was obvious that something had to give. It seemed I could make a complete career of teaching alone. I could not do everything. We were planning to build a home in the estates at Palisades Highlands, which demanded time.

People asked which I liked most, the clinical treatment of patients, the research, the writing, or the teaching. My answer was that they were like four children, and I loved them all. I could help train someone to do the clinical work, but research, writing and teaching would be difficult to delegate.

The practice had reached a plateau. After moving into a new building in 1978 I was no longer aggressive in building the practice further. It was obvious it needed better attention, because I was being pulled in too many directions.

I had two young men assist me, both U.C.L.A. graduates. Dr. Ken Fischer was developing his own practice in Orange County. He was an excellent worker and a good researcher, and has remained a loyal friend. He became manager of the Foundation for Orthodontic Research. Dr. Hilgers from Northwestern had stayed only two or three years, and continued to teach our philosophy. Dr. Rick Jacobson became very interested in the broad aspects of our whole movement. With his enthusiasm, he seemed to be the best candidate to continue that particular practice. I felt he was almost like a part of the family and I sold him the practice.

Recapitulation of the Deterioration of the 1970s

As we entered the decade of the 1970s I had foreseen many problems facing America. As it ended, citizens needed to take a long look at the direction our culture was shifting. The problem of drugs had sneaked up to bite painfully.

We were not aware of the ravages of stress. The Cold War had us contracting. It was a whole world involvement. Anxiety accompanied our daily decisions. We suffered a series of embarrassments as a nation. Moreover, arguments were increased at the intellectual level. Morality itself came to be argued regarding war, abortion, and religion. The divorce rate rose to about 50% of the frequency of marriages. The liberation movement for women and the frustration of race and color issues all added to the problems.

Technology had also played a large role in the shift of the culture. Live television brought everything newsworthy, including hot wars, into our living rooms. Our culture became entertainment-oriented. News became an entertainment form. Anything bad or hideous became news. Interpersonal conflicts made news and ripe and juicy rumors became immediate attractions.

Computers meant high speed; computers demanded more attention, and created more stress because of increased competition. Many feared computers, associating their high speed with car accidents caused by recklessness. But computers give information which necessary for prudent decisions. They become a full-time working assistant that wears down only when the power is turned off.

During the 1970s we suffered possibly the greatest price increases and inflation America had ever known. This led to some economic panic. With the emergence of foreign goods of superior quality we began to pin blame on our own manufacturers. It led to frustration. Even our national security was questioned.

But the greatest of all problems, as I saw it, was the change in attitudes of the American public. Democracy and freedom demand responsibility and accountability for a personal conduct. If an amount of disorder is required for that freedom of choice to be exercised commands that tolerance for others' disorder be granted. I saw intolerance being manifested in many ways.

People grew disturbed at the slightest inconvenience. Children had no ability or capacity to tolerate any discomfort whatsoever or any inconvenience. We were supposed to be pain-free and problem-free society. We grew softer in many ways. The word "wimp" became a popular buzz word.

We not only grew irresponsible about ourselves, we didn't care about others. We didn't graciously ask, we demanded. No one made a decision without first asking, "What's in it for me?" **The typical child did not want to push himself to learn.** The ethers were supposed to bless him with knowledge, as he imagined someone else was responsible for learning for him. We began to depend on gadgets.

All this lack of personal fortitude led to the alibi and to the blaming of others. "If it's not my fault, it's got to be someone else's fault," was the thinking. This in turn led to litigation-conscious society. The other person even though he did his best "goofed up" - therefore sue him. This further led to a plethora of malingerers and deliberate fault-finders.

Thus, not only was the "American century" slipping away economically, the "American character" was being lost. Something drastic needed to be done!

The old homestead, ca. 1904 (six years before my parents' marriage). Dad is behind my grandmother on left. Mom is in background in center. Uncle Tom is in background on right center. Great-grandmother is in center holding child. The bay window was where Mom struggled to keep some green plants alive in winter. The house was leveled by a midwest tornado in the 1950s.

The old barn and silo, ca. 1940. Cement works beside old John the mule was the foundation of an older silo blown down. Jocko, our little mule, is in the foreground heading down to a stream.

Dad (on tractor) and Tom and a neighbor with my brother Joe, ca. 1915.

Five of us with a litter of pups. Brother Joe was elsewhere. I'm in black bloomers at about age three.

My brother Jim and I on knees in front of two neighbor friends, ca. 1927.

Dad and Mom on a Sunday afternoon in the front yard, ca. 1942.

PICTURES IN HIGH SCHOOL (1934 TO 1938).

Wearing "K" sweater, with two school mates.

The 1936 Kokomo High School basketball team was the only one in history dismissed for striking against a coach. I'm #4 on front row at age 16.

COLLEGE LIFE AT INDIANA UNIVERSITY

R.O.T.C. uniform: I'm with Mom on right. On left, Joe Dewberry, a roommate, who was killed leading a platoon in Bougainville two years later.

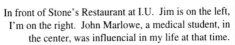
In front of Stone's Restaurant at I.U. Jim is on the left, I'm on the right. John Marlowe, a medical student, in the center, was influencial in my life at that time.

Our family in front yard, ca. 1944. Notice the high tank in the background which still functions for Kokomo Gas Co. From left to right: Esther, Mary, Mom, Dad, Jeanette, Jim, and me.

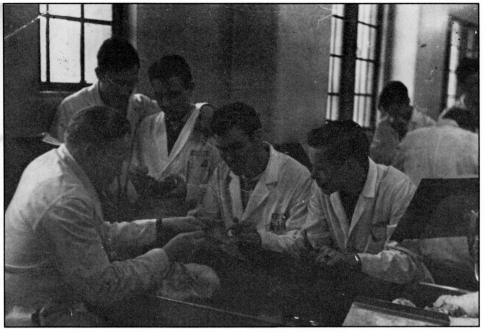

Five of us are dissecting a cadaver in dental school, 1943. Only half the class graduated.

As a private
in the U.S.
Army ASTP
Corp, 1943,
age 23.

e dentists and
r corpsmen at
mp Sheldon,
ginia, 1946.
second from
right.

Jim and I as officers in the Navy in 1945.

On a long boat with my corpsmen at Key West
Submarine Base in 1947. I'm on the right. Truman
made this base his holiday quarters.

Our starting graduate class in orthodontics at University of Illinois. [Pruzansky, Walters, McGonagle, Kincaid, Wood, King, Schaeffer, Ricketts, Rogge, Wong] Notable professors sitting. Brodie, department head, is third from left.

Cutting up with straw hats at a picnic, 1949. [Dan Watkins, Sam Pruzansky, Ricketts]

A party with our mentor Dr. William Downs, Jerry Borden and Harvey Cole, later, 1961. (I'm on the left.)

The home we built on Rimmer Avenue in Pacific Palisades, 1955. Note the cement roof.

LIFE IN CALIFORNIA

With my first family in front of the home [Patricia, and children Robin, Gale, and Craig] 1960.

The children later: Gale, me, son-in-law Mike Machette, Craig, and Robin Machette, 1975.

My life was occupied with research, practice, teaching
and writing. Someone, it seemed, was always
observing.

Central
carousel,
original design
1962, for
work theatre.

Planning La Colina Professional Building, 1959. (I'm seated at center.)

The original planning staff for UCLA School of Dentistry, 1959. (I'm on the right.)

with Dr. Henry Kawamoto and Dr. Paul Tessier, the world-recognized plastic surgeon from Paris.

with the author and playwright
Robert Ardrey

with Dr. Hans Selye of Montreal, Canada, finder of the stress syndrome

with Dr. Janet Travell, John Kennedy's White House physician

The Board of Directors for the Foundation for Orthodontic Research (FOR). This private organization has contributed over one million dollars to research. Ruel Bench and I, front center, are honorary co-chairmen.

Vic Benton, Dick Starr, Hugh Simms and me at a practice organization meeting in 1975.

with Rolf Diernberger (L) and Ernst Hosl (R), two colleagues responsible for orthodontic education in Europe.

Receiving the Hinman Award in Dentistry with Dr. Ron Goldstein 1977.

A talk show with Dr. Allan Brodie and Dr. Cecil Steiner, 1974. Dr. Robert Payne is in the background.

Studying a computer printout in 1973.

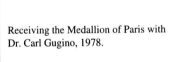

Receiving the Ketcham Award in Orthodontics with Dr. John Rathbone, 1975.

Receiving the Medallion of Paris with Dr. Carl Gugino, 1978.

With a group who lead the Ricketts Study Club in Japan.

Entering the ballroom with Bunnie for wedding celebration, 1978.

Bunnie and Anastarr.

With Bunnie dancing with our daughter, Anastarr, and niece Amanda Machette.

With Juan Canut, autho friend and disciple, in S

With officers of Rocky Mountain Orthodontics. R, Martin Brusse, President; C, Dan Van Straten, Vice President.

Singing with Victor West, Department head at Melbourne, Australia, a dear friend.

With Dr. Clark Jones, instigator of the Rickett Library.

With founders and officers of the Ricketts Society of Italy.

With planning committee of the Ricketts Library at Loma Linda, California.

At a meeting seated with coach and commentator Dick Vermiel, a widely admired motivator of people.

With Betsy and Col. Oliver North at Christmas party in the home of Dr. Robert Sears, 1991.

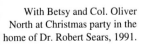

The Reappearing American

11
REBOUND, RESENTMENT AND REEXAMINATION
(1980 - 1990)

How quickly we forget the past. How inviting is the tendency to ridicule and find fault in hindsight.

Our Situation in 1980

As America came into the Eighties there was still anxiety that the Cold War could become hot. Former presidents in both parties had supported the modernization of Iran under the Shah with the objective that this Persian Islam population would be a buffer against Soviet imperialism. When the Shah was overthrown in 1979 during the Carter administration, and the exiled Khomeini returned and put down all opposition, all blame was thrown at America. Faces of hatred were shown on our television screens.

With the downfall of the Shah, the Soviets had invaded the adjacent country of Afghanistan. Under the purges of a holy war, Khomeini had encouraged the Shiite rebellion against Saddam Hussein in Iraq. In effect, this started the Iran-Iraq war in 1980.

Our country was also confronted with fear of terrorism. Khadhafi in Libya based his theories on Mao Tse Tung and was suspected of training terrorists for international disruption as a part of a major leftist movement. We started X-ray luggage checks at airports. Anyone traveling to Europe grew accustomed to seeing armed soldiers with automatic rifles at exits leading to the airplanes.

Evangelists such as my friend Hal Lindsey were predicting that this might be the beginning of the fulfillment of the book of Revelation (16:14), the battle of Armageddon, the final conflict between good and evil.

A Democratic Congress had complied with 80% of Carter's requests. The defense budget had been hammered down for the sake of more social benefits, not for reduction of taxes. When hostages were taken at our embassy in Teheran, our inept military attempt to retrieve them was a joke. Morale, equipment and leadership in the armed services was pitiful, coming as it did after the public derision of the Vietnam affair.

The delegates of the Republican party sensed they had made a great error in 1976. Now in the new election it was Ronald Reagan all the way. They called him just an actor, but he had been successful for two terms as Governor of the state of California. He was a shrewd business man and had served as president of a union, the Screen Actors Guild. The gross national product of his state, if taken as that of an individual country, would be the sixth largest in the world. He was a good manager. And a good manager delegates authority! Many criticized him for delegating, but on the other hand, who in his right mind would attempt to handle all of the details of running the Federal government except an out-and-out dictator-like person who trusted no one.

We needed leadership as never before. When Reagan was finally nominated many thought he was as ready as anyone to tackle the job of the Presidency. I personally felt he was our best shot. I wrote a letter to Reagan to warn him about the buffoon climate in Washington and how they would try to make a clown out of him. I further described the earlier social programs as Stage One of a rocket propulsion and that Carter had ignited Stage Two, the momentum of which we had not yet caught full force. **The inevitable deficit spending required for those programs alone would keep skyrocketing.** Having met Reagan and talked privately, I liked the man very much, yet had anxiety for him.

What Could He Do?

Reagan's campaign promises were to restore the national defense and to bring some respect back for servicemen and public officials. He also promised better efficiency in government and a change in the prevailing economic conditions.

It has been my observation that anyone working for the government tends to become oblivious to costs. "Goofing off" by government workers is a classic occurrence. As in a union, the "stringing out" of a job becomes an art. "Cost plus" contracts are hedges for sloppiness and inefficiency. "Time padding" was a trick of most trades.

Anyone going to Washington soon discovers a jungle of entanglement. As I heard columnist Jack Anderson describe, a new senator will come on the beat and be full of enthusiasm and try to fulfill his ambition and make a difference. He soon discovers, however, that the whole thing is run by bureaucrats having Civil Service status: since they are not elected they almost cannot be fired. No sooner is the senator settled than the desire for entrenchment sets in. He starts re-running long before the next election.

It's always been a mystery to me why candidates spend millions of dollars to be elected to jobs that pay only thousands. There must be some perks or kickbacks coming from someplace that we don't know about.

When I began to look at what Reagan alone could do, it was really not much. His main thrust was to communicate with the people, and influence the Congress. As the executive branch of our government, the President had only a privilege to suggest and has a right to veto bills.

As Commander-in-Chief, the President has certain control of the military. He also has power, somewhat, in education. But **all spending is approved and controlled by Congress**. The President merely makes the budget proposal.

There always has been and always will be a conflict between the Chief Executive and Congress. This becomes ever more a difference when the Congress is Democratically-controlled and the President is Republican. Maybe the public intuitively senses the need for brakes to be applied on the traditional penchant for social spending on the part of Congress which never stops. Even Republicans, allegedly conservative, are spenders. Please read Goldwater's "Conscience of a Conservative" written in 1960, and find how correct he turned out to be in some of his views.

* * *

We Were Still Rich

Despite World War II, the Korean War, the Vietnam encounter, the fiascos of the Middle East and our role of supplying an international police force, we were still rich in 1980. The reasons for this may be speculated upon. One factor was that we had become accustomed to deficit spending which had been started by Roosevelt in 1938. We were borrowing money, partly from ourselves but foreigners could buy our government bonds, and buy they did. In addition, foreigners could buy our real estate, businesses and securities. **This all continued to pump capital into our economy.**

Many foreigners were concerned about government instability in their countries. To foreigners, investment of capital was deemed to be a better prospect and safer risk in America. In fact, when I was in South America in 1961, it was rumored that much of the millions given to South American countries in Kennedy's Alliance for Progress did not go to the people, but instead had been worked into private hands and was within weeks reinvested back in the United States. In my trips to Europe, as well, colleagues would privately inquire regarding good investments in the U.S.

But it was obvious in 1980 that our own core economy was at risk. Journalists like to call our great century the "smoke stack" industrial period. The moving belt assembly line methods had been copied abroad. Japan bought our scrap iron. Their automation and our high labor costs were driving us out of competition.

One other serious problem was that most American people had misconceptions about the profits and stability of our major industries. This was also reflected in the willingness of Congress to tax producers. These taxes had to be tacked onto the sales prices in order to turn a profit and stay in business. The result was the tendency of the American companies to make cheaper products. No one seemed to understand this. Finally, unions demanded medical care. If the government didn't have socialized medicine, then "someone should take care of me", and it was anyone with deep pockets. "Health for me is someone else's responsibility" was the attitude.

Also, people were demanding more regulations. If people could not accept responsibility for fairness, then they must be controlled. This meant agencies and new taxes for their supervision. People who try to stretch the limit of the law must be controlled by tighter and tighter regulation. Smog and pollution control, emission control, and literally hundreds of regulations continued to be enacted because businesses and individuals were not responsible for themselves. When Reagan suggested deregulation of the airlines for the promotion of competition there was a howl. When he turned against strikers, air traffic controllers, and civil employees there was a stiff reaction by unionists.

Experiences at Age 60 (1980)

In May it was time for another decade celebration of my own birthday. This time I planned an even greater celebration: a three-day affair. For the dinner dance and banquet we took over the ballroom at the Riviera Country Club. Friends from four continents came. A whole group from Germany arrived with a large crate that had been air-shipped with their flight. It contained a beautiful six-foot high antique armoire built in 1826. They opened it at the party with a lovely ceremony. What a thrill -- true friends indeed. I am lucky.

Dr. Paul Tessier

The Foundation for Orthodontic Research meeting that year was in Monaco. A European Foundation was starting. For that meeting we had on our program the world's foremost plastic surgeon, Dr. Paul Tessier from Paris. I had met him in 1978 and taken his course previously in Chicago. During and after World War II, Tessier had been engaged in reconstructing faces after traumatic injuries. He had studied the work of previous French surgeons and had created techniques to literally take the whole skull apart, eye sockets included, and reassemble the parts into a beautiful order. Thus, the children with hideous congenital deformities in many kinds of distorted features could be put into society as acceptable members.

I had by now more than a 30-year track record of care for some of these conditions, but never had met anyone as heroic as Tessier. He was magnificent. He presented his material first in 1967 and, like many others with new ideas, was rejected by his local society as being utterly unrealistic. Now he is known all over the world and has taught many of his techniques which he continues to improve. I have spent days studying the long-term results in his office in Paris.

For posterity, I made a two-hour video interview with him. I knew that he had to have come from something exceptional in his background. I myself had been a farm boy. His father had been a blacksmith! How often it is that productive and innovative adults have in their youth been closely associated with the earth.

Rediscovering the Divine Proportion

As a youth on the farm, I first conceived of a relationship which I later learned was called the "golden section", where a line could be divided so that the smaller section would be in the same proportion to the larger section as the larger was to the whole line. It has been known since the time of the Egyptians and probably before. This was also called the "divine proportion" by Pacioli, a teacher of Leonardo da Vinci.

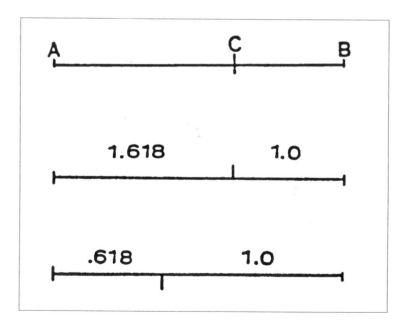

One of the objectives of a computer study of facial growth in the side view, made in 1966, was to ascertain if possible a "center" or a single point in the face from which growth would diverge. By 1968 a radial point was located. This meant that there was an underlying phenomenon on which any point lying closer to the center would move less with growth and more distant points would correspondingly move a greater amount in order to maintain the same form. This was a sort of "big bang" idea -- the order of the universe, and the order of the growth of sea shells. I called it the "polar growth phenomenon", as if behavior radiated from a magnetic pole.

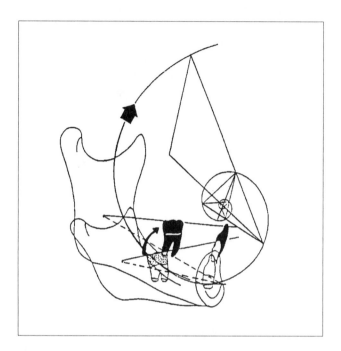

Still another finding by 1971 was the discovery of an "arc" or curve on which the lower jaw growth could be predicted over several years. Nature tends to grow in curves. It took some months to find the most reliable curve. This was first published in 1972.

I continued to wonder about these fascinating observations and continued to improve the science by acquiring more details. I tried at the same time to review my plane geometry and trigonometry, but I needed to know solid geometry for study of a three-dimensional object such as the human head and face. My mathematical analytic ability was not up to my observations.

I remembered that a colleague, Dr. Melvin Moss in New York City, was knowledgeable about analytic geometry. He was head of the Anatomy Department at Columbia University and also at the time Dean of the Dental School. My daughter Gale lived in New York, and on one visit there in 1979 I was graciously received by Dr. Moss and his wife Lettie in his laboratory at the university. He was already familiar with some of my work and previously, without knowledge of my arcial discovery, had described a logarithmic spiral of growth for the lower jaw which I supported.

When I told him that I observed a relationship of some order in growth as a 1,2,3,4 proportion he immediately barked, "I wish you had said 1,2,3,5!" I inquired why.

"That's Fibonacci numbers. You know that, don't you?" he asked.

"Well, I'm a little fuzzy. Tell me more."

"You should know all about the Divine Proportion and the Fibonacci numbers." With that he reached up on a shelf nearby and drew out a small paperback copy of a book entitled

"The Divine Proportion -- A Study in Mathematical Beauty" by H. E. Huntley, who was a teacher of mathematics and physics in England. As I opened the book (which had been published in 1970) and glanced only at illustrations, I shouted, "This is it! This is what I've been seeing!"

The divine proportion is an extension or application of the golden section. It is a principal key to beauty. But more than that, it is a key to functional arrangements of muscles and bones for maximum mechanical efficiency.

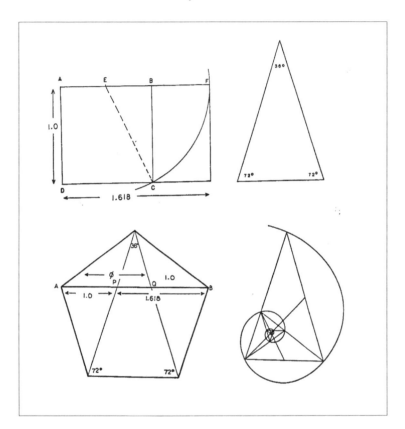

This ("Fibonacci") proportion is 1 to 1.618. When it is used as the larger to the smaller unit, it is 1 to 0.382. It was called Phi (ø) in honor of an Ancient Greek sculptor named Phidias who used it in his work. It is a unique number, establishing a link between geometry and numbers.

0	1	1	3	3	5
1	1	2	3	5	8
1	2	3	5	8	13

In a series   when the last two

numbers in a series are added, soon each increase will be 1.61803 times the last number. This principle was discovered by Filias Bonacci, a son of a Roman customs agent stationed in Africa, and named FIBONACCI. It was he who in 1202 introduced Arabic numbers to the Roman world.

Beauty and Esthetics

Beauty and esthetics have been thought to be subjective and difficult to describe. Beauty pleases the senses and charms the intellect. Esthetics is the study of beauty and its psychologic responses. When judged by the individual, something is not truly beautiful until it arouses an emotional feeling.

It is thought that within the constellation of the nerves at the very center of our primitive brain there is stored a property for esthetic appreciation, genetically endowed and biologically derived. This is a center for sorting the sensations of sight, sound, touch, smell and taste, and is called the limbic system, or the reptilian complex. It is contained within what is described as the reticular formation at the base of the brain.

It was fortuitous that I came upon this phenomenon. My whole outlook on our world suddenly changed. I began to see beauty where I had never recognized it before. I saw grace and splendour in things that formerly were common. For a time my life became a poem. Color took on new meaning.

Beauty was seen in the branching of trees and bushes. Sea shells had their secrets of beauty unlocked. Delicate flowers displayed God's handwriting. The intervals in birdsongs became natural music understood. My love for beauty in the natural world was aching for expression.

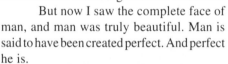

This reaction occurred despite the fact that thirty years before I had already been the first in my field to set parameters and standards for harmony and balance of the lips and mouth with the face for esthetic guides for treatment.

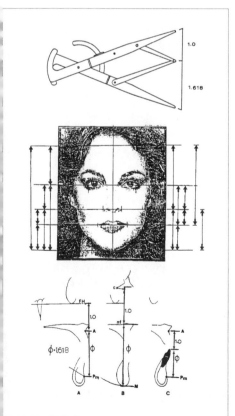

But now I saw the complete face of man, and man was truly beautiful. Man is said to have been created perfect. And perfect he is.

Probably most attractive is the human face. Man's face is a complete medley of divine proportions from any angle it is observed. We are assembled and grow harmonically. The human face presents a vision of beauty unadorned.

With the background of so many years of study, it took only days for me to unravel the congruity of the face. Beneath the surface was the bony structure supporting the face, the proportions of the base of the human skull and the elegance and the golden majesty of the order of the jaws and teeth.

When two parts were related in a divine proportion arrangement I described them as being "golden".

When lovers cuddle they hold and adore hands. The human hand is a remarkably beautiful structure and an instrument of perfection. Each segment of each finger is golden to the next. Making a fist forms a logarithmic spiral from the forefinger through the thumb. The extended hand is golden to the forearm and the forearm is golden to the center of the shoulder blade This arrangement provides efficiency in buttoning the shirt or tying a tie.

The foot is golden to the foreleg and in turn the foreleg is golden to the top of the hip -- a functional unit. From the top of the hip the rest of the body is golden to the top of the head Thus the whole body is composed in regal golden splendor. It goes down to minute detail because form is determined by the arrangement of cells. The lower front tooth is golden to the upper front tooth. Even the twisted staircase models of the DNA molecule display these golden characteristics.

Three more geometric figures are of interest in the "golden cut" connection (1.0 to 1.618). (See page 222) The first is a rectangle with the base and altitude being Phi (ø). Interestingly, it is the proportion of a credit card. The second is the triangle with the two sides and base forming a 72°-72°-36° figure which gives a base of 1.0 and sides of 1.618 proportion. When the base angle is bisected it produces another triangle of identical shape. When its points are connected with a curve it forms a logarithmic spiral. The third is the pentagon, the form of which is seen in the core of an apple and the base of a star.

How was I to explain this vision? How could I not be excited about its practical application? It became my tool for diagnosis of deformities and became a medium through which planning for correction of the face could be conducted.

An instrument had previously been designed, a divider with two interconnected parts in proportion so that it would widen and maintain the proportion at any length. I redesigned this caliper for the facial dimensions; it then applied for dentistry, orthodontics or for facial surgery as a guide for the positioning of parts. Unattractive faces with orthodontics or facial surgery were transformed into faces of positive beauty through its use.

Starting in 1980 I lectured on this principle before many audiences in orthodontics and plastic surgery. It is a joy to take a beautiful lady or gentleman from an audience and explain why they are so attractive.

We also built a home in Pacific Palisades based on many of these proportions (described on page 244).

* * *

Two other very important medical events took place in 1980. One was good, one was horrible.

The good was the announcement that smallpox had been eradicated. The bad was that AIDS was discovered and was incurable; and worse, it was suggested to be a disease only found in homosexuals.

Shocks in '81
Prior to Reagan's taking office, Iran released its 52 hostages. Reagan took over in January, and in March was wounded by a gunman. In May, Pope John Paul was also wounded. Streets everywhere were no longer safe.

Professional Experiences in 1981
Due to the developments with the Divine Proportion, we started courses in Orthognathic Surgery with Dr. Henry Kawamoto, a plastic and reconstructive surgeon in Santa Monica and U.C.L.A. who had been trained by Tessier in Paris.

I had accepted the job of program chairman for the American Association of Orthodontists convention to be held in San Francisco. My old graduate school classmate Dr. Robert

McGonagle of Euclid, Ohio was president. We wanted a bang-up program with a mix of practical and theoretical subjects. I pulled in several friends as a committee and arranged the program which included about 40 speakers. I felt very strongly about the role of nutrition at that time (and still do) and obtained Dr. Lindon Smith, a very well-known pediatrician from Portland, Oregon, to be the keynote speaker for the convention. He wrote "Feed Your Kids Right", had been on several talk shows on television and was very entertaining.

We attracted the largest attendance ever at a meeting up until that time. Since the divine proportion application was so new I took the liberty of grabbing a spot on the program myself. I am accustomed to being put last on the program in order to hold the audience until the last day. But it's unpleasant to see people leaving a lecture early to check out of hotels or to catch a plane.

At national or local meetings it is customary for committee members to wear certain colored ribbons on their name tags so that visitors and members can easily get information and advice. Some committees may wear a certain type of jacket as a uniform for identification at a convention. This time, because the meeting was held in a cosmopolitan city, I asked my assistants to wear top hats. I thought it would be fun. When we all showed up for the meeting, I was the only one with a top hat, so wear it I did! People wondered who the strange character was walking around the convention in the daytime with a top hat. They must have thought I was an Englishman fresh from the Derby.

The entertainment chairman had called one day and explained the plan for an evening of dinner and entertainment in the Galleria in San Francisco. Several hundred would be in attendance. A band was hired and a floor show was to be presented. One of the acts was to be a jitterbug contest, and he wanted me to be in it. I rejected the idea, busy as I was, but at his insistence I finally agreed. It was necessary to work out a routine, so I went to San Francisco on two visits just to practice with a group from the dance studio contracted for the performance. It was different from what I had taught 40 years before. We worked out to canned music. I hid a plaid jacket, loud red tie white shoes, and straw hat and slipped backstage after the dinner. We dancers took our positions and as the cue for the dance was given we rushed on stage.

Now it was a big live band sound with the old swing! I couldn't remember even how to start the routine I had rehearsed. I therefore grabbed my partner and said, "Let's go -- just follow me!" I moved up front and went into an old routine that came back to me from years before. We brought down the house. Backstage, when we finished all the young people in the act came up to me and asked where I had learned to dance like that. I had stolen the show. Not bad for age 61, I thought.

Futuristics

Prior to that meeting our Foundation had a meeting in Monterey. I had prepared a long paper on "Futuristics" wherein I outlined fifty new movements in the field in the social, biological, clinical or mechanical sciences. In addition, I had worked up a television interview with another well-known orthodontist, Dr. Reed Holdaway from Provo, Utah.

I had packed my tuxedo knowing that a formal dinner was planned for the committee people at the American Association of Orthodontics convention. My wife, Bunnie, wanted to visit the sites around the ocean there and this delayed our drive to San Francisco. The dinner was to honor me together with others, but my secretary had not noted it on my calendar which was loaded. I kept thinking there was some reason for me to be there early. As it was, we never got there until late at night. The next morning McGonagle called me in disgust for missing the evening. I was heartsick to have disappointed my old friend.

The second awkward experience was a surprise. The national meeting is usually the first week of May and my birthday is the 5th of May. Some of the young men on the committee had gone around insisting to others to be sure to be in the main hall at a specific time for a big event. Prior to one of the lectures I was called to the podium and all at once everyone sang Happy Birthday.

But that was only the start. Very soon a lady and a gentleman came in. She dropped her coat and went into a wild belly dance with the appropriate music. But it didn't stop there. One of the fellows tied an apron around my waist and gave me a couple of fun gifts and then told me to lift my apron to hold them. Concealed under the apron there dropped out a huge cloth penis over a foot long. This was in front of the whole society, foreigners and all, and was in poor taste for that occasion. I tried to make as light of it as I could, but later I received nasty phone calls from some members saying it was my fault and my idea. I was more embarrassed than anyone.

Developments in 1981

In January Reagan had taken office, with a Republican majority in only the Senate. We sensed a profound change by the end of that year. The country was on a rebound, it seemed, but many were disturbed with the prospects of deregulation and the threat of dropping some of the farm subsidies. The influence of the Cold War was still with us; Poland imposed martial law.

A Changing Pattern

At our Foundation meeting in Hilton Head, South Carolina, I delivered and later published three papers. One was on the convergence of attitudes among various workers in the field regarding the diseases of the jaw joint. The second was on the present beliefs of orthopedic or skeletal change possible. The third was directed at the waning interest I began to detect with professional people and their societies. I used "The Lives of a Cell" by Lewis Thomas as backdrop in a paper entitled "The Mutual Interdependence of Societies With Their Members".

Perhaps the reader would enjoy some thoughts expressed in that latter paper published in the Proceedings of the Foundation for Orthodontic Research, 1982:

> For best progress, we in the health sciences need to be connected, for man is the most social of all social animals. However, it is difficult for us to feel our conjoined intelligence. Zimon points out that "The invention of a mechanism for the systematic publication of fragments of scientific work may well have been the key event in the history of modern science."

> Thus, the gathering of modest contributions to this store of knowledge is the secret of western science, and achieves a collective power far greater than one individual can exert. This fact justifies the existence of research organizations and forums for expression of professional ideas. As we report and cry out our findings and observations, maybe we have our own pheromones.

> To be sure, enthusiasm is catching. We continue to be stimulated, but maybe it is more than just a simple situation. There may indeed be a chemical bonding that takes place among us because we affect each other in remarkable ways. This is witnessed by observations of young women living in close

quarters in dormitories who spontaneously synchronize their menstrual cycles. In fact, we have witnessed this with our own assistants in common at the chairside.

There are forces which drive humankind together just as surely as the lower social animals are obliged to work together. Organisms join into communities and communities into ecosystems. If this is the way, we may view genes for chemical marking of self and perhaps the reflexes and responses of aggression as secondary developments in evolution which are necessary to control and modulate symbiosis in the first place. Thus, we live together in mutual interdependence. It is the nature of all living things to pool resources and to fuse when possible.

In *The Lives of a Cell*, Thomas brings to light further the problems involved in clinical medicine on a current basis. Hundreds of billions of dollars are currently involved in the managing of disease, and history has shown that the costs seem to have no limits. It seems to be continually changing, and it is difficult if not impossible for each of us to keep pace with all the new developments in our fields of interest.

There are, in fact, three different levels of technology so unlike they may be considered unrelated. The first level is "non-technology" to be equated with supportive therapy in a disease or the so-called bedside manner. Norman Cousins in his book *The Anatomy of an Illness* projects the placebo as a force on the mind great enough to actually reverse the effects of a drug designed for another specific reaction. This placebo effect may be important to us in the care of temporomandibular dysfunctions. But, in orthodontics, this may include the whole field of motivation, the caring for and standing by in which we all are engaged for the success of our patients. The cost of this kind of "non-technology" is higher than most would imagine because it involves time. This kind of time is not often counted as doctors' time in our practice, as lawyers count their time, but advice is all the lawyer has to offer in the first place.

The next level is "halfway technology". It refers to procedures "after the fact" in efforts to compensate for things we are unable to do much about in the beginning. The transplantation of organs or artificial organs is viewed by the public as the equivalent of high technology and the media presents each new procedure as a triumphal breakthrough. But in medicine we ought to know how to prevent and reverse cardiovascular disease rather than perfecting bypass procedures or developing artificial hearts. Surgery, radiation and chemotherapy are directed at already established cancer and not at the mechanism by which cells become neoplastic in the first place.

In orthodontics, we resort to reconstructive surgery; and while it is highly sophisticated, it is at the same time profoundly primitive and must be continued until we genuinely understand the mechanisms of dysplasia and the underlying causes of skeletal disproportions. Our own regular orthodontic therapy is aimed at already preexisting, developed conditions. Our relapses speak for our inability to produce routine desired perfection, and they further show us that we reside in the state of "halfway technology".

The third type is "full technology" which attracts the least public attention, and tends to be taken for granted. This technology may be exemplified best by the immunization against childhood diseases and the effective antibiotic treatment for infections such as syphilis and tuberculosis. This technology came as a result of great understanding of diseased mechanisms. When such knowledge comes, it also becomes the least expensive to a society.

Thomas in his book declares communication to be a basic gift to mankind. As a biologic property of the human mind, we are all born with an innate capacity to use language. Language is the core of our existence and a ground substance holding us together. Art, music, dancing and singing may be a part of that same genetically determined phenomenon of language as a special gift.

The desire for beauty, for precision and for esthetic harmony also falls into this basic of all human qualities. This must mean that we possess genes with special strands of DNA for the discernment of speech, language, music and the arts.

Thus, professionally, 1982 comparatively was a slight shift in emphasis with a turn to greater concern for society as a whole and the whole person.

Other Events in 1982

On an international scale: Princess Grace died in a car accident with some mystery about it. Brezhnev also died. The Falklands War occurred. My impression was that the military in Argentina needed to divert some attention elsewhere and engaged the United Kingdom over sovereignty of the Falkland Islands. This precipitated the downfall of that Argentine government. I had already had an invitation to go to Argentina in 1983, and was anxious to talk to my friends there about their situation.

At the beginning of that war I learned something that confirmed the writings of Ardrey. When the soldiers boarded their ships to take the long trip from England to the tip of South America, our T.V. showed them singing. When asked where he thought he was going, one soldier replied, "We're going to a party." They apparently thought a war would be fun. I'm wondering how those felt who were in one of the modern ships which was sunk with great loss of life.

I'm also reminded of the classic movie "Gone With The Wind" of the young farm boy who couldn't wait to "whip those Yankees" and thought the war would be over in six months -- not four years.

Will we never learn?

Prestige Restored

By 1983 many people were digging in, working hard for a rebound of the economy and hoping for a restoration of American prestige. We had lost in Vietnam, we made an aborted attempt to rescue our hostages, we had endured the Watergate humiliation, spies had been discovered, Carter had given away the Panama Canal, our embassy in Moscow was bugged, a 747 whose passengers included 61 Americans had been shot down by a Soviet jet pilot, and Communism was invading our "underbelly", the Central American countries. We were walking in space again after nine years and Reagan tried to raise our spirits. But we needed some sort of sign. That sign came when Reagan declared enough was enough and put his foot down in Granada in October. Maybe things could be turned around.

* * *

Professionally in 1983

One pleasant occasion in May was being again on a program in at the F.O.R. meeting in Phoenix, Arizona, and having an interview with my friend Dr. Phillip Tobias from South Africa. It had been eleven years since I had been with him but we had corresponded in the interim. He had continued his graduate programs and had new ideas. I prepared a paper on evolution, also taking skulls of the ape and Neanderthal and Cro-Magnon and demonstrating the change in form through the evolutionary process. He elaborated on his concepts which were unique, and my respect for him was reinforced.

My international teaching was once more in Holland and Germany, and in September a large congress was held in Buenos Aires where 300 were in attendance for a three-day course, interpreted by my dear friend Dr. Juan Canut from Madrid. This opened even more doors to South America. They were still chagrined over the Falkland Islands episode and the senseless expense of it, and had thrown out the military rulers. Inflation remained rampant, but they all had high hopes of improvement.

Alive or Dead

A drop-off of interest in our movement among orthodontists in 1984 was manifested by fewer requests for the advanced seminars. I had never advertised, they were all put together from inquiry and word of mouth. With that lag, I took the opportunity to call a Colloquium for all the teachers and in April brought together by invitation 60 people who were now engaged in teaching our philosophy.

Meanwhile, some of our competitors who had their own ideas to defend had spread the rumor that our "Bioprogressive" movement was dead. I was invited to lecture by Dr. Charles Burstone, then head of the Orthodontics Department at the University of Connecticut, who had arranged a large meeting in which devotees of all the popular methods were to present their ideas at one meeting so that comparisons could by made by an audience. The meeting held in March was closed at 300 participants.

In order to make the assignment, it was necessary for me to stop off in Hartford on my return from an eight-day lecture trip to Amsterdam and Baden-Baden, Germany. I was to be the last speaker and Master of Ceremonies for the day was to be my friend Tony Gianelli, head of the department at Boston University.

My flight was to take me through customs in New York, with a connection to Hartford. When I arrived, however, there was a blizzard and Hartford Airport was closed down indefinitely. The buses also were stopped. The only option was the train. It was evening, and I had planned one day in Hartford possibly to listen to other speakers or to focus my own lecture. Therefore, with six pieces of luggage and equipment I taxied to Grand Central Station and boarded the train to Hartford. I arrived at 3:A.M. dead tired from the time change. The snow was very heavy. I immediately tried to call a taxi but could get none. I continued to try for two hours. Finally at 5:00 A.M. someone arrived at the station in a taxi, and I was able to get a ride to the hotel with all my bags and cases. When I got there I crashed.

I slept until noon, unpacked my lecture material and procured a program to become oriented. My talk was to be the next morning and to last three hours. Being the last speaker thought maybe many attendees would have gone already, but because of the storm no one could leave. The room was packed.

At one point, about two-thirds of the way through my lecture, the idea came to me to check the deadness of my techniques. I therefore described one of its features. Ninety percent of the audience were using it. I described a second feature. By guess, seventy-five percent were using it. With that I said, "It doesn't look like Bioprogressive is dead. It's more like it's just beginning to be understood and is alive and kicking." And that was the end of that rumor.

I was surprised that Burstone was not there to greet me for the lecture. He was actually on his way to Europe to lecture, so our flight paths probably crossed. Some time later he called me to apologize and explain. "Sorry I wasn't there, Rick. But if it's any consolation, you won. They liked your stuff the best." I thanked him and remarked that I would have liked to hear all the rest. One of the speakers was put out because he thought that I had snubbed him.

It was obvious in these years that jaw surgery was exploding as an interest among orthodontists. It was appealing to set the teeth up in each jaw and then section and move the jaws surgically. My courses in surgery were becoming popular. Adult orthodontic treatment likewise was now becoming a rage.

The American Plan

The Cold War was still on, the Soviets withdrew from the Olympics. Andropov died and was replaced by Chernienko. We were rebuked by the United Nations Security Council for mining the harbor at Nicaragua. But we as a country were beginning to stiffen more. Reagan and Bush swept aside Mondale and Ferarro, but the Democrats still held Congress.

American society as a whole was witnessing competition on an international scale. We had shared our knowledge and techniques. Other countries, however, did not share our national altruism. Our core industries were finding it hard to stay in business.

When automobiles, trucks, buses and farm equipment are put together collectively, they make up a major part of our core industry. A minor part is household appliances. There always is the need for steel for bridges, girders of buildings and plates for ship construction. In 1985 there were 8 million passenger cars sold together with almost 3.5 million trucks and buses. When all of the small parts, ceramics, hoses, electrical wires and tires for vehicles are considered, that's a lot of core jobs for a lot of people. We had the industry in our hands.

However, American manufacturers became greedy for profits instead of quality. remember in the 1930s a car after 35,000 miles required an overhaul or reconditioning of the motor. Tires lasted 10,000 miles. It became a habit to buy a new model every two years, perhaps sensing that cars could not last. The models were always changing anyway, so some decided to make the change every year. Detroit had been spoiled. In order to make the bottom line look better they began to skimp on quality. The slam of a door on American cars sounded less secure than that of a German or Japanese car. In addition, theirs were better detailed. We began to slip.

When profits were reported the stock would rise and the CEOs seemed to be preoccupied with whatever it took to make that quarterly profit. But also the public and the politicians looking in at the profits, wanted a larger tax bite. In addition, the unions demanded more if not in salaries, in health care and pension funds. In order to manage and keep profits up quality was further cut and, worse, **research and development budgets were cut**.

Everyone blamed Detroit when better cars started coming through our ports. But we should all be ashamed of our greed. We and our politicians were blinded by the successes of the mid-eighties.

Germany and Japan had built new factories after the war with more modern technologies. Japan had steadfastly applied computerized automation. We were just as capable of doing these things, but didn't. Look at the automation at Disneyland if you doubt our ability. Look at our technology required to put Neil Armstrong on the moon in 1969. It was not a technology shortage, it was application! Now it was apathy! It was complacency! I saw it in my own field as I witnessed Europeans, Japanese, and even Latin Americans displaying more driving interest in my new techniques than my colleagues in America.

What were the reasons? Perhaps it was still a preoccupation with the Cold War. But perhaps it was more. Did we really care? We didn't care about a lot of things. America was becoming spoiled with affluence, the affluence of deficit spending. It was blamed on the military budget of Reagan's administration, but was that really it? Was it not that our social control and our regulations were beginning to eat at us?

I noticed it earlier in the attitudes of students. When I was in dental school we wore ties, kept our hair orderly and behaved with respect to those offering their time to teach. We were alert and attentive. But further, it was respect for the profession that we felt. In fact, 40 years ago we cleaned the floors and waxed and polished the cabinets ourselves. Now, however, long hair, blue jeans, shoes without socks, unshaven faces and even sitting posture, with one leg propped in the air, displayed a disrespect for literally everything including the education itself.

On a further national and international scale, some positive things were happening in 1985. Margaret Thacher addressed the Congress and endorsed Reagan.

However, the terrorist activity on an Italian cruise ship, with the killing of an American, "raised our dander". Reagan, in an attempt to create better harmony, visited a cemetery in Germany where S.S. troops had been buried, and received the wrath of the Jewish people. We were encouraged when Mikhail Gorbachev at age 54 was elected, the first premier ever in the Soviet sphere to have had a college education. The Summit in November between "Ronnie" and "Gorby" seemed to thaw some of the ice, as Reagan had always been a staunch anti-Communist.

Foreboding Quiet

In September of 1985 I was giving one of my courses in Mexico at the Centro Medico, a beautiful round clinical building with several theatres. At a break one morning I came out of the lecture hall to a dark sky and hail such as I had never seen before. It had been blown into a corner of a wall to a depth of more than a foot, and looked like snow. The sky was filled with black clouds. But all was quiet now.

I stood there for a moment and had a premonition. There was going to be an earthquake! I felt it. I even expressed it to one of the students. It is said that dogs and other animals suffer unrest before earthquakes. I also almost felt something. That evening when I returned to the California Hotel only one block from the Medical Complex, I studied the location of my room and where I would go and what I could do to escape in the event of a catastrophe. My room was inside; all I could do was to find a strong doorway jamb for protection.

On my return to the U.S, I was to meet my wife, Bunnie, in Fort Worth, Texas, for help in a TMJ course. I have, since 1947, been a believer in fortifying patients biologically with proper nutrition and gentle counseling of life style and attitudes to reduce stress and grinding of their teeth. We had started a nutritional supplement supply company and had worked out specific programs for various conditions. She was to present the logic and the research behind the program. She was in the process of earning her Ph.D. at the time.

During her presentation I picked up a local paper on one of the desks and saw the headlines of a major earthquake centered exactly where I had been standing only three days before! The hospital had collapsed during the shift of personnel. Later it was estimated that 10,000 had died. A few months afterward I drove through the area to see the destruction. The variety of twisted and collapsed buildings defied description.

In November a volcano erupted in Colombia, leaving 25,000 dead. Could there have been any connection? I wondered.

Reagan's Dilemma

By 1986 Reagan had started to take steps to stop terrorism. The assets of Libyans were frozen. On the domestic front, Voyager II reported on Uranus. We were all set back and saddened when the space shuttle Challenger exploded, killing all on board. Our luck had held out too long. Naturally, everyone wanted to know what and who had gone wrong.

The House of Representatives rejected Reagan's Star Wars policy that I thought they should have endorsed for a number of reasons. I still think that eventually we will be flying routinely in supersonic jets. That technology will be of great advantage.

By April Reagan reacted to the terrorists. He ordered U.S. planes to knock out the terrorists' centers in Libya, which pleased everyone -- it was time to stop that insanity.

When I was in South Africa in 1972 I had addressed a Rotary Club there. I also had discussed their problems with several people privately. They wanted to be left alone, and said in time their solutions would be worked out fairly for everyone. After that visit I wrote another letter to Reagan expressing my observations and findings on South Africa. I was therefore disturbed when Congress overrode his veto on economic sanctions against South Africa which hurt us as much as them. Most of the politicians were playing the popular role for civil rights in *our* country with little knowledge of the conditions there and the fact that much of the conflict was black against black. I had, in my speech, alluded to the dearth of television among the lower class community. I was told by one businessman that Americans should mind their own business because they couldn't see all the problems. Events, however, have shown that perhaps sanctions forced quicker defeat of apartheid.

* * *

One of our greatest shocks was the nuclear power plant explosion at Chernobyl in April. This confirmed the fears of many regarding nuclear energy. The damage extended to many neighboring countries. Was it Soviet bureaucratic carelessness or was there a threat so great that this form of energy production must be abandoned? Certainly inspection and management should be tightened under all circumstances, everywhere.

Three other events in 1986 disturbed me greatly and in different ways. One was the torturing of a U.S. narcotics officer by Mexican police. This event was an indicator of the growing menace of the drug problem. The second situation was the manner in which the press publicized our covert action for diverting funds from arms to Iran to the Contras to help contain communist murders in the mid-americas. The third move, however, intuitively bothered me the most. It was the sweeping revision of our tax code with a simultaneous removal of capital gains and the denial of tax credit for interest on borrowed investment capital.

Reagan was in a spot. The deficit was increasing. He had opposed Mondale on the matter of tax increases. The majority in both houses was Democratic. When bills by Democrats were presented to mask income tax increase he signed them. My taxes went up. Moreover, the incentives for expansion and risk-taking for new businesses was destroyed. The enactment of that bill meant less expansion, less research and development, more regulation, and *fewer jobs*. I could see it immediately, and I'm no economist. This was not a double dip -- it was a triple dip. Maybe not immediately, but in the foreseeable future it would destroy our American dream. And it did.

It was another ploy, another tactic, another treacherous plot by politicians to take more of our money without reducing spending which was the real base of the evil. Fortunately, they had something else to divert our attention: it was the venom displayed toward Col. Oliver L. North.

* * *

Early in 1986 I was a part of a meeting in Singapore, and stopped off in Melbourne to put on a short three-day course under the auspices of the University of Melbourne. My good friend, Victor West, head of the department, has for many years been as close to me as a brother. Men do not tend to have intimate friends, but I can truly say that this man is my intimate friend.

There was an interest in Asia in my new developments. I hadn't been to Singapore since 1964 and it was interesting now to see it 21 years later, as it is becoming prepared to replace Hong Kong in some way as a commercial center. It seemed to have become quite modernized since my last visit.

My lecturing schedule was less full because I was busy writing on my major books. I had one advanced course in Pacific Palisades that year, and another in Caracas, Venezuela. In Palm Springs I talked at a reunion meeting of my alma mater, The University of Illinois, and reviewed the 40 years of orthodontics since I had started my training at that institution. It was of interest to reflect on the various movements that had occurred and were still occurring.

Through the recalling and restudy of many patients I had worked up the most common conditions which led to stability of results. In the developing of a new appliance or new wrinkles on old themes, I formulated the concept of a therapeutic ideal which I called "The Fourth Dimension Appliance". We were trying to build in some automatic features in the hardware itself to prepare the patient for better stability over a period of time. Hence, the fourth dimension: time.

I was again on a program with Paul Tessier for the Great Lakes Society meeting which was being held in Williamsburg, Virginia. I had been based nearby in Camp Perry and dated some ladies at the William and Mary University there in Williamsburg. So in a sense it was "old stomping grounds". Having lectured at the University of Pennsylvania earlier in June, I began to detect a shift in the characteristic of the orthodontic profession. Orthodontists were becoming more biologically oriented. They were beginning to look at variability in patients and also beginning to think more in terms of growth. I wondered then, when I had time to ponder the impressions I had gathered, whether or not it was a general movement in the profession or whether my work had finally made a difference after so many years. It really didn't matter who was responsible, but I saw the whole profession of orthodontics moving forward. We were doing better, and that was good.

The Divine Proportion and our work in esthetics had perhaps made an impression. Now, after 15 years the computer was no longer feared. It was no longer a threat. Other people were starting to develop computer programs, and all of our hard work was showing signs of being integrated. I took a deep breath, and said to myself, "It's about time."

The Big Books

With the gain that had been made, and with some of the most difficult work behind me, I began to return to a project that I had started in 1962. Although I had contributed to numerous chapters in other textbooks, and together with other colleagues had published three of our own, I still held a vision of a complete works in the field. It had never been done. From time to time I had picked up the outlines and reviewed them, and developed the notion or the vision of the complete works. It actually meant nine volumes, divided into three main parts with three sections in each part. Therefore, on airplanes, in random available time periods, I set about to finally pull the whole thing together.

The first books began with the social and biologic sciences. Most of the illustrations I made myself. I did my own photography and in fact did many of the layouts. We had started with one computer system and had difficulty with its integration for use by the publisher. Therefore, after much work, we had to go through a conversion process which meant more time for editing. In 1985 and 1986, much time was spent in writing and making illustrations and organizing.

Through my long association with Rocky Mountain Orthodontics in Denver, Colorado beginning in 1955 I had developed a working relationship. For some years I had been a paid consultant with their company for continued advice on technical matters. They had developed a communications branch in their firm and with artists and illustrators began to do jobs for outside firms. They felt prepared, then, to handle a much larger book of this magnitude. If a professional person writes a textbook, usually it is a grossly un-profitable venture, except perhaps for the publisher. The writer of the book commonly gets from the publisher about an 8% override on the wholesale price of the book. Since the number of sales is usually limited, if the writer gets his cost back he can usually feel rather satisfied. If a book goes to the general public, with greater production, the cost can be reduced and the author will get a greater share. Even so, for scientific publications there is very little profit to the writer. We tried to make an equitable deal for production of the books. The main thing was to do as fine a job as I could.

Good teachers in all the professions are very difficult to come by. Many times a teacher may be good in one subject, but poor in another. It was my objective, then, to put together a whole set of books that at least could more or less tell a story, and perhaps lighten the burden on the teaching institution and be of benefit to mankind on a world basis. Thus in 1985 and 1986 this was the main activity.

A Christmas Conception

On Christmas Eve of 1985 we had had about 30 guests in to our beautifully decorated home in the Palisades Highlands for dinner and gift exchange. Bunnie is a woman consumed with the Christmas spirit. If she doesn't decorate the house to its maximum she doesn't feel it's a season to be jolly. She personally cooked for the 30 people, giving of her time and energy for several days before the event. After most of them left, late on Christmas Eve night, we had to clean up and were quite weary. A couple of guests had stayed overnight to leave on Christmas morning.

So we found ourselves all alone with the huge tree and the house still flooded with Christmas music and spirit. We had a very comfortable lounge over to one side of the room in front of the television, and I had lain down and propped my feet up. The time was about 2:00 in the afternoon. I had dozed off when I heard a pop from the kitchen and glasses clanging. In walked Bunnie dressed in scanty attire with a smile.

"I know I've been neglecting you for some time. Do you think we can make up for it?" she asked.

"Right on," I replied.

So we lounged together, sipping champagne, next to the 14-foot Christmas tree decorated in all its grandeur, and things happened beautifully. She became pregnant with our beautiful daughter Anastarr on that Christmas afternoon!

A few weeks later she asked me if I remembered what I said after we made love that day, and I had forgotten. She reminded me: "When you finished that day you said, 'Boy, if that one takes it's sure going to be some kid!'"

And it sure was! Anastarr was born nine months and three days later, in the early morning of September 27, 1986 at a birthing center in Upland, California. I helped her. We had contemplated a water birth, but Bunnie had a partial placenta previa so there were some minor complications. She gave birth in a squatting position beside the bed in my arms. I helped catch Anastarr and gave her her first bath to clean up the birth coatings. And I elicited her first smile, when she was only minutes old.

I doubt that there are many people who know exactly what day and what hour their children were conceived. Anastarr means "messenger from Heaven", and her middle name, Miliani, is taken from the Kahuna in Hawaii and means "love greater than all loves".

So here I was, at the age of 66, after I had sold my practice to Dr. Rick Jacobson, starting over again with a new family. I must say, Anastarr has been an absolute delight and an abundant cheer.

Warrior Ollie

I was in Hawaii on a vacation with my first and second families, including grandchildren, when the Oliver North hearings were held in July of 1987. My son and daughters were glued to the television. I was disgusted. The record of proven spying by the Soviets, the acts of terrorism and the animosity of so many against America for no reason other than our success, was forgotten. Covert action has been a function of many governments. The role of a fellow Palisadian, Peter Graves, in "Mission Impossible" on television and the whole series of Ian Fleming's James Bond movies were based on that substance.

Covert means secret and hidden. It means concealed and, above all, sheltered. Little did I realize that within four years I would be calling North a friend. In 1987 I was impressed with the manner in which he conducted himself. There was no hesitation in his speech as he expressed himself from his heart. Somehow, the covert action had been exposed. In someone's drive to be magnanimous we wanted to show to the world our own faults. We in America apparently want to give our opponents our game book and in addition stupidly even give them our individual game plan.

From what I could gather, North had been a tremendous leader in Korea. He had shown unusual organizational talents; otherwise why would he have been selected for the job of retrieving our hostages? Wasn't that what it was all about? He was already assumed guilty of a crime by a tribunal of public opinion.

No president or leader of a government could condone terrorism and the taking of hostages. To frankly admit that ransoms would be paid to retrieve those captured would open a floodgate of abductions of our tourists on a world scale. Carter and Reagan would therefore be forced to announce "No deals."

Privately, however, as North explained, there are only three ways that such a situation can be terminated. First, they can escape (six in Iran did with the aid of the Canadians). Second, they can be killed (William Buckley). Third, someone cuts a deal, which must be done covertly for obvious reasons. (In June 1985 thirty-nine remaining hostages were freed in Beirut.)

Thus, when self-righteous, opportunistic, pompous and arrogant Congressmen and lawyers attacked North as the fall guy it bothered me. I could see it all plainly. Worse yet, Colonel North's defense had to come from his own pocket. He and his family were at risk of his life for doing the job he had been instructed to do. Why not have his house secured at government expense? In August, Reagan accepted the responsibility for the Iran-Contra mistake.

After thousands of hours of community service as punishment, North's conviction was overturned by the Appeals Court. By now his defense had cost between three and four million dollars. He had been fired and had no job. Having a deep Christian faith, he remained strong.

* * *

My Big Move

Throughout 1986 and through the pregnancy Bunnie developed a compulsion to leave Los Angeles. Our large home was quite expensive to keep up. We had built it with many of the features of a Divine Proportion. People would go along the street and stop just to look at it. It was very pleasing to the senses. The architect was Douglas Phillips.

But with the changing of the demands of teaching in Pacific Palisades and with my extension abroad, and with a child to raise, it seemed sensible for me to start looking for another location to live and consider a shift in my career. I wanted to get back to writing. My publications had fallen off rather extensively due to more research and the time needed for teaching, as well as practice. And I felt by moving that I might be afforded more time.

Bunnie also was in fear of another more severe earthquake, after the one that had happened. The traffic problems in Los Angeles were becoming quite dense, and we had been spoiled. It took more and more time to get anyplace. There was a fear of gangs, a fear of more riots, and murders were taking place very close by. And so I agreed to start looking around for a better place to live.

Ultimately I found it in Scottsdale, Arizona, in the Pinnacle Peak area. We looked all over the country and had it narrowed down to Colorado and Arizona. Some of our family was in the San Francisco area, and I considered Monterey, but that was still in the earthquake area, which caused a great deal of anxiety for Bunnie. So we narrowed it down to two places, one in the mountains at Telluride, Colorado, and the second one in Scottsdale, Arizona. Therefore, in consideration of the five reasons (with a child, with the crowding that was taking place in Pacific Palisades, with my need for more time to write, with the expense of living in the Los Angeles area, and finally with the finding of an even better place to live), I decided to make the change.

In the previous five years Bunnie had begun to love skiing, and we had gone to several places, but we didn't think of getting one specific place that we liked well enough to go to regularly. Dr. Mike Churosh, a friend of ours in Phoenix, insisted that we stay at his condominium in Telluride. We had never been to Telluride before, but the minute we got there and saw the little village in a box canyon, and the mountains that were my closest reminder of Switzerland in the United States, we knew that this was it. We therefore began to look for some vacant property on which we could build a log home, and found one in the Ski Ranches. I pooled some of my money and bought it. I went over 300 plans of log homes, finally drew one up and gave it to an architect. We got the plans drawn, had the geologic survey done and part of the lot cleared, and were ready to go with the more or less full-time home with perhaps then a condominium in Scottsdale.

The log home was to have a full basement with a work center and perhaps a small teaching center. That would have really meant a change. John Naisbett lives there and is a writer working there, and several people by way of computers and FAX machines find it very convenient to run their businesses from there. It is a most delightful spot in the mountains.

Before that became consummated, I had been lecturing in Scottsdale at a meeting, and one day took the afternoon off. In a rented car I started looking around the North Scottsdale area. Having lectured in Carefree many years before, and making a swing now through that area, talking to some realtors, it was obvious that the kind of living and the kind of home that I was interested in would be found in Desert Highlands. I am a golfer, and had been a member of Riviera Country Club for 35 years, and had known about Desert Highlands as being the first site of the famous Skins Game. When I saw it I knew that this was the place wanted to move if I was going to move anywhere.

There were three or four houses on the market for sale, all of which I felt were overpriced - not for Los Angeles, but for the Phoenix area. So I thought I would build again, and began to select some lots. I called Bunnie from Scottsdale and told her I thought that this was the place I wanted to go and that I wanted her to get over here! In the next few weeks she repeated my investigation of the area and drew the same conclusions. The next time we both came together to look at the area and again look at the houses. We still owned our house in Pacific Palisades and were not in a position to take a double risk of owning property in Arizona and also in California. We went back and sat for a while. That was about 1985.

Throughout 1986 we still had the yearning to move to Scottsdale, and had seen particular house that was available, designed by Mr. Bill Toll, which had been built by Mr. Bernie Ziegler. One day I was rummaging through some folders in my study and came across the brochure for Desert Highlands. The house that we liked was one of them shown in that advertisement, and having the number available I called to see what was going on. The asking price for the house we liked had been reduced. I made the decision. I wanted that house. I called Bunnie and said, "Get ready, next week end we are going to go to Scottsdale with the baby." We arrived and saw the house once more and envisioned some changes to our liking, and made an offer contingent on our being able to sell the house in the Palisades.

We went back to California and put it on the market with an agent who specialized in houses of that calibre. The crunch for homes in the area was going on, and although we did not get to sell our house at the market's peak, we sold it when everything was on the rise to the very first person who looked at it. When that was concluded, we purchased our house in Scottsdale, arranged for some changes to be made, and were free to move in November of 1987.

We had to set up an office for my secretary for the management of my teaching programs, the nutritional supplement company we had started, and Bunnie's business, which meant renting an office/warehouse. We found this in the Scottsdale Air Park, in North Scottsdale. To move everything that I had accumulated in the 35 years in California, with the research records, the library books and journals, was a difficult task. Five years later I was still sorting out and re-filing and putting in order much of that material.

In November of 1987, I was to lecture in Palm Springs, so I loaded as much as I could in the car and started the drive from Los Angeles to Palm Springs. The traffic was bumper to bumper almost all the way to San Bernardino. It took me two and a half hours to get a distance that I formerly could have made in 45 minutes some years before. I thought to myself, "I am getting out of Los Angeles at just the right time."

In a few months I had rented an office in the Pinnacle Peak business district, and had some courses in this building, using it as my study and work area for writing. I maintained this for about a year, until I later decided to build another house at Ballantrae Ridge at Troon, which was just a mile away from our home. It is used as a study for the present, but could be sold some day as a home.

Settling in Arizona

My busy lecture schedule continued into 1988, and when I got to Scottsdale I found myself busier than ever. Many people in the pediatric dental field were eager to learn about growth forecasting and in May of 1988 I gave a major address at the American Association of Orthodontists on an analysis of the subjects of that meeting and prevailing trends in orthodontics, with the expressed request to summarize everything in the whole field.

I had been quite busy in the previous two years writing and wanted to put a lot of data in it, and found myself precipitating 27 different studies on the characteristics of arrangement of normal teeth and their variation. From that came a new design, or in fact three new designs or formulas for adaptation of the teeth to different types of faces.

The first book by now had grown too large to be carried in one bound copy, so it was divided and became Part I and Part II of Book One. It was exciting to get the galleys back and see the fruit of the labor. My secretary, Sallie Coyle, was indispensable in this effort.

No amount of my thanks would suffice for the effort she put forth, in the proofing of the material. When the book was published in 1989, I could find only one mistake, which is rather an accomplishment in dealing with over 1000 pages.

The 50th Year Class Reunion

I had graduated from high school in Kokomo, Indiana in 1938. A few of the old classmates still there in the area arranged for a 50th year class reunion which was held at the country club and which, to my surprise, included a group of our old teachers who still survived. About a third of the class had already died. There were two or three days of activities, one of which was a tour through the old school which had now been converted into a junior high school. There were about twelve of us who made this excursion and it brought back a lot of memories.

It was very interesting to see that the hierarchy that had been established was still there in their minds 50 years later. It was as if everyone took on the personalities they had had during that time. I, of course, was the "dumb jock", I had lettered in both football and basketball. I really had no scholastic motivation then.

But now, 50 years later, things were different. I looked at everybody in an entirely different light. I almost volunteered to give a talk but it didn't seem appropriate. One of the girls in the class changed the tempo of the meeting entirely too much by focusing on her personal religion. It was her chance to preach. The ceremonies were pleasant, but in the end quite boring. The most encouraging was when someone from the local "Kokomo Tribune" seemed to want to find out what that class had accomplished as a whole in the 50 years.

Then it was time for the dance. I had enjoyed dancing all the way through school, and because Bunnie had chosen not to accompany me back to Kokomo, I was there alone and sat with a couple of other people whose spouses had also not joined them. Some, in fact, had lost their spouses and were there alone. I thought it would be nice to get re-acquainted and dance with several of the girls I had known in school, two or three of whom I had dated. The first one I danced with was quite a lovely lady who had lost her husband, and we had a nice time. I asked another lady to dance, and after half of the number, she said she would have to sit down, she just didn't have the strength to continue. I asked another one, and she said she had a bad back, and didn't want to risk trying to dance. Still another one I asked said that she had arthritis so bad in her knees that she didn't choose to dance, but thanked me, and so we had some nice conversations instead.

I then saw another lady who had lost her husband and went over and asked her to dance, and she accepted. When I had known her in high school I had liked her very much. She had been one of the officers in the class. After a minute or two I took the liberty of asking her why it was that she had never accepted my invitation for a date while we were in high school. I asked her if she remembered that. She said, "Of course I do." I said, "Well, why was it that you would never go out with me?" She said, "Well, I thought that you were the dumbest kid in the class and perhaps the least likely to succeed." She said, "I know now how wrong I was, because you are probably the only man in the class of letters and advanced degrees with the kind of record that you have, and I certainly was wrong." I said, "But going out with me didn't mean that you were going to marry me!" And she said, "Well, I didn't want to date anybody that I thought that I might not want to marry." I said, "Then who did you marry?" "I married a very nice man, but his health wasn't good, and now I'm all alone." I expressed my sorrow for her. She was, as I had anticipated, a very lovely lady and extremely well adjusted.

Having run out of sources of dance material, I then went back to the girl I had danced with first, and asked her to dance again. But she said No, she couldn't. I asked why. She said "Well, if I dance with you again people will start talking." I said, "About what?" "Well they will think that something is going on and it will become a rumor in the community and I can't let that happen." At the time I laughed. I had forgotten conditions in a small Indiana town, and my first thought was, "Let me out of here!"

Everyone still in their sixties was talking about their age and what they couldn't do any more. One of the things that was most appalling was the condition of their teeth. When was a student in high school, of course I never noticed what their teeth were like. But now I did!

What bothered me most with this reunion, and another reunion almost at the same time of my dental class, was that everybody seemed to be more interested in their financial security than the security of their health. It was as if a whole generation equated longevity with economics rather than a state of mind, great attention to a diet, and the value of exercise. After I had had this experience I was glad that I hadn't given a talk, because the one that I had contemplated giving would have been entitled "Sex, Salad and Scotch" as a take-off on a lecture I had heard from Dr. Robert Samp a researcher on centenarians in Wisconsin a few years earlier.

Sex would stand for the vigor of human intercourse, not just sexually but the whole idea of altruism, the idea of continuing to do something for someone else and remaining active They found that people living past 100 were very busily engaged in trying to do something for someone else, and did not lie in bed anticipating death, but chose to live. **Salad** stood for frugality, the idea of all things in moderation. **Scotch** stood for resilience and the idea that a person can spring back from catastrophic disasters in their lives. In other words, it was an attitude of life; people who lived to 100 did not let things get them down. On my trip back I suppose I was a little chagrined that I didn't go ahead and give that talk because I think my classmates could have used it. (See Appendix.)

Agony and Heartbreak

The last two "Reagan Years" were 1987 and 1988. In the elections of 1986, the Republicans lost the majority in the Senate, so Reagan was now faced with a completely Democratic Congress. Problems on a national scale (domestic policy) and internationally (foreign policy) had escalated. I could see the dilemma. Nationally, despite the efforts to reduce a federal dependency, people wanted more centralization. It was as if they wanted someone specifically to blame. They accused him unjustly of having no foreign policy.

The Cold War was continuing. The Soviets launched the most powerful rocket ever known. I remember Reagan's firm dealing with Gorbachev at the summit meetings where the bargaining hinged on the "star wars" program. Gorby knew more than the American public. He was fearful of its success because it meant 40 years of futility with armed power and would lead to Soviet submission. It was the first time I sensed a change! Reagan had done it!

I cannot resist quoting Goldwater's last paragraph in his "Conscience of a Conservative" written in 1960:

> "The future, as I see it, will unfold along one of two paths. Either the Communists will retain the offensive; will lay down one challenge after another; will invite us in local crisis after local crisis to choose between all-out war and limited retreat; and will force us, ultimately, to surrender or accept war under the most disadvantageous circumstances. Or *we* will summon the

will and the means for taking the initiative, and wage a war of attrition against them -- and hope, thereby, to bring about the internal disintegration of the Communist empire. One course runs the risk of war, and leads, in any case, to probable defeat. The other runs the risk of war, and holds forth the promise of victory. For Americans who cherish their lives, but their freedom more, the choice cannot be difficult."

It took us 30 years after Goldwater wrote these words until our war of attrition was won. Signs of internal disintegration were evident now and Reagan stood firm.

There were also encouraging signs as five regional presidents in Central America agreed on a peace accord. During these years, we signed a trade agreement with Canada, which I supported. I argued among friends at the time that we should also strike harmony with Mexico. If we couldn't reach accord with our next-door neighbors, how could we expect agreement with those on other continents? Thus the Cold War was now in the "cooker", thawing completely.

While terrorism was lessened, the killing of William Buckley, the abduction of Col. William Higgins in Lebanon, the death of nine tourists on an Aegean cruise, the bomb on a PAN-AM flight over Scotland killing 270 people, and other assassinations all plagued Reagan.

The Israeli problem with the PLO bothered us, and our Jewish friends even more. An Iraqi missile killed 37 sailors on the U.S.S. Stark in the Persian Gulf. Kurt Waldheim was refused admission to the U.S. The Middle East situation was not improving. The Iran-Iraq war dragged on until 1988 with an uncertainty regarding arms build-ups. It was strange to us -- though far away it involved our energy.

Our educational levels continued to slip despite more money applied, which bothered me immensely. Basically something was wrong.

The drug menace was becoming a drug culture and a drug economy.

Reagan was having difficulty with Congress. They rejected Robert Bork for the high court. They overrode his veto on civil rights. They rejected his "Star Wars" defense program.

It seemed that now the media and the public had become paranoid over civil rights. The Rotary Club was forced to take women. The Supreme Court ruled against restrictions in private clubs. I wondered if the right of free assembly could be regulated also.

In addition, in this same two-year period, Reagan signed a bill to compensate Japanese-Americans interned during World War II. We were still paying for World War II and Japan now was still closing markets to our products. There was a new amnesty law for illegal aliens. Heated debates privately and publicly centered on gun laws because of the increase in crime.

Ironically, everyone blamed Reagan for it all because of Reaganomics. But perhaps the source of his greatest faulting, now that he had become meat for the journalists' grist mill, was in two major areas. First was the huge deficit and the increase in the national debt. The second was the loss of our core economy and balance of trade particularly with Japan. It was as if he were blamed for the decision in Detroit to make profits rather than quality. It was as if he were responsible for Japan making better cameras and radios than anyone else.

We had a lead in the microchip industry, but they said he was bored and indifferent. Journalists said that his countrymen asked only that he make them feel better and that he complied.

Many people agreed that credit was wrong, but each year the uses of credit increased, a
if he were commanding it.

Fear and Mistrust of Japan

In 1982 I wrote Reagan another letter explaining what I had experienced in Japan. W
had previously exported dental X-ray equipment to Japan. First they started making all thei
own mountings, balancers and controls. But still there was profit for us to be made in th
X-ray tubes. So starting from absolute scratch they set up a division to make the whole
X-ray tube. The next thing we knew, they were exporting as good a product but with
slicker and more marketable look to America.

In my letter, I asked Reagan to pass on the need for all manufacturers to improve quality
How could we compete, with our marginally educated and profit-minded workers in ou
industries and our companies in conflict with our government, with an educated populatio
that was quality-minded and whose government subsidized products to break in and stea
our markets? Halberstram said, "Reagan was a kind of therapeutic, no-pain conservatis
for a therapeutic, no-pain society." Why not then blame society at least equally? I agre
with Halberstram that "we have separated economic realities from the political process"

Iran-Contra and Hostages

Yet beyond even all this there was Iran-Contra. If I had been Reagan, and many hav
shared the same opinion, I would have done what was done even if I had known the plan

Wives, relatives and children of the hostages were on his mind constantly. They wer
calling, writing, and on television pleading for him to do something. How could a perso
of his conviction not have made some effort?

I heard him in a press conference declaring that they could find no responsible person o
group even to deal with. There was no hope of a rescue because nobody could even fin
out where they were located. They kept trying to explore all channels.

If it took some repairs and sales of obsolete arms to make a deal -- let's do it! He coul
not -- nor would I have, as the Commander-in-Chief -- say he would pay ransom, which i
actually was. But if a process of exercising pressure on the fanatic group responsible coul
be worked out, why risk more American lives?

Once the money was received, what was to be done with it? Where would it go? It hac
to remain covert. Therefore, why not divert it to a cause that would help protect the country
Even I with no more than common intelligence could see that.

On two occasions he admitted it was a mistake. Most liberals and socialists wanted t
make it another Watergate. In fact, some called it a "Contragate". Let some of those
objecting so self-righteously be forced to listen to the pleas of hostage families and face
such problems in the White House -- and they dare to talk about consciousness!

Reagan had calculated correctly that respect for the military had to be restored and tha
pride in the country had to be rekindled. He recognized we had to have a strong leader. He
was a great communicator. Everyone laughed at his Star Wars program until we saw the
little Patriot missiles knock down big Russian SCUDS in the Gulf War. The country was
bursting with pride under Bush, but it was Reagan who had set that process in motion. Tha
as much as anything, in my opinion, was a factor in bringing Gorbachev to the table with
the new policies of the Soviet Union and the end of the Cold War.

Europeans didn't give us credit. We hadn't been shooting hot bullets with the Soviet
Union, which is why it was called a Cold War. The same people who voted for all of the
programs and deficit spending under Johnson and Carter now took turns in condemning

deficit spending under Reagan. Admittedly, it was larger now, but largely because of the momentum that had been initiated by their administrations.

There was a so-called lowering of taxes but taxes overall rose. Reagan did everything he could to reduce government spending within his power except for the military which he considered imperative. With the Cold War in which we were outnumbered in missiles, with the problems in the Middle East, the drift in Latin America, and the unrest in the Philippines, we needed a strong defense. He attempted to shift as much of the Federal program as he could into the private sector. To lower taxes without cutting the programs, of course, probably wouldn't work.

In order to balance the budget, he proposed that many of the unproductive Federal programs initiated before be abandoned. How many working on a government payroll were willing to freely give up a soft job? Per capita income in Washington, D.C. is the highest in the country.

* * *

The election in the Fall of 1988 pitted Bush and Quayle against Dukakis and Benson. I remember well an incident between Quayle and Benson in which Quayle had remarked also on the youth and inexperience of Senator Jack Kennedy in defense of his own relative youth. Benson said, "I knew Kennedy, and you're no Kennedy." I thought at the time it was a low blow. Quayle should have quickly retorted, "Maybe not, but Dukakis is no Bush, and that's what this election is all about!"

When Bush ran against Dukakis, who was suggesting raising taxes again, he ran on Reagan's record and won. This time, however, in contrast to Eisenhower's lackadaisical support of Nixon, Reagan was active in his famous speech "George was there..." With that background, Bush proved to be one of our ablest statesmen.

Personal International Scope

After having given some courses in Madrid, I was being driven to the airport by Dr. Juan Canut. He is one of the most unusual of my many international colleagues in that when we first get together we make it a point to talk about anything but our profession. One of our conversations, I remember, was a discussion of romantic love. Another was on why people sing. Many pertained to cultural differences, and the most recent was on esthetics.

While he was driving along, he said, "You know, of course, your life is not your own." I replied, "That's a stupid thing to say." He quickly added, "Oh no it isn't. You belong to us. You belong to the profession. You will go to help people wherever it is they call."

I thought a moment. "I see what you mean," I said. "It's rather like that now. I find myself running around trying to put fires out. People want information which I have and ask for it — and how can I refuse them?" "See what I mean?" he said.

The last four years (1989-1992) have manifested that notion on an international scale more than ever before. During those years I have lectured before 55 groups and 60% were to people outside the United States. This doesn't include my lectures at universities to students.

The traveling to Europe, South America, North America (Canada and Mexico), Australia, and Asia gave me a perspective. The differences among peoples are not subtle.

Probably the most serious-minded and intense are the Japanese. When I first met them as students they were distant and reserved. They were prompt and courteous, but were not accustomed to my smile. As I became acquainted through the last 30 years they have warmed up. I hope it's not just catching the "American disease" as some of the old senior in Japan fear.

The Japanese students as a group go back to their hotels at night, even after late sessions and compare notes and recreate my lectures. They are present bright and early the next morning, and seldom a head drops. They try to get the most out of their time as if their time is the most precious commodity. The current Japanese tends to be mechanical. I find Asians are fun-loving and enjoy a good time. The men mix with the women in a more awkward manner than do Americans.

In February of 1991 I had completed a three-day lecture course in Osaka which one of my students, Dr. Hiroshi Nezu, had arranged. I was giving my concluding remarks when I noticed slips of paper were being handed out to the group of about 100. Presently they brought the sheet up to me and on it were the words to the song "My Way" printed in English for the group. He then requested that I lead the singing, as the music now came on in the audio system for the room. So on we went:

..."and now the end is near; it's time to take a final curtain. My friends, I'll make it clear, I'll state my case of which I certain. I've lived a life that's full, I've traveled each and every by-way, and more much more than this, I did it my way." etc. etc.

When we finished the song, with most all trying to sing, I took the opportunity to really give them some American spirit: I became a cheer leader. "Okay! Let's hear it! Let's hear it for Japanese orthodontics -- Yea, Yea, Yea!" I thought, the Japanese love baseball, so why not loosen them up? It worked. Everyone was smiling. They work hard, and the young are learning to play. I've come to respect and like them.

The antithesis of the Japanese are the Mexicans. Their heart is in their hand. They are open. Time is of little value. For a group of 80 I would wait to start a lecture until 40 were present, and in an hour most would have arrived. Some would not make it until after lunch. They love life. The present is to them what counts. What good is a great tomorrow if today is sad and stressful? They are grateful and respectful. Their emotions are not put on. Tears are in their eyes with a good-bye. How loving.

The whole of Latin America is not far behind. I suppose it takes a "mañana" attitude for survival with the inflation they have and the endless turnovers in government and the struggles in poverty. True, they need discipline, and could take some lessons from the Japanese, but I would hate to see that beautiful spirit lost. They can have that spirit and still be hard-working. My very dear friend Carlos Montt in Chile is an example. He started from scratch after the communists were ousted and created jobs for thousands. He is the husband of Dra. Reni Muller, one of my best students anywhere. She and Raul Carvajal of Santiago are tremendous workers.

Next in line with a fun-loving zest for life are the Italians. They are a complete enigma. They enjoy fine cars, fine dress, fine food, and the finest things in life. Yet they seem to be relaxed. They love to talk. They love to discuss things, and they want to know. Last April I gave a two-week course in a majestic, immense old Medici hunting lodge just outside Florence. My interpreter was my old friend Franco Magni, and we had about 25 students. One Sunday we took a trip around through the rolling country, and visited Leonardo's birthplace, and the museum at Vinci. It was a profound thrill to think of his presence there and the struggles the whole culture underwent at the time of the Renaissance. As a gift I was given a book by Pacioli who taught Leonardo the Divine Proportion.

All of Europe has a different pattern than ours in America. A quick review of European history suggests that the American presence in Europe has had a more elusive benefit than we in America have been told about. A part of the European philosophy has been to live better than us. They take time for vacations and holidays. On the other hand, since wars have been so frequent, they must make as much money as they can while they can.

Europeans are intense business people. From the end of World War II to 1990 was forty-five years, which is longer than any period in the last 200 years that Europe has not had a serious conflict. Our presence there as a peace-keeping force, together with NATO, has functioned to the advantage of all of Europe. In fact, in my opinion, it has granted the stability to permit the formulation of the European Common Market, which is a United Countries of Europe.

Because of our presence, their outlay for defense has been minimal. Their young could devote themselves to engineering, business and production. Their businessmen walked their streets in suits and ties while our young men walked their streets in uniforms. In some places in Europe I detected an arrogance, particularly among the young. How soon, indeed, people forget.

A Peg for Each Hole

My views about other people and other countries do not overshadow my views about America, they only accentuate them. During the 1980's I detected a growing resentment. As with all countries, one attitude does not fit all people, but my underlying concern was becoming manifested. America was beginning to be anesthetized, and we needed to be wakened up.

Our young had been preoccupied, from Elvis Presley on, with hard rock and clattering cacaphony in the name of music. Our dance was really not dance, it was an individual wiggle halfway between the grunt and jump of the Watusi and the series of hip movements displaying a sexual expression. There was more of an erotic release rather than grace and joy in such dancing.

For boredom and escape or a search for some feeling of self-worth, drug experimentation became common. A decay in moral values was evident as frequency of sexual experience and pregnancy in the young continued to escalate.

But probably the most dangerous sign I saw was the evidence of a peculiar mind fix. We had become mechanistic to a fault. Perhaps it was the influence of television. Our minds were being shut down. Mechanistic means to be automatic or as if run by machine. We were becoming robot-like. Things were done as if seemingly uninfluenced by the mind or emotion. Technicality in petty matters took precedence over thinking things out.

Each problem represented a hole, and it was up to anyone to simply find the peg that would fit the hole. Medical diagnosis was put on the computer, and once all the symptoms were entered (making the hole) then the disk spun to find the peg that fit it. This is fine for information, but we became slaves to the production without using it as information for a higher level of reasoning. I was chagrined, however, to learn that the computer was correct more often than the general physician in making the diagnosis.

Children were not taught arithmetic and were lost without a calculator. Why should they learn to read when they could see television? The virtue of a good education was in a long slide downhill. Our young made poor conversationalists.

The mechanistic mind always looks for the easy way out. When a peg didn't fit there had to be something wrong with the hole. So we began examining the hole to alter it so the peg would fit. We altered the problems to fit our answers. For example, we demanded smoother roads rather than sturdier cars.

Americans are not lazy. In order to make ends meet, pay taxes, and live nicely, many work long hours (often two in a household or one with two jobs). They do their own housework and do many odd jobs themselves as in no other country I know. The ubiquitous "Home Depot" is proof of this. The hard work probably helps account for the resentment of taxes and the frustration of inordinate regulation. We are still a huge middle-class majority. Four out of five new jobs are not core, but in the service industry which is highly unstable -- hence more resentment.

Thus, when answers are not forthcoming we want to blame someone, and it usually is the government. They should have the proper pegs to put in our holes!

* * *

The Surprise Bash

The American Association of Orthodontists met in Anaheim, California, in 1989. At this meeting I was told they were planning a roast for Dr. Carl Gugino who continued to be our main lecturer in Europe, but who practiced in Buffalo, N.Y. It was to be a formal affair. I was asked to prepare a talk as a roast for him.

I should have suspected something when Bunnie told me to stay in the hotel room and rest. I should really have been alert when she bought a white sequinned gown. Further, there should have been a clue when we hired a sitter for Anastarr. It was in the Anaheim Hilton Hotel, and when we came down I saw the registration desk in the anteroom to the main ballroom and Jana, one of the assistants of Dr. Duane Grummons, alone at the desk. I thought that was a little odd, but she escorted us to the ballroom and as the doors were thrown open I was greeted by 150 friends. It was a tribute to me.

I was completely and absolutely surprised. People had gathered from five continents. I was speechless. I couldn't believe it.

Everything was planned. A large dance band was hired. We had a most unique comedian and Harriet Reisser had letters and cards mounted on a folding cloth from 27 people who had worked for me over the years. I was roasted good! All my children - Robin and Mike Machette, Craig and Jennifer Ricketts and Gale were there, with the grandchildren. Dr. Grummons and Dr. Clark Jones and several others had been working on it for months.

As I said previously, I had my library and work studio at Ballantrae Ridge at Troon, in North Scottsdale. A colleague, Dr. Charles Mitchell from Orange County, California, had for many years collected old books, paintings, equipment and documents in the profession. It was without a doubt the finest collection in our field. My students, friends, and commercial companies had raised a library fund to the amount of $60,000 for the purchase of that collection and provision for shelves and cabinets for its preservation. Added to my own, it is undoubtedly the best orthodontic library collection now in the world.

I also have about 80 human skulls that I have accumulated, as well as an anthropologic assemblage of primates and lower animal skulls, and many memorabilia. Together with records of thousands of patients, this will all go into a Ricketts Library at Loma Linda University as my books are completed, one by one, and I no longer need them to be readily available to me. In addition, the goal is a clearinghouse for international communication by computer to many universities.

The testimonies and the love shown at that tribute brought me to tears along with many others. They piped into the sound system a conversation with my brother Jim in Kokomo and my sister Jeannette in Terre Haute, Indiana. They tried to get Reagan to phone, but he had a pressing engagement and sent a telegram. I was only 69 but they celebrated it for my 70th, probably sensing I would throw my own a year later. What a marvelous and wonderful occasion! It warms my heart every time I recall it. That's the stuff life is all about.

The New Ball Games
Starting in 1989 it was evident on an international scale that communism was in deep trouble. I had caught a clue when I visited South Africa and saw the problems impending when knowledge of the outside world is concealed by news media. They had no television.

But we are today living in a wired world. Transistor radios and live television prevented the Soviets from suppressing conditions outside their curtain. Lies were now no longer believed. The Soviet Union was held together by fear of the United States and hate for the West. Their people began to doubt those accusations. When it started with the Polish people backing Walesa and Solidarity, an opposition was one against a combined people. That was the spark.

Five years before it had been unthinkable that the Soviet Union would collapse in my lifetime. People within East Germany, as well as the Soviet Union and other states took delight in their power over others in their society. It was a block-by-block police state. How could it be broken after 70 years of entrenchment? The people trusted no one, not even their family members.

Yet when the Berlin Wall was torn down in November of 1989, and the East German people by the thousands poured into the Western sector, it was expected that they would feel nothing but elation. However, they were enraged. Food, clothing, lodging, transportation and a free society had been within miles all those years. Who was responsible for keeping it from them?

One by one, in rapid order, we heard of changes in various Iron Curtain countries. Ceausescu and his wife were executed in Romania. When the Soviet communists began to relinquish power collapse was inevitable. Only a small taste of freedom was all it took. "Just to think," they said, "we will be given a choice of parties rather than a dictatorship of one party." Dealing with the former Soviet Union meant a whole new ball game.

Thousands of Chinese demonstrated for freedom and thousands were killed in the traditional mold of crackdown that reminded us of Hungary and Czechoslovakia. We expected it. They were running true to form. Was it an ideology they were protecting or was it again just another form of oligarchic dictatorship exercising a continuation of power? I thought the latter.

Nelson Mandela was freed after 27 years in prison in South Africa. The ball game was changing there too. The world was watching. We need their markets and their raw materials.

Another ball game was forming nationally. No sooner was Bush in office than his appointee as Secretary of Defense, John Tower, was rejected. This to me signalled a new power play between the branches of government. In addition, Oliver North was convicted and the Iran-Contra ulcer was still festering with many others also indicted. People were glued to their television sets in anticipation of a prison term. North's conviction involved the burglar protection system of his home and the destruction of incriminating papers. Yet he had acted in response to his superiors, doing the job to which he was assigned.

But another game was forming in the Middle East. Iran and Iraq after eight years had negotiated a cease-fire. Both countries remained armed, with millions in uniform. The burden of that protracted war against Iran (Persian) had been borne by Iraq (Arab). Other Arab countries such as Kuwait, I was told, did not pay up for the conflict, and this is what led to the Iraqi invasion of Kuwait. Our intelligence indicated that Saudi Arabia was next in line. Therefore, in August of 1990 Bush sent troops in haste to prevent Saddam Hussein from striking into Saudi Arabia. The United Nations Security Council encouraged an embargo by force. We were at war, with 500,000 troops available. The Iraqis vowed to "teach us a lesson".

Congress passed a bill to raise taxes and cut spending, but the Democrats still won more seats in the Congress in the midterm election. How were they to reduce a deficit without spending unless taxes were raised "on the rich"? Only two weeks later Bush ordered 150,000 more troops to Desert Shield. The Security Council authorized the driving of Iraq out of Kuwait, but as in Vietnam were to stop at a certain point.

On January 16, 1991, the most devastating air assault in history was waged. Who could forget that fateful night with the sky lit over Baghdad? The ground war began on February 24. Iraq was smashed in four days and capitulated on March 3.

Perhaps the most senseless and sick final act was Iraq's igniting of over 500 oil wells in Kuwait. What kind of minds! what kind of treachery and blind impulse! what disrespect for natural resources!

Again we won, but at what price? This time the troops returned as heroes. We had learned our lesson after ridiculing the Vietnam veterans.

The Last Shot

When I realized how long it would take me to complete all my books -- a sort of professional career memoirs of sorts -- I found that it would be some years before I could cover all the subjects. I sat down in 1989 and listed all the projects I was committed to and the articles I wanted to write. The list was 40 in number. I then proceeded to finish chapters for four books (for others) and sent them off. I finished four papers for the European journals and two others that had been hanging. This left 30 yet to do. I rough-drafted eight and had Sallie Coyle type them. The ninth was on the present status of forecasting growth of a child's face to maturity. Much of the decision in a child's problem is related to the long-term natural development of the face.

I was into the writing of it when I realized that the reluctance of the educational community to accept the forecasting theory and practice might be based on two reasons. One was that I had not submitted enough scientific data. The method for long-range prediction had been discovered twenty years before; it was reported and had grown through trial and error use to what I and many others considered a very acceptable level for clinical application. The second factor was that the manual or hand-generated procedure was very technical and time-consuming. We had other methods on the computer which were useful, but we wanted it to be of the finest quality and utilize the latest information. This meant a major new program with the computer. We first needed data.

The whole idea had been ridiculed and derided from the podium by practically all educators. The cynicism and sarcasm had sometimes become caustic. One teacher told one of his students that I was the most dastardly person to ever appear on the orthodontic scene. I looked up dastard: it means cowardly or one who commits malicious acts. Then, in turn, it followed that I looked up malice which means to desire to see others suffering or having an intent to commit harm with no justification. It was impossible for me to understand how these terms could apply to me. How was I doing harm by discovering truth?

As I listened at meetings I attended it seemed that those who scorned the idea were resupporting each other and finding strength in repetition of the limitation.

In July of 1989, therefore, I decided to do a major investigation, perhaps my last big shot at major research. It would take the help of others, so I started to enlist colleagues I could trust and who would be honest.

I had developed the first method in 1950. In 1960 I had tried, unsuccessfully, to simplify it for the average clinician to use. In 1970 I discovered a spiral on which the lower jaw grows. In 1980 the principles I had found were augmented by the findings of the Divine Proportion as a law of growth. So in 1990 I wanted to determine the accuracy of the technique and add any new findings for its final perfection.

Dr. Thomas Christie had taken my course in 1972 when I first started teaching the method. He saw its potential and had worked on it for improvements since that time. I called him to engage his help for the project.

I received X-rays from Dr. Donald Joondep at the University of Washington, Dr. Harold Perry at Northwestern University, Dr. Alex Jacobson at Alabama, Dr. James McNamara at the University of Michigam, Dr. Arthur Lewis at Fels Institute in Ohio, and Dr. Spiro Chiconas at U.C.L.A. In all, I was able to locate the records on 133 children. Fifty of those were treated by myself and Dr. Christie, and 83 were not treated.

Each X-ray was to be traced and then predicted. The original copy was sent to Dr. Christie for his prediction with his methods. Each prediction and the original were sent for analysis with the computer. The finals were later traced for accuracy of comparison.

Data and composites were then compared. The prediction worked. There were small details that were discovered from both our methods together with the new findings. It resulted in a method that was outstanding. I wrote seven papers on the project.

Little did I realize when I accepted the challenge to try to predict facial growth that it would take 40 years. I never even dreamed then that it would be done better by a computer as developed by Dr. Christie. But such is the new life in the 21st century as we progress in all things.

The Resentment of Trade Barriers

A sovereign state is an organized society which has power over its body politic. That being the case, its leaders want it protected both physically and economically. One tool for advantage economically is the use of tariffs.

A duty imposed on imported goods used or sold within another country is a tariff. When goods are purchased on foreign grounds and brought back into the country, then the duties, tolls, or imposts are collected as "customs". In fact, **for many years customs and tariffs were the only source of income for running the American government** before income taxes were levied.

Even today, our customs are lenient compared to other countries. Americans can bring in duty-free up to $400 worth of items acquired abroad. Anything up to the next $1000 is taxed a flat 10%. Taxes on alcohol and tobacco are limited also.

All imported items pass through Customs in order to protect the health and the welfare of the U.S. or other countries. Duties are charged for items at the port of entry. The four leading ports in the U.S. are New Orleans, New York, Houston and Long Beach and Los Angeles together.

Items leaving the United States for another country may also be taxed.

The United States, in its smokestack industrial era, had a positive balance of trade. This meant that items sold in other countries exceeded those sold in this country. The Commerce Department supervises this aspect of the government.

It seems to have been forgotten that our national policy and the will of the American people was to help the war-torn countries and the Third World countries rebuild after World War II. The Marshall Plan under Truman in 1947 extended aid of twelve billion dollars over four years to Europe alone. We willingly exported our know-how without considering the consequences.

Foreign labor was cheaper than domestic labor. In addition, foreign products were made with better workmanship and style, which appealed to the American consumer. Hence, German automobiles, English automobiles, and ultimately Japanese automobiles were made to be attractive and more lasting. As robot- and computer-automated and controlled core economies developed in other countries, our companies stood complacently by, still looking at only the bottom line of profits rather than facing the reality of quality. It was not that ours wasn't good or even improved. It was just that theirs was better.

In 1985 our trade deficit with Japan alone had jumped to almost 50 billion, but still only one-third of our total deficit. By 1988 our total deficit had soared to 3.2 trillion.

When it was discovered that Japan was selling semi-conductors and computer memory chips at below their costs in order to corner the market, the Omnibus Trade Bill was passed in August of 1988. Later Bush called Japanese practices "unjustifiable". In January of 1992 a trade delegation with Bush and CEOs of big manufacturing companies in the U.S. went on a Pacific Rim visit and came back with only token tariff concessions.

The feeling has been that American altruism has been unappreciated. Our openness to our markets has been met with closed markets. For instance, American cars are taxed almost 100% of original costs in some countries. This has given rise to resentment and sooner or later possible conflict. They probably resent our intrusion in their affairs but after all, fairness should be practiced by everyone.

Seven of the world's eight largest banks are now Japanese. They are not just larger, but three times larger in assets. We have been accused of an empire objective, while Japan has quietly built an economic empire.

We should remember it is not just Japan but the whole world that we must contend with. We all need each other in the new era ahead.

A Look in the Mirror

The Changing American emerged with World War II when we became global in Europe, Africa, Australia and Asia. After the war England was exhausted and with the dismantling of that empire we substituted as a police force without asking for territory. We still had to revitalize ourselves and convert a war machine back into a domestic society.

Under Eisenhower we maintained our military protection and yet at the same time had positive years in the payment of national debt. The 1950s were to me our greatest glory years, with no wars and a steady, growing economy.

But those years were not satisfactory to the socialist-minded. They wanted things and they wanted them immediately. Enough of conservatism! The public clamored to "get going again". They remembered the glory we had seen in the recovery from a war economy.

We began a shift toward over-spending again with "The New Frontier" of Kennedy. When he was murdered, Johnson took his programs as his own and renamed them "The Great Society". The programs were rammed through Congress despite the warnings Nixon had given not to move so fast that debt would be accumulated without order.

Our conflict with communism was preoccupying. The domino effect of one-by-one knocking over countries in a planned manner was real. Therefore, when the North Vietnamese attacked our ships in the Tonkin Gulf in 1964 a long, unwinable, defensive war was started against the advice of previous generals. The American public was duped. A partial war economy gave rise to an illusion of wealth. We lost our posture.

The question is what we would have done with Vietnam if we had "won". It is not within American character to take over other countries. We would simply have turned it over to any group that would have pledged a democracy and asked them to be a buffer against Communist expansionism.

Nixon was asked to restore our prestige. But the damage had been done. Our country was divided. Nixon's opening of the door to China was a breath of relief. But the cover-up of the bugging at Watergate put us back into mistrust of our leadership. We had lost the glory of the "American Century".

I have depicted the last twenty years (since 1970) as essentially representing our present. This is not only based on movements within my profession, but 1969 was also the last year that we enjoyed non-deficit spending. In 1975 our Federal debt was 533 billion, which amounted to $2500 for each person.

The Reagan years in the 1980s witnessed the greatest economic boom in history. It was characterized by tax cuts, deregulation, "junk bond" financing, buyouts, mergers and increased defense spending. Four Reagan-Gorbachev summits led to treaties. We had won the war of attrition against the Communists, but at a very heavy price. We were, in 1990, 3 trillion dollars in debt, or now about $13,000 per person.

Let us look in the mirror again.

No longer are we the wealthy. Our wealth has been transferred to the oil barons of the Middle East and to the electronic culture of the Pacific Rim.

We have increases in pollution and our protective ozone layer is threatened. Crime and homicides climb daily. Our prisons are packed to the brim and new ones are contracted for daily. Viruses infect our oceans and our computers.

Each day there is a greater clamor for health care by the Federal government, but who is to pay for it with a debt already greater than that of any nation in history?

Our education standard continues to decline. Students are unruly and without desire and motivation to learn. We argue and become emotional over hand guns and abortion. Our courts are packed by citizens suing other citizens. The illegal use of drugs spreads by the hour.

In the Clarence Thomas hearings the playing of a Perry Mason role by a lawyer determined to get his man was only upstaged by Congressmen wanting camera time. The details of sex acts shown to the world in a rape charge only served to sell air time. We didn't have to get into the gutter, it was brought to us.

Americans want only to be entertained. Why learn to read when everything can be explained by a glittering TV personality?

But worst of all, look at our freedoms. We talk about freedoms but the Congress despite Bush and Quayle has shown an unabated growth of regulations. Nearly 4,900 Federal regulations have been written, or about a 25% increase, since the Reagan years. Already signed by Bush are the Clean Air Act, Disabilities Act, laws on airplane noise, oil spills, food labelling and others. Very few were enacted under Reagan. The point of it all is that they became necessary due to negligence by the manufacturers who now need to correct their mistakes. Regulations multiply because of people not willing to cooperate on their own.

Each new law means a new regulatory agency and cost of administration and adds to the cost of doing business. Environmental regulation costs are annually now 123 billion and by the year 2000 are expected to be 171 billion. The Clean Air Act will cost our industries 25 billion each year. And so it goes. Everything has its price. Will other countries clean their air as we must do and still stay competitive? It's a world dilemma.

Yet, as I see us in the mirror, we still are the envy of the world. We still have to build protection to keep people out, not fence our citizens in. Our system is not perfect, but it's still the best. We must improve it.

Let's look forward to the Reappearing American of the future, which is the challenge of Part III of this narrative.

PART THREE

THE REAPPEARING AMERICAN

Introduction

In Part I, "THE DISAPPEARING AMERICAN" and Part II, "THE CHANGING AMERICAN", I tried to relate some of my personal experiences and express reactions and feelings to American and world events as they took place.

This third portion, Part III "THE REAPPEARING AMERICAN," will borrow from many of those occasions. Now I turn scenarist and endeavor to contemplate the possible conditions America may undergo in the next decade and millennium. In addition, projections are made to indicate directions for action that Americans may consider as guides for the molding of our future.

Chapter Twelve will explain the concept of principle. Chapter Thirteen will deal with near certainties for our future. Chapters Fourteen and Fifteen will cite probabilities in the future for several aspects of society. Chapters Sixteen through Eighteen will deal with the possibilities of a New Renaissance. And Chapter Nineteen will list challenges.

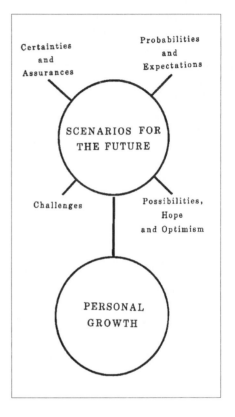

On many occasions I have been asked by colleagues, in a serious vein, to comment on what will happen in the next decades. Outside of one or two major miscalculations or mistiming of events, my track record makes a passing grade. My relative place in society may be somewhat unique when compared to other writers, other workers in the social fields or the science of socio-biology. There are several factors which give me an advantage, perhaps, that might be worth consideration by the reader, to wit:

#1 - Because I have been in close contact with several thousands of patients, I have seen their willingness to accept treatment, ask questions, and their ability to pay their bills --all as a sort of hidden barometer for the changing social and economic conditions. Health services are frequently the first to reflect **economic shifts**, lying as they do at the bottom of the totem pole in terms of absolute necessity. People feel least threatened by not paying the doctor's or dentist's bill and kneejerks in the economy are detected immediately.

#2 - My monthly costs yielded the sense of movements of **inflation**. A continuous probing for the fees parents thought my service was worth produced an intuitive perception of **economic drift**.

#3 - The third factor was my experiences as a regular member of a Rotary Club. We met each Tuesday for lunch at Riviera Country Club in Pacific Palisades and were privileged to listen to talks on a wide variety of civic, **national and international interests**. This was my contact with the "outside world" from my profession. This further afforded me the opportunity for intimacy with a cross-section of our whole society in services and industries.

#4 - I was responsible for numerous changes and improvements in the technical aspects of my field by working directly with manufacturers. This offered a first-hand exposure to **technology** with the advent of new materials, and new processes. It also prompted me to be mindful of management and labor problems. I kept in touch with the metal and plastic industry. I formed five companies and learned much of the background and problems of current American business.

#5 - The nature of my research and developments, made from both a biologic and a technical standpoint, gave me the opportunity to **lecture extensively both nationally and on six continents**. This provided good contact with people in many parts of the world. I could probe their true thinking and their own conditions and their views of America.

#6 - I was forced to organize my life in order to permit me to continue research, writing, teaching, running a successful practice and raising a family. Motivation and a continued good patient relationship was imperative, and this required an understanding of the nature of mankind. I therefore embraced the field of **socio-biology**, which meant interest in all the social sciences. Caring for patients with locomotor problems of the head, neck and jaws forced me also to examine the stresses of society causing distress in the body.

#7 - Almost 30 years ago, I became one of the pioneers in the clinical application of the **computer and automation** technology for the dental field for diagnostic and prognostic services. This afforded an insight into the progressive developments of computer technology.

#8 - I found time to design and build three homes and two commercial buildings, which kept me in touch with the pulse of architecture and the **construction industry**, and problems with labor unions.

#9 - Because I was quite busy and was faced with sagacious competition, efficiency of operation was necessary. I did time and motion studies in my practice as a result of which I **designed equipment** and layouts which became patterns for work and for office designs by others.

#10 - My early exposure to farm life has kept me mindful of the role of **agriculture** as a benefit for the entire country.

All these experiences developed conditioning for a broad look at American society. While that by no means makes me an authority, it does perhaps make for more concrete opinions and ideas.

Part III, consequently, deals with the realization that all Americans can be a part of a future structuring of our society. I offer my contribution for whatever it is worth, and pass on what little I have learned. I have tried to communicate in a simple, straightforward manner some of the directions in which we may perceivably go.

* * *

At the time of the ancient Greeks, there was a man named Xenophon who trained horses and observed that they feared fast approaches and unusual environments. Perhaps his name is connected with the origin of the term xenophobia. Or perhaps the word is what its Greek roots literally mean: xenos=foreigner, phobia=fear.

Xenophobia, a word first coined in 1903, is a term employed to express fear of a stranger, fear of the unknown, or fear of anything that is strange and different.

Maybe this is one reason why some yearn for the "good old days". They would feel more comfortable in an older familiar state which they would feel more certain about. **If we fear the unknown and the future is unknown, then we fear the future.**

If, however, we can understand what greatness the future may offer we may have less anxiety, greater confidence, and much greater hope!

*   *   *

Let me therefore try to (1) organize the factors, (2) contemplate first the unlikely changes, (3) speculate on likely alternatives in American society, and finally (4) view the possibilities of the future.

12

PRINCIPLES FOR SPECULATION ON THE FUTURE

Always in communication there are problems with semantics or the meaning of words and concepts as employed by the writer or speaker. Some clarification is therefore indicated.

The Future

Whenever I am asked about the future of our profession and the future of America, my answer is, "America? our future will be what we make it." This is sometimes shocking to the inquirer because of a set notion that "everything is out of control". Some view America as an uncontrollable monster that will display godzilla-like movement, and believe that we must stand back and wait to see which direction the monster will move. To predict, then, would be simply to anticipate its next step. I do not intend to stand back and be an observer rather than a participant in this major game: the future. Hence this writing and my own actions. Each person can be a force.

* * *

The Hypothesis of Corollaries

Certain happenings in one area are harbingers of attitudes reflected in the whole society.

A corollary is something that incidentally or naturally accompanies or parallels something else, or undergoes a similar phenomenon. Theoretically, an experience in one aspect of our society probably reflects basic problems, or parallels other events in society at the same time. Many aspects of society probably march to the same drumbeat. Trends in one sector of society influence trends in others.

* * *

Impulse

The word "impulse" technically means "force times time". It usually is taken to mean something producing sudden motion. Some events make a high impact in a very short period of time, and therefore have a high impulse. Who could forget the sight of a missile directed through a window in Baghdad followed by another missile through the same window? Such events have a very high impulse due to an immediate impact on the consciousness. But, if the definition is true, what would seem to be a very innocuous occasion when or if it persists over a long period of time can result in an impulse that is tremendous but difficult to detect because of its low attention level despite a long duration. Some movements take place a bit at a time, and suddenly become recognized when the public becomes shocked by sudden reality.

* * *

Liberal Arts and Scientists

Some readers may not have gone to college, and only by sheer determination and guts did I manage to do so. As a Freshman I took a beginner's course in sociology and also one in economics. I have had an interest in civic affairs since high school when I was president of the Civics Club.

Liberal Arts in colleges are composed of languages, philosophy, history, literature and some of the abstract sciences, all of which are intended to develop the general intellectual capacities and promote good reasoning and judgment as opposed to the learning of professional and vocational skills. With the attention required for learning a technique and developing a working skill, often the mind is confined to mechanistic considerations. The big picture of society under such a learning process becomes clouded.

The true scientist must experience the broadest kind of presence in philosophy, in the liberal arts as well as the sciences. This too is necessary for any comment on the future.

Centricism

During my course in Sociology the term "ethno-centricism" was met. The word "centric" means toward the center. It is a term we use in dentistry with relation to a person's bite. During swallowing the jaws are closed into a centered position which is called the "centric" or "habitual" bite.

We don't realize that we all have a "centric" in our personalities. The word "ego" refers to self. People with high self-esteem are often considered to be "ego-centric" or self-centered.

Mankind from his very beginning, perhaps, when he compares himself to lower animals, thinks he or she is pretty hot stuff. The word for this is taken from anthropology and is "anthro-centricism".

Ethno-centricism means an ethnic or a racial feeling of "hot stuff" or superiority to neighbors. This feeling expresses itself in pride for the local baseball team, the football team, or the Olympic team of the country as a whole. The concept extends to patriotism and even to the protection of the territory. It further may go down to one side of a city block. Youths form gangs in order to "belong". They earn their stripes within the group and become centered. Thus, gang warfare is for identity of the group.

I didn't realize when I first heard that word how much it would actually mean to an understanding of men and women in the future. Presently the struggle for ethnocentrism is seen under the guise of nationalism in former Iron Curtain countries.

The Development of Principles

My first principle is:

Our whole culture will improve as we get back to the basic principles that made the great American century.

Many people may have a similar message but express it differently. Conflicts of opinion may occur, not with an idea, but with the manner in which it is presented or connected. Semantics can be manipulated and so can statistics. But new ideas are often put down or ridiculed because of xenophobia.

Charles Kettering, once president of General Motors, made a statement on why ideas are killed:

> "Man is so constituted as to see what is wrong with a new thing . . . NOT WHAT IS RIGHT. To verify this, you have but to submit a new idea to a committee. They will obliterate ninety per cent of rightness for the sake of ten per cent of wrongness. The possibilities a new idea opens up are not visualized because not one man in a thousand has imagination!"

During my graduate education I was taught that when an argument or disagreement arises it cannot be settled on a superficial basis. Any issue must first be broken down into its components or brought "back to basics".

A basic, or a basis of something, is considered a foundation, a fundamental, or that which serves as a starting point.

We also hear of a "basic principle"; the basic idea would now have principle added, which would suggest there are basic, intermediate and advanced principles.

In sports, when a team continues to lose, the coach or manager will often say, "We've got to get back to fundamentals", or "back to basics", or "back to principles". **This means getting back to working on general principles rather than the practical game application.** It means getting back to the central important things, back to its minimum constituents without which a thing or a system would not be what it is in the first place. **This may be needed for our country as a whole**, unrelated to political parties.

But the word "principle" is often confusing or taken for granted without being understood. Certain definitions and usages must be related in order to enhance better communication for the following narration concerning speculations on our future.

Idea, Ideology, vs. Principle and Philosophy

An **idea** is a conception, a thought, a notion, or something that exists in the mind as a representation of a thing comprehended or formulated. It may or may not be true, or only imagined. When a group of ideas or concepts are connected, it is said to form an "ideology". Thus, **ideology** is nothing more than a body of ideas often somewhat integrated which may be based on supposition. This differs from principle.

"Principle" comes from *principium* which means a beginning or a base. It means a primary source or origin, and it usually is employed as a basis for the structuring of something else. It is based on a truth or something which is right or correct. This accounts for its confusion.

However, if we accept the definition of L. A. Allen that a principle is **"a general truth that is usually trustworthy but not without exception"**, we can use this term more successfully. A truth with no exception is a law. In biology and the social sciences, due to the diversity of Nature, there are few absolutes and certainties and laws.

What, therefore, can we use as guides for our thinking? The principle simply has to be basic. It has to be a truth and one that can be trusted in a most general manner. But still it must be realized that such truths may not be absolutes due to the variance of the human biologically and vagaries of our social condition. When a group of principles are integrated they form a "body of principles" in a consistent manner. These are the conditions which in my mind form a **philosophy**.

It is the philosophy, regarding women, men, and children, that we want first to examine before we can dare to prognose future circumstances. We will, in the following pages, attempt to examine many of the different aspects of the current American society, and further develop principles on which we can speculate regarding our future.

Paradigm

There are many terms either formulated in the computer world or employed in computer jargon that have become common words in our present lexicon. One such word is **cybernetics** (feedback). Another such term might be **servo-control** (interval control mechanisms). Yet another term popular today is **paradigm** which comes from the act of something being shown side by side. But paradigm means an example or pattern, or something that is an archetype which is a sort of **simulation**. In practical use, paradigm means the building of a model which can be constructed which in turn can be subjected to several conditions in which certain principles can then be applied for testing of the situation.

This generality is used for the present application of the computer with regard to the growth of the human head and neck. The computer is programmed for the orthodontist to predict the adult face from the head X-ray of a child as young as four years. This becomes a model or a paradigm for the treatment plan.

But several sociologic paradigms can be created just as the dynamometer is used for engine testing or the simulator for the training of an airline pilot. We will try to reduce many of the unknowns and questions regarding our future into principles, examine them, and make estimates and speculations.

Abstraction and Reductionism

Maybe another word would also apply; it is the "reductionist". To **abstract** is to take a total entity and shrink it down to a sort of an abridgement or some shortened form. But to **reduce** is different. It is to pick out the key factors, or those which are the most significant, and integrate them or resynthesize them into a more appropriate form. The reductionist is, therefore, the person most useful to a society.

All the foregoing thoughts are taken into account as I relate what I consider to be our present circumstance. In order to respectfully cover the matter I have grouped subjects into Philosophy, Art, and Science.

The Organized Thought Form

In searching for a method of presentation, I tried to organize the aspects of the current human experience and started with the format of the "USA TODAY" newspaper. The old established journalist ridiculed a shortened version of the news and especially the "factoids" in a square in the lower left corner of a news sheet. I appreciate the condensed reports and find the displays in the factoids educational. "USA TODAY" has four sections: General News, Life, Money, and Sports, and occasionally a special section. Analyzed and said in another way these are **society**, **economics** and **entertainment** plus current national and international events with sometimes some geography and history.

But for this discussion a better format was needed, one more specific. I chanced to find it in the Hutchinson Pocket Encyclopedia while browsing in a bookstore in Brisbane,

Australia, in June of 1991. Some fifty-six people in London had collaborated and done most of my organization job for me. I tried to relate to that group by dividing the subjects into Philosophy, Art and Science. They had grouped subjects into Society, Art, Science and Technology.

In the words of Will Durant,

> Science seems always to advance, while philosophy seems always to lose ground. Yet this is only because philosophy accepts the hard and hazardous task of dealing with problems not yet open to the methods of science -- problems like good and evil, beauty and ugliness, order and freedom, life and death; so soon as a field of inquiry yields knowledge susceptible of exact formulation it is called science.

> Every science begins as philosophy and ends as art; it arises in hypothesis and flows into achievement. Philosophy is a hypothetical interpretation of the unknown (as in metaphysics), or of the inexactly known (as in ethics of political philosophy); it is the front trench in the siege of truth. Science is the captured territory; and behind it are those secure regions in which knowledge and art build our imperfect and marvelous world.

> Philosophy seems to stand still, perplexed; but only because she leaves the fruits of victory to her daughters the sciences, and herself passes on, divinely discontent, to the uncertain and unexplored.

Many of the aspects of total society, when it comes down to it, must be dealt with as philosophy. As I considered these subjects the material was rearranged into about thirty different major facets of modern life listed under society or philosophy. I therefore reduced them and formulated some eight divisions of art and sixteen subjects under science and technology. Yet they needed to be reduced further for better organization and communication for our purpose here.

Classification of Subjects

The function of classification is to establish order and break down facts so that **the mind can handle them**. It therefore appeared that better groupings would help because a prediction of the future is based on a prediction of individual components as they contribute to the prediction of the whole.

Accurate predictions cannot be made until trustworthy explanations are made first. Explanations can be made only when the forces underlying a phenomenon can be identified and then evaluated. Contemplating such a complete viewpoint, I therefore set about to do some mind-mapping so that a fresh look could be made of the whole complex of subjects that may have a bearing on the outcome of the future. When I listed them randomly there were more than fifty and required organization for handling by the mind.

Society (philosophy)

The human race has produced many thinkers with ideas. There are many who have speculated on man's behavior, further offering reasons for his actions, and often suggesting solutions for his problems. As a starting point we may begin, in the broadest manner, with the eight main branches of philosophy as seen in Map I and as compiled from Will Durant and Manly Hall. (See Map I)

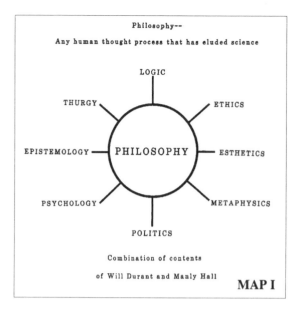

Philosophy--
Any human thought process that has eluded science

LOGIC

THURGY

ETHICS

EPISTEMOLOGY — PHILOSOPHY — ESTHETICS

PSYCHOLOGY

METAPHYSICS

POLITICS

Combination of contents
of Will Durant and Manly Hall

MAP I

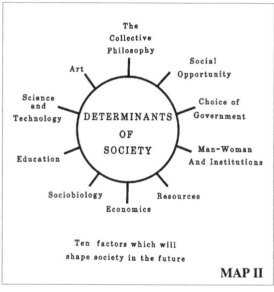

The
Collective
Philosophy

Art

Social
Opportunity

Science
and
Technology

DETERMINANTS
OF
SOCIETY

Choice of
Government

Man-Woman
And Institutions

Education

Sociobiology

Resources

Economics

Ten factors which will
shape society in the future

MAP II

It is difficult to separate philosophy from society as a whole, and therefore we won't try. Many of the aspects of philosophy overlap sociology. And with many of the modern world thinkers such as Norman Cousins, Buckminster Fuller, Edward O. Wilson, Robert Ardrey and Will Durant, all from a universe of their own, the field of sociology embraces biology. With so many of the factors now being studied, and coming under the whip of a scientific discipline, it is indeed sometimes difficult to determine when a subject crosses that floating barrier that fluctuates between philosophy and science. We therefore offer another rendering for a perspective of the determinants of future American society. (See Map II)

Science

First of all we must perceive what science really means. It is systemized knowledge, and the assemblage of facts and truths with a provision of discovering new truths within its own domain.

Science employs the scientific method which when broken down has essentially only four steps: observation and organization; the production of a classification and the asking of questions; the construction of a hypothesis or a guess, hunch or supposition; and finally proving it or disproving it by means of experiment. Science is conducted in many subjects, but the fundamental ingredients are always the same. Anyone can be a scientist, it's just a matter of being exact and properly inclusive.

Another natural ingredient is the proper intellectual background for the subject. The final characteristic needed for the greatest success is an insatiable curiosity to learn and find answers to the puzzles. It is always necessary that the scientist be supremely honest. It is also better when he or she is a good communicator.

Therefore, let us look at the sciences. Because technology is such a vital part of American culture, all its various aspects provide major headings, as shown in Map III.

Art

My perception and appreciation of art was greatly enhanced by reading Robert Henri's book "The Art Spirit". He starts out as follows:

> Art when really understood is the province of every human being. It is simply a question of doing things, anything, well.

His field was in the visual arts, painting and sculpting. Many would not put sports in an art category, I am sure, but the art in sports can be appreciated as an art form and today is a strong part of the entertainment industry, and should be recognized as such. Therefore, Map IV is proposed for art.

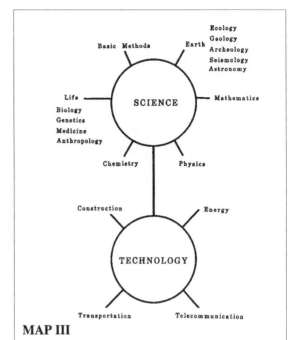

MAP III

Principles in Philosophy, Science and Art

To remind the reader again, as employed here a principle is a general truth that is usually trustworthy but there may be an exception. So the principle, in this sense, can be perceived as the central tendency of a bell curve of distribution. The outside tails are the exceptions and the general truth is the main body of the curve.

We shall use this approach in the analysis of the present situation

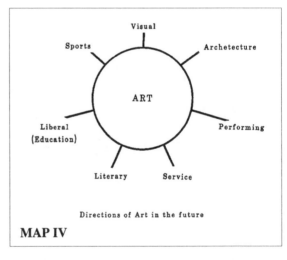

Directions of Art in the future

MAP IV

and a forecast of the future. **The general truth or principle will not change**. Its application may change, but if it falls under the definition of a principle, it is an unchanging truth or else it would not be a principle.

Law

From a principle we might dare to take the final step in some circumstances to defining a law, or applying a law. To remind ourselves again, a law is a truth that has no exceptions. It is a constant, and is a bedrock foundation. From this base of laws and principles understood, we can then move forward for speculations of the future.

13

SOLID FOOTINGS FOR PROGRESS

Some things are too firmly based to be shaken by ordinary forces. There is an old statement: "There is nothing new under the sun." Some things don't change, and it is truly amazing how often a thing conceived by the mind had been conceived long before in another mind.

Often all that is new is the different interpretation of an old idea or a concept modified by application of new technology. But nothing remains absolute forever in any society, and modifications and circumstances do change. Therefore, a principle exists:

Change itself is predictable and trends and fashion exemplify such changes.

Changes are only predictable to the extent of chance or to an experience following some factual or impressive event. A trend is a vogue, a change in style, or a general tendency toward a specific direction. Consideration of trends permits the offering of another principle:

Regardless of efforts to stabilize and hold things as they are, trends will continue to occur.

We shall therefore start our discussion of the future with phenomena which will most likely remain relatively constant in the future. Many of these are connected with our genes and with the basic nature of mankind.

On Human Nature

In his book "On Human Nature", E. O. Wilson quoted the American anthropologist G. P. Murdock in 1945 who listed the recorded characteristics of any human culture that had ever been known to history. Some 67 characteristics were common to all people on the face of the earth:

Age-grading, athletic sports, bodily adornment, calendar, cleanliness training, community organization, cooking, cooperative labor, cosmology, courtship, dancing, decorative art, divination, division of labor, dream interpretation, education, eschatology, ethics, ethnobotany, etiquette, faith healing, family feasting, fire making, folklore, food taboos, funeral rites, games, gestures, gift giving, government, greetings, hair styles, hospitality, housing, hygiene, incest taboos, inheritance rules, joking, kin groups, kinship nomenclature, language, law, luck superstitions, magic, marriage, mealtimes, medicine, obstetrics, penal sanctions, personal names, population policy, postnatal care, pregnancy usages, property rights, propitiation of supernatural beings, puberty customs, religious ritual, residence rules, sexual restrictions, soul concepts, status differentiation, surgery, tool making, trade, visiting, weaving, and weather control.

[N.B.: Eschatology is the study of death.]

The anthropologist and pioneer in sociobiology Robin Fox was even stronger in projecting the probabilities of development in children reared in total isolation. To quote: "I do not doubt that they could speak and that, theoretically, given time, they or their offspring would invent and develop a language despite their never having been taught one. Furthermore this language, although totally different from any known to us, would be analyzable to linguists on the same basis as other languages and translatable into all known languages."

But if these children could survive and breed, Fox theorized they would produce a society which would have at least the following 21 characteristics:

Laws about property, rules about incest and marriage, customs of taboo and avoidance, methods of settling disputes with minimum bloodshed, beliefs about the supernatural, social status, initiation ceremonies for young people, courtship and adornment of females, symbolic body adornment, certain activities set aside for men, gambling, a tool-weapon-making industry, myths, legends and story-telling, dancing, adultery, homicide, suicide, homosexuality, schizophrenia, neurosis and psychosis, and various healers.

If all these characteristics have occurred in every culture of the past, and in theory a human society would be compelled to develop certain patterns, the force is too great not to be expected for the future. I would predict all these characteristics to continue in the future, plus others with continuing modern developments.

Fraternal twins differ more than identical twins or triplets. Studies of facial structure analysis clearly show identical twins to be quite similar. This suggests a strong hereditary factor in form and shape of our bodies. From such studies geneticists have shown also that certain traits implicate heredity beyond our physical bodies and that these traits affect social relationships. The list includes:

- ability with numbers
- verbal fluency
- memory
- timing of language learning

- spelling
- sentence construction
- perceptive skill
- psychomotor skill

- extroversion-introversion
- homosexuality
- age of sexuality
- neurosis and psychosis

All this would suggest a more powerful connection to our genes than behavioral psychologists would like to admit.

Ardrey

I have mentioned before some of the ideas of Robert Ardrey. Now perhaps in connection with genetics it would be well to go into his life and teachings in more detail. Before his death I sat for many hours talking with him. And I appreciated his genius.

Ardrey's first book, "The African Genesis", was published in 1961. He had spent six years in its research and writing. Because he had been a playwright and a screen writer he had a tremendous insight into human behavior and psychology. He went to Nairobi for a story about the causes of the nationalistic movement and the formation of so many different African countries, but ended up in 1955 in Raymond Dart's laboratory in the medical school in Johannesburg where he was introduced to the workers in the field of anthropology and archaeology. There he learned about the discovery of Australopithecus.

The human did not originate approximately 6000 years ago as the Bible would suggest, nor some 35,000 years ago with the development of Cro-Magnon Man, but our beginnings from animals of human characteristics date back to from 2,000,000 to perhaps as much as 14,000,000 years ago. That's a long, long time.

In "African Genesis" his first idea was to describe roughly the physical development of man in the uprighting of posture, and like other scientists he remarked on the freeing of the hands with the development of bi-pedal or two-legged locomotion. He recognized the associated evolutionary bend in the base of the skull which we in our field call the "hafting zone" (or the bones located halfway between the face and the brain).

The second part of Ardrey's book dealt with the behavior of humankind. The hypothesis was drawn that while man was a food-gatherer he also was a hunter, and therefore a killer. One of early man's favorite weapons was thought to be the bone of the foreleg of an antelope. In groups he clubbed his prey to death. And he was not loath to feasting on members of his kind.

The third part of "African Genesis" dealt with the origins of human motivation. He made the case for the human's innate or instinctual drives being far, far deeper and more ancient than anyone had previously concluded. In Ardrey's view Freud was wrong, in that he didn't go far enough, and Marx was wrong, period.

Ardrey's reasoning was that behavioral characteristics are locked up in our genes and transmitted in codes in DNA molecules. We are **not a solitary result of our culture** or environment as would be imagined by the behaviorists. He cited many examples of characteristics that had been thought to be distinctly human that were found in lower animals. He quoted scientists in the field of ethology (the science of ethics) as well as psychology as backup for such beliefs.

Ardrey agreed that mankind was, of course, driven by the four forces that Freud had described. These were the individual's provision of protection for survival, the drive to search for food, the love and care of progeny for the future of the race, and finally sex. But if there were only four, then any frustration or disturbance that would upset a human being that couldn't be easily identified in the first three simply had to automatically fall in the fourth, which was sex. Sex then became the wastebasket for receiving many varied frustrations. Sex was blamed for many things for which it was not responsible.

Animals were shown to fight for territory or for dominance, which is another form of territory. Male animals fight for status which automatically attracts the female. With ethology as a background, Ardrey described at least four more drives that human experience manifests. These were **territory, status**, the **need to belong to a society**, and the **acquiescence** to the characteristics of that society.

With the discovery of these other drives, and with the suggestion to behaviorists that something should be added, Ardrey caught their wrath. A group headed by Ashley Montagu, a British psychologist, without consulting him or inviting him for discussion, got together and published a condemnation of the idea. Ardrey was not highly respected by them because he had no degree in anthropology and had perhaps scooped many in the scientific fields with the suggestion of other human motives.

However, his writing perhaps did more to expose the field of anthropology and contemporary psychology to the public than did any other offering. Being a playwright, he was a master of the anecdote. It caused many to recontemplate the true nature of the human species.

Once that train of thought was set in motion, it went through the generations of the derision, gradual consideration, and the gradual incorporation into a body of knowledge. After "African Genesis" Ardrey backed up, licked his wounds, went back and reinvestigated all his material and in 1966 boldly published another work, in part discussing the objections to his notions, and deliberately called it "The Territorial Imperative". Humans not only desired private property, their psyche demanded it and drove them.

"For it was not just a matter of *Australopithecus* and the predatory transition; there were alpha fish and pecking orders, gene pools and displacement activities, exploratory behavior and ritualized aggression, and all had bearing on the human condition. Above all there was territory.

"Not only had the new anthropology produced a revolutionary interpretation of man's emergence from the animal world; not only had the new biology begun a revolutionary interpretation of the behavior of animals in the world from which we came: also, as I was now to discover, our time of high stress was producing a revolutionary class of human being. A new human force -- a force anonymous and unrecognized, informed and inquisitive, with allegiance to neither wealth nor poverty, to neither privilege nor petulance -- was silently appearing on earth. And the class was massive.

"There is nothing so moving -- not even acts of love or hate — as the discovery that one is not alone."

While his first book attempted to gather a long perspective of man's evolutionary nature, his second book brought into focus a single aspect of human behavior, a consequence not of choice but of inheritance -- it was territory. From his writings we may venture the opinion that there were certain principles on which further knowledge could be based.

Three Faces of Janus

Probably Ardrey's greatest gift was his use of reductionism. While he had taken from other people's work, he logically further reduced human drives to only three factors. This was in my mind most brilliant. These three sources of power were brought out in the last chapter of "The Territorial Imperative" (which he labeled "The Three Faces of Janus"). People in old-world cultures put the image of Janus (a god of the beginnings, with two faces) at the doorways to their homes, one image facing inward and one outward. One was symbolic of the face put on when confronting the public in the outside world. The other was a face for the family and inside the home. It was a beautiful concept. It would be nice to rejuvenate the idea. There may be a fortune in it for somebody! If so, I want a piece of the action.

But Ardrey said there were three faces, which were symbolic of the three drives in the total human experience. Each of these represented a face, and they had a hierarchy of importance.

Identity

The first in the scale was identity, the second was stimulation, and the third was security. But conceptually, these ideas were difficult to appreciate until their antithesis was understood. The antithesis of identity is anonymity. Stated very simply, man has, as the foremost need, **to be somebody rather than a nobody**. It may be the one underlying cause of frustration and cause of depression in teen-agers, as one in three currently have considered suicide.

How can young people be somebody and have an identity until they have done something? It is almost as if students feel identity is something to be learned rather than worked for. It is as if their thinking follows the idea that a person is supposed to inherit identity, that something is missing in the school system that a student is supposed to learn rather than earn.

The truth is, identity comes from other people. Only when a man, woman, or young person does something for society or does something for other people, or something for greater personal satisfaction, will they be recognized and discover identity!

If a youth is not appreciated in the family, then he or she can be appreciated or receive identity in a gang. The pattern is that he may have to do something criminal or extremely exceptional to reach the recognition of that group. This is a form of identity.

Identity is a primary drive, and it won't change. The underlying principle is:

When identity is related to other drives it ultimately becomes the highest in rank.

The sooner identity is recognized as a drive of every human being the better for the future of our children. It is the underlying cause of ethno-centricism, racial centricism, and even ideologic centricism. In prediction of the future, therefore, it is extremely unlikely that anything in the next millennium would alter this human condition.

Stimulation

Ardrey's second face, stimulation, is best understood by its antithesis which is boredom. Anyone knows a child becomes bored very easily. It is the good teacher, social worker or camp counselor who has an endless number of projects to keep a child busy. It could be a part of our reptilian complex which is the base for our preparation for action; people seek "kicks". Life must have interest; everyone needs stimulation. Why is jail a punishment?

Stimulation must of certainty be, as Ardrey explained later, one function of art, as art is for the stimulation of life. It raises interest in things and people. It stimulates the brain. It is pleasing to the senses. It gives one an appreciation of beauty. It lends an appreciation of adventure. Some people become addicted to their pleasures and can hardly get enough stimulation.

Maybe the need for stimulation is an underlying factor in drug abuse, that extra "kick", that super-stimulation through no effort however phoney and false it might be.

Stimulation is the secret to our entertainment society. We don't want to participate quite often; we are stimulated by just watching and perhaps the vicarious counterpart.

Books are written on games people play. Love stories, love triangles make stimulating stories, as any writer knows. People always want something new because they become bored with the old. Madison Avenue takes advantage of this human characteristic as new products constantly are presented to attract attention. Like identity, the need for stimulation will not change. And it represents another principle:

People are driven to sources of stimulation.

I have heard it said that the average person in the United States goes through five career shifts in a working lifetime. Why? Other studies have shown that even salary levels take a second place to job stimulation. People will work for a lower salary if it's more fun. This is even doubled when people can see in a job a contribution to the welfare of others and to the good of society, which now adds identity to a job. All of these ideas have been proven, but maybe they have never before been approached with Ardrey's "three face" analysis.

It's a good wife who makes life interesting for her husband. It's a good husband who charms and continues to stimulate his wife. This is the substance on which a marriage thrives. It is the coal that drives that locomotive.

Security

Like identity, and stimulation, security can be misinterpreted. At first glance people might put it in the first level of hierarchy rather than the lowest. Security is better understood when the concept of its antithesis, anxiety, is analyzed. Anxiety means fear. It means frustration.

I have already discussed xenophobia, which means a fear of the unknown and the natural fear of a stranger. Therefore, security in a job would suggest that a person is free from the fear of being unemployed. Health means that the individual is free from the fear of being ill. Perhaps people's desire for national health programs is a misinterpretation of security. Having a love relationship means that the lover is free from the fear of not being loved. Therefore, a person with no job, no income, who is ill and who is unloved is in a life at its lowest ebb.

Consider the drunkard on skid row, and realize the problem, and understand why alcohol overtakes him in order to in that way overcome his anxieties. Now we have another principle:

Man basically will react to fear.

This is part of our flight or fight phenomenon, basically set up by adrenal hormones in our glands. Fear and anxiety causing stress can upset the body's systems as much as many disease states. This principle will not change.

No matter how much health insurance or social welfare is available, it is not going to change the psyche of anxiety. It may blunt it, but it won't change it. I would therefore make this recommendation: national health insurance should be absolutely limited to only major diseases. I have been told by seasoned veterans in their medical practice that only a few of the people who go to a physician will have a life-threatening disease that really needs their attention. I might make another recommendation: alternative methods for prevention should be explored as a method of full technology in the prevention and treatment of disease. No-technology as an example is use of surgery or radiation for a cancer. Full-technology would be the recommendation for the patient to get out of the sun to prevent skin cancer in the first place. Medicine wallows around somewhere in the field of half-technology, except when vaccines are used, when fluorides are employed for dental decay, when proper foods are recommended and when tobacco is eliminated and alcohol is used in moderation.

Abraham Bernowsky
Ardrey's thesis is, together with that of Edward O. Wilson, and I would have to say that I would be in agreement with them, that we are much more alike than we are different. Secondly, they argue that our genetic pool which permits us to stand, walk and run upright with our arms free for labor, art and weaponry, with our big brain hovering over our faces and the capacity for articulate speech, gives us so much in common that as a major principle

Man as a species is distinct.

But Bernowsky stresses inordinate variability. From the outset I would therefore add another principle:

Man is infinitely variable but only within the framework of that human uniqueness.

I believe this to be true in a structural or morphologic sense, but also in a behavioral sense.

Leroy Garn
Garn wrote a book on motivation in selling, entitled "The Magic Power of Emotional Appeal" in which he described four types of individuals that a salesman was likely to encounter. He also described how people carry around themselves an invisible shield, and before a sale could be made that shield had to be penetrated so that the salesman could get to the person and gain their confidence. I would describe that shield as xenophobia as it is superimposed on Ardrey's triad.

People have likes and dislikes and to be sure, certain types of personality exist. In an effort to gain their confidence the seller or a person trying to influence another could most easily reach them by analyzing which particular type is most prominent in their individual characteristic. Without any scientific basis, let us say that a community is made up evenly of the four types.

The Self-Preservationist
Garn did not place the types in a hierarchy, but the first person he described was a "self-preservationist". Persons like this are high in security need! They want an established order in their lives, and they prefer routines. They seek great order because they do not want to be upset. They love minute detail. They like a personal freedom and if their clothing is too tight or a room too hot or too cold they will be bothered. Loud noises will frighten them exceedingly. They tend to be highly religious, sometimes are hypochondriacs or vegetarians. They will keep a tight time schedule. They will be on time and will be very disturbed when others do not meet such obligations. They pay their taxes, they have loyalty, they are good law-abiding citizens. The reason is they want to feel secure. By recognizing this type of person the salesman will have a good start on obtaining a good customer. We all have a survival drive, but these people have a high level of self-protection.

The Romantic

The second type of individual is the antithesis of the self-preservationist: it is the romantic. Many things that characterize the self-preservationist are exactly the opposite in the romantic. The romantic is bent on stimulation. This type of person likes to be where the action is. Art is stimulation, and these are the artists. These are the entertainers. This is the Don Juan or the Donna Juanna. This type of person prefers blue jeans to a black tie. They love to travel, to meet new people and see new places and try new languages. They are the sky divers seeking new thrills. He or she will own a boat, an airplane, and will love to make over old cars or redecorate the home. They often will move from one avocation or hobby to another.

The romantics are not too bothered if a check bounces -- so what? tomorrow's another day, let's eat, drink and be merry right now, because right now is all that counts. These types are the NOW generation and tend to demand instant gratification in just about everything they do. Playing games and participating in them particularly is rewarding. They love to snow ski but soon become bored with the same slope and maybe the same resort. The game is the thing. The romantic disdains a schedule and likes to be his or her own boss. They are also the dreamers, innovators and inventors, and they make their lives exciting and are exciting to others.

The Recognitionist

This type of individual thrives on identity. They prefer quality to utility, they want to be identified with the best! They tend to be more proper. But also, in seeking recognition, it may be the school teacher, the clergyman, the president of a society, the boss of a business, and above all the politician whose ego must continuously be fed and who has a tremendous appetite for it. We see recognition in sports where the baseball player or basketball player will want to be the highest paid in his sport, not because of the salary but just to make him recognized as the best. They suffer drastically with losing self-esteem and self-confidence. In a personal relationship when that person is put down, it becomes a severe blow and a harbinger for the end of a marriage.

On the basis of identity the Nobel Prizes were born and other awards are sought. If a housewife is not recognized for the making of a good meal or the cleaning of the house, and keeping things nice, she is hurt that her efforts go unnoticed. People in this category require a lot of attention and identity is the foremost need. Recognitionists make excellent workers because they take a lot of pride in their work, because they want to recognize themselves. Perhaps this need is the highest in most of us. Do we understand it?

Moneyist

The final type of person is the money person, who is materialistic in all things. Money is their security, money is stimulation, and money is identity. That being the case, money is constantly in this person's thinking.

Moneyists like to hoard their money. Even though they may be prepared best to pay a bill, it's the romancer who will often pick up the tab first, because the moneyist wants to keep his money. Some people want to haggle and haggle to get the best price possible while others would be embarrassed to do so.

The moneyist is not comfortable paying full price for anything. Unless these types can make a deal, it's no deal. Even after the moneyist has made a deal, this type of person is a stickler for quality. They will make absolutely certain that the price paid is full value. The reason for this is because they consider business a game also. Moneyists get tremendous joy out of pulling a fast one on someone else. Money is their game, money is their fun, money is the goal. It can be the empire-builder, or it can be the little lady who sews bills in her mattress.

Bernowsky, without classification, talks about the need for variability in the human species. It is of such stuff that a free society is made. We are not Pavlovian dogs!

The Social Contract

With the idea of variability, we can now return to Ardrey and his third book "The Social Contract", published in 1970. In his second book he had made the case for territory as a form of identity and also showed that it was the most propertied male who naturally most attracted the female. Countless examples of this are also seen in the human experience; traditionally, in many of the old cultures, marriages between families had a purely economic or social basis. In old Europe, even kings took as brides princesses from other countries in order to seal economic relationships between their countries.

Status

But another form of identity is status. If man is a social animal, then his ranking within that society is a strong part of his needs and drive. Ardrey's "social contract" is one that grants a person an individual expression. There should be enough order or enough regulation to have a stability of the society, but a principle is involved:

Too much regulation and too many restrictions take away the chance for individual expression and a pursuit of excellence.

The opportunity to seek the level that is within his inherited genetic endowment must be guaranteed in that contract. Some people want to be led, others are not satisfied unless they lead. The concept of the need for individualism or the need for freedom of variation can give rise to another principle, which is this:

Man's need for freedom is not economic or even political, it is social. That will not change in the future.

Success breeds success. The successful wants to be even more successful. The loser may find himself in a rut, never to get out. Such are the problems in life.

Batra

In 1990 I was exploring stations on the radio of my car while traveling in Phoenix, and by chance came upon someone's interview with Mr. Ravi Batra, who teaches economics at Southern Methodist University in Dallas. He was predicting a strong recession or depression in the 1990s which he had previously (in 1987) correctly predicted. He had also correctly predicted the downfall of the Soviet empire on an economic basis. He predicted that capitalism itself would fall on hard times. As I listened, he piqued my interest, and I obtained his books. So far as I could determine, he made an adequate interpretation of the different schools of belief in economics. I can well understand differences in economic theory because there are three major schools of belief in my own field of orthodontics, each with emotional advocates of their particular ideology.

Insofar as possible Batra attempted to make the field of economics a science, principally through the study of cycles and the tendency of economics to be cyclic in major moves through distinct time periods and minor moves in shorter time periods. Things cannot keep going up, up and up forever, nor down and down forever, and try as we may, there is no such thing as a steady state in economics.

I remembered from my college course in economics the forces of supply and demand. But I was a little bit hazy about supply-side economics vs. demand-side economics, what it really meant to be a monetarist, and I was happy to have it explained in his books. I think everyone should know in present-day world circumstances all these different theories, as we now are moving into a world economy, not just an individual national economy. This movement to a world economy is probably not going to change. Nor do I think the cycles will stop any more than do the seasons of the year.

What Batra did, however, was to adapt and explain what has happened in whole cultures in the past, and what is still happening. He used, as his brief, the writings of one of his Hindu masters from India, by the name of P. R. Sarkar. Sarkar, a most unusual and brilliant philosopher, had analyzed history. His analysis, all new to me, was that societies as a whole go through four stages which are cyclic, and can be picked up and discussed at any stage, because all societies go through four stages.

We can begin at the lowest stage, which he called the **laborer** society. This starts out, particularly in the past, in an agricultural and even an industrial community, with the masses of the people crying for economic welfare for their survival. They are the workers, they are the helpers, and if there are no jobs they look to the state to provide them. When jobs are not available they look for state welfare however it can be arranged. But in the laboring ranks there is usually limited education. They also lack leadership. In order to obtain leadership they will submit to some kind of authority. That authority, then, is the second level, or the second stage which Sarkar called the **warrior** stage.

The **warrior** mentality is that everything can be achieved with physical effort. If hard work isn't enough, the warrior works harder. But with the warrior now also comes violence -- power obtained by violence. In the past it has been a warring king, or a dictator, or even an oligarchy of generals such as we have seen in some present-day South American countries. With armies come controls and regulations. A police state and the threat of violence subjugates the laborers into a controlled or regulated society. Generals thrive on war, it makes them important. It gives them identity, and it gives them an even greater power particularly in modern warfare -- the power of the tank operated with computers; the guided missiles; the ability to shoot down a plane without seeing it -- all provide absolutely awesome power. As General Schwarzkopf said, "We'll go over 'em, under 'em and through 'em, whatever it takes to kill 'em." Thus, the laborer always becomes subjugated to control by some sort of an authority.

But sooner or later within the ranks of the warrior or within a society itself the **intellectual** emerges. In the past, history shows that this role was filled by the clergy, when church and state were the rulers, and the intellectual with his cunning and with his knowledge manipulated the warrior. Today it doesn't have to be a clergyman, it can be a college professor, or anyone with knowledge. So we see a third power source: education and knowledge giving rise to power and ultimate control through legislation often in favor of those in power.

But usually the intellectual cannot resist taking advantage of a position of authority, and in order to improve the economy it takes the businessman, whom Sarkar labeled the **acquisitor**. What he meant was a stage in which a society is dominated by business people or those making money and accumulating wealth, ultimately, the wealth to buy things and buy people. Thus, under the protection of the warrior, under the sanction by the intellectual, the acquisitor through wealth gains the power. Laws are drawn up and enacted for his benefit, and as long as jobs are produced for the laborer, and as long as the warrior has his power with the threat of violence and intellectuals hold respect, things run smoothly. As long as the intellectual is pulling the strings in politics and the acquisitor is gaining wealth, usually a society is on the rise.

Where, then, does the problem start? What puts an end to that cycle and starts a new one? It arises, according to Batra, when an extreme majority of the wealth in a society ends up in the hands of too few acquisitors. This takes the wealth out of circulation and **limits the laborer as a consumer**. When poverty gets great enough, when the pangs of hunger get strong enough, and when a status gets too low for even the merest human dignity, anarchy erupts. The laborers rebel, the people rebel, but they don't know what they are against or what they are for. Witness the armed bandits in Somalia. A revolution ensues, led by the best organizers. In order to put down a revolution or actually run in front of the group and lead a revolution, the warrior emerges and the process goes through another cycle.

Sometimes these cycles are very rapid, and sometimes they can take hundreds of years. But because it has been repeated in history so many times, both Sarkar and Batra strongly believe that it is a profound principle and perhaps even a law of cyclic change. I would make this statement as a principle:

> **Without control and recognition of its problems, a society will probably undergo the Sarkar-Batra shift.**

* * *

[For an interesting forerunner of one aspect of Batra's thought see the quotation from a War Department Training Manual dated 1928 in the Appendix].

Ephemerality of Technology

A correct principle has a strong degree of immortality. That is a principle within itself. But another principle quite the opposite is:

> **Techniques and technology are ephemeral.**

We are obliged to look at art, science and technology as the avenue of change. There will no doubt be cultural modifications, but they will probably lie within the frame of reference of the foregoing principles.

Philosophy's Stability

Let us ponder certain aspects of the field of philosophy, such things as good and evil, life and death, the proper roles of government, ethics, the place for religion, and man's ultimate purpose. These subjects will remain in philosophy until they come under the scientist's dissection and a scale of measurement. To that end they will still be present in the future.

Physical Man and Woman

As a long-time student of prediction of facial growth, I have often been asked what our race will look like in the future. The first thing that pops into my head is that we will be prettier. I base that on the theory of the process of natural selection, and my work with the Divine Proportion. Structurally, man will change very little unless we are bombarded with cosmic irradiation or environmental catastrophe.

For more than 200 years we have been increasing in size, as is evidenced from the recorded size of soldiers and sailors in the War of Independence, World War I and World War II, and at the present. Mighty Captain John Smith was barely five feet tall. Each era has grown larger than the last, and we can only speculate as to the cause. This growth is almost uniform on the face of the earth, and there has been a hypothesis that it is some environmental factor in the earth itself such as cosmic irradiation. However, anthropologist Dr. Philip Tobias of South Africa has found tribes in which no change has taken place, which suggests the presence of more local environmental factors.

In bigness there could be a process of natural selection operative. Natural selection works like this: if an animal, by way of having an advantage in a given environment, can survive and be selected for mating, those genes will be a part, then, of the genetic drift of a given population. If he is unable to survive or is inferior, he will therefore not live to reproduce his kind and will be eliminated. His kind will then become extinct; and indeed if widespread enough the whole species will become extinct. Whatever small property it is that gives man his success within the society will contribute to his survival, and in nature it is the strongest and the one with the best fitness for that environment that will be selected for the propagation of that species. Maybe females choose larger males more than we recognize!

If my hunch about the Divine Proportion is right, being attractive for beauty is an advantage in the survival game, but also body part arrangements in this proportion yields superior mechanical efficiency which can be a factor. If this is true, slowly but surely there will be a drift towards those proportions with the process of natural selection.

However, the fact that the female tends to select from the ranks of the propertied and in essence is not selecting on the basis of beauty, would definitely make that hunch wrong. Today, with orthodontics, with surgery, with cosmetology, the selection of a mate may have a concealed genetic dysplasia and in fact end up being a shock with the birth of a family of ugly children. But by and large, if our pre-natal care improves, our knowledge of nutrition improves, and even applied to the present level of knowledge, world societies in the future will become more and more beautiful as well as larger.

Weaknesses

My mother once confessed that even if someone fell down and broke their neck, she would probably laugh. From Charlie Chaplin through Red Skelton, to many later comedians, a good fall on the prat was always worth a laugh. When the monkey urinated on Johnny Carson's head it made headlines. So there seems to be some delight in looking at a fault or a misfortune in another.

Maybe such a human tendency is a part of our survival mechanism which makes us feel better when someone or something has been shown that is obviously inferior. People fall because they are clumsy and instinctively we feel that we are not. How else would it be that some take delight in watching a boxing match, or the violence in a football game? Someone has to give, and someone has to take, the hit. We usually delight in appraising the hitter rather than the hittee. This gives us a sense of strength in our own psyche. The winner is praised, the loser is booed, the winner makes us feel good, the loser makes us feel poorly. This attitude is a part of human traits and will continue.

* * *

The bedrock foundation for prediction of the future starts with the understanding of humankind. Our human characteristics lie deep in our genes, and have a base of millions of years of survival experiences from the past. Genetic dominance far overshadows all other factors in our body form as well as our socio-biologic disposition. Variability and individuality is a part of that genetic expression. In this light, as stated by Halberstram, "History punishes those who come too late to it."

Mankind is inherently driven by many behavioral forces. Yet there will not be a change in the need for recognition, the desire for freedom of thought together with the pursuit of enjoyment and finally the demand for security.

Each person will intentionally pursue a small part of earth and a proper place in society. These drives will survive and they will transcend any economic, political or social condition to come.

The simple fact remains: certain biologic principles are so solid and so widespread that they are unalterable. We found, for instance, an arc of growth for prediction of the human face in all races and all types. This tells us that there is a basic starting point. Man will still be man whatever his society.

14

HANGING SUSPENDED

In many aspects of society we are left hanging: which way will the wind blow? By chance will we be twisted and turned? Will it be a placid wind that moves us gently and comfortably, or will it be a strong wind that tears at our moorings and shreds us in violence?

In the previous chapter we alluded to the endowments of mankind that make up our resilience, our ability to spring back to a previous likeness, and factors in which we will most likely remain as we are. These were biologic in nature, both physiologic and psychologic, and based on genetic stability.

There are, however, conditions which can go either way -- forward or backward, upward or downward -- or explode completely in American society. Let's look at them.

Making Predictions
Correct predictions are made when explanations of phenomena run true to form. Forecasts formulated from the framework of a changing philosophy, art, science and technology might be of value. Our basic theme will be to again integrate principles in a synthesis for the forecasting of the future of America.

Chance
If there is one thing that is predictable, it is the prediction of change itself in economics, politics and vogues and style. The one thing that can be certain is that the element of chance will always be working. In fact, we ourselves are the result of chance in the original fertilization of the ovum, because an ovum at the time of impregnation may be surrounded by several candidates for conception.

When contemplating the future a prediction can be made from the analysis of the circumstance, and the odds of the same reactions repeating when similarities exist. But chance always enters into the equation. History, as it is recorded, is filled with important events or great changes by **catastrophe**, or calamity by upheavals in social, economic, political, or religious aspects of a society, or major **discoveries** in science and technology.

History is the sum total of all the people who ever lived and all they ever did. Ordinary, mundane, everyday affairs do not make history. Even major acts of benevolence make back page news. On a day-by-day basis, it is the outstanding, unusual situations or major conflicts in personal relations that attract the human psyche.

Politics and Parties

Probably foremost in the immediate future is the question of politics, about which more will be said later. America has a long history of a two-party system. Splintering could occur in the future, as one almost did with Ross Perot.

Experiments toward socialism still are common. But the breakdown of communistic socialism, based on history, was predictable. Even the rapidity with which disintegration took place could be based on experiments when it was first attempted in the colonies of America when it lasted only two years.

Politics is said to be the procedure whereby man gets along with his neighbor. Its essence is good will and better friendship, reciprocity, and the satisfaction of mutual interest. In addition, it is said to be the art and science concerned with guiding governmental policy.

But there is a certainty regarding man's desire for dominance. Dominion is related to the sense of pride, but also it is a sense of superiority, exemplified by classic ego-centricism and ethno-centricism. When national groups want to dominate, it becomes natio-centricism. Politics forms the basis of all governments. Governments mean power to those governing, granted by those to be governed. Power means control. Power means the attainment by some way of exercising a will over others.

Power Sources

According to Toffler's thesis in "Power Shift", there are three main sources of power. The first is by force, or **violence**, and the more awesome the violence or threat of violence the greater is the power. This has one facet of effect on hegemony, and now that the Soviet Union has disbanded it leaves America with an intact armed force, probably the greatest the earth has ever known. This will no doubt be cut back, but lessons from the past suggest a powerful defensive posture will probably need to be continued in the next century.

The second source of power is **wealth**. Everything has a price, it seems. Therefore, if power cannot be gained by violence, with enough money it can be bought. Therein lies the problem on an individual basis, as well as the collective basis for nations. Having wealth permits a buying of support, even at the intuitive level.

Particularly during the accumulation of his wealth Donald Trump made news. Every move he made in society was monitored by the press. People were interested because he had wealth. What else did he have, except perhaps an ability to make big deals? Wealth is power, but it can go as quickly as it is achieved. On an international basis, seven of the eight largest banks in the world are Japanese. They in effect have cornered to a degree the financial control of other nations. In fact, their wealth has influenced American politics and world politics.

The truth is that now America does not have the wealth it once had. One factor is the World Wars, I and II, the Korean and Vietnamese conflicts, and the debacle in the Middle East. The second is the fact that we have continued, now for 40 years, to maintain an international police force. It has not just been to support the armed services abroad, but all of the local services that are needed at the military bases in foreign countries.

The third factor to deplete our wealth is that we have also been the greatest givers of aid in the history of the world. This has reduced our wealth in proportion to other countries. We still have wealth because we are so big, but when wealth is put on a per capita basis we don't stack up as well as we formerly did among the First World nations. Just travel to Europe or Japan and see how far the U.S. dollar goes as of 1993.

Toffler's third source of power is **knowledge**. Going back to Sarkar's thesis, this would be the power gained by the intellectual. Knowledge is not isolated, it is collective. The power of knowledge permeates every facet of society. Certainly knowledge in a given field, particularly when combined with consummate skill in its use, gives power in that field. With America's technology, our front-running in space exploration, the early development of our computers, and particularly in the aircraft industry, we in America had abundant power in knowledge.

But instead of creating more knowledge we in effect wanted to take our profits. In fact, Americans borrowed against the future to have a party for ourselves today. We became complacent. The complacency ran from the very top to the very bottom of our society and no one person was to blame.

We talked about the need for better schools and education and it was almost unanimously agreed. But our children weren't listening. They wanted to be injected with knowledge rather than earn it. There was an assumption that education could be bought by wealth. Certainly such was not and is not the case. Greater investment did not produce better students. More pleasant surroundings have not produced more Ph.Ds. Education comes first by will, by desire, by determination, by hard work. It should be obvious, but many have missed the point. The principle is:

Good luck occurs when knowledge, opportunity and willingness to work come together.

Therefore, when one is prepared and the opportunity exists, success is achieved, major advancements are made. America is falling behind and will continue to fall still further behind unless a major attitude change takes place, not by the powers-that-be but by the grass-roots of our whole society. It starts with better parenthood. It must start with the family! We hang suspended — let's get our families together. Dads, let's get tougher over the education and work ethic in our children's learning.

* * *

Women and Men
Conflicts within ourselves arise from indecision and uncertainty. Yet greater conflicts occur from dealings with other people, particularly those between woman and man, husband and wife.

If there has been one remarkable change in this century it is the change in the manner in which men view women and how women view themselves. But we are still left hanging suspended.

I would anticipate the changes in these perceptions in America are not yet finished. In order to speculate it would be necessary to develop some principles based on the thrust of the feminist movement itself.

Biologically, men and women will not change, regardless of the culture. The genetic pool runs too deep to anticipate much alteration in the next centuries. Females will always bear the babies.

A look at the history of mankind shows that the men have a greater body size and greater strength than their female counterparts. Men in most past cultures used that strength for absolute domination. In primitive societies, there was an inconsistency and a dilemma. On the one hand, women were often treated as slaves and wives were even traded for working animals. Yet, going back to the most primitive, there was always a respect for motherhood.

It happens even in tribes of baboons that mothers during childbirth are protected and given privacy. Some of the most ancient art work, sculptural and ceramic, often displayed a pregnant mother, or an object with life and maybe the earth goddess. Boy children were much preferred, and a woman was not honored until she gave birth to a son, or even sacrificed one to a war for protection and preservation of the territory. In fact, genocide was practiced on female babies. Even in this day, the selection for abortion may rest with the sex of the child in cultures where early detection is available.

Marriage Historically

As Western civilizations came into being, marriage came to be respected and honored and given grace in the church and sanctioning by the state. Marriage has had one essential purpose, to guarantee the perpetuation of the race. With marriage, however, the male assumed the female as his property, and she in turn submitted herself to his ownership. With the agricultural revolution, large numbers of children played a role in family survival. They were used as laborers on farms, and large numbers were needed since always a certain percentage of children would die of disease. A dozen or more children in one family were not uncommon. Of my four grandparent families, the range was from seven to fourteen children. From marriage to menopause some women spent almost half their time in a pregnancy state. With motherhood representing a respected condition, and the family desiring to be preserved, laws were written for a wife's protection. These rights gradually increased in most Western societies. Some question the fairness of older laws today.

But the greatest change occurred when the Industrial Revolution took the woman away from the family kitchen and the parlor and put her elbow to elbow with men on the assembly lines for industry. Even with that, it took a long time before she was permitted to keep any of the money she earned for herself.

She became privileged to be educated in the universities, where she held her own or excelled. With her ability to concentrate, together with the recently discovered greater connection of the left and right brains through the corpus calossum in her brain, and with her earlier development, she has continued to demand a greater respect in the work place. She slightly outnumbers the male.

Through woman's willingness to organize and communicate, more changes in her favor may occur in the future. She already has assumed responsibilities as her own provider, and will more and more.

A woman's relationship with a male will of necessity change still further. This may not be easy or comfortable. The reasons for it, of course, go back to biology because the sexes are born with independent instincts and men and women differ in predispositions. Perhaps sex is to the adult as play is to the child. In many, particularly males, it can become a preoccupation, and some women can become addicted to romance. Others may be completely passive.

Human Drives and the Sexes

Ardrey proposed in the 1950s that man is driven by at least eight factors. Earlier, however, in the 1920s, Durant had almost paralleled those same conclusions from an entirely different vantage point.

Ardrey called the first drive survival. Durant called it the tendency for fight or flight, both of which were for individual protection and preservation in order to provide genes for future progeny.

A second instinct or inborn natural drive was parental care. Ardrey called this the love and protection of progeny. The third factor was the provision for food or food procurement, or food gathering, which anyone can understand who has had an empty stomach. The fourth drive was sex. These four drives had been identified by Freud and because all could be readily acknowledged as a personal individual impulse, no one argued.

However, one fault with Freud was that he limited drives to those four, and if a frustration or a need arose and could not readily fit into one of the first three, it must necessarily fall in the sexual reference which means relationship between the sexes. Psychologists came to focus on problems of sexual expression, or the relationship of a child to his mother and father as a source of frustration completely out of proportion to an appropriate scale. Ardrey took issue with three resulting specialties based on that kind of Freudian thinking. He described the behavioral psychologist, the cultural anthropologist, and the environmental sociologist as the three blind drunks thinking they were holding up the lamppost when in fact they were all holding up each other.

Probably Ardrey's main contribution was the unveiling of territory as being inborn and instinctual. Territory could take on numerous forms; one, of course, is property. But it could be enlarged to the concept of power itself. When a person has a property it gives a certain amount of feeling of power, of ownership. In fact, if history and the old Western movies are considered, it is always the villain trying to take over the rancher's property. Power is achieved, then, with wealth and accumulation of private property. This instinct goes all the way down to a possession of a child, of a toy, and the conflict when another child wants to play with it without permission.

But man is also driven by other instincts which Durant called gregariousness, or the desire to be around other people. Ardrey called it a society orientation. It is therefore clear that there is an underlying need of man to be a joiner. People want to become a part of a group or a society which may strengthen their odds for survival. Within that society there is still another instinct, which Durant called love of approval, but which Ardrey called status. Some people are not content to be in a second position and continue to seek a dominant position of control. Other people are quite willing to accede to the control of a state or a dictator or a higher power, simply out of a feeling of impotence and lack of knowledge or lack of will for their own preservation when the protection of themselves and a community can be handed to someone else.

One final drive listed by Ardrey was that there is an instinctual will to obey the rules of a society. It might even include the idea of altruism which he referred to as another inborn characteristic. This may be due to an underlying need for the urge to preserve the group as a basic instinct. In other words, an acquiescence to the order of a society may give rise to another principle:

The preservation of a society may be a basic ingredient of our instinctive attitude towards politics itself.

I find myself a disciple of Ardrey, who condensed all of these interests and drives of mankind into three concepts: the need for identity, the search for stimulation and the desire for security, in that order and in that hierarchy. Everybody wants to be somebody, they want to have pleasure in life and they desire freedom from the fear of losing their rights and opportunities. All the rest are a part of this whole complex. These forces can be better understood if society as a whole undertakes this kind of concern.

Vive la difference

Now the big question arises, how do men and women differ in these instincts and where do their priorities lie within these concepts?

First of all, there is the more direct role of the female in the generation of life and the perpetuation of the race. With the birth of the child the man must stand aside and be an observer. It is her work and her flesh and blood. Both her modesty and coyness, which aided her in being selected by the male sexually, have now declined. The mother who may have been shy previously now openly may nurse her babe in public.

Women are endowed to be more clever in love than men. The woman's desire is somewhat less intense and may obscure her judgment less. More than a third of females can be indifferent to love, and in fact seek not physical delight at all. Men must remember in dealing with a woman that her first need is indiscriminate admiration. The human female delights in lavish attention to her needs and wants. To be needed is fundamental to her survival. Many women's greatest pleasure is the sheer sense of being desired. There is more of a spiritual element in love for her than for a man. The stories regarding a Romeo's success in seduction are amazing. They tend to follow six rules: 1. Be bold, 2. Create a romantic atmosphere, 3. Go first class, 4. Listen, 5. Go slow, 6. Display an interest.

In some women love is more maternal than sexual. The feeling of affection that binds her to a man arises less from sexual impulse than from instincts for the need to adapt to her partner.

Man's love is different. Some psychologists and philosophers suggest that his love finds memory in the desire of a mother's breast. On the other hand, some women live only when loved, and the woman's requirement for attention becomes a vital medium. Man, however, suffers egotism to an infinite degree! It is the smart woman who never tries to outshine her male mate.

Women start earlier and surpass men in the art of love. Men surpass women in friendship. Hence, women can be catty and men more competitive.

Women in general have more difficulty in entertaining themselves and seem to experience the greatest stimulation when they are talking about men! Their feeling is once they have felt love, ordinary existence is rather insipid. Love may be a whole existence to a woman; to a man, however, it can remain a thing apart from the rest of his life.

Jealousy in a man can be very intense, but may be short-lived. To him a broken love affair is more like the loss of a possession. In fact, once this is overcome he has a feeling of victory and a sense of competition with a loss only of copyright. He may seek a personal umbrage but his jealousy is less prolonged. The male, prior to contemporary times, was anxious to procure a mate who had never been possessed before. But now so few women are candidates, it could be thought of as hopeless. Yet still this underlying and sometimes unconscious desire may be what stirs his attraction to younger women.

The female, on the other hand, is less anxious to secure a mate with no experience. Woman's jealousy may be of another lover, but perhaps the combination of all the other factors is to her a more severe problem. She may be jealous of his male friends, his pipe, his love of a book or the newspaper, his work, the Monday night football game, any other preoccupying hobby. Men should understand that she needs gentleness. Maybe this is the origin of the word "gentleman" in the first place.

America's Opportunity

Perhaps man-woman relationships can be one aspect of society where Americans can quietly lead the world. Formerly, and in some circumstances today, families were kept together primarily for economic needs. The male felt a responsibility for the female and the children. With woman's emergence in modern culture it has become obvious to many psychologists that females have often felt pained, frustrated, and resentful from the experience of dependency on the male. Contemporary psychological studies clearly show that children develop better confidence and independence when they receive proper nurturing from **both parents** early in life. Young couples with that information can be more deliberate in their decisions on rearing children in the future.

Dads of the future will need to accept the responsibility as a provider and manager of the household. ("Husband" originally was defined as "manager".) Too many men of any race or color abdicate their moral responsibility and abandon their wives and the children they produce. The statistic that is so bothersome is the number of fathers leaving young mothers. The freedom to breed and spread genes is inherently connected to caring for the brood. Some men, I have heard it said, do not feel they are matured until they have made a woman pregnant -- how sick indeed!

Women, on the other hand, in our speeded-up society need now to be stronger and better prepared than ever before. They must fulfill the important role of housewife and mother and as a partner in the joint venture of the home and the raising of the family while maintaining a loving relationship. Like it or not, the avoidance of pregnancy is the woman's responsibility. Many men are willing to spread their seed with abandon. After all, it's her body. Her acceptance of this responsibility still hangs suspended.

Modern Male-Female Relationships

What we have been talking about so far are some older principles. Maybe these principles can be extended still further, as we consider the more recent past and the future. In some past cultures it was obvious that men preferred a double standard. He was protective, wanted to acquire property, but also to remain adventurous. Since he didn't marry for love he could behave as he could afford. He left the nest, to procure food, and became an agent for nutrition while the woman remained the instrument of reproduction. She was attracted to his wealth because it offered assurances for food and the feeding of her brood. Some say that men are less fond of women than of eating and drinking. A look at the broad beams in blue jeans walking the streets in Disneyland suggests to me that women have as much trouble in pushing themselves away from the calories as do men.

While in the past women were seekers of shelter rather than war, and were less pugnacious and more patient than men, they have become more aggressive, even desiring to serve in the armed forces in combat.

Still, my clinical experience has suggested that some women may find secret pleasure in illness and discomfort. It is as if it is a respite in some sense from her endless toil and her plight in life. Men, on the other hand, bear illness more restlessly.

Women probably are pugnacious vicariously, and delight in the protection of a masterful man. As women become more self-sufficient and self-protective, it would suggest that they also would become more pugnacious. Thus we hear the expression among men, when they refer to a woman with pugnacious tendencies, "She's a tough broad".

Men's Attractiveness to Women

Women instinctively are attracted to a man who can firmly command with confidence. When man loses his leadership and desire to manage and arrange for a woman, he abdicates his force of character and becomes less attractive to the female. This attraction is being lost and will continue to be lost more in our society as aggressiveness in the female is now obvious even by the teen years. As Durant put it, "Perhaps the stupefying routine of industry and the enervating artificiality of intellectual life have habituated men to slavery and worn their courage away." Woman, however, looks to strength for protection and provision, but still she despises being dependent.

Women need nurturing also. While the man assumes the woman will cook and scrub, she too needs nurturing. She had a mother too. The principle is:

Future man will need to simulate a role of both mother and father as well as lover to his wife.

Women's Characteristics

Women win their way with persistence whereas man yields for the sake of peace. She will repeat and be tenacious because she is rich in subtlety and endowed with patience. When the woman cries the man loses his resistance. The idle woman can be dangerous to a man because she has time to plot.

Socially women excel. They are drawn to things most popular or to events best attended by others. But women also intuitively require protection and they delight in being led despite their gregariousness.

There is no doubt that the typical woman is more perceptive of signs and feelings in others and is more expressive of emotion than the typical man. There is also some resentment of man due to her uncertainty. Her economic dependence on a man weighs most heavily upon her. Economic problems tear people apart, most at the divorce court.

Women in general maintain a passion for social approval which extends to the depth of their behavior and choice. Women are caught by the appearance of their image in the minds of other women and maybe occasionally in a man's. I have often thought that women at mixed parties dress more to please or stimulate other women than their man. This becomes obvious when women remark so candidly about another's dress and only rarely regarding a man's clothes other than the look of expense. Women comment frequently on other women's jewelry. Most men are not stimulated by that kind display in excess, considering it to be vulgar.

Women's expressiveness leads to gossip. Their eagerness to rise in society leads to hunger for a better position. They desire to be superior and dominate the man and perhaps others as mothers to their children. Yet, they are more polite, kind and sympathetic than men and in addition are more considerate, gentle, and have a better disposition to nurse and help the ill. Females tend to be more altruistic and intuitively have better morality. Perhaps these qualities in American culture -- if they are maintained -- will continue the trend for women to outlive men, which is unbiologic because men take longer to develop and should outlive the female.

In addition, all these qualities of mind tend to make the female more religious. Her intuition makes her more keenly sympathetic to bereavements that sadden life. The longing for a reunion with the deceased makes her more susceptible to the concept of immortality and things of the spirit. Because nature is such a sublime mystery she is enraptured by divine guidance. While man kills himself with abuse and neglect, she may throw herself on the mercy of God.

Men's Characteristics

There are some qualities in which men excel. Man is more critical, analytic and scientific.

He tends to be more skeptical and less subject to dropping off the deep end following an emotional high. Being less desirous of emotional reaction, he is more flexible and adaptive. Men take lessons from hard experience.

Men tend to select beauty. It gives them great pleasure. Beauty is a banner for vigor and for health in which a man delights. It works well in society because women in turn love to be possessed. But men soon tire of a chronically weak, sickly and nagging woman, which the woman should remember. A little sympathy by a man goes a long way in his mind.

Men occasionally need the friendship and support of other men, and it becomes a comfort and a pleasing memory to share a joyful experience. They tend not to want to be leaned on consistently, however. I think it's great and fruitful for women also to bond and share with each other, but men often lack adequate intimacy among themselves.

Marriage Difficulties

There is a change in many social patterns which makes marriages difficult and threatens the future of America. Currently many women work outside the home. They marry later and postpone child-bearing until their thirties and some even to their early forties. As explained by psychologists serving as marriage counselors, a woman cannot perform three roles successfully. Some females, I have found, will argue about this, in self defense. But it is claimed that she can be a mother and a wife without a career. She can be a wife and have a career without children. She can have children and a career but is now a very poor wife. If she has children and gives priority to her career, it is the dad who suffers. This brings hardship to the typical marriage and he may look elsewhere.

But even in the late-developing families, children ultimately grow up and go to college, leaving home while the parents are still quite active. This leaves the male and female with a life of another thirty to forty years which often poses a crisis for the marriage with the kids gone. The second period in a marriage partnership may be longer than the child-raising period. The birthing and nurturing of children take a woman's energy, which must be understood by the male who is also dependent on her for sexual needs as well as his own nurturing needs, which continue.

Women's Wants

What males don't understand is what women need most or what women really want! The question is often heard by the counselor: "I've provided her with everything, what does she want?"

The principle is:

Females want the same thing that males want!

The male wants to be nurtured and in his chronic ego state he wants to be praised, to be cared for, listened to, looked after, and catered to in all his needs after the pattern of his own mother's devotion and love. This attention serves to give the male a sense of identity and self-worth. Unfortunately, he intuitively resents a wife when she can't fulfill that profound need in the relationship.

What men (and also many women in their frustration) don't realize is that **women have the same psychologic dependency and ego needs as men**. If she is dependent for her economic needs, she now in her married state has a doubled dependency which can lead to further resentment when unfulfilled. She too needs the nurturing of a mother, often without recognizing it as such. Her sexual attention needs are also present, but her real "wants" go further, into true nurturing and love, respect, and almost spiritual partnership. This she is asked and expected to give abundantly, yet so often fails to receive in return. But she may not even be able to receive love graciously without first understanding herself. What nurturing she gets is often in a form indistinguishable from the closeness and confessions to other women friends or neighbors in similar situations.

I remember the closeness of my own mother to her friends Jose Kenny, Ann Hillis, Maude Miller, Katherine Harris, Roxy Randolph, and others. Each morning Mom could expect a call from someone to check each other's feelings that day. Little did I realize it was a form of womanly love, taking care a little bit of the nurturing for each other which they all needed. When I was a teenager I remember hugging my mother, and often telling her how very important she was and how much I loved her. She lived to be 93 and outlived most of her friends who died much younger. I hope my loving helped.

Out of frustration and out of exhaustion a wife or a woman may neglect herself. Men will also, but in a different form of self-abuse. Both sexes in American culture may become gluttons, grow fat and inactive. They then lose the attraction of a mate which particularly adds to the woman's dilemma. The still aggressive male, by chance of circumstance exposed to a younger and more active and energetic female in the business world, becomes a target when he is successful. "Soap opera" affairs happen again and again. He offers the excuse that he's nagged at home, as the wife steadily increases her stellar demands for attention. Testimonials of prostitutes tell the same story. Finally, under great stress, they separate, which is always a severe tragedy when children are involved. You can divorce each other, but children -- never. Ironically, both parties then repeat the same pattern, because men and women are essentially more alike than commonly imagined throughout the world.

Stress in Human Relationships

In 1961 Thomas Holmes and R.H. Raye developed a stress rating scale based on histories of thousands of patients in the hospital at Washington University, St. Louis. They were able to put stress factors into a hierarchy, with the death of a spouse or a mate receiving the highest count and traffic violations and even vacations being at the lower part of the scale. (See the Stress Rating Scale in the Appendix.)

It is of interest to abstract this chart and note first that **any change**, particularly one that is not elective, produces a psychologic trauma, stress, or tension in the human experience. But scanning down through the whole list, the major aspects, when added together, are those involved with **inter-personal conflicts**. It is true that people need people, but it is also true that people make other people sick and kill people. Sometimes there is a short span between love and hate, as battered women and battered men seek shelter. What a woman can't do with her fists she does with her tongue!

Another principle is indicated:

The simple reality of life is not politics, not economics, but human relationship.

It is the relationships among man, woman, family and neighbor. Problems with family can sink deeper into the heart than economic strife. Studies of people on their deathbeds, who reflected back on their lives, have suggested that in the end their happiness lay not in their possessions, not in their position, not in their power, but in the gift of love and the return of that love by others be they friends or within the family. This whole respect for marriage and family will continue to be lost until it is recognized for its importance and appropriate attitude changes take place. We are hanging suspended.

Marriage Functions

First of all, it is obvious that marriage never has been and, obviously now more than ever, is not merely a license to make love. **Marriage should be looked upon as an opportunity to improve a quality of life.** Not only does it function for a life quality, but for the better care of the offspring that a marriage produces.

There is one profound principle that can be gained from all societies of animals, and it is that:

A society that takes poor care of its offspring will not long survive.

Nature bound the male and the female in service to the child, which became a family vehicle for the strengthening of a race. Why else would we have licensure, marriage ceremonies, moral condemnations and taboos, and courts of law regarding divorce if not for the guarding of the family and the better guarantee for replenishment of human life in a society? **But marriage was never for the guarantee of happiness ever after.** Its function was for the proper rearing of children. Probably this was most important in the agricultural revolution, tempered significantly in the Industrial Revolution, but now undergoing horrendous modification in the cybercultural revolution.

Several factors will alter marriage and the family still more in the future. With the possible lengthening of life, and with the promise of longevity into super-senior ages, parenthood is reduced to an early phase of life. There is no longer a premium on large families because of the cost of educating and rearing of children, even some of our most sacrosanct religious institutions are having to take a new look at birth control and perhaps abortion. The question is, will marriages be considered in the long run a means for race continuation and for a society elevation?

American society is becoming a less well-knit society and more of a collection of individuals. In fact, the frequency of young people living together prior to marriage has become the custom. Even oldsters within the eighth decade of their lives now practice mutual live-in arrangements rather than undergoing the problems involved in legalized marriages and property settlements resulting therefrom.

Polygamy

Several writers and serious investigators have shown that man is partially, at least, polygamous. Otherwise, why is prostitution said to be the oldest profession? In ancient Ephesus, one of the Asia Minor cities visited by St. Paul, the brothel was only a few steps away from the court house and library. More primitive cultures bought and traded wives. Families chose wives or husbands for their children on an economic and cultural basis in order to preserve their future welfare.

Love did not emerge as a force for selection until the romantic days of the Renaissance. Marriages were made in Heaven, and adherence to vows was a puritanical guarantee for the survival of the family. Life spans were short, and marriage was sanctified by the church almost for its own propagation. Sex itself was labeled as shameful and sinful, and children were "accidents in the night". But hormones changed the females' desires; and labor in the birth room, combined with labor in the kitchen, further cooled her ardor for a male. Biologically speaking, nursing is to last from two to four years, and during this time males become impatient.

Some cultures and some religions encouraged polygamous marriages when affordable. In Saudi Arabia men can still have four wives if they can afford it. But in Western culture man was expected to be monogamous -- against his intuitive desires and natural instincts. It became also the role of women to try to keep him interested at home, even while she breast-fed the baby.

Men fantasize about women in a direct relation to their hormonal push. Boys play games as children, and find it hard not to play games with mating when they come of age. As they mature more, it is not only the act of sex they crave, but often they feel the need of a stroking companion. Almost any acceptable woman is desired, or anyone who particularly will continue to feed a man's ego and his conceit. Furthermore, in marriages or live-in conditions, boredom begins and routines lose attraction. Nagging and discontent enter into a relationship, while in urban cultures when new opportunities are presented the head is turned and the heart may follow.

Fantasies

When marriage takes place, men supposedly lose their fantasy for conquest. Meanwhile the female on the other hand acquires her fantasy for a home and to be possessed by a male. It is only then, in modern American culture, that the **challenge to keep romantic love alive begins**. The maintenance of respect becomes the key. Those surviving must match at the soul as well as at the thighs.

A stable marriage and family is one of America's greatest challenges in our increasingly urban culture. Promiscuity in sex has its excitement but carries its risks. In my opinion it is the female who makes the choice, with humans as well as with lower animals. She must be receptive. After all, a man needs someone to do it with; it takes two to tango. A man's sexual drive can be turned off easily by the woman. His pursuing nature will make him look elsewhere if he is not interested in the bridal suite. My hunch is that man will show an even greater polygamous tendency in the future. Our enquiries into the lives of political candidates have proven that, and it's probably not new.

Thus, our culture today is faced with the problem of a tendency toward polygamy in males in particular, and with many females as well. In the old days in primitive societies the cave man took his club and stole a mate. This was replaced by peace and in Biblical times the male gave presents or offered service to the father for a female. Marriage by purchase then replaced the capture and gradually there evolved a strange mixture of capture and purchase. In the old days war was frequent and death came to many males. Polygamy then was the crude way of taking care of the more numerous women left behind.

Women usually abstained from sexual relations until the child was weaned. Thus the male in many cultures had a wide variety of partners to take care of his sexual demands and an abundance of offspring was a blessing for the race survival when men succumbed to accident, disease, and war.

Monogamy Necessity Historically

Monogamy developed when it became an advantage to the propagation and protection of children, for their care and their love, and for the provision of more abundant food. Man consequently concentrated his interest and endowment rather than scattering his wealth. In many cultures man found himself still free to indulge his desires. But despite the double standard, monogamy served as an advantage to women. It gave them a certain biological equality and a modest leverage for positions in society. Since that time marriage has been a struggle between women and property, wealth and love.

A principle emerged:

Promiscuity was replaced by the concept of romantic love.

Surveys of females still show that she would prefer to marry for potential property rather than for the troubadour. But as romantic love came to the front, the male began to soften his brutality and he began to see qualities in the female beyond those which originally lured him to her lair. American civilization came to be built on the superstructure of poetic love. Relationships of soul-to-soul came into fancy. The world may never see such 19th century love again.

Marriage in the American Future

If the thesis that identity, stimulation and security is a requirement of both sexes, then a new principle obtains:

Marriage itself must lie within these drive confines.

We can consider a number of conditions with which we are now faced. Let's look at our young American male of the 21st century. He has received an education, he aspires for individual security which is being depleted as his demand for social security is increased. Perhaps he can look forward to a safer physical life, but as he feels all of the potency from the elaboration of his testosterone he is brave and impetuously conceited. Now his first love comes. It attacks him at the very core of his being. It arrives when his pockets are empty. Only a few dare to marry at this time. Eventually the flame may die, because she may not wait for his pockets to fill.

So love comes again, now more weakly. He is still economically ignorant, so he loses again. Still later he waits, and in our culture today his opportunities for sexual expression are many. He is frustrated, confused, disillusioned, and disappointed with life. I saw it happen in my own son and many of his friends. Love comes yet another time, but now with only a fraction of the freshness and so -- maybe reluctantly, at a time when he is bound into a career -- he finally decides on marriage. Many now joke about "tying the knot", but intuitively a man considers marriage to be a celebration of the death of love. He instinctually feels an obligation to a family, but never does he feel prepared.

Contrast this scenario with the urban woman, who has also been cycled. Her intense love comes even earlier, and its breakup may be even more disturbing. She gradually has tried everything except the wedding ring, through sexual favors and display. Her needs are for attention, entertainment, attire and champagne. If she delays too long, due to her own career accomplishments, she may find herself in increasing disfavor with a male who risks a relationship with one as learned as himself and one more accomplished in the art of love than he. No wonder the male is frightened.

Throughout my now almost 50 years of practice, I have hired probably 50 females. How often I have privately been asked by females even from 20-25 years of age or older how they could attract a young, decent man. Now consider the situation in these urban cultures. Sometimes -- most of the time -- only after a trial period, they at last marry, often not in a church and without any moral code, and establish a business contract which from the beginning they both feel can end. They rent an apartment amongst the smog, stone, steel and the cacophony in an attempt to improve the quality of life for both. If children are to be a part of it, they will have to wait. To the man it is little change from his bachelorhood except for a more voluntary restriction. The woman soon becomes disenamored because there is nothing new, nothing to grow on. Their marriage is a sexual association and they are lucky if it is a bonafide friendship. Poetic love, spiritual love, and the open giving of love in altruism often retracts into individualism. The desire for conquest in the male reappears because she has nothing new to give. She yearns for his departed tenderness and begins to neglect her allure in her actions, speech, and appeal. This is followed by sexual incompatibility which becomes a barrier.

Quarrels over money begin and love further slips away. Resentment ensues, jealousies may occur, and they become boring to each other. There is no sanctuary where the soul can find peace and solitude in their environment. Days are filled with conflicts, and nights are only temporary respites. Each becomes distant-minded. She still craves the flattering of his desire. Divorce comes, and the cruelties are exaggerated for justification of the strife.

In 1990 there were 2,448,000 marriages and 1,175,000 divorces in the U.S., making nearly one divorce for each two marriages (48%). This was up from 2,158,800 marriages and 708,000 divorces in 1970 (33%), an increase from one-third to essentially one-half. If this same trend continues, by 2010 we will see two-thirds as many divorces as marriages. Some wonder why marry anyway, except to have children. The problem lies in the fact that without a moral "society" code, and without a binding sense of responsibility to each other, and without a knowledge of each other's needs, many unhappy marriages exist even with children. Probably only a fraction of those unhappy and discontent end in divorce.

Arrangement, Alliance or Circumstance

It was my conclusion years ago that many human relationships were due to chance -- a chance meeting, a chance to get to know and respect another, or timing when both parties have a need. In a discussion on male and female relationship with a mixed group, one male in his forties contrasted his attitude about sex to that of his father's age group. In the son's opinion, sex was a very big deal to his father. Sex was a preoccupation, allegedly because of his father's early experience with women who played hard to get. To the son, sex was just "okay", and it was no big deal. There really was no conquest required. Women were easy. Women were looking for a spark and for attention. Thus the son, rather than the female, had experienced the position of playing hard to get!

As he spoke, I wondered if the struggle for career success had taken away from his male character. I wondered also if another principle was not formulated:

Women really are degrading themselves by arrangements and alliances to move in and out of a relationship on the basis of compulsion and convenience.

A true loving relationship is a thing of beauty, and "arrangements" seem to be a throw-back to primitive satisfaction rather than personal fulfillment. Women, or females in general in the animal kingdom, seem to behave in any way necessary to satisfy the male of the species once her choice is made. The female will also choose excitement over boredom when given the choice. This will help with her fulfillment, but also cheapens and undermines the woman's position in the contemporary society.

15

PROBABILISM AND PRESUMPTIONS

Certainty is almost impossible in science, and we must therefore look at probabilities that are great enough to establish presumption but not absolute proof.

Biology in the American Future

Although Biology should be listed with the sciences and technology, it crosses over so many of the social aspects of society that it is considered here together with human relations. Biology is the science of life and the living.

Biology dates to Hippocrates at 400 B.C. but did not develop until the free inquiry of the Renaissance in the 16th century. Today the study of human living beings involves sociobiology (human behavior and its consequences), ethology (instinctive behavior), together with the emphasis on ecology (or living organisms affected by the environment). The study of biology therefore is fundamental to any study of society as even evolution (the change of life forms) may be affected by the environment.

Ecology

Our consideration is America, but biologically we are faced with a principle:

> **The industrial and technologic explosion has caused a world involvement and America is only one of its members.**

The nuclear plant accident at Chernobyl, for example, caused international fallout. Acid rain from industrial plants in America affects the forests in Canada. Acid rain from the Ruhr Valley in Germany affects neighboring countries such as Norway. The ozone layer is being depleted by vaporizers and air conditioners all over the world, which affects the ultra violet radiation in Australia. Melanoma is on a frightful rise. The deforestation of Brazil may also be affecting the world's oxygen balance. We are filling our whole electrical and magnetic air wave length physical spectrum with television, telephone and radio, which even penetrates subsurfaces of our earth (as explained by Robert Becker in "Crossed Currents").

Much is not yet known of these contaminations. Above all, in urban cultures particularly, we experience water and noise pollution. As a principle:

We are caught in a dilemma regarding progress for the future and our future destruction.

Thus, biology is a vastly important consideration for the future.

But for some reason, to laymen and some professionals alike the expression of the word "biology" is a social turnoff. It may bring to people's minds things too scientific or too theoretical and not practical. Biology searches for reasons or the "why" for behavior and phenomenon. The typical mind says, "Don't bother me with facts, just give me the answer and tell me what to do." Some people want the "fix" without the reason.

Throughout the natural world, animals and plants have adjusted to an ecologic balance. The number of grazing animals was limited to the savannah and the predators (carnivores) were limited to the meat available from the grazing animals (herbivores). In the ocean the plankton formed the beginning of an ecologic chain. Food from the sea has been dominant in man, since many of the earth's large cities are within one hundred miles of a major body of water. The large Rhine River of Europe extends all the way from Switzerland to the North Sea. The Mississippi drains from Canada to the Gulf of Mexico.

Many factors in the last century have affected that ecologic balance, often dramatically. Imbalances have been produced by industrialization and population growth. Pollution has become the buzz word. Near Tucson, Arizona, an experiment is under way for production of a second biosphere, earth itself in ecologic balance being the first biosphere. Four men and four women are airlocked into a sealed building to test the ability to survive under natural circumstances in "Biosphere II". Much is being learned if the seal can be depended upon to be perfect. There is concern for the health and welfare of our planet, as evidenced by the Rio de Janeiro summit in 1992.

Our oceans are so polluted that fish near our shores are not edible due to the presence of mercury. Birds are becoming extinct because of pesticides. Smoke and smog make life unpleasant and endanger our lungs and immune systems. Tobacco is being banned in public and work places. Our forests are dying from the contaminants and chemicals in the air. Deforestation threatens to bring not only oxygen imbalance but also soil erosion. The greenhouse effect of burning fossil fuels may alter earth's temperature catastrophically, although this is still being debated. Noise in urban communities invites ever-increasing stress. Nuclear waste and nuclear war is a constant concern and even a phobia to some. Water recycling lies in our future and, even worse, there will be a shortage of it. Electrical pollution may prove to be even more serious than other contaminants. This threat will increase in the new electrical age of the future.

The principle is:

The quality of life on earth will be reduced unless America, and all other nations as well, take these ecologic problems seriously.

The conditions of pollution exposed in the Soviet Union and Eastern Europe are appalling. Not only America, but the whole world, needs to clean up its act for the future of our children. Thus, biology is a vastly important consideration for the future.

The Biologic Basis of a Medical Practice

The basis of the field of medicine is exactly that of biology. It is anatomy (structure and form) and physiology (the study of the body's functions).

A medicine is a substance used for the treatment of disease. A professional practice involves diagnosis, prognosis, planning and monitoring and the application of modern expensive tools. It further may involve anything from radical or heroic surgery to simple counseling on a social problem or the treatment of an infections disease or a vaccination. But other options to conventional medical practice are emerging as greater complication and expense escalates. These are often referred to as **alternative** choices in the care of the body and may also be termed either curative or more preventive in nature.

For instance, advice in dietary nutrition in America increases each year almost on an exponential scale. The reason is another principle:

Most people feel better when proper nutrition is followed.

Chiropractic and osteopathic approaches have worked when drugs have been ineffective for certain disorders. Acupuncture, homeopathy and physical medicine (massage and exercise) also are growing complimentary services to the medical field. On the basis of these now entrenched additions to Western medicine a principle is proposed:

The future of medicine will gradually become more preventive-oriented than merely treatment-oriented.

New drugs, however, will continue to emerge in the future as they have in the past. Most of the drugs on pharmacy or chemists' shelves were not there in that form ten years ago.

Health Care Movements

Long before AIDS became known, immune deficiencies were well studied. Lupus erythematosus was associated with the body's inability to differentiate its own tissues. Transplantation of organs was studied for immune reactions. Mysteries still surround the question of why a cold virus may infect only a few people out of a group. Older people losing their immune systems may decline to death very fast. A principle is involved:

The future of medicine and maintenance of a reserve for energy and health lies in the protection of the immune system.

Several other major aspects of society in the future in America are related to biology. These include a movement toward nationalized health care or continued private care, the whole field of psychology, the complication of drug abuse (alcohol, opiates, cocaine, anti-depressants and stimulators), the causes and consideration of homosexuality, the recognition of mildly polygamous man, the increasing role of stress, the tendency for altruism in man, the scourge of AIDS, and even the biologic association of crime and violence in American society.

* * *

In Chapter Thirteen the difficulty and improbability of a change in the basic genetic gene pool of man was emphasized. The predictive changes in the future will be those regarding society's methods to deal with these basic instinctual conditions with his continued demands. This prompts another principle:

Stress in our society will continue to involve the struggle to protect or achieve a self-image, the path to escape boredom, the search for excitement and the struggle to acquire a freedom from the fear of disease or poverty.

As Hans Selye showed almost 50 years ago, common reactions to stress were ulceration of the stomach, shrinkage of the thymus and lymph glands and enlargement of the adrenal glands. There are two avenues open to the treatment of pathologic reaction to stress. The first path, taken by some psychologists, is to change the environment or life-style. Some are now adopting methods to relieve anxiety and high blood pressure by relaxation meditation. However, the opposite method is more biologic. The body's systems to resist stress are enhanced by better nutrition, better thought control and better understanding of the underlying factors. In other words, treat the body's weakness rather than treating the symptom, because stress is unavoidable in modern life.

Conflict around these basic drives probably will increase in the future with population density and even greater competition. This is due to the greatest factor of all -- stress due to forced changes and interpersonal conflict and the growing segmentation of our population.

The Impact of Sociobiology

Man's evolutionary behavior has deep roots in genetics and is spread throughout the lower animal kingdoms. The behaviorial psychologist, the environmental sociologist, and the cultural anthropologist all claimed man to be solely the product of the environment -- in error, in my opinion. Mozart's talents were not an environmental product. I would object to the psychologists' stance and the assumption that the human brain owes little or nothing to a complete evolutionary experience. There are innate censors and motivators in the brain that unconsciously affect our ethical premises. **Morality as well as altruism therefore may well have evolved as an instinct.**

If population (group) genetics of man and lower animals is studied as a route to the evolution of behavior, the question I would consider is the **possibility of the consequences of brain damage by drugs, accidents, disease or chance which may alter attitudes regarding moral issues.** The senseless murder by drive-by assailants on the Los Angeles Freeway must certainly be the loss of morality and a usually inherited sense of ethics and respect for human life and conscience. Something is missing in that human brain. These people cannot be treated as normal humans.

Probably the most dramatic studies in sociobiology were those of Edward O. Wilson who made extensive investigations of the behavior of social animals (the bee, wasp, termite and ant colonies). He conceived of a conjunction of biology with psychology, anthropology, sociology, and economics. Our behavior has evolved from natural selection and is constrained by genes and predictable human reactions to given situations therefore exist.

If genetic directives operate, man's basic nature will change very little. However, a principle exists:

When damage to these directives occurs or when they are overridden or dominated by circumstance, man will be altered in his behavior.

This is seen in wars. Even wars have such a long history the scientist wonders if it can be changed.

The psychologist busies himself studying the regions of the brain, searching locations for the so-called cognitive processes (recognition of environmental conditions or awareness).

Such information is used to understand and treat mental problems, phobias, depressions and obsessions which are on the rise in American society. The problems of sex, marriage, drug and alcohol dependence ever increase. We still are suspended.

Homosexuality

I doubt that I'm different from many others in the difficulty I had to overcome in my attitude towards homosexuality. I read stories of Ancient Greek men taking young boys as love partners. In the beginning it turned my stomach. From exposure to the medical sciences in the formulative days of my career, there was no evidence -- at least in my exposure -- that it was a genetic or congenital problem and it was therefore considered an acquired phenomenon. That made matters worse.

Now, fortunately, that has changed. Some significance is attached to sickness of the mother in the early stages of pregnancy, which suggests that neural connections and hormonal triggers were defective in the formation of the usual sexual determinants. It appears that even completely asexual (no preference) personality traits are not as uncommon as would be imagined.

However, if it turns out that no biologic reason exists for homosexuality other than a biologic compression and that it is a totally acquired characteristic, there may be cause to reject the pornography in movies and magazines. Not that pornography and homosexuality are connected, but the vulgar public display of homosexuality at least should be carried on in private. The question is, how far will pornography be permitted in American culture?

There is little doubt that homosexuality will increase, and I accept it as a right for the personal preference of some people. Many of our greatest scholars and artists were and are homosexual.

National Health Care

National health care is a carrot dangling in front of the noses of American politicians. A health care panacea is proposed which needs to be considered carefully for a mass of 260 million people with open borders to the world. Already under present limited programs health care is a gigantic expense, increased by hospitalization and a plethora of tests for the protection of the doctor against being sued. Remember we are suffering a litigation-conscious society, and one putting blame on others and, further, one having too great a confidence on gadgets and a false impression of the sophistication of medical knowledge and expectancy of miracles.

It is predictable that with socialized medicine some will sue the state. When service is free, lines of people with minor complaints block the chances of treatment for emergencies or others urgently needing care.

Many years ago when I first started practicing, a semi-retired surgeon from Texas began a practice at the same time in the Sunset Medical Center on Sunset Boulevard in Pacific Palisades. Because we both had time to ponder, we often found time to talk. One day over a cup of coffee I inquired about the nature of his life as a physician and surgeon. I wanted to know about the patients he had saved and those he had lost. "You know, Rick," he said, "one of my old teachers, who was a great surgeon, said ninety-five per cent of the patients go to the physician when it's not needed, and the job is to find that five percent that need you and really do something for them. In my experience that's been pretty well confirmed. Most of my losses occurred when people waited too long and came to me too late."

This conversation, among others, led me to the idea that the good doctor of the future will be oriented toward prevention. It will mean an even greater cost (in time) of monitoring his patients and advising patients on home care and medical prevention. This is being done in certain areas such as the dangers of smoking and excessive exposure to the sun. But the whole field of medicine needs to be even more conscious and take lessons from dentistry which almost put itself out of business with fluoridation of the water supply and insistence on better home hygiene.

Immunology

As the population is better protected against infectious diseases more will reach the senior status past sixty years. Stress will increase and immune systems will be more depleted. Cancer will increase also as a result of loss of resistance. AIDS will continue to rise unless a cure or preventative vaccine is found. Diabetes will also increase as fat in the diets of our young will take its toll.

In medical and nutritional circles we talk about the Big Five and the Big Eight diseases. The Big Five are: (1) Heart disease, (2) stroke, (3) cancer, (4) diabetes, (5) arthritis. Add hypertension, obesity, and pneumonia and it becomes the Big Eight. About 50% of our population dies of cardiovascular disease, and about 25% or more die of cancer. That means if these two can be avoided the odds of longevity have been greatly advanced.

Orthodontics in the Future

In my own field I can make certain projections with greater confidence. Malocclusion will probably not increase significantly. We make the faces of our population more beautiful and attractive which increases the odds of sexual selection to perpetuate the genes of the original facial deformity. However, increases in jaw size of the offspring we have witnessed probably will offset that factor. In an American population only one-quarter will have superb occlusion (fit of the teeth) naturally. About another quarter will have bites and jaws good enough to contraindicate any correction. A third quarter could use some correction with braces for improvement upon request. This leaves about one in four children needing more or less extensive help in the development of their bite and their face.

With currently about four million new births each year, that means about one million each year as candidates for braces of some sort. Socialized orthodontics to take care of this load, with projected inflation in the coming decade, would cost the government four billion dollars each year. To include another quarter which could be improved, add another four billion. That would be only a part of the cost of socialized dentistry, and what cutoff with sophistication will be granted? What will be the cost of administration and monitoring of those in the health service? -- add another billion or two.

This brings up another point in biology regarding the physical stature increase in the population. Scholars have searched for reasons regarding this increase which has caused some shock waves in many industries such as clothing, furniture (especially beds), automobile space and other aspects of society. Are we still going to increase more?

If my projections are correct, my little six-year-old daughter will be six feet tall. Her mother is five feet seven and I at my tallest, at age 18, was just over five feet eleven. Is my daughter's height due to better pediatric care, with less childhood disease? Is it due to better heated homes? Is it due to richer and more plentiful food? Can it be the antibiotics and hormones used in farming and in the dairy industry? Will it continue? The principle is:

Sizes of children will continue to increase until we reach a full genetic potential in America.

In other words, the environmental influences will be at a maximum unless catastrophic hazards to health are encountered such as massive irradiation or massive starvation.

Probabilities With Science and Technology
Science
The modern scientific movement probably started with the invention of the printing press. Peasants could lay down their hoes and learn to read and become educated. Science emerged where there was darkness before.

The essence of science is the search for truth. The scientific method is simply observation, hypothesis experimentation and verification. That revolution, starting about 1650, made many contributions to the quality of life but also led to nuclear war.

For our purposes, to gain perspective for the future, this subject has been divided into technology and the basic sciences, earth sciences, and life science.

Basic Science
Pure science and pure research is conducted for its own truths with no reference or research to application elsewhere. Basic science is fundamental but oriented to relate to something else. Applied science is the taking of the pure and basic sciences to a practical application. In the future these processes will probably escalate.

Most modern science, world-wide, if not originally reported in English is summarized or abstracted in English. As the developing countries of the world emerge, the few scientific minds in each country will become many. Research will broaden in the "Pacific Rim" and all continents. Europe, North America and Japan will not be alone in research. This gives rise to a principle:

The problem in the future will be not the discovery itself but the assimilation and application of the facts and new truths discovered.

Earth Sciences
Earth science particularly will probably flourish in America. With the Soviet Union's demise their scientists, like the Germans after the Hot War, will cooperate with those in America and other countries in space research and astronomy.

Our sun is spinning almost 93 million miles away. It is composed of 70% burning hydrogen, turning it into helium in its center. It is calculated to be almost 5,000 million years old, and will die in another 5,000 million years, so our earth is doomed eventually. Astronomy will continue to attract attention. Most laymen are still intrigued by the prospect of unidentified flying objects. There are an estimated 20 billion, billion stars, each of which is a sun with potential planets around itself.

Physics
Physics is concerned with the laws which govern the structure of the universe, matter and energy. It has many branches which include electricity, magnetism and thermodynamics, which play basic roles in modern electronics in the computer industry. The thrust of research will continue in all branches of physics. New engineers will have opportunities with quantum mechanics, quarks and leptons, still trying to find the secret of light itself. High temperature superconductors were not discovered until 1986 and have ignited much research and development since.

A major problem in America and elsewhere will be radioactive contamination. Robert

Becker, originally searching for favorable or healing effects of electricity phenomena, warns about a dangerous clogging of our wave spectrum and potential cancer hazards as our human body tissues are surrounded and bombarded by physical factors from electric wires, motors, radios, television and computers. Our modern quality of life is connected to electricity, starting with the door opener to our garage.

Chemistry

Chemistry is the other side of matter. It deals with the formation of matter from atoms. Inorganic chemistry, composed mostly of acids, alkalis, salts and oxides, deals with all elements except carbon. Carbon becomes the basis of organic chemistry and is concerned with living tissues of all kinds. The wedding of physics with chemistry -- physical chemistry -- deals with the changes materials may undergo when acted upon by physical conditions.

Organic chemical research had its thrust from the products from oil which are the remains of infinite microscopic marine living organisms from millions of years ago. The carbon atom will continue to be investigated and alternate fuels will continue to be sought, especially alcohol. Our fuels are already braced with ether. Efforts in these directions will continue.

But an even greater thrust will be in the organic chemical composition of the human body. This will escalate in the **search for better nutrition and the factors for enhancement of immunity as a secret of health** and a long productive life. The effects of drugs for medicine will come under greater and greater scrutiny.

More research is needed in the mechanism of drug dependence and the biologic effects of steroids. Who knows what new menaces to health will be thought up or discovered in the future?

Agriculture

There is no other part of human existence more important yet more taken for granted in America than agriculture. More and more production of fruits, grains, nuts, vegetables, and animals are required for an expanding population of 260 million according to the 1990 census. When I was born in 1920 the population was about 120 million. The number now to be fed has more than doubled, while at the same time much of the very best farm lands have been turned into home sites. Our complete farm south of Kokomo was sold to a home developer almost 50 years ago. Farmers are asked to produce more with less space. The old rail fences of my youth are long gone. As fences are wiped out, rotation of crops has almost ceased.

Soils are treated with fertilizer. Animals are fed hormones. Chickens are kept under artificial light for better egg and flesh production. Roadways also take space, and in the next century we may need to stack transportation routes on top of each other despite the tremendous cost involved. One great problem is transporting food to where it is needed. Transportation improvement is consistent with the advancement of technology.

A projection of a principle seems appropriate:

Food producing earth in the future will need to be protected from the clamor for homes by our citizens and the developer with his bulldozers.

We will need to go vertically with our construction, not out horizontally.

One saving grace for the obtaining of farming land has been the developments in efficient irrigation. Lands formerly untillable are brought into production, particularly in the Western states. All this takes us into ecology.

Technologic Projections

When I was a youth we boys were all gadgeteers. The Indianapolis 500-mile Memorial Day race was only 50 miles away. We all were crazy about automobiles, and by age 15 we were good drivers, possibly because most of the farm kids started driving trucks at age 12 and tractors even earlier. If we were big enough to do a man's job on the tractor, we sure could drive a truck on the farm. We learned about motors and technology as well as lessons from the animals in life sciences. Many Midwest farm boys were innovators later in life.

From Alexander Bell, Thomas Edison and Henry Ford, invention and innovation became typical of America. Everyone sought to do it better and cheaper, which helped elevate our living standards by making products and services within the economic range of the masses.

But in the future technology will move on a broad world front. America has been generous in sharing many methods for the betterment of mankind. As we face the future, the little experiment in a garage here, and a little trial of an idea there, still typifies American industry and new developments.

Technology is so broad it would be difficult to cover it all. The major fields of development are listed only for projection in the future as follows:

- Energy   - Communication   - Construction
- Transportation   - Computerization   - Medical

Energy

On our farm in the early 1920s we had no central heating, no inside plumbing, and no electricity. It was a blessing when we could afford coal, because it burned hotter and the room was warmer. It was even better when people could burn oil from a tank which could store a winter's supply. It was still better when gas could be used, because it burned even more cleanly.

Strong running streams were unavailable for water power, so water was pumped from wind mills. Our sorgum press was pulled by a mule attached to a large pole circling the press. Piston-driven gasoline engines have replaced the old steam engines that I remember watching with such fascination. Our lamps and lanterns were lit by kerosene. Our first crystal set radios were powered by large batteries not unlike those in automobiles today.

Electricity transformed rural America, and the world. Sources continue to be developed for electrical production of heat. These include solar panels and windmills to run generators. Geothermal underground heat may be piped to a home. Tidal waves and water pressure from dams are used as natural forces. Nuclear fission used to produce steam for turning turbines is utilized for electrical generators or the propelling of a submarine. The search is on for more and cleaner sources of energy.

The world was alerted in the 1970s to the fear of using up oil reserves, but more is being located continuously and an oil glut still persists. Although many petro-chemicals from oil are fractionated off, gasoline is the most important ingredient of oil. But with our carburetors in automobiles, buses, trucks, and tractors, unburned hydrocarbons pollute the air we breathe.

I predict pollution coming from automobiles will be controlled, and soon. Already the technology exists for a different form of fuel processing for the engine. Gas emission will be almost eliminated, even better than that called for by Federal standards. In addition, these processors will provide for cold start of an engine on alcohol. Alcohol burning has been a problem because it will not burn at a low temperature, and this has been solved. With these developments, plants can be raised agriculturally to be converted to alcohol. We will grow our fuel on the ground and not pump it out of the ground. America will no longer rely on the Middle East. A whole new American industry will form as new engine designs will follow the new fuel processor. Electric engines will be successful on a limited basis. The use of magnetic energy is in its infant stages.

Transportation

A garage with a car in it is still the dream of most Americans outside the metropolitan centers. But transportation is a vital essential for the prosperity of a community. Commercial exchange is the backbone of economic welfare.

Mankind has moved from traveling by foot to animal, to canal, to river barge, to sea, to carriage, to rail, to motor car, to airplane, to jet, and now to rockets in space. Jet travel will become faster, more comfortable and more efficient. The time between continents is already reduced to but a few hours, which brings America ever closer to Europe and the Pacific masses.

Without roads, rail travel was the method of choice. New speeds of 250 miles per hour by rail and new modes of rolling may bring trains back for efficient travel between nearby cities. Cross-country travel will continue to be by jet, although as costs escalate other means will be considered.

As I write this I am in Europe. We arrived in Milan, Italy, and rented a car to travel about three hours to Pordenone, just north of Venice, where I put on a six-day course. I have been accustomed to seeing trucks on the highways on our West Coast. Route 10 between Los Angeles and Phoenix is quite busy with huge trucks. But never have I seen trucks almost bumper to tailgate moving at 70 miles an hour in a solid stream going both directions as I saw in northern Italy.

After flying to Brest, France, and back to the University of Strasbourg, I was driven to Frankfurt. Almost the same density of trucks was seen. The traffic in the opposite direction was worse. One telescoping accident was seen involving several trucks and cars on the highway, and we judged about 6 miles (10 kilometers) of back-up traffic to be completely at a standstill with some people sitting outside their cars on the fenders having a smoke.

At least visually the diesel trucks put out the most smoke and probably the most pollution. Perhaps with the new fuel processor and with better efficiency diesel will be replaced in the future by larger, stronger, and cleaner piston engines.

Another possibility may be the revival of the air-ship. The explosion of the Hindenberg at Lakehurst, New Jersey, in 1937, put an end to that development. New synthetics and light-weight, stronger metals, together with non-explosive helium may bring back the use of the air-ship commercially. They cause minimum noise, very little pollution, are economic on fuel, can carry enormous loads like an ocean ship, and they can travel over sea or land. They would be sitting targets, however, in time of war or sabotage.

Oil transports will continue to dot the oceans and large goods will likewise continue to be transported by sea. Still, the faster the better, and the most economical transport will be the one to survive.

Communication

In the modern era the development of radio and television for world simultaneous communication has probably made the greatest impact on society. The problem of television waves travelling in a straight line was managed by placing a satellite travelling at exactly the speed of earth's rotation at a fixed point at the equator so that signals could be reflected from it back to earth. This permitted world instant communication and viewing. The viewing of a live war in Baghdad made an unforgettable impact. It was not a fireworks display, it was for real.

Fiberoptics is capable of carrying 80,000 simultaneous messages. Personal telephones small enough to carry in the pocket which now prove to be a business advantage will become a necessity. Everything is the "now" and speed in our new age ahead.

Developments have been so rapid we take them in stride. It wasn't until 1975 that Sony developed the first video cassette. Tape recorders date only to 1956. High definition TV only became available in 1989. Telephone TV is just around the corner.

Computerization and Industrial Use

In his narrative on "Power Shifts", mentioned earlier, Alvin Toffler pointed to knowledge as the new power source. When information cannot be stored in the brain it can be stored in the computer. When knowledge cannot be retrieved from the brain, it can be retrieved from the computer. Even some intelligence with cybernetic feedback can be built into the computer. Without the computer, international banking would be impossible in today's speeded-up society.

A doctor, dentist, or orthodontist uses the computer for diagnosis and treatment planning aid. Growth forecasts of the skulls of children are programmed on the computer with 250 feedback loops for the best accuracy. The face is adjusted by imaging for planning facial corrections by orthopedics or surgery. All these developments have reached perfection. The principle is:

The most successful business or profession in the future will be the one who can utilize the most information, perform with the greatest knowledge and efficiency, and communicate in the most complete manner.

The value of the computer is its thoroughness, its storage capacity, and finally its lightning speed. Yes, we are headed for the symbolic generation, which brings up mathematics.

The broad subject of mathematics includes geometry, algebra, calculus and trigonometry, as well as applied mathematics for many branches of physics. It has been vastly aided by the computer as three dimensional models are commonplace. Paradigm is the buzz word and the creation and manipulation of models is becoming as common to engineers as the pocket calculator is to the housewife.

One of the beauties of mathematics is its use for the expansion of thought processes. One of the fears of computer use is that it may restrict mind development and the personality required for a broad view of life. This fear has been expressed by some educators in Japan.

Construction

For a practical scenario, there are four basic needs which will continue in the future. The first is the automobile, or overland vehicle, the second is housing, the third is routes for transportation, the fourth is the business establishment. All construction starts with mathematics and engineering.

The automobile will probably remain a four-wheeled carriage. Technology will be pooled and due to competition manufacturers will continue to improve their product. The new fuel processor mentioned before, and use of alcohol, will remarkably reduce pollution.

Truck, bus, and train motors will take longer to convert from diesels. New metals, new synthetics and robot construction by computer will keep competition ever keener. New safety devices will be mandatory.

Housing developments will be limited, due to shortage of land near the large cities. Multiple storied buildings in metropolitan areas will go higher and higher, and garages will go deeper and deeper.

In the future with ultimately less wood or stone and raw materials available, the geodesic dome composed of triangles will be employed more. Maybe not too much can be improved on a dome, but the idea can be compounded for architectural and esthetic acceptance.

To own a private home has been and will be the American dream. The housing industry uses much labor and materials, and continued construction fuels the American economy. New prefabricated modules will increase in popularity because of their cost-efficient construction.

For commercial small buildings, the sequence is much the same. However, preconstructed steel girders, prestressed and preassembled concrete and premanufactured windows are assembled on the job.

Now the challenge is to move the workers to their work place, to move products, and materials and customers. This takes larger bridges, larger roads or freeways and more tunnels or cuts through mountains.

The remarkable tunnel under the English Channel has been envisioned since Napoleon's time. Technology of pressure and preconstructed panels made this achievable. As more and more metro undergrounds are desired, tunneling will improve.

Airplanes also wear out and become obsolete. Continued vibration loosens attachments. Continued bending makes some materials more brittle and subject to break. Designs change. Aerodynamic improvements continue and commercial aircraft continue to be quieter and more efficient. The principle is:

People will want to get places faster and will seek out the best method of transport.

The question is, will rocket transport (vehicles carrying their own fuel and oxygen for burning) ever find commercial use? Supersonic travel (the Concord) permits the traveler to have breakfast in London and another breakfast with a customer in New York City. Perhaps face-to-face telephone conversations will cut down on the need for extended business travel to some degree.

Medical Technology and the Future

One of the chief complaints about current medicine is the cost and extent of tests. One justification for this is the need for more complete information, but another is for the protection of the doctor. If, for instance, an X-ray isn't taken or read properly and complications develop, the doctor is liable and sued. His cost for insurance goes up and his fees rise accordingly. The same is true for hospitals.

But technology continues to improve and to become more sophisticated and expensive. The discovery of a vaccine for AIDS would be full technology. Half technology is the use of antibiotics to cure disease, early cancer detection and surgery, and a broad array of treatment modalities for various diseases and complaints. There may be blood pressure control and anti-coagulants plus an array of drugs for mental problems.

No technology occurs when surgery, irradiation and chemotherapy are employed for advanced cancer. It occurs when by-pass procedures are used for the heart or transplants are necessary. In dentistry, metal implants for missing teeth are of great benefit but prevention might have saved the tooth in the beginning.

Each new technology and modality is often heralded as a large medical breakthrough and receives attention in the media. In fact, however, it may be little more than another addition to the no-technology level. No-technology procedures for treatment are always more expensive.

Technological improvements will, however, continue. These will include better application of M.R.I. (magnetic resonance imaging), X-ray tomography and the application of fiberoptics in diagnosis and surgical conditions. Laser surgery has a strong base. Laser is particularly applicable to dentistry, soft tissue surgery, the etching of teeth, evaporation of dental decay, sterilization of pocket infection, and sterilization of root canals.

War Machines

Already war is so sophisticated the fighter in an aircraft may be shot down without ever seeing the enemy aircraft or a structure blown up by an object-seeking missile. It becomes more computerized and more sophisticated and expensive year by year. Let us hope that, now that the Cold War has ended and the power of devastation has been demonstrated, the money spent on research for such weapons can be put to human good.

16

THE NEW RENAISSANCE -- THE POSSIBLE CHANGES

Something possible applies to that which lies within the known limits of realization or attainment regardless of chances for or against its actuality.

The Old Renaissance

The original Renaissance in Europe meant a new start or a new beginning after the so-called Dark Ages. But the Byzantine culture of those centuries, between the time of the Roman world and the reawakening, may not have been so dark after all. There had been great movement in art, science and technology. The new movement was probably thrust forward by the invention of the printing press in 1456 which resulted in the first printed book, the Holy Bible. Education previously had been limited to the elite and the clergy. Commoners were laborers, and were restrained, suppressed, and illiterate. The church held dominion over the state. With printing available, the lay person could learn to read and write, and could also start thinking in a different light! The Protestant movement became entrenched as some people desired to worship God directly and "protested" against being interceded for by the priest or bishop.

Printing in essence led to education which in turn promoted intellectual freedom. This freedom of thought and experimentation gave rise to science. Discoveries then laid the foundation for the "Industrial Revolution".

The New Renaissance and the Reasons For It

Through the amplification of an applied scientific process, and with the willingness to produce, the glory of America can continue with the new millennium. We can take a lesson from the benefits that the printed word, reading, education and the scientific method has produced for the previous eras of prosperity.

America can ostensibly undergo a new Renaissance of her own. This is made possible by several factors and conditions, as follows:

First, there is a spiritual "new age" philosophy among many **young people** that is stronger than most recognize.

Second, our **children** seem basically better oriented in many ways even though scholastic tests show a slippage.

Third, the application of the **computer** with the availability of information has opened up previously unavailable business and scientific possibilities. This is verified in my own personal research because manual work to acquire the same information derived from the computer technology I employed would have taken several lifetimes.

Fourth, the termination of the Cold War has permitted **efforts** to be **concentrated** in new directions. Some of our soldiers can now don business suits and compete with Japanese and German businessmen, while others can put on lab coats for research and engineering.

Fifth, the availability of a large trained and **energetic work force** from the defense industries is a hidden source of American economic power.

Sixth, a **positive, imaginative and innovative younger generation** is waiting in the wings to tackle new world-wide business economics for this New Renaissance.

Seventh, the horror of a nuclear war makes any country reluctant to drop the first bomb and gives us a better sense of freedom -- except from the ongoing crisis in volatile countries in the Middle East.

Eighth, there is great need for housing, transportation, food and a better quality of life in Africa, Asia, South America, and even North America when all the constraints are lifted -- these offer opportunities.

The Collective Philosophy

America is still the land of freedom with abundant opportunity and resources. She will excel if she doesn't (1) overtax the middle class, thereby restricting consumerism, or (2) spend herself out of a position of international economic strength. The American idea is alive because America still is a melting pot of peoples and cultures; only the racial and ethnic types have changed over the years. America continues to attract the ambitious and hard-working youth of the world. America therefore will continue to be a leader. We remain a model and a paradigm of the largest kind. But two principles exist:

> **We can and must change ourselves in certain areas, primarily those involved with morality and common sense, if our dream of a new Renaissance is to become a reality.**

> **We must instill the concept of honesty and morality in our children in the schools, temples, churches, mosques and ashrams.**

* * *

Middle Class Life

The typical middle-class life is still the goal of the majority of Americans. A typical man is married in his twenties and in his thirties usually wants a home to own privately. Both a man and a woman want a good, trustworthy, intelligent partner in life for father or mother for their children. They would prefer to live in a suburb of a large city or a smaller community with good police protection and **a community free of violence**. Their needs will be an automobile for the husband and a van or wagon-type for the mother and children. The husband will seek a steady income or a career capable of providing for two or three children. This couple will seek local friends to invite to their home and expect reciprocation to share good times and enjoy recreations of their choice. They may want a local place of worship. Most will select a home in a neighborhood having a good school system, a handy library and nice parks. They hope their marriage will last against an almost 50% failure according to statistics.

A contemporary man expects to help with the children, even the babies, and will also encourage his wife to maintain personal interests and perhaps hold onto a delayed career. They hope to enjoy leisure hours in mutual interests. They will invest in insurance programs and try to put something away for retirement. When the family plays together it usually stays together. They need to support each other, especially spiritually, or culturally, if they are to maintain their role model for their children.

This family of the future, particularly in all but central urban societies, will make up the principal individual philosophy of typical America of the future. While they may have been liberal or socialistic-minded in their youth, with maturity they often turn more conservative in their attitudes as private property is acquired. The reason is that they will want to preserve their home and better ensure a good social opportunity for their children. They tend to vote against higher taxes except for local education.

As this scenario of an individual philosophy adds to the collective philosophy, the attitude of middle America will be pushed toward conservatism and will support continued free enterprise for its opportunities.

There will, however, be a frustration. On the one hand, they will feel the compulsion to conserve and preserve their life style, but on the other they will want insurance against catastrophe. This is protection against two types: loss of income because of economic cycles and secondly, losses due to major health problems. One theory holds that extreme wealth has been accumulated by too few because more than one-third of the wealth is held by only 1% of the families. These pose major dilemmas in the American politic now and in the future because it takes away buying power of the majority of consumers. This prompts a principle:

If America is to continue to lead we will somehow need to develop employment insurance in the future based on ability and education similar to health insurance.

Qualification for employment insurance would be based on a work experience record, education, and work ethic. I also believe that somehow individual character would need to be assessed.

Private vs. Public Education

Private schools will escalate in the New Renaissance. Many parents seek private schools for their children for two reasons. First, they feel they will get a better education from selected teachers of higher caliber. Second, they hope that the environment of other children is more disciplined and less subject to drugs and other acquired behavior which is undesirable. This same notion was in the mind of the public school system in Los Angeles, as leaders hoped that busing from long distances would be practical not only for school opportunity but for a better racial mix. Remembering my own busing years, however, I hated every minute of it, and all children complain of the loss of play time.

One-Language Advantage

This brings to light still another principle:

A society will succeed better when a single language or dialect is available in the educational system.

Traditionally, foreign immigrants in America were required to learn the English language. With Latin American infiltration, many insist on making the educational system bilingual so they can maintain the Spanish language. This can only complicate a school system, and will not be conducive to advancing American society at a pace required for future world competition.

Yet we should also prepare children for communication as is practiced in Europe, with the learning in early years of second and third languages. The real concern of many is that we don't do a good job of even learning English. What needs to be accomplished here is improvement in the teaching of the English language **in addition to** the introduction of foreign languages.

It is a pity that so many in America do not avail themselves of the free education offered by our society. Are they lazy or simply too ignorant to realize what education has meant historically? If young Americans can be made to realize the advantages offered by the reading and the writing of the English language, they can overcome a major future frustration in their lives. It is the tool for self-education!

A few years ago I happened to be motoring with Italian friends, enjoying country roads between Milan and Rome. We stopped at a small village for snacks, and the waiter-owner was called to the telephone. I heard him shouting. I asked my friends what all the excitement was about. The man came back disgusted and annoyed, and with a loud voice said, "How in the hell is Italy going to get anywhere when people only six blocks away can't understand one another?" Another Italian had telephoned to ask directions to a certain place and couldn't understand what he was saying in their common language.

America's advantage is the one English language. As I lecture world-wide and as interpreters or translators are used, I must speak slowly. This is not just for their understanding but also because more words are necessary to convey the thought in other languages. More print is needed to say the same thing. Therefore, English is an efficient language.

Computers are programmed in English. Air traffic on a world basis is conducted in English. Scientific journals are published or abstracted in English. Eighty percent of international phone calls are in English. English is the language of the future, like it or not.

All U.S. citizens should be obligated to learn English, and neither indolence nor ethnic background should be an excuse not to learn English at the grade school level. Is bilinguality in America promoted for political reasons only? In order for America to continue, we must have literate people and smart people as we face the future.

Yet a dilemma exists. We need people conversant in foreign languages to take advantage of business opportunities. We need to produce cars to drive on the left side of roads in order to obtain foreign markets.

Education for the New Renaissance
Discipline in Students

For the past 20 years, article after article in newspapers and magazines has expressed the weakness of American education. There is a ubiquitous fear of losing ground even to some third world countries, despite the clamor by foreign students to be accepted at American universities. In the past America has had more Nobel prize winners than any other country.

Some point to lack of money for education as the problem in our system. Others point to poor teachers. Still others list the cost of college education. But university professors note the absence of preparedness in students enrolling for higher education.

Most of all, grade school and high school teachers point out the very poor discipline of children and their lack of compliance with home assignments. Child labor laws protect the young, and corporal punishment has been prohibited. Parents are accused of not having an interest in the discipline of their children, dumping them at the school with a relief of that responsibility.

As a teacher myself, I know how exhausting it is to teach unmotivatable students who have no respect for a teacher's efforts. Meanwhile, our test results for language capability, mathematics, history and geography all seem to progressively decline. We struggle for answers.

It is difficult for me to believe that poor showings of students of any race are due to deficient brains. One factor not appreciated, however, in hyperkinetic children incapable of concentration is a bad diet, or incorrect nutrition. Too much free sugar can, according to some scientists, block brain pathways and destroy concentration.

One of the most revealing works regarding the growth of intelligence was "Magical Child" and "The Bond of Power" written by Joseph Chilton Pearce, a teacher who became an investigator in the development of intelligence. He stressed several aspects of learning and emotional development, referring to a matrix (or mother) as a place of comfort and a sense of a safe place to return. "Matrix shifts" were described from birth through babyhood, to the juvenile and adolescent, to bonding to lovers and finally to a personal confidence or individual matrix. When a matrix was rushed or not carried through to its fulfillment, it allegedly led to fixations and frustrations and altered personalities.

Children need to run, play and utilize their imagination. This keeps many of the abundant neural pathways exercised and available for association. Sitting in front of a television screen can be damaging to the development of the learning processes because these pathways are closed down with sedate behavior.

Attitude Toward Education

The question is, "If our children are getting larger, are they developing earlier and getting smarter?"

Most societies around the world have compulsory education from six to sixteen. While the Chinese had systems of education three thousand years ago, the Greeks in 400 B.C. educated only their elite. But the pattern of European and American compulsory plans for all children dates to Prussia at about 1750. The basic "three R's" (readin', 'ritin' and 'rithmetic) were a part of early American folklore, and the school "marm" or school "master" was a respected and dignified person in the community, with a status that rivaled the minister.

Education must become a demand by those seeking knowledge before it will change. One principle, therefore, is that:

American education will decline so long as the public attitude toward it continues to degenerate.

By this I do not mean a degeneration of the teacher (although I sometimes wonder about the dedication of some teachers who look on teaching as only a job). I mean a lack of will, a lack of pride, and a **void of respect by the students**. Good teachers can motivate, but they can only do so much with their material. A coach cannot win games without some talented players. Teachers cannot teach when preoccupied with maintaining order in the classroom and when their time is spent in disciplining pupils.

The solution is not for the government to spend more money -- that has failed -- because the problem is not one of education availability (supply), it is one of demand. **The problem is the dearth of ordinary American students hungry to learn.** Education for the majority of students must be earned by hard work. It strikes me as interesting indeed that refugees from foreign countries will come to America not knowing our language and soon achieve marks that lead a class. The reason for this achievement seems to be the involvement of the *whole family* in the student's progress. Father and mother hover in the background, doing chores, as the student struggles at the dining room table with his books, also helping younger siblings with what he has already learned.

Thus, another principle is:

Too much television has hindered the creative processes in the learning experience.

Brain and Skull Growth

From my own work it is clear that learning readiness at age six is not accidental. For the first six years the brain is growing, as evidenced by the increase in the skull. The size of the brain case is about 90% complete by age six. The skull bones thereafter grow thicker for brain protection and superstructure for the facial orifices, but the brain at age six is essentially grown and is now ready to learn.

During these formative years there are channels open from the senses coming from the brain stem. Children's physical play action and contact with the earth set learning pathways. Kindergarten means "children's garden" for play as a learning experience.

Entertainment Craze a Detriment

But today children and grown-ups alike are an entertainment-crazed society. Instead of exercising creativity, exploration, and imagination, the child wants now only to sit long hours before the "boob tube" being entertained. This breeds an attitude in children of having things done for them rather than their doing things for themselves. In the long run, as another principle:

Too much and the wrong kind of television can restrict the work ethic, and the altruistic basis proven to be beneficial to happiness and health.

Some television programs are constructive, but display of sex, violence and high-action films do little to produce a balanced and cultured society. Even four-year-old children become addicted to television which, of course, is taken full advantage of by the media and the advertisers. Sexy shows and smutty comedians searching for something different go deeper into the gutter. I recently heard Steve Allen on a radio talk show expressing distress about the moral slippage of fellow entertainers.

Another detriment to education may be in an indirect way the influence of heavy rock music. As the senses of the young become more conditioned for impact, the amplified loud pounding and screech of the steel is necessary to stimulate senses deadened by the continual bombardment. Contrast that scene to the beauty and serenity of a quiet Japanese garden or the joy of a walk along a country lane or a babbling brook. Contrast the reactions to a smoke-filled rock show locale with the ability to appreciate a symphony. Part of the educational process is to prepare for the understanding of fine music.

Motivation

Probably the foremost need of children, something not widely understood by adults, is the same need they have -- for identity. Kids delight in competition. Winning gives them a sense of achievement. Identity simply means being a somebody, not a nobody. Therefore, as a principle:

Any little thing that produces a sense of individuality, success, achievement or even attention (which is a form of recognition) is hungered for.

For instance, as a seven-year-old I took pride in being the fastest runner. One boy may be better with his fists. The little boy in our class with poor eyesight and thick glasses took pride in being the best scholar. Every child needs some small thing in which to excel for his identity. Some girls and boys may want to dance or perform. Even very young little ladies love to play bride or put on Mommy's high heels. Imagination is a beautiful tool for mind preparation. Television or just watching entertainment alone yields no identity value.

As time goes on, learning accumulates into knowledge, and yields confidence. The growth of knowledge seems also to build individual power and confidence. This is exemplified in the feeling of power of the 18 to 19-year-old boy who senses his invincibility. Finally, accumulation of knowledge plus the experience of mistakes makes wisdom.

Lessons on Learning

Processes

Growth of intelligence, or learning in general, goes through three processes. First, information is received by the mind in the **abstract** or a general, separated, or disassociated idea. Second, that information, when contemplated, may become a part of an immediate experience and becomes **concrete** or takes on a reality. More detail is learned and the gaps are filled. Third, the idea solidifies and becomes knowledge retrievable in the mind when it undergoes **application** or is actually put to use.

Some people are memory experts. Years ago at our Pacific Palisades Rotary Club we had a memory expert as a speaker. When we arrived for the luncheon meeting we were greeted by our Club president at the door and introduced to this man. With the introduction the president explained who each member was and said something about his vocation and his career. There were about 65 people at the meeting that day. When, about 30 minutes later, the memory expert was introduced to speak, he arose from his chair, went to the podium and recalled the name of each person in the room, recognized where he was sitting and remarked about the individual's characteristics. We were, of course, dumbfounded at the capacity of his brain. He, however, went on to explain the keys to a long-lasting memory (which I have remembered, because I took notes and reviewed them several times).

Impression

The first key was an **impression**. In my own experience I would liken this aspect to the **importance** the student may assign to the information he is receiving. If a person thinks something is important he will give it his concentration. Impression is made if a telling image or some impact is made on the senses, the mind or the conscience. If the shock or impact is great enough, it will create a new channel in the nerve network in the brain and will penetrate to the outer cortex memory bank and be recorded to a state where it can be retrieved on command.

I always felt that if a subject were worth my time it was important to remember, and therefore I should be impressed. I heard one of my grade school teachers say (about her pupils), "I just felt like grabbing them and shaking them to wake them up to reality!" It's as if they need to be shocked into being impressed. Impression is also related to urgency and **emotional intensity** such as cramming for finals for the purpose of a grade and not necessarily with the idea of retention for long memory.

Repetition

Repetition as the second key has been shown to be necessary for new ideas or new subject matter. There may be no shortcut; it must be rehearsed again and again like the lines in a play. Like an athlete practicing his skills over and over, new information must often be repeated again and again. Studies have indicated the average mind needs **seven rehearsals**. That's not seven repetitions at one time. It means leaving and coming back to it later, seven times.

The problem with children (or adults) may lie in the decision that it requires too much effort. Students may decide the reward is not worth the bother to learn. **They consequently do not have that information to build on when required for a later application.** They then lack an intellectual background for further growth.

Having been in stage shows and having taught ballroom dancing as a vocation to get through dental school in Indianapolis, I can testify that in order to remember it takes rehearsals.

"If you can't tell it you can't sell it!" quipped Kenneth McFarland, one of America's greatest salesmen and speakers. In order to "tell it" a person must "learn it". This takes repeated attempts and time commitment, which many students are not willing to give. I often say, "If you can't show it, you don't know it."

Association

The third key to a long-lasting memory is **association**. When a fact or phenomenon is already known, there is an existing channel in the brain network to the cortex. Association utilizes information already in the mind. If a new piece of information is now hauled over that existing channel and connected to something already known or fixed in the mind, it is like adding another detail to something previously known. This would suggest another principle:

Previous knowledge begets new knowledge.

When something is learned sensory pathways form a succession of unions through the nerves in the brain and an imprint is made like a computer program. Rehearsal strengthens these neuro-electrical pathways and then, when an idea or a feeling can be attached to a previous pathway or imprint, it is said to be associated and can be remembered in this manner. For instance, to remember a person's name, you may mentally print their name on their forehead and associate it with their hair, eyes or face. Association is a process of stacking new knowledge on old knowledge already owned.

My Personal Challenges

I have often been asked by my students how I became motivated to learn so broadly in my field. "How can you retain so much information in your head?" they ask. At first I didn't have an answer. But on reflecting and examining the source, I recognized four basic principles. The first principle was:

A person cannot learn without an intellectual background.

The mind needs something to build on. This is probably the reason for so-called vertical learning. Basic information is needed to appreciate and understand more complicated or detailed facts. This means knowing the history of a subject and achieving an understanding beyond just words or events!

The second principle was:

Continued learning requires an insatiable curiosity.

There must be an intense desire to know; otherwise, there would be no motivation. It means a desire for knowledge for the sake of knowledge itself that reaches a state of excitement. It involves ingenuity, skill and above all an inquisitive nature.

The third quality is **persistence**. Probably no greater statement was ever made than that by President Calvin Coolidge who held office from 1923 to 1929 (when I was a small child, aged three to nine):

> **Nothing in the world can take the place of persistence. Talent will not; nothing is more common than unsuccessful men with talent. Genius will not; unrewarded genius is almost a proverb. Education will not; the world is full of educated derelicts. Persistence and determination alone are omnipotent.**

The fourth principle was:

Application requires imagination.

Imagination is the process of lateral thinking, as described by Edward De Bono. Facts must be put together by teleologic reasoning. This is the secret of creativity and the innovation of new ideas. The pursuit of knowledge becomes the challenge and is stimulating and invigorating in the process. An enthusiasm for any subject makes the good teacher! How dull indeed is the professor who has no motivation within himself or herself.

Thus, learning starts with the mastering of fundamentals in a step-by-step laborious procedure in the beginning. A bright future for America will be certain if enough of this kind of labor is performed by our young. Cut it any way you choose -- children must work! It is truly child's labor, and perhaps our child labor laws have some negative aspects after all. It has been said that success breeds complacency. Still another principle obtains:

> **America's leadership in the future is guaranteed as long as its doors are open for the foreign students with their strong ambition, desire and work ethic.**

Left and Right Brain and Memory Qualities

Educators also attempt to produce mental exercises which will utilize the left and right sides of the brain for a better holistic value. Females have been shown to possess a larger corpus callosum than males, which connects the two basic hemispheres. Females seem to be more intelligent in some ways than males. Males are less assumptive and tend to go deeper into subjects.

Another *a propos* statement adapted for our purpose is by Vince Lombardi, an original teacher who was to become one of the most famous professional football coaches.

> The spirit, the will to learn, and the will to excel, these are the things that endure. These are the qualities that are so much more important than any of the events that occasion it. And I want to say that the quality of a person's life has got to be a full measure of a personal commitment to excellence and to victory regardless of what field it may be.

The following idea was expressed by the Rev. Katherine Reynolds:

> Knowledge is useless until it becomes inventive and inspirational. This occurs only through individual effort. It cannot be just handed to you. Exposure won't help unless you listen and apply rules to your pursuit.

Answers

I have no pat answers to problems of education for the New Renaissance. If I thought that money alone was the answer I would barnstorm for that objective. Probably it must start with making education a worthwhile contribution to our society, something of value in our eyes and our hearts. **Identity and respect should be gained by those with scholastic achievements** rather than back-page factual notations alone. **Also, teachers must receive recognition.** I have always gained respect from private practice, but what of those who toil unnoticed? We should invite teachers to our homes and learn from their wisdom and give them some attention.

But teachers should not feel they simply put their time in for the state, or that teaching is just a job. They are not there to entertain, to give pleasure to students, or amuse them. They are there to teach, and they need family support.

I can recall in my own education poor teachers, good teachers and great teachers. The truly great were those who had the following basic qualities: (1) They knew their stuff!; (2) They were enthusiastic and exciting!; and (3) they were organized and could present the subject to make it interesting and applicable to a student's life! Teachers, hear this!

When President-elect Clinton decided to put his daughter in a private school in Washington, D.C. it prompted an article on our educational woes in USA TODAY for January 11, 1993. Problems previously associated with inner cities now were hitting the whole community. Many dedicated teachers were quitting. The reasons were numerous: children's suicide attempts, mentally retarded children misplaced in regular instead of special-ed classes, teen-age pregnancies, children led from a class in handcuffs for selling drugs, students threatening murder, students with mental breakdowns, anorexia and bulimia all were listed as problems. Teachers complained, "We're not teachers any more, we're managers." Half of all teachers -- after only two years -- consider that children are coming to school with too many problems which interfere with learning. They cite chiefly a lack of parental support as the reason for seeking another career. Soon the empty seats aren't going to be the students'!

Problems in the current educational process start early. By first grade some children with kindergarten or a home exposure background already know numbers and letters, while others can't recognize their own name. Some children have the will and the learning capacity during grammar school and up through high school but are held back by inferior students who reduce the whole process to the level of mediocrity.

As an answer perhaps a tier system is indicated, not just two but three levels. The disruptive and uncooperative students should be segregated. The capable, hard-working and talented students could have their own segregation. The middle group -- the plodders who are cooperative but slower -- could be the third tier. Such a system would no doubt be difficult to manage, and expensive. But what is more expensive than the waste of effort under the present procedure?

Mind

The mind is our source of perception, thinking and will. It is the seat of consciousness and intelligence. It is our regulator for sanity. It is our reactor to our drives for identity, pleasure and freedom. It constitutes the mechanism for the establishment of goals and the appreciation of the virtue of achievement. **No mind can make another mind happy.** It is our own mind that is our key to personal happiness. Society does not owe our mind anything!

Society cannot accept the blame for the riots in Los Angeles. White people can't fix the minds of their own poor, or the blacks or the Hispanics. Those people cannot blame their condition on the middle class or people in the upper income levels. It's their own problem and if necessary they must build their own society. They must do what they can to earn respect. We will help all we can!

One fact is certain: we are in the information age and beyond. The need for science and technology skills has surfaced as the base for the future. There will still need to be workers, repairers, and service people. They deserve equal respect and should maintain an attitude of support for the community as well as those in the higher levels.

If America is to still lead the world in the New Renaissance, it must move ahead with acquisition and application of knowledge. It must start with personal will. In our New Renaissance, the human factors and qualities just covered are to be communicated and better understood. Communication means education.

Romantic Love and Harmony of Life

The New Renaissance will have people learning to live in good relationship. This means living in harmony with family or friends, acquaintances, co-workers on the job, customers, or with any person in any way. Poor relationships and anxieties lead to a loss of energy, ulcers, poor self esteem and general frustration and failure -- all symptoms of distress.

When that hot, burning love and intense caring relationship is entered into in a marriage, it slowly fades -- frequently as the family comes along. Dad and Mom now need, also, some quality time together privately for mutual nurturing. Intelligent people will bring in the grandparents or friends, or hire help when it can be afforded, in order to share some prime time together. **Romantic love puts the other person's interests first.** The preservation of the family is America's backbone, and it starts with love and respect between the parents.

Making Decisions

People need to heed the words of Dale Carnegie who 75 years ago laid down a plan for important decision-making in any aspect of life. He felt that procrastination and indecision lead to frustration and build up distress. I have modified his basic plan for my teaching, but the central matrix or core applies to any problem in life, of any kind -- even to the diagnosis

of a condition. It is a procedure to help "clear the deck" and solve problems whether they be marriage, family business, or social relationships. The steps are as follows:
1. Identify the problem (on paper);
2. Expose the intuitive feelings;
3. List various possibilities for the solution;
4. Critique each option;
5. Select some of the best answers;
6. Decide on one solution;
7. Commit to a plan and act;
8. Monitor and stay in control, with continued update.

* * *

It may seem redundant to the reader that I keep returning to the three human drives conceived by Robert Ardrey. These pertain to motives or forces directing actions for both men and women everywhere on earth, and are the drive for identity, stimulation and security. Many problems can be solved and mutual understanding reached if this hierarchy is kept foremost in the mind in all human inter-personal relations.

Each person demands respect and needs dignity. Each human seeks joy and happiness. Each man, woman or child wants to be free of worry about poor economics and poor health.

In Dale Carnegie's short course six rules were laid down:
1. Don't criticize or complain (takes away stimulation).
2. Make others feel important (identity-recognition of others).
3. Try to see things from their view (security).
4. Praise the slightest improvement (identity).
5. Don't carry negatives -- stay positive (security).
6. Put enthusiasm into your complete life (stimulation).

These among others are keys to success in living a happy life in the future American society. Various authors have laid down rules but so many contain the same theme.

Honesty is required by each party, yet each citizen must protect himself or herself from the weasel who may be dishonest, one who makes a livelihood of cheating and taking advantage of those with integrity.

Some readers may be amused, but it has been proven that being married and having a family provides the greatest happiness, health and longevity. Studies of altruism or giving to others show that the greatest benefactor is the giver, particularly when what is given is his or her time, and this applies to the family also.

Happiness comes with setting goals and reaching achievements and then making new pursuits! Goals for identity and self worth, goals for stimulation and enjoyment of life, and goals to find peace and freedom from poverty and illness are all forms of worthwhile pursuits.

Probably the greatest lesson America has shown the world is the importance of doing things for someone else. The principle in achieving a happy life is:

When in doubt, do something for somebody else!

The Future of Art in America

In the history of a Renaissance, attention naturally turns to art. During the 15th and 16th centuries art was no doubt appreciated by the masses as well as by the elite, as reflected in the frescoes and statues still visible in the cathedrals. All through Europe at that time masters in art emerged. Their works are glorified in America because the purpose of art is, and always has been, for the stimulation and enjoyment of life.

Human beings have always appreciated fine things. There has been a growing demand in America for things done well, whether it be a good ski, a good golf club, a fine chair to sit in, or fine music to listen to. America has more recently become progressively good-quality-conscious, rather than accepting products that just get by. Our schools are teaching art and encouraging art expression, whose purpose Americans should better understand.

When I finish a patient's orthodontic treatment, it is a piece of art. When the jaws are in harmony with each other and when the teeth are in unity with each other, the resulting smile deeply touches my senses of pleasure in a most rewarding manner. That's beauty! That's my art! The joy is in the job well done!

The pursuit of excellence is becoming a buzz idea.

The Five-Way Test

The Rotary Club recommends to its members a four-way test in business and personal affairs, which goes as follows:

Is it the truth?

Is it fair to all concerned?

Will it build good will and better friendship?

Will it be beneficial to all concerned?

These cover some basic issues in philosophy, but esthetics was left out. I would therefore add one more question:

Is it done well and in good taste?

This does not mean that each person should become an esthete or a pretender of fine taste and artistic culture, but it does mean we should develop an esthetic sense of enjoying the principles underlying beauty in all things. I sense in our New Renaissance that more and more people will achieve the perception of beauty and good taste as Europeans did in their Renaissance.

Arts Function

If art is for the pleasure of people, it may be an escape from boredom. The Circus Maximus Hippodromes of Rome were for the appeasement or diversion of the mobs. If beauty touches the senses on a deep emotional level, then performances of all kinds can exhilarate the emotion. Think of the outburst of the crowd at a baseball game when a home run is hit, or the sheer beauty of Michael Jordan hanging in the air with his art of handling a basketball. Sports as an art form gets the attention of the masses, and businesses spend millions for advertising sports on TV and radio, which explains the players' immense salaries.

Art must have as its goal the stimulation of life. It is for joy and the breaking of boredom. The artist as well as others enjoys the product of his imagination and skill.

Robert Henri, one of America's greatest artists, explained to his students that art is doing things, any thing, well. "When the artist is alive in person, he is interesting to himself and interesting to others." Most artists are romantics. Artifacts of art have been used to study the history of ancient peoples. Much is learned of a society by examining their art.

* * *

Plato discussed his understanding of art in its broadest sense in the following extract from "The Republic". Socrates is describing his conversation with Thrasymachus:

Is the physician, taken in that strict sense of which you are speaking, a healer of the sick or a maker of money? And remember that I am now speaking of the true physician.

A healer of the sick, he replied.

And the pilot -- that is to say, the true pilot -- is he a captain of sailors or a mere sailor?

A captain of sailors.

The circumstance that he sails in the ship is not to be taken into account; neither is he to be called a sailor; the name 'pilot' by which is he distinguished has nothing to do with sailing, but is significant of his skill and of his authority over the sailors. Very true, he said.

Now, I said, every art has an interest?

Certainly.

For which the art has to consider and provide?

Yes, that is the aim of art.

And the interest of any art is the perfection of it -- this and nothing else?

What do you mean?

I mean what I may illustrate negatively by the example of the body. Suppose you were to ask me whether the body is self-sufficing or has wants, I should reply: Certainly the body has wants; for the body may be ill and require to be cured, and has therefore interests to which the art of medicine ministers; and this is the origin and intention of medicine, as you will acknowledge. Am I not right?

Quite right, he replied.

But is the art of medicine or any other art faulty or deficient in any quality in the same way that the eye may be deficient in sight or the ear fail of hearing, and therefore requires another art to provide for the interests of seeing and hearing -- has art in itself, I say, any similar liability to fault or defect, and does every art require another supplementary art to provide for its interests, and that another and another without end? Or have the arts to look only after their own interests? Or have they no need either of themselves or of another? -- having no faults or defects, they have no need to correct them, either by the exercise of their own art or of any other; they have only to consider the interest of their subject matter. For every art remains pure and faultless while remaining true -- that is to say, while perfect and unimpaired. . . .

But surely, Thrasymachus, the arts are the superiors and rulers of their own subjects?

To this he assented with a good deal of reluctance.

Then, I said, no science or art considers or enjoins the interest of the stronger or superior, but only the interest of the subject and weaker?

He made an attempt to contest this proposition also, but finally acquiesced.

Then, I continued, no physician, in so far as he is a physician, considers his own good in what he prescribes, but the good of his patient; for the true physician is also a ruler having the human body as a subject, and is not a mere money-maker; that has been admitted?

Yes.

And the pilot likewise, in the strict sense of the term, is a ruler of sailors and not a mere sailor?

That has been admitted.

* * *

Divisions of Art

Durant insisted that all ideas start as philosophy, go through science, and end as art in their application. It would seem to me that Americans enjoy art as much as any group, but little do they recognize how many art forms surround them daily -- even in the form of art for advertising. The basic intent of advertising is to appeal to the senses and stimulate a desire, and art forms are used to achieve this.

We may therefore divide art into essentially four types for discussion of the future. They are visual, performing, servicing, and literary.

Visual Arts

The classical sculpture forms of the Greeks and Romans and the realism of the Dutch masters may never return in our plastic generations of the future. But new innovations in architecture, landscaping and interior design will continue to flourish. America has excelled in the field of photography. New sight and sound techniques will be found in many mediums. Product design is recognized as an art form. Visual arts, therefore, include ideas for marketing -- a field in which Americans excel.

Architecture will reflect modern trends, but some designs will return to old patterns. All Americans will express more and more the divine proportion because of its pleasure to the human psyche. This movement will extend to home design and decoration and to the advantageous use of color in all of commerce.

Performing Arts

First coming to mind in performing arts are, of course, drama and musical performance. The popularity of movies and television will decrease but little in the future. Live theatre will need more stimulation from the public. I long for some good old classic musicals and concerts with that old band sound which was as exciting as anything ever was. Crosby, Sinatra, Como, Sammy Davis, Nat King Cole, and many others will continue to sell because they are classic.

Formal ballet will continue. But ballroom dancing, as ever, will continue to change, with new fads or trends in music and new combinations of moves.

The circus performer has existed since the days of early America. Of interest to me is the fact that the first circus brought from England to America was a Ricketts Circus which performed before George Washington, went broke, was shipped back to England, and perished in a storm on the Atlantic.

Performing sports are not recognized by many as an entertainment form, but try to tell that to a sports fan! Long hard work and development to perfection of a talent is required by the professional athlete. Perhaps they receive the highest incomes of any performer on stage or screen outside of such artists as Pavarotti.

Participation sports are a form of recreation, and people also enjoy watching amateurs try. But art is required to ski, dance, race, skate, shoot an arrow or a gun, or throw a ball well.

Servicing Arts

A beautiful flower arrangement is a work of art. The design of beautiful fabric is art. The design of a beautiful dress or suit likewise is art. Any beautification process in the home such as decoration is an art form. Art is pleasing! Art is stimulating! The preparation of a beautiful dish of food is art. Who can deny the taste of fine food prepared by an accomplished chef or the taste of a fine wine given perfect care?

Literary Art

America has had its share of great authors in almost all branches of society. Books, journals and tabloids will continue to increase in number. Just on the horizon, however, are computer publications and more and more teaching with visual aids as an art form -- even with the computer.

Art Forms

While considering art in its totality, some other subjects came to mind. If art is creative effort in music and dance, in fine arts, in literature and other branches of academic learning (as liberal arts are distinguished from the sciences), then a principle obtains:

Efficient knowledge acquisition becomes an art in itself.

Finally, the application of intelligence and wisdom gained from knowledge in the end is art.

Such natural behaviors of each race and culture such as courtship and dream interpretation also must be placed in art. Effective speaking and oratory and the mastering of language is another art in such analysis. Words become tools of thought for expression and communication. In the end, effective writing or literary art is no easy task, and requires consummate skill just as all the arts in order to do it well.

All these aspects of art become challenges in the New American Renaissance.

* * *

The future of the arts in America is quite secure because Americans have an increasingly high desire to be entertained, as in music and dance. Entertainment breaks boredom. Furthermore, it is a kind of effortless stimulation as the observer or spectator may receive either direct exhilaration or a subliminally pleasant impression. If fine art is for stimulation it also breaks boredom. My secretary, Sallie Coyle, senses that art which engages the mind and soul of a person, as in a painting or a piece of music, or a dance, or a piece of writing -- whether the person does it or merely observes it, thereby participating in it -- touches something deeper in him than almost anything else other than religion. There is a spiritual factor here that for her is not present in pure entertainment, which has an aspect of gratification. Some people enjoy different aspects of art, and the sports fan jokes about the "long-hair" just as some with a cultivated knowledge of opera disdain the sports lover.

Big businesses also support "the arts" as well as sports. Consider the advertising on TV for all types of programs.

Probably as shorter working hours permit more time for employees' personal pleasure, entertainment, and recreation, a wide variety of "arts" will fall under the interests of big and small businesses alike. The future of art is secure.

In 1992 the Western States Arts Federation offered $5000 fellowships to 20 artists, and in addition will have new students' work represented in a catalog for galleries, museums and collectors. Art is not dead in America. Arts and crafts exhibits on the sidewalks on week ends offer proof of its health.

The Total Perspective of Art

If art is anything done well, it therefore permeates all aspects of a society. Who would argue with gymnastics or ice skating, especially ice dancing, as an art form in the Olympics?

In my travels to many countries, even the most remote areas, to my great surprise and pleasure I have heard American music played and witnessed American dancing. If there is one impact that we have made on the world this is it! I'm not happy with the heavy rock and ear-splitting sheer noise, but it attracts the young. Each generation will find its own expression. But I long for the smooth band sound of Glenn Miller and Tommy Dorsey and many others, and the need for learning to really dance with a partner rather than wiggling alone on a floor displaying moves with the buttocks. Maybe beautiful partner dancing will return. It has started in Country Western.

Symphony, opera and pop orchestras will continue to find popularity in the New Renaissance. Formal music may have a brilliant day as many people may try to find escape from the pandemonium.

Together with the effect of American music is the influence of American films. Almost everywhere also are seen American productions with voice overlaid in other languages. It is sometimes extremely strange to see "shoot-em out" westerns played in other languages, even those of the orient. A favorite example of this is a scene in a Gary Cooper western, showing in Paris, where Cooper struts into a saloon, throws a coin down on the counter and says, "Gimme a slug of Red-Eye." The French subtitle read, "Un doubonnet, s'il vous plait."

However, I'm concerned about the violence and bloodiness and the vulgarity of movies and television which has been increased to make an impact. Who can ever forget the screams of a man finding his bloody horse's head in his bed in "The Godfather"? We are living in a progressively more violent society, and this is one sad part of the American culture. Some serious studies are indicated.

Arts such as those dealing with body adornment will find greater acceptance in the New Renaissance. Clothing will continue to go through trends and fads -- skirts short, then long, and ties narrow, then wide, over and over again. Facial make-up and anti-aging products will improve. Plastic surgery demands will increase and insurance programs will be pressed for payments in all body improvements.

We have covered anticipated problems, but it should be recognized that chance is always an unforeseen factor. Speculations are fun and sporting. Let's hope that I'm correct in some predictions and hopefully wrong in others.

Science Probabilities

The world today probably has about seven million scientists divided into almost 700 different divisions. **Most scientists seek to find ways for improvement and betterment**

of life. Some may be considered crackpots and accused of prying into things which are thought to be none of their business. But through their efforts, people live healthier, happier and longer lives.

I have found those I respect most in science to have a passionate interest, a profound intensity and a displayed excitement not seen in other callings. A continued interest and study certainly keeps me in the swim. Each go-around has broadened my view. Each orbit made has revealed new possibilities that were not apparent in the original work. And so on and on it goes!

The nature of science makes me ever more intensely critical of my own theories and more expectant of criticism from colleagues. My moments of truth have occurred when the theory survives and becomes a foundation for still greater progress.

It is my hope that many young people can catch this scientific spirit during the New Renaissance.

Classification of Sciences

Even though science varies almost with impunity and scientists come from all types and races of people, the whole scientific realm can be listed under four main branches: mathematics, physical sciences, life sciences, and social sciences.

In a more refined manner, sciences may be divided into seven major divisions: mathematics, physics, chemistry, astronomy, and earth, life and social sciences.

Mathematics started first with geometry and then much later included arithmetic. It developed algebra and analytic logic, and later statistics, and then higher mathematical logic. It will no doubt continue to be a basis for all science in the New Renaissance.

Physics, consisting of optics, mechanics and thermodynamics, graduated to atomic physics and quantum mechanics. Radio, television, jet and rocket power and computers are all its products for mankind. With the force of its momentum new discoveries will continue to open up new possibilities. Let us hope that it can be more useful for peace-making purposes rather than for those of war.

Chemistry started with the melting of metals and the use of herbs for medicine, but the periodic chart of elements did not come until the 19th century. Organic chemistry with carbon and the benzene ring also was not spun off inorganic chemistry until the 1800s. Quantum chemistry and chemistry of the nucleus of a living cell with the discovery of the DNA molecule was chemistry's recent contribution. Chemistry gave us antibiotic drugs and awareness of vitamins and minerals.

Probably the greatest need in the future is for an attack on pollutants and treatment of wastes. **Chemical engineers are needed to discover methods to neutralize many of the chemicals used in the manufacturing and farming industry which threaten human drinking water, the air, and the ozone layer.** These are foremost challenges for the New Renaissance.

Astronomy is now connected with radio astronomy and astrophysics. Space exploration will continue in order to yield information about our planet and the weather. Satellite stations for our communications will continue to improve.

Earth Science has captured the imagination of many of our young people because **they want to protect their environment for their own future**. Geography must be better known by our students in whose background it is sadly lacking at present. Paleontology, minerology and geology with the availability of fossil fuels are a part of that future. The role of fossil fuels will change. Geochemistry and oceanography are vital subjects for the New Renaissance.

Ions in the air affect people's mental and physical health. Food is raised in the earth so soils must be better preserved. One-half the original rain forests have been lost to man's commercial needs. Success with organic farming should be better known. We will need to share our knowledge with Africa where savannahs are being turned into deserts by cattle.

Life Sciences could be likened to biology or the study of all living things, man in particular. Medical science and all its allied disciplines are found here. Molecular biology with biochemistry has attracted our greatest minds. From comparative anatomy and phylogenetics to modern genetics, life sciences will be extended. The effects of ecology and ecosystems and the health of man in the future will be a paramount interest. Probably prevention will be a stronger part of medical practice through nutrition and awareness programs.

Social Sciences are a product of a long history of philosophy and governments. Social sciences mainly deal with society and its elements of family, race, state and institutions influencing man's life as a member of an organized community. This large division includes also economics, psychology or man's adjustment to society, and cultural anthropology, his total social environment. Politics and metaphysics are a further part of social considerations. Finally, archaeology, physical anthropology and ethology contribute to a new wedding of the social and life sciences to form sociobiology. When a consideration is made of the effects of excessive stress on the human health, the formulation of sociobiology is appreciated and increasing attention will be paid. It will become more and more difficult to separate life sciences (biology) from the social sciences.

In fact, there is a cross-over or overlap of many subjects in most of the seven branches just described. The field of medicine, for example, may have disciplines in all the sciences.

As I sat in my studio on April 30, 1992, I saw a lesson in social science. On TV I witnessed the violence, the riots, burning, looting and anarchy in Los Angeles of supposedly sane American people. They say they have been incensed and enraged. But my intuitive sense is that, as in Saigon at the close of the Vietnamese War, there was opportunistic seizing of property characteristic of human nature. The result, nevertheless, is inexcusable. It would seem those older and young of both sexes were in a frenzy of excitement exercising the chance to take someone else's property without an apparent fear of punishment.

As explained by some of the jurors who were queried about the decision to acquit the four police officers, the beating as shown again and again to the public on television was not the whole story. It was apparent that they found it terribly distasteful but within the law as they interpreted it. They didn't feel those public service people should be sent to prison. Reading between the lines, it was a message that people are to pull over and stop when a siren is heard or the red light is flashed, which was not done.

There were actually two faults and two problems, but only one was sensationalized by the media. The first and major problem, of course, was the over-extension of force, which had to be weighed by the jurors. But the second, being further exemplified by the hordes of people looting, was total disrespect for law and authority. The failure to cooperate with officers charged with enforcing the law and placing their own lives at risk, together with that of other citizens, in a 115 miles-per-hour pursuit on a freeway, and an 80 miles-per-hour race through street crossings in residential areas, plus the physical resistance to arrest was forgotten by the public. In addition, the person was suspected at the time of being on drugs. We can never condone such a beating. Neither, however, should we condone risking other people's lives, as I have explained in my earlier remarks on freedom.

Now, people in that local community say they are frustrated and want to do something? What can be done?

Los Angeles Mayor Bradley blamed the Federal Government for not supplying jobs. **Are they asking for a socialist state where everyone would be poor?** The Congress played politics with every request made by Bush for the relief of the recession.

The Rodney King beating was only one factor precipitating a deep-rooted problem in society vs. social science. Although unintended, Mayor Bradley's speech was a harangue and was a vehement appeal to passion. It contained disputation of a court's decision and was combative in nature.

As a solution, education seems to be the only avenue to explore, but that takes work, and time, and dedication by many people. Even education will not prevent opportunistic looting by any group. Are we dealing with an unprepared culture?

Conclusions on Science and Lateral Thinking

Having **knowledge** is a state of understanding or apprehending with the conscious mind. It is the ability to separate truth from falsehood and be in possession of facts. It means things committed to memory but with an awareness also of their meaning. The work of Science is never finished. If young people are wondering about their future and seeking a place to make a contribution to society, they may look to careers in all of science. By the new millennium at year 2000 there may be as many as a thousand branches of science. Youths with intelligence may make their own opportunity. All they have to do is search the literature, find a statement where it says "it may be assumed that..." -- and stop right there and start digging.

However, make sure to develop lateral thinking. De Bono said, "The greatest authority may be the person with the deepest dry hole." He also quipped, "If the hole is dug in the wrong place, no amount of improvement is going to put it in the right place. But unfortunately, the greatest amount of scientific effort is directed toward the logical development of the same accepted hole." He also joshed, "It is not possible to look in a different direction by looking harder in the same direction." And I have often said in my lectures that all the mathematics, all the physical laws and all the powerful statistical tools mean nothing if you are measuring the wrong thing.

We will perceive many of these individual subjects as a preparation for opening of our minds to the possibilities of the New Renaissance. It should be remembered that science also becomes an art when it is done well.

* * *

One objective of graduate school is to teach the scientific method. Masters and Doctors of Philosophy theses are for this purpose. Often the student will undergo the process and make a worthy contribution to the body of knowledge, but some works only verify older ideas. And we have but few with the scientific discipline among practitioners making continuous contributions from a private practice environment. This is unfortunate because every science needs open-minded scholars with continual experience.

At the request of those around me it was deemed to be of interest to lay people or students to outline a recent research project, showing the processes by which science works as applied to my field.

Please bear with me the following sequence of events and my participation on a scientific basis. The study and its reporting are still in progress.

In July of 1989 four factors prompted me to initiate a large study. First, other scholars in the field disclaimed the merit or reliability of forecasting of the child's face to maturity with our method, and we needed scientific data to satisfy the intellectual community of its accuracy. Second, long-term growth studies to maturity had not been conducted with our methods, and we needed a long-term base for comparison of treated patients. Third, our present computer base data needed reconfirmation and updating after 25 years of application. Fourth, short-term changes during treatment had shown dental and skeletal alteration, and these changes needed to be assessed through to maturity. This, then, constituted the four-fold purpose of the study.

The first step would be to acquire the material and establish the scientific method. Oriented skull X-rays were obtained from eight institutions on 73 growing children who had not experienced any tooth or jaw correction. Ten more were examined who had experienced tooth removal due to severe crowding with no other attention, making 83 children on whom no mechanical treatment had been performed and for whom X-rays were available from young ages to maturity. This would establish a control base. For a treatment comparison the X-rays of 50 children, half boys and half girls, were employed after having received different treatment modalities. In addition, long-range behavior was compared to four other samples of long-term treated patients by four institutions.

In the total of 133 subjects studied, 74 were males and 59 were females.

For the method the original or beginning X-rays were to be carefully traced on acetate film without reference to the final X-ray taken about 10 years later. Copies of the tracings were then sent to a commercial data processing center for digitation and entering into the computer. A second copy was sent to Dr. Thomas Christie of Fairfield, Connecticut, a colleague with an improved method for forecasting without treatment. Each was also forecast by myself, and all forecasts were sent to the computer for data analysis.

Following this, the final X-rays were collected, traced and also submitted to the Rocky Mountain Information Service for data processing.

Composites were constructed by the computer to represent the sample as a single entity. The whole group was broken down into 20 sub groups, as separated by age, sex, type of malocclusion, type of treatment, and source. For statistics, standard computer programs were applied.

The next step was to report and assess gross findings. This was followed by a discussion of the relative significance of the different data, whether it confirmed older theory or whether new considerations were indicated.

The final step was to draw conclusions. The nature of the study required seven papers. The gross findings and background were reported. The base of the skull, the lower jaw, the upper jaw, the teeth, nose, lips and chin were analyzed. Comparisons were made of the forecasts and analysis of long-term treatment changes were reported. Some thirty-eight profound contributions resulted from this study.

This is the value of research.

Technology

Technology refers to technical methods, materials, procedures and their utilization. Science and technology go hand in hand when sciences advance as new materials and processes are discovered.

Computers

One of the most arresting technologic discoveries in my lifetime has been the silicon computer chip in which such vast information can be stored on so little space. It has changed the manner in which society works and lives. Computers really have existed for only some fifty years.

In 1964 Alice Mary Hilton, in looking at methods of production and contrasting them to the earlier Industrial Revolution, labeled the new movement the "Cybercultural Revolution". Before paradigm (a model to simulate) was the buzz word, cybernetics (feedback) was a term generated by the computer industry and adapted for explanations of the mode of the working of the human brain.

The agricultural revolution took place when man was freed from the hoe and harnessed animals for energy. The Industrial Revolution was propelled by the use of fossil fuels such as coal, gas and oil, in what later was referred to as the "smoke stack" economy. The further freeing of utilization of heavy labor was through the use of electricity which resulted in automation through the application of computers directing robots, which journalists have called the "Super Symbolic Society". The nature of many industrial jobs has changed. If a person cannot manage a computer he cannot qualify for many jobs.

The main advantage of computers is their speed in addition to the handling and storing of prodigious amounts of information for later retrieval and association. Small pocket calculators have unfortunately actually taken the place in many young people's minds of their need to learn mathematics. My little daughter played games with the computer before she was even in kindergarten. Such are the conditions already for the New Renaissance.

Statistics are employed routinely at the public level. Odds on the weather are predicted in percentages. Polls taken are expressed by giving the "margin of error" or percentage in a finding. People want information with immediate updates and business reports. Stock market analyses done by computer are requested by the minute.

The New Renaissance will indeed be even more of a "now" generation business-wise. Business management in serving industry or in manufacturing of products, their marketing, advertising, sales, packaging and delivery, are all connected with computers.

Yet if a business is not successful, after keeping records with a pad and pencil, adapting to a computer with the hope of building a more profitable business is nonsense. Computers per se can stifle the mind. They must be kept in perspective!

Energy

As stated, the need for human and animal muscle energy was lessened by wood and coal which made steam energy. Water pressure power was used to turn mills and together with coal was used to turn turbines to make electricity. Nuclear energy was then employed. For travel and transporting goods man went from steam engines to gasoline piston-driven engines and diesel engines and others to jet engines. Rockets carrying their own oxygen and hydrogen were used for space exploration.

The New Renaissance will find a greater use of alcohol for energy, or "fresh fuel" rather than "fossil fuel". Solar energy, wind energy, hot springs, volcanic energy and tidal energy are also available for greater exploration. And they are cleaner!

Ecology

Before we can consider change we need to be aware of the circumstances. People need to be transported. They travel to work and shopping, by car, rail and air, and goods need to be delivered. The use of fuels burns oxygen and is not without contamination of the environment. Smog in big cities threatens human health on a progressive scale with automobiles and trucks and fossil-fueled motors as the greatest offenders.

Traffic accidents account for thousands of deaths per year. But the pollutants caused by traffic pose a greater threat. In Mexico City, a part of North America, the foul air is composed of ozone, carbon monoxide, carbon dioxide, lead, dried sewage, dried particles of fecal matter, smoke, dust, and soot. It is caused mostly by 3.5 million vehicles.

A new industry is being born for reclaiming many of the city rubbish wastes. Plastics that don't decompose are the greatest headache. But the main challenge is from sewage. In America, overloaded sewage systems dump billions of gallons of untreated bacteria-laden effluent into our waterways, particularly after big storms. In New York it's the Hudson River, in Chicago it's Lake Michigan, in Philadelphia it's the Delaware, and in Cleveland it's Lake Erie. Not only does it threaten the lives and livelihood of people but also the habitat of the rivers and lakes. It requires separation of the drainage and sewer systems which alone may require 100 billion dollars for correction.

Earth Day 1992 dealt with the swelling earth population, climatic changes and endangered animal species. Problems exist from the top ozone layer to underground water supply. Air pollution causing acid rain endangers our agriculture and erodes stone buildings. The spread of deserts, resulting from improper land usage, makes drier air as well as greater heat, and endangers many species. This is aggravated by the clearing of rain forests at a rate of 28 million acres per year.

America generates 240 million metric tons of hazardous wastes per year, almost half of which goes into landfills and one fourth of which is dumped into sewers. Another major culprit for contamination is agriculture with chemical fertilizer and pesticides which leach into the soil or drain into rivers, accounting for 64% of the pollutants alone! Mining also accounts for almost 10% of hazardous wastes.

In addition to water contamination, the waters have been overfished to the point where fishing grounds have been severely restricted or closed. Scarcity of fish has caused fish to be one of the most expensive foods. The poor fish at one time had a chance. Now they are located by sonar and netted by computer operations. Larger and more ecological fish farms are needed for greater food production.

The New Renaissance will address these problems, but first they must be recognized by the populace as they are.

Bioengineering

For the New Renaissance in the earth and life sciences, bio-engineering and genetic engineering are both wide open avenues for the future. Several companies are improving products for food. These vary from raising ripe tomatoes for extended shelf life to production of safe bioinsecticides improving food value in vegetables and extraction of the herbal Taxol from plants as a possible cancer cure and inhibitor. Plant genes are being changed to give certain life forms particular commercial traits, or avoid a trait which may lead to cancer.

Physical Science Technology

Probably the most dramatic alteration that has occurred in the field of communication is the cellular telephones that are now pocket size. Satellite dishes make it possible for world communication and fiberoptics makes monstrous telephone traffic possible. Television itself has changed the world. Computers have penetrated almost all aspects of our every-day life, even including the brakes of our automobiles. These applications will continue in the New Renaissance.

Improvements should continue in the construction industry. Light-weight materials and prefabrication techniques have yet to reach their potential. The work of Buckminster Fuller with the triangle and the geodesic dome has yet to reach its full practical application.

Biology and Medicine

Biology is a science dealing with the study of living things. But from a practical standpoint, biology to many people pertains mostly to their health and to their physical welfare. The definition of health, as described by the World Health Organization, is: "Health is not an absence of a disease or an infirmity, but it is a **state of complete physical, mental, and social well being.**

In the New Renaissance, the emphasis of medical care must change. Medicine in the past has dealt mainly with the treatment of disease and the saving of lives. The New Renaissance will have an emphasis on prevention and maintenance and preparation of patients to stay away from doctors rather than totally relying on them. It will focus on the immune system.

Medicine has made great strides in the vaccination and inoculation against diseases, and immense progress in infectious diseases. But while we hear of life extension, the odds of a person living a longer life and a more comfortable life are not much more favorable than with those older people alive in 1910, or about the turn of the century. In other words, the American Century has done little towards the prevention of the degenerative diseases.

In fact, medicine in general has opposed vitamin, mineral, herbal and food supplementation and only recently has accepted the role of exercise as having any preventive potential. The choices of food recommended by the N.I.H. changed vastly in 1992. The new pyramid as suggested by Pritikin 30 years ago put grains at the base, vegetables and fruit above that, dairy and meats less, and oils last. Why did it take the government so long to overcome the bias of the medical profession which may still put fat beef and fat dairy products first and most basic to a proper diet? The public should consider the economic gains and the work of lobbyists in Washington that influence our laws and attitudes about public health.

Heart and cardiovascular diseases kill one-half the population. About 25%, and probably coming to 30%, can expect to die of cancer. Most favorable statistics in cancer deal with early recognition and treatment, but most of the modalities for the curing of cancer are particularly disheartening. Taxol from the yew tree is giving promise in some tumors. A new missile-like agent appears to have been discovered which targets cancer cells. The synthetic material is an enediyne, a compound found in soil bacteria. The natural molecule kills healthy cells, but the synthetic version seeks out and destroys cancer growths.

Realistically, if a person can prevent cardiovascular diseases, including diabetes, along with cancer, the prospect of living to a ripe old age can be improved 75%. At the present time AIDS has changed our culture, as did poliomyelitis before the advent of the vaccines, and smallpox before that.

What confuses me is the trouble that Federal programs in health and the Surgeon General's office go to, to protect America's health, and still do not come down hard on people who smoke. As of 1992, more than 20% of the developed world's population estimated to die will succumb to the effects of smoking. That's 250 million deaths, of which five to six million are in the U.S. Smokers are fewer in the U.S. but still far too many. Non-smokers are bothered immensely by smokers.

The widespread obesity of our population, together with the physical indolence as well as the gluttony, is deplorable. When my friends from other countries visit America, the fat men and women and even children walking our streets are a source of laughing derision.

Yet, it is these same unhealthy people who are crying for socialized medicine to protect them in the event of inevitable sickness ultimately to come from such conditions. To me, these factors are totally inconsistent. In the New Renaissance people will have to have more of an attitude of being "their own doctor". Food selection, exercise, and a positive mental outlook will go along with the New Renaissance. (Please see Chapter Twenty.)

In the New Renaissance it will be accepted that some responsibility will be expected, perhaps even by the government, for the selection of foods. Earlier I mentioned the factors of genetics and environment and in those we included physical factors, nutrition, disease state, psychologic state, ecologic conditions and endocrine or hormonal factors. People are stuck with their genetic or hereditary endowment, but these environmental factors are more or less within the control of the individual. What people put in their mouths depends on their choice and their ability to bend their own elbow to put it there.

Speed

From a biologic standpoint, stress resulting from social factors is an agent of disease. Management of interpersonal conflicts rates as a most significant factor in the maintenance of health. Many pressures are also brought on by the drive for speed. Our whole life is speeded up. We are all in a hurry. Half the crowds in Dodger Stadium in Los Angeles leave in the 7th inning so they can beat the traffic. Everyone in urban communities is in a hurry. There is always pressure from urgency. Everyone talks about personal hygiene. What about mental hygiene?

Dental Technology

As I contemplate technologic developments in my own field of dentistry, they include anesthesia, fiberoptics, TV monitoring, new antibiotics, anti-coagulants, ultra-sound, electro stimulation laser, immuno assays, tomographic and magnetic resonance imaging (MRI), new ceramics and bonding agents, new metallurgy, computer application to diagnosis and planning, the application of the Divine Proportion from mathematics, food supplementation, microbiology and new knowledge regarding nerve and muscle systems. Even restorations of the teeth will be carved by computer-generated robots.

Problems in Some Technologies

Probably the worst thing that has happened biologically is the growth of illicit drug use. Steroids are used by athletes, many of whom are role models for our children.

Much work is needed for the biologic study of the causes of homosexuality. Greater human understanding of those experiencing the same sexual preference must occur.

The whole subject of abortion which crosses biology into the social sciences must be met. The compacting force resulting in problems of overpopulation, health care and child care will ultimately win for women a free choice of abortion. No matter how much abstinence and celibacy is preached, it will not reach the ears of the teenagers who have little fear of pregnancy and contracting venereal diseases or AIDS. Morality is the issue, and safe sex must be weighed against old traditional values of self-restraint and selection.

17

ECONOMICS FOR THE NEW RENAISSANCE

In my innocence I thought that taking a course in economics in 1939 at Indiana University would help me to "economize". Maybe learning something about economics would help me make money or save money for my old age some time in the future. To my surprise it had nothing to do with placing money away for savings, but dealt with major factors in business and commerce.

Economics

There were three lessons I remember from that course. First, economists sought a balance between supply and demand. It was, in other words, a relation between the availability of food, clothing, and products desired for a personal life, and what people could afford or were willing to pay for them.

The second lesson was the charts, the statistics, and the cycles. There was no steady state of supply and demand nor of economic conditions.

The third observation was that economics did not seem to be an exact science. Economists seldom agreed on anything. With such a wide berth, anyone's opinion was just that: a good feel, and one guess seemed as good as another.

Chance, in human relations, is very risky to predict. Vogues and styles may produce either weak or strong trends. Why cycles of good times and bad?

When money becomes involved good friends can become enemies. Psychologically, money (or wealth) means an insurance against starvation and survival, two basic instincts. Some people, already wealthy by conventional standards, are penny-pinchers and misers perhaps intuitively. To them money is a preoccupation and it means power. Good times reflect periods when people buy goods and services without worry of ability to pay. Because businesses and factories are busy, help is needed, so jobs become abundant when growth and expansion occur.

In bad times, people become fearful. They accumulate savings rather than risk consumption of a product without assurance of being able to pay for it in the future. When "times" become horrible, businesses shrink, and help (or a job) is not needed, many enterprises fail and jobs are lost. People then look to someone to blame, and it's usually their government. This is because of a principle:

In good times the government grabs too much of the economic share for itself and gets away with it.

Those in the government, in control during a recession, are therefore automatically blamed when things go wrong.

Credit Use

Since World War II America has become a nation of borrowing. We live on credit. For four decades wealth has not often been measured in savings, but in the amount of credit an individual or a business could obtain from those willing to lend.

Non-payment of debt in the past was a serious offense. Prison terms were levied on those borrowing and not having the ability to repay. Many immigrants to America had developed the habit of paying cash as a result of those laws. Purchases were not made until they had saved up enough to pay in cash. Those people insisted on quality for their money, and something that would last.

Norman's family

In 1955 a family came to me with a boy named Norman, age 11, who had a very deformed problem of the teeth and jaws and a speech impediment. I took the usual diagnostic records, made a growth forecast and a design of the likely result, showed the goal on treatment in a drawing, and presented my plan. I gave them my lowest fee of $750 for the complete job. I was disappointed when the father said he would get back to me later -- maybe. I assumed they had gone elsewhere, but no one asked for the records to be transferred, so I let it pass.

Two years later the mother and father, together with Norman and his sister, appeared in the office with a cloth bag. They poured out its contents on my desk. It was coins and small bills they had saved as a family for Norman to get his teeth straightened. My heart went out. Now he was 13 years of age. I worked very hard from many physical and psychologic aspects with that young lad. I believe I changed his life, and eventually reported his case in the literature.

One day I was told by my nurse that a visitor was asking to see me. I went to the waiting room and there was Norman, now aged 17. He had found a lovely young lady, and he proudly introduced me to his wife. He had become self-sufficient as a garage mechanic and somehow was starting his own service station. Formal schooling for him was over, and he was now ready for his own family. What a joyful experience it was to have helped him on his way to such a successful life! By contrast, many young men still "play around" when double Norman's marrying age. How many want fat jobs with big pay and with little or no preparation? How many are so spoiled by willingness to borrow that they insist on support and identity without saving and earning it?

Causes of Downturns

Many writers in economics have a story to tell. Some boldly proclaim that there exists a cause and effect of the downturns in the economy. For our mutual enlightenment, and if we are not to be frightened by terms not usually understood, let me see if I can, in short order, present a scenario of the present and the future by considering the last 5000 years of the history of mankind.

Nations have wars. Wars are expensive and must be paid for. Agencies in government increase their control over the people. Taxes are raised and more paper money is printed.

This causes inflation. Government is then asked to further control wages and prices due to overprinting of money. All this ultimately results in limiting the choices of the people -- in short, restricting their freedom. This reduces morals, inhibits prosperity, reverses cultures, and the quality of life recedes. Governments are then asked to provide benefits with even greater minimization of choice by the people. Ultimately another war occurs, which puts people back to work to support the armed services. It's an old story.

When freedom of choice goes down, taxes, agencies and national regulation go up. The value of money goes down while there is a rise in disturbances and unrest in the people. Price fixing is attempted, the black market and tax evasion occurs. The masses of people then blame the problem on big business and the rich individuals. They are increasingly taxed. The result is a further contraction of personal rights. As freedoms are more and more restricted, moral standards drop and living standards shrink. As this **"economic disease"** spreads the people cry for even more controls. The rich are further taxed and the means of production of money (capital) is even more reduced. People often submit to a dictatorship by one or a few under many forms. The principle is:

More government power results in less individual freedom.

Anarchy is the final consequence.

Another historical sequence described by Ravi Batra deserves repeating:

The large laboring class takes over by revolution or is suppressed in a reign of terror. The warrior type comes to the rescue. Violence becomes the power and a measure of order is restored. Warriors rule, but are then controlled by intellectuals. Those with knowledge manipulate and pull the strings. Greed in man shows its face. From the ranks of the warriors (generals) and the intellectuals (statesmen or religious leaders), business men emerge. These types start to acquire wealth and accumulate property, and are labeled acquisitors. In the beginning they create jobs and are accepted. But when wealth becomes concentrated into the hands of only a few, the capital is contracted. The means of investment for creation of new business is reduced. New jobs and new industry are curtailed. People rise up against the wealthy, and the cycle is repeated.

Situation 1992

Batra's study of cycles suggests that major downturns occur in America every sixty years. As I wrote this section in February of 1992, the whole world was in a state of contraction like a massive bowel movement. Every country I visited except Chile had the same story. In February of 1992 I was between lectures in Northern Italy and watched it happen. Europe was having economic problems. The British blamed John Major for their local problem, while a few months earlier, when I was in Australia, people there were calling for the jugular vein of Bob Hawke whom they ousted in favor of the comptroller Bob Keating, a member of the same party, with the same policies. Frustration leads to a change without reason.

In America they now wanted the blood of Bush, blaming him for the loss of jobs as if one person, or one group, was the cause of a sixty-year cyclic phenomenon (1930-1990). In his 1992 State of the Union message, Bush again offered ten suggestions for the quick fix. However, the Democratic Congress criticized his effort, and ignored it.

And so economic cycles go, as political advantage is taken by those out of office at the time of a crisis. Periodic progress is marked by retrogression and stagnation. The problem is that no one wants to pay the bill in good times. Many continue to gripe and do not distinguish the good times from the bad times.

Each generation, it seems, cannot learn from the previous one when economic lessons are taught. People become drunk with the intoxication of inflation. Small twenty-year-old homes in Pacific Palisades that sold for $19,000 in the 1950s were fifty years old in the 1980s and sold for $300,000. The quality deteriorated while the price went up by more than a 1500% increase.

Economic Principles

Are there no useful economic principles? There are principles which relate cause and effect like a medical diagnosis, but the farmer is at the mercy of the weather and a drought or a freeze can change his whole economic condition. The objective is to choose the correct medicine to achieve a desired result in the most effective manner. Can economic rules be accepted and applied? (In the past bad times were treated by human or animal sacrifice to the unhappy gods.)

Tony Fisher described six methods of making economic decisions. These were (1) superstition (cults), (2) reaction to wrong assumptions, (3) guesswork and luck, (4) experiments of the past (socialism), (5) the pragmatic method (experience) and -- finally -- the only one that is prudent: (6) the scientific method (determination of cause and effect). This ladder includes the classic results of cultures throughout history such as instincts, dogma, personal emotions and religions.

Good solutions require education so that future generations can benefit from our present. If wrong assumptions are made, society becomes the victim of guessing and superstition. It is necessary to determine, over the long run, what factors produce the most favorable consequences with the least effort and cost to society.

Marx and Smith

Any layman in economics should at least be apprised of the different theories. For instance, Karl Marx (1818-1883), on perceiving the problems of the Industrial Revolution with the sweat shops, made the false assumption that work alone creates wealth. Value in a product was, he claimed, directly related to the amount of labor socially necessary to produce it. There were two errors in this conclusion. The first was related to the effectiveness of the work in production; if the machine does it there may be no actual human labor, and the product should therefore be free. The second error is the desire or craving of the product by a customer. Marketing and selling are performed by appeal to desire and comfort of a customer, not to needs for survival alone.

Adam Smith (1723-1790) was a Scottish philosopher who wrote "The Wealth of Nations" in 1776 at the time of the American Revolution. He had, a century before Marx, advocated the free working of individual enterprise together with free trade among nations. He claimed that consumption, not production, was the purpose of production in the first place. Without consumption where could a product go? Therefore, demand rather than labor was the determinant of the value of anything!

For two hundred years it has been demonstrated that the greater the satisfaction in choices a system yields for the individual the richer he or she and the whole society will be.

The natural desire of people to make things, to transport goods, to exchange one thing for another, enhances a wide spread of wealth. The principle emerged:

Voluntary exchange is the most fundamental source of economic progress!

Wealth in Early Italy

As I sit here now, a few miles from Venice, I am reminded that in past history two port cities on either side of the large peninsula called Italy stood out as economic successes. Venice on the east side and Genoa on the west were harbors where exchange could be made at the underbelly of Europe. Artisans developed fine glassware and many other products, but these two immensely successful locations thrived mostly on exchange!

Free Enterprise

Every man and woman wants to better their condition. The drive for opulence exists at private, public, and national levels and is a powerful force for natural progress. It is plainly obvious to anyone who will take notice that in order to better ourselves and our social situation we need to be **free** to make the best use of our own labor to produce what others may want or (need to) consume! The second principle in the exchange is:

We must be free to spend our income on what we desire from others.

It becomes a mutual affair, a fairness to both parties. If the deal (exchange) does not benefit both parties, one will withdraw and it's no deal — no sale — no profit — no economic progress. Reciprocity means fairness to both sides. How can one country expect in the long run to maintain open markets in other countries when it excludes from its own markets the goods of the other countries?

Another factor, which is hidden, is restriction of free choice by the labor union. Working people tend to view themselves only as workers or producers or investors — not consumers. The people want protection as producers, not as a consumers. Yet everyone exchanges; money (cash, check or credit card) is the medium of exchange. The principle is:

The value each person attaches to his earnings determines its worth.

Something of less value (money) is exchanged for something desired more (food or goods). Another principle is:

The function of government in essence is to provide law and order to permit these exchanges.

Honesty and integrity (quality) form the basis for the outlet of natural effort (labor) so that each person can better his or her condition. Thus, competition increases everyone's wealth.

The purpose of mass production is the satisfaction of the needs of the masses! In America, for some strange reason, big business became an enemy to our government. Yet the business successes were made possible only because they satisfied the needs of the masses! Mass production meant quality goods at less cost.

If it is the duty of government to provide a condition for maximal individual choice, all members of society must be protected equally. Legislators must be fair and realize that not only must voluntary exchange be maximal, but also that **this system must permit a wealth accumulation by many or all of the people who are capable.**

If all of this is true, then the opposite must surely be a true principle as well:

Reduction of choice leads to economic tragedy.

Reduction of choice by over taxation leads to chaos, bewilderment, confusion, anger, frustration and to final disorder, black markets, and deals under the table.

A successful system demands competitive hard work and thrift, as we learn from the Japanese. Competition insures constant development in technology. The competitor finds new ways of making products better, and thus through competition still another principle is derived:

If there is no competition it is impossible to establish better efficiency.

Government-owned monopolies usually become economic disasters and demonstrate why prudent governments have learned to turn over every public service they can to private institutions in competition. Inefficiency in government assures that inflation will soon follow!

No business can long survive without honesty. The savings and loan corporation experiences have proven it. This prompts yet another principle, which is:

Success in the competitive marketplace is related to true caring about others.

Other Theories

What I have tried to do, in a layman's manner, is to reduce economics to some basic principles, at least so I could try to understand them myself. No discussion would be complete without reference to certain other theories in history. Thomas Malthus (1766-1834) was a British cleric who argued for population control. He observed that the population in the eighteenth century was increasing at a faster pace than food supply. He missed the mark entirely — it was not a matter of food shortage, it was a problem of transportation. Observe our population explosion since 1800, and still there is food available with no shortage. It was, rather a question of the ability to buy or otherwise obtain transport. The Malthusian movement caused, unfortunately, a wide movement in societies to control population.

John Maynard Keynes (1883-1946), a British economist, had a profound effect on Franklin D. Roosevelt during the Depression years of the 1930s. He advocated the control of financial crises and unemployment by adjusting **demand** through government control of currency and credit (macroeconomics). Government spending was advocated in dire times, but in good times the accumulated debt was supposed to be paid back. The problem was that the payback never happened.

Joseph Schumpeter (1883-1950) warned that Western capitalism was possibly an evolving form of socialism. Large firms become separated from personal ownership and are considered to be undermining the traditional objectives of wealth accumulation. Large firms must continue to be contributing factors in society.

Currently, Milton Friedman, from the University of Chicago was the foremost exponent of "monetarism". This meant the control of the economy through the **supply of money** by the government. The problem lay with the unwillingness of the legislatures, for political reasons, to apply the necessary controls. The preoccupation of members of Congress is to be elected again and again. They will **not** risk cutting government spending and consequently risk the decreasing of government employment.

New Economics

Thus politics, governments, policies and human exchange are a progressively conflicting mesh. **Capitalism as it has been known in the past probably will be forced to change.** A world economy is at hand. No country can be isolated as principles of the new computer age are applied to the means of production in the generations ahead.

Regardless of the movements in the future, one final fundamental principle will probably remain:

> **Each political system must guarantee the opportunity for free exchange to provide the best chance for economic success of individuals, communities and nations.**

Sooner or later, and probably sooner, I predict either a tax rebellion or massive cheating! People by instinct will continue to be associated in communities and will acquiesce to the rules of that society for survival. The form of those associations will tend to drift toward nationalization and freedom for instant international communication.

Freedom will take on new meaning, and democracy and justice will undergo new interpretation as economics becomes a more pressing aspect of government. Economics will be better related to sociology, anthropology and the psychologic disciplines in the future. Thus the processes of government will continue to be remarkably influenced by economics.

Government means power. And power is either granted or taken away within a society, which may be a monarchy (one ruler), an oligarchy (group rulers) or democracy (majority rule). A modern view, however, distinguishes the types as (1) liberal-type democracies (more than one party), (2) totalitarian states (all power in one party), and (3) autocracies (army — with reliance on force). For economic and progressive systems a presidential and parliamentarian system will be attractive to emerging nations, and will continue where such exists. (See Chapter Eighteen.)

Worth and Wealth

Following the exposure of the C.E.O. (Chief Executive Officer) salaries of the group that accompanied President Bush to Japan in 1992, many of our citizens were disturbed to discover the amounts paid by firms to their top executives who were responsible for the preservation of the automobile company and for the maintenance of profits for the shareholders. This later was found to be only a pittance when compared to the salaries and perks that corporation executives other than motor manufacturers received.

Surveys of laborers indicated they thought a multi-million-dollar salary much too much. Many considered a $100,000 yearly salary to be more in line with their worth. Yet athletes can earn several times that in one season even without a college education; at this time one baseball player is holding out for seven million for one season of eight months — almost one million per month. Rock stars can achieve that almost with a single performance. A near-illiterate fighter can command $12,000,000 for a single bout, which may last only minutes. Consequently, to limit a person whose responsibility it is to oversee a major corporation which hires thousands of people, and must be kept operating at a profit, to a salary in the $100,000 range displays a profound weakness in knowledge or perspective.

When people make more money, they usually buy a better car, buy a better home, or a second home in a resort, send their children to schools at higher tuition, go on longer and more expensive vacations, and make investments which create jobs for someone else. All of these extra endeavors put other people to work all the way up and down the ladder. Also, when people have large incomes they make investments. They are in a better position to take risks, and the higher the risk the greater the expected reward. This is usually the way business deals work, and it has been the route of American economics.

I discussed economics as a primary factor in the choice of political systems. The major mistake made by the Soviet Union was that they tried to control supply without paying proper attention to demand or the consumer. Ability to purchase is generated by a person's wealth. **If there is no wealth there is no demand.** The basic law of economics is still supply and demand. This has been so as long as money has been available as an exchange in any society, and dates back to the time of the Egyptians. Money conveniently takes the place of other goods or products for barter or for exchange. Money is the supply that makes the demand when in the hands of many people. Factories make products which are exchanged for money which in turn is used to pay their employees and their stockholders or owners.

Economics as an Imperative

Successful economics makes a government work or fail. **In the final analysis, perhaps after freedom, economics is the principal issue for a society.** Traditionally, at a scientific level, the subject of economics is manifested in a consideration of government management. This is by control of supply, by control of money, or control of trade barriers to prevent slippage of money out of a system.

But economics to the typical American does not mean all of that complicated theory. It means having a job or a business and being able to pay for a home, clothe, feed and educate a family. It means a decent living standard, a comfortable life style and a satisfactory quality of life.

Evolution of Economics

In olden times in Europe and around the world there was an elite, privileged class which was also the ruling class. Armies were garnered and paid by the king, emperor, or dictator as loyal supporters to keep the ruler in power and control the people in serfdom. In actuality, it was slavery. People were attached to the soil and even sold with it to another elite purchaser. People were therefore subject to the will of the owner. There was essentially no middle class.

In 1992 I lectured for one week in France and was motored from Paris to Clermont-Ferrand. We passed through the Loire area and on each large hill, it seemed, were remnants of an old castle. The Crusaders gathered in Clermont for the movement toward the Middle East. This was a sobering reminder of the days of kings, lords, barons and serfdom.

The beauty of America was that a middle class emerged by opportunity for ownership of land, factories and private businesses. The Civil War was fought by those holding to the principle of freedom for the slaves, who in America were mostly Afro-American but in other parts of the world were white or yellow. Millions of slaves of all colors are still at this time held in many parts of the world.

In early America there were rich landowners, manufacturers and entrepreneurs, bankers and traders who accumulated wealth, but there was no nobility and no caste system by birth. Fortunes were, however, passed on to offspring. The opportunity was always present for ascending the economic scale. The opportunities will still be as great in the New Renaissance, but many claim the golden age for America and other countries is over. This I reject as rubbish!

Capitalism

Capitalism is a social, economic and political system consisting of a distribution of income from the results of free enterprise. The idea was that the best quality of product at the lowest price would be produced by free competition. This was the classical theory of capitalistic economics and worked well for rural cultures.

The survival instinct has been deemed to be a virtue. The belief further was that if a person worked hard and achieved success the state should not interfere. As urbanization occurred, and industry and factories dominated, the theory became modified. People saved money or bought property, taking cash out of the system. Foreign goods entered the system which also took money out of the economy. Counterbalances to such "leakages" were then introduced by the Federal and state governments. Exports were promoted in order to counter imports. Government borrowing (by bonds) was expanded. Huge government spending was intended to create jobs from income taxes expected from successful businesses. In times of depression a deficit was to be permitted. In times of inflation or prosperity, the policy was to be a **budget surplus** in an effort to maintain an overall equilibrium. The problem was that the masses demanded more services, and more regulatory bodies became necessary, so **government spending showed deficits**.

Other Batra Theories

Ravi Batra has described three situations as always parallel. First, inflation precedes depressions; second, excessive printing of money precedes that inflation; third, a move which goes with both is an increased regulation which spends more and more for government agencies. A principle is that:

> **The New Renaissance must be characterized by greater honesty and more deregulation which helps to check inflation.**

All these principles foreshadow the real problem in American economics, and perhaps the world, -- the concentration of wealth in the hands of too few citizens. In 1929, for instance, 1% of the families held 36.5% of the wealth. The cause of the Depression was simple. When the buying public had no money, a demand suffered, prices fell, supply went up and factories laid off help, people couldn't buy products or pay debts, and banks failed. When an economy tightened, savings went up; and as consumption went down the wealthy hoarded more. Another principle is:

> **The New Renaissance must find a way of releasing the concentration of money and property by the wealthy —**

— hence the policy of dynamism I propose later.

Problems

There are fundamentally two major problems facing the economics of the New Renaissance. The first is an old saying, "It takes money to make money." Success breeds success. Capital (money) is needed to start a business, and profits are needed to pay help to operate it and expand it for even more jobs. Studies showed, for example, that America's middle income group ($20,000 to $50,000) increased 44% over the 1980s. Those making $200,000 to 1 million increased income 697%. Those making more than 1 million increased more than 2,000%, but there were relatively few and inflation is not counted, both of which factors makes it sound more than it actually was.

Capital accumulation is inevitable in successful businesses. But, in my opinion, wealth accumulation should not be stolen from the prosperous by taxation. However, if Batra's thesis is true, the very rich should be obliged to release some of their wealth to other job-promoting enterprises. To have it taken away by taxation just for more bureaucratic expenditure by politicians would not correct the job situation, but would put more on welfare. Forced loaning to the government for new projects may be one solution for prevention of job scarcity. However, such programs would require excellent management! -- and a new section in government headed by a person the calibre of a Ross Perot.

The second problem which faces America is that many of those acquiring greatest wealth are investors from outside the United States. This means that America is a microcosm of an economic macrocosm -- a global economy. If a thesis of boom and bust is correct, the frustration will sooner or later be on a global scale, as we are presently witnessing.

Bartlett and Steele

According to a recent study by Ron Barlett and Jim Steele of the Philadelphia Inquirer, there were only 183,000 people in 1989 with incomes of more than $500,000. Ownership of property or a business represents wealth but not cash in the bank or hoarding. Holding stocks in a company represents wealth but that's not hoarded cash. Therefore, the thesis of wealth accumulation must be tempered by actual **accrued money taken out of circulation**. If their statistics are correct, the average yearly income of the top 1% of American families is $560,000. Take away the thousands of athletes and entertainers and the thousands of lawyers and some of the CEOs and I wonder who is left except the oil barons. At any rate, **tax all those by 66% of their income and it would be less than 70 billion for a budget of a trillion dollars**, and that's only 7% of the total budget. Taxing the rich may be excessively self-defeating.

Levels in American Society

Classification of anything has a useful purpose. It enables the mind to sort and handle groups of things with common characteristics as a single condition. The human mind can easily manage three groupings such as large, medium and small. But beyond three divisions, many minds often become confused. Therefore, in societies it has been common for people to refer to the upper, middle, and lower classes.

It's undignified to speak of college professors as being in the lower class simply because of lower income. And further, it's ridiculous to place a multi-million-dollar-per-year athlete with maybe not even a high school diploma in the upper class when he may not even speak English or any other language correctly. Class income levels, therefore, have nothing to do with quality and integrity. Let us henceforth speak of five groups of income levels, not classes:

Level I   The homeless and jobless, by choice or by necessity, pay no taxes; may earn $0 to $6000; may be a school dropout. Poverty levels by latest 1992 estimates are at $12,000 per year.

Level II   Laborers or workers who pay taxes, earn less than $20,000 per year, may own a car and personal effects and can only afford to rent an apartment, condominium or small home; saves a little; may have at least a high school diploma.

Level III   The middle level, considered to earn from $20,000 to $50,000 (actual 1992 mean: $36,000); owns two cars, personal effects, and owns or is buying a typical American home which costs about $100,000; sends two children to college; tries to save for a pension; tries to obtain stable income; often has some college education.

Level IV The upper middle level; earnings from $60,000 to $200,000 per year; may own three cars, and a home in the $500,000 range or up; probably owns income or investment properties; probably but not necessarily has a college degree or advanced degrees.

Level V The upper 1%; mean income of $560,000; may own multi-million-dollar home; usually has an investment counselor and managed portfolio of investments; usually has investment capital with which to risk.

The Psyche of the Wealthy Person

All people are not the same, there are financial gluttons in all cultures. Money to this type of person represents all their drives. They think money is most important in gaining respect from others. Wealth to them is a guarantee of having food and shelter. Wealth to them is a source of power! They can buy anything they need. Competition in big business serves as a stimulation for them. They think that with money they can also pay the best doctors to keep them healthy and pay the best lawyers to keep them out of trouble. They can buy friends. Money, they conceive, is the avenue to all needs.

The lawyers in America often work themselves into a position of being the very rich. Many lawyers also go into politics. There is a sort of code that goes along with being a member of "the bar" (a barrister is a counselor-at-law admitted to plead at the bar). Lawyers generally are those who make the laws. They also have a hard time legislating against themselves. There is always much truth in the many jokes, and reference to sharks, snakes and thieves, in stories referring to lawyers in current society. It is obvious that the future will be influenced by lawyers and their integrity must be purified if we are to move into the next Renaissance.

Reaganomics and the Deficits

There is a tendency to blame the 1990's deep recession on Reaganomics. Studies show that since the late 1970s the upper class increased its wealth by a large percentage, the middle class increased by less, and the poor stayed the same or become poorer. Reagan's policies of lowering taxes moved more money into the economy so most businesses thrived. Opponents criticized deregulation, yet it brought lower fares for the people as airline passengers and made businesses more efficient in the free marketplace and helped reduce inflation. Was it Reaganomics or was it big mergers and money manipulation at high levels that created the greatest wealth?

The Savings and Loan businesses were not started by Reagan but became a popular banking form under both Democratic and Republican administrations decades before. Making capital available for borrowing was a tool to fuel the economy as far back as Truman and was even utilized by Roosevelt. Thus, instead of money trickling down, **many people trickled up to a higher income level**. More became wealthy to the chagrin of the poor and less fortunate. The irony was that taxes were to be lowered, but when the Congress changed the laws somehow my taxes went up.

Because I owned my home and some commercial property, I would be classified among the rich or the upper middle level. I have never, however, considered myself to be anything other than an ordinary citizen of the so-called middle class, having risen from poverty, from the level of a poor farmhand out of the 1930s Depression.

Leave Channels Open

At present I am 72 years of age and enjoy living at Desert Highlands Country Club in Scottsdale, Arizona. I was able to trade for a home here in 1987. I enjoy golf, but even though I live next to the course, I am able to take time for it only about once a month. I enjoy bicycling through the trails. My wife Bunnie also works full time as a nutritional counselor, and we therefore can afford to keep our daughter five-year-old daughter, Anastarr, in a private school. It might be of interest to the reader how I got to where I am financially.

The first key was probably my **education**. When I started a private practice at age 32 years I had spent 13 years in college, graduate school and research. That's in addition to the 13 years of grade school, junior and senior high school. It meant, therefore, 26 years of preparation for what I was to contribute to society. I felt I owed a debt to the public school systems in the states of Indiana and Illinois for my long though arduous opportunity. I have never resented one bit my taxes for education funds to local or state institutions, even though all my children were put through private schools which I considered superior not as a scholastic guarantee but because of individual attention they received.

Thus, when I started I had a confidence in my knowledge and my competence, and a positive attitude about an ultimate success.

The second key to my economic growth was my **ability to borrow money**. It started as a little at a time. In order to borrow, from any banker or any personal lender, a track record was needed. Debts were paid on time! The 1992 check scandal in the House of Representatives Bank is an indictment of that group of the highest caliber. Banks must make money or go under. If an individual friend loans a person money and it isn't paid with interest, the friendship is lost. This condition was expressed by Shakespeare in Polonius' advice to his son, Laertes ("Hamlet"):

POLONIUS: Yet here, Laertes! aboard, aboard, for shame!
The wind sits in the shoulder of your sail,
and you are stay'd for. There; my blessing with thee!
And these few precepts in thy memory
See thou character. Give thy thoughts no tongue,
Nor any unproportion'd thought his act.
Be thou familiar, but by no means vulgar.
Those friends thou hast, and their adoption tried,
Grapple them to thy soul with hoops of steel;
But do not dull thy palm with entertainment
Of each new-hatch'd, unfledged comrade. Beware
Of entrance to a quarrel, but being in,
Bear't that the opposed may beware of thee.
Give every man thy ear, but few thy voice;
Take each man's censure, but reserve thy judgement.
Costly thy habit as thy purse can buy,
But not express'd in fancy; rich, not gaudy;
For the apparel oft proclaims the man,
And they in France of the best rank and station
Are of a most select and generous chief in that.
Neither a borrower nor a lender be;
For loan oft loses both itself and friend,
And borrowing dulls the edge of husbandry.
This above all: to thine own self be true,

And it must follow, as the night the day,
Thou canst not then be false to any man.
Farewell: my blessing season this in thee!

My interpretation follows, a father talking to his son who is going away to college:

POLONIUS: Now listen to me. You are prepared, and you have my blessing. Remember these few things:

Don't speak out of turn, keep your character. Don't yield to negative thoughts.

Be familiar with friends, but don't be vulgar. Those proven friends should be held bonded to you. Therefore, select your friends carefully.

Don't seek to quarrel, but once involved make yourself heard.

Listen to everyone, but talk to but few.

Take criticism and don't react.

Make as good a presentation with your appearance as you can afford, but don't be gaudy, because your clothes often speak for you. People in cities most appreciate good attire.

Don't borrow and don't lend, because you won't be paid back and you will lose a friend, and it will make you a poor manager.

Above all, be true to yourself. Don't mislead yourself, and as surely as night follows day this will make you a genuine, true and respected person.

Good-bye and good luck.

* * *

I started my practice on borrowed money. My father had sold a part of the farm in Kokomo, Indiana, for a housing subdivision and offered to lend me $25,000 at 6% interest with the admonition that the interest was to be kept up monthly and that the principle could be retired as I was able. I paid interest monthly and took 10 years to pay off the loan. In the meantime, I established credit with the Santa Monica Bank in Pacific Palisades, California.

I started out living in an apartment on Sunset Boulevard. We had two children (Robin and Gale) by 1952. I saved to buy a lot for $5000.00 just above the Presbyterian Conference Grounds. After three years, with the help of my father-in-law, Harry Rickert, we built a modern home at the end of Rimmer Avenue overlooking Sunset Boulevard and the ocean. With the lot paid for I borrowed to finance the house. I helped build it, put up retaining walls and landscaping. The whole project was contracted for $35,000 but went to $55,000.

My son Craig arrived in September, 1955, just as we moved into this house. We were three years in getting furniture and fixtures for the inside. It was there I lived for 20 years and raised my first family.

Lesson From Cycles

A lesson of supply and demand and inflation can be gained from my experience there. When in 1977, twenty-two years later, my Rimmer Avenue house sold after a divorce for almost ten times the cost of building it, I was able to roll over that profit into building a house in the Palisades Highlands, together with my wife, Bunnie, in 1978. We decided to move to Scottsdale, Arizona in 1987, selling that house for about double our cost. In effect, therefore, with an initial investment for a lot in 34 years I had, through borrowing, and paying interest and principle, increased its value 200 times. That's the story of real estate, and many, many people have graduated up the economic scale in this manner. Yet real estate can fluctuate immensely, and many have lost. I was lucky. Each time, inflation was the key.

Some have done the same with commercial property. Others have invested in stocks, and others in businesses. But in free enterprise, there is always the chance to lose as well as to win. In several projects during this time I lost! In fact, several friends have ended up with very little and some are bankrupt after a life of effort. Any investment is always a gamble! It's a game of odds. We always hear of the successes and people are envious, often even bitter, without realizing the risks of loss, which no one braggs about.

The Head Start Toward the New Renaissance

A poll reported in May, 1992, indicated that people around the world look to America to lead the way into the next millennium. Forty-two percent of those in the 16 countries polled named the U.S. first and Japan second (20%). Not everyone wants to live in America, even though we are the most admired.

The value of U.S. real estate in 1991 was 8.7 trillion dollars. Of that only 0.5 trillion was in factories and warehouses, and 2.1 trillion in offices and retail stores. This meant a whopping 6.1 trillion, or 70% of American wealth was in residential property.

The goal of most Americans is to own their own living space! A three-bedroom unfurnished apartment in Asia is more than twice the rent as in America, but America is about 10% more costly than South America. Seventy-eight percent (78%) of American married couples own their own homes. Of the single people, only 46% own a home. Only 35% of single parents own their living space. Thus, about two-thirds of single parents, mostly young mothers, must rent and the majority probably need welfare help.

American workers are not lazy. Time on the job is essentially on a par with Japan. But in 6% of households both parents may work and some have more than one job. Seventy-one percent (71%) of males and 67% of females between the ages of 26 to 46 save for retirement. Farm income increased from 20 billion dollars in the early 1980s to 47 billion in 1991. Potatoes remained the most commonly consumed food, but rice raised to 16 pounds per person per year, and bananas to 25 pounds per person in 1991.

Poverty levels **decreased** from 17.3% in 1965 to 13.5% in 1991. During the Carter administration of 1979, inflation hit 13.3% while in the Reagan years it hovered around 4%.

Many with envy and malice complained of the rich getting richer, forgetting that everyone did better in the 1980s except the very poor and the lower level, many of whom pay no tax. But they suffered from inflation and higher costs. Financial help doesn't transform a non-skilled worker into an engineer. The problem is the inability to employ unskilled labor in this, the new information age.

Women still complain of getting a raw deal in business. Only 2.6% (1 in 40) top executives in the "Fortune 500" are women and one in ten executives in the apparel industry are female, as is true of the photographic and publishing industry. In 1980 women only purchased 36% of the new automobiles sold, but in 1991 it was 49% or essentially one half.

Although car sales were reduced from 1990, there were still 10.6 million sold in the U.S. in 1991, with about one-fourth of those from Japanese companies.

While some big businesses have fallen on hard times, their contributions to charity have not slackened, and in 1991 amounted to 6.2 billion. Even the savings and loans in 1991 made their first profits since 1986. While about 1000 banks failed from 1980 to 1990, still 2900 new banks were chartered.

A shift in retail buying patterns emerged in the past 20 years. Outlet stores, Price Clubs, and Home Depot stores with low merchandising and advertising costs have thrived, while Macy's in New York sought bankruptcy protection. People expect to save 30% or more on retail prices in outlet stores and are willing to wait on themselves there and at the gas pump.

Credit cards and plastic money are the growing medium of retail exchange and will increase. Citicorp alone did 31.5 billion in 1990 while the next four banks combined did 33 billion. Buying other than retail seems to continue to focus on home appliances, a new car or a new home. Taxes, together with the problems of product liability, killed the boat and private airplane businesses.

In 1983 there were 6 million personal computers, but by 1990 there were 24 million. Cameras, tape recorders, television and microwaves are so common as to be considered standard in the home.

Our factories still work at only three-fourths capacity. Job security is a problem and lack of guarantee for work shakes confidence in the future. Many people seek to establish personal businesses so at least they can't be fired. I look for personal businesses to increase.

With miniaturization of many household items, the need for raw materials continues to be reduced. This trend will continue as exemplified by hand-held cellular phones. Recycling will increase.

Deregulation brought cheaper air fares to the U.S. Mergers brought efficiency as 40% of the travel is by American, Delta and United Airlines. I am amazed at the high cost of air travel in Europe and other countries. We are spoiled.

When interest rates declined the people and the banking industry were hurt by lower real estate values, and people opted to withdraw savings and put them in the stockmarket. This gave rise to a 35.6% increase in the market in 1991 alone. Japan's investments in the U.S. contributed to inflated real estate prices. Yet Europeans hold five times the stake in American interests that Japan does.

The Oil Industry

The "great American century" was made possible by the abundance of available natural resources. One advantage was the availability of oil throughout the Southwest. Millionaires and billionaires made overnight with the drilling of a gusher are legendary.

During the Carter administration it was obvious that a plot to raise gasoline prices was set in motion because of the gullibility of our Federal government. An oil well in Texas will free flow for some time, and then require a pump. The production may run to around 200 barrels a day, per well, until the well is depleted. In the Middle East, however, as demonstrated by the fires in Kuwait, there is such pressure within the oil field that the oil will be free-flowing at a rate of 10,000 barrels a day, or much more.

The availability of this kind of oil production and over such a wide area made oil cheaper to produce, and with massive oil tankers to transport it back to the United States, in effect made oil exploration in the United States uneconomical. Production still continued in the 1980s and oil reserves were contemplated in the event of a major world catastrophe.

But, the buying of foreign oil drained billions of dollars out of the American economy. Oil is not used exclusively for gasoline, kerosene, diesel or fuel oil, but feeds a whole petro-chemical industry. The heaviest part of a barrel of oil, for instance, is used to make asphalt for the building of roads. It is obvious that much oil will still be needed for American industry in the New Renaissance, despite the increase in fresh fuels such as alcohol.

As explained before, natural petroleum was produced by the natural process of breakdown of vegetation. Oils are found in shale, and oil can be extracted from coal. The question arises, "If vegetation produced hydrocarbons in the prehistoric times, why cannot fuels be produced by natural vegetarian growth processes?" The answer is that they can! Alcohol can be made from almost any plant in the form of methanol and ethanol. The problem with the burning of alcohol in automobile engines is that it has been difficult to vaporize at low temperatures. Gasoline itself in a liquid form does not burn. It is the vapor that burns. As the vapor is mixed with oxygen, which makes things burn, it will ignite and drive an internal combustion engine.

In the New Renaissance there will be a secondary method for processing of fuels which will permit alcohol to be sufficiently vaporized at a low temperature but in addition it will burn much cleaner than the present hydrocarbons, although aldehydes will still exist. The technology for a clean-burning fuel, which will solve much of the smog problem in urban cities all around the world in the New Renaissance, **already exists**. With that available, a new industry will spring up in America and around the world for the growing of certain plants which will have high yields of alcohol. This will make America less and less dependent on Middle Eastern oil and will indeed change world politics. The greater use of this kind of technology, plus the continued discovery of oil reserves on all continents, will render the cost of fuel ever more cheaper, relatively, to the average consumer.

Service Industries

The American public has become more and more demanding of quality goods and also of quality services. The old days of "take it or leave it" are over. Without customer satisfaction and product dependability, a business or a personal service will fail. People want to be taken care of. This means service at the grocery store, at the hairdresser, in the doctor's office and at the automobile center.

Service industries will escalate to a very pressing need in the information age of the New Renaissance. Information regarding a product can be put on a personal computer, and the client or patient can be educated in order to understand the value of a product or the nature of a service.

With the slackening of the manufacturing giants and with automation of machinery replacing a very large work force, many of the jobs created in the United States deal with services. Many people receive on-the-job training, but loyalty to a company has been replaced by the benefits for the dossier that a person can accumulate by working at a particular task or a particular job. A person capable of managing a computer has a distinct advantage over a person who does not. A person with experience in an industry will continue to be at an advantage over one who has had no experience.

Everyone does not have the proclivity to be a professional. Every person cannot be an academic scientist. Therefore, in order to prepare people for the new industries ahead, **vocational schools will need to be more popular**, with just enough Liberal Arts included to round out the thinking capacity of a student. There are literally thousands of kinds of jobs in this category, all of which can aid in bringing about a better quality of life for all in the New American Renaissance.

Five World Economies

John Naisbett claims that today the Pacific-bordering countries are undergoing the fastest period of economic expansion in history, at a rate five times that of countries during the Industrial Revolution. "It's the best thing to happen to the world since America," he says.

By the new millennium, in my experience of world travel, there will be five economies in the world that will need to work together. The **Pacific Rim,** particularly when including

China and perhaps India, becomes an economic target for the world at large. **Europe,** when East Germany and the former Soviet Union are added, becomes another major economic unit. **Africa** is another potential, and with the developments in South Africa that continent as a whole, vastly rich in natural resources, may be an economic unit once the cultural shift and the movement towards nationalism has run its course. The countries going to majority rule are producing poor records, however.

Then there is South America. Brazil has a land mass to rival the whole United States. Brazil has come under close examination by many conservationists as a result of the deforestation that has taken place. It is very rich in minerals and has a remarkable potential. If the same thing could happen in South America that has taken place in the unification of Europe, it could also be a major economic force in the years ahead.

The problems with education, with cultural differences, and with ethno-centricism need, of course, to be managed and overcome. Again, as with many countries in the Pacific Rim, there are millions of people in South America needing goods and services and a better standard of living and quality of life.

America

This leaves the fifth continent -- **North America**. One major economy in America is at hand with our freedom of restrictions and free trade, first with Canada and now with Mexico. Mexico has 80 million people, with about one-fourth of that population in Mexico City itself. Mexico has natural resources, many minerals. And Mexico has oil. Mexico has an extremely large labor force with many capable of being skilled technicians. In many parts of Mexico housing and transportation are inadequate. There is consequently a vast potential need for goods and services right at our doorstep.

For the past thirty years I have lectured to and made friends with many persons in Mexico, and have found them to be a delightful people. They are a far cry from the image of the sleepy peasant sitting asleep under a large sombrero. Many of my friends there (such as Dr. Carlos Guttierrez and Dr. C. Morrett) have candidly joked that it's too bad when the United States purchased or acquired the Southwest that the whole country of Mexico wasn't thrown in.

In the New Renaissance it is my feeling that with the addition of Mexico as a consumer the economy of the United States will develop more than many politicians now imagine. As it is, when Mexican workers are hired for the farming industry and other jobs in the United States, a good bit of their money already goes directly to Mexico. On the basis of world trading in dollars and other currencies it probably is not a significant amount, yet that money slowly and continuously leaks out of our economy.

Even the old Renaissance required some wealth. Someone had to have money to order Michaelangelo's and Leonardo's works, and support the talents of the great composers. Economics is the tail that wags societies at all levels. Status is achieved in some cultures by the number of cows owned or the number of wives supported. Money represents property and makes exchange easy. When governments run well and fairly the **white market** thrives. In poor times, the **black market** and bartering replace free exchange. When taxes get too high, people try to cheat for their survival. It's an old, old story. Let us hope that America's markets will remain white and that all will be able to live in dignity.

18

GOVERNMENTAL CHOICES IN THE TIME TO COME

Although there are speculations, no one is certain that major earth changes will occur. However, the summit meeting on ecology in June of 1992 in Rio de Janeiro, Brazil, forebodes factors that may dominate many decisions in other aspects of society and government in the future.

Social Opportunity, Human Rights, and Morality

Probably the greatest dilemma in the future facing America, and perhaps the world, pertains to human rights. The democratic principle suggests majority rule. One-person one-vote means one adult has as much voice in the affairs of our nation as any other. But further, the democratic idea of a majority can be a very small fraction, with essentially one-half of the population forced to go along with the other half on major, complicated decisions. Clinton was elected with much less than one-half the popular vote.

Under pure democracy there is no protection against many conditions. First, there may be a **protest vote** against one single issue, candidate, or party out of the whole gamut of a total philosophy. The vote for Carter was a protest against Ford's favorable treatment of Nixon. Second, the people may be swayed by the best salesman of an idea and may vote emotionally on issues without being informed or having full familiarity with a total condition. The "confidence-man" or hustler persuades people in cases of fraud. It amuses me how newspapers will publish the questioning of many people who have no knowledge of the issues, but only opinions often based on prejudice. Polls are headlined as major earth-shaking events. Bush, for example, is blamed for the recession which was predicted before he took office and is world wide. Further, it is one which the Congress, not the presidency, is in charge of in the first place.

But in addition, pure democracy leaves people unprotected because the majority may not have the foresight to evaluate the long-term implications of an impulsive decision at the voting booth. It was obvious that people in Chile who voted for communism didn't realize the freedoms they gave away. It took several years of a military oligarchy to break the vice that a communist police state had imposed. With the leaders exiled, there were still those waiting for a chance to return to power, as was seen in Lithuania. The same will be true for Russia and the other states of the former Soviet Union.

Democratism at first seems fair and also appeals to many psyches, particularly the poor who come to demand an equal share of the public largesse. There develops from the one-vote principle the idea also that each citizen owns a like percentage of the nation and that another's private property thus becomes their "right". In addition, strict democratic theory leaves no protection against mobs or anarchy and loss of necessary regulation. Finally, when the economic tide goes out people lose respect for government. Yet, human oppression has a history as old as mankind itself.

The Constitution -- A Republic

It was with this knowledge that our forefathers formed a republic conceived in liberty. They have been criticized by some theorists because most of the organizers were land owners and business people said to be intent on protecting their property and their enterprises. But the idea of a republic historically goes all the way back to Plato, 400 years before the birth of Christ. In order to protect a nation from the mob, who may take control from passion for their own interests, he advocated an electoral system. In order to provide the necessary regulations for a society the founders of our government laid down a constitution with three branches of government for the protection of the people's rights and the preservation of the nation.

One major error in the interpretation of that effort is the declaration that we are all equal. This pertains only to spiritual recognition in the eyes of God. But we are all born physically unequal, with different talents and levels of capability. We are unequal in many ways, otherwise every child would be blessed with straight teeth and congenital deformities would not exist or, further, we would all be geniuses. The Constitution wanted, as much as possible, to guarantee **equal opportunity**. A child born in poverty and from an alcoholic or addicted parent has tremendous problems to overcome.

A further dilemma is that **equal social acceptance is not guaranteed**. Identity, self-worth, self-esteem, self-confidence, pride and many of the social blessings that people seek **must be earned** and cannot be granted by laws. Power and prestige may come from inherited wealth, but some of the saddest and unhappiest people are those given wealth without earning it. Recognition by our fellow man must be deserved.

This was and still will be the American objective in the New Renaissance. When a little black girl was asked during the Watts riots what she thought the burning was all about, she replied, "I guess we would rather be hungry than be a nobody." The issue was social acceptance, not economics when compared to the poor in other countries. Despite that, Johnson poured millions of dollars into the situation he saw as an economic problem alone. It wasn't the answer. The burning was repeated in 1992.

To return yet again to the human drives, all Americans want and deserve identity and recognition as a part of the human race. One group of Americans cannot look down on another group. Each must overcome the ethnocentric inclination which still is a basic human trait. An example of this is the current long drawn-out conflict in Ireland even with one color and one race as a starting point.

Perhaps it's time for the Afro-Americans, the Hispanics and others to take some lessons from the Asiatics. Refugees from the Pacific rim come to America not knowing the language. Parents in a short time set up successful businesses. They spend time as a family helping their children. Their children soon learn English and lead public school classes scholastically. Maybe it's time our American children of all races quit belly-aching and get to work to educate and prepare themselves for our New Renaissance. When I went to college I took on five part-time jobs at one time to make ends meet. Some earned me only a few cents.

A student is often heard to express the idea that he or she is trying to find out "who I am". Unfortunately, identity cannot be gained until a person does something to earn it. Identity cannot be found -- it is developed from successes within the individual. Young people and even those older should stop complaining and prepare themselves. Most have a wealth of talents to draw from. Even a cleaning lady can find joy and satisfaction in doing the job well. They should analyze and collect their virtues and stop comparing themselves to others and resenting those already successful.

One major achievement of Soviet communism, which led to its downfall, was that it educated its people. As people became educated and learned abut successes in other countries, they sought freedom from domination and sought individual opportunity. The demise of communism was aided by television exposure to the world outside the Iron Curtain. People could no longer be lied to about the superiority of their own condition. They lost trust and faith in their leaders.

Freedom, Virtue and Truth

What is freedom anyhow? To be absolutely free simply means without social restraints of any kind. Some people may think that freedom means abandonment of all regulation. They would run red lights or take liberties that risk themselves and others. The meaning of freedom in America is the right to vote, the right to bear arms in defense of the country. It means freedom of speech and freedom to worship as one pleases. It also means the right to live wherever one chooses or can afford. It means freedom to choose friends. It finally means freedom to choose a career and an avocation, or not to work at all if some means of support can be found. Freedom is an ideal.

But also it should be understood what freedom is not. Maybe our populace should take a second look at the Ten Commandments or canons offered by faiths other than Christianity or Judaism. All have a sort of code or rules. Freedom does not mean freedom to steal, maim or destroy another's property, be it personal or business. Freedom does not mean the right to murder. Freedom does not mean the right to cheat in business or any other social enterprise. Freedom does not give the right to lie and bear false witness. The cause of freedom gives no license to put another's life at risk or endanger the welfare and freedom of a neighbor.

In absolute freedom there would be a society of survival of the fittest. The law of the jungle would prevail. The weak and the old, and perhaps the honest, would have no protection. A functional society requires regulations. The principle obtains:

The more dishonesty and irresponsibility in the society, the greater the need for regulation.

In primitive cultures the regulation was performed by a chieftain. The rabbi was the manager of the Hebrew clan. The old European kings and Asiatic emperors maintained a regulatory power over their subjects, which in turn bred "Robin Hoods" when they were too oppressive for too long. The rise and fall of Rome was related to the sagacity of its emperors. The function of any regulatory body should be to check, control and be fair, but above all be honest.

The Progressive Decadence with "Payola"

A problem exists in many societies by way of "payola" to those in positions of control.

People in authority in regulatory offices are in a position to be paid off and will hold out a hand even for the privilege of providing honest and normal regulatory situations. They are bought off under the table for favors requested which are against their own laws. Certain countries are well known for the political graft associated with their regulatory commissions. America also has experienced such shenanigans, but in some countries it seems to be an accepted standard, or at least seems a hopeless situation to their populace.

These kinds of dealings, however, go all the way to the top levels of government. They may deal with huge government contracts and immense public programs.

If America is to lead the world in the New Renaissance, then **honesty, morality and virtue** must be the hallmark of any official of any kind! "Throw the rascals out!" became a 1992 clamour. Otherwise, like the person who steals money from his company to gamble, always with the idea of paying it back after a big win, the graft continues to go deeper and deeper. I remember in 1949 a friend paid a Chicago policeman money for a traffic violation to keep it off his insurance record. I often wonder why politicians spend millions to become elected to government offices that pay only a few thousand! Is it for power, and does that power result in economic payola?

The New American Renaissance can serve to lead the world in morality if enough citizens pull together and expose such dishonest fraud by individuals and severely punish them. **It's our system that needs protection.** Maybe it should start with an examination of the honesty and fairness of lawyers.

Taxation

One major issue with morality is taxation. The definition of morality is related to honesty and justice. How much taxation is fair? Who is to judge? Shall a hard worker be progressively penalized for his knowledge, energy, enterprise and work ethic? In the final analysis, the decision for taxing rests with the regulating bodies of a society. At the Federal level it is totally in the hands of the Congress. In addition, the individual states impose taxes and finally the local authorities collect taxes.

It would seem that, as an agency, the U.S. Congress is masterminded by those who continue to determine how they can lift more money out of the pockets of the people. The appeal to give it to the poor and needy is virtuous. I fully agree that the truly poor and homeless should receive help. But when programs run through the Federal, state and local administrators, plus the inevitable graft by those along the way even down to selection of the correct recipients, a surprisingly small percentage goes into the intended needy hands. Even when it gets there, how is it monitored? Government aid becomes a gift, and who wants to criticize someone's management of a gift? Welfare support should not become a way of life!

Prevarication

It has been shown through scientific studies that the human will instinctively lie. Children will tell "tall tales" and it doesn't stop when they grow up. People will invent excuses, and it is said that we now suffer from "the age of the alibi". People try to avoid guilt and fabricate excuses. In a recent radio talk show the speaker estimated that two out of three college students cheat in their schooling.

The purpose of a government is to preserve order and provide public services. The purpose of religion or any other spiritual organization is to **teach moral conduct and glorify individual virtue and honesty**. However, breaking the law is a challenge to some people and becomes exciting. Honest and forthright citizens are the ones damaged.

American society needs to more mightily protect the virtuous and not justify the criminal. Courts have degraded to the place where the person robbed or assaulted is less protected than the suspect who is often the guilty party and who hires a clever lawyer. Our courts often do not represent the principle of justice, but rather demonstrate which lawyer is the most capable of swaying a jury.

In the final analysis, a principle evolves:

> **If a free society is to exist, it must be accompanied by the acceptance of responsibility by its citizens for their own individual conduct.**

Thus, for the New Renaissance one of the fundamental objectives of our families, schools, Sunday schools, churches, synagogues, mosques and ashrams should be to teach the virtue of honesty, trust and moral attitudes for our coming generation. **If that is not present nothing else will count anyway.**

Parenthetically, the future of American justice will be directly related to the **individual philosophies** of the future citizens. If everyone in our society always seeks to work some angle for advantage, then our leadership role will fail, and we will die a dishonored country.

Choices of Government and Politics

One of the first recorded attempts at classification of government was made by Aristotle. At that level of knowledge (circa 350 B.C.), he divided the regulation of society into three processes: monarchy, oligarchy and democracy. He referred to each as starting with idealism, with the possibility of degenerating into tyranny or oppression by either an elite group or a mob. His teacher, Plato, had in turn honored his own teacher, Socrates, in the "Republic" in which he formulated a conception of the perfect state.

"Politics" has become distorted in the modern world. Historically, Durant and other philosophers have classified politics as a branch of philosophy, together with logic, ethics, esthetics and metaphysics. Politics in their view was the attempt at **an ideal system for creating good will and better friendship**. A good politician, therefore, will often say things that the majority of people want to hear. Some politicians, however, weak in personal integrity, will wait for polls or straw votes and then declare the most popular position. They will then proudly announce themselves as the champion of views of the highest number, run ahead of the group, and in effect say, "See, here I am, your leader." In this way they try to make the people have confidence in their intelligence for thinking like the majority at that one point in time. This tends to be a characteristic of many of the current politicians.

The statesman, by contrast, thoroughly examines all the problems and on that basis makes personal wise decisions. By so doing, a statesman declares a position on his principles. He then says, "I have come to this conclusion and if you agree you may support me." This counterbalances the pirouette nature of those politicians who shift with the wind in an attempt to remain popular and stay in office.

Maybe trying to be more statesman-minded is the reason I personally have antagonized so many in my own profession. My research often resulted in a challenge to popular beliefs. I had to make the decision early in my career either to try to be popular or to stand firm and defend the truth as I found it and interpreted it. Often the things I said made others uncomfortable and even provoked their xenophobia.

In the New Renaissance it is my hope that the younger people will be statesmen and true leaders.

The Sovereign State

A sovereign state is a prescribed territory with an organized people submitting to a common rule and regulation. A government's purpose is to regulate such a formed society with laws. A community needs services such as police protection, schooling for children, electric power service, street and highway systems, traffic control, sewage disposal, court systems for the administering of justice, and agencies for regulation. The collective society usually will contribute also to a national armed force protection of its boundaries and also to the regulation of trade and traffic with other sovereign countries.

Traditionally in the U.S. the Federal government has had a President and several different divisions headed by Secretaries who report directly to the President. With the working of the Congress, laws are enacted for the regulation of the country as all branches try to operate within the restrictions of the constitution. The Supreme Court interprets the law.

Government's Role

Through my friend Dr. Robert Sears in Washington, D.C., Colonel Oliver North agreed to discuss, in one of my courses, the current professional and public problems in our society. I introduced him with the question, "What should the government today do for the people?" His quick answer was, "As little as possible." With that he launched into a history of societies and the Constitution of the United States. We were spellbound for two hours.

In America there continues to be a major debate on the role of the Federal as well as the state government. I heard the major arguments presented in 1992 by William Buckley in his "Firing Line" program. There is some confusion with the word "liberal" because its original meaning was to liberate or obtain freedom, which has now become a dichotomy. The word, I suppose, now refers more properly to a liberal spending of funds for social programs. The liberal cause, as explained by writer James Michener in a recent magazine article, is sympathetic to the poor, to public projects rather than private.

It is my conclusion, right or wrong, that many Americans really do not understand what they stand for or even what the political parties running our government stand for. From the writing of this personal narrative the reader may have reached the impression that I am a red-hot Republican and an arch conservative. I would, however, classify myself as a progressive conservative, as I think many others are -- even many who are registered Democrats.

It has become clear that about one-third of the American public are quite solidly conservative. Even against Roosevelt, Landon drew about 35% of the vote. Bush garnered only the same general number in his election loss when running against Clinton and Perot. Possibly if Reagan had not at one time been a Democrat he would not have swung as many votes. The Democratic base is much stronger because they identify with the common folk and the poor, while the Republicans are claimed to be a party of the rich. That's odd because at the same time the rich are termed the top 1% of the country; where does that leave the other solid 32%?

I also quite seriously doubt that the top 1% in income are all Republicans. I know several whom I would assess to be one-percenters who are staunch Democrats. There must be more to the difference between the parties, therefore, than income levels. Perhaps some simple clarification can be made of the differences in ideology.

Liberal Thought

Certain liberal thinkers consider that they have a license on ideals for the "revival" of our country which are not shared by a "conservative ruling party". It's also strange to me that a Republican president opposed by a dominating Democratic Congress, during most of the past thirty years, would be considered a "ruler".

Consequently, let me see if I can precipitate the differences in ideology in a simple manner for those not focused in current politics to understand, and for my children's consideration.

Two writers state the case succinctly for the liberal cause. One is Micky Kaus, a lawyer in Washington, in his book "The End of Equality", published in 1992. The other is the well-known author James Michener who at age 84 declared his views in the previously-mentioned article, "We Can Create A Decent Society" (Parade Magazine, November 24, 1991).

I find it difficult to object to Michener's views. Our differences would be in the method to be employed most effectively and permanently for the solution. If he is a humanist, so am I. If "humanist" means having a respect for the nature, dignity, interests and ideals of man, then I am with him. He describes himself as a knee-jerk liberal when he sees a penniless widow with children to feed, or funds cut off from libraries, or education budgets reduced, lunches for children curtailed, health services denied to the poor, and particularly when the state of Texas produced two teachers for calculus and 500 football coaches. Yes, I'm with him. My knee jerks too. Does that mean I'm a liberal? This whole book is aimed at encouraging a better quality of life.

Kaus asks what liberals really want. More than anything else, egalitarianism seems to be the common goal. This would suggest that each person have equal rights -- politically, socially and economically. However, in order to fulfill that we would have to dump our whole capitalistic system -- whose very inequality is what makes it succeed. People work hard, take risks and deny themselves for the opportunity to either get rich or go broke. He asks several fundamental questions which liberals had failed to answer: what should society be that it isn't?, what compassion is necessary?, what is fair? and what is meant by affirmative government? The difficult question is, do liberals really want "money equality" by the forced lowering of the standards of the upper levels through taxation or several other scenarios? Kaus stresses that what they really desire is a more "civic equality" if they truly examine all the alternatives. It struck a note in me when he analyzed that social inequality is at the core of liberal discontent. Throughout my narrative I have stressed the importance of identity. Isn't that it?

When the rich (or anyone, for that matter) flaunt their possessions, act smug, or act superior in obscene and repulsive manner, then we have a problem with society! When less fortunate people are made to feel inferior they rightly have a cause to develop hostility.

In my personal opinion, the real measure of greatness in a person is not the achievement of great notoriety or accumulation of wealth, but rather in the manner in which a man or woman respects the rest of mankind.

Conservative Thought

On the other side are the conservatives. Very simply, they hold that the greater the regulation the less the individual freedom. The greater the regulation the greater the need for taxes to administer and monitor the regulating agencies and the less production for its people. The more centralized the power within the Federal jurisdiction, the more immense the government and the more difficult and costly it becomes to manage. The conservative view is: the less the Federal government can interfere, the better for the country.

The irony in America is that both the conservative and the liberal-minded are members of the two major political parties, Republican and Democratic, but the Democratic Party is generally more "liberal". The South is Democratic, but Southern members of Congress traditionally have tended to be conservative, and may vote on issues with Northern conservative Republicans. As Members of Congress must continue to appease their constituents, the liberal factions tend **to drift more and more to socialism which, as history shows, tends to stifle economic progress in a country**.

Thus, several issues are open to debate constantly as the political parties continue to maneuver for positions of advantage for their ideologies and seek methods for their own propagation and for enjoying the spoils of the system.

Our Republic

So successful has been our republic idea that many Americans want to share the system. But our Constitution and form of government have been copied by other countries less successfully. When I first went on a lecture tour to South America in 1961 I visited Brazilia, the new capital of Brazil. It had been built in the jungle miles inland and was a new city. Brazil was the United States of South America, with the executive, legislative, and judicial divisions represented by three magnificent, large, new and modern buildings. The country, however, was failing. Inflation was rampant. It declined to an anarchy within three years, which led in turn to a take-over by the army followed by military control of the country. They did not make our form of government work, at least not at that time.

Many are heard to say that our republic system is outmoded and not in step with modern times. True, our population is larger, technology is advanced, and communication is immediate. But there is no difference whatsoever in problems in human relationships. In the final analysis, that is what it's all about.

Frustration Regarding Representation

No matter which party leader is in the White House, the pattern of government goes on. Most Americans forget that the greatest power by far resides not in the President but in the Congress. Since 1930, roughly 60 years, the Congress has been controlled by Democrats for 50 of those years, or 85% of the time. This is perhaps because the laboring person considers the Democratic party more favorable to his or her interests and also minority groups feel they can go farther with their interests in that party. When they combine they form a majority. The Democrats, therefore, fill significantly more seats in both Federal and state congresses.

The people try. Frustrated local voters elect a new, energetic person and send him or her to the Congress in Washington. Full of ambition, they instill new vitality into the process, but they are assigned to committees and must rely on the entrenched and immovable civil service bureaucrats who, according to columnist Jack Anderson, really run the machine. Everyone must represent the people who elected them while still promoting their own personal ambitions.

The shock is that one Congressman knows so little about the details of the transactions of other committees. The new Congressman or Congresswoman will attempt to write new bills and to **do things for the people, which ends up costing the taxpayer more**. Any attempt to do away with agencies even after they have fulfilled their purpose is several times more difficult than creating them. Some say it is impossible. It is because jobs would be lost and power would be taken away. The frustrations continue as the tentacles grow.

Mutual deals are cut again and again, and often sneaky moves are made by tacking things onto major bills so they are hidden.

The people back home are even more perplexed. They see taxes increase while their quality of life seems to be compressed. Many look out of the corner of their eye and grow envious and jealous of others more successful than they. Soak the rich! the poor say. And so they do. But the rich grow relatively richer because the material costs increase (due to inflation), escalating labor costs, and strikes all occur due to higher living expenses. The cycle continues. Increases in production expenses cause large companies to take their factories to foreign countries where labor is cheaper (and more dedicated), where taxes are cheaper and where the governments are more cooperative with the problems of management.

America, wake up! What would you as an individual do if you were responsible for a business that had to survive in the present world economy?

In the New Renaissance demand for good quality of work will take precedence over expediency as our young people will see the difference.

Wisdom of Voters

Wisdom is defined as the power of judging rightly or following the soundest course of action. Wisdom is based on experience, knowledge and understanding.

To be wise, knowledge is first required. The question is, how can a person have knowledge without the experience? How can the young be informed if they can't read, or refuse to read and study? They must rely on the news commentator to do their thinking. The thoughtless mind may go something as follows: "The easy way for me is to vote for the person or government who holds the greatest promise for having the government take care of me! This means an inevitable yielding of control of my life, it means the surrender of my own personal choice, and therefore of my freedom. But I don't care. I need these things now! I'll let the future take care of itself!"

Some may argue over the foregoing scenario, but listen to the rhetoric of the politicians and the news media (who are themselves in the upper 1% of income) and prove it wrong.

Big Government or Small

What is a government? What is meant by "Big Government"? What kind of governments do Americans have as an option?

We could start by looking at local government and go up, or start from Federal and go down.

The first function of all governments at the highest level is to protect a sovereign nation. In America our President is Commander-in-Chief of our armed services. It would therefore seem proper that our Commander-in-Chief be somewhat based in military orientation if he is to command rather than blunder.

The second major role of a government is to provide a platform for laws of regulation of society. The argument then ensues as to what needs to be regulated. A free society is not really free. People in a free society must assume responsibility. When in their childishness they cannot be trusted they must be regulated, for the protection of the rest of society. If they do not voluntarily accept the moral responsibility for their own conduct they must be forced by law. This is where the great expense comes.

* * *

Politicians have an unquenchable thirst for recognition. They are embarrassed beyond tolerance when proven wrong. This is why they struggle so for radio or television time, or will actively try to keep their name in print. The public must be aware of this fundamental type taking the political avenue to fame and often, sadly, seeking fortune from the spoils.

All too many politicians are more interested in recognition than in being the honest servant for the public. "Recognition" voters would probably be influenced by the most popular or socially accepted person as a candidate. Their voting pattern probably has no order or party loyalty and they may vote for economic reasons alone.

Big Government and Disrespect

In my adult life experience it seems to me that the moral fiber of America suffered its greatest setback under the leadership of Lyndon Baines Johnson. In retrospect, I felt he was perhaps the most ruthless leader we ever had, and even when he was Vice-President we witnessed the Billy Sol Estes matter and other shady operations. His questionable character in the highest rank of office, together with the pitiful nature of the Vietnamese War leadership, did much to produce disrespect for politicians and for authority. The escapades of Johnson reported by some authors make Watergate look like child's play. Other situations in the Congress led to not only disrespect but humiliation and disgust.

Many people also hated Reagan, but at least he turned around the attitude of American people toward public servants in spite of still having to deal with the Cold War. Probably more than any other single President he contributed to the Soviet empire's demise. His eight years were tarnished by the Iran-Contra conflict which was solely an effort to obtain release of our precious American lives held in hostage. The first years of Bush did much to restore respect for the Presidency, and the quick victory in Iraq reestablished in a sweeping stroke the hegemony of America.

But as the election of 1992 approached, a loss of respect for our public servants again was sensed, particularly in the Congress. Disrespect started with the obvious opportunists in the Oliver North and Poindexter hearings. We aired our dirty linen, now by way of international television, before the whole world. Attitudes regarding this situation closely followed political party lines.

When the Kennedy brothers practiced their polygamy, almost flaunting it publicly, no one dared cry out. But sooner or later opportunistic journalists, looking for a righteous cause, took a new attitude, and Gary Hart and Donna Rice became the brunt of barroom jokes. The supermarket tabloids make their success on inter-personal conflicts and if none exist they are invented.

I doubt that there is significant difference between men in Congress on either side of the aisle. Maybe extra-marital affairs go along with going to Washington. But Republican and Democrat alike are now monitored, not only for their political attitudes but for their bedroom behavior as well. It makes great copy.

When the issues of sexual harassment arose in the Thomas case, involving the Supreme Court, literally the very highest level in our government, when the details of the excursion in the Kennedy-Smith rape trial were aired on television, and when the Clinton 12-year experience with a female entertainer was related — when all these things happen, I see again a slip in respect. It is a loss of respect for our Congressmen, our mayors, our governors, our bureaucrats and our businessmen which seem to be a part of that nature and which I don't think will change very rapidly, but will just become more discreet.

With 100 reporters in the room, any Congressman or President must constantly remain on vigil against any remark that could be interpreted in a way to make it offensive for someone. Due to our insistence on free speech and the advantage of a scoop for the aggressive reporter, this is a way of life that I doubt will change unless freedom in America changes itself, and this I would resist with all of my energy.

Relabeling and Formation of Parties

Maybe we are headed in the future toward possibly a relabeling of our political parties, or adding new ones. In fact, there is not a sharp difference or often as much choice between the parties as would appear. The reason for this is that most of the government is actually run by civil service people, and the public demand more and more services. The government is so tremendously large that one part is totally out of contact with another. The Congressmen seem to throw around a million dollars as if it were a single dollar.

When Bush in a State of the Union address suggested that some 240 agencies be dropped, it did nothing but bring frowns to the faces of the Democrats. In the future, it would seem to me that the parties must more closely represent a true separation of ideologies and be strong enough to break the common trend.

In the beginning there were in both parties conservative and liberal wings which kept both parties from being too radical. Today, the Democratic Party is caught between an appeal to the poor and an out-and-out socialistic doctrine. We already have Social Security which by the year 2000 is projected to be bankrupt. As our population ages there will be more projected recipients than there will be contributors. As inflation ensues, it will ultimately be proven to be pitifully inadequate.

The next drive by socialists will be towards socialized medicine. Liberalization in the courts regarding damages against physicians is driving many honest practitioners out of the profession. Opportunistic lawyers also dominate politics and therefore the preservation of that system for lawyers' fees is practically guaranteed. In 1992 there were 133,000 lawyers in California. It is the lawyers who make the laws, and it is the lawyers who protect the lawyers. That will continue.

Lawyers have indeed, together with other folk heroes, lost respect.

19

AMERICA'S SIX MAJOR CHALLENGES

The future can be directed only when enough force and influences are applied. This should be appreciated by all Americans.

Six Challenges
The problems ahead for a New Renaissance in the final analysis concern primarily the most appropriate role of the Federal and state governments and secondarily our relationship to other countries. The Federal government holds the most power. But with its Congressional members based in Washington, it may be too far removed from the people. Governors of states and mayors of large cities have a better sense of reality because they are closer to the people and their problems.

Our Federal power has continued to increase, the bureaus expanding as if malignant. The decisions for the New Renaissance rest, in my opinion, on at least six main challenges, in the following hierarchy:

Challenge 1   Preservation of Capitalism, Freedom and Free Enterprise
Challenge 2   Size and Power for Taxation by Governments
Challenge 3   Morality and Solutions by the People - Sexual Revolution, Abortion, and Legal Systems
Challenge 4   Drug Abuse, Crime, Violence and Prisons
Challenge 5   Federal Deficit, Social Security, Health Care and Welfare
Challenge 6   Protection of Resources

* * *

Challenge 1: Preservation of Capitalism, Freedom and Free Enterprise
In order to preserve the system of free enterprise, capitalism and freedom, Americans must consider and react to the best forms of regulation of society. The principle is,

Where the America of the future will stand will be related to how much freedom will be the final demand by the people.

I discussed a process of decision-making earlier in Chapter Sixteen. Perhaps the interested person could apply it here to make their choices of government and their voting for the future. I list the problems in writing. The next step is to consider the intuitive feelings and the alternatives, and then to ponder decisions.

Ten Choices

There are essentially ten steps or choices on the ladder to individual freedom. One, as we shall describe later, is Dynamism. It is my own invention, based on history, but others have no doubt considered it as well. These are listed in the hierarchy from the least to the highest degree of freedom for the individual, and translated to "isms":

1. Monarchism
2. Communism
3. Fascism
4. Islamism
5. Oligarchism
6. Socialism
7. Democratism
8. Republicanism
9. Dynamism
10. Anarchism and Cooperatism

Monarchism

Probably the least amount of freedom was found in ancient serfdom where people were subjugated by a king or an emperor. Almost all the efforts of a society of that kind were directed toward the welfare of the king and his family, and indeed in some instances the tyrant would proclaim himself to be a god, to be worshipped. The beheading of the wives of King Henry VIII in England indicates the absoluteness of such tyranny. The common person was not educated and, in fact, was enslaved in such a condition. There were, however, sometimes benevolent kings.

Communism

Communism not only steals all of the methods of production, but steals individual properties. The records of the individual spying on a neighbor, exposed after the fall of the Soviet Union, is almost unbelievably sickening. Adults were like little children in a family when one happened to get a fuller glass of milk than the next.

Communism brings out absolutely the worst in human nature. It is the ultimate example of greediness in man, while claiming to eradicate the greediness of the industrial lord. Any communist regime can only survive under the threat of violence while masking itself under the ideology of a benevolent and fair and absolutely egalitarian state.

The irony of communism is that it espouses freedom. But in order for it to continue all efforts must be made by the people to support the state. Its survival depends on a fundamental weakness in human nature, jealousy. Underlying this is the idea that no person, despite the will to work hard and create for a society, is entitled to more than a specific share of return. Communism is successful only as an absolute police state when every person is against or will report every other person who seeks an advantage or expresses discontent. While communists talk of liberation, millions upon millions have been sacrificed under the veil of humanitarianism and an absolute, ugly form of egalitarianism. Complete control, government ownership of literally everything, and centralized manifestos by one central party are essentially as tyrannical as a single monarch.

Communism's biggest error in the information and cybercultural age lies in the idea that the worth of goods is directly related to the amount of labor used in their production. Were that the case, a product constructed with computerization and robot manufacturing should be dirt cheap while one inferior, for the same purpose, made manually would cost much more. In a free market place, the manual producer of goods is soon out of business. Therefore, a program for "economic determinism" in modern society is grossly in error with the new technology. The dictatorship of the proletariat (working class) is to be the means of an authoritarian control.

Foods, goods, supply (matter) are said to exist independent of thought. All develop an opposition which becomes a proclaimed prime factor in the theory (dialectical materialism).

Fascism
Fascism claims, "We don't want to own your property, but we want absolute control of it. We want to tax you with impunity, and you must be a part of our system or else you will be eliminated." Because of its nature, Fascism requires a Hitler or a Mussolini, and in current times perhaps a Saddam Hussein, as a dictator. Fascism emerged from the economic and political crisis after World War I. It was based on the creation of scapegoats such as Jews, foreigners, or blacks. Today many people (mostly demagogues) use the Americans as a scapegoat to rally their people in hatred.

But fascism for the most part does not take over ownership of the productive means of a society. It demands the ability to take all profits and to control all the branches of industry. Fascism with its police forces in the night becomes absolute in power. They take away wealth, they control by violence or the threat thereof, and they gain control of the intellectuals.

Islamism
Islamism is a type of government combining state and religion. Islam, one of the world's five great religions, is significant in the Middle East, the Arab world, in Pakistan, Indonesia and Malaysia and in parts of Africa. It has had a resurgence since World War II and is often fanatically opposed to the ideas of the West. It is a mixture of statism, socialism, and religious dogma, holding its people in allegiance to rather strict codes. Freedom is limited, as opposition to its doctrines evokes extensive discipline.

Oligarchism
The old kings were monarchs who were in effect dictators. Oligarchies, or rule by small groups or committees, could also be given such broad powers and have been typical of some South American countries.

There is a pattern that usually unfolds, almost as a revolutionary cyclic process, when a country meets with poor times, and people become discontented. This is followed by anarchy, disobedience and destruction; looting and killing result. Members of the army are sworn to support the generals who activate the army in order to put down the revolt. Curfews are established, general meetings of people are curtailed, and the generals come to power and establish regulations. If it is a single general, often a dictator will emerge as did Castro in Cuba. But if it is done by committee, several generals or self-appointed leaders take power. These are usually the leaders of a political party or an idea.

The oligarchy is thereby established, such as those seen in Brazil, Argentina, Chile and many other countries throughout history. A certain degree of freedom may be granted, but all opposition is quietly crushed. Oligarchism continues with some success in a country and some freedom of enterprise is successful. Perhaps the exception is the long-lasting right of assembly. Oligarchism, however, is usually not a permanent form of rule.

Socialism

Socialism is a creeper. Socialism steals from the citizen the private ownership of all sources of industry. In socialistic states it is the government that owns the power companies, it is the government that owns automobile manufacturing, it is the government that owns the railways which are taken from private ownership. Businesses are no longer taxed because they are owned by the government in the first place. Therefore, socialistic systems inevitably **have to tax the individual heavily** for the ordinary operations of the government.

Worst of all, any business administered by the government historically and characteristically and almost uniformly is very inefficient because of irresponsibility and unaccountability. Thus, the bigger the government the more regulatory bodies it contains, the more completely entrenched it becomes, the more inefficient it becomes, and the more expensive it becomes.

Socialism has as its goal egalitarianism (or equalitarianism). It is sometimes confused with communism. Communism is a dictatorship of the proletariat. Socialism, which is sometimes confused also with laborism, ideologically consists of government ownership of the means of production and the mechanisms of care for the social welfare. Under Socialism, everyone works for the government. Ultimately there is no incentive to excel or surpass anyone else because it would be to no personal advantage. Upon retirement each individual literally becomes a ward of the state. In some countries, older people have been cared for but little, because they lose their usefulness to the state.

The best way to gain understanding of total socialism is to consider the experience a person has in the armed services. The soldier is told where to go, what to do, and what he is to be paid. In Socialism a whole country is regimented. Probably there are those who are content to spend careers in the service and willing to let superiors direct their lives, but freedom is limited.

Statistics seem to indicate that in Socialistic countries alcoholism is extremely high and suicide rates are among the highest. Socialism breeds hopelessness and because the state is supposed to care for everyone a person can literally ignore his neighbor. Socialism may work to take care of general medical problems, but Socialism as a system leads to unhappiness, often to frustration and certainly to a loss of incentive.

Democratism

Democracy, or democratism, is very simply "the highest number wins". If an issue comes up today, through the medium of television a persuasive speaker even with false information and inaccurate presentation will overwhelm a gullible television audience. If hysteria sets in even among a few members of the populace, then a majority vote can be achieved. Under the absolute democratic process democracy could become "mobocracy". When Johnny Carson joked that there was a shortage of toilet paper suddenly the supermarkets were emptied -- as if most said, "To hell with you, I'm taking care of me." It is in such a way that a dictator can be elected, and once in power he can make the rules. Heaven forbid that America, priding herself on democracy, would be led to its absolute application.

Democratism is one step above socialism. Democratism is associated with free enterprise and freedom in the marketplace. Democratism extends to private ownership of property, private ownership of the factories, and private means of production and utilities. But the fix of the democratic mind strives also for egalitarianism. Just a fraction above 50% of those holding a particular view can demand that the other half to go along with their decisions, which is a restriction of the freedom of the second half.

One danger in democracy is the influence of the mob. A certain group may take freedom in their own hands. If a rampant majority rules, order and fairness can be discarded. Freedom of religion, freedom of assembly, freedom of speech is permitted. Democracy, however, also puts heavy pressures on the government to provide, and it is really one step on the ladder above Socialism.

"Liberal democracy" was coined to separate Western types from other systems purporting to be democratic. Its features are more than one party, open processes of government, open political debate, and segregation of government powers.

Republicanism

In the Athenian Empire, during the time of Pericles, and during the empire of Alexander the Great, most commoners could not read or write. Things had not significantly improved during the Roman Empire 500 years later. There was in effect a special group of intellectuals who also had procured wealth by virtue of their inheritance or their knowledge. From the ranks of the masses or plebians were chosen representatives for government. A group of what were called Tribunes represented the common mass of people. A republic was formed and operated so that each locality could select a representative to vote and speak for them collectively, and therefore the responsibility for judgment for their group was placed on their shoulders. All the members of the senate in turn would select the most acceptable rulers until finally, through organization, a titular head or authority and major decision-maker would be chosen with such a representative-type government. This, with the exception of the plebians, was a prototype of the government planned for the United States and has been the fairest and most respected. It had checks and balances and protection against radicalism and overthrow. The Roman Empire lasted 800 years. That of the U.S. is little more than 200 years old.

Historically, when society could finally dispense with wars temporarily, and when the production of a society could thereby support the intellectual, thinkers could emerge. Such were the days of the ancient Greeks with Pythagoras, Socrates, Plato, and Aristotle. Reasoning about human problems involved different types of regulations for a society. Plato advised that in order to protect from the mob, and to prevent temporary calamities from destroying order, the common people should elect representatives to a government to speak for them. The system was to work in such a manner that the most intelligent or educated, and allegedly the wisest, be chosen to govern, and this was the **intended nature of the republic**.

In America the republic form of government was a form designed to guarantee the greatest amount of individual freedom possible. But through the years, particularly with the adoption of social security and a welfare system, the creation of the Federal Reserve Board, and the advent of the Keynes philosophy of government spending, the power of the Federal government continued to increase enormously. Both democratism and republicanism by American standards, became altered. Federal regulations, state bureaucracy, and perhaps the size of government have, a bit at a time, eroded away the original freedoms.

At the present (1992) pay rate of a middle class salaried individual, with between $25,000 and $50,000 a year income, taxation amounts to about one-third of yearly earnings. In effect, this is the amount of money each pays for government services -- or for the common welfare. As more and more Federal spending is required for regulations, higher and higher taxes are levied, and one woman (a school teacher from Montana, who was a seatmate on a recent flight) claimed that apparently we are, in this process, headed for a type of serfdom all over again.

There was a taxation revolt in California in 1978 headed by Howard Jarvis, which was amazing in its effect. The people rose up and said, "Enough taxation on a private home is enough!" The result was that alternative measures were taken by the state legislature in California. This movement was looked upon favorably by many other states. In 1992 California is headed for eleven billion dollars deficit and this will probably raise their state sales taxes yet again. People do not flock to Los Angeles to enjoy the smog. They hope for a free ride.

Dynamism

As we have seen in the subject of economics, good times are mixed with bad. Theory holds that economics is cyclic and that depressions occur every 60 years in the history of the United States, and perhaps even in the world.

Consistent with that theory are the findings that one of the factors is the accumulation of wealth by too few. When a large percentage of the wealth gradually falls into the hands of only one in a hundred, money is taken out of circulation. With the progressive downturn effect, periodic recessions occur, which in two years lead to a wave of major depression.

In order for jobs to be created, investment capital is required. As investment capital availability is lessened and risks are declared too great for resulting gain in the economy, problems develop in the country. The processes of the current government are then blamed. This is the argument for capital gains tax breaks to be returned.

If accumulation of wealth in a country goes into the hands of too few, then some means must be found to put it back. But taxation only puts the money in the control of non-productive and non-return situations by the government. Some solutions should be considered in order **to protect capitalism and to protect freedom** while at the same time protecting a system which would provide the most jobs and the highest standard of living for the most people.

We may speculate on one avenue, therefore, to satisfy these conditions in the New Renaissance. Money may be loaned to the Federal government by the rich for a very small return. But what would government do with such funds? If they simply put them into all the usual schemes of programs, it would only add another government bureaucratic department. A separate loan arrangement would be necessary for small businesses which create jobs. Remember, for a job to be created an owner has to need assistance in the running of a business. Typically a service, a productive manufacturer or one of the thousands of businesses in American industry would be the receiver.

The principle of dynamism is **"keep the economy active and moving"**. Dynamics is the antithesis of statics. Statics means stasis, or things held in place with no action. The idea of dynamics is not mere change but progressive change, because all change may not be favorable.

Another idea is progression. It is a principle meaning that:

Everything cannot be expected to occur ideally and under control simultaneously.

Things must happen in sequence, things must be kept in order, and it is in this sense that we use the word "progressive". Progressivism further means a series of events aimed toward a common goal and a common conclusion. I would therefore use the word dynamism in the sense of progressive dynamics.

It indeed seems unfair that because I spent time and energy in preparation, work harder and earn more, and because I am productive and successful, I should pay more accordingly or a greater percentage of my labor for taxes than the person expending little effort to be educated, less thrifty, and less contributory to society. It is not morally correct. It is, in fact, resented by those who are taxed higher for their labors than those who are less ambitious and productive. Yet, if the whole country is to succeed, and we are not to revert to anarchism, some plan, some mode should be available to keep our economy thriving.

I would be in favor of a plan to make it mandatory for the wealthy not to hoard their money. It is unfair just to take it away from them, but by the same token it is not their right to sit on it at the expense of society as a whole.

But wealth can be lost more quickly than it is gained, and the rich do not always stay rich. Inflation is ever increasing, and even in good times the inflation rate is **4%**. The very rich might be assessed for their property owned in the form of a very low interest-bearing loan to be returned from a controlled fund to them if ever there was financial ruin in the future. One problem is investment in art, precious stones and coins which are difficult to locate. This is a wild idea, but what are the alternatives?

Anarchism and Cooperatism

The words anarchy and anarchism are very frequently misunderstood. Anarchy means the absence of law and order, or a general revolt, a general state of disorder and confusion. But anarchism as a political theory holds that individual freedom should be absolute and that all government and all law is evil. In complete anarchism, capitalism and private property would be abolished, which would mean that it would rely on individual voluntary cooperation without any government at all. It's absurd except in Shanrgi-la.

Anarchism is further complicated with religious types of anarchism, exemplified by the early organization of the Christian Church and expressed in modern times by the philosophy of Gandhi in India. It probably could never work for long periods, because of the inevitable genetic nature of the human character.

* * *

In the years ahead, America will tend towards either a more complete form of socialism or may go towards what I have termed dynamism. With modern communication and modern international ventures, and with the demonstration that some sort of a free enterprise is needed for the best method of feeding people and providing for dignity in human welfare, it is my belief that some sort of international dynamism may be appropriate and perhaps some cooperative order must occur on an international basis in order to remain at peace and in progress.

In America in the future we may have a division of our two-party system. The first would be made up of a laboring party, although from the ranks of the laborer there will be but a few intellectuals. The second party would be a liberal-democratic group which should perhaps be more properly labeled socialists. The third would be progressive conservative, and the fourth would be a traditional libertarian or conservative party. Maybe the ideologies of the first two and second two would be the result, but a better separation is needed.

* * *

Challenge 2: Size and Power for Taxation by Governments

At the time of the Great Depression in 1930, income taxes were virtually non-existent. How was the Federal Government paid for and how was it run? This was done by excise taxes and customs tariffs which constituted the principle form of income for the government.

But with the adaptation of the Keynes philosophy to establish work projects, which was noble on the part of Franklin D. Roosevelt, and with the establishment of the Social Security system for the care of older people, the income of American citizens had to be taxed. Sales taxes were imposed by states, and the citizenry came to demand more services from the national, state and local governments. The idea, or the impression, was that the benefits by the government were something for nothing!

As World War II ensued, higher taxation for social programs was concealed by the cost of the war. Even with recovery, three Eisenhower years (1957, 1958 and 1960) were surpluses for the government. Social programs were hidden under the costs of the later wars and further the cost of social programs was confused with the armament build-up connected somehow with space exploration in the confrontation with the Soviet Union in the Cold War, and the issues against international communism.

In the face of all of this the American people, as it turns out, have been the most altruistic nation in history. We have had enough people who would "knuckle down and work" manually to take two jobs, or a husband and wife both working in order to reach their economic and social goals, and at the same time support the government. The government itself has continued to print money, and we have undergone inflation, which also means a greater cost in administrating government programs. Therefore, everything continues to escalate.

In the New Renaissance this must stop. In the Theory of Dynamism which I have proposed, there must be a limit and enough of our citizenry must agree to it and it must be done quickly if our Renaissance is to express itself in full force. As long as Congress, in the name of doing things for the people, continues to hammer away at the citizenry and the I.R.S. agents make a personal vendetta of squeezing money out of the populace, the respect for government will continue to decline. Black markets will start, and thrive. As in other countries, bartering will increase, people will hide income in order to protect their families and their personal economic welfare.

Putting a lid on taxation should indeed help, but in its present state, no matter how it is conceived, taxes continue to increase and they seem to be out of control. The individual is buried in a sense of hopelessness. The idea for a maximum for taxation is not new. All it needs is enough common agreement to put it in order in our free country.

If it doesn't happen, I personally am fearful of the next decade and particularly the next century. People work hard to make ends meet for the day, or for the week, or for the month. Many have nothing left for savings or investment. This is made even worse by the raising and the cost of education of a large family. These are the problems of facing the New Renaissance. (See discussion of inflation in Chapter Ten.)

* * *

Challenge 3:   Morality and Solutions by the People --
Sexual Revolution, Abortion, and Legal Systems

This is a broad subject and covers many aspects including honesty, ethics, the institution of marriage, the sexual revolution and abortion. When Vice President Quayle said that the TV story of Murphy Brown who was a single mother represented a bad role model and was degrading to our male responsibilities, he became the brunt of jokes. Democrats loved to ridicule him and made mockery of his defense of the family and his plea for a stable moral condition for our future. The TV program writers said they were only satisfying the will of the public. However, when the majority of the public sided with Quayle, they were chagrined. They were the ones with the decadency! Hooray for the backlash! Decency is within reach after all.

In the days of the first Renaissance, honesty, virtue and character were highly prized. The challenge to a person's integrity might result in a sword-fight or a duel to the death. As America was settled, honesty was a necessary characteristic, because neighbors needed neighbors to survive, and without fairness the culture could not succeed. To be honest was to be good, honorable, trustworthy, true and upright. A person who is honest is disposed to act with regard for the rights of others in matters of business or in relation to property.

Honesty is closely associated with **honor**. One who is honorable observes the dictates of a personal honor so high that the demands of a contract or public opinion take second place. The antithesis of honesty is deceit, falsehood, fraudulent actions, treachery and unscrupulousness. To be honest, therefore, is to be just, morally right, and virtuous. Where is the father of Murphy Brown's child?

Virtue is moral excellence, and the abstinence from immorality and vice. Particularly in women it means purity and chastity. Plato classified the four cardinal virtues as justice, temperance, prudence and fortitude. The Christian scholastic moralists added faith, hope and charity (or love) to Plato's list. In addition, admirable qualities such as merit or accomplishment constitute virtues, as well as patience. Virtue is goodness that is victorious through trial, temptation and conflict.

Morality is conformity to moral laws in action, whether in matters concerning ourselves or others, whether with or without correct principle.

Integrity is moral wholeness, particularly used as applied to contracts and dealings, and has reference to inherent characteristics, character and principles. In the New Renaissance, **the young people of America must bring back a respect for honesty and virtue**. Youth, hear this!

Ethics is a branch of philosophy which deals with ideal morals, right principles, and is often defined by a given system of behavior or professional conduct. In a sense, ethics is somewhat described by the culture itself.

One problem lies in the acceptance of guides and laws which are unrealistic. It amuses me that so often speeding limits are violated particularly when the streets are empty. Yet one feels compelled to sit at a stop light in the wee hours of the morning when there is no car in sight in any direction. The breaking of the law, a little bit at a time, opens the door to possibility of greater and greater chances to be taken with the law.

When marriage vows are spoken there is a covenant made with the church that each partner will be loyal so long as they both shall live. Yet anyone can plainly see that such promises are broken not only one time but many times with the role models of some movie stars. Vows have no meaning.

Closely allied with this is the common practice of the modern culture in which people choose to live together out of wedlock for convenience. There is some argument that perhaps the getting to know each other sexually is an advantage for the possibility of the permanency of a marriage if it is to occur later. Certainly if two people can't get along, it is better to know it in advance rather than after children have come on the scene. Many women consider sex only immoral when it is without love, or when sex is performed on a physical basis only. This is pure tripe!

In earlier cultures marriage occurred at young ages. The function of marriage was for economic and survival purposes, and it wasn't until the romantic period that people married for love. However, with the postponement of marriage age, often up until the thirties, our laws are not realistic, and there develops an intense conflict with our moral codes. Perhaps this situation needs to be addressed by the clergy.

Abortion

Abortion is one of the most highly debated subjects on the present political scene. I find myself tremendously torn on this issue. At the time of conception, a human organism starts to form. Within seven days, it implants into the uterus and becomes an embryo, which is a living being. The organs are formed, the face is developed, and the parts are in place by the end of the second month, or thereabouts. From the third month on the baby is a human being and simply grows inside the womb. Therefore, the taking of that embryo or foetus constitutes, in fact, a murder on a biologic basis. I am torn, consequently, between that moral issue and reality.

If the child is not wanted and will not be cared for, then there is an issue as to the wisdom of bringing it to a full development or to a full expression. If, on an economic basis, the child will be born in poverty, and in some cultures 25% of the children are dead before age three, then it makes little sense to simply postpone the time for a more violent death.

Our moralists and our religious people argue with regard to when the soul actually enters the body. Some theories hold that it is only when the child actually expands the lungs and sees the light of day. Under this view there is no argument with regard to abortion, even on a religious basis. On the contrary side, some religions, almost as if for the propagation of the religion itself, have initiated and taught doctrines glorifying the birth of children and a large family. I take no issue with large families when they can be loved and nurtured, afforded and educated. However, in some societies or in certain urban ghettos when teen-aged mothers are still unwed and have three or four children before age twenty, they more than likely will need to be supported by the state, which taxes the upright moral and ethical citizenry and in itself becomes unjust for them.

Probably the worst situation of all exists with the mother who is an alcoholic or a drug addict, and is weak of mind. The odds of her child being normal are greatly reduced. The odds of that child being cared for properly are minimal. And in such situations on a scientific basis, should abortion be plainly legalized and practiced for the good of the state and for the unborn child itself? Is the slogan "woman's choice" adequate or does it give her freedom for promiscuity only?

I am not concerned about the earth being able to support more human lives. As I mentioned before when discussing economics, the British cleric and economist Thomas Malthus argued in 1803 for population control, since people increase in a geometric ratio and food only in an arithmetical ratio. He suggested moral restraints and sexual abstinence. But the production of food seems to have kept pace with population growth. It is not a matter of the production of food but rather its transportation and the ability to purchase food on an economic basis which ultimately constitutes the problem. Distribution is also the problem, and population control from the standpoint of food production does not seem to be a strong component of the argument in my opinion.

Euthanasia

The last issue in the arguments of moral integrity in the New Renaissance deals with euthanasia. Here again I am torn, because miracles are sometimes heard of, and as the saying goes, "Where there is life there is hope." On the other hand, when a person's immune system is riddled, when their body has been taken over by malignant cancer, when they are in constant pain and suffering, begging for it to be put to an end, no one could sit by and watch a lower animal suffer so. Yet our moral codes, our religious doctrines and our virtuous laws would make anyone assisting them to their death a murderer and subjected to the criminal laws.

Care should be exercised in judging who should be assisted in the death wish, because it could be offered as an excuse for the voluntary killing of another person. Perhaps it could be placed in the hands of judges or people with wisdom, and in the interests of humanity maybe euthanasia could be legalized. Sick older people spend all of their life savings and much more in hospitals hooked up to instruments of high technology! Intensive care wards require nurses around the clock, which absolutely makes no sense except to bring income to all of those attempting to save the life, and fills the coffers of the hospital's bank account.

Courts and the Legal System

I previously mentioned the growing litigation-conscious society. The prevalence of lawyers (133,000) in California is seen in the ratio of nearly one for every four hundred people. Is it our Perry Mason movies that have had an undue influence? Is it the impact of malingerers seeking opportunities for a free ride at others' expense? Or is it lawyers wanting to get fat?

I also mentioned interpersonal conflicts as the greatest stressor in ordinary life. These conflicts happen during marriage, divorce, inheritance settlements, breaking the law or problems with neighbors. Other factors are home or travel accidents, insurance claims, boundary disputes and product liability. Finally, there is a plethora of medical and dental grievances.

All the foregoing conflicts involve money! All charges against medical practitioners involve disagreement regarding standards of care. All involve income for lawyers or to people seeking remuneration in money. Why is the law profession so attractive to career oriented students?

America's judicial system is a mystery to many people. Everyone knows from the movies about a judge and a jury and a trial, but few know the whole process. Lawyers, in particular, as with most folk heroes, are no longer held in high regard for virtue and honesty. Many lawyers will do whatever it takes to make money. A lawyer will argue one side of a case in the morning and accept the opposite side of a similar case in the afternoon. The final verdict of a case is not necessarily the truth. Lawyers are now going back to school, not to learn the law but to drama school to become effective actors to plead their cases. Movie videos are reviewed in search of the most effective influence for the voice, gestures, and facial expressions.

In many cases, truth and justice in our courts may have little to do with honesty and integrity. They have little to do with truth, as a wrong impression has to be squeezed out of a situation by the use of misleading questions which can cast a witness in poor light or even place him at fault. It's little wonder people do not want to cooperate in legal situations. If a case has poor merit, a slick lawyer may try to discredit an opposing personality. To lawyers it's part of the game! In fact, delay after delay permits them to clock up more time, which starts clicking from the moment they say "Hello" on the telephone.

Due to involved experience in my field through the years, I continue to be asked to serve as a witness in many cases where patients have sued practitioners regarding treatment. I have found most of the cases involve expectations of service which was not received. Only once have I seen cause to testify against the practitioner, but I have advised some to return the patient's money and be rid of the complaint.

Throughout my career I have continually done the best job I could do under the circumstances of a patient's limitation and my technical capabilities and knowledge. After almost half a century with no litigation, in the last four years I have suffered six suits, all of which were in my opinion unfounded. In every instance the people had odd quirks in their personalities. Three had history of psychiatric care. Two were lawyers themselves who seemed to know how to take advantage of the system.

Before a complaint can be registered there must always be someone available who, following another ideology or belief, will testify against another doctor. When they are handsomely paid, and particularly when they suffer an ego problem regarding their beliefs, they become willing participants to the game.

Let me explain my impression as to how the game or the system works. Every doctor has insurance against accidents or unfortunate experiences. The cost of insurance is based on probabilities and chances like ordinary insurance tables for health, occupation and age. A complaint is made after consultation with another practitioner. In fact, certain doctors take an additional law degree and set themselves as authority within their own profession. Also, lawyers specialize in certain problems. Lawyers from the accused's (defendant's) insurance companies are engaged. Depositions (testimony) are then taken from the complaining person (plaintiff) and from a doctor supporting the complaint. The purpose of the deposition, under oath and with sworn statements taken down by a court reporter, is to obtain information for the arguments pro and con. This seems to be a good system.

A referee, usually a retired judge, will be brought in to make a preliminary decision before a trial is set up before a jury. After this a settlement (out of court) is to be considered by both sides. But here is where this "system" hurts society. If it's cheaper to give the plaintiff an award, the insurance company's lawyers will advise to pay them off rather than bearing the further cost of a court defense. It has nothing to do with truth or fairness. The defendant will often agree to the settlement for the sake of time, for the cause of peace, for the avoidance of a further harassment, and for the freedom from anxiety over a strange experience.

In criminal cases another factor in our law is the protection of the accused. Because innocent people have been put in jail or executed, our court system tries to be exact and certain. In addition, it is expensive to the state to "keep" people in prison. The whole parole system is now under examination because some are returning to criminal practices upon being turned loose in society. There is a movement to dispense with parole altogether, as successful rehabilitation in prison is questioned.

Finally, our system is based on the mercy of the court which tends to be more liberal than conservative and will react against any company or individual "with deep pockets".

In the future our efforts should be to find a way to settle disputes without suing each other. More arbitration is needed before even bringing lawyers into a conflict. Maybe a whole level of sub-lawyer personnel will develop -- a sort of clergy consultant strata in our society to help settle disputes as referees.

In addition, speeding up the legal process will save great expense as well as anxiety and grief by parties engaged in the process.

In our large urban cities rather than increasing the police force we should establish mandatory meetings of all those in the community. All resident citizens should be forced, under penalty, to participate in the local educational process regarding crime. It might take the form of a positive town hall affair. It would bring the local citizenry together. The parent-teachers association could serve as a paradigm. Local citizens could rotate on a council for their community which would be egalitarian in function.

With the change in attitudes regarding neighbors, and the tendency to find fault, our court calendars are flooded. Many of our courthouses were built when our cities were small and our populations less. With the increase in population, together with the public attitude, the situation has become desperate.

Finally, the following listing of the various courts is provided, information which is not well known by the American public in general.

Courts of the U.S.
Supreme Court of the United States
Plus the following judges, all elected for 4-year terms:
>   Court of Appeals
>   Court of Claims
>   Court of International Trade, U.S.
>   Court of Military Appeals
>   District Court
>   International Court of Justice
>   Juvenile Court
>   Small Claims Court

* * *

Challenge 4:   Drug Abuse, Crime, Violence and Prisons
Drug Abuse
According to an article in "Fortune" magazine the size of drug traffic on a world scale was considered large enough to challenge America's gross national business product. Despite all efforts to curtail entry into the U.S., drugs seem to increase continually. In fiscal 1991 almost 400 million dollars were spent in an effort to curtail the entrance and abuse of drugs.

The biology of the drug problem was addressed previously in this narrative in Chapter Ten. It is not only a major social problem, it is killing our people. Some say if a person is that stupid let them kill themselves and good riddance! However, when it kills the child of your friend who is a leader in your community it looks quite different. When users kill innocent people, including children, it cannot be condoned.

A principle applies here:

> **When the profit is great enough the risk of being caught will be taken by a dealer.**

As long as this condition exists, drugs will find a way to the user.

I agree with Colonel Oliver North that the problem can be solved only one way. **Fine and punish the user more severely than the seller!** When enough adults are punished extensively, their automobiles taken away from them or stiff penalties invoked, then the kids will get the lesson quickly! Are some of the lawmakers themselves the users? Maybe enough adults do not see the problem or do not take drug abuse seriously.

High school seniors say it's quite easy to get drugs. Of those questioned, 84% say marijuana is easy to get, and 55% find it easy to obtain cocaine; for crack it's 42%, for LSD 41%, and 18% found it easy to buy heroin. Virtually all say alcohol acquisition is no problem at all.

A question arises regarding legalization. Legalize use in children? -- unreal! The legalizing of drugs could make highway accidents worse, and they are bad enough now because of the use of alcohol. A young father, age 36, left a country club after a number of cocktails, and his Corvette became airborn after hitting one of the dips in our local road, throwing him to his death against an oncoming vehicle. While legalization may curtail profits for the trafficker, it would put more intoxicated people on the highways and would not reduce the number of addicts. It would also fill our hospitals with legalized addicts. Countries legalizing drugs have witnessed horror. Forget it!

Crime and Violence

One of the functions of any organization of humans into a society is to establish order and make laws for guiding conduct. One basis for education should be to teach the principles of ethics and fairness and respect for property both public and private. Traditionally, the service of religion has been to help man overcome savage instincts and inclinations. Many faiths have something tantamount to the Ten Commandments and the Golden Rule. **Human beings have normally an inherited sense of right and wrong, and a sympathy, empathy, and altruism for others.** This is our conscience.

But some people seem not to be normal with regard to a conscience. Biologically, some animals are simply mean and behave off the normal curve of distribution. It is possible, I repeat, although I know of no scientific reference, that **drugs over time may alter the brain so much as to lose that protective altruistic character** of man toward his fellow man.

Some people probably are born without the protective strata in the brain cortex, for serial killers are discovered in all societies. Can some people become conditioned or addicted to crime of various sorts? People can become addicted to gambling, and gambling may lead to crime in the loan racket. Why could not forms of crime be addictive? Crime also entails the thrill of the possibility of *not* being caught.

The New Renaissance must consider such possibilities because crime of most sorts continues to increase at a rate greater, proportionally, than population growth. Much crime we know is triggered by needs for drugs by those addicted. The female turns characteristically to prostitution, but females are also copying male crime practices. Both sexes may turn to theft or larceny or fraud in order to procure money. Fraudulent scams involving an older person's savings are most deplorable.

If Ardrey's argument is correct, man evolved as an offshoot from a terrestrial hominid who was a hunter and a killer. In this light, killing is in our genes. "Take No Prisoners" is a popular saying in sports games. Further, lower animals also cheat. Birds steal other birds' nests. Honesty and morality must therefore be learned as a factor against natural tendencies to prevaricate, to commit assault and battery, to maim and to murder.

A **misdemeanor** is a breaking of the law subject to fine or censure. Shop-lifting increased 70% in 1980 to 1990 and these were only the caught and reported. Some well-off people are addicted to shop-lifting.

A **felony** is a more serious crime punishable by jail sentence or worse. Per 100,000 in our population, 140 persons were serving time in prison in 1980 and this more than doubled in

1990 to 293. Prison parolees for females also doubled between 1988 and 1990.

A **theft** is the taking of another's private property with intent to deprive the owner. **Burglary** is a break-in and **robbery** is with a gun or use of force. A **larceny** is stealing without a break-in. A **homicide** is murder or the slaying of one person by another or the taking of another's life with malice aforethought.

The murder tide is still rising. In 1990 the projected number of homicides in the U.S. was 23,700. In the Phoenix area homicides went from 179 in 1990 to 226 in 1991, an increase of 26%. One incident was a traffic altercation between two young men and a gunman in a parking lot at a prominent Scottsdale resort. It reflects a national trend and reminds us of movie stories of the Old West.

Crimes of passion are those conducted under intense emotional stress which should, nevertheless, be no excuse for injustice to another. Mafia-type killings and acts in adult gang warfare are usually premeditated.

A **fraud** is cheating and tricking by intentional perversion of the truth in order to induce someone to part with their possessions. It is a deception. Cheating on income tax is a type of fraud.

Suicide is the taking of one's own life. Per 100,000 youths age 15 to 24 years, the rate has increased from 8.8 in 1970 to 13.6 in 1990 and continues to rise. Recent surveys suggest one in three teen-agers have considered suicide, and one in seven in high school say they have been raped.

Police violence is either being discovered more and reported more, or it also is increasing, possibly as a backlash to increased pressure. Charges of abuse have been claimed along the U.S.-Mexico border, involving the Border Patrol, the Immigration and Naturalization Service, U.S. Customs, and local authorities. The rewards for sneaking into the U.S. are very high, and people continue to make the attempt.

The rise in violence has been attributed to the "Four D's": drugs, dealers, deadly arsenals of assault weapons, and demographics in violent teen gangs. No city is spared. In New York on a summer night 17 people were slain in one 24-hour stretch.

Prisons

Each time I drive on Route 10 between Los Angeles and Scottsdale I pass a state prison on both the Arizona and the California sides of the Colorado River. It makes me conscious of the "system". I heard a radio interview with the warden or representative of the prisons regarding the tremendous overcrowding. Across the nation Federal prisons are also jammed.

I remember when I lived in California the difficulty of selecting sites for new prisons due to local citizens' resistance to having the site near their communities. I remember also a talk at Rotary a few years ago in which it was explained that because of the number of appeals and the court costs to convict, it was more costly to execute a person than to give them a life sentence.

Courts of law and prisons are something the typical American does not want to learn about. How they work and how they are managed is a mystery. Yet they pose one of our greatest problems in the future.

In addition, great debate is occurring relative to the deterrent effect of a sentence. Some propose that all terms be carried to the limit. Others propose paroles for those rehabilitated. Scientific data needs to be developed in order to make prudent decisions. One thing is sure, the public is alarmed when parolees are set free and repeat a crime. If they are released and commit a crime they would have to be convicted all over again. The answer may be to always let them out one day early -- on parole in any case.

Repentance and "going straight" have their virtues, but the legal system is perhaps incapable of making the individual distinctions.

At the present rate, bigger and bigger prisons will be needed in the future, if only for the population increases (assuming equal odds of criminals).

Answers

The answer in the New Renaissance is to **go back to the family** to provide role models and education for children who are now unsupervised. When the girl reaches 12 and the boy is 14 it is too late. Education toward self-esteem is working to some extent in the high schools. Marijuana was reduced from 48% use in 1980 among high school students to 27% in 1990. Cocaine was reduced from 12% to 5%. But what about the drop-outs?

The offspring of the baby boomers are alleged to be the greatest offenders. The retail trade in "crack" placed large amounts of cash in the hands of young men who have bought assault weapons. With the shrinking of drug use among the white affluent population, gangs and dealers battle over fewer paying customers, and deaths result. A Los Angeles Police officer blames narcotics for the record killings but says, "With gangs there is another element: just plain old meanness." Disputes that were once settled with fists are now concluded with guns.

Prevention of delinquency, failure in school, and sexual promiscuity are all allied with drug use and are everybody's problem. A good principle to follow is:

Muster respect in yourself and respect for others.

Parole and supervision systems are proposed as an answer to our overcrowded prisons. The releasing of people from prison with promises to go straight has not worked in too many cases. The non-professional parole boards are not successful. A mean person is a mean person and may not possess a normal brain. How can they be allowed to run free in a society? The New Renaissance must insist on more competent parole board members. A near-unanimous parole board opinion must be obtained, and some permanent prison penalty for parole offenders must be exercised.

* * *

Challenge 5:   Federal Deficit, Social Security, Health Care and Welfare
Federal Deficit

In 1969, for one year of all those since Eisenhower, the Federal Government took in more than it spent. In 1987, the spending was over 1,000 billion and income about 875 billion. In 1991 the income was 1.054 trillion and spenditure was 1.323 trillion dollars. The deficit in 1991 was 268.6 billion dollars. That is over 268 thousand million dollars ($268,000,000,000) we were short!

Spending by the Federal Government in billions in 1991 was: Defense 298.3, interest on debt, 288.7, Social Security 266.4 and health care 166.1. All other spending put together was about 243 billion.

With the Cold War thawed, a defense-reduced spending will move up the payment on debt and social security to the top of Federal Government costs. With the clamor for health care, that cost has risen steadily, and the way it is headed could easily become the top government expense.

Spending on defense was necessary to win the Cold War and help preserve peace in Europe and the world for half a century. In essence, however, it was done at America's expense and achieved by borrowing. Our people, as well as foreigners, bought government bonds. They invested in our future. Our Federal debt has become astronomical. Have we borrowed from our children to live high since World War II?

Social Security

The Social Security system in the United States was initiated in the 1930's under Franklin D. Roosevelt. As I remember, it started out as a good idea, and theoretically was supposed to stand as an independent program with funds going into a specific account separate from taxes. With everyone paying into it, it was supposed to be a sort of insurance program, together with unemployment benefits. It was a move toward some insurance against retirement by laborers and a program to take care of older people upon retirement.

However, the temptation was too great for the politicians to simply keep that money out of the regular tax revenue. And instead of the program growing with funds being available for perhaps even loans to other parts of the government, or to individuals, the funds paid into it were eaten up by other branches of government spending, and it came to be treated as another tax with future benefits to come out of future taxes on the younger people still working. With the using up of the money, this put the burden on the future taxpayer. By the year 2000 there will be an estimated large increase in older people in the U.S. Whatever the retirement age, it is mandatory to take Social Security benefits by age 70.

I think that Social Security is a good system, particularly for those who reach an age where they are unemployable and have not been fortunate enough, after the raising of a family and financing children through college, to set enough aside for retirement or who, by the same token, have lost their life savings in either poor investments or by a health calamity which has used up their funds. It is obvious that the majority of Americans feel this way, and the Social Security system would be most difficult to dispense with, like it or not. But, when the statistical curves are extended and a standard expected rate of inflation around 4% each year goes on and on, every ten years that 4% becomes 40%. In 20 years it becomes 80%. What was intended to be a provision against poverty by way of inflation and not consequent adjustment may prove inadequate. But in addition increases may burden the wage-earners by increased taxation to the extent that the country would be held back and stifled.

Health Care

By latest calculations in 1991, U.S. expenditure for health care per capita exceeds that of Germany which is socialized. It also exceeds Japan's. The problem with full socialized medicine is that too many feel entitled to the ultimate in care, crowding out the truly desperately needy in terms of emergency and urgent care. A national health insurance program, like automobile insurance, should have a minimum, even for the poor, if the system is to work. Major hospitalization for cancer, major surgical conditions such as cardiac by-pass procedures, and other major aspects of high technology for kidney disease and the like should be covered.

One other burden with health insurance is that which is supplied by industries in the United States, paid out but not through the workers' pay envelope. These amounts are deducted from the earnings which the average worker usually doesn't count as income in his mind. Therefore, he talks about "take-home" pay on the job rather than true pay. Such programs, in addition to union benefits, price many American products out of the international market. Small wonder, then, that whenever possible industries will tend to put in robots and automation on the assembly lines rather than using people who also are subject to human error.

Health care and other benefits are a great part of the motivation for laborers in modern industry. There are many people pushing for national health care, and in the beginning it sounds idealistic. One unmarried male computer worker (sitting next to me on an airplane) said he would be willing to give 35% of his income for national health insurance. That would be 70% taxation, leaving him 30% for all his other needs. Is that realistic?

But, in the end, long lines wait and wait in hospitals. Incentives are lost by health care workers. People working in the health insurance service learn to put their time in as in other jobs in any socialized system. Working for the Federal government ultimately is non-efficient. Examples of this in other countries are too notable to be challenged.

Welfare Programs
Welfare programs have usually been within the jurisdiction of the state. Analysis of programs across the country as late as 1991 showed that the following divisions, rounded out for ease of memory, as follows:

Education	37%
Welfare and Health Care	28%
Highways	9%
Debt interest	4%
Prisons	3%
Other processes of Administration	19%

When Education and Welfare are put together, they account for essentially two out of every three dollars spent by state governments. This is the reality of running the state, with only one-third left for actually all the state's services other than education and welfare. Such is the present situation.

State taxes continue to rise in addition to the Federal taxes, with a ceiling only when the public says "I've had enough!", which is beginning to happen. With regard to issues of taxes and welfare, I believe a principle applies:

> **When a father and a mother can no longer feed themselves or educate and care for their own children, they will not sacrifice to feed someone else's child.**

State taxes, like Federal taxes, have continued to grow, and there is a generalized revolt for the gradual increase in the cost of welfare. I refer to some of the writings publicized and some of the moves by certain politicians in an effort to manage the problem. Most decent people have empathy for the poor and needy. Most of the time the picture painted is the young single woman trying to raise a child or two, while holding down a job or going to school, and provide for living quarters, food, and clothing on what a monthly welfare check would supply.

The State of California has the highest cost welfare program with "Aid to Families with Dependent Children", which is shortened to the A.F.D.C. program, and also general assistance programs. In that state, starting with the two billion dollar bill for welfare in 1980, aid has risen to 4.3 billion in 1991. A family with two children could get a grant of

$663.00 each month. Welfare recipients both with children and without children have been subject to ridicule mostly by the middle class people who are paying the bill.

Wayne Bryant, a black Assemblyman in New Jersey, calls the system a modern-day slavery. He refers to the system enslaving his people for the rest of their lives, and has offered bills to the state government in New Jersey to serve as a model for other states. For instance, a woman who marries now loses. In order to encourage women to marry he suggests keeping them at a higher level. In addition, he suggests cutting extra benefits in welfare to mothers who have more children, who are already on the Aid to Dependent Children. The Federal law at the present time provides child care and health care for one year after a mother gets a job. He would extend it to two years. The bill further pushes education and vocational training to adult recipients. His issue is that **education is required to take the poor out of poverty**.

From the Howard Jarvis organization for tax revolt, people in states other than California have begun to take a stance. In 1991, 82,000 were taken off the welfare rolls in Michigan, which was in addition to a 13% cut in aid to families with dependent children. In Massachusetts welfare to childless adults was reduced by 56 million dollars, which took 10,000 people off the benefits. In Maryland, the aid to children was cut 12%, with recommendations for a 30% cut in the next year. In Illinois aid was cut for 110,000 adults, to only nine of the twelve months of the year. All this was taking place while eleven states actually raised their benefits.

In 1991, seven states in the United States have more than a billion dollar shortfall in their state budgets. State politicians and governors are coming to reality. In New York the budget was 30 billion. In the state of Maryland it's 12 billion. In Massachusetts and New York the shortfall is 3.6 billion, which is more than 10% short of expenses. With the total budget of only 13.4 billion, Massachusetts is short 1.6 billion. Thus, New York and Massachusetts are short in their states about 12% of their total budget. And so many governors, as for example Oregon's Roberts, face a one-billion shortfall of almost 17% in the six-billion budget. Nearly all of the states, as well as most of the nation's cities, face budget deficits. Most expect state and local tax collections in 1992 to fall far short of estimates. As reported in "USA TODAY" of May 22, 1992, Pete Wilson, Governor of California, has a budget of 60.3 billion, and a shortfall of 11.0 billion. His welfare reform initiative would slash payments about 25%.

Many see higher taxes as the solution. The reality, however, is that the goose that lays the golden egg has now reached the age of infertility, and there are no more geese that politicians can engage.

The New Renaissance will not deny aid to poverty-stricken people. The welfare proponents will come to the realization that taxes cannot be raised another 10% to cover the shortfalls of state governments, as is proposed by many politicians. If people insist on living on subsistence, I can see communes or localities put together where the job can be done far more economically than is done at the present time. I would suggest another principle based on history:

Programs should be turned over to private enterprise to manage.

The state would give to a private organization the limits of the money they can give to that program and let it be handled in the most efficient manner that way. Such programs are not available. It takes private enterprise money to create the kind of efficiency that would be appropriate for such programs. People could move in and out of such programs with ease, and jobs could be made for people within the program itself. Some people may say that's beneath human dignity, but it's reality, and it's a lot better than starvation.

The very worst part of high costs is that businesses are also taxed, and it is another factor in driving factories and businesses out of a state, and also out of the country.

* * *

Challenge 6:   Protection of Resources

The factors that made the "great American century" (1890 to 1990) were related to its resources. A resource is a supply that can be drawn on when needed. It is something to fall back on or turn to for support. America had fertile farm lands. She had minerals, coal, oil and gas. America had waterways for electric power, for transportation and for irrigation. She also had great forests dotted with lakes for recreation and fish. She had seas with sea life. The air was clean and healthful. Then the smokestacks came, together with the automobile -- and pollution. Throughout the century some of the land was eroded and valuable farm land was turned into homesites. Much timber was cut and much more damaged by acid rain and smog. Minerals were used up and many oil wells have been water-fed and pumped dry. A shortage of polluted water is anticipated even with recycling. Noise and electromagnetic airwaves are almost filled to capacity and their detrimental biologic effects are speculated to be immense.

There are many people, particularly those New Age-oriented, who are deeply concerned about not only American resources, but the resources of the entire planet. They are particularly concerned about deforestation on a world basis, contamination of the oceans, the change in the natural food chains, the extinction of animals, the turning of farm lands into deserts, and the protection of the ozone layer. In the New Renaissance of the future, these people as they mature into middle-class adults will demand a stronger voice in some of these issues.

Products such as automobiles, hairsprays, even the by-products of coolants for refrigerators, will be more critically evaluated. Chemists must work harder. More time and effort will be spent on education, and research will be conducted in the New Renaissance, not only to stop its loss but to replenish the ozone, to maintain our plant life for the production of oxygen. More research and development will be done to remove smoke and fume contamination.

One of the major areas of research will also be in electromagnetic phenomena to help protect the population from increased irradiation. It is anticipated that pollution-free, or nearly so, engines will be in production within the next five years.

* * *

Challenges for the Young

Many older people are frustrated and tired. The New Renaissance is therefore in the hands of our youth and our children. They are the people to whom I address these ideas. May they be wise as angels, steadfast, and strong as Sampson and as kind and patient as Job.

PART FOUR

PERSONAL GROWTH

Introduction

The pursuit of knowledge is endless. In my teaching it has always been an objective to keep a student motivated and inspired. No one can learn for someone else. Neither can a person develop another's personality.

The principle remains:

Each person is responsible for building his or her own character.

This final part entertains the question regarding the pursuit of happiness and the search for a fitting quality of life for the individual. It also deals with factors to be considered in personal growth. Lives change. Continued growth is a task that never ends so long as a mind is active. This is a great part of the joy of being human!

20

PATTERNS OF LIFE

Quality of Life

Norman Cousins put it best: "Death is not the greatest loss in life. The greatest loss is what dies inside us as we live." The objective of every person, recognized or not, is a quality of life. Scholars have debated exactly what is meant by this abstract idea.

Quality refers to a sense of highest order and good. It denotes a degree of excellence. Many Americans, unfortunately, associate quality of life only with affluence. But the quality of a whole life is made up of the quality of each part. Each component contributes to the whole, hence the need for a "balanced life". Without an ideal concept people are confused and act on the impulse of the moment, or hold values in conflict with quality itself.

To maximize a quality of life means to move beyond the ordinary. Each person is unique; no two are exactly alike. The principle is:

Quality of life requires a continued pursuit of personal growth.

Complacency leads to idleness and a bland existence. In order to continue to grow there must, ironically, be a measure of discontent with present knowledge and present circumstance. When satisfaction sets in, excitement ceases and quality of life drops.

Quality of life means vitality: it means dynamics. A person who does nothing eventually becomes a blood-sucker on society, expecting only to be entertained by others. Life is an experience and a quality person must be greedy for its last drop. People who have lost self-esteem have lost desire for a better life.

The first business of one who wishes to learn more and increase the value of his life is to part with self-conceit. Of two people with equal talents and tenacity, the one who contemplates his experiences and weaves them into harmonious patterns will be of greater use to society and enjoy a better quality of life.

Any person's life needs reinforcement by becoming involved with something. Sitting back and waiting is to watch life's parade pass by. An emotional participation is required for maximal life quality, even if it is perceived in quiet solitude. People need mutual support if they are not to be frustrated.

Instead of standing dejectedly on the street corner, a young person should aggressively sit in a library learning human worth, or be busy participating in life by helping others.

Quality of life is not a stuffed stomach or a belly full of beer. Quality is the enjoyment of the natural stimulants of life: good air, good water, the scents of nature, the song of birds, the presence of a child, the touch of a loving hand, the beauty of a true friend, the exchange of feelings, the pursuit of an honorable endeavor, worthwhile achievements, and the love and respect of a partner.

Happiness

The goal of every person is happiness. This auspicious state is so broad it may be confusing. Happiness is connected with success in life. It is the antithesis of frustration. Both happiness and success are complicated because they are made up of at least five principal factors. All these components are arranged in different magnitudes in each individual. It makes each person an entity unto himself or herself. These constituents are characterized by desires for (1) self-preservation, (2) romance and excitement, (3) ownership of property, (4) recognition, and (5) identity and appreciation of noble things of the inner self, often referred to as altruism or spiritual essences.

Succinctly stated, people struggle for acceptance, achievement, joy, freedom to pursue their desires and, further, to seek contentment. Underlying all this is the necessity for health and a long life of vitality, perhaps a part of the survival instinct. Quality and excellence are consistent ideas. The ultimate goal of a pursuit of good knowledge is wisdom. Wisdom can overcome fear! This leads to the ability to make wise decisions from clear reasoning. Excellence results from deep thinking. It is a choice between good and evil, truth and falsehood, beauty and ugliness, and the worthwhile over the trivial.

It is necessary for a quality of life to obtain a clear image in the mind. Such visualization through imagination is a key to memory and growth. Clear reasoning is based on good memory.

Quality and excellence exceed, stand out, and are beyond the ordinary. All people have some quality in which they can excel. Each must examine his or her talent and continue to improve it for personal growth. In the pursuit several characteristics are essential for success.

Numerous books and articles on success, self improvement or happiness are available, and they all have similar advice stated in different ways. From six writings ten qualities were found in common which seem to characterize the successful happy person, as follows:

1. Be positive; don't worry, be optimistic and enthusiastic and take initiative.
2. Set goals; organize; aim high; use imagination; make decisions; and don't procrastinate.
3. Display altruism; be outgoing, give time to others.
4. Be friendly; be yourself, live each day, don't be overbearing or talk too much.
5. Remain active; work hard, maintain discipline.
6. Face reality; evaluate, have perspective, maintain humility.
7. Have patience; be resilient in adversity.
8. Select a meaningful purpose; do things that are beneficial and important.
9. Earn respect; do not expect to be applauded for mediocrity.
10. Recognize your uniqueness; develop confidence, believe in yourself.

Building Your Own Character and Relationships

Dictionaries can't seem to describe love adequately. Such words as deep or tender feelings, profound affection, strong liking, attachment, devotion, benevolence and passion are used, but all fall short of love's true meaning and value. Yet, love has existed as long as civilizations have been recorded. Eros was the god of love in Greek mythology. Cupid was the Roman god of love, was the son of Venus, and was displayed as a naked cherub with a bow and arrow to penetrate the heart. Each Valentine's Day Americans are reminded of that history.

Maybe the confusion about love exists because there are several types of love, as the feeling is expressed. We would list these as parental and sibling love, brotherly love, animate and inanimate love, love of approval, and romantic and spiritual love. The latter type is perhaps of greatest interest.

Romantic and Spiritual Love

Probably more dramas, epics, poetry, songs, and literature has been written regarding sexual love than any other subject.

How are physical feelings transformed to true love? In many primitive societies marriage was taken without celebration or even attention. It was hard to recognize love at all. What happened with later cultures? Was it the development of greater protection for the mother, for the insurance of human survival, that made their daughters more inaccessible?

In Durant's words, "If men are braggarts, traitors, hypocrites and strutters, then women are vain, faithless, treacherous, and artificial. What then makes a union between these two imperfect creatures so sublime and given holy recognition?"

Is it the delay in consummation of marriage that makes it more precious? Does the development of that love or resistance work to build up a spiritual connection? Is it the secret feelings unconfessed and held personal that magnify the affection? Men will move beyond normal drives in order to provide economic leverage in hope of better gaining their choices, but seldom will admit it even to themselves!

Courtship raises the level of love and gives time for selection. The male plays a game of advancement and the female retreats modestly, strategically and subtly. A woman becomes his prize. It is a contest. He tries with a flare of property prospects and display. She chooses!

The immodest woman is attractive only passively. It is perhaps this factor more than anything that has caused young men of the present generations to progressively disrespect the female. When is she a lady and not just another "broad" in a passing parade? Her economy of gifts raises her appeal, but does she so recognize?

Mating is mastery and with familiarity brings its problems. But with the flowering of the family, love rises again, yet differently now. With the echo of the laughter of grandchildren it is more solidified. With the imminence of death love even yet takes on new life. Finally and scientifically, the greatest distress an older person can bear is the death of a spouse.

Understanding and Preserving Your Personal Health Comes First

All the body's tissues are composed of cells each of which is a tiny living organism itself. The health of the body is only as good as the health of each individual living cell. Long healthy life is very simply a process of maintaining homeostasis (equilibrium) for all the tissues and each cell.

The basic cellular needs, whether they be outside cells (epidermal), muscle, nerve or fiber cells, are a supply of oxygen and nutrients, and the maintenance of acid-base and electrical balance. A fifth requirement is the means of elimination of wastes or toxins. If any of these processes is disturbed, disease and death of cells ensues, and the whole person then becomes ill and quality of life deteriorates. All the tissues are connected through the blood and nerve systems.

The blood supply is the source of the life force. Cells do not have direct contact with the blood but are fed by a separate fluid that runs among the cells (intercellular). Oxygen and nutrients are present in the blood plasma which is transported to the surrounding fluid of the cells. Held in the connective tissue are the threaded strands of fibers that hold the body parts in place. The nutrients are moved from the fluid from the connective tissue into the cell for the production of energy. **This movement of nutrients and oxygen from the (interstitial) fluid into the cells is a key to health.** Further, the elimination of toxins or by-products and wastes is another essential function of this central mechanism. A cell cannot survive in its own excrement.

Contemporary nutritionists describe the techniques for periodic detoxification aimed at purging the cells of their toxins. Maintenance of the balance of the three body fluids -- blood plasma, serum between the cells, and fluid within the cells -- enhances the immune system and is the objective of the good doctor and of persons attempting to help themselves to keep their need for the doctor at a minimum.

The Patterns of Life

The keys to happiness are organization, understanding, faith, patience, time and the pursuit of ideals. Happiness is found in dealing with other people, with the whole being, and understanding of each other person, as a friend.

I have observed that maturity and continued study bring about an inquiry into philosophy of life no matter what the calling. Great thinkers in all ages past have wondered about human relations, life extension and human needs. Each person has his own pattern or make-up in emotion, desires and a personal grouping of factors for happiness.

After analyzing the nature of this subject, I formulated a triple triad shown in the accompanying diagram. It is offered as an aid to considering the life needs of each human individual, each friend or to better understand each foe. At the center of the diagram is **the individual pattern of life which is composed of a mix from three main sources.**

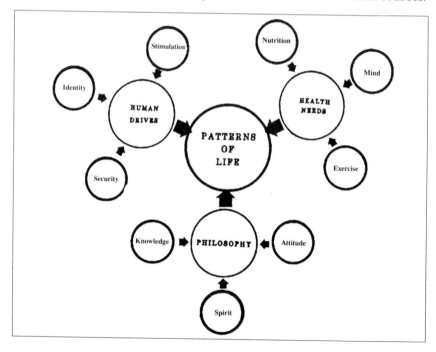

Health

The first source for happiness is **health** and an implied life extension. A sick person, or a person not feeling well and fit, is of limited use to society. Ill people drain a family or a community force. I like the Olive Garvey Institute's definition:

> **Health is having the reserve to do what you need to do and want to do with energy and enthusiasm.**

Without health life is limited. Consider perfect health and fitness as 100% and death as 0%; where would you rate your health on this scale at this moment?

Human Drives

The second source of happiness resides in the **human drives**. Whether these are inborn or acquired they constitute a force behind human actions. These are tremendously powerful motivators that can cause conflict and even wars or when understood can lead to tranquility and peace. But these are thought to be instinctual and should be recognized as **deep limbic impulses which are to be controlled**.

Philosophy

The final source of happiness is rooted in **philosophy**. "Philosophy" according to the dictionary means a love of wisdom or dealing with thought and reason. It concerns the nature of the universe and the nature of human relationships. Logic, ethics, esthetics, politics, epistemology, metaphysics mostly constitute its domain. It can contribute to life fulfillment and without it life is an empty existence only. Philosophy is an integrated body of principles based on truths as perceived by each individual.

Each of these three major aspects are in turn broken down into three categories for consideration.

Nutrition

The first need is an adequate supply of oxygen and nutrients. Foods must be available to the body and in a form or combination that can be absorbed by each particular person. Fats, protein and sugars taken in excess are stored for future utilization. This is deposited as fat in the body connective tissues and stored as minerals in the bone. Many vitamins, enzymes, amino acids and fatty acids are, however, not stored or manufactured in the body. For optimal daily body performance and health of the cells, and for life extension and vitality, some people benefit from supplementation, particularly when the body is depleted. Proper diet and nutrition is the one factor in the environment over which a person may exert some self control. We cannot change our genetic endowment. We must play the cards we are dealt.

Health, or equilibrium of all the body organs, cannot occur without proper nutrients. Cells wear out and die and new cells replace them. Without a source of building materials the foundation for health and life extension is insecure. Growth of cells is a continuous replacement process until death.

Ironically, scientific studies suggest **the single most frequent cause of early death from the environment is the use of tobacco**. Even being chronically in the presence of secondary smoke is almost as dangerous, and people in the work place as well as in public places deserve healthy air.

Physical Exercise

The second contribution to health is **physical exercise**. More than one-half the population according to present data will die of cardiovascular problems; one-quarter to almost one-third will die of cancer. The blood is pumped by the heart and the vessels carry oxygen and nutrients to all the cells. When that goes the life processes cease to be adequate, life of all organs becomes exhausted.

A proper amount of exercise has a number of functions. These include toning of the muscle walls of the vascular system, clearing wastes, enhancing oxygenation and building skeletal muscle as well as producing chemical by-products which protect the system. In addition, a person by exercising builds up the body in preparation for handling acute physical demands whenever they arise in an emergency. **A fit person is also in a position to help others and to help himself.** Healthy people look good and feel well!

Mind

The third health contribution comes from the **mind**. This probably comes first because it is manifested by desire or will. There must be an intense motivation to want to achieve and want to live and want to contribute to life. A person must strongly desire to eat correctly and maintain a level of fitness. There must be activity in the mind that makes life worth living abundantly. There must be a purpose causing a person to eliminate those things bad for the health and **to select and do those things which are beneficial for life's continuation.**

Mind plays a major role in health; the effects of placebos are well known. **Fear** is a major biologic deterrent to health. **Stress is in the mind and usually occurs with forced change and mostly from interpersonal conflict.** The chemical relation of the brain to the body suggests the brain to be perhaps the most powerful controller of the hormonal glands.

The combination of mind, exercise and nutrition, all in harmony, protects the immune system so that serious disease cannot take root.

Human Drives or Motivations

The second triad, **human drives**, at one time were considered by Freud to be only a quadrangle which consisted of survival, desire for food, love and care of progeny, and sex. Later, the drives for territory, society orientation, status and acquiescence to cultural codes were discovered. These were condensed to the three drives shown as identity, stimulation and security. They can be easily understood and are valid.

Security

The lowest drive is security. Many would think it to be the highest, but security is the antithesis to fear or anxiety. People want to be free of fear of economic need and of being unloved. Security means freedom from not being taken care of, and therein lies the desire for social security. **Security does not, however, buy happiness or contentment by itself.** Loneliness can be a disease to some.

Stimulation

The second most important drive is stimulation. Its antithesis, boredom, is the tool employed by society for punishment in a prison cell. Most people need other people for stimulation and fun. Games, plays, movies, books, music, dancing and all art collectively, including esthetics, **is a stimulation of life and a weapon against death**.

Identity

The third and highest need in the hierarchy of drives is identity. Its antithesis is anonymity. **Very simply, people like recognition.** They are flattered when another person remembers their name. Their sense of well-being and self-importance is bolstered by achievement no matter how small. There is always something in the life of the meekest person of which he or she can be proud. Lack of showing respect (or identity) is the single most common cause of interpersonal conflict. Lack of receiving rewards from a spouse is the shortest route to the divorce court. Thus, identity and self worth lie at the very heart of every person's needs in their pursuit of happiness.

Philosophic Essentials
Knowledge

First under **philosophy** is knowledge itself. **Epistemology** is the study of origin, nature, and limits of knowledge. Curiosity and the desire for the understanding of the nature of things is a guiding and compelling element. Witness the questions asked by the child and the joy upon understanding what is received. It has been said that **the pursuit of knowledge is life's greatest conquest because it can never be fully achieved**. The pursuit of knowledge is a sword against boredom. **Knowledge is power.**

Attitude

The second part of philosophy is **attitude**. Looking on the bright side of any issue has a way of producing factors for achieving success. **There is always more possibility found when a belief in the positive presides as a fundamental.** Negative people are generally unexciting and lead dull lives. They continuously re-examine each of their organs or the weaknesses of others to find faults. The negative person becomes ill easily. The happy-attitude person beats the odds on fatal diseases. Anyone must believe the brakes are going to work or else he would not risk driving the car. Life is full of risks. Cheerfulness, joy, humor, good will, and positive moods make for happiness.

Spirit

The third but highest rank in philosophy is **spirit**. Philosophers take on subjects not yet measurable by the scientist's weights, calipers and analysis and which must therefore be approached by logic and reason. A philosopher acknowledges that every subject goes from philosophy to science and through it to art. **The subject of spirit is therefore a philosophical question** and metaphysics constitutes one of its branches.

The theosophic philosopher would reason that a limitless universal force exists. People in primitive cultures worshipped the universe, the sun and the moon and all of Nature's elements. One function of most religions has been to ease people's minds of the fear of the unknown by providing some explanation for life's purpose and existence. Compared to the billions of years of the existence of the earth, the entire history of man is but a snap of the finger. Light, reaching our planet, was emitted from suns thousands of light years away, distances incomprehensible to our minds. Our earth's rotation around the sun is like electrons orbiting around the nucleus of an atom making up a mass. Electricity and magnetism are describable but inexplicable.

All the five great religious doctrines teach about a hereafter. There is the promise of a happy life forever as a spiritual essence. But if there is a hereafter in spirit, many believe that there must also be a herebefore. If life is believed to be a continuing unit of existence, then reincarnation and past lives must also be believed.

In chemistry a monad is an atom or element having a valence of one. In biology, a monad is a simple single-celled organism. In metaphysics, a monad is an indivisible and indestructible entity that is the final constituent of the universe.

Whatever the belief (altruism to be an inherited biologic program or altruism to be a desire to do good as a part of a learned culture, or altruism as the Good Samaritan, part of a religious belief), men and women must live in harmony with their neighbors, or unhappiness and resentment will prevail. A spiritual essence may help comfort a person and has been known to heal when all else has failed.

Egocentrism

Many people accuse others of being egotistical. Several factors should be evaluated, however, in considering personal ego. "We" are not better because "they" are different! We may not know of another person's past, their present condition, or their destiny (which some confuse with "karma"). We tend to judge on the basis of our personal standards which may often be grounded by our own limited perceptions and bias. There is a dimension of love or understanding that transcends ordinary human consciousness. To make judgments and find fault with others' beliefs is very egotistical.

I am, after fifty years of study, considered to be quite knowledgeable in my field. Yet, when I realize how really superficial is my knowledge I am embarrassed. Many members of the public often have a notion that doctors know everything or that science is conclusive, final. Fortunately, we do have ways of helping others in need. But when we consider in physics the gravity in black holes being so strong it contains the light, and in chemistry the basics of the single atom, together with all in biology which includes the formulation of life and the assorted behavior of humankind -- for all our progress we remain profoundly ignorant. We still debate our origin and our ultimate fate. That mystique will continue to provoke the human to contain the ego in the millennia ahead.

The Balance in Life

Each individual creates his or her personal pattern of life. For a healthy, vital and fulfilling life, a balance is needed. This would seem to be composed of the body, mind and spirit with human sensibility, sincerity, dependence, freedom, physical and mental health, ethics, goals, honesty, trustworthiness, pride and sensitivity all entwined as the foundation for success in life.

By understanding our body we can promote its health. By understanding our drives we are in a position to understand the sources of stress and problems in human society. By possessing knowledge and an attitude of positive and optimistic thinking, we can stand strong and earn and receive respect. By having an inner spiritual essence and a powerful source of strength, we can work with principles and develop a philosophy that is profound, dynamic, and consistent. Indeed we can come back from failure. We may recover from tragedy and we are empowered to escape from despair.

If we cannot begin, we cannot finish. Order begets order once progress is put in motion. Each person can touch another, to help direct toward a positive path of life.

Our Mother Earth

In this book, particularly Part III, I have tried to paint a positive picture of our world to come. I would like to think that when I go I would have left the world a little better than when I came. I would hope that my children, grandchildren, and their children will find a progressively better quality of life from the gifts of Mother Earth.

But Mother Earth is becoming ill. We have shredded her outer cloak. We have removed her protective forests; she is becoming bared and exposed and will crack and wither. Her contaminated waterways are like sludge in her veins. One day, and maybe not too far away, she may have a seizure and convulse. She is shocked into frustration by contamination of her electro-magnetic spectrum. She will vomit lava and try to shake herself free of the pain we have wrought. Man for all his technologic skills will be hopelessly inadequate at her retching. We must nurse her back to health.

* * *

In December of 1992 I was again in Rome to lecture and had two days to rest between courses there and in Saudi Arabia. I went alone back to Romolo's Restaurant on Via Garibaldi in Trastevere near the great bend in the Tiber River in the heart of Rome. This was where I spent the first hours with my old friend Robert Ardrey. I silently raised a glass of red wine to him in memory and with thanks for the years he had made me think. The waiters were young. A bearded man and a lady with large gold earrings sat gazing into each other's eyes and kissing hands. A pipe-smoking gentleman walked in escorting a beautiful lady wearing a fur. A fuss was made to find her a table, seemingly where she could catch the most eyes -- eyes of the other ladies, to be sure, as I observed. Nothing had really changed.

I contemplated that Rome was timeless and still stood, and that there would be more like Ardrey and me in the time to come. Each of us is expendable. But maybe, as Robert Henri put it, each of us should put down on paper our thoughts, our ideas to serve as stepping stones for others -- to step on or to avoid. Henri said:

> This thing that I call **dignity** in a human being is inevitably the result of an established order in the universe. Everything that is beautiful is orderly, and there can be no order unless things are in their right relation to each other. Of this right relation throughout the world beauty is born. . . .

> Everywhere I find that the moment order in nature is understood and freely shown, the result is nobility . . . . Nearly all children have nobility of impulse. This orderliness must exist or the world could not hold together.

Our greatest possession is our imagination, through which we create wonders and stimulate lives. There are no limits to this creative power of the mind.

* * *

The Ricketts Creed

I will release the past, let go resentment and remember good.

I will respect the dignity and identity of each human being.

I will be joyfully aware of the whole world around me.

I will grow little by little each day toward honorable pursuits.

I will strive always for excellence and try to improve my performance each day.

I will appreciate the benefits of the accrual of knowledge.

I will be selective in curiosity with a penetrating mind.

I will maintain integrity and not feign honesty or uprightness.

I will assure my body of its life sources of oxygen, food and exercise.

I will resist all negatives.

My stream of consciousness will result in a positive power.

My prayers will be first of gratitude and thanksgiving.

My life will be a manifestation of love.

Robert M. Ricketts

APPENDIX

INTRODUCTION

The human appendix is a small "extra" part of the gut that hangs downward from the large intestine. It has been described as being a remnant of evolution and has no particular function as it is often surgically removed in cases of appendicitis with no functional consequences.

An Appendix in a book is also an "extra" that may either contain afterthoughts or subjects not easily fitting in the main body of the book. I have been encouraged to relate certain particular experiences in my life that may be of extra or unusual interest.

The following disassociated subjects are thus included:

    I.   One of my letters to and answer from Mr. Ronald Reagan when he was running the first time for the governorship of California

   II.   A statement by L. R. Schwedes on a comparison of a democracy with a republic

  III.   The stress-rating scale of Thomas Holmes and R. H. Rahe analyzed for consideration by the public

  IV.   Stress management

   V.   One patient's experience

  VI.   Factors in living past 100 years

 VII.   The mystery of the origin of romantic love

VIII.   Clarification concerning the prostate gland

  IX.   Social sciences unraveled

   X.   The catastrophe of the savings and loan companies

  XI.   More American problems

 XII.   A letter to President William J. Clinton

* * *

I
ONE OF MY LETTERS TO AND ANSWER FROM MR. RONALD REAGAN

This author's opinions concerning appropriate directions for America to take have been gleaned and nurtured for many years. The two letters that follow, from May of 1966 (one from the author to Ronald Reagan when Mr. Reagan was a candidate for Governor of California, and the other his reply) reflect my concerns about America nearly 27 years ago.

Mr. Ronald Reagan
1669 San Onofre Drive
Pacific Palisades, California

Dear Mr. Reagan:

Your fund-raising party at the Palladium was a tremendous thrill. You should be very proud. I'm sure you realize your responsibility.

You are a breath of fresh air and a hope on the whole American scene for serious-minded people. How can I, as an individual, help? Maybe to begin I can put some thoughts on paper and make a few suggestions for your consideration.

1. <u>You must become a teacher.</u>
Constitutional Republicans (notice: <u>not</u> conservatives) talk far above the heads of the average voter. <u>Too much credit for knowledge is given to the audience.</u> Personal experience with job applicants for orthodontic personnel positions leads me to the conclusion that the public at large is so unsophisticated that we can't reach them with the usual appeals because <u>the average person does not possess the background of history to comprehend.</u>

An alarming percentage of high school graduates are incapable of passing a very easy test of simple arithmetic percentages. Most young people don't have the foggiest notion of the workings of local, state, and federal government, and they couldn't care less. It must be assumed that parents are not far ahead of them. As Kenneth McFarland says, "We've got to quit assuming that because children are born and raised in American they automatically know Americanism . . . . They've got to be taught. . . . Each one teach one."

Only last evening my 13-year-old daughter asked me to help her for a test and we entered into a discussion about a democracy and a republic. She said her teacher stated that the U.S. was a democracy -- at least that is what she understood, and the text book stated such. I spent over an hour with her looking up articles on the subject from my files and carefully explained that the Constitution set up a Republic -- it is in our Pledge of Allegiance. I even underlined, in red, certain statements and sent her to school with them. The driver of her car pool also insisted that we are a democracy -- I hope you see what I mean.

How old is the pure democratic idea? Count its number of failures. Apparently we can't assume either that the schools teach Americanism, patriotism, or moralism any longer.

When I was President of Pacific Palisades Rotary Club, we had a joint meeting with the Beverly Hills Club and I sat beside Senator Alan Cranston. He talked about the voters of

California giving the Democrats a mandate for all the social reforms. He said everything that Governor Brown was doing was the will of the people. He put the blame for all his programs on the public because 50.1% rules in a democratic state.

The people must be taught to go slowly and weigh changes carefully. People must be charged with responsibility in selecting leaders who will uphold the laws and Constitution and not make a new set by their own majority rule with their own expedient aims. This ends in mob rule.

2. You must teach in simple terms.

Even with my college background, I had to use a dictionary to understand some terms familiar to Adlai Stevenson but not familiar to me. After looking up egalitarianism and seeing it meant equalitarianism I still didn't understand what he was talking about. In fact, it wasn't until I understood that democracy usually stood for total equality while constitutional republicanism stood for individual liberty that I could see the difference. Further, I didn't realize that equality should be limited to a concept of being created equal in the eyes of God and on moral grounds and that man must have social inequalities in order to be free. All this is implicit before understanding what the philosophy of egalitarianism is all about. Truly all slaves are equal. Freedom is when a man can move up or down in his society. It's got to be taught.

We need a teacher. The greatest teacher in history used simple language and allegories to His followers. Things can be explained as an image of another more simple thing. We need to explain that democracy has dangers and that the constitution of a republic protects us and gives us freedom and liberty. The antithesis or opposite of freedom is slavery. Are we not sending our children into slavery? Sovereign power must reside with elected bodies with checks and balances for control even at the state level. The unions are grabbing power far above their numbers and relation to society.

3. Identify with all groups.

Make sure that people understand that both parties stand for representative government and there are great similarities. You have been in both parties. Explain to all levels of intellect the differences as you perceive them! (You do a great job here, with your warm, homespun, and wholesome attitude.) But remember, don't take it all too seriously -- there is magic in your eternal smile. Man is deprived of his senses when he allows himself to become frustrated or to experience hatred. Emotional explosions cause greater loss than gain. Love reflects love . . . a politician must take hate and reflect love.

4. Fight the stigma of a lack of social consciousness by Republicans.

As far as I'm concerned, you are running for Governor of the state now, not Governor of the Republican Party. We must accept social welfare -- it's already on the books. The argument is, what level? We can't take it all back and we shouldn't want to. Maybe we should use it intelligently but handle it properly. Keep in mind that the word "republic" means "affairs of the public", the whole public, all the people.

But, the problem comes in taxes, which you do a fantastic job of explaining. We need schools and education -- with their research, physical facilities, good well-paid teachers -- and its traditions for the future of our country. Make it clear that you are for all of these --

not against any of these except for waste and extravagance. However, as you stressed, free handouts and a system so developed that it pays more _not_ to work is most unfair and will lead to ruin.

More than once I have been asked by incompetent dismissed employees to make fraudulent statements to enable them to continue on unemployment benefits as a paid vacation.

How far can we go with <u>social consciousness</u>? No one likes to see people starve, nor likes to see them sick. But neither is it fair to give them free money for anything above absolute need. What kind of dignity does this promote? In my opinion, no one is entitled to that status without earning it. When people do earn it, they have no trouble in acquiring status in society no matter what color the skin. Above all, a personal respect is gained -- while on the doles they cannot gain self respect, self worth or identity.

5. <u>Explain that the Constitution still applies to problems today.</u>
This is the big one! The cliche that the Constitution is outmoded is a tool of the enemy. It's like saying that capitalism is a failure when it not only is the best but the <u>only</u> system that has ever kept all of its people from starvation when people always have starved. Even in the depths of the big depression, food was available in America.

What are the changes in our society since the Constitution was written? We <u>communicate better</u> with radio and television, jet air mail, dial telephones with satellite transfers, and lazer beams are just around the corner. We can <u>travel faster</u> and more comfortably in modern autos by wide swift freeways, and no place in our country is more than four hours by jet. We have <u>more home conveniences</u> which add to <u>comfort and an easier life</u>. We have made truly fantastic <u>technical advances</u>. But our basic nature and instincts have not changed -- evolution is slow, very slow compared to known civilization.

All these changes have brought on some different problems, however, which must be recognized. The big one mainly is <u>urbanization</u>. We are becoming a country of more city dwellers than country dwellers, and even our country folk are no longer isolated. What is the difference?

In past years the American rural families often lived miles away from their neighbors. They lived from the soil. They were almost <u>independent of society as a whole</u> and wanted to remain free. Their social and cultural contacts were their church and school. Although <u>independent from large societies</u>, these people were more <u>dependent upon their neighbors</u> for help in time of need. Good neighbors were loved and cherished because they often <u>needed each other</u>. Since property was hard to come by, everyone respected the other person's property. They needed a faith and an outside strength to survive the hard life.

Today the city dweller lives close to his neighbor but is independent of his neighbor while dependent on the larger society. The larger society provides food, clothing, housing, transportation and now entertainment. The larger society caters to protection for the business welfare of the society. This society feeds on the masses for survival because it needs society collectively rather than individually. Children as well as many adults have come to disregard and disrespect others' private property.

Man historically has needed to be led. His history is one of almost continuous war. Thence from democratic representative government we ultimately arrived at "constitutional republicanism".

Now the big question: does the Constitution still apply to this kind of society? The answer is <u>Yes, but even more so.</u> Without his neighbor for protection and help, the individual is completely at the <u>mercy of society</u> as a whole. Without a Constitution to protect that society, how can it long endure until it becomes a socialistic state? The danger lies in giving elected officials a blank check.

I believe you will be the best governor California has ever had. I want you to believe it, too.

I can't believe that someone in the swim in Washington can see the needs of individuals at the community or state level. It is a little like asking the caddy to give you the line or roll of a putt. He can tell you the average line, but he doesn't know how hard you are going to hit it; in other words, no one on the outside can tell you the exact nature of personal needs.

6. <u>Beat them at the semantic game</u>.

To be democratic is a term that has been made to sound good. It sounds fair and appeals to a right sense of equality. But words are merely tools of thought. Thoughts cannot be conveyed until they can be understood. The ten-year-old mind can't conceive the difference between democracy and constitutional republicanism. Let's make republicanism sound fair and for the common people, and for the good of all with no strings attached. It's the back-bone of human rights.

Certainly the founding fathers realized the dangers, because socialism and communism were centuries old and were not new when the Constitution was written. The scholars of those days were informed of the disasters of pure democratic societies in the long run.

Each individual must be led toward a personal interest in government. The public must be made aware of the wisdom and good judgment of a republic with free enterprise and fair competition. Many imagine the Republicans as the snooty, the filthy rich, the affluent blue bloods, or the independent, selfish, and egotistical business man. This image must be destroyed. Republicanism must be explained as a policy fair for all, and as the best way for the progress of a complete society.

7. <u>Explain the long-range implications of the welfare state</u>.

Under the pure democratic philosophy, people conceive of short-range benefits, better living standards, and apparent higher prosperity. Many really don't understand the meaning of the word capital. The truth is, many are mortgaged and living on borrowed money and can't see the long-range results. Our modern business philosophy is to work around taxes and hedge for inflation rather than following prudent business practice.

Today, credit is needed to create markets, but taking on too much debt is shackling some of our young people. It will be bondage for them. The alarming increase in bankruptcy, the taking over of home and business mortgages, and the necessary tightening of the reins are felt. Savings and loan companies were granted license to steal -- in their own words. There's something wrong someplace.

The results are inflation or uncontrolled deflation. This is your baby. But this doesn't mean much to the man on the street. To him there's no problem in living on borrowed money -- living high today but finding it tough to pay back later. It means the money must be paid back, with interest, by tougher taxation or limitation of spending at a later date. Some say, "It's okay for my children to pay for these debts since they are going to reap the benefits, aren't they?" The fact is, people can no longer comprehend the billions. They think in some ethereal manner of juggling money at the higher levels and that it doesn't mean anything. This fallacy should be pointed out.

While I was in South America in 1961 on a lecture tour I spent a week in Brazil and made some friends there. During seven days (the week of the Bel Air fires) I saw the cruzerio drop from 370 to 375 to one U.S. dollar. The bank tellers were on strike and business was at a halt. Businessmen were frantic. Cost accounting was impossible. People were secretly sending money outside the country, buying American stocks and Swiss currency. The importance of the U.S. to the whole free world scale was emphasized when they related to the U.S. dollar in values as their own money changed.

At that time, governments were rising and falling in South America with the stability of their currency. Peron, as a dictator, had played Robin Hood. He allegedly had robbed the country's higher classes but had shipped carloads of gold to Europe after taking care of the inside group. The recovery of Argentina in 1961 was dependent on slow restoration of their currency. While in Bolivia, I cashed a twenty-dollar bill and got more folding money than would comfortably fit into one pocket.

The story does not end there. We were visited last winter by a colleague from Rio de Janeiro. He had stood manning a machine gun during the uprisings of last year when the Communists tried to take over. The women (his wife and daughter) had paraded in the streets in prayer to prevent open gun fire. The cruzerio had rocketed to over 2000 to one U.S. dollar -- the country was bankrupt and in chaos. Only by the will of the dedicated constitutional defenders and the control by certain army generals was it saved at all. It thus became an oligarchy.

They said it couldn't happen there, but it did. Many say it can't happen here -- look at the anarchy of only a few people in Watts.

8. Explain anarchy.
   Explain the need for laws and the function of order in a society. The mob violence is like the survival in a jungle and does not reflect civilization, but is a throwback to disorder. We must belong to a society and be bound by an order for the preservation of that society.

Now, these are some of the thoughts of a professional man dealing with society. They are confounding, and offer the challenge faced by many generations past. We must accept them and move forward toward freedom, not socialistic slavery.

Sincerely yours,

Robert Murray Ricketts

Robert M. Ricketts, D.D.S.

To which he replied:

RONALD REAGAN
Pacific Palisades

May 25, 1966

Robert M. Ricketts, D.D.S.
La Colina Building
984 Monument Street
Pacific Palisades, California

Dear Dr. Ricketts:

This is just a quick line between campaign trips to acknowledge your good letter and to say that you have offered some very constructive suggestions. I am deeply grateful. We only have two weeks to go now and as you can imagine, we're all working very hard.

Thanks again for taking the time and trouble to write and again, thanks for your support.

Sincerely,

/s/ Ronald Reagan

/s/ Ronald Reagan

RR:ss

* * *

II
A STATEMENT BY L.R. SCHWEDES ON
A COMPARISON OF A DEMOCRACY WITH A REPUBLIC

When quoting the passage appearing below in the Rotary Club Bulletin of Santa Monica, California, L.R. Schwedes also quoted Prof. Alexander Fraser Tytler who wrote as follows over two centuries ago:

"A democracy CANNOT EXIST as a permanent form of government. It can only exist until the voters discover they can vote themselves largesse out of the public treasury. From that moment on the majority always votes for the candidate promising the most benefits from the public treasury, with the result that democracy always collapses over a loose fiscal policy, to be followed by a dictatorship."

The following data is quoted from War Department Training Manual No. 2000-25, dated **November 30, 1928**.

"DEMOCRACY:
A government of the masses. Authority derived through mass meeting
  or any other form of 'direct' expression.
Results in mobocracy.
Attitude toward property is communistic - negating property rights.
Attitude toward law is that the will of the majority shall
  regulate, whether it be based upon deliberation or governed
  by passion, prejudice and impulse, without restraint or
  regard to consequences.
Results in demagogism, license, agitation, discontent, anarchy.

REPUBLIC:
Authority is derived through election by the people of public
  officials best fitted to represent them.
Attitude toward property is respect for laws and individual
  rights, and a sensible economic procedure.
Attitude toward law is the administration of justice in accord
  with fixed principles and established evidence, with a strict
  regard to consequences.
A greater number of citizens and extent of territory may be brought
  within its compass.
Avoids the dangerous extreme of either tyranny or mobocracy.
Results in statesmanship, liberty, reason, justice, contentment
  and progress.
Is the 'standard' form of government throughout the world."

* * *

III

THE STRESS-RATING SCALE OF THOMAS HOLMES AND R.H. RAHE ANALYZED FOR CONSIDERATION BY THE PUBLIC

In 1961, Thomas Holmes, a psychiatrist, and R. H. Rahe published a "Social Readjustment Rating Scale" based on 15 years of documented study of thousands of patients' records. They corroborated what others had found -- that patients presenting with ill health, in a variety of diseases, had **in the previous 12 months** experienced severe social and personal problems. They listed these in a hierarchy of 43 categories.

When a person scored a total of 150, only a 37% chance of illness was expected. Between a score of 150 and 200 it rose to a 51% chance. When over 300, the patient was facing odds of 80% of becoming ill. (See chart)

Event	Value	Your Score
Death of spouse	100	_____
Divorce	73	_____
Marital separation	65	_____
Jail term	63	_____
Death of close family member	63	_____
Personal injury or illness	53	_____
Marriage	50	_____
Fired from work	47	_____
Marital reconciliation	45	_____
Retirement	45	_____
Change in family member's health	44	_____
Pregnancy	40	_____
Sex difficulties	39	_____
Addition to family	39	_____
Business readjustment	39	_____
Change in financial status	38	_____
Death of close friend	37	_____
Change to different line of work	36	_____
Change in number of marital arguments	35	_____
Mortgage or loan over $30,000	31	_____
Foreclosure of mortgage or loan	30	_____
Change in work responsibilities	29	_____
Son or daughter leaving home	29	_____
Trouble with in-laws	29	_____
Outstanding personal achievement	28	_____
Spouse begins or stops work	26	_____
Starting or finishing school	26	_____
Change in living conditions	25	_____
Revision of personal habits	24	_____
Trouble with boss	23	_____
Change in work hours, conditions	20	_____
Change in residence	20	_____
Change in schools	20	_____
Change in recreational habits	19	_____
Change in church activities	19	_____
Change in social activities	18	_____
Mortgage or loan under $30,000	17	_____
Change in sleeping habits	16	_____
Change in number of family gatherings	15	_____
Change in eating habits	15	_____
Vacation	13	_____
Christmas season	12	_____
Minor violation of the law	11	_____
TOTAL		_____

Analysis of the stress-rating scale may permit the following conclusions:

(1) Change forced on a person unexpectedly or any alteration of routine life may bring on undue stress;
(2) Economic problems, debt or factors associated with finances are accumulative;
(3) Interpersonal conflicts seem to bother people most.

In essence, those closest to a person such as a spouse, the family, neighbors or fellow workers may be the major source of distress. Each person should recognize that the potential cause of major stress lies in these areas and attempt to sustain the best harmony in inter-personal relations.

* * *

IV
STRESS MANAGEMENT

As Hans Selye showed almost 50 years ago, common reactions to stress were ulceration of the stomach, shrinkage of the thymus and lymph glands and enlargement of the adrenal glands. There are two avenues open to the treatment of pathologic reaction to stress (which he called distress).

The first path, taken by some psychologists, is to change the environment or life-style. Some are now adopting methods to relieve anxiety and high blood pressure by relaxation meditation. However, the second or opposite method is more biologic in the long run. The body's systems to resist stress are enhanced by better nutrition, better thought control and better understanding of the underlying factors producing tension. In other words, treat the body's weakness rather than treating the symptom, because stress is unavoidable in modern life. Getting rid of one problem only leaves the next for stress reaction if the body is weak.

— • —

The following was received in the mail one day:
"The ready acceptance of the stress and strain concept is understandable. It nourishes the ego of the believer and it is readily acceptable to the unfortunate victim and his relatives. It places coronary heart disease in the position of being an unjust reward for virtue. How much nicer it is when stricken with a coronary thrombosis to be told it is all due to hard work, laudable ambition and selfless devotion to duty, than to be told that it is due to gluttony and physical indolence."

(Author unknown)

* * *

V
ONE PATIENT'S EXPERIENCE

Throughout the course of history it has been noted a single individual can entirely alter the life of another individual, even masses of individuals. I am among the masses whose life was altered, in a most positive and meaningful way, by Dr. Robert Ricketts. He was first my doctor, then my most avid encourager, helping me believe in myself. He was my mentor in the knowledge of science and the psychology of life.

Here's how it happened. For many years as a child I needed orthodontic work. I came from a large family of nine children and my parents couldn't afford that luxury. My teeth were turned inward so badly that I was often teased by other children. I was even called "bulldozer-blade teeth", and it hurt. I became quite an introvert, absorbing myself in studies. I didn't have many friends because I didn't like the teasing.

When I was about nine years old I was in a Christmas play, and with costume and make-up the other children loved me. I thought then that what I would love doing most in life was acting. I became very good at it, but when it came to auditioning for major parts, opening my mouth to talk or smile, I simply withdrew. I was paralyzed with the fear of being teased or ridiculed and decided to go into another field that didn't require a beautiful smile to make a living. I chose medicine, and I had a good mind for it, but my heart was with the performing arts.

As I grew older I decided I would get a job and pay for my own orthodontic treatment. I was dismayed when several dentists said they would have to pull several teeth to accomplish results. I didn't want that, and gave up the idea.

And then in 1971 I was introduced to Dr. Ricketts by a mutual friend. He did the orthodontic work without pulling one tooth, and as a result of his brilliant work of art I received a beautiful smile. What is most memorable of Dr. Ricketts during the time of his treatment of my teeth was his ever positive words of encouragement. He always told me that I was special and that the new smile would be a finishing touch. He seemed to have the innate ability to evoke the best in everyone around him.

I did become an actress and just last year, 20 years after treatment, I did a commercial for which I was selected because I have a radiant smile. This may be true, but a light within burns brighter for me because of Dr. Ricketts' having touched my life with hope and compassion. For that I will be forever grateful.

Vangel Creech

* * *

VI
FACTORS IN LIVING PAST 100 YEARS

Studies of the characteristics of older people, who have kept on going until 100 years of age, revealed some interesting findings. These were studied and explained by Dr. Robert Samp of the University of Wisconsin in a concept of "Sex, Salad, and Scotch", discussed before and now emphasized here related to health.

Symbolized by "sex" was the characteristic that these centenarians retained a passion for life. They were giving and outgoing. They continued to be "turned on" by the whole world around them. They genuinely loved and appreciated other people of both sexes. They remained physically active, even sexually, past a century of living. They were altruistic to the end.

The "salad" symbolized a simplicity of life. A balance in life meant a dearth of excesses. It meant a moderation in the diet -- they were not gluttons. Moderation in habits was also implicit in their lifestyle. They were sensible in their living patterns, no matter what their education, vocation, genetic predisposition, or economic level. Large meals before bed was a factor in early death. Samp didn't mind people smoking so long as they did not exhale -- yes, exhale!

The "scotch" represented people who are able to partake of recreation between crises in life. Everyone has failures and tragedies, but these centenarians, studied from their histories, bent with the wind, yet didn't break. They enjoyed their rewards in between bouts of catastrophe. There was no evidence that people who had only one drink a day died younger than teetotalers. Meditation was shown to be an effective method of relaxation and a factor to help, to heal, and to thrive.

Stress was a destroyer. Thirty percent of their population didn't make it to 70 years. Those who survived established priorities. They retained a marvelous sense of humor. Further, and most significantly, they maintained a positive attitude.

* * *

VII
THE MYSTERY OF THE ORIGIN OF ROMANTIC LOVE

The basis for this discussion was prompted by Will Durant in his "Pleasures of Philosophy".

When a single-celled animal grows, its volume increases more than its surface. The outside of the cell functions for nutrition, the inside of the cell operates for its survival and for its reproduction. From its surface it obtains its oxygen and nutrients. As the size increases a change is required in the ratio of its internal materials to its external surface. The whole mass must be divided in order to grow. Like a balloon squeezed in the middle, two new cells are formed as the old disappears.

Ironically, as primitive one-celled animals or colonies progress they tend to wither and become rejuvenated when blended with another cell or colony. In other words, organisms tend to need other organisms.

Cross-breeding is employed in animal husbandry to bring out the strongest elements in both partners. The sexes became divided for the strengthening of genetic power.

In insects the female dominates by far in size and strength. The queen bee is an example. In fact, as soon as many male insects finally are able to find her in the mood she may be modest and coy; and as soon as their nuptial delight is consummated she will quickly devour the poor fellow.

In fish and amphibia a plethora of eggs is spread and covered with billions of sperm for natural selection. A wide berth in excess is needed because of no parental care and low odds of survival. As the evolutionary scale was climbed and care for the young became practiced, Nature produced a more efficient ration of eggs to the final surviving offspring such as bird and mammal.

With one-on-one copulation finally only those males having the strongest drive for pursuit sought and found the chance to spread their genes and leave progeny. The female, doing the choosing since the time of the insects, sought the strongest and most powerful as offering the best prospects for success of her brood. The male animal in the wild fought for dominance and territory — not for the female. His conquests were against rivals for status and the females were only a part of the reward. His attraction became a part of his identity.

Physiologically and psychologically, male and female children are different at birth. Most boys soon are attracted to mechanical tools, and most girls to color, design and dolls. Most boys later seek sports, action, companionship and competition, while most girls delight more in art, dance, music, and things pertaining to home and children. By age four, little girls have already learned how to manipulate their fathers' weaknesses by their charm and coyness, and they become preoccupied by stories of princes.

Our research has suggested that by age six the average size of a boy's face was more than one year ahead of a girl's. By their prepubertal period, boys and girls start to become a mystery to each other. The boy at age 10 to 12 may often exclaim, "I hate girls!" which is a way of proving he is vastly aware and may be frightened about his feelings.

Physiologic Love

With the sprouting of hair, the observation of greater muscle mass, the lowering of the voice, and the increased sensitivity of the penis, the young male finds his own New Renaissance. Each new chest hair is counted. (I was mortified when at age 13 my brother-in-laws put me down and pulled out my few chest hairs.) Boys secretly flex their muscles in front of a mirror and observe their throbbing male organ with a new-found ego. They realize their days of conquest are about to start, but they are frightened.

Pubic and axillary hair also come to the female. Her widening buttocks and soft contours start earlier. She watches impatiently for nice breasts to form, knowing full well their luring value to the male. She often seeks another female friend for comparison of physical changes and exchanging deepest psychological shocks that her estrogen has produced. Her nights are filled with stars and her days are broken by dreams of romantic adventure. She feels trapped between bobby-sox and high heels.

At this time lads are quite awkward and lassies have learned to blush. Their curiosity for the whole world explodes. It's also a difficult time for the development of reason. They are ready for a matrix shift. Nature has accomplished its plan for survival of the species -- the reproductive organs have matured.

Romantic love is a caring so deep that the interests of another person are placed first. It has its origins in physiology and hormonal push and lies deep in instinct.

Ardrey, in "African Genesis", talks about "love's antique hand" and describes several birds that create life-long attachments. Probably in human conclusion we have been lured into belief that the male is the sole aggressor. This is despite the full brilliant plumage of male birds and magnificent antlers and sleek muscled body of the male herbivore. Perhaps we have been pushed off course, in our human understanding, by tradition and morality in assuming the female to be passive. In Ardrey's words, "If it is the behaviour of the female towards a particular male that awakens his full sexual response, then we must conclude that the power of sexual choice rests largely with the female, and that sexual competition is not so much between males for the female of their choice, as between females for the male of theirs. And so the male becomes the sexual attraction, and the female in her response the sexual aggressor."

It may appear undignified to liken man to lower animals, but this is the path from which our instincts emerged. Tie instinct together with human imagination and romantic love loses its mystique.

* * *

VIII
CLARIFICATION CONCERNING THE PROSTATE GLAND

The mammary gland in females is openly discussed socially. Palpation for "lumps" is common knowledge in feminine hygiene and causes no embarrassment. But for some reason the prostate, a male gland also related to the reproductive system, is shockingly avoided in parlor conversation and even in the barroom as well. My concern for the prostate gland is due to its involvement with my father, myself, and the death of six friends and close colleagues by cancer of this organ.

Most laymen know less about the prostate than any other gland. In fact, they may even misscall it the prostrate! Male hygiene knowledge is virtually non-existent. I wish, therefore, to reflect on the lessons I learned from Dr. Roderic Turner, a well-known urologist at U.C.L.A and also on my own understanding from experience.

Glands are usually composed of clusters of sacs with a lining of cells that manufacture substances which are secreted. Sweat glands for perspiration and temperature control and mammary glands for milk production are classic examples. The pituitary, thyroid and adrenal, endocrine glands producing potent chemicals are other examples. The prostate gland functions to elaborate a fluid which protects and delivers sperm to the cervix of the female uterus for fertilization. It is the main constituent of semen.

The prostate remains dormant in a boy until acted upon by "gonadotropic hormones" at puberty. When hair grows under the arm and on the male chest, when fuzz appears on the face and the voice lowers, it becomes a signal that this gland has sprung into action.

Located at the base of the bladder, the prostate is composed of three lobes: one underneath and one on either side of the urethra (the tract for flow of urine from the storage in the bladder). In the young male each lobe is small, about the size of a kidney bean. With age, in most males the lobes continue to grow. (Testosterone [a male hormone] from the testes, which is stimulated from the pituitary, is elaborated into the bloodstream hourly and daily, and this causes the prostate to grow. Enlarged prostates have never been found in eunuchs.) Constrained tightly in the perineum they enlarge to the size and shape of a horse chestnut, thereby restricting the lumen of the tube and inhibiting the flow of urine to a dribble. Three events then may follow.

First, an increased pressure to force out fluid builds up the muscular wall of the bladder, making it smaller and less capable of containing a normal volume. Consequently urination needs to be more frequent. This also may cause a restricted flow from the kidney to the bladder and lead to toxic accumulation in the kidney and impaired function of the whole body. It causes early uremia because the blood cannot be filtered.

Second, the enlarged gland may experience less blood supply, limiting oxygen and nutrients and reducing cellular waste elimination of that tissue. Hence, it may more easily become infected. I was told alcohol and spicy foods, particularly pepper, stimulate and irritate it.

But third, and of most serious consequence, the individual cells within the gland through biologic restriction may lose their immune capacity. With that they may become cancerous.

When detected early the more serious complications can be avoided by surgical resection with small instruments through the penis. The operation, which is performed endoscopically rather than with open surgery, takes about 45 minutes.

Three problems should be kept in mind regarding this gland. One is that serious problems can develop with minimum pain or discomfort. Second, the "macho" male, bearing illness restlessly and possessing a profound ego, will try to ignore it. Third, "business as usual" will prevent him from stopping for consideration of his own health and welfare.

Detection is made by palpation by the physician through a rectal examination. A PSA blood test for a "prostate specific antigen" identifies cancer presence. An ultra sonogram also is used to give information regarding the prostate size and suspicion of malignancy. In addition, a needle biopsy, causing no discomfort, is performed as an office procedure. The gland should be relatively soft, like the web between the thumb knuckle and the forefinger when a fist is made. When the gland more resembles the hardness of the joint of the thumb a tumor is suspected.

My first personal bout with prostatitis was at age forty-five when I felt a fullness and discomfort in the area. Like an infection of the tonsil in the throat, the gland when infected can become painful and swollen. This condition is not classified as a venereal disease. However, some urologists believe that bacteria can be transmitted to the male from the vaginal environment of the female. Scientific experiments with married couples suggest the transfer. In my case the acute condition was treated successfully with antibiotics. It fully subsided and yearly examinations revealed nothing alarming.

Twenty-three years later, however, at age sixty-eight, I became aware of great difficulty in urination. It also became more frequent with a more pungent odor. After returning from a lecture tour in Mexico where I had eaten spicy foods I developed a fever and became ill. I easily diagnosed my own acute infection of the prostate. It was again treated with antibiotics, a sulfa drug, but this time the gland remained enlarged. I consulted Dr. Turner, and my prostate remained so firm he was alarmed. Also, my PSA was slightly elevated to a level of concern. An operation was recommended. I also remarkably altered my nutrition and partook of supplemental therapy for three months while fulfilling lecture commitments in Germany before the surgery.

I was lucky. No cancer cells were found after thorough examination of the removed tissue of the gland at biopsy. There was little discomfort -- only the nuisance of a catheter in place for three or four days during recuperation, with some back pain due to immobilization and possibly the spinal anesthesia. I felt like a new person, relieved physically but a greater salvation mentally.

After the whole process I became somewhat angered at society as a whole and the medical field in particular. Here I was, a professional person in the healing arts and yet so uninformed and taken to the "brink". For this reason, I want to share the experience with all middle-aged or senior men. It is a pity that many men at an age where wisdom is accumulated, at a position as patriarch of a family, and where they can make great contributions to society, are taken by an avoidable malignant disease.

Mr. Robert Dole, a Republican leader of the House of Representatives, did much to publicize the prostate problem. Several signs and symptoms need to be recognized and detected early. Having personally experienced the progress of the condition, I offer the following as a course of male hygiene:

1. Recognize that we are all different and symptoms and timing of problems may occur at different ages.
2. Be alert for fullness or pressure sensation deep between the legs on jogging or sitting, particularly on long automobile trips.
3. Take note of any change of flow in urination or time required to empty the bladder.
4. Take account particularly of dull aching pain following urination.
5. Take note of the caliber of stream: if the stream is interrupted or not steady this is another sign of a problem. [When, at a half-time at a game, there are lines at the

urinal, never get in a row of white-haired older people -- get behind kids!]
6. Particularly notice waking up during a night's normal sleep with the need for urination.
7. Seek yearly examination from an informed physician or specialist.
8. Do not delay too long if your urologist recommends an operation. Contemporary methods do not cut nerves and destroy sensations or performance.

For prophylaxis several measures are offered from various health advocates:
1. Some studies suggest supplementation of zinc, and other nutritional factors may offer some hope for preservation and function of the prostate.
2. Some physicians recommend prophylactic ejaculation.
3. Enlighten yourself and discuss hygiene factors with your mate.
4. Realize that the prostate is a part of the human body and adult males should not be embarrassed to consider its health for the welfare of the whole family.

Men have the erroneous conception that anything done to the prostate will destroy their sexual ability. "This is pure balderdash," says Dr. Turner.

— • —

It has been now almost five years since my operation. I'm told that I'm still capable of procreation, and I'm still active sexually. I say this to help prevent the anxiety that others may have with regard to their own personal problems with the male organs.

* * *

IX
SOCIAL SCIENCES UNRAVELED

At the risk of being too pedantic, I feel it will help in communication to refer more specifically to the social sciences because many people find this broad science to be confusing.

The essence of **social science** is the study of a person's existence as a member of a family, a state, or any institution within a community. For my own use I divided the broad subject of social science into ten sub-subjects. The following first five are considered primary and the second five secondary:

Economics deals with production of supply, its distribution and the satisfaction of people's needs and wants. It has a major impact on all societies exemplified by wars over hunting and gathering territory in the most primitive cultures.

Sociology pertains to the relationship of people, their organization and the processes of change in a society.

Cultural Anthropology deals with the contrasts of different societies both past and present.

Politics involves the most ideal methods for the promotion of good will and better friendship among people and between countries.

Metaphysics attempts to explain the nature of reality and the ultimate benefits from relationship with others and with God.

Physiology, a secondary but nonetheless important subject, addresses the intrigue of interpersonal relationships as they affect mental and emotional processes and mankind's adjustment to his environment.

Ethology is the scientific study of animal behavior as it possibly relates to humankind.

Sociobiology is a relatively new field which brings together many of the foregoing aspects of society, particularly as they relate to stress in the modern culture.

Management is also a new field which entails the processes of motivation of others toward the achievement of common goals.

Esthetics is usually classified under philosophy but as mathematical analysis of beauty is possible, particularly with the Divine Proportion, esthetics is brought under science and involves humankind to a remarkable extent.

* * *

X
THE CATASTROPHE OF THE SAVINGS AND LOAN COMPANIES

To most of us the failures of the savings and loan institutions was a mystery. Most people have their own problems. They go about their business and use a bank or a savings and loan company to deposit money so they can save, create a margin for emergencies, draw on it to write checks, or use a credit card. They know little or nothing, however, regarding the principles of the workings of the banking industry.

Money lenders have operated as a business throughout the history of mankind. Any reader of the Bible knows that Jesus kicked them out of the synagogue.

Each working person earns a wage or a salary. That pay becomes a profit. The money received can be considered a property that he now owns. In a free country that property (money) can be exchanged for other property (goods) or the property of skill (services).

When that property (money) is deposited in a bank they pay you a fee for the use of your money. In essence, they are going to use your property so they will pay you a "rent" fee. By the "renting" of your money to them, you have given them the right to use it. For that permission, a rate or a percentage of its value will be paid to you as "rent", which is called interest. In small amounts, the interest is paid by the banks as costs for management. This is usually the small checking accounts in which the bank's use of your money pays for the processing of the checks. This is the reason why they need a "balance" so that such costs are covered, and this is why they charge for a withdrawal when you have exceeded your deposit -- now they are renting you their property on which you fairly should pay a rental fee.

Now this is banking in its most simple form which any school child should understand. Let's see further what the bank does.

As I have tried to explain throughout this narrative, capital (money from profit from someone) is needed to create a business. When businesses grow they need help and in this way provide jobs. **A "job" is very simply an assistant or help to someone else to get work accomplished or a project completed.** In asking for a job, the question often asked is "Do you need any help?" Hence the posting of the sign "Help Wanted".

Many workers miss the whole idea of "helping". If the business fails, they are no longer needed for assistance in running it, and they lose their jobs. Therefore, the goal of any worker or assistant should be toward the stability and the success of their company! There should be pride in the work! The product they make should be as good as possible, or the service they render should be as "tops" as they can possibly accomplish!

If the demands of the helpers and the cost of their service is too high, then the business (management) will not thrive. A squeeze on the profit leaves four problems. First, there is no enlargement of the business (expansion) to create the need for more help (jobs). Second, there is no profit to spend on research and development (R & D) for the creation of new products for the marketplace or to meet competition. Third, equipment wears out and new technology develops, and the old may need replacement, and profits are needed for maintenance. But fourth and foremost, the product itself may be reduced in quality in order to squeeze profits out and the company will no longer meet competition.

All these conditions are a part of the banking system and we don't realize it. When expansion is desired, when new machines need to be installed, or when marketing and promotion (advertising) need to be improved for the health of a business, a company or business may need to rent more money (borrow from a lender).

When a person or a business needs to borrow (rent money), they go to an institution which is designed for that purpose. They are charged a rent fee (interest) that is greater than what is paid by the bank (as rent) to the person who deposited those funds. The difference in the rents paid to the depositors and the rents charged others (borrowers) is the profit made by the bank. It is called the "spread".

Banks have essentially four different kinds of accounts, or different types of depositors. The ordinary checking account is understood. The second type of account is also simple -- it is a savings account, in which the rent fee paid is somewhat higher because the cost of the bank's operation for drawing checks is not needed.

The third type is a "money market" account, which has a higher rent fee to depositors on a short-term basis. This is connected with money rented by the government. The nature of these accounts fluctuates with the economy.

The fourth account is a certificate of deposit (CD) which is a long-term account, the rental or interest rate of which is fixed.

There are other ways a bank makes money. If a person or business wants to build a house or a commercial building, the bank will appraise the property and the plans and risk the rental of their money in a "construction loan". They will pay the money to the contractor in installments as the work proceeds. The bank management will make a charge for this service, and they will charge "points" which is usually by percentage of the loaned amount, that is: one point/one percent.

Due to the competition among banks and the nature of their business, the rates for renting people's money and the rates for which they rent their money out varies with the economy. Therefore, not knowing what the economy will be next year or five to ten years later, the bank cannot risk the rent fees coming in or going out over long terms. They therefore want someone else to spare them this risk. This process is called a "take out". The bank will then become only a broker or a middle person to reconnect their customer to a different kind of customer. This is where the Savings and Loan institutions come in.

The first savings bank in the United States was in Boston in 1816, so they have been around for one and three-quarters centuries. Savings and loan banks were designed for long-term risks. Their deposits were principally for savings and security alone. They rented their money out on 20- to 30-year conditions and naturally, for that risk, made their rates accordingly. Usually their "spread" (the difference between the rent paid and the rent charged) was commensurate with the risk of the particular circumstance.

During the Depression (25% jobless) in 1931 alone 2000 banks failed and suspended business. One group of economists (monetarists) believed recessions (10% jobless) to be due to money supply. The stock market crash resulted in a wave of uncertainty and people withdrew their cash from the banks. This brought ruin to the depositor who didn't get his money out in time. Spending was slowed to a crawl, which added to the decline. Thus, the drop depleted money supply in the economy. It was argued, however, that money supply was not the factor and that it was the drop in supply of goods and services that was the problem, because although the banks in Canada and England were rescued by their governments the Depression was just as bad for them.

But a worse situation prevailed. In order to balance budgets, for the operation of the government, the tax rates were increased. These further lowered consumption and the domino effect wiped out many businesses and personal funds as well as banks.

Nevertheless, something needed to be done. Therefore the government started regulation of the banks and savings and loan companies. This became the F.D.I.C. (Federal Deposit Insurance Corporation) and the F.S.L.I.C. (Federal Savings and Loan Insurance Corporation).

The idea was to federally protect the depositor of money in the event of a catastrophic run on the bank or the savings and loan company, as I understand it, to the amount of $100,000.

The customer for a savings and loan company would keep a pass book with a guaranteed 3%-4% "rental fee" and this would be compounded (the interest would accumulate and be added to the total). The regulation for the savings and loan companies further stipulated that no more than 4% could be paid by anyone in the system. This meant for a period of 20 to 30 years such a regulated income was essentially guaranteed. The amount charged for loans to homeowners would range around 7%. Therefore, the difference between 7% and 4% was their "spread" and was considered safe. Small companies knew the 7% was the limit of their interest expense because it didn't vary. They could therefore take higher risks than banks whose rates floated with competition and the business climate.

In about 1957 I was approached by the father of two of my patients. He flashed a large, fat roll of money and asked me to make an investment with a group to obtain the charter for a new savings and loan business. I confessed I knew nothing about the business but when he said, "It's the greatest license to steal ever invented!" I smelled a problem. That feeling was intensified when I also learned that in order to obtain the charter in California a sizable portion would go to a bank in another state. I gathered that it was "payola" to the powers-that-be in the chain of the state government. To me it stunk, and I rejected it.

Many home loans and the construction of commercial buildings were the common risks of savings and loan companies. They were the tool for expansion of the economy. The politicians loved them. Throughout the Fifties until the Seventies these companies thrived.

However, they got greedy. Cronyism came into the picture. Poor risk loans were made, and some of them couldn't pay the lender back. In order to protect the system, the officers supported the election of sympathetic political candidates -- hence Keating's Five with members in both parties. The savings and loan companies loaned on poor properties on which "inside" appraisers would beef up the values so that higher loans could be granted.

But the banks didn't like the S & L's advantage. They felt it wasn't fair. Their competition and business conditions would make them pay less for their rented money and pay more to their customers. Therefore, in the Eighties, the savings and loan companies were deregulated. The ceiling was lifted on the saving rates paid to customers for savings. Banks and savings and loan companies could now pay more for deposits. S & L's would now have to compete with banks for deposits. **They now had to pay 7% to rent money which they had already rented out at the same or a lower fee.** Considering the bad risks that many had made, most had to fold.

Keating had taken funds and formed an investment company which then speculated on "junk bonds" that were very high-risk. The whole thing was legal except there were no watchdogs for speculating with such capital, and officers in the firms took inordinate risks with depositors' money.

Federal Reserve Bank

Now where did the Federal Reserve Bank come in? There were both state and federal regulators for state and federal banking companies. They use what is called a "discount window" in times of a problem they could borrow from the Federal Reserve. Large banks such as New York Chase and Citicorp could therefore set the pace for discount rates as an indicator for interest rates in general.

With rates raised and with a drop in the economy and the decrease in values, the banks and savings and loan companies would call on a customer to put up more cash as a security, which the customer couldn't do. The savings and loan companies and banks were left holding the property which they would sell at a loss to partially recoup their investment. Thus, the savings and loan companies or the "thrift" industry became a national disgrace.

Because the government insured the depositor they now had to pay off the depositor, they now had to pay off the losses to the insured amount. This was a major woe for the Bush administration but was not of his doing. The birds had come home to roost.

* * *

XI
MORE AMERICAN PROBLEMS

The American public often hears rumors of foreigners sneaking into the United States. People have a tendency to shrug their shoulders and think "so what?" Perhaps they would react differently if they knew some facts.

John Brechtel of the U.S. Immigration Service revealed the following information in a Rotary address in January, 1993. A record 14,000 illegal people were apprehended in 1993. However, estimates in Los Angeles alone go as high as 25% of that population being aliens. Sophisticated production of false documents, including all necessary identity including Social Security, can be readily obtained. State-of-the-Art forgeries of anything needed has preempted law enforcement. The high profits outweigh the risks for convicted forgers. Drug trafficking also boosts the value of the risk.

Still another problem is boatloads of hundreds of people asking for asylum who get in and disappear into anonymity. These people need jobs and seek social welfare. By falsifying Social Security information they get into that system without the normal contribution.

Our hearts go out to the unfortunate people starving or being brutalized in other countries. In times past, our shores were protected and when the economy was thriving we could absorb great numbers. However, our states are now going broke and already citizens and businesses are jeopardized. Our society is being split.

Probably the greatest risk is the underworld element cashing in on the whole situation. Yet, as I have said before, many of these alien people are industrious and capable of making a contribution. It bothers me when good people cannot get into America legally while others, less desirable, get in by fraud, deception, and cheating.

One answer might be to help Mexico and the Central American countries to prosper to the point where living there would be a choice. Again, I see no long-range solution to the drug trafficking problem until the demand is curtailed by punishment of the user rather than the dealer. There's just too much profit for it ever to be controlled at the borders. Sooner or later individuals must group together and take action.

* * *

XII
A LETTER TO PRESIDENT WILLIAM J. CLINTON

20 January 1993

The President
The White House
Washington, D.C.

Dear President Clinton:

I am writing to you now because I have a concern about the future of America, a concern based on history. You have declared you will cut our deficit in half in four years. My hope is that you will not, like so many in history, try to pay off our debt by simply printing more money.

It doesn't take much study to determine that the death of a country is tied more than anything else to inflation. The British Empire vanished with the value and security of the pound sterling. Travelling throughout the world as a lecturer it is plain to me that our money is becoming devalued at an increasing rate. Too many examples, on five continents, are present to even mention them.

Like you, I'm concerned about our poor. History shows that class separation is made wider by the disastrous result of devaluation of currencies. It was put in motion by Johnson and a Democratic Congress and really brought to fruition under Carter and a full Democratic Congress. Now, what will it be with you in the same situation?

In Dr. Pick's "All the Monies in the World" every study of inflation resulted in twenty listed reversals in economic and social structuring. Among these are soaring prices, rising interest rates, horrendous budget deficits, drooping production, paralysis of savings, massive social unrest, decapitalization, rampant speculation, manipulation of exchange rates, towering trade deficits, smuggling, flourishing black markets, and economic strangulation. Worst of all was the loss of faith in their country by people saving for old age and the loss of insurance companies.

There are many models of inflation in my lifetime starting with the German mark in 1923. The story is repeated -- of central bankers who issue pious platitudes while silently expropriating the assets of citizens who believe them. How soon will it be that we will be printing larger bills and eliminating our pennies which people don't even bother to pick up on the street any more?

For 600 years the bezant gold coin held together the Byzantine Empire. Rome died when its currency was debased. When authorities debase money the end of a nation's greatness is not long in coming. Contrariwise, when a nation obtains sound currency its future is guaranteed!

My plea is for you to play the correct role for our future. Congress would not work with a Republican in this light. Set our dollar at some value --any value in gold, silver or metal of some kind -- and leave it there! It's that simple. At the present value say one dollar is worth 1/350 of an ounce of gold.

Let's restore America's greatness. Tell me why not! Some day I would enjoy meeting you. Good luck in your efforts. I don't envy your job that lies ahead.

Sincerely yours,

Robert M. Ricketts, D.D.S., M.S.

BIBLIOGRAPHY

Ardrey, Robert: African Genesis, Dell Publishing Co., New York, NY, 1961.

Ardrey, Robert: Territorial Imperative, Atheneum, New York, NY, 1970.

Ardrey, Robert: The Hunting Hypothesis, Atheneum, New York, NY, 1970.

Ardrey, Robert: The Social Contract, Atheneum, New York, NY, 1970.

Barnett, Lincoln: Treasure of our Tongue, Alfred A. Knopf, New York, NY, 1964.

Batra, Ravi: The Downfall of Capitalism & Communism, Venus Books, Dallas, TX, 1990.

Batra, Ravi: The Great Depression of 1990, Bantam Doubleday Dell Publishing Group, Inc., New York, NY, 1987.

Becker, Robert: Crossed Currents, St. Martin's Press, Los Angeles, CA, 1990.

Bronowski, J.: The Ascent of Man, Little, Brown & Co., Boston, MA, 1973.

Browne, Harry: How I Found Freedom in An Unfree World, Macmillan Co., New York, NY, 1973.

Cheraskin, E., Ringsdorf, W.M., and Brecker, A.: Psycho-Dietetics; Food as the Key to Emotional Health, Stein and Day Publishers, Scarborough House, Briarcliff Manor, NY, 1974.

Clason, G.S.: The Richest Man in Babylon, Hawthorne Books, Inc., New York, NY, 1955.

Cousins, Norman: Anatomy of An Illness, W.W. Norton & Co., New York, NY, 1980.

Cousins, Norman: Human Options, W.W. Norton & Co., New York, NY, 1980.

De Bono, Edward: The Mechanism of Mind, Penguin Books, England, 1969.

Durant, Will: The Pleasures of Philosophy, Simon and Schuster, New York, NY, 1929.

Durant, Will: The Story of Philosophy, Garden City Publishing Co., New York, NY, 1938.

Eibl-Eibesfeldt, Irenaus: Ethology -- The Biology of Behavior, Holt, Rinehart and Winston, 1970.

Fisher, Antony: Fisher's Concise History of Economic Bungling, Caroline House Books, Green Hill Publ., Ottowa, IL, 1978.

Fuller, R. Buckminster: Critical Path, St. Martin's Press, New York, NY, 1981.

Garn, Roy: The Magic Power of Emotional Appeal, Prentice Hall, Inc., Englewood Cliffs, NJ, 1960.

Ghyka, Matila: The Geometry of Art and Life, Dover Publications, New York, NY, 1977.

Halberstam, David: The Next Century, William Morrow and Company, Inc., New York, NY, 1991.

Hall, Manly P.: Secret Teachings of All Ages, Philosophical Research Society, Los Angeles, CA, 1978.

Hambridge, Jay: The Elements of Dynamic Symmetry, Dover Publications, New York, NY, 1967.

Harriss, C. Lowell, ed.: Inflation: Long-Term Problems, The Academy of Political Science, New York, NY, 1975.

Hayakawa, S.I.: Language in Thought and Action, Harcourt, Brace & World, Inc., New York & Burlingame, 1964.

Henri, Robert: The Art Spirit, J.B. Lippincott Co., Philadelphia, PA, 1960.

Hilton, Alice Mary: Logic, Computing Machines and Automation, The World Publishing Co., New York, NY, 1964.

Holmes, T.H. and Rahe, R.H.: The Social Readjustment Rating Scale, J. Psychosomatic Res., IL, pp. 213-218, 1967.

Huntley, H. E.: The Divine Proportion, Dover Publications, New York, NY, 1970.

INFORMATION PLEASE 1992 ALMANAC (Otto Johnson, Executive Editor), Houghton Mifflin Company, New York, NY, 1992.

Kaus, Mickey: The End of Equality, Harper/Collins Publishers, New York, NY, 1992.

Kraus, Bertram S.: The Basis of Human Evolution, Harper & Row, New York, NY, 1964.

Kuebler-Ross, Elisabeth: Death - The Final Stage of Growth, Prentice-Hall, Inc., Englewood Cliffs, NJ, 1975.

Maltz, Maxwell: Psycho-Cybernetics, Simon & Schuster, New York, NY, 1970.

Mandino, Og: The Greatest Miracle in the World, Bantam Books, New York, NY, 1975.

Mann, John A.: Secrets of Life Extension, Harbor Publishing, Inc., San Francisco, CA, 1980.

McFarland, Kenneth: Eloquence in Public Speaking, Prentice Hall, Inc., Englewood Cliffs, NJ, 1961.

Michener, James: "What I Believe", Parade Magazine, New York, NY, 11-24-92.

Naisbitt, John and Aburdene, Patricia: Megatrends, Warner Books, New York, NY 1982.

Naisbitt, John and Aburdene, Patricia: Megatrends 2000, Morrow, New York, NY, 1990.

North, Oliver L.: Under Fire, Harper Collins, New York, NY, 1991.

Pearce, Joseph Chilton: The Bond of Power, Dutton, New York, NY, 1981.

Pearce, Joseph Chilton: The Magical Child, Bantam Books, Inc., New York, NY, 1980.

Rees-Mogg, William, Crisis of World Inflation, Baxter World Economic Service, Greenwich, CT, 1975.

Runion, Garth E.: The Golden Section and Related Curiosa, Scotts, Foresman & Co., Glenview, IL, 1972.

Salk, Jonas: Survival of the Wisest, Harper & Row, New York, NY, 1973.

Selye, Hans: Stress Without Distress, J. P. Lippincott Co., New York, NY, 1974.

Slavkin, H.: Developmental Craniofacial Biology, Lea & Febiger, Philadelphia, PA, 1979.

Smith, Adam: An Inquiry into the Nature and Causes of the Wealth of Nations, Random House, New York, NY, 1985.

Soyka, Fred: The Ion Effect, Bantam Books, New York, NY, 1977.

THE HUTCHINSON POCKET ENCYCLOPEDIA (Michael Upshall, Editorial Director), Century Hutchinson Ltd., London, 1987.

THE WORLD ALMANAC, 1991 (Mark S. Hoffman, Editor), Pharos Books (Scripps Howard), New York, NY, 1991.

Thomas, Lewis: The Lives of a Cell, Bantam Books, Inc., New York, NY, 1975.

Toffler, Alvin: The Eco-Spasm Report, Bantam Books, Inc., New York, NY, 1975.

Toffler, Alvin: Future Shock, Random House, New York, NY, 1970.

Toffler, Alvin: Power Shift, Bantam Books, New York, NY, 1990.

Weaver, Henry Grady: The Mainspring of Human Progress, The Foundation for Economic Education, Irvington-on-Hudson, New York, NY, 1947.

Wilson, Edward O.: On Human Nature, Harvard University Press, Cambridge, MA, 1978.

Wolford, R.L.: The 120 Year Diet, Simon & Schuster, New York, NY, 1986.